DSHIRE

D1138470

Long Road from

Jarrow

A journey through Britain then and now

STUART
MACONIE

EBURY
PRESS

1 3 5 7 9 10 8 6 4 2

Ebury Press, an imprint of Ebury Publishing
20 Vauxhall Bridge Road
London SW1V 2SA

Ebury Press is part of the Penguin Random House group of companies
whose addresses can be found at global.penguinrandomhouse.com

 Penguin
Random House
UK

Copyright © Stuart Maconie 2017. This edition published in 2018.

Stuart Maconie has asserted his right to be identified as the author of this
Work in accordance with the Copyright, Designs and Patents Act 1988

Quote from 'Brexit is the only way the working class can change anything',
p14, © Mckenzie/Guardian News & Media, used with kind permission.

First published by Ebury Press in 2017

www.penguin.co.uk

A CIP catalogue record for this book is available from the British Library

ISBN 9781785030543

Typeset in India by Integra Software Services Pvt. Ltd, Pondicherry

Printed and bound in Great Britain by Clays Ltd, St Ives PLC

 MIX
Paper from
responsible sources
FSC® C018179

Penguin Random House is committed to a
sustainable future for our business, our readers
and our planet. This book is made from Forest
Stewardship Council® certified paper.

For Tracy Brabin and Jo Cox, Members
of Parliament for Batley and Spen, West Yorkshire

CONTENTS

PROLOGUE

'Going far, son?'

I turn to meet the voice, somewhat awkwardly since I'm still getting used to the graceless choreography required when travelling laden with a large, bulky modern rucksack. It's made in Colorado and according to the manufacturer, 'delivers serious function while looking great, featuring Axiom 5 technology, front entry and stretch mesh front and side pockets'. It can hold '65 litres' should I ever be tempted to fill it with liquid. Nonetheless, it's this highly visible piece of kit which has presumably prompted the question from behind me. That and my remorseless, solitary plod along an unlovely stretch of northern trunk road on a quiet weekday morning.

'London,' I answer.

'Bloody hell!' he replies.

He's a big man in his late fifties, I'd guess; Geordie accent, close cropped hair, brisk, active. He moves alongside me, clutching a thick rope leash wound around his wrist at the end of which strains a large German Shepherd dog; enthusiastic, curious, increasingly aware I feel that there is half a meat and potato pasty in either the stretch mesh front or side pocket (I forget which) of my great-looking, yet seriously functional pack.

It's 5 October 2016 on the A167 between Pelaw Grange and Chester-le-Street. A rinsed fresh autumn morning in County Durham; a sky of rippled, downy cloud and a low gauzy sun over the far blue smudge of fells. Nearer to hand, less lovely, the buffeting, thunderous, continuous rush of articulated lorries along the noisy arterial road.

'London?' There's pity in his voice, with a hint of disbelief and perhaps a dash of admiration. 'Elsa!' He yanks the boisterous dog to heel.

'Yes, I'm retracing a famous journey ...' I pause. 'If I were to say "the Jarrow march" to you, would that mean anything?'

He smiles and looks me up and down, as if wondering what kind of response might go down best. Over the next month of walking almost the length of England, I'll ask many people this question and get all kinds of responses to that word 'Jarrow' and the famous march of 1936. Some will be knowledgeable, some vague, some apologetic, some impassioned, many wildly inaccurate. A few faces will be blank and sheepish, offering an embarrassed shrug or a wild guess. Others will have learned about it at school, especially up here on this first northern stretch, where many will have treasured, polished stories to tell. Some will have had family members on the march. Others will claim to.

I'll meet people whose granddads cooked the marchers breakfast in a drill hall in Leicester and a lady whose mum watched them stride past her cottage down a country lane near Bedford. A taxi driver in Darlington will talk of knowing old miners who had walked with them through Manchester and Birmingham. A sweet, older woman in Newton Aycliffe will tell me that she still has a tent peg that she found as a girl left behind after they had taken down their camp in her village. They didn't pass anywhere near Birmingham or Manchester and they never pitched a tent in Newton Aycliffe but as Frank Lloyd Wright once said, 'the truth is more important than the facts'.

The man on the A167 between Pelaw Grange and Chester-le-Street thinks for a second or two, then with a jutting jaw, a sly look and an eye on my reaction says, 'Aye, it means something. A bunch of bloody left wingers who went to London to stir up trouble because they had nothing better to do.'

Certainly the last of this is true. It was having nothing to do – no work, nor money, security or purpose, just long, empty repetitious days of hardship, boredom and despair – that sent the marchers all the way down to London 80 years ago. In a sense then, my dog walking companion is absolutely right. He registers my surprise though, which is genuine. You don't find many north easterners who'll 'trash' the Jarrow marchers. Respect for Jarrow's great collective effort is coiled into the DNA of the region, embedded in its still proud sense of self.

'Every bugger in County Durham claims their dad or granddad or budgie was on that bloody march. Sorry, son, but I'm a bitter man. Worked in the steelworks in Consett and it was never the same after nationalisation in '67. Labour let me down. I'm a rarity round here in talking like that. This is Labour country, Country Durham. Mining country … with no mines. Well, I wish you luck. You'll see some places … I almost wish I was going with you … Cheerio, son.'

He crosses the road gingerly, Elsa recalcitrant still, odour of pasty still lingering on the breeze perhaps. As he gets to the other side he yanks on the dog's chain, halts her and turns around on the opposite verge. He shouts something across the road back at me with a wry grin.

'I hope you get a better welcome than they did anyway … all five hundred thousand of them.'

A joke. A good one. I want to ask him more, but a speeding convoy of huge vehicles flicker and rumble past like a strip of film, and when they have passed he too is gone. But to answer his first question, which I don't think I did: yes, I am going far. Three hundred miles, give or take.

To London. A long road from Jarrow.

*

They denied us the future we wanted, but that doesn't
mean they can deny us our past ...

Matt Perry, *The Jarrow Crusade: Protest and Legend*

'Who cares? The world's moved on ...'

Software Consultant, Kent, via Twitter

The *Shields Gazette*, established in 1849, is the oldest evening
paper in Britain. It still appears nightly, in print and online,
and remains the voice of home and the journal of record for
generations of Geordies, Mackems, Wearsiders and for thousands
across the north east of England. On New Year's Day 2013,
in amongst details of the Queen's Honours List and drunken
revelry in Hebburn, it carried these notices:

SHIELS Con. Died aged 96.

Dad, you had a long life. We are so proud to have been
a part of it. Love and miss you always, Moya & Brian x

Dad, you will always be near us. Con, Eileen, grandchildren
and family.

Con Shiels, a widower of Jarrow, South Tyneside died on Boxing
Day 2012 after a short illness, mourned by his son, two daughters
and several grandchildren and great-grandchildren. He'd been a
fitter by trade and had served 12 years in the Royal Navy. But it
was the events of one late October day in 1936 that Con spent
the rest of his long life being asked about, interviewed by earnest
academics, TV comedians and politicians, appearing on scores of
documentaries, speaking to classrooms full of eager schoolchildren.

On 31 October 1936, aged just 20 and enrolled on a work
scheme in London, Con joined his father, an unemployed
riveter, and nearly two hundred other men from his home town
to walk the eight or so miles from Edgware to London's Marble

Arch. They were on the final leg of a protest over the decision to close their steelworks, to publicise the plight of their dying town and to ask for government assistance in creating new jobs. They'd been on the road on foot for three-and-a-half weeks and covered almost 300 miles by the time young Con Shiels joined them. The youngest present, he went on to outlive every other man on that walk and thus when he passed way, he held a claim to be the last of the Jarrow marchers.

A decade before, on 14 September 2003, another nonagenarian and another 'Con', Cornelius Whalen of Hadrian Road, Jarrow, died at the Queen Elizabeth Hospital in Gateshead. He was the last man alive to have walked the whole 291-mile route from Jarrow to London amongst that famous body of men. In commemoration, the Jarrow Brewery named a beer after him, the Old Cornelius. But it was Con Shiels who was actually the last survivor to have walked among them, if only for that final dour, rain-lashed day along the Edgware Road. At a packed requiem mass for him at St Matthew's RC Church, Jarrow, parish priest Father Peter Martin said: 'This is the closing of a chapter of history. There can't be any others who can say they took part.'

Except that there might have been. There might still be even, though this is extremely unlikely of course. The truth is we just don't know. The Jarrow march of October 1936 is an event which, although lit by fires of memory and the glow of romance, has many an obscure and shadowy cranny and corner. That's decidedly strange when you consider that we are not amongst the Vikings or the Saxons here. We are not in the realms of Camelot or Sherwood Forest. We're talking of twentieth century Tyneside and modern Britain. Here is an event that happened relatively recently and within living memory, had two 'embedded' journalists in its number and was covered by the national press, radio and newsreels. It was a fairly straightforward undertaking; a three-and-a-half-week march to deliver a petition to parliament. But it has attained the status of a national myth akin to the stories of Robin Hood or King Arthur, and like those, has become negotiable, malleable, debatable. While its status is unarguable, its details are anything but.

For instance, above my desk as I write this is a laminated copy of the original schedule of the walk drawn up by the organisers and lodged at the time of the march with the BBC and the National Archives. It is hard to conceive of a more august or official document of the trip. It is also quite wrong. Two overnight stays are recorded in Thirsk and Boroughbridge. These never happened. The marchers didn't even pass through these towns, though they did lodge in nearby Ripon. Ripon, however, doesn't appear on the itinerary. During his 2005 bid for leadership of the Conservative Party, David Davies claimed his grandfather had marched with the Crusade from York to Aldermaston. His grandfather may well have marched somewhere with someone. But the Jarrow marchers passed through neither York nor Aldermaston.

Famously, a dog accompanied the march. Many of the press reports dwelt somewhat sentimentally on this adorable pooch, presumably to provide some cute human (or rather canine) interest and distract from any awkward political dimension. Depending on whose account you read, this was either a setter, a retriever or a terrier. But even a cursory glance at the pictures would suggest that it's actually a Labrador. Whatever its breed, this plucky, uncomplaining companion was called Paddy. Or perhaps Peter. Then again, some people say it was called Blackie. Others say Jarrow.

Anyway, what is certain is that it walked all the way with the men, all 200 of them. That's 'two hundred' according to the police and the march organisers in any case. We can only find corroborating evidence and names for 176. And when I say 'names', there's another complicating issue here because many of the men gave false ones so that they wouldn't have their benefit stopped by the National Assistance Board. For instance, marcher Thomas Downey was probably actually Thomas Dobson.

While the marchers covered the miles, their equipment went ahead in a van. No one knows the driver's name or the make of his vehicle. On arrival in London, they were taken on a river boat trip and the 10,000 signature petition they had carried in a box for the entire route was hurriedly taken from them at the House of Commons. It has never been seen since. No one knows where it is, or if it still exists. It might be mouldering in a forgotten cabinet in the bowels of Westminster, or lying in its wooden box on the muddy bed of the Thames.

Some may find all this vagueness and fudge dispiriting. But apart from that last properly shameful detail, I think it entirely in keeping with the march and its legacy. 'Jarrow' (the whole matrix of events reducible to one word like 'Aberfan', 'Hillsborough' or 'Orgreave') has become mythic, storied; a thing of lore and romance as much as hard fact, one whose details and legacy are still debated today. Many of the 'facts' surrounding the march may be opaque or contentious, but the 'tru' of the Jarrow march, its emblematic significance as a piece of Britain's social history, is as enduring as it's contested. D Douglass in the *New Statesman* in 1996 said, 'it is a story told and retold …. The ghosts of Jarrow's Crusaders still march into Jarrow's consciousness.' The Jarrow march casts a long shadow, and you invoke the name lightly at your peril.

In 2000, a collective of disgruntled road hauliers, the self-styled 'People's Fuel Lobby', announced their plans to send a slow-moving convoy cum blockade of lorries down the A1(M) from Jarrow to London to force the government into lowering duty on fuel thus safeguarding their profits. Spokesperson Andrew Spence declaimed, 'I don't know if anyone has heard of the Jarrow Crusade? Well, it's starting again, only bigger. We want as many vehicles on the road as possible.' Spence's crass attempt to usurp this icon of working-class struggle for such selfish, disruptive, acquisitive ends was a PR disaster. Denounced everywhere, it lost the People's Fuel Lobby what little public support they had.

Whilst the 1930s produced many marches, protests and outpourings of anger and dissent, none are as well remembered, beloved or lionised as the Jarrow Crusade. When discussing the

Jarrow march, be it with Geordies, Labour movement stalwarts, working people of the north or British people of a certain vintage generally, it's wise to remember that you're on hallowed ground and dealing with emotive, if not entirely accurate, memories. Tread softly, as W B Yeats asked the famously unfussed Maud Gonne, for you tread on my dreams, or in my case, lacing up my Size Nine Meindl Respond GTXs and treading on a whole romantic cultural icon, over community and place and memory.

I have no connections with Jarrow. I've no link to the march or any of the marchers. I'm from the north west, not the north east, and Geordie friends have never tired of reminding me that my bit of 'the north' is more like the Midlands to them. But something appealed about retracing the Jarrow march.

Firstly – and I wouldn't want to downplay this element – I just fancied going for a really long walk. I liked the idea of passing through unfamiliar landscapes, experiencing the character and thrill of towns, villages and cities never visited, meeting, eating, drinking, soaking the country in. I like Britain and British history. I like the people and I like hanging out with them. I like random eavesdroppings, chance meetings and unexpected encounters and I had many on this journey, from the rosy cheeked Women's Institute ladies who gave me a bag of apples to Albanian builders tearful on grappa late at night, and from concert pianists to chip shop waitresses.

Being British, I was also drawn to the notion of heroic failure. At the end of his life, the last surviving man of the march Con Shiels said of it that it 'had made not one ha'porth of difference' and been a 'waste of time'. But some think the constant, largely supportive publicity for the Jarrow march, the effort and endurance of the men and the focus on the plight of the town and conditions in industrial Britain, helped shape public attitudes into a fresh and keen desire for change. This new national mood may well have contributed to the Labour landslide of 1945 and thus to the setting up of the Welfare State and the NHS, those imperilled secular sacraments of modern Britain that are part of our self-image and identity. As long as Jarrow's remembered, 'the struggle' goes on. Even growing up half a century later and a hundred miles south, my nana would bring up the Jarrow march whenever industrial disputes or economic crisis were in the news, which they often were in the seventies and eighties. It was a crusade; the men were heroes, their treatment a scandal. These days, we didn't know we were born, us modern softies with hire purchase fridges and central heating. We hadn't known the deprivation and squalor of that grim decade, the 1930s. Even the term 'the thirties' has a ring to it, and it's more a tolling bell than a dainty tinkle.

Unless you're one of those enormously irritating people who says 'before my time!' when receiving a question about the Marx Brothers or the Suez crisis in Trivial Pursuit, certain decades call forth an immediate mental image. The eighties: a girl with a bubble perm in legwarmers listening to a Walkman on rollerskates, or a yuppie banker in Sloane Square with a brick sized mobile. The seventies: a bovver boy in half-mast trousers eating a Findus Crispy Pancake during a power cut. The sixties, a couple in kaftans singing Donovan's 'Catch the Wind' round a campfire, or pushing flowers down a National Guardsman's rifle barrel or rolling naked in some mud whilst doolally on acid. And so on. The 1930s, should they conjure anything, will suggest a downcast man in clogs, flat cap and muffler standing on a street corner. At his knee, perhaps, two filthy kids who look beseechingly into the camera whilst playing with a hoop and stick or a lump of coal. Words and phrases that spring readily to mind might include 'Means Test', 'Rickets', 'Hitler', 'Diphtheria' and, of course, 'Jarrow'.

The thirties get a really terrible press. Though recent revisionist historians have proposed a different view of the decade citing the relative affluence of the south and such, this has yet to gain much popular traction outside academia. 'A low, dishonest decade' was W H Auden's famous verdict, badmouthing the thirties almost before it was over in his poem 'September 1, 1939'. That poem was written on the eve of war of course, and our view of the end of the thirties is inevitably coloured by it being the grim prelude to years of global carnage. In 1973, Claud Cockburn called it 'the Devil's Decade' which quickly gained purchase as the accepted view of the times. In 2009, Richard Overy named it 'the morbid age'. Most recently, Juliet Gardiner in her hefty, magisterial study *The Thirties: An Intimate History* claims, 'the thirties is a statement as well as a decade because whilst those years are gradually slipping from our grasp what they have come to represent are ever more present; confusion, financial crisis, rising unemployment, scepticism about politicians, questions about the proper reach of Britain's role in the world'.

With no grand regnal designation such as the Elizabethan, Georgian or Edwardian age, the thirties have become simply part of what we blandly compartmentalise as 'between the wars', suggesting a hiatus, a pause, an interval between the two great defining conflicts of our modern world. But there's another point of view, one building up a credible intellectual head of steam that cites the thirties as the shaping decade of the world we live in today. It's the decade in which we started to voraciously consume mass media such as the new-fangled BBC, which was powered by the smart new National Grid; one where we become obsessed with personal fitness, fashion and sport and greatly more hedonistic, going to the movies, drinking, dancing, 'clubbing' and staying up late. The thirties in some ways start to look very much like Britain today, once you've wiped away the snot and coaldust.

Other thoughts occurred to me too, casting Jarrow's legacy in a different and less rosy light. In a modern world fixated on anniversaries – happy and tragic – and in a cultural milieu where the passing of a moderately successful pop musician or minor sitcom actor creates the torrents of grief once seen for dictators (and with sometimes, it seems, the same whiff of compulsion), Jarrow's eightieth anniversary made barely an appearance in my 'timeline'; no hashtags, no videos, no campaigns. Jarrow's anniversary was not trending. It was not going viral. We had not reached peak Jarrow, or anything like it. For this reason alone maybe, it was a trip worth making.

Of course, any writer with a gleam in their eye and a nose for a good 'state of the nation' story will find rich loam in this doleful era, and richest and most fertile of all is the seedbed of the Jarrow march. It resonates down the years and like all good myths you can bend it to your own ends in any era. From the moment the Crusade reached Marble Arch, writers and commentators have been finding echoes and parallels in their own age, and I clearly am no different. But even so, the particularly weird, fissile state of England in October 2016 seemed to have so much in common with the England of 1936 that a notion long nagging at me suddenly became compelling. When I realised that a significant anniversary loomed, I had the idea to re-trace the walk on its eightieth anniversary day by day as the marchers did, visiting the same towns and comparing the two Englands of then and now.

Some parallels between then and now suggest themselves immediately: A Conservative government recently returned to power with an increased majority. A Labour Party led into disarray by a leader widely seen as divisive and incompetent. The rise of extremism here and abroad fired by financial disasters, a wave of demagoguery and 'strong man' populism. Foreign wars driven by fundamentalist ideologies leading to the mass displacement of innocent people. A subsequent refugee 'crisis'. The threat of constitutional anarchy with conflict between government, parliament and judiciary. Manufacturing industries, especially steel, facing extinction. Marches and mass rallies resurgent as popular but questionable forums for political debate. Explosions of new forms of media. Inflammatory rhetoric stoked by a factionalised press. Football a national obsession; its wages, profits and morality constantly debated. A country angrily at odds with itself over its relationship to Europe, the elephant in the nation: Brexit.

David Cameron's decision to hold a snap referendum on our membership of the EU on 23 June 2016 was both for him and, so many think, the nation a disastrous, vainglorious mistake. Margaret Thatcher hated referenda, feeling that they gave up parliamentary sovereignty and put national policy at the whim of a protest vote. This is precisely what occurred. Misreading the national mood entirely (and not helped by Jeremy Corbyn's near-invisibility) the Remain campaign ignored concerns over immigration and talked dryly of economic competency and trade tariffs. Saatchi and Saatchi designed two stunning posters for the Remain campaign; one showed Boris Johnson looking twerpish in a woolly hat knocking on the door of Number Ten with the caption 'Be careful what you wish for', another featured a grinning Nigel Farage lying smugly in a crumpled bed captioned 'Don't do something today that you'll regret in the morning'. Strategists think they could have proved decisive. But they were never used.

In the aftermath of the referendum vote to leave the European Union, the reaction from some liberal metropolitans was disbelief, disgust and not so much rage as a kind of pricked hauteur. Those boors and idiots up north had gone and spoiled it for everyone. This generalised shock and bafflement was not shared by those of us who come from these towns or had spent any time outside London and the home counties this decade. In the run-up to the vote, and in the absence of any genuine, cogent explanation of the issues involved, the intelligentsia, especially on the left, had simply snorted their contempt and dismissed any opposing views as 'racist' and held only by 'little Englanders'. In truth, whether your England is little or large and whether you want its borders iron clad or porous, Brexit proved that one thing is not in doubt: we are a divided country, chiefly along lines of geography and class.

The referendum result was so truly appalling to some in Britain probably because they had grown used to viewing the world through the filter of their Twitter timeline, hearing only the echolalic voices of those who thought like them. Thus was assumed a general soothing consensus about race, nation, work, power. The only dissenting voice I heard from the creative industries post Brexit came from socialist comic Jeremy Hardy who said, 'the centre of British politics is so incredibly Europhile. They seem to base their entire view of the EU on the welcoming attitude to children in continental restaurants.'

Brexit was such a shock to the metropolis because it broadcast and amplified the authentic voice of an England they had nothing to do with and probably didn't much want to; not the warming, agreeable multicultural glow that came with chatting to your Senegalese neighbour, Nepali shopkeeper or Latvian plumber, but a different, chillier, altogether less genial acknowledgment of diversity that is the realisation that not everyone thinks, lives or acts like you do. Brexit proved that there is not one England. We are not all sweetly alike really when you get down to it. We are not all in this together, and in that too, we have much in common with the fractious and divided 1930s.

As the shampoo ads once had it, here comes the science bit. The Gini coefficient was developed by an Italian statistician in 1912 to describe the income distribution of a nation. It's the most commonly used measure of inequality. Before 1979, inequality in the UK was actually fairly low in terms of income, but through the 1980s income inequality began to rise. Apart from a brief pause during the recession and financial crisis of 2008–2010, the UK's Gini coefficient has steadily increased to an all-time high. We are now the most unequal country in Western Europe and at a level of income inequality unheard of since the setting up of the Welfare State.

Just as in 1936, the old centres of industry in the north – Britain's 'rust belt' – have been hardest hit. Not everyone and not every town has felt the bite and sting of austerity or experienced the raw downside of globalisation and technology as keenly as some have. Thus metropolitan Britain could scarcely believe that the post-industrial north would be so insular as to baulk at warm notions and comforts as easy travel, study and work opportunities, access to continental markets and affordable mini-breaks to Budapest and Lisbon. However, having never properly enjoyed any of these, it was easy for Wakefield, Oldham and Skegness to reject them.

A brilliant but atypical article in the *Guardian* by the LSE sociologist Dr Lisa Mckenzie bucked the trend, asserting in its title 'Brexit is the only way the working class can change anything'. In it, she wrote:

> As a group of east London women told me: 'I'm sick of being called a racist because I worry about my own mum and my own child,' and 'I don't begrudge anyone a roof who needs it but we can't manage either.' Over the past 30 years there has been a sustained attack on working-class people, their identities, their work and their culture by Westminster politics and the media bubble around it … In the last few weeks of the campaign the rhetoric has ramped up and the blame game started. If we leave the EU it will be the fault of the 'stupid', 'ignorant', and 'racist' working class. Whenever working-class people have tried to talk about the effects of immigration on their lives, shouting 'backward' and 'racist' has become a middle-class pastime.

In the midst of the post-Brexit hand-wringing, navel-gazing and fist-shaking, this struck a bracing chord. Whilst no Brexiteer, I'd been dismayed at how whole areas of Britain and all kinds of people I'd grown up with and lived among could be so easily, so lazily, so insultingly dismissed. When I saw that the Jarrow area had voted 'leave' by 62 per cent, I wondered what the Jarrow men would have thought, how they'd have voted and why, and what the world would have made of their march then. Heroic stand for the native community, or petty protectionism maybe?

One enraged tweet I saw frothed about how the inhabitants of 'these boring towns' had done us all a terrible injustice and inflicted an act of suicidal revenge on blameless London,

Brighton and the likes. Another message I received when I stated my intention to 'do' the Jarrow march again was the response from the software consultant quoted earlier, viz, 'Who cares? The world's moved on.' Our Kentish friend may well be right and, if so, I was about to find out exactly how. But I wasn't so sure. As for those derided 'boring towns', in many ways, this is their story. But for me they are only boring if you are bored of history, people, politics, sex, death, religion, art and culture. Life, in other words. I'm very much hoping you're not.

The 1930s may have been a dire period for Britain's coal mines, shipyards and steel mills but they were a boom time for travel writing and the solo literary traveller. Adventurous young men like Patrick Leigh Fermor and Laurie Lee packed tiny knapsacks of pitifully small litreage with neither Axiom 5 technology nor front entry mesh and stomped across Europe. Leigh Fermor trekked from Rotterdam to Istanbul getting into scrapes, sleeping in hedgerows, monasteries and the odd inn, sketching, talking, drinking and generally having a wonderful, character building time that would later make him a famed war hero. His magical account of his teenage odyssey *A Time of Gifts* is a classic of the genre. Laurie Lee 'walked out one midsummer morning' and that was the title he gave to the book of his journey, one that would ultimately take him to the battlegrounds of the Spanish Civil War. That bloody conflict was a darkening stain across Europe as the Jarrow men marched through England.

At home, two colossi of English letters were making journeys through England that would prove just as vivid and celebrated, if less gilded, with smoke and rain and muck instead of wine, fruit and Mediterranean sun. In the first half of 1936, just before the Jarrow march, George Orwell spent three months in the north of England researching what would become *The Road to Wigan Pier*. Orwell lived in Wigan, Barnsley and Sheffield but his experiences in these towns – in whose deprivations and squalor he immersed himself completely – are those of Jarrow too. The remorseless, sapping, daily grind of poverty is described to haunting effect and those middle-class, left-wing intellectuals who will not dirty their hands with it are excoriated in a closing tirade which his publisher Victor Gollancz was extremely nervous about. (I would have loved to have read Orwell on Brexit and its treatment; he was an internationalist but he was both a patriot and fiercely supportive of the working people of England.)

Orwell took some of his inspiration for *The Road to Wigan Pier* from a very successful and similarly motivated book of three years previously. J B Priestley's *English Journey* was one more comfortably travelled than Orwell's road (by chauffeured Daimler and pleasant hotel room rather than the trams and tin baths of Wigan) – but the sentiment was the same. The two writers, of different backgrounds and mien, laid bare an England of harsh contrasts and lives of constant desperation, one in which the plight of the industrial working class could only be remedied by democratic socialism. The success and impact of both books, along with and the Jarrow march, may well have contributed to the Labour landslide of 1945.

So with both *The Road to Wigan Pier* and *English Journey* as daunting, humbling antecedents, I decided to embark on the *Long Road from Jarrow*. I wanted the title to have an echo of both and a hint of the metaphorical as well as the actual. I would start the walk eighty years to the day after the Jarrow marchers did, 5 October, and cover the route day by day as they did, staying in the same towns. I would do it on foot by and large, but if I needed the time to research and explore those towns – some of their daily stages covered 22 miles – I'd hop a passing bus if it took their route. I didn't have a chauffeured Daimler but I did stay in hotels with reasonably fluffy duvets, trouser presses and complimentary tea-and-coffee making facilities. I would aim to get to London on 31 October and hopefully succeed where the march was fobbed off, not to say duped, by getting inside the House of Commons and actually meeting an MP. How this eventually turned out was sadder and sweeter than I could ever have imagined.

My intention was to compare the England of now and then, to see if the shadow of 1936 really did fall across 2016, but also to get to the heart of England today first-hand. Commentators and chatterers across the media are fond of airy generalisations in think pieces composed in what Priestley described as, 'warm, well-lighted book-lined apartments'. These 'state of the nation' prognoses and editorials are often written from one very particular part of that nation, and with a view partially obscured by the Gherkin and the Shard. I wanted to see, hear, smell even what England was like close up by walking it, moving along its length at a speed where I could look it in the eye, shake its hand, maybe buy it a drink. You can cover the distance I would travel on a high-speed train in three-and-a-half hours. But I was going to take three-and-a-half weeks; still brisk going on foot, but with time to linger, delve, look around and 'mooch', to use a good, descriptive old dialect word.

This is not then a book about the Jarrow march as such, in the way that Matt Perry's excellent aforementioned study is, or the powerful, evocative *Jarrow March* by Tom Pickard (out of print but findable). What follows here, and what I'm more interested in with this book, is where we have been since then and how we have got here. I'd like to know what the country looks like now from the roads, tracks, streets and riverbanks they walked, and to see the pews, pubs, cafés and halls they visited; a picture of now overlaid with a filter or gauze of 1936. If a journey of nearly a month can be said to be a snapshot, then it is that; a picture of a country with a long history, a volatile present and an uncertain future – vivid and real, if sometimes blurry and breaking out of the frame.

'THE TOWN THAT WAS MURDERED'

You can tell a great deal about a place and a time by the names it gives to its tower blocks. In the Futurist architectural reverie of the 1960s, when designing the new estates was as much 'civic art' as 'town planning' and more about 'cities in the sky' than reeking stairwells and intermittent lighting, they were given titles as lofty as their elevated walkways.

In the opening shots of the 2011 alien invasion thriller *Attack the Block*, the names glimpsed on the map of the sink estate where the action takes place (Wyndham Tower, Huxley Court, Clarke Court, etc.) tell us that director Joe Cornish knows his classic British sci fi. The renaming of the Peckham tower block in *Only Fools and Horses* from Walter Raleigh to Nelson Mandela House cleverly reflects changing British cultural touchstones. This trend was parodied in the Judge Dredd comic books where tower blocks are named with desultory ordinariness after Enid Blyton, Ricardo Montalban, and Rowdy Yates of TV western *Rawhide*.

When I was a teenager, I hung out with two punk girls with vermilion hair who lived in one of the three 16-storey tower blocks that loomed over my council estate. These impressive edifices were called Dryden, Thackeray and Masefield House respectively and were clearly christened by a council apparatchik with eclectic taste in literature and a touching high-mindedness (in every sense). Similarly, Dublin's heroin-ridden Fatima Mansions were named after a miraculous visitation of the

Virgin Mary in rural Portugal. In the decaying concrete heart of Ordsall, Salford, stood the fabulously misnamed Orchards, comprising Apple, Peach and Pear Tree Court. These sardonic anomalies and juxtapositions were once common and many remain. Unless you live on a Shetland croft or in a thatched Cotswolds idyll, there will be a tower block somewhere in your town called Rembrandt Court, Coleridge House or Johann Sebastian Bach Gardens. It will be covered in crude drawings of genitalia and the lifts will be out of order.

In the centre of Jarrow, by the squat red brick town hall, stand two bulky, neatly kept, cream and red concrete tower blocks. These are small by the standards of my old estate but they still dominate the skyline as the shipyard cranes would once have done. One bears the name Ellen, the other Wilkinson. We will come back to why. But they stand almost in the centre of a tough, embattled town, the sort you find across the north of England, maybe the north of everywhere, maybe everywhere. It carries in its streets and its stones the enduring sense that it has taken hard blows in what was not a fair fight, and, whilst unbowed, is still bloody from the fray.

Some hard facts about a hard, defiant town then. Jarrow sits on the banks of the Tyne, watered by tributaries of the Don, nine miles east of Newcastle reached by travelling along the busy A1058 then the A19, or seven stops of the Metro line. In the past, it boasted a nine-hole golf course, squeezed in between Hebburn Lakes and the slag heap, although it did not possess a single set of traffic lights until the late 1960s, when this modern flamboyance was installed at Carrick's Corner. Even further back, the world's oldest complete Bible, written in Latin and to be presented to Pope Gregory II, was produced at this monastery – the 'Codex Amiatinus', now under lock and key in Florence. Jarrow's population was 43,431 at the 2011 census, over 97 per cent of which were white British. It is the least ethnically diverse area of Tyneside and its unemployment rates are significantly higher than its neighbours'. Jarrow is not just geographically distant from London (let alone Florence), it is financially, ethnically and culturally remote from the capital's habits and ways of life and walking from one to the other would show me what Britain had in common and what divided it. Ellen Court and Wilkinson Court, 'the Jarrow flats', stand sentinel in the middle of the town at a flat intersection of two main roads. They look down on a Masonic lodge, the town hall, a typically British parade of charity shops and pizza outlets. They hint at no worse and no better than a thousand similar blocks across Britain and look rather smarter than many. Ironically, recent refurbishments were financed by the European Union. Jarrow will not be seeing money like that again any day soon, if ever.

There are other Ellen Wilkinson courts and houses around the country; in Poplar, Dagenham, Bethnal Green and Tower Hamlets for example. Across Britain there are girls' schools named after her and university halls of residence. But here her memorial is most relevant, most rooted in place. Whenever anyone here in these neat ten storey blocks gives their address, they pay tribute to one of the most colourful, significant and enigmatic figures in post-war British politics, the woman who coined the two most memorable descriptions of Jarrow: 'the most famous town in England' and 'the town that was murdered'.

'Red' Ellen Wilkinson, as every biographical note including this one mentions, had fiery auburn hair and politics to match. Born into a poor family in Ardwick, Manchester in 1891, she was a bright and dynamic girl who became a socialist in her youth and a communist after the inspirational events of Russia in 1917. An active trade unionist and feminist, she entered parliament in 1924, one of only four women MPs at Westminster. Part of the National Government during the Second World War, she became Minister of Education in 1945 in Attlee's Labour administration. Always plagued by ill health and bronchial problems, she died of an overdose of medication during the bitter, iron winter of 1947. The coroner declared it an accident but doubts have always swirled around the facts of her demise.

She was worried about losing her post in a cabinet re-shuffle and possibly depressed at the end of an affair with Herbert Morrison, intriguingly a stalwart of the party's right wing.

But Ellen Wilkinson is seared into the popular imagination because of her tenure as the MP for Jarrow and her strong involvement with the Jarrow march. Having become the town's MP the year before, she symbolically led the march – albeit often dashing away to other engagements – and became an icon of it. If you're looking for an insightful exploration of the background to the march and the political climate of the time, you can do no better than her little book *The Town That Was Murdered*. I have it in front of me; a faded red first edition from 'The Left Book Club' bearing the stern injunction 'Not for Sale to The Public'. Wilkinson had a glittering second career as a journalist and her gift for the punchy phrase is evident from the off: 'Jarrow's first export was not battleships but Christianity'.

With this brilliant opening line, Wilkinson reminds us of what made the town famous before it became a byword for industrial decline. She's referring to another of Jarrow's famous old boys, in fact its original local boy made good, not Palmer the millionaire shipwright or any of the marchers but a writer called Bede, who came to the monastery of St Paul at Jarrow in AD 684 as a boy and long before anyone called him Venerable. 'First among English scholars, first among English theologians, first among English historians, it is in the monk of Jarrow that English literature strikes its roots … he is the father of our national education.'

She goes on in her brisk entertaining style to describe the ebbing and flowing of different waves of capitalism and industrialisation on the spunky little town; often watched jealously by its large, overbearing neighbour Newcastle. She describes the coming and the going of the pits and mining life. She notes with a narrow, suspicious gaze the arrival of the 'vain and vigorous' Charles Mark Palmer the shipping magnate and the various moguls of steel. For Red Ellen, these men were not the admirable civic benefactors who now lord it paternalistically from statues and pedestals all over our towns, but avaricious fat cats for whom profit was all, even when they weren't up to the job. 'Business men denounce the very idea of planned socialism as inefficient and wasteful. But under capitalism, shipbuilding seems to be as wasteful as could be.'

Palmer's shipyard gave the town work and a great and dirty deal of it between 1851 and 1933. But Sir Charles was no Titus Salt, no George Cadbury or Lord Lever. He gave his town little in the way of concert halls or public baths, no temperance bars, nurseries, libraries or clinics, no carillons playing merry tunes on Sundays in well-tended parks. He stretched to a tea stand that would sell them a hot drink while they queued for work at five-thirty on freezing winter mornings. Jarrow was no Saltaire, Bournville or Port Sunlight built on decent principles, non-conformist faith and a desire to do right by one's fellow man. Here the religion was profit and Sir Charles's god was Mammon.

Wilkinson's verdict is damning:

> There is a prevailing blackness about the neighbourhood. The houses are black, the ships are black, the sky is black, and if you go there for an hour or two, reader, you will be black … Sir Charles Palmer regarded it as no part of his duty to see that the conditions under which his workers had to live were either sanitary or tolerable.

Like many of his peers, Palmer made the task of making a living as hard as the men could stand. 'Lying like a dockyard clock' is a phrase you can still hear used by some old timers in the region, referring to those exploitative and unscrupulous owners who would keep the clocks slow to wring more labour out of the men.

Pretty bad even in the 'good old days', life was about to get appreciably worse for the working folk of Jarrow. By 1933, profits were down in the shipyards due to overproduction and cheap imports, and Palmer's yard closed. When Jarrow's one main industry was destroyed, in Wilkinson's ringing phrase, the town was murdered. In an attempt to rein in the 'excess capacity' in British shipbuilding, 37 other yards were to suffer a similar fate. None though was left so damaged as Jarrow. In a harsh twist that was impressively badass even for big business and government, the shipyards were not only closed and dismantled; powerful vested interests then 'salted the land' in a manner that Hannibal and the Assyrians would have whistled approvingly at. Government and bosses colluded to set up a body called the NSS, the National Shipyards Security Ltd, to protect profits by closing and dismantling sacrificial yards like Palmers (the word 'security' here carries a certain black humour). The NSS, the government and the shipyard owners decreed that once yards like Palmers were closed, none could be established again there for forty years to keep ship production low and profitable nationwide. The earth was salted. Jarrow was murdered. (Eighteen months later, with war looming, there was a shipping shortage. The orders went to Belgian shipyards who had bought first-rate machinery from yards like Jarrow at knock down prices.)

Unemployment soared to 80 per cent. Houses were overcrowded and infested with vermin. To the misery of unemployment was added the humiliation and degradation of the Means Test, a harsh inquisition intended to determine whether the unemployed deserved any benefit. Government inspectors would come to the house armed with lists and notebooks, spying into the family's material circumstances in the most prurient and invasive ways. Mothers were checked to see if they breastfed their babies; if they did, their meagre benefit was cut. If one member of a family worked the others received less, so families split up to avoid starvation. So much for the preservation of family values. G K Chesterton, no pinko by any stretch, wrote of it, 'For the first time within mortal memory, the government and the nation has set out on a definite deliberate attempt to make the poor poorer.' Forty years later, as a child in the seventies, watching *Crown Court* or *The Cedar Tree* with my Nan, any mention of the Means Test would make this reasonably genial old lady scowl and curse contemptuously. I shudder to think what she had seen as a girl.

The future Edward VIII had declared, shocked, that 'something must be done' when he saw the plight of the working classes in Wales and Tyneside. When Priestley visited Jarrow just before the march he saw a town ruined and a vision of urban hell on earth:

> Wherever we went men were hanging about, not scores of them but hundreds and thousands of them. The whole town looked as if it had entered a perpetual penniless bleak Sabbath. The men wore the masks of prisoners of war. A stranger from a distant civilisation, observing the condition of the place and its people would have arrived at once at the conclusion that Jarrow had deeply offended some celestial emperor of the island and was now being punished. He would never believe us if we told him that in theory this town was as good as any other and that its inhabitants were not criminals but citizens with votes.

Decades later, Ritchie Calder, one of the journalists 'embedded' with the march, recalled the state of the town that they found. 'In the story of Jarrow, we have the story of the face of hunger … you weren't seeing it on a poster, you weren't seeing it on the telly, you know, Biafra or the Congo or something like that. You were seeing the face of hunger in your street. Or even in your own mirror.'

Whatever your politics, it's hard to conceive of a more perfect stitch-up and sell-out of a community than the one perpetrated in Jarrow in 1934. When a delegation of workers from the shell-shocked town met with the head of the board of trade, Walter Runciman (in Wilkinson's words, 'a figure of ice … apparently completely indifferent to the woes of others') his response to their requests for aid was to coldly announce, 'Jarrow must work out its own salvation' – a remark described by historian Ronald Blyth as 'the last straw in official cruelty'. Runciman's chilly indifference and callous response 'kindled the town', according to Wilkinson.

In July 1936, a packed council meeting convened in the town hall at which Ellen Wilkinson, Mayor David Riley and councillors like Paddy Scullion all spoke. The town should ask again for government help, specifically in the form of a new steelworks, but this time the appeal should be backed up by a petition. Signatures should be collected from Jarrow and beyond. While the meeting debated what to do after this, an unknown voice in the crowded public gallery shouted, 'Let's march down with it.' Within days, plans were afoot to do just that, to the acclaim of Jarrow and to the shrinking terror of the Labour Party, the Trade Unions and the socialist Establishment. The Jarrow march was on.

Hunger marches, as they were known, were very much in vogue in the 1930s. Communists, ex-servicemen, blind communists, blind ex-servicemen, strikers and the unemployed of Rotherham, Sheffield, Bolton and all points north, agricultural workers from East Anglia, all could be found criss-crossing the nation under various banners demanding various reforms and with varying success, i.e. usually none. Though support was immediate and widespread for Jarrow's march to London, there were a few dissenting voices from within the working-class community, and perhaps for good reason. Councillor Dodds of Jarrow was one of many unconvinced about what merely marching could achieve:

I am not so ready as I was to support an ordinary march to London. I am willing enough to march, God knows, and there was a time when I would have suggested that we put the women and children on buses while the men of the town marched with the Council at their head. But now I think we should get down to London with a couple of bombs in our pockets. Oh Christ, yes, I am perfectly serious. We should go down there with bombs in our pockets. These people of Westminster have no use for us anyway. These people do not realise that there are people living in Jarrow today under conditions which a respectable farmer would not keep swine. Do not put any limits on your demonstration. Get down there. And I think we should go to the absolute extreme.

In more conciliatory mood, and with reference to the other political protests that had gripped Britain, David Riley later admitted that he felt that, 'Hunger March would not be a very nice name to have and Crusade would be better. And of course we adopted the idea; called it a Crusade instead of a march. At the time, there was quite a number of marches being held all over the country and they weren't being too well received in many places.'

Riley was a decent and principled man but his words show how, right from its planning stages, the organisers of the Jarrow march were obsessed with public relations and fearful of offending or antagonising the media or Establishment. 'Crusade' also struck the right churchy note of piety and godliness. Perhaps it's understandable that the marchers should have worried about how the Conservative Party and its press would receive them. In fact, they should have been more concerned and dismayed at how the Labour Party would react. Essentially, Labour washed their hands of the march, as they did its predecessors, panicky about possible infiltration by communists. The Trades Union Council actually issued a circular denouncing it. Ramsay MacDonald, the Labour leader, begged by Ellen Wilkinson to offer support, said wanly, 'Ellen, why don't you go and preach socialism, which is the only remedy for this?' She called this bland response 'sham sympathy'.

And so Jarrow marched, and stitched itself into the warp and weft of British history. Questions on the march or 'crusade' have been included in the British Citizenship Test and it remains a central module of the GCSE syllabus and the Learn English network. In

Jarrow: Protest and Legend, Matt Perry cites some of the crazily varied array of items the march can be said to have inspired:

> Five plays, two musicals, an opera, three pop songs, two folk songs, several paintings and poems, a short story, performance art, a mural, two sculptures, glassware, four television documentaries, four radio programmes, a children's story, a cuddly toy, a real ale, a public house, an election poster, street names, innumerable pieces of journalism and historical references and of course hundreds of often reproduced photographs.

Popular art has kept the name of Jarrow and its complex associations – struggle, hardship, heroism, failure even – alive down the decades. Nevil Shute's 1938 novel *Ruined City* concerns the plight of a town in the north east called Sharples, a thinly disguised Jarrow, left devastated by the closure of the 'Barlow' shipyard which is clearly modelled on Palmers. Decades later in 1974, as an economic and energy crisis gripped Britain and the lights flickered on and off in offices, homes and factories, the nation's pop pickers cheered themselves by singing along to Alan Price, formerly of the Animals, and the most famous musical tribute to the Jarrow marchers. 'Jarrow Song', which reached number six in the charts, came from an album called *Between Today and Yesterday*, in which Price delved into working-class life in the north east for inspiration. Born just six years after the march and an old boy of Jarrow grammar school, Price's jaunty brass band number masks a message substantially more militant than the ethos of the march itself. It starts with Geordie McIntyre, whose wife tells him to go to London, where:

> . . . if they don't give us half a chance, Don't even give
>   us a second glance
> Then Geordie, with my blessings, burn them down.

Actually, the notion of burning anything down, or indeed any inflammatory or revolutionary fervour, was something the march organisers were desperate to avoid. Price's lyric though has no such qualms and ends by concluding that 1974 finds the working-class north as disadvantaged as it was in 1936 and in the same need of salvation.

There's a musical, *Cuddy's Miles*, based on the Jarrow march, written by John Miles: a seventies rocker probably best known for his grandiose hit 'Music', whose granddad Cuthbert (or Cuddy) was one of the march's two cooks. Just in case you think the kids are missing out, a New Zealand company produced a cuddly bear toy called Jarrow which the little 'uns could play with whilst reading *The Road to London*. Andrew Matthews' slim book was produced in conjunction with the National History Curriculum in 1997 and tells the tale of Clogger, a little lad from Jarrow who stows away on the march. While loosely based on real events, the real stowaways never got out of the north east and certainly didn't make it all the way as Clogger does. Along the way, he gets a few terse lectures about the essentially inequitable nature of capitalism and specifically the failings of Stanley Baldwin's Conservative administration. Produced just as New Labour were sweeping to power, the tone of the book is decidedly partisan. It ends with Clogger's dad explaining Baldwin's refusal to meet the marchers (you can still pick up the book quite easily on eBay, so clearly not all were pulped by incoming Conservative education secretaries post 2010):

> 'He's frightened. The whole governments afraid there'll be a revolution like the one they had in Russia ...'
> On the train back to Jarrow, Clogger was quiet for a long time.
> 'Dad,' he said eventually, 'isn't there a way of sharing things out, so that rich people aren't quite so rich but people like us have enough to get by?'

On the small screen, Peter Flannery's epic TV drama *Our Friends in the North* began life as a stage play for the Royal Shakespeare Company in 1982. As writer in residence when the RSC staged a cycle of Shakespeare's history plays, Flannery was seized by the thought that his Newcastle background – the legacy of the Jarrow Crusade, housing, industry, corruption – could form the basis of a large-scale work based on life in England in the 1960s, 70s and 80s. Initially keen, the BBC then dragged its feet for years. Flannery said later, 'I remember pitching it to BBC executive Alan Yentob as a drama about post-war social housing, probably because I'd spent the day writing one of those scenes. He looked alarmed. Two days later, I'd have said it was all about sex and Soho. It got through eventually.' When it did come to the screen, it was recognised instantly and widely as one of the greatest achievements of British television of any era and made stars of its young cast Gina McKee, Mark Strong, Christopher Eccleston and Daniel Craig. Thus the Jarrow march can claim to have indirectly shaped the future of two other legends in the pantheon of British romantic myth, *Dr Who* and James Bond.

In the opening episode of *Our Friends in the North*, it's 1964 and Nicky, played by Eccleston, has returned to Tyneside after a summer's activism in the USA with the civil rights movement. Almost immediately, his new-found political zeal brings him into conflict with his disillusioned dad Felix. Felix shows no enthusiasm for the future Labour government that seems likely after the forthcoming election. 'The Labour Party of which I was once proud to be a member were the first to condemn the Jarrow marchers as hooligans. They stabbed us in the back before we got to Durham. We were sold down the river long before you were born, son.'

Nicky's reply across the kitchen table echoes the dog walker on the Pelaw Grange road.

'Here we go. It never takes long, does it? ... The Jarrow march.'

Flannery is from Jarrow, had family members on the march, and the scene is clearly drenched in memory and meaning. About four months before setting off on my march, I spoke with Peter Flannery about representations of working-class life in the media. *Our Friends in the North* treated such people with a Tolstoyan depth and, despite that note of exasperation in Nicky/Peter's attitude to his father's generation, there's a real pride and loyalty to the values of an older era which drove Flannery to get his work on screen despite the misgivings of commissioning editors in offices in W1.

> One very famous controller of BBC 2 said, 'Does it have to have the word "North" in it? And does it have to be about the Labour Party? They're failures. I don't want it to be about failure.' So isn't it interesting that they only agreed to make it when Labour were almost in power and fashionable again? In our hearts, we knew that my dad's generation were right but we didn't want to trade on the old gripes and grudges. I looked at my parents – why are they so gloomy and cynical about political purpose when I felt so optimistic? In my youth it felt like a sea change was coming. Doors were opening in your own head. We felt on the brink of something better, not like Jarrow, but a real change. But you can't divorce that from an era that's gone now – the era of funding. That's what makes things possible. What made it possible for me wasn't my role models like Courtney and O'Toole and Richard Burton, brilliant though they were, it was the fact that Durham County Council were willing to give me a grant of twelve pounds a week.

Thanks to social media and a few posts of mine, I had some new friends in the north. Their tweets and messages ping into my timelines over the weekend. Graeme Fenwick tells me that his 93-year-old next-door neighbour waved off the marchers as a little girl in a Jarrow street. Laura Perlmann remembers being hugely proud to play Ellen Wilkinson in her school play about the march. A few correspondents, like Peter Flannery, actually had relatives on the march. Joanne Hackett-Smith's granddad, John 'Smiler' Harney, wrote a poem about his experiences on the march that she says she'll send me a copy of. Iris Walls wrote:

> Hi Stuart, my uncles Edward Stead and Sammy Needham were two of the marchers. Sammy looked after the dog which joined the march and stayed with them right throughout the journey until back in Jarrow. Are you going to be at the Civic reception on 5 October at Jarrow Town Hall? It's only 60 or so yards from Christ Church. It starts at 12.30, Wednesday.

I wonder whether I should use my years of rock journalist expertise and savvy to 'blag' my way on the guest list. Perhaps not. I'm not on 'official business', nor am I 'Beefy' Botham stomping along mob-handed for charity. Nonetheless I jot down the time and venue in my brand-new Jarrow notebook specially purchased for the journey (with small concealed pen in the spine), place it with laptop, shoes, soapbag, maps, carefully rolled and folded shirts and trousers, phone, chargers, cables, replacement contact lenses and other assorted paraphernalia inside my rucksack. Noting with some satisfaction that I still have several litres to spare, I settle back as the train makes the long pull over Shap Fell from my soft north of silent mills and damp valleys into the high lonely north of sea and mountain and, once, of steel and ships.

PRE-AMBLE

There are some cities one never enters without a gladdening of the heart and a quickening of the pulse. Newcastle ranks high among them, possessing that dazzling alchemy of fine buildings and big, open water that always works a certain magic trick. Just as no man ever felt more glamorous or sophisticated than when rounding a corner in his water taxi motor boat with a wake of foam, turning onto the *Gran Canale* and seeing the *palazzos* of Venice or the bridges of Rialto or Accademia rise up before the prow, so (in a quite different way admittedly) it's always a palpable thrill to cross the Tyne by the high line over the King Edward VII bridge and see the best-looking city in England today spread alluringly below me as the weekend begins.

The train is indubitably the best way to arrive. All the 'Toon's' most thrilling features crowd and elbow each other sideways to get into shot like those daft excitable kids you see behind sports reporters on TV. At the Ouseburn end there's the stately brick edifice of the Baltic Warehouse, now a fabulous art gallery, glowering grandly across at the huge, sleek, curvaceous silver snail of the Sage Concert Hall. In between is the posh apartment block whose two adjoining rooftop penthouse flats are owned – so a Geordie once told me – by local lads made good, Ant and Dec, which is probably far too cute to be true. The star of this particular show though, as always, is the Tyne itself and its various bridges – graceful and slender, muscular and imposing, funky, functional, old, new – each echoing its neighbour along the broad, silky muscle of the river.

In four days' time, my Jarrow march starts in earnest and I've arrived in the north east early to meet people, do some research, attend a couple of events, mull, acclimatise, buy plasters and toothpaste and generally do all the things that I'm sure I won't have time to after I stride optimistically out of Jarrow on Wednesday morning to spend the next month trekking the long miles to London. I breakfast at a busy greasy spoon tucked below the giant arches of the Tyne Bridge, built by Dorman Long of Middlesbrough between 1925 to 1928; pure architectural Gotham in green metal and tensile steel. Two council workmen come in, paint spattered and chalky – that's their appearance, not their names – and proceed to put themselves efficiently and remorselessly outside two large breakfasts whilst gutting and filleting the morning's tabloids. They dispense swift, terse, unrepeatable judgements on Theresa May, global warming and Ken Bruce's PopMaster. I ask them if they have they heard of the Jarrow march. They tell me they know the song, and after some debate and rehearsal, proceed to sing me a challenging, atonal version of 'Fog on the Tyne' by Lindisfarne.

I head from the waterside to town proper up the steepening curve of Grey Street, the most elegant thoroughfare in England according to John Betjeman. I pop into Newcastle's finest department store Fenwick's for last minute supplies. Foot balm, a flat cap (a nod of solidarity to Jarrow's marchers), some new socks and some shaving oil. This being the modern world – and me wanting to keep people apprised as to my progress – I tweet a picture of my purchases. A trollish home counties dentist posts, 'If the Jarrow Marchers could see this, they would give you a righteous shoe-ing.' No they wouldn't, I tweet back, tetchily perhaps. This sort of stuff riles me though; the implication that one should 'know one's place' and that working-class people deserve no better than spittoons and scrag end. I attach to my reply my favourite quote from Nye Bevan when challenged about his love of lobster and champagne, 'Only the best for the working class'.

Once installed in my room, I go through a long-practised routine. Turn off the wall mounted TV with the boomingly loud dance music satellite channel the chambermaid had on, boot up the MacBook and log on (oh, the simple, unalloyed joy of hotels that don't require you to fill in an online questionnaire or decipher those weird hieroglyphics), turn down the aircon temperature (you can grow rubber in most British hotel rooms, and in those that you can't, you could cryogenically store Walt Disney). Then I start an afternoon of research. This begins with a dip into the labyrinthine depths of the BBC's fabled Redux website and archive.

The British Broadcasting Corporation was still a fledgling operation in 1936. It was gearing up to broadcast its first television programmes during the march, actually commencing them the day after the marchers reached London. Perhaps this is why the BBC appears to harbour such a crush on the Jarrow Crusade. This has shown itself through many documentaries, plays and features down the 80 years since. Looming large during the corporation's formative years, the march is now bound up in some way with what Hollywood would call the BBC's 'origin story'. The Jarrow Crusade fits well with the BBC's remit and ethos: national stories that emphasise consensus and moral example rather than conflict, dissent and entrenched interest. A more cynical take on this might be that Jarrow is the BBC's favourite protest because it was the meekest and most obliging to the powers that be.

Redux is one of the BBC's more secret services. When I was first tipped off about it, it was very much Auntie Beeb's Fight Club, in that the first rule of Redux seemed to be that you didn't talk about it. A verbal invite was whispered to me in a TV green room by a producer friend and after that I had to apply to join by writing to the shadowy cabal of technocrats who administer it. After a week or so, I received an anonymous email saying that I was in. I was elated. I felt like I'd been accepted into a more benign version of the Freemasons or a less metrosexual Groucho Club. The Magic Circle perhaps, or Big Chief I-Spy's Club.

Redux is an archive of BBC TV and Radio programmes. But what an archive. Invented by boffins in the BBC's hidden techno-lair at Hook Norton on a day off from the official corporation business of spreading communism and undermining decent British values, it is a vast, bottomless resource for nerds and pros. Firing up my laptop, I enter the search term 'Jarrow march' and look up the most recent result on the subject, a BBC TV documentary *The Road From Jarrow* on the march and its legacy dating from 1996.

It was with the most profound sinking of the heart that I make out, through the juddery visual tape hiss, the unmistakable features of presenter Sir Bernard Ingham, Margaret Thatcher's former press secretary and once ubiquitous bluff pontificator of the loony right. Much of my dismay rests on aesthetic considerations. Sir Bernard is a hard man to gaze comfortably upon for any length of time and such discomfort is only heightened by his belligerent, nasal 'Zippy from *Rainbow* on helium' vocal delivery. My other complaint is more substantive, however; namely that inviting a right-wing ideologue to author a piece on a leftist protest is perhaps not the best guarantee of fairness or accuracy. (A reader called David Walker tweeted me wryly about the choice of Ingham as presenter on the Jarrow march: 'Blimey, did he advocate using unidentifiable policemen on horseback to break it up?' – an Orgreave joke.) This perverse booking would seem a perfect illustration of a malaise of the modern media, that of 'false balance', the notion whereby kneejerk gainsaying is equated with truth. At least they just give Michael Portillo documentaries about old railway lines and steam engines.

Anyway, it's not long before Sir Bernard deviates from historical analysis into one of his trademark riffs of irascible windbaggery. 'Discipline has given way to indiscipline. Family, the one thing that sustained the Jarrow marchers, has gone to pot.' When Ellen Wilkinson is mentioned, it is through gritted teeth, and she is described as 'Fiery Helen' or 'Wee Ellen' when her nickname was universally 'Red Ellen', a designation that presumably stuck in Bernard's throat. It soon became very clear that not only was this rubbish, it was self-serving, ahistorical rubbish, although there were some good contributions from Peter Flannery and marcher Con Shiels. A few minutes though were enough to make me blithely unconcerned that the other two episodes of this have been wiped. I make another 'advanced' pass though the archive and happily I find a more recent and insightful looking radio documentary about the Jarrow march from 2008. Naturally, it is presented by Michael Portillo.

Despite the perverse choice of presenter once again, it is really very much better; more sociological, less opinionated, and in essence a consideration of why the Jarrow march lives on whilst the many hunger marches of the era have been forgotten. The documentary touches upon what would seem to me to be the obvious explanation: the men of Jarrow essentially came politely and with cap in hand, without the dangerous whiff of revolutionary sulphur of the older communist marches.

That night I walked in the dusk across Newcastle to one of its cultural and historical landmarks, the Literary and Philosophical Society. Newcastle is proud of the Lit and Phil and it's as much a part of the cultural fabric of the city as the Big Market, St James' Park or the Angel of the North, and rather older than any of them. Established in 1793, it is the largest private library outside London. It is where Joseph Swan first demonstrated the electric light bulb. It received Britain's first wombat and duck-billed platypus and notable current members include Alexander Armstrong and Neil Tennant. In the beginning, it was styled as a 'conversation club', albeit one in which discussion of religion and politics was strictly forbidden. That has since been relaxed and so there are no awkward moments or angry shushing tonight during Matt Perry's lecture on Ellen Wilkinson, of whom he has written a comprehensive biography. It's compelling stuff and Matt doesn't gloss over some of the anomalies of her career and mysteries of her life: though initially a staunch supporter of Indian liberation, when in government, she thought we should put the troublesome Gandhi in gaol, and of course there are the vague and cloudy circumstances of her sad premature death.

Matt kindly gives me a copy of his book and tells me I should visit the Jarrow Crusade eightieth anniversary exhibition at South Shields Museum that he's curated. We also make a tentative arrangement to meet at an event I am very much looking forward to, the tempting if queerly named Jarrow March Eightieth Anniversary Fun Day at Monkton Stadium in the town. How could anyone resist? Tombola, food, brass bands, stalls, activist fun and special guest star, one Jeremy Bernard Corbyn, MP for Islington, leader of Her Majesty's Opposition, the Labour Party, and saint or fool depending on your point of view. I tell Matt I'm looking forward to it.

Geordies are proud of their Metro transport system, and Jarrow particularly so as it was the brainchild and passion of Michael Campbell, the so-called Statesman of Jarrow, leader of Tyne and Wear council who managed to champion the project to completion at a time when Britain was in hock to its eyeballs and could barely keep the lights on. When work began in 1974 it was the biggest urban transport project Britain had attempted in the twentieth century. Tunnels were driven beneath the city's streets and viaducts thrown airily across the Tyne and Ouseburn valleys. It has always been non-smoking and wheelchair friendly and classical music was piped into stations to improve the 'passenger waiting environment'. It opened in the summer of 1980 to instant acclaim and popularity. When my Geordie mate Stod came back to college for the autumn term that year, he talked of little else.

The Metro's sixty stations are a potted history of British transport architecture from late Victorian at Tynemouth and art deco at West Monkseaton to the1980s minimalism of Park Lane and Ilford Road. At South Shields station, a fruit and veg stall has blossomed under its brutalist steel girders which is a neat bit of civic adaptation. Having certainly got the rucksack capacity but not the desire for a few heads of cauliflower, I pass it by and head to the South Shields Museum and the Jarrow exhibition.

Celebrations of local culture are of variable entertainment value, as anyone who's ever broken their leg at a Gloucester cheese rolling or attended a potato picking festival in Kent can attest. But they seem ever more crucial as municipal Britain takes wave after wave of battering from central government. Despite grand speeches about 'devolving autonomy' and a 'northern powerhouse', we are the most centralised country in the Western world. Westminster has the nation's purse strings in a grip of iron and for every pound raised by tax, 91p is allocated by central government. Towns like South Shields and Jarrow have been hardest hit.

Put baldly, the north east is the poorest region in Britain. In an essay of December 2016 entitled 'The Strange Death of Municipal England', Tom Crewe states that, 'almost a billion pounds have been sucked out of its economy since 2010 [and] it has the highest percentage of deprived neighbourhoods in the country ... Newcastle City Council has reduced its budget by £221 million with another £100 million in cuts planned for the next two years. Leader Nick Forbes told the *Guardian*, "people went white ... at the prospect of it".' So this is a northern power house that cannot afford the electricity bill.

At South Shields Museum though, however embattled, there's a flutter of excitement among the staff as a film crew from the BBC's *Look North* magazine show are upstairs in the exhibition hall. 'I'm afraid that the museum is closed to the public at the moment,' says an earnest, diligent, young staff member. 'Ah, I see ...' I say and produce my BBC pass, always a useful thing to have in one's pocket, even if the picture makes one look like Alan Titchmarsh's idiot younger half-brother. I am waved through under false pretences which makes me feel rather

a heel and so, once upstairs, I lurk outside the inner door until
the filming is over.

The interviewees are Matt Perry (who's having a busy week)
and Tom Kelly, a local writer and poet who along with Matt has
been working with school kids in the town to produce some
excellent, inspiring work about community and history. Matt is
a boyish academic in mod casuals, Tom a genial silver-haired
Geordie in a stripy jacket. Matt and Tom are hoping not just to
keep alive the memory of the march but to use it as a springboard
for all kinds of creative activities. A workshop in which:

> Pupils will examine archive material, photographs and
> personal accounts to bring the story to life as they think
> about the lives, hopes and feelings of the men, as well
> as thinking about the general morale and conditions.
> Afterwards, they will put themselves in the shoes of
> the marching men, to write either a poem, diary entry,
> song or newspaper article. The day can also include a
> session making banners, posters and badges.

It's easy to mock such well-intentioned efforts at educating kids
about 'people's history'. But after one workshop, five kids came
back and said they had found out that they had relatives, great-
grandfathers and great uncles on the march and that it had made
them feel 'ten feet tall', and had sparked long conversations
between generations in the family. I remember grim, pointless
field trips spent brass rubbing the tombs of long dead viscounts.
Keeping the stories and culture and sacrifices of their granddads
and grandmas alive for these kids is surely just as valid a way to
spend a Tuesday afternoon.

In the exhibition, portraits and testimonies bring the
marchers vividly to life. James Henry Walters hadn't worked
since being gassed twenty years before at the front (62 per cent
of the men were First World War veterans) and was keeping
a wife and four children on 36 shillings a week. Touchingly,

he commented, 'The march will be a success … the country's behind us.' Philip McGhee was one of the lucky ones in that he had only been out of work two years when the march took place. There is a sweet picture of the youngest and oldest marchers: John Farndale who at 18 had worked two weeks since leaving school at 14 and Geordie Smith, 62 and a veteran of the Boer War. Framed on the wall is the original of John 'Smiler' Harney's poem (my correspondent Joanne's granddad), touching in its defiantly high spirits.

Playing on a continuous loop are the two brief fragments of surviving newsreel footage of the march; the men on their way to Darlington ('great sympathy for this orderly march' says the narrator, plummily) and their sodden final entry into London. The Metropolitan Police had originally tried to prevent all filming of the march fearing it would create too much sympathy for the men but in the end they grudgingly relented. Seeing Ellen and the tired, soaked phalanx on this grainy monochrome film, trudging across London in the dreary, pouring rain, water cascading from their antique sou'westers and capes, reminds me of just what I've got in store over the next month. I make a mental note to check the long-range weather forecast, through splayed fingers possibly.

The morning of the Fun Day though dawns bright and warm across the north east and, though I don't know it yet, it's a herald of a mercifully mild October to come. There is for sure a rich, easily mined irony in styling the commemoration of a hunger march as a 'Fun Day'. Wags across social media have clamoured to point this out when I mentioned the event. 'Relive those heady days of the Means Test and rickets with a go on the bouncy castle and a jumbo hot dog' and so on and so on. They have a point. I thought it was important that I was there though. I wanted to sense the mood of the community, I wanted to see how Labour's newly re-elected leader acquitted himself and I really like hot dogs, especially the al fresco variety.

Having initially been distinctly cool on the idea of the Jarrow march, not to say positively obstructive, the Labour Party, like the Beeb, have spent much of the intervening eight decades getting enthusiastically on board. The Jarrow memorial in the town (one of them anyway) has been unveiled not once but twice by successive leaders Michael Foot and Neil Kinnock, both seeking glory by association and presumably glossing over the lack of party support back in the day. Carrying on in this vein, the Labour ruling executive of 2016, unlike that of 1936, are keen to express their solidarity with the sacralised memory of the march. So much so that they have sent their top man up from London for the job, rather like the dispatching of Michael Caine in *Get Carter* except hopefully without anyone getting pushed off a multi storey car park or shot and dumped in a massive coal scuttle.

The Jarrow Fun Day on 1 October 2016 is the first public appearance of Jeremy Corbyn since being re-elected as leader of the Labour Party with an increased majority a week earlier; which is a sentence that no sane person could have envisaged reading or writing before 12 September 2015. Though an MP for over 30 years, he had never held any position of authority or responsibility, and during the party's 13 years in power, when he might have been expected to help with the business of government, Corbyn voted against the whip 428 times – more than any other Labour MP. Then he was regarded, as one unnamed Labour insider told the *New Yorker*, as 'a quaint irrelevance'. His relevance may be arguable but his quaintness is not. In a paroxysm of either stupidity or optimism depending on one's point of view, Labour introduced a system whereby three quid bought you a vote in their leadership election. Corbyn was washed to power on this unleashed tide of activism, and some mutterings of chicanery.

Many of those who'd been vaguely aware of him as a bearded antediluvian spear-carrier of Labour's London left have been baffled, not to say appalled, by Corbyn's ascent. Not just by his rise to power – stranger things have happened in Westminster – but his elevation to Che Guevara–style counter-cultural icon among some young and not so young. (I gave the piece I wrote for the *New Statesman* on the Fun Day the title 'JC Un Rock Star' but they didn't use the headline, perhaps unfamiliar with Bill Wyman's solo hits.) Corbyn is a phenomenon that seemed to have disappeared along with Benny Hill, Red Wedge and student union bars named after Steve Biko. He's a variety of political animal most thought had become extinct, a Spartist dinosaur reeking of hummus and hemp and definitely not the smoky fires of industry.

As a Corbyn agnostic with a strong disposition towards downright atheism, I wanted to see how the north east took to the new Messiah. Over his first year in the job, I'd found him weak and disengaged, especially on issues close to the heart of the working-class north. He had been almost silent on Orgreave and Hillsborough: both emotive events back powerfully in the news. Conversely, you couldn't shut him up on the Middle East and Arab–Israeli matters, and believe me I had wanted to.

There was another flavouring in the mix. Tony Blair was the longstanding MP for nearby Sedgefield. Many in the north east still regard him as one of their own and had never enjoined with the now prevalent view of him as slick warmonger. The New Labour love-in of 1997 now makes some rather embarrassed. Power corrupts, but it also makes others uncomfortable, particularly those who'd prefer a state of continual carping but largely impotent opposition. There was much muddled and dubious logic surrounding the Iraq war. But Professor Peter Clarke, author of the *The Locomotive of War* put it well when he told *BBC History* magazine, 'Blair took a very moral view of why the British and Americans should invade Iraq. Something he had reason to rue afterwards but even if it was a terrible mistake, we should not doubt his sincerity'. Many brilliant voices of the secular left – Christopher Hitchens most famously – thought that, in essence, it was a just war. Also it seemed to me that in the revisionist rush to excoriate Blair and his legacy, we had forgotten SureStart schemes for working-class families, the now-abolished AIM education grants that supported many poor ethnic minority students, the introduction of the minimum wage and many other achievements which no one should be ashamed about.

In this conflicted, sceptical state of mind, I make my way through the sunny, pleasant suburban streets of South Tyneside between Hebburn and Jarrow to Monkton Stadium. Along Dene Terrace, the houses and gardens are well kept, the streets clean, the people busy. Eighty years ago, when the last-minute arrangements for the near military planning of the Jarrow march were taking place here, Dene Terrace would have looked and felt very different. The faces thinner, the streets grimier and the houses grimmer. Monkton Stadium wouldn't have been here either, since this fine local landmark and resource was built as a direct result of the Jarrow march. In June 1937, unemployed men from the area (including some marchers) rebuilt a derelict sports ground with money from the Surrey Fund, established after the Jarrow march by Sir John Jarvis, MP for South Shields. In the years since, it's become one of the crucibles of north-eastern athletics and distance running, training ground of Steve Cram and more.

When I arrive at the gate to pick up my wristband from councillor Audrey, I am told, a little breathlessly, that 'he' is already here: 'We gave him a dinner at the Lakeside pub last night. I think he enjoyed it.' Inside, there's a low-level buzz of activity. As well as the usual Fun Day stalwarts – stalls selling smelly soaps and wonky home-made craft items, the aromatic burger van and the little kids serenely orbiting in giant teacups – there's a tangible if cordial political dimension and presence; trade union groups hoping to save the local hospital, a lively contingent of ladies from Women Against State Pension Inequality dressed as suffragettes. Various local politicians are waiting for their chance at the mike, but they all know that they are the support act. The star here is slightly younger than Mick Jagger and has become a slightly odder kind of rock star politician.

The stands are full-ish of Jarrow and Hebburn families. Many have the names of a Jarrow marcher on small placards that they wave. Congratulating myself on recognising her from her tiny Twitter profile photo, I spot '@JoHack', or Joanne Hackett-Smith, one of the first people to contact me when I 'reached out' (in the modish parlance) for people with Jarrow march stories. Jo is smart, blonde, 30-something and rightly proud of her march associations. She's a civil servant, a local girl, and her great-grandfather ('Granda' as Geordies have it) was John 'Smiler' Harney whose sweet poem is in the South Shields exhibition. He lived in Lime Street Jarrow with wife Eleanor and was father to ten children, though only eight survived (at the time of the march, Jarrow had one of the worst infant mortality rates in Britain).

When Smiler reached London, he met a woman who said she could offer his family work, particularly his daughter who could clean for her. He continued to write to the woman and he eventually received a fancy coat in the post. She said if his daughter wore the coat and travelled to London, she would hire her as a live-in housekeeper. 'This was a bribe I suppose,' reflects Jo.

'So he sent Florrie, my granny, aged 13 to London on the train alone. She arrived at a posh house in London where the lady of the house was a doctor's wife. They had one child and the mother didn't work. She was awful to my grannie apparently; she had to scrub all the floors before she would feed her on a morning. She was also made to eat alone, with no interaction with the family whatsoever and she could only use the tissue paper from oranges for the toilet.'

Florrie was desperately unhappy, but didn't dare tell her father John because she knew the family back in Jarrow needed the money. Such experiences were not uncommon. Many young, working-class girls from industrial Cumbria, Lancashire, the north east and Wales were sent down into domestic service with well-to-do London families that was effectively little more than slavery and certainly not as benign as the world of *Upstairs Downstairs* or *Downton Abbey*. Eventually, one day, some old Jarrow friends also in service in London called for Florrie and the doctor's wife refused to let her leave the house, demanding she went to her room. 'Imagine the anxiety and fear of a 13-year-old girl being controlled by a complete stranger,' says Jo.

The Jarrow girls went to the local bobby on the beat and explained the situation. By happy coincidence, he was from Sunderland. He went to the house and demanded Florrie come to the door with her suitcase packed. Florrie went home to Jarrow and lived into her nineties. 'But granny always said she was "sold down the river for a bliddy coat!"' remembers Jo. We could have talked much more, but at this point I had to take my leave of Jo as, with a discernible rustle of excitement, the Fun Day's main attraction was passing beardedly amongst us.

While it would be wrong to say that Corbyn's presence created the same scenes of unhinged mania that might attend the arrival of Beyoncé, or Barack Obama or one of the judges on *Strictly Come Dancing*, there was a definite buzz in the air. As he was led around the grassy enclosure, patiently and amiably nodding as various things were pointed out to him, a small but intense knot of admirers tailed him closely. I fell into their wake and together we circumnavigated the arena like a clump of drifting frog spawn.

If I was expecting dazzling bon mots, Bevanesque oratory or high wattage charm, I was to be disappointed. His visible mood as he was corralled into several selfies was that of a man who would much rather have been at a polytechnic sit-in or an airless council chamber in Haringey debating sanctions against South Africa, both of which I imagined he did enthusiastically 'back in the day'. Eventually, with a flourish by the brass band, activities proper commenced.

The host of the event was a local TV anchorman who was well known to the crowd, and by far the best dressed of the various people to take the stage that day. His daughter, a budding pop chanteuse, also provided some musical entertainment, although the song she sang was one of those enervating John Lewis advert ballads rather than 'The Red Flag' or an inspiring anthem about Soviet steel production, both of which I'd have enjoyed more.

Jarrow's MP Stephen Hepburn gave a doughty and on-message speech by way of introduction to the Labour leader which was as much about JC (Jeremy Corbyn) as JC (Jarrow Crusade). This reached a weirdly obsequious climax as he evoked the trials of the marching men. 'Had he been at the side of the road when those marchers passed by, Jeremy would have shared his sandwiches with them,' he said, and at least one audience member found the faintly Christ-like tone of this eulogy somewhat creepy.

The *New Yorker* compared Corbyn to Chauncey Gardiner, the simple-minded gardener embraced as a guru in Peter Sellers's *Being There*. But soon after the man himself takes the mike it becomes very clear to me that JC is not so much Chauncey or that other JC (Jesus Christ) as JP (John Peel), the late radio presenter and alternative music guru. The two men have many things in common. They share a physiognomy; both bearded, softly spoken, mildly drony. Both were educated at private school in Shrewsbury and acquired greatest affection and fame in middle age. But there's more than that. JC and JP deftly cultivated images as principled mavericks and saintly rebels despite long, comfortable careers in two of the cosiest berths in the British Establishment – the BBC and the Labour Party. All the while though, they presented to the world a much-admired resistance to being sucked into the mainstream, even whilst being at its very heart. (There are few places more mainstream or 'Establishment' than the Palace of Westminster or the *Top of The Pops* studio.)

Both exhibit(ed) a haughty disdain for the shallower, slicker elements and personalities of their chosen worlds. Peel routinely made sport of people like Tony Blackburn, a genuine soul fan who did more to promote black music on BBC radio than anyone else in his era, and the admittedly sickly/sinister Bates/Edmonds axis at 'wonderful Radio One'. In Corbyn's case, he has billed himself as polar opposite and antidote to the stage-managed spin machinery of New Labour, Blair and Alastair Campbell. By hiding their not inconsiderable egos behind a gentle wooliness, Corbyn and Peel are 'National Treasures' for the kind of liberal who bridles at the idea of national treasures, considering them painfully 'little Englander' and celebrated by the likes of the *Daily Express*. My grumbling discontent (occasionally flaring into incandescent rage) with Corbyn is that it is not his beard, allotment or even politics that make him the polar opposite of Blairism but his electability. (As I write this, before 2017's snap election, his poll ratings are miserable, though admittedly the last year has taught us to be wary of the pollster.)

JC's speech was cogent and thoughtful if short on emotional fireworks. He gave a genuinely fine tribute to 'Red Ellen' whilst brandishing a well-thumbed first edition of *The Town That Was Murdered* from the Left Book Club. He went down well of course; this is Labour's heartland and these people are loyal. In private, a few I spoke to were downbeat about his electoral clout and competence but others said that they found him fresh and inspirational. I acquired a coffee and a bag of doughnuts and decided to listen to the other speeches before going back to the hotel to pack.

Next up was an executive of public service union Unison who'd come straight from central casting circa 1984 with a strident, staccato delivery and a range of 'off the peg' agitprop ('and let us be clear that we say as a movement to THIS Tory government'). There followed a smooth LibDem, then a pleasant lady from the Greens whose lengthy factual re-telling of the march read from a piece of paper was lovely whilst smacking of an earnest school project ('This term we have been studying the Jarrow Crusade which took place in October 1936 …'). Funniest by far was the nonagenarian Conservative candidate who sat on a folding chair beaming and said, 'I am from Jarrow and I live in Jarrow and naturally I haven't agreed with a thing I've heard here today ...'

I watched as Jeremy was hustled very gently into the changing rooms and I assume out to a waiting car, since I didn't think even a cyclist of his commitment could have come on his folding Brompton. The week before, his share of the Labour members', vote grew to 68 per cent. A huge influx of new members have made Labour the biggest political party in Western Europe. All this proves to some that he is destined to be our next Prime Minister. As many have pointed out, however, this is rather akin to saying that Liverpool will win the Premier League because the Kop want them to. As I set off for my three-hundred-mile trek to London, Downing Street seemed a long way off for me and JC.

STAGE ONE

JARROW TO CHESTER-LE-STREET

5 October, 12 miles

We are a nation besotted with statuary. Latterly, our near immediate response to the passing of a beloved celebrity is to demand a disturbing, generally unrecognisable facsimile of them somewhere of local significance: Eric Morecambe leaping like a salmon on that town's seafront, Harold Wilson pipeless outside Huddersfield station, the John Lennon with the tiny body and alarmingly large head outside the Cavern, Liverpool. At the time of writing there are campaigns to erect statues of Victoria Wood in Bury, various suffragettes outside Parliament, and David Bowie in Brixton, Bromley and seemingly everywhere he ever booked into a Travelodge for the night. There was briefly a campaign to commission a 300-feet-high golden statue of former Dr Feelgood singer Lee Brilleaux in Southend which sadly failed.

For every 'controversial' abstract bronze on the windswept piazza of a new town, or geometric fibreglass scalene triangle in front of a Midlands police station that creates local kerfuffle, there are thousands of silent sentinels that we pass by every day without a thought. And, ignoring the occasional celebrated Peter Pan or Sherlock Holmes, most of these stolid figures are the sons of empire: straight-backed, moustachioed, mercantile, magisterial, military and nearly always men (only 2.7 per cent of

British figurative statues are women and they are mostly either allegorical, royal or nude).

The statue of Sir Charles Mark Palmer on the main street in Jarrow leaves you in little doubt as to who once bossed this town like a personal fiefdom. He stands above the main street puffed and proprietorial, gazing out over the hard little town. Below his feet is a lengthy, boastful CV graven into the stone: 'Sir C Mark Palmer, baronet, born South Shields, November 3rd 1822. Founder of the Palmer works and of the town of Jarrow of which he was the first mayor in 1875 ... originator of the first steam screw ... Member of Parliament for North Durham ... this statue erected in 1903 by the workmen of Palmer's company and a few friends commemorates a life devoted to the social advancement of the working classes, the prosperity of Jarrow and the industrial progress of Tyneside ...' Whether the working classes of Jarrow would still have coughed up for a statue to Sir Charles 30 years later is very much open to debate.

The Jarrow marchers have their own memorials of course, scattered around their home town: a crude and often vandalised mosaic in a grim underpass, a bronze of Red Ellen at the head of a group of men in Morrisons' car park. (At its unveiling, surviving marcher Con Whalen was persuaded to wear a Morrisons' badge for the pictures.) There's a stark metal silhouette of marching men at Jarrow Metro station too. But while these form part of the everyday street furniture of the area, none is as grandly prominent in Jarrow as Sir Charles surveying what once was very definitely his domain. Everywhere in the town are shades and echoes of his marshalling of the long defunct yards; Palmer Street, the Palmer Hospital, the Palmer Nursing Home, even the Palmer's Tavern pub.

I was last in Jarrow a decade ago, researching an earlier book called *Pies and Prejudice*. I was, I hope, honest and fair but what I wrote was no puff piece or tourist blurb and I've always thought that the least I could do was come back and explore again. A passing Jarrovian in the street reminds me of my earlier visit. He passes by with a wry, not unfriendly smile, a handshake and a swift nod. 'I hope you like it a bit more than last time, Stuart'. And I do. There is still the faint echo of neglect and decline, of hard times being resisted and there is none of the easy, comfortable atmosphere of content that I'll increasingly find as I travel south. But there's life here and people going about their business on a glorious October morning and no sense of a town cowed or beaten. There are, however, signs of Britain's remorseless and bizarre 'hipsterfication', something else I'll see much of on my journey. Jarrow now boasts retro emporiums where a fellow about town can get his tache waxed and his beard mascara'd. You can buy cupcakes and smoothies. Most noticeable of all for me is the transformation (from the exterior at least) of the pub that so unnerved me last time. The Jarrow Crusaders then was a dark, forbidding cave of gassy, pissy lagers, giant booming TVs and clanking fruit machines where everyone stopped talking, *American Werewolf in London* style, when I entered. Now it's McConnell's Gin And Ale House and has wood panelling, posh spirits and micro-brews. Who knows? It may still be a place a chap could get a thick ear but at least he could enjoy a chilled Masons Dry Gin (distilled from a small copper alembic still) whilst acquiring it.

It was the early hour rather than nervousness that stopped me popping in. And I was distracted by the appearance on the street corner of a man in a blue serge boiler suit carrying a large tray of sandwiches augmented by what may well have been vol-au-vents and bound for the side entrance of the town hall. This I took as a cue that the Jarrow eightieth anniversary civic reception was about to begin. A local and well-connected contact of mine (who shall be nameless) had tried to wangle me an invite to this event but had encountered stubborn resistance among the local council to 'journalist types'. I wasn't slighted by this at all but I did find it a little strange. From the embedded journalists of 1936 through BBC documentaries through various anniversary pieces, the press treatment of Jarrow's march has never been less than positive. In fact, one might even say, sentimentalised and gushing. So exactly what scandalous and profligate fillings were in those sandwiches. Caviar? Songbirds? Cruel and exorbitant pâtés from endangered species? Just what had they got to hide at that buffet?

Denied entry I may have been, but there was little chance of me starving to death in Jarrow. You would have to be extremely poor or painfully shy for this to occur. Little greasy spoons, prim cafés, pizza outlets, pie shops, chippies and cake shops abound. Rosie's Café. Hetty's Tea Room. Even butcher David C Hodgson ('purveyor of quality meats') will wipe his bloodied hands on his apron and seat you in the window by the hanging sides of beef for a 'delicious Saveloy, pease pudding and stuffing – £1.40' or a 'Full House Bellybuster – £2.95'. Pavement and café society is alive and well in 'Jarra' on a Wednesday mid-morning.

I plumped for beans on toast in Rosie's where, above the sizzle of bacon, the local radio news bulletin was reporting on yesterday's speech by recently installed PM Theresa May, asserting that the Tories were now 'the party of workers', occupying the centre ground vacated by Corbyn's Labour Party. Next was an item on Home Secretary Amber Rudd's proposal to force companies to disclose how many foreign workers they employ, which some business leaders called 'divisive and damaging'. Then it was back to the DJ who was trying to get a phone-in item going on what people thought was the most inspirational sandwich filling. I checked the website of the *South Shields Gazette* where a nice young journalist had written up an interview with me alongside a report on the Fun Day. Against all common sense, I broke an iron habit and dipped 'below the line' into the comments section where the dark things lurk. There was nothing nasty there – this is the north east after all – but one contributor, writing under the name 'Old News', reminded me that many are waiting at the keyboard to grind their personal axe.

There is no comparison between the desperate lives that our ancestors endured in the 1920s and 30s and today's luxury. They had NOTHING – but now even sanctioned lazybones STILL get state and voluntary aid despite being undeserving. So much so that today's Britain has been stupid enough to lavish money and houses even on to 3m workshy foreigners. The poor souls shown above got on with life after their march. Only the Labour Party seeks to profit from their poverty now.

On the way up the street I paused to look in Blackberry Estates's window to check local house prices. A three-bed new build semi is on offer for £110,000 billed as a 'must view', 'perfect for first time buyer, no chain'. Very different from the vertiginous London prices often in the news. But then, as I was going to find, I was a long way from London. I stopped off in Boots to buy some spare batteries and paracetamol and headed up to Christ Church for my 10.30 ceremonial start.

When you consider the loathing and contempt their local bishop held them in, starting the Jarrow march in an Anglican church with a service and a blessing might seem odd, grovelling even. Though a man of the cloth, Hensley Henson, Bishop of Durham, is one of the undisputed villains of the Jarrow mythos. This pillar of the Establishment and virulently anti-socialist member of the Lords regarded the marchers as a revolutionary mob and condemned several fellow bishops and clergymen for their warmth towards Jarrow and its plight and their 'foolish utterances'. In Jarrow, his condemnation of the march is well known and well remembered.

But then this was a 'crusade', and keen to be seen as such rather than a hunger march or anything similarly inflammatory. The mayor had wanted a minister with a crucifix to lead the march from the front but none willing could be found, which with the benefit of hindsight seems a good thing. Still the pews of the church were crammed with marchers and their wives plus various dignitaries resplendent in their chains of office, wigs and gowns and the clergy of all Jarrow's denominations; C of E, Catholic, Baptist and Presbyterian. From the pulpit, the men were encouraged not to 'drink the wine of violence' en route. They were then blessed by one of the many clergymen present and sent on their historic way to the rousing strains of 'Onward Goes the Pilgrim Band'.

Eighty years later the church is locked and barred so I can't even get in to see the little plaque commemorating the march. There's no signs of life, just a faded cardboard sign for the day nursery and toddler group in a grimy window of an outbuilding at the rear. An elderly lady passes with her dog which sniffs me listlessly, closely followed by a young Romanian mum with a buggy who tells me that the church doesn't open today. Maybe they'll do something special here for the hundredth anniversary, I hope. When I'd been planning my trip, I'd regularly been asked if I was having any kind of send-off or whether anyone would be walking with me. No, I'd answer, perhaps a little piously. This wasn't a sponsored walk or high-publicity charity event. It was research, exploration, discovery with maybe a little adventure along the way. I didn't want any hubristic palaver at the start. But as I stood alone in the deserted back street, the young mum, the old lady and the listless terrier all long gone, I couldn't help thinking that maybe just a tiny bit of palaver would have been nice.

The start of the original march had palaver galore. Almost the whole town turned out to see them off, police forcing crowds back behind cordons on to the pavement. Those lucky few townsfolk who had jobs and watched from their office or factory windows were reprimanded and told to get back to work. For the first time in years, the public gallery of the local court, usually a popular source of warmth and diversion for the unemployed, was empty. A thousand men had applied to be marchers and the round number of 200 were chosen, as well as the Mayor of Jarrow, three councillors, two journalists to record the journey and two supportive medical students to check health and administer any first aid. A second-hand bus was purchased for £20 and converted for their needs. This would go ahead with supplies, cooking gear, sleeping kit and sundries. Every man was provided with waterproofs, 1s 6d. pocket-money and two 1d. stamps a week. Sam Rowan was detailed as 'mail man', collecting and sending post for and from the men in every town (this was an England of four cheap postal deliveries a day where an invite to lunch could be sent at breakfast).

Outside the church, after the service, Mayor Thompson inspected the men. Seven of the original cohort had dropped out, most because of ill health or family pressure, with one fortunate chap having found a job. Substitutes were found quickly though including two neighbours, Bob Burns and Billy Beattie of Morpeth Avenue. Billy's wife was out so he left a note on the mantelpiece saying he'd set off for London and would see her in a month. Nowadays of course he'd text her, Facetime her or leave a post on her Facebook wall. Mine and Billy's Englands are similar in many ways, but only if you discount the astounding advances in everyday technology. I'd be helped in my journey by strange new forces: Google maps, Spotify, YouTube, Dark Sky Weather apps, Uber and Twitter. I was keen to feel resonances of 1936 and so I donned the flat cap I'd bought in Fenwicks and, with a nod to the marchers' mouth organ band, put Vaughan Williams's 'Romance for Harmonica and Orchestra' on my headphones as I left the little houses and narrow streets of Jarrow behind me.

Unexpectedly, the first few miles are lovely. You might even call them leafy. Very soon out of Jarrow a green walkway leads me away from town through Campbell Park, a verdant tract reclaimed for the community from what was once called 'the Crusher', a huge slag heap resulting from smelting iron ore at the Palmer's shipyard. An information board has an aerial shot from the time of the march which shows a vast, scarred muddied tract of prefabricated buildings and hulking machines. Now, in the caption's words, it has 'returned to field' and on this sparkling morning, the sound is that of coal tits and blackbirds rather than grinding and crushing.

I've given myself a few rules for the trip. As said, I will begin and end every day/stage in the same towns they did. I'll walk as much as I can but if a meeting or adventure suggests itself I'll buy time by hopping on a bus for a while as long as it covers the route of the march. I've decided that as I walk, if I can find a pleasanter path than the verges of a busy road I'll take it, provided it runs at least alongside their route. So I walk along the Bowes Railway Path, following the track of the old Bowes line, built by George Stephenson in 1826 to shift coal from the Durham pits to the River Tyne. When the marchers passed by, it was a busy, noisy and viable line and they'd have seen and heard the comings and goings of smoking and laden engines. Now it is part of our post-industrial heritage culture, quietened and retired into a long gentle walking and cycling route.

Springwell Bank is the village and cutting where the marchers made their first stop for lunch on that first day. They arrived by one o'clock to the cheerful light tenor of Councillor Gordon, 'the singing councillor'. They drank a couple of gallons of tea and ate corned beef sandwiches that involved forty pounds of corned beef and fifty loaves; this was a trip requiring military logistics. I stop, sit on a tree stump and try to catch the radio news on my phone, wondering about the social and political context of my trek compared to theirs. I catch the end of a radio magazine show and hear two items; one is about the current craze for spriralising vegetables, the other is about the protocols of group chat on WhatsApp.

I stomp the Bowes Railway Path for several more congenial miles through which, if you ignore the distant thrum of the A1(M) and the Sunderland Road, you get a real sense of how beyond the big population centres, 'the great north' is vast and wild and empty. Eventually this enormous silence and emptiness of green moors and distant hills gives way to the urban edge of Sunderland. This is the land of the Mackems, the nickname supposedly reflecting their manufacturing heritage and gift to the world, as in 'we mak'em and they tak'em'. This was a name given in Sunderland's heyday of mining, shipbuilding and glass – all gone now of course, but the city has seen massive regeneration in recent decades. Nissan came here famously and reset the region's economy. Danish mechanical engineers Grundfos and various service industries have relocated at Doxford International business park.

I walk though Crowther Industrial Park between the large striplit units of Schiedel Chimney Systems and Ronbar Flexible Conduits and Accessories, emerging onto the main road from a subway and into the prim bungalows and mock Palladian columns of Picktree suburb. Somewhere around here, 80 years ago today, borrowing a football from schoolkids who'd bunked off to greet them, 40 or so of the marchers played football in the street. The north east was and is football mad and was once a hotbed of British football talent, even if the area's giants are snoozing a little too soundly for local satisfaction these days. A prominent sign advises that I am entering into County Durham or 'Land of The Prince Bishops'. The Prince Bishops were a ruling class of noble clergymen of the fourteenth century onwards, but they always sound to me like a sixties beat group with bowl haircuts, white sports jackets and winklepickers.

After another hour down the roaring road, I finally enter Chester-le-Street as the sun drops low and slants blindingly across the quiet town. I'm about an hour ahead of the marchers. They arrived at 5pm to be met by local councillor Mr Robson and the women's section of the local Labour Party, who came to greet them with bread and jam. Marcher Sam Rowan said later that he would 'remember to his dying day' that he'd 'never seen men so disappointed in their lives' – presumably at a second round of sandwiches. Ungrateful perhaps, but then these men were tired and hungry and the contrast with the exultant send-off from home must have been marked. Was Chester-le-Street jealous or grudging of its local rival's new fame? Certainly some of the most generous and sympathetic receptions the Crusade would receive were in places you would least expect it: Yorkshire's Tory strongholds and comfortable southern villages.

Though the men felt their reception here was 'cheerless' and 'ambivalent', pushed and 'packed like sardines' into the tiny parish hall for their supper, the *Shields Gazette* put a distinctly upbeat spin on proceedings, mindful of the effect on morale amongst families back in Jarrow. Chester-le-Street's own weekly paper though, the *Chronicle and District Advertiser*, only found room a week later for a brief mention of the marchers in the 'We Know' column, buried amidst Mothers' Union meetings, exam results, the Dean of Peterborough's visit and an in-depth investigative report on the trade in stolen leeks from local agricultural shows. (This apparently silly story had a serious dimension. Allotments were a vital source of food that unemployed men could feed their families with and, as writer Arthur Barton put it, provided 'a refuge where he could get away from the accusing faces of his children and his wife's incessant "will ye now work again?"') Regardless of Bernard Ingham's homilies, the truth is poverty divides and wounds families and communities, rather than bind or strengthen them.

I enter Chester-le-Street slowly, footsore, squinting, my flat cap pulled down over my eyes against the glare of a brilliant dusk. I fancy I cut rather a dash; a Clint Eastwoodesque man of mystery, making curtains twitch and causing owners to pull down the shutters and spin the signs to 'Closed' in Lloyds Pharmacy, G W Horner's general store and Bridge End Kebabs and Burgers. My first day's march is over and I'm ready for something long and cold. There's a café open on the square and I stride in as they are wiping down the tables and upending the chairs. Sensing my disappointment, the two ladies say they can stay open for a few minutes more (and a few dollars, well, quid more) and I take a seat. One lady brings my order and I launch into an explanation that I hope will prove an overture to an informative and wide-ranging chat.

'I'm a bit hot and thirsty, you see, because I've walked from Jarrow. I'm retracing the Jarrow march. The Jarrow march!'

'Oh have you? Very good. That'll be £2.65 please. I'll be locking up in ten minutes.'

Deflated, I take a long draught of my mango and apple crushed fruit cooler, something that neither The Man With No Name or The Jarra Lads would have ordered I'm sure. But at least I'm on my way.

STAGE TWO

CHESTER-LE-STREET TO FERRYHILL

6 October, 12 miles

On 6 October 1936, the day after the Jarrow march reached Chester-le-Street, Ellen Wilkinson headed north to Edinburgh for the Labour Party Conference which opened that day. In this bald statement is a very striking illustration of one difference between then and now. In the new, devolved UK and particularly since the election of 2010, Scottish Labour could probably hold its conference in a small branch of the Edinburgh Woollen Mill outlet and not unduly inconvenience any customers.

Writing three years later, in *The Town That Was Murdered*, Wilkinson's burning frustration with her 'comrades' in the party still smouldered.

> It was a queer experience, that Labour party conference in Edinburgh in 1936 ... Having got the men well started on their road I dashed to Edinburgh for a couple of days for the unemployment and distressed area debates ... I went from the warm comradeship of the road to an atmosphere of official disapproval. The Trades Union Congress had frowned on the march and the Labour party followed the lead.

There were other good reasons for Ellen to make sure her voice was heard at conference. High on the agenda for debate was the worrying rise of the far right both here and abroad. In Spain, Franco's Fascists were waging war on the democratically elected government and their own people, helped by Hitler. Closer to home, the very day before the Jarrow Crusade set out, Oswald Mosley's Blackshirts, or the British Union of Fascists as they were officially known, had attempted to march through predominantly Jewish areas of London's working-class East End and been beaten back by anti-fascist demonstrators, socialists, Irish republicans, Jewish groups and ordinary Londoners in what would become known as the Battle of Cable Street.

According to the *News Chronicle*, 'the greatest East End crowd in living memory – some estimates say 300,000 – awaited the Fascists.' This huge and diverse contingent faced the Blackshirts with a chant of 'They shall not pass', a deliberate echo of the *No Pasaran* battle cry of the Spanish Republicans. All police leave was cancelled and 6,000 foot and mounted police were assembled to escort the 2,000 Blackshirts, at least until the full force of the opposition was known. Tram drivers parked their vehicles across Aldgate to block the Fascists' intended route. Off-duty seamen opened their storage sheds and turned lorries on their side to form barricades. Women flung the contents of chamber pots over the Mosleyites from upstairs windows. Eventually persuaded to abandon their route through Jewish areas, Mosley's crew were escorted by police through deserted back streets. Later Mosley complained that, 'it was the first occasion in which the British government has surrendered to the Red Terror'.

Wilkinson though did not arrive in Edinburgh in time for the conference's morning debate. At it, her secret lover Herbert Morrison (grandfather of Peter Mandelson) condemned the anti-fascist contingent and praised the police, in the same spirit which had seen the parliamentary Labour Party wash its hands of the Jarrow marchers. Morrison and Red Ellen were certainly unlikely paramours, which tells one something about the capricious workings of the human heart as well perhaps as other organs.

Minus Ellen, the marchers were up and off from Chester-le-Street by 7.30am after what seems a fairly cheerless and uncomfortable night on the cold floor of the church institute. I was up bright, if not quite this early, and over a cappuccino in Mr Pickwick's café (random Dickensian posters, brisk mid-morning trade of chatty oldsters) I looked at the news pages of 6 October 2016. Unlike the BUF, the modern British far right were keener on breaking their own heads than that of their enemies. Nigel Farage, a strangely ubiquitous media figure for a man who has failed seven times to be elected to parliament, had once again taken control of the chaotic UK Independence Party following a punch-up in the Strasbourg council chamber which had left MEP Steven Woolfe in hospital needing a brain scan. His alleged assailant, a fellow UKIP MEP, later described the incident as 'handbags'. Wolfe replied that the party was 'ungovernable' and in a 'death spiral'. Elsewhere, more literally and more tragically, a hundred people were killed in a hurricane in Haiti.

I checked my texts, tweets and emails and there was encouraging stuff from friends and strangers alike. My old mate Andrew Collins pointed out that as I was doing this for a book, I was following very much in the Jarrow men's footsteps: a northerner walking to London and hoping to get some work out of it. Other contributors suggested good places to get 'bait' if I was 'clamming' at various pubs and cafés here and in Ferryhill, today's final destination. Strolling through Chester-le-Street as noon approached, I summoned the effort of will required to forgo the tempting if dyspeptic offer advertised in a pub window. 'Pint of Crushed Berries Bulmers served in a glass with ice, cheese burger, chips, onion rings and our home-made coleslaw, all for £7.95.' In the same glass, I wondered?

Today's stage, 12 miles from Chester-le-Street to Ferryhill, would take me through a series of evocative-sounding places.

There was the curiously named Pity Me, lonely and harsh-sounding Framwellgate Moor and Neville's Cross, the site of a famously vicious battle between the English and the Scots. Soon out of Chester-le-Street, the original marchers had discovered two stowaways, a couple of 14-year-old lads from Hebburn who were put on the next bus back home but whose tale inspired the kids' book about Clogger that found its way onto the national curriculum. It took the marchers a while to notice them among the throng, certainly longer than it would have taken me to spot extra companions as I walked alone through County Durham. My spirits were high though. A tweet from a correspondent called Anne Graham said that she would look out for me as I passed through Pity Me and, even if she missed me, I should call in at Taylor's the butcher for 'the best pork pie in the north east'. Surely this was a claim no red-blooded, mildly peckish northerner could ignore. I narrowed my eyes, scanned the horizon and paced another mile or three of long, straight road.

Neither Pity Me nor Framwellgate Moor are as forlorn or desolate as their names suggest. They meld into one; two long, straggly urban villages clinging to the sides of the major road from Newcastle to Darlington. According to the Oxford Dictionary of British Place Names, there are various theories on the origin of Pity Me. It may indeed be 'a whimsical name bestowed in the nineteenth century on a place considered desolate, exposed or difficult to cultivate'. Or it may be an anglicisation of the Norman *Petit Mere*, a small or shallow lake. Most wild and romantic are the folk tales that say the coffin of St Cuthbert was dropped near here en route to Durham, at which point the saint implored the monks carrying him to take pity on him and be more careful (which must have come as a surprise), or that a group of monks, who were similarly surprised to encounter some raiding Vikings, sang the fifty-first psalm, 'Miserere mei, Deus' or 'Pity me, O God'.

Nothing so rum befell me as I made my way along the parade of shops that form a kind of retail border land between the two villages. In a consecutive run come the Ebony Salon, Look Lush Lucy's Nailbar and Terry's Barber Shop. In 1936, these sites would presumably have been hardware stores and grocers, bakers or cobblers and there are two ways of seeing this shift, both of which seem to me partly true. Yes, we have become an image-fixated, self-absorbed, adorned and decorated nation, for sure, but when times are tough, people still want to look good – or at least striking, almost as an act of defiance – and that may be no bad thing. After all, we have been doing these things to ourselves with woad and kohl and pelts almost as long as we have been hunting and skinning stuff and so, appropriately, at the end of this array of beautification, I find the much-vaunted Taylors the Butcher.

The staff in their nylon housecoats and jaunty hats are gearing up for lunchtime but it's already busy; a young goth couple, a clutch of workmen in flecked blue overalls, a man in a suit buying several pasties. I mention my journey and that I've been recommended here by a local gourmet and one lady disappears into the back. A few minutes later, a hearty bespectacled man appears wiping his hands before shaking mine. John Green, head butcher, and I chat by the purple flicker of the Insectocutor. He's well up on the Jarrow Crusade ('it was a time of real deprivation and they were marching to London to show their willingness to find work') though, like many, he places it ten years earlier than is the case, presumably to chime with the General Strike. John lives in Ferryhill where I'm headed today. 'Eight miles you've got left I'd say. Straight down, you can't miss it.' He tips me off about a good pub, the Manor House, and sends me on my way with a pie which is not only gratis, always a splendid seasoning, but hot. Midlanders regard this as sacrilege but it's the way the north likes them. For what can give more solace and joy than the feel of hot grease dribbling down the chin whilst dining on foot *al fresco* and *en plein air*, as our continental friends would have it? Afterwards, freshening up on a bench with a packet of wet wipes bought from the Co-Op, I reflect that this may well be the second best pork pie I have ever had. (The first will always be the one consumed one winter's afternoon in Cromford, Derbyshire in the street outside the pie shop and to which no words can ever do adequate justice.)

On a milky, muggy October morning at a busy intersection around which a few pubs, tanning salons, some maisonettes and the Bella Mamma Italian café bar cluster untidily, one would have no idea that this is a place not only steeped in violence and bloodshed, but one with a very real significance in the history and composition of the modern United Kingdom. What happened here at Neville's Cross 670 years ago still shapes England and Scotland's fractious and intense relationship.

It happened on an October day too, the seventeenth of that month in 1346. Following English King Edward III's resounding victory over the French at Crecy in the summer, the French King Philip invoked the terms of the Auld Alliance between the Scots and asked King David II of Scotland to avenge him and retaliate by invading England. The Scots had it their own way for several days, rampaging south through Northumberland sacking and looting as they went. But when they came near Neville's Cross, a settlement named after the old Saxon Cross here, they camped and waited to be paid protection money that was promised for the next day, unaware that the Archbishop of York had mobilised 7,000 men of northern England into a fighting force that lay in wait in the autumn mists of County Durham.

With favourable ground and better tactics, the English routed the Scots army. Many Scottish nobles perished and the rest fled the field, abandoning King David II and his bodyguard. Legend says that they escaped and hid under a bridge over the nearby River Browney but were given away when their reflections were spotted by a detachment of English soldiers. Already hit twice in the face by arrows – one of the metal tips could not be removed and gave him pain and headaches for the rest of his life – King David was captured and imprisoned for 11 years, and whilst most of southern Scotland subsequently fell to the

English, David's sacrifice and stoicism was seen as instrumental in securing independent nation status in the long term.

The cross has gone, relocated to Durham town centre now, and the actual battlefield has been developed and built upon; studio flats and garages where a generation of high Scottish nobility was cut down by blades and hails of arrows. But a network of paths and an information board will guide you through a quiet pasture which once ran with blood. As I walk the length of the land on this journey, time and time again I will be reminded that every postcode, every OS square, every parish boundary is packed and freighted with history at its densest and darkest. Another legend of Neville's Cross has it that the English were led into battle by a woman, the dark-skinned Queen Philippa, Edward III's consort of Moorish extraction and a leader every bit as loved and exotic as Red Ellen at the head of her band of men.

A quick glance at the various Macs and Mcs among the roll call of marchers shows that many of Ellen's men were either Scottish or of Scottish lineage and were rubbing alongside their English brethren a deal better than in the fourteenth century. Scottish migrants had been drawn south by the promise of work in the mines, steelworks and shipyards of Jarrow during the town's boom years. Between the wars, Scottish unemployment was always higher than in England, and even when some parts of England (though not Jarrow, for sure) began to experience some economic upturn in the mid and late thirties, Scotland remained poorer. Much of the available work had also been relocated to England where the workforce was seen as more amenable and malleable. This labour drain sapped not just Scotland's economic and industrial vigour but its self-confidence and pride. By the time of the Jarrow march, Scotland was widely viewed south of the border as the sick man of the union – a basket case in modern parlance. But for years this was slow to solidify into any real organised support for nationalism or independence.

Prior to the EU referendum of June 2016, the last convulsion in British politics had been the bitterly, narrowly contested vote on Scottish independence in 2014, which brought forth a turn-out of 84.6 per cent – the highest recorded for any election or referendum in the UK since the introduction of universal suffrage. Its aftershocks were still being felt on the day I arrived in Neville's Cross. Nicola Sturgeon of the SNP was suggesting in that day's paper that Scotland's clear 'remain' majority in the EU vote meant that she had a mandate for a new referendum on independence. Scotland want to be part of Europe, even if England don't. Let's call the whole thing off.

The afternoon was shading into a golden, glorious early evening as I paused on a bench at an intersection provided by Durham City Council 'for the benefit of residents and visitors alike. Pause for a while and enjoy the area'. I tried, DCC, but there's only so much enjoyment to be gained from watching articulated lorries thunder by. But the thought was there. Once rested, I'm off again to the sound of birdsong and down a quiet stretch of road at the bottom of which a little cottage has a pretty sign framed and hung on a gate. It reads, 'Come My People. Enter thou into thy chambers and shut the doors abut thee, Isaiah 26 20. Leave The EU.' I read it several times, undecided whether it's an ironic sneer at 'little Englanders' or a genuine plea for 'drawbridge up' isolationism. This is the weird new febrile, uncertain England I walk through.

A sign tells me I'm five miles from Spennymoor, one from Durham, 12 from Bishop Auckland and 13 from Consett. Ferryhill, my destination, is not mentioned. This is disconcerting. I decide to take a minicab from here to my nearby hotel, drop my bag, and then return and pick up the Jarrow route into Ferryhill proper. I call a local number and the man who comes to pick me up is a Scot. 'If you want a recommendation for local pubs, I should say that I don't go drinking in Neville's Cross. Old habits die hard. It might be another ambush.'

In the taxi, along empty rural back lanes to the soothing backdrop of Smooth FM's liquid melding of Elton John, the Bee Gees and George Benson, I fall into an easy, knackered kind of conversation with the driver. He's smart and funny, silver-haired at the margins of a shiny dome, 60-ish, resembling a more genial Larry David. 'I've always worked away or long hours. Used to work on the pipelines. My wife finally got fed up and decided she wanted me to retire. She says, "I've been married to you for 34 years and only seen you for 18 months." Well, I says, you can either have the big money or me in the house. So I retire and I stay at home with her and we go shopping and on wee errands … well, she soon got sick of that, so here I am again, on the roads.'

Unlike the waitress in the Chester-le-Street café, my driver has not only heard of the Jarrow march but is positively interested. 'I was born 17 years after the Jarrow march but I suppose like them I came south looking for work. A group of mentally disabled people – is it special needs? Learning difficulties? Sorry, I don't know the phrases – they did a stage play about the march just recently. It was in the local papers. Industrial history's a bit of a thing with me. This used to be mining country, County Durham. They say you could once walk from Black Hall colliery just near here all the way to Workington, coast to coast, completely underground in the old mine tunnels. In Ferryhill you'll see a pub called the Dean and Chapter, everyone knows it as the Black Bull, but they changed its name to that of the old pit here. Nice gesture I suppose. Yes, lot of changes in those 80 years …'

At this very moment we hit a pothole and my head grazes the vinyl roof.

'… But the council hasn't finished the road yet.'

He drops me off at my hotel, a queer, rambling but intriguing-looking place in the outlying countryside. 'You're actually slightly closer to Sedgefield here, Blair's old constituency, you know. The Dun Cow is where he took George Bush and 20 armed security officers for lunch. They had the fish and chips I believe. Good pub. Minister's Indian restaurant, that's a nod to him too, superb. Enjoy! Hey you know, we had an oyster festival here last week, and a Bavarian stomping band ... Oh, it all happens round here,' he says with a wry smile. Then his radio crackles and he is called away to Pelaw Green.

With a parting, over the shoulder wave, he leaves me to Ferryhill in the dusk. With the sun dropped behind the distant treeline of Thorpe Larches, it's turning distinctly cold. The lights are on in the bus that pulls into the station, disgorging its homecoming workers back from the factories of Sunderland or the offices of Durham, a gang of kids from the big college there or in Spennymoor. I take a walk along the main street where, up at the eastern end, there's a 'Europe Beacon', a stylised and somewhat ironic gas lamp, considering that this corner of Durham voted overwhelmingly to leave the European Union with the only substantial Remain vote coming from the students of the famous and prestigious university. Outside the Post Box pub, a lad in kitchen whites blows on his hands and pulls on a fag; a real one, increasingly a rarity in the land of outlandishly named vaping outlets. Already I am finding that there are new constants and fixtures of every English high street today, 80 years on from Jarrow, when it would have been tobacconists and butchers. Now it's e-cig shops, retro barbers, cupcake bakers (often defunct, a bewildering craze on its way out), pizza shops where a moustachioed eastern European man stands behind a teetering tower of boxes waiting to be filled, and tattoo parlours. Ferryhill's is called Comfortably Numb, which is actually rather good.

My dog-walking ex-Consett steelworker told me that Ferryhill was 'a pit village with no pit'. It's a simple statement of fact that, like the famed 'pub with no beer', suggests a certain melancholy. The town has a tough and insular air, sitting on a limestone ridge on the former Durham coalfield, its jaw set against the world and the coming winter. It's quiet today, but on

Friday things get livelier for the market and in summer, fetes and galas parade the old miners' banners and celebrate the town's heritage. At the Dean and Chapter pub – the former Black Bull – a young woman sips a bright blue drink as she feeds the kaleidoscopic fruit machine, and a hefty, older man sits hunched at the bar over his pint and *Gazette*. From the outside, it is a north-eastern Hopper scene. The exterior has been redone vividly and rather forbiddingly in slate grey and coal-black livery with ghostly silhouettes of former miners. The legend reads, 'The Dean and Chapter, this pub is dedicated to the 73 miners who lost their lives at the colliery from 1904 when production began until 1929. The colliery closed in 1966.' A long time gone, but where work has been hard, the memories are long too.

Night is properly here now, cloaking the town. The marchers got their first hot meal of the trip by the roadside at Neville's Cross – a stew of lentils, carrots, leeks and turnips. I get mine in a curry house down one of the dark ends of Ferryhill's main drag and where, as I'm the only customer, the waiter comes and sits with me as I finish my carafe of house red, admiring my recording device ('what is that, man?!') and listens thoughtfully as I tell him why I'm here.

'You've walked from Jarrow? From Jarrow?! Today?!'

Yes, and I'm going a lot further. He's never heard of the march but is fascinated and horrified that the men went all the way to London. 'Times must have been hard. I don't think anyone would do that now. Too far. They'd be on their phones haggling on Uber!'

He lives in Sunderland and gets the bus in every day to Ferryhill. 'It's not my restaurant but I sort of manage it. It's owned by my uncle.' He nods towards the kitchen from where some clattering, sizzling sounds and pungent, heady aromas are emerging. 'He's been here five years. I've been here ... hmm ... about two and, to be honest, now I'm getting ...'

He searches a little mournfully for the right word.

'Restless?' I offer.

'I just have this feeling that there must be something more, something else out there ... see a bit of the world. But I suppose I'll stay here,' he concludes with a small resigned smile.

'Well, the food is lovely,' I say, not entirely truthfully. 'The Jarrow marchers wouldn't have eaten bhuna and bhajis.' 'No,' he laughs, and then, in case he thinks I'm presuming them bigoted, I quickly add, 'I mean I bet there was no hot food in Ferryhill at night then.'

'Well, there is now,' he laughs, 'if you like pizza. And they could certainly have got their hair cut,' alluding to the town's glut of cheap independent pizza shacks and mock Edwardian barbers.

The streets of Ferryhill are dark and deserted tonight but things were different 80 years ago. The welcome here was as warm as it had been muted in Chester-le-Street. A message chalked on the road as the marchers arrived read, 'Welcome to the Jarrow Crusade. We are in solidarity with you.' In a letter home from the road, the Crusade's cook, Con Shiels' dad (also called Con, confusingly) said, 'We got a better welcome here, as all the town was out.' After placing the oak petition box (lettered in gold leaf paint from Woolworths costing a penny) in the council chambers and holding a public meeting in the street, the marchers were fed on scones and ham sandwiches in the Miners Institute. In a famous incident, one marcher was seen carefully lifting the ham from his sandwich and posting it back home. When asked, he explained that his family had not eaten meat for six weeks.

The Manor House has been here several hundred years, but with their strict discipline, I doubt any marchers popped in for a pint. I'm pointed in its direction by two twinkling ladies in their eighties tightly linking each other for warmth as they make their booteed way along. 'You can't miss it! We've just come from there!' they giggle, and perhaps their tight embrace is for reasons of stability as well as warmth. I lift the latch and find the pub empty except for a little lively, amiable knot of drinkers at the bar. I find a spot a discreet eavesdropping distance away and order a pint which I promptly knock over, spilling the contents all over the bar. This is embarrassing but it does effect a dramatic entrée into the conversation.

At the bar in a loose circle with pints and white wines are a couple in fleeces, a hearty solo male drinker and a mother and daughter with a fascinating dynamic who I chat to in earnest. Mum is in her forties; denims, check shirt, casual and smart in an alternative, relaxed style. Her daughter though is immaculately coiffured, glamorously made up, salon tanned, tall and catwalk elegant. The differences between them are not just aesthetic I'll find, but both are bright, chatty and personable. Mum moved to Ferryhill some years ago, but was brought up in Jarrow and remains a proud Jarrow lass.

'It's an anniversary tonight, isn't it? They passed through here and stopped the night. They were marching for jobs, not handouts. They wanted to work. And they were given no support at all except from the ordinary people. Their Labour MP pushed their case but the rest of the party didn't want to know. They ostracised her for it. Ellen Wilkinson, she was called. Now everyone wants to claim them for their own. Have you ever studied the Jarrow march, Robin? Robin's doing Government and Politics at college. She'll give you a different view I imagine.'

Daughter Robin tells me that she's a Conservative, 'and that makes me proper weird round here. You never meet anyone who's a Tory. Or at least who'll admit to it. Of course, there are lots of different types of Conservative. There is for instance (and here I think Robin is quoting from her course notes) the One Nation Conservative who believes in the Welfare State and in helping the vulnerable and the less well-off. But even they aren't naive. You have to face the fact that some people are just … higher than others. There's a natural hierarchy among humans.'

Really? I say. Is there? Listening back to the recording they kindly let me make of the conversation, I realise that the speed at which I snapped this back at Robin was ungallant to say the least. But Mum is with me.

'Is that right? A natural hierarchy? So the rich are rich on merit, are they? Not because of inherited wealth or their old school ties or ...'

Robin knows Mum has the better of this rally but attempts a lobbed return. 'Mum, you can't say that ... that ... a teacher, say, has the same intelligence as someone on the dole ...' She drifts back to the baseline as Mum closes in at the net.

'Well, they might well have. And anyway, it's not about where you end up. A society should have equality of opportunity. Look at me and you. When I went to college, I didn't have to borrow or beg from my mum and dad. I got a grant and went to university and I got a degree. You're a bloody talented drama student and you can't tell me that you wouldn't go to uni and study if it wasn't for the money. And, love, I can't afford to pay for you to go ...'

'I don't want it,' interjects Robin, quickly but not completely convincingly. 'We went to Parliament on a college trip and some of the politicians told me it was a waste of time. The assistant chief whip of the SNP hasn't been to university, you know ...' she tails off.

My feeling about this is the same now as it was in the pub that autumn night. It may well be right that university is not for everyone, but I would surely like to meet the men in Westminster who, having had the best education money can buy, tell working-class girls from the north east that university is a waste of time.

Inevitably, as talk, beer and wine flow, the conversation glides inexorably towards one topic. 'They're all saying round here this Brexit is a great thing,' says Mum. 'They'll learn. I don't think it's a great thing at all. My cousin is in medical science, he's researching a disease of the feet, not a very serious one but an unpleasant one that could be cured. The research is funded by the EU. Or was. Straight after the referendum, £600,000 of investment cut instantly and 20 people out of work.'

As I leave, each drinker except Robin – who to be fair hadn't heard of it – offered some positive thought about the march that passed through here 80 years ago.

'I don't know if Jarrow would happen again. People standing together, women, children with their husbands, you think – wow! But are we like that any more? On the news tonight they were saying, yes, it's all romantic and all but did it achieve anything? Well, I think it did. It achieved something in that we're talking to you about it now.'

This is the notion that Matt Perry addressed in his lecture; that if Jarrow and by extension the Labour movement forget the march then it certainly has failed. But not if it is collectively remembered. They can take away the future that working people wanted but they cannot deny them their past.

Just down the road from the Manor House there's one minicab in Ferryhill's taxi rank and I take it back to my hotel. The driver is a handsome woman in her fifties, but her eyes are dark and lined and her face is flecked with little scratches and nicks. These are not signs of abuse necessarily, but of someone who isn't looking after herself as well as she should. She asks me what's my business in Ferryhill and when I tell her I'm researching a book, her own story starts to emerge.

'I've thought about writing a book, just to tell about my life.'

After 32 years of common-law marriage and two kids now at university, her partner left her last year and she seethes, 'The bastard is now trying to get me out the house, the house and the home I've built for 32 years. It's dragging through lawyers now. They say you've got rights, but have I? That's why I'm driving this cab. You think you know someone but you don't. I said to the bastard, "All these years, what was I to you?" I know that people split up but he wants me out on the street. It's my home, it's my kids' home. My son wants to kill him. So,' she glances at me in the rearview mirror with a sad smile, 'you think anyone would be interested in my story?'

Maybe, I say. As she's pulling over and reading the meter and I dig for change, I suggest that she starts a blog to see how that feels and to perhaps find sympathetic readers with similar experiences. She turns to me puzzled, awkward. 'What's a blog?' And so I get my phone out, lean into the little space between the two front seats and flip through a few blogs randomly: musings about spiralised vegetables and vinyl records, with a nice but angry lady from Ferryhill that I've just met.

'Yours doesn't have to be like this, of course,' I say. 'People blog about family, divorce, kids, all kinds of things.' As I leave, she stays parked, and as I reach the door of the hotel, I look back and see her looking into her lap still, her face uplit in the chilly northern dark by her phone. Perhaps she's found an inspirational blog from a woman sharing her similar story with the world. Or maybe she's just buying a copy of Donovan's 1971 *Mini Monster* EP on Pye. Either way, it was an interesting trip.

I'd noticed while scrolling though the blogs on my phone that Matt Perry had emailed me. So, having kicked off my shoes and with one eye on *Question Time* on the tiny wall-mounted TV in my room (the kind specifically designed for you to bang your temple on), I read his message. At his lecture, we'd been talking about the Jarrow march in the context of other 'iconic' events in Labour and working-class history, prompted by the fact that the 1984 miners' strike is back in the news with calls for a debate on the clashes of Orgreave. The strike was initially about the pit closures enforced by National Coal Board chairman Ian MacGregor doing the bidding of Mrs Thatcher. Matt has been reading MacGregor's memoirs.

Hi Stuart,

You might have missed the topical connection between Orgreave, MacGregor and the Jarrow Crusade. And might want to use it. In his memoirs, he recalls getting a job in 1936 with Sir James Lithgow, who established

the National Shipbuilding Securities that bought
Palmers and put a 40-year ban on shipbuilding on it.
'Of the half dozen or so men who have influenced my
life, he was the one – my first great mentor ... I did
not take on the Coal Board in order to butcher the
industry, or to smash the miners. But there was no
way I was going to let their leadership stand in the
way of establishing management's right to manage the
business and make it a going concern.'

At this very moment I look up and catch a glimpse of *Question
Time*. When I was a child, this was the BBC's flagship political
debate programme, where union and parliamentary titans
clashed under the withering basilisk gaze of Sir Robin Day.
These days, tuning in, you are more likely to be treated to the
political insights of some unspeakable and deranged reality
TV show flotsam or the dim but loquacious lead singer of a
minor 1990s pop–soul ensemble. But speaking at the moment
is Leanne Wood, the leader of Plaid Cymru, who has been
pricked into passionate scorn at mention of Theresa May's claim
that the Tories are the party of working people. 'I worked as a
probation officer in South Wales during the miners' strike,' she
says, white-faced with quiet rage. 'I saw the human cost and
the legacy of closing those pits. They will never be the party
of working people. We should never forgive them. Never, ever
forgive them.'

I turn off the TV, turn over, and fall asleep in the quiet arms
of a mining town with no pit, just like scores across the land,
where the lights are going out. 'No longer a going concern' and
definitely no concern of some.

STAGE THREE

FERRYHILL TO DARLINGTON

7 October, 12 miles

Breakfast in Ferryhill must have gladdened the Jarrow marchers' hearts as it hardened the arteries: 70 pounds of bacon, 140 loaves of bread for frying, three boxes of tomatoes for same, all consumed in the Miners Institute. On leaving, they were also given 120 pounds of cherry cake for the journey, and the reporter from the *Shields Gazette*, Selwyn Waller, noticed that some were already putting on weight. Before they set off at 9.30am, some of the younger marchers had an impromptu dance with the girls of Ferryhill in the market place.

Not having been asked to dance, not liking cherry cake much and, moreover, none being forthcoming, I skip breakfast, leave town and pause for elevenses from a van by the roundabout at the Eden Arms in Rushyford. Someone once wrote that a man never feels as free and alive as when he jumps on to the back of an old London bus in motion. I would add the similar feeling engendered by eating a bacon butty and drinking coffee from a Styrofoam cup on a road never taken before and headed somewhere new.

Seated at a plastic table on the layby, I listen back on my recording device to Robin and her mum exchanging views in the pub last night and think about the youngest of the Jarrow lads, early twenties I guess, dancing and flirting with the girls of Ferryhill before setting out with a wink and a spring in their step that October morning in 1936. The year before, the school leaving age had been raised from 14 to 15, but children could be exempted if they could find 'beneficial employment'. This dismayed educationalists but was welcomed by those working-class families who needed the extra wages of their teenage offspring.

Of course they weren't 'teenagers'. No one would have called them that as that designation only really arrived (and then across the Atlantic) with the Second World War, the ubiquity of the automobile and the growth of leisure industries and the mass media. The lads and girls who danced in Ferryhill market place were young men and women; 'youths' as they were called. They were not a separate tribe, there was no generation schism. They were merely younger, sillier and more carefree versions of their mums and dads. But essentially their sights were set on the same targets – houses, jobs, children – and they took the same, long-established route to get them.

Most of the Jarrow marchers were well out of their teens since juvenile unemployment was always low even during the worst of the twenties and thirties slumps. 'Youths' were cheap to hire and pay and easy to get rid of. They were physically different too. According to Branson and Heinemann in *Britain in the 1930s*, the average 16-year-old then was more like a child of today. Most 12-year-olds of the 1960s were as big and strong as a thirties' 'youth' and their lives were similarly constrained and slight compared to the teenager of our times: 'Their horizons were limited, their lives rather bare, their opportunities for enjoyment meagre ... there were no special teenage fashions in clothes or cosmetics, no teenage magazines to speak of, few teenage activities or entertainments laid on. It was not the custom to interview teenagers on the radio or to solicit their opinions or explore their attitudes.' While things were slightly better for the 18–25-year-old group at whom much culture, entertainment, sport and recreation was aimed, they were still a marginal section of society compared to the powerful middle-aged middle class who held tight the reins of the law, the economy and the polity.

Eighty years later, that situation would seem to have changed. Pippa Norris of Harvard talks of a 'generational cleavage' running through the new politics and the new populism, young people being (or asserting to be) globalist, progressive and more interested in issues like LGBT rights, multiculturalism and gender equality than the old blue collar concerns of community solidarity, nationhood and working conditions. Jon Cruddas, influential Labour MP and thinker, has talked of a shift in the power centres and bases of the left away from the industrial working class and towards what's called 'Globally Oriented Network Youth'. This new 'radical' sector tends to be found in cities, is well educated and easily embraces technological change, leisure and internationalism. 'You can see it around Corbynism. But if you build a public philosophy and a politics around this network, one that discounts the working class, where are they going to go politically? They're not going to regroup around this new fashionable left. They're going walkabout on the right.'

That's the walkabout that took us away from Brussels, and whilst I don't agree with that decision, I can understand it. In the three months between the seismic shock of the Brexit vote and me setting out from Jarrow, I read and heard countless leftist commentators and writers airily, and I think snobbishly, waving away some of the concerns of older, non-metropolitan working-class voters as racism and bigotry. I couldn't agree with Stephen Bush, a writer I generally much admire, when he said that white working-class people in England had no right to talk about being vulnerable and marginalised. He didn't 'buy it', as he put it. The only people who could legitimately feel this way were, say, Mexican workers in San Diego or Latinos in Miami or ethnic minorities in the UK. Whatever you think of this, this dismissiveness will win you no friends among the old blue collar labour heartlands, as was proved on 23 June to the apparent bafflement of some liberal observers. Belatedly perhaps, some have come to see the error of their ways. As Adam Shatz, *London Review of Books* contributing editor, said of the liberals' response to the new populism and the white working class, 'Most of us have found it easier to hate than persuade.'

Such thoughts occupy me as I stride along, though with admittedly less strength than my regret at deciding to wear some rather raffish knee-length shorts on what has turned out to be the first grey, overcast and chilly morning of my trip. A sign points right to Newton Aycliffe and, fancying the warmth and buzz of civilisation for a while, I detour toward it. The marchers lunched at Aycliffe Village just down the road and I'll head there later, but Newton Aycliffe is its brasher, younger brother. The largest new town in the north of England, it was founded in 1947 around a major wartime munitions base which brought workers from the surrounding regions.

In 2015, against the prevailing economic mood, Hitachi opened an £82million train-building plant here, bringing the glory days of rail construction back to the north east, continuing the grand engineering traditions of George Stephenson and creating 700 jobs. It was feted by then prime minister David Cameron and was to be at the heart of George Osborne's plans for the much vaunted Northern Powerhouse. Cameron and Osborne are both gone, distant as figures from a bygone political era like Disraeli or Stafford Cripps. But the trains are still being built. Head out to the site and you can see the huge, sleek beasts under vast white sheets awaiting their imminent roll-out. In Hitachi's promo video for the project on YouTube, you'll find gleaming hi-tech vehicles, besuited captains of industry smiling and handshaking through a flickering storm of flashbulbs and accompanied by a beautiful and elegant female Asian string quartet in white silk. All dazzlingly glamorous, but it will I fear give you an unrealistic expectation of Newton Aycliffe, especially if your first port of call is the town centre, or what passes for one.

The architectural style known as Brutalism is beginning to find favour again amongst some critics after years of hostility from the likes of Prince Charles. The north east has more examples of this harsh but powerfully dramatic style than anywhere else in Britain. You won't go far here without chancing upon looming concrete towers or raw, uncompromising brickwork: Redcar Library, Darlington Town Hall, the Apollo Pavilion in Peterlee, the Wilton Centre, Teesside, Billingham Forum and Owen Luder's iconic, divisive, now demolished Trinity Square car park in Gateshead.

Newton Aycliffe is a whole town built in this rugged and unsentimental mode, a style which divides people. Supporters of Brutalism like the writer Owen Hatherley admire 'its rough surfaces, heavy forms and dissonant, often monumental compositions', and see it as 'an attempt to recharge a modernism considered increasingly ingratiating and polite'. Sometimes though, a little ingratiation is no bad thing, especially towards the people who have to live in your brave experiments and your rough, heavy, monumental dissonance.

The journalist Merrick Winn called Newton Aycliffe 'the town that has no heart' in 1957 and you do feel on arrival at this bleak, windswept promenade that the people here deserved something better. It's hard to imagine anyone but those that created it on a drawing board having much affection for the Thames shopping arcades – the nearest thing Newton Aycliffe has to a town centre. But with the ceaseless energy that people have, for better or worse, the townspeople have colonised this dire space and made it their own. An old chap on a mobility scooter chats about 'regeneration' with a lady with a B&M Bargains bag and a small, angry dog. Office workers dash by with soup and salads and mobile phones held end on away from their faces in the style they've seen on *The Apprentice*. Two goth girls sit giggling on a hideous concrete planter. Given a choice, I doubt this is anyone's idea of a pleasant spot to spend your lunch hour. A regular town centre in all its higgledy-piggledy organic confusion would be preferable to this regimented chilliness.

I find more warmth in every sense in the public library, as is often the case. I sit and leaf though a lever arch file full of pictures of the town's construction and inauguration. Every computer terminal is occupied with people doing whatever it is people do on them all the long afternoon. A young blonde woman in boots and a leather jacket comes in. She's just moved back to Aycliffe village and wants to send a fax to her new employer's head office in New Zealand. While she and the ladies behind the counter establish whether they have the technology to do this, they ask how's she's finding the old place after her time away and I schmooze my way into the conversation by asking about my destination today.

'If you want to know about Aycliffe,' the newly returned young woman tells me, 'go down to the village hall. Every month, there's a community club there and you can get a late breakfast. Ask for Harry Moses. He knows everything there is to know. He's written books.'

Harry isn't around when I arrive at the village hall an hour or two later. But I get a cuppa and a warm welcome from the ladies of the Women's Institute. Brenda, Anne and Gill Atkinson are running a bring-and-buy stall. They all know of the original march and Anne has an actual souvenir. 'I believe they stayed here overnight and camped in the field opposite. When I was a little girl I found a tent peg in the field that must have belonged to them because no one ever camps there. I've still got it. If Harry were here he might tell you more. And one of our members, Muriel, is 95 and sharp as a pin. She might remember them coming through as a girl.' A few phone calls establish that, like Harry, Muriel is away for the weekend, but we manage to rustle up David Lewis from the village's local history society and he takes me on a whirlwind tour of Aycliffe.

It's a pretty place, once on the old Great North Road and hence squarely on the route of the Jarrow march. I mention to

David that I didn't like to contradict Anne, but the marchers didn't overnight here. 'No,' he agrees, 'but they did, as she says, have their lunch in the old cabbage and potato patch just opposite the hall, so they might well have put up some kind of tent or awning. They would have had to come here as there was no bypass then.'

The modern bypass, though, means that the village green is a delight; sun dappled and serene on this warm Friday morning. The only activity is a prowling, indolent cat and a gentleman in a fleece and trainers pottering along to his front door with a pint of milk. David has hit his stride. 'The church is older than Durham cathedral, Anglo-Saxon ... that little red building there is the old toll house ... you had to pay to use the old North Road ... that pub, the Royal Telegraph, would have been here then. And that one, the County. Tony Blair went there for lunch with the President of France, there's the blue plaque. And that river running by is the Skerne.'

David has a story that relates how unassuming Aycliffe has another unique place in industrial relations history beyond being where the Jarrow marchers had their butties.

The village hall used to be a school, opened in 1898. There was a church school here on the green but the head teacher and the vicar's wife were in constant conflict, basically because the head was his own man and wouldn't simply do the vicar's wife's bidding. She was always meddling and criticising him and she managed to get the head sacked by the vicar even though the village liked him and he did a good job. So the villagers got together a petition that said Thompson, the head, had been sacked 'ignominiously and without valid cause' and demanding his reinstatement. It was signed by 162 parents representing 449 children. When that got nowhere, the people were so angry that they built a new school on land bought with their own money. But

the interesting thing, historically, is that the dispute was
one of the first to be taken up by the National Union
of Teachers, one of its very first industrial disputes. It
went to parliament and in the end the head was re-
appointed.

Our circuit of the village has brought us back to where the
school once stood and I slurp another tea before hitting the
road. Brenda from the WI sees me off in the bright sunshine
and gives me a bag of apples for the journey, which strikes me as
nicely 'old school' and makes me feel like a peddler or man of the
road in a Thomas Hardy novel. I munch a couple myself (apples,
not Thomas Hardy novels) and give the rest to some friendly
but skittish horses in a field on High Beaumont Hill, and this
encounter is the only eventful moment on an afternoon's gritty,
noisy walk along the big new A167 into Darlington. I've never
been to 'Darlo' before so I'm looking forward to exploring and
from the stuff I read on Wiki last night in the curry house, it has
several interesting quirks and claims to fame; the Brutalist town
hall, comedian Vic Reeves, Quakerism and the coming of the
railways.

If you have ever been hugely, vexedly distracted from the matter
in hand by the twee recorded message about what is permissible
to flush down the toilet of a Virgin train, or sat becalmed in a
Hertfordshire field, the victim of a failure of lineside equipment
near Leighton Buzzard, then in some senses you have Darlington
to blame. It was the pressing need of the people of Darlington to
get themselves and their stuff to Stockton that birthed the railways.
By 'stuff' we mean specifically coal, the chief reason hotshot
Geordie engineer George Stephenson established the world's first
public railway between the two towns, primarily to bring coal from
Killingworth colliery to the port of Stockton. This was the really
important cargo. People were relegated to being dragged along
behind in open carts. For these pioneering rail users, there was

also the nagging worry widely reported that one might asphyxiate at the high speeds – in excess of ten miles per hour – that the loco could reach. This was a falsehood encouraged by wealthy canal owners desperate to keep their investments profitable and propagated by their press baron friends.

Work began in 1822 laying track on the 12-mile route between the two towns. Three years later, the railway opened to great fanfare. Large, eager crowds flocked to watch Stephenson himself at the controls of the 'Locomotion' as it pulled its 36 wagons – 22 of coal and flour and 14 of workmen and guests. During the final descent into Stockton, it unexpectedly reached 15 mph, surprising one passenger who fell out of his wagon and was badly injured. Add to this the fact that a few years later, on the maiden voyage of the first regular passenger service between Manchester and Liverpool, a high-ranking MP was run over and horribly killed, and one begins to realise just what excitement and faith there was in this new mode of transport. People like Stephenson were determined to make a success of the railways, whatever the cost.

It seems the accident outside Stockton did not sour the mood a jot. Spectator John Sykes recalled, 'The novelty of the scene, and the fineness of the day, had attracted an immense concourse of spectators, the fields on each side of the railway being literally covered with ladies and gentlemen on horseback, and pedestrians of all kinds ... By the time the cavalcade arrived at Stockton, where it was received with great joy, there were not less than 600 persons within, and hanging by the carriages.'

My entry into Darlington was more low key, it has to be said. Night had fallen and there was a chill in the air. But there was some of that old frisson of transport-related danger. Darlington, like most of our town centres, is now thronged with boy racer cyclists criss-crossing at speed, buzzing pedestrians and proffering the odd obscenity for seasoning. Even the most pacifistic among us surely find themselves fantasising about administering rough summary justice on these occasions, but at least these unlovable scamps have youth and stupidity as mitigating circumstances. Even just three days into my trip as a pedestrian, I am already reserving most loathing for those bulky middle-aged men, often in upsettingly snug lycra and with a little ribbed plastic hat, who ride their bikes on the pavement scattering old ladies and children, being too wussy and precious to ride on the highway as they are legally required. The punishment commensurate with this arrogance is yet to be devised. But I'm working on it.

Such retributory thoughts would not have sat well with some of Darlington's most eminent founders. Quakerism was born in the turbulent England of the Civil War when a young man called George Fox, a firebrand and electrifying preacher, toured the north of England spreading the word about a vision he had had on Pendle Hill in Lancashire. Fox's revelation was that the light of God was within everyone, discoverable within oneself and needing no formal or credentialed hierarchy of clergy. This was a radical notion which brought him into conflict with the established church who hauled him before various inquisitions for blasphemy. As Fox recalled, 'They were the first that called us Quakers, because I bade them tremble at the word of the Lord.' Quakerism grew from its beginnings in the English north to become a global religion and, along with other Nonconformist strains of Christianity like Methodism, part of a radical, dissenting, even socialistic strand in our history. Where Anglicanism and Catholicism are ultimately two different faces of the same conservative coin (and I say that as an ex-altar boy), Nonconformism, as the name suggests, is predicated on a lack of trust in the vicar or the priest, the dog collar or the surplice, on what Larkin called 'the vast moth eaten brocade' of the Establishment religions. Methodism and Chapel are indissoluble from the great Labour traditions of Wales, whilst Nonconformism made Manchester the great radical city of the industrial age.

Nonconformism also made towns like Darlington rich. Prohibited from entering the military, church or university by the powers that be, Quakers in England threw themselves into business and commerce, albeit with a caring and positive attitude to their workforce that set them apart from much of capitalist enterprise. Quaker family businesses created some of our best loved brands, brands redolent of Englishness itself: confectioners like Rowntree, Cadbury and Fry's, Clarks the shoemakers, banks such as Barclays and Lloyds. And in Darlington, Quaker industrialists and bankers like Jonathan Backhouse and Edward Pease supported Stephenson in the creation of the modern railways and a world transport revolution.

Making a TV film about Quakerism a couple of years back, I attended a meeting at the Friends House on the Furness Peninsula that is George Fox's old haunt and the crucible of Quakerism worldwide. Quaker meetings are not like church services; there's no leader, no palaver, no incense or droning, no 'vast moth eaten brocade'. Attendees sit in silence until someone feels moved to speak, and if no one does, that's fine. At mine, some 25 minutes of silence in, a man chirped up with a fairly anodyne remark about world peace and that was it for the whole hour. The film crew said they found it uncomfortable. I thought it was the most relaxing and nourishing hour I'd had in years. And I enjoyed my second visit to a Quaker House here in Darlington even more, especially as they were playing 'Brick House' by the Commodores thunderously loud when I arrived and someone speedily handed me a 7.6 per cent strength New World IPA.

I am indebted to Twitter correspondent Judith Sykes who led a chorus of similar voices in steering me to The Quaker House, Darlington which, as you may have guessed, is these days a pub. In fact, one of the finest pubs I've ever set foot in, and as you may have guessed yet again, there've been a few. It's tucked away in the Mechanics Yard, one of the maze of little alleys and ginnels that bisect the town. When Google maps proved wanting, I just let myself be lured by the throb and clamour of music.

'Brick House' by the Commodores was quickly followed by 'Ace of Spades' followed by the Isley Brothers' 'Behind a Painted Smile', to which most of the glamorous, beaming female bar staff and their adoring clientele cut various kinds of rug and threw a range of alluring shapes. It is hard to say just what the pub's chief selling point is, be it the staff, the beer, the live music, the attitude or the home-made onion bhajis. It is even harder to say after a few pints of the 7.6 strength New World IPA. But let us consider them one by one.

Shelley has run the pub for three years and worked here for seven. She heads a team who clearly love their pub and their job. Tonight the music is recorded rather than live – I have no problem with this at all I should say – and is played by DJ Rob who's seated at the 'wheels of steel' in a rather cramped and ungainly fashion in a corner of the bar as one leg is encased in plaster ('Don't ask'), jutting out at an angle designed for a sitcom mishap. However, this in no way affects his performance this evening. The eclectic opening musical salvo is followed by a selection of infectious northern soul tunes that coax some hard-looking middle-aged blokes in Ben Sherman and Farrah on to the postage stamp of a dance floor. The looks of rapture worn by men who've spent lives doing tough jobs in tough towns, whilst dancing to songs of unrequited love, devotion and heartbreak, is one of the many things I love about soul music and soul fans.

It's Friday night and this is the beginning of a weekend of gigs across the country (I had no idea until Shelley and Rob told me) called WSO or We Shall Overcome and designed to raise awareness and money for charitable causes all centred around the notion of 'anti-austerity'. 'Austerity' and 'austere' used to be words I liked. I applied them to the bleak beauty of upland moors and the poetry of R S Thomas. I hadn't realised that 'austerity' apparently means closing libraries and stopping vulnerable people's benefits. The staff at the Quaker House, in keeping with the traditions of their name, are amongst those generous, decent souls not accepting that the weak should suffer most when times are hard, especially when little of it is their fault.

'This is our second WSO anti-austerity weekend,' explains Shelley. 'There are 260 WSO gigs going on across the country this weekend but there has been no coverage in the press. Help spread the word. We want food for the food banks, sleeping bags for the homeless. Darlington has been massively affected by "austerity". We're a working-class town and the cuts have hit us hard. People simply not capable of work are being told they have to.' Here is another quietly smouldering impetus for Brexit that many commentators have either failed to notice or chosen to ignore: after the economic crisis of 2008, one largely brought about by the wickedness and greed of bankers, it has been ordinary people who have borne the cost, in reduced services and savage cuts. Rightly or wrongly, the EU is seen as aligned to that protected cabal of affluent and seemingly untouchable financiers. Brexit was an attempt, however clumsy and misguided, to land a punch on them.

Battling against the joyous racket of Frank Wilson's 'Do I Love You' (if you've got one on the Soul label, congrats, it's worth about 25 grand), I chat with a clutch of gregarious regulars. Marty's been drinking here for 17 years and has missed just six live bands in all that time. I'd heard that Darlington was becoming a boom town, with some people commuting to London. 'A boom town?' He takes a thoughtful sip. 'Well, there are now 12 pubs in the city centre serving real ale,' he says, this clearly being Marty's quality of life index. Francis is a beaming Indian man who is clearly loved by all. 'I am Francis! I am the Curry King! I ran a restaurant in Darlington for many years. I'm 72 years old and I've been here 45 years. In 1972 I came to run a building company, then I did a job for a restaurant and he asked me to come and partner him. When someone first say you should go to Quaker House I say, 'Oh no, I'm not religious,' but then I found out it is a pub. And they soon converted me! I have embraced it well! Now it is my religion!'

Francis' long squealing laugh at this is ridiculously infectious, especially if someone seems to be continually filling your glass of 7.6 strength New World IPA. 'I'm retired now but I always come and hand out onion bhajis all over pub. For free of course! And if they want curry I cook curry. For nothing. Everybody enjoys it! This is a great pub! This is a great town!' And through a warm enveloping, caressing fog of loud music, strong beer and aromatic bhaji, I hear myself agreeing, woozily but heartily, as the evening slips gently away from me.

STAGE FOUR

DARLINGTON TO NORTHALLERTON

8 October, 16 miles

I wake, much later than intended, with a red rubber band emblazoned We Shall Overcome on my wrist and a carefully wrapped but now damply flaccid onion bhaji on the bedside table. Gifts from the previous night; I smile at the foggy memory. It turns out though that smiling hurts my head so I assume an expression of dazed blankness – which isn't hard – as I proceed with my preparations for embarkation on day four.

After about an hour under a shower as volcanic as the clanking pipes of my odd hotel can muster, I am ready to leave. I spread my OS Landranger 34 on the floral duvet. Today will take me into my third county of the walk. Yorkshire, or more specifically North Yorkshire, since despite a shared, uniquely Yorkshire cast of mind – shyness, modesty, a certain easy-going frivolousness – I consider the Ridings of this big county to have subtly different temperaments.

Northallerton is North Yorkshire's county town and it's my destination today. I'll head loosely south following the new A road, crossing the Tees at Croft and then down towards Great Smeaton where the marchers rested a while and Con Shiels Snr and Cuddy Errington rustled up another al fresco Irish Stew. Before my tracing finger gets this far south though, it passes through several villages of North Yorkshire that set me off playing the game that's amused me on many a long car journey: spotting any English villages or hamlets that could believably be the names of English supporting film actors of the 1940s and 50s. I will pass by many today and they are always a delight; Hutton Bonville, Lazonby Grange, Appleton Wiske. ('And now on ITV 4, a Rank Organisation classic from 1948, *The Vainglorious Heart*, starring Margaret Lockwood, Michael Redgrave and Appleton Fiske as Group Captain 'Sniffer' Daniels).'

This nostalgic reverie of a classier, more courteous age of stiff upper lips and perfect manners is abruptly curtailed by a quick dip into the morning's papers over tea and toast beneath the clock tower. The Republican US Presidential nominee Donald Trump, by his every utterance further revealing himself an odious human cocktail of self-regard and idiocy, has apologised – albeit in a graceless, insincere manner – for some vile and coarse remarks about women. I won't repeat them here, you will surely recall them. With the blustering disdain typical of his kind of man, he's dismissed them as 'locker room' chatter, as some British men seek to excuse their nastiness as 'banter' or, worse, 'bantz'. Many commentators of a liberal bent have sought to sum up Trump's essential nature but none so succinctly as Alan Bennett who has called him 'a lying, bellicose vulgarian'. This has just the right blend I think of elegance and scorn. Watching Darlington go quietly about its Saturday morning business of bakeries and newspapers, it is baffling and more than a little terrifying that Trump could conceivably be the next president of the USA and thus the leader of the free world. Surely not, one's rational self thinks, but then one remembers that alongside the brilliance, vigour, sophistication and dynamism of Americans is a corresponding trait of sometimes behaving like overgrown and wilful children.

America was also about to go to the polls back in October 1936 as the Jarrow men marched south. The Great Depression was entering its eighth year and this giant of a country was still on its knees. But Franklin D Roosevelt's New Deal, a progressive programme of relief and social security, had inspired the country, giving it hope and even a kind of unity that was reflected at the polls. The election, held just as the Jarrow Crusade arrived at the gates of their own political capital in Westminster, proved to be the most one-sided in US history: a landslide in which only Maine and Vermont didn't go with FDR. It's staggering that the American political system can have gone from fostering FDR to Donald Trump in 80 years, but then it's just as difficult to conceive that it's gone from Barack Obama to Trump in a matter of months.

However, as FDR won that pivotal election, Ellen Wilkinson, the Jarrow men and the British political class were looking not to events in America but Europe. Russia's Communist regime and its consolidation of power divided opinion here amongst the intelligentsia. From Spain, stories of fascist outrages committed by Franco and his army against their own people were beginning to emerge. Also on the agenda (literally) was the Middle East. Wilkinson was still in Edinburgh where she spoke to the Labour Conference on the subject of the fraught Arab–Israeli relations. There was a general strike in Palestine which the conference failed even to mention, let alone support. Wilkinson attacked this timidity. She then went on to excoriate the party's line in instructing local Labour Party branches not to support Jarrow and other hunger marches on the grounds that communists were involved. She openly mocked the TUC General Secretary saying, 'When Sir Walter Citrine gets to the Pearly Gates, St Peter will be able to reassure him that there are no communists inside.' In retaliation, Labour apparatchik Lucy Middleton said that Wilkinson had sent 'hungry and ill-clad men on a march to London'. This was a downright lie in every regard that angered the marchers greatly.

As the marchers passed along the lanes between Darlington and Northallerton, locals from the surrounding villages came to meet them with baskets of apples and pears. Brompton is as lovely as I had been told. It's early on a Saturday afternoon and there's just the low murmur of occasional traffic as a van, saloon or country bus pass the big triangular village green overlooked by a couple of attractive pubs, the Crown and the Three Horseshoes. St Thomas' church has stood on this green for a thousand years. Brompton is one of those quietly enduring English villages, like Adam Thorpe's fictional Ulverton, that offers a compacted nugget of the English story in miniature and microcosm through waves of history: Saxons, Vikings, Normans, Civil War, Enclosures, Industrialisation, Mills, Suburbanisation.

A sign erected by the Brompton Heritage Society nearby promises two alluring delights: the Linen Workers Memorial Seat and the Anglo–Danish Hogback Stones. The latter sounds to me like a UK–Scandinavian tribute to Jagger and Richards but are apparently a historic artefact that 'draws visitors from all over the world'. This visitor from Wigan via Jarrow couldn't get in, sadly, as the church was locked but the elusive stones and the Linen Workers Memorial Seat will always remain a brief and tantalising memory of my Saturday sojourn in Brompton. (The stones, by the way, are remarkable examples of Viking settler sculpture that are apparently well worth seeing. But pick the right day.)

On the outskirts of Northallerton, a plum-coloured vintage car passes me sounding – from the spluttering and wheezing of its antique engine – to be in a spot of bother. It's a Vauxhall of Luton (a town which awaits me further down the long road), registration DS89 34 and made in 1928 and so very likely to have been on the road, maybe this road, when the marchers passed by. 'Nice car,' I shout as the driver pulls up aslant the roadside, gets out and disappears under the bonnet. 'Can I have a word with you about it?'

'Now isn't really a good time,' comes a disembodied voice accompanied by a furious percussive burst of hammering, some ominous clanks and the occasional vivid swear word.

'Grand car that,' remarks a stout Yorkshire fellow in a flat cap passing by slowly and regally on a mobility scooter. 'Worth more than these modern ones,' he states solemnly. Not at the moment, I think, as I cross the road into the centre of Northallerton.

By 1936, the car was king of the road. Horse-drawn carriages had practically disappeared from our streets, confined to the odd brewery wagon or coal cart. Trams, once popular and mooted as the transport of the future, had been largely abandoned; a trend that would be successfully if expensively reversed in the 1990s. There was a tragic human cost of the new ubiquity of the motor car though. The powerful road lobby were keen to assert the primacy of the car over pedestrians. Under pressure from the AA and the RAC, the government had abolished the 20 mph speed limit and there was a huge subsequent rise in road deaths. (*The Listener* claimed that more people were killed on the roads in the first two years of the 1930s than in the entire Napoleonic war.) In response, Tory MP and 'colourful' character Colonel Moore-Brabazon huffed, 'What is the point of such concern over 7,000 road deaths a year? Over 6,000 people commit suicide a year and no one makes a fuss about that.'

Despite walking down busy roads for the most part, none of the marchers fell foul of a speeding motorist or lumbering lorry, although presumably Colonel Moore-Brabazon would have shed no tears if they had. It seems the spirit of *Top Gear* was already flourishing in Britain in the thirties.

In Northallerton, Rosie, Ruth and John, here on a shopping trip from nearby Stokesley, have been watching the car's erratic progress too and are waiting for me at the pelican crossing. 'Is he having some trouble? Do you think he should get a new one? You can get a Ford Focus as a runabout very reasonable on finance in Northallerton.' None of the trio has ever heard of the Jarrow march but all are warmly enthusiastic about Northallerton. 'It's a lovely place. You'll have a fine time. Plenty of nice pubs up those little streets.'

Those little streets radiate in a series of yards off a grand central boulevard. In the heyday of coaching and droving, this street would have thronged with traders coming down from Northumbria and Scotland. There were four annual fairs a year where you could sell your mother's prize cattle for magic beans and get a thick ear when you went home, or celebrate driving that hard bargain on a crate of cauliflower in one of the four inns along this main street. They're all still here though the names might have changed and all are busy on this fine market day. My room is at the Golden Lion where, under my window as I go through my unpacking ritual, I hear a broad Yorkshire voice attempting to lure the ladies of Northallerton to part with their hard-earned brass. Never an easy task in Yorkshire.

'Eight bunches of bananas, all for a pound, sweet juicy strawberries, luscious pineapples,' and from further down the street, 'Chinese spare ribs, lamb chops, twenty pounds for all them lamb chops, missus, gammon, bacon joints, make a lovely Sunday dinner, love.'

This is the prime time for bargain hunters as we're approaching the end of the long market day. The stalls are packing up, the trestle tables are being folded and the big white vans loaded, and I am watching the clock for a very good reason. My home town rugby team Wigan Warriors are playing in the Grand Final of the Rugby Super League, essentially the highlight of that sport's year. Whoever wins this can rightly claim to be the best team in the land, or rather lands, since in another modern development – along with words like 'Warriors' and 'Super Leagues' and 'Grand Finals' – French and Spanish teams now take part as well. The match kicks off soon and I know that on a Saturday in the football season and in the posher 'county' end of Yorkshire where they hunt, shoot, fish and play a different (inferior) kind of 'rugger', I will have my work cut out finding a pub that has the game on. But I have a plan. I will adjourn to a curry house – with a kindly and obliging maitre d' I hope – and, in return for a guaranteed hefty spend at a corner table for one, will hop on to their wifi network. Then, whilst working my way through a lamb dhansak, I'll watch the match on my iPad which will be propped against the first of several pints of lager. It is a plan almost beautiful in its elegance and simplicity.

Unlike so many plans – personal, national, political – this one actually works out. Aroma on Zetland Street is filling up with early night-outers and late market shoppers but they squeeze me in the window (as in, they find me a little table at the front of the restaurant, in case you thought that sounded weird). Happily, the waiter is a rugby league fan too and goes along enthusiastically with my plan. He arrives with the wifi code on a piece of paper on a silver tray and despite it being a lengthy, bamboozling string of random numbers, asterisks and hieroglyphs (always) I get it right first time and a small but crisp image of chunky men in cherry and white hoops on the greensward of Old Trafford, Manchester, appears above the poppadoms.

The next hour passes extremely pleasantly indeed. It's a tight, hard fought encounter but in the second half Wigan gain the upper hand and with it, to mix metaphors horribly, begin to turn the screw. At the bar, a couple waiting for a takeaway sink cocktails and bicker in a brittle way like a couple in a Noël Coward play before leaving with several white plastic bags of food. In the dying seconds (of the match, not the argument), Wigan score a late and conclusive try that clinches it and involuntarily like the oik I am, I half rise from my chair and growl 'Come On Wigan'. As you can imagine, when a solitary strange man does this in a curry house full of locals who know one another, it's quite the conversation starter.

It draws me into a chat with the big cheery group on the middle table. I tell them why I'm here and, this time, all of them have heard of the Jarrow march. They all know at least roughly what it was about and means, and I record our conversation over the increasing hubbub of a Saturday night curry house in a northern town.

'Protest … desperation … dignity … in the face of
Conservative bastards – come and have a beer with us!'

I perch at the corner of the table and am given a quick
resume of Northallerton and its character, 'It's a market town,
livestock market Tuesday and Wednesday. Always been a big
agricultural community and there's still that feel to the place.
That's why it's such a Tory town. They say round here that
in Northallerton they'd vote for a pig if you put it in a tweed
jacket. They voted to leave you know [I don't need to ask what].
The farmers think they're going to get more money. One of my
students is from a farming family and he keeps saying, "we're
going to be rich". Baffling … he's got a bloody shock coming
to him. It's the county town of North Yorkshire too so there's
always been that big admin sector, government offices … that's
a big employer. Rural payments agency used to be here but
that's gone now.'

What's still here though is the 'Pongo', as all the town calls
it. Its proper name these days is Club Amadeus: 'but everyone
calls it the "Pongo" and nobody knows why. When we were
kids in the seventies and eighties it was Sayers Disco. It was
effectively two garages concreted together. Awful but great.
Sticky carpets. That sort of thing. But there was nowhere else
to go. There still isn't. It's still in two parts. The middle-aged
people turn left at the door and the young 'uns turn right.' The
gentleman who told me all this can claim a certain authority.
He was one of the rumoured and select band of just ten people
who were in the audience in the most famous night in Pongo's
history, one that fixed Northallerton's premier (and only) night
spot as a footnote in the pop history of these islands.

On 19 May 1976 the Sex Pistols played at Sayers Disco
in Northallerton. Sending the fledgling band into the lion's
den of the northern club scene was part of manager Malcolm
McLaren's plan to toughen up the band and presumably provoke
outrage. On the fortieth anniversary of their famous show at the
Lesser Free Trade Hall in Manchester, I'd spoken to bassist Glen

Matlock about those early sojourns. 'I went into a chip shop and I asked, "What sort of fish have you got?" 'Cos in London you get rock, skate, whatever. The bloke just looked at me and said, "Are you taking the piss? We've got cod".' Drummer Paul Cook said that the furthest north he had been up to this point was Hampstead.

McLaren would give the band just enough money to get to the shows and the band would exist on stolen chocolate bars and chips, then having to badger the clubs themselves to get their money. 'It was vile, horrible, a nightmare. No chance to relax ... nothing ... awful nylon sheets ... utter total boredom,' recalled John Lydon, who would nightly bait the largely unresponsive audiences. Their van couldn't manage hills so Matlock would use the Ordnance Survey map to plot the flattest route possible, even if this involved enormous detours.

In Northallerton they supported the Doctors of Madness 'a real record company band' remembers Pauline Murray of the Ferryhill punk band Penetration, one of the rumoured ten in attendance. 'The Pistols wiped them out, they wiped a lot of bands out ... I saw it happen.' Not everyone was so keen though, as I was about to find out. Declining yet more offers of beer from the wonderful folk at the curry house, I leave them to their poppadoms and head for the Little Tanner pub. 'It's quirky,' they tell me, 'and Brian who runs it put the Pistols on at Sayers.'

The Little Tanner is definitely quirky, one of those strangely likeable new pubs or bars that have sprung up all over Britain in what feels like front rooms or old sweet shops or printers. Now the spaces are occupied, not unhappily, by luxuriantly bearded graphic designers wearing vintage US seed merchant baseball caps and drinking botanical gins and Sri Lankan pale ales. Even if these people had existed in 1976, they would not have been the kind of folk who went to see the Sex Pistols. Their audiences were largely either curious hippies or oikish 15-year-olds like me obsessed with the music press, hormonally restless and for whom liking punk was the cultural equivalent of smashing up a phone box.

The hipsters aren't in tonight but the nice barmaid Louise (or perhaps Lucy; the man with the phlegmy laugh and the large Gordon's at the bar called her both during my brief stay) tells me with an apologetic smile, 'Brian's not in tonight I'm afraid, he's in Thailand. But I know that he didn't put the group on. He was the DJ. I think he said he had to wake them up in the dressing room to come onstage and play. I don't think there was a stage, just the dance floor. And Brian thought they were rubbish … well, most people did then. It was very new, very different. Certainly for Northallerton …'

In 1936, the biggest single employer of musicians and the greatest patron and commissioner of music in the land was the BBC. The 'Beeb' would have been the way most of the Jarrow marchers listened to music. Lord Reith believed that light music, along with comedy and quizzes, was 'lowest common denominator' fare and not to be broadcast at all on Sundays. But at other times, thanks to wiser and less snobbish counsels, it vied with classical music as the bulk of the BBC's output. At 10.30pm, every night (except Sunday) there was a broadcast of an hour-and-a-half of music from a West End dancehall with bandleaders such as Henry Hall and Lew Stone and 'crooners' like Al Bowlly. Reith's deputy described crooning as 'a particularly odious kind of singing' but the audience loved it. They deluged the Corporation with bags of fan mail to the surprise of BBC mandarins and musicians alike.

By the mid-1930s, that august, now defunct publication the *Melody Maker* reckoned there were almost 20,000 dance bands in Britain, playing in various palais, lidos, theatres and hotels. The year before the Jarrow march, at a holiday camp in Great Yarmouth, Percy Cohen's band played to 1,500 people a night. British dance bands tended to be either 'sweet' or 'hot', playing music that was essentially romantic and lush or quick and infectious. No British bands ever really 'swung' though in the way that their American jazz counterparts did, like Benny Goodman. Nonetheless, in the UK, dance bands and light music were a phenomenon that cut across all classes and ages, despite the out of touch scorn of men like Reith and his deputy and the ever-reliably wrong-headed conductor Thomas Beecham who declared with all the confidence of the mistaken that 'the performance of music through the wireless cannot be other than a ludicrous caricature'. It seems the public have yet to twig this.

The bar of the Golden Lion ('OK but a bit seventies' was the curry house jury's verdict) is full and raucous as I settle in with a last whisky. There's what looks to be a wedding or at least a hen do; girls in scarlet and cream silks tottering to the toilets laughing. There's a few couples sipping wine and at the bar a cliché made flesh – quite a lot of flesh actually – a group of loud, hearty florid middle-aged men in tweeds, Barbours, a gilet or two and those shirts with the thin-lined patterning that you can only buy in 'country outfitters'. They seem amiable enough but then I can't hear what they're talking about. Maybe if I was a couple of tables closer I wouldn't be so generous. Or maybe I'm just being prejudiced.

I'd definitely felt a slight but perceptible change in landscape and mood as I came south from County Durham into North Yorkshire. No chimneys brood over the landscape of the north east now (or few anyway) but the Durham coalfield still carries the tough, ingrained feel of mining country. Towns like Ferryhill are very different in mood to Northallerton, especially on a busy market Saturday. No official reception met the Jarrow men here in 1936 and no councillor came to shake their hand. The council would not allow them to sleep in any school or council-owned building and so they took cold and uncomfortable shelter in the drill hall, just across from the Little Tanner. Drill halls were once a fixture in every town, as meeting places for army reservists. 'Thank God we found decent clergy in Northallerton,' said marcher David Riley. The *Northern Dispatch* for its part said the men had 'groused' and that the welcome was every bit as warm as strange folk from up country could have wished for. The war over Fake News had some of its initial skirmishes in the 1930s maybe, I thought as I drained my Aberlour, negotiated a teetering girl in high heels with a Chardonnay and made my way up the anaglypta-ed and horsebrassed staircase to bed.

STAGE FIVE

NORTHALLERTON TO RIPON

9 October, 19 miles

When I was a teenager, quite an odd one perhaps, I loved the party conference season. Unlike the youthful William Hague I never went to one, but I much enjoyed them vicariously. The telly was on all day providing, for skiving students and dole-ites of which I was from time to time both, a genuine alternative to horse racing or *The Sullivans* in the form of a kind of engrossing live theatre. Several different kinds of theatre actually.

The Conservatives' was always the most tightly scripted, directed and stage managed, with hardly any surprises – except for 1980 of course – and with the only variable being the toadiness of the cabinet, the hair-raising stridency of Mrs T's speeches and the length of the North Korean-style standing ovation that would inevitably follow them. The Liberals or SDP or Liberal Democrats or whatever they were called that year were always homespun and pleasant but mildly disorganised, like a CND jumble sale. Labour generally provided the great box office conference moments of the 1970s and '80s Dennis Healey in 1976, sweating like a prize fighter, pummelling his way through the boos and catcalls to finally earn a standing ovation; Kinnock taking on Derek Hatton's entryist Militant tendency in 1983 raging, 'You start with far-fetched resolutions.

They are then pickled into a rigid dogma … irrelevant to the real needs, and you end in the grotesque chaos of a Labour council – a Labour council – hiring taxis to scuttle round a city handing out redundancy notices to its own workers.' Militant bayed and sulked. But more cheered; it was clearly the start of the long fight back to power, even I could tell that from a sofa in Wigan. And I could tell that the personable young chap I watched in the late 1980s with the proto-mullet and thin lapels and skinny tie à la Duran Duran, new Shadow Trade Secretary Tony Blair, was going places.

By 2005, things had changed in all kinds of ways. My days were no longer my own and thus I could no longer slump all day in front of speeches, motions, resolutions and shows of hands. Tony Blair's days had got busier too. Labour had eventually ousted the Tories, a government that seemed as permanent as the ice caps during my twenties, and now he was giving his third conference speech as Prime Minister to the Labour faithful in Brighton. Looking back now, his words ring hollow with a conviction and sense of rectitude that proved fairly groundless.

> I hear people say we have to stop and debate globalisation. You might as well debate whether autumn should follow summer. They're not debating it in China and India. They are seizing its possibilities, in a way that will transform their lives and ours … The character of this changing world is indifferent to tradition. Unforgiving of frailty. No respecter of past reputations. It has no custom and practice. It is replete with opportunities, but they only go to those swift to adapt, slow to complain, open, willing and able to change.

Around that time I interviewed Digby Jones, the former head of the CBI, on Radio 2 and it proved one of only two occasions that I've ever lost my temper on live radio. Jones's position was essentially the same as Blair's, but expressed with even less sympathy for his countrymen and women. 'The British worker is going to have to change and work harder and be more productive and more flexible. Because otherwise there are thousands of workers in India who are going to steal their lunch.'

Neither the ice caps nor Tony Blair turned out to be permanent, and both Blair and Jones turned out to be wrong – as blithely wrong in fact as Francis Fukuyama was in 1992, in his once-influential book *The End of History*, when he confidently predicted that we were entering the final phase of human social development, a serene universal shift to liberal democratic government and an end to geopolitical conflict. Even as he wrote, in Jalalabad or Khartoum or a cave somewhere in the Tora Bora mountains of Afghanistan, Osama Bin Laden was planning the holy war on those same liberal democracies. It is a war that still rages today and has brought murder and mayhem to the cities of the east and the west. As Jon Cruddas now says of the imperious but naive assertions of Fukuyama, Blair and their ilk, 'This sink or swim view of humanity is alright for the winners. Rule from 35,000 feet is fine if you're in the first-class cabin.' Soon even those in that cabin wouldn't be safe, literally or metaphorically.

Similarly aloof, the Labour Conference of 1936 had little cheer to offer the marching men of Jarrow. After a frugal breakfast of bread and jam in the town hall, trudging from Northallerton in the teeming rain, spirits were further dampened by news from the conference that the Labour Party had decided not to support the marchers by protesting the National Assistance Board's decision to stop their benefit. The NAB had come to this decision as the marchers were 'technically not available for work'. David Riley, mayor of Jarrow and the march marshal, broke the news to them saying that it was 'a stab in the back'. A telegram was sent to Edinburgh to the conference delegates saying, 'We, the sons of England's most famous town, resent the unsympathetic attack on our members and the deliberate attempt to pauperise our crusaders.'

Perhaps it was this muted and unhappy start to the day that has led to some confusion about where the actual march went next. According to the official route lodged with the authorities and the BBC, they headed for Thirsk and Boroughbridge, making an overnight stay in each. But this is clearly wrong and no one seems entirely sure why. Did they deviate from the original route? Was the itinerary drawn up incorrectly? Anyway, I know where I'm headed. I'm bound for Ripon and I leave Northallerton on another golden autumn morning in North Yorkshire – an egg yolk sun and a faintly speckled Cadbury's Mini Egg blue sky to the gentle clamour of church bells. The *FT*'s cheery headlines are ringing in my mind too; 'Chill wind blowing through corporate landscape ... the pound in freefall ... protectionism returns ... Jeremy Paxman on writing his memoirs ...' I pop the *FT* in the recycling bin in Northallerton Market Square and head south on the Boroughridge Road.

The miles that stretch between Northallerton and Ripon pass through the most conventionally pretty scenery to date. They offer a peek into Herriot country and a hint of the quintessential Dales. As the road curls gently south west it nuzzles against the River Swale until, at Skipton-on-Swale, it leaps the slow, blue, viscous river at a fine little bridge. Eighty years after the marchers crossed this (breaking step in order not to set up potentially dangerous vibrations, as every schoolboy knows) I leaned here a while, watching the Swale whirl and pool around the reeds and disappear through trees across rolling fields.

At the big, handsome village of Baldersby where the road bends towards Ripon, I stopped for lunch on the village green, my pack beside me on a bench. There was not a soul about and I couldn't tell whether The Smithy was a pub, a garage, a tea shop or a garden centre. In any event it was closed, but this mattered not as I had had the uncommon foresight to bring my own lunch. Everyone I'd met in Northallerton had told me that I simply had to visit the artisanal deli of Lewis and Cooper.

Indeed, everyone I'd met in Northallerton was either headed there or just leaving it when they said this to me. The few that weren't were already in there. But through sharp elbows and enormous patience, I had emerged with some jamon serrano and a chunk of Gouda with cumin. 'Only the best for the working class!' I thought again, as I opened and carved the delicious fare with my Swiss army knife and ate it off the blade, feeling very much the carefree and seasoned man of the road stepping out one mid-autumn afternoon.

It was a very pleasant 20 minutes, watching the occasional light aircraft drone gently overhead and brushing the odd cheesy crumb from the folds of the OS map. It was so unseasonably mild, balmy even, that stretched out with my pack behind my head, I might even have dropped off. But then a thought occurred. Whatever The Smithy was, it was closed because it was Sunday. And if it was Sunday then there was a chance that, even if there wasn't honey still for tea, there was choral evensong at Ripon cathedral soon. A spot of light Googling revealed that it would indeed be happening at 3.30pm in Ripon cathedral, the very place where the town's Bishop welcomed the marchers. Ripon was a comfortable market and agricultural town in the thirties, as it is now, and the Jarrow marchers met a pretty indifferent response here, it's said, except at the cathedral. I thought that the least I could do was symbolically return the favour (I've started to see myself as a marcher) and pop in for choral evensong.

I quickened my pace across the amiable and easy pastures of North Yorkshire. What hills there were were far-off charcoal smudges in the hazy distance and I caught a glimpse of them from the appropriately named nook of Pennine View. Then on again, past Carlton Miniott and Ainderby Quernhow, two more splendid entries for the Villages That Sound Like 1950s Character Actors Game ('... and who can forget Carlton Miniott and Ainderby Quernhow as the two bungling policemen in *Mayhem at the Vicarage*').

Above me and above the rolling dales, the skies had darkened and around 2.30, I felt the first unwelcome splashes of rain since starting off. Soon it came in great, soaking gusts and I was grateful for the shelter of a petrol station awning. Inside in the shop, a gentleman called John Lyndley chatted to me as we both perused the Hula Hoops and Skittles. John told me that Ripon was a lovely old town and he also passed on a cherished family tale that his granddad had known a bloke who'd been on the march who had declared on arrival at Ripon that his 'boots had broke down' and made a new home in that cathedral city. I was hearing many, many stories like this on my travels and whilst they may not all turn out to be quite true, that's really not the point. King Arthur and Robin Hood didn't exist but they are still culturally enduring; potent and vivid ciphers for our country, lenses through which we see ourselves. Jarrow did happen, even if some of the stories are pure and righteous romance.

Remarkably soon, the rain was gone. The clouds became ragged and then dispersed in a stiff wind leaving skies wide, clear and blue as I raced to get to Ripon for evensong. I'd decided at the outset that the book came first, and if in search of a good story or an interesting encounter, I needed to use motorised transport for a short distance, I would, so long as it stuck to the route of the march. But it was Sunday of course and since bus deregulation in the 1980s, rural services in places like this must be long gone. One of Mrs Thatcher's many apocryphal remarks (my favourite is 'happiness is a ticked-off list') was 'a man who, beyond the age of 26, finds himself on a bus can count himself as a failure'. I was happy for Mrs T to think whatever she liked of me from wherever she may be. But she had seen to it that there were no buses for me that Sunday.

Now absurdly keen to see my plan through, I upped the pace to a mild trot, which isn't easy with a rucksack the size of a child's wardrobe. Still, it all felt very 'ecclesiastical race against time', à la *The Da Vinci Code*. I've never seen or read *The Da Vinci Code*, but I have seen the films promoted on the sides of buses (which is where I get most of my movie marketing from) and they generally seem to involve Tom Hanks dashing through a cloister or transept looking quite determined followed by a pretty girl 30 years his junior. Tom presumably makes these films at gunpoint whilst visualising the cheque.

When I was teaching sociology to likeable scallies in Skelmersdale new town in the late eighties, the standard line on 'the sociology of religion' trotted out in the textbooks and syllabi was that we were living in an 'increasingly secularised society'. The theory ran that church attendance was falling, the teachings of religious leaders going unheeded and religion itself, once such a potent force in people's lives, was dwindling to the extent that soon it would be no more influential on society than chamber music or mime. With the supreme confidence of the deluded, no one foresaw the rise of Islamic fundamentalism or that of the Christian right in America, the constant rows over anti-Semitism in the Labour hierarchy or even the brief revival of Catholic churches in England driven by devout young Polish immigrants. The predictions of experts often carry no more weight than the prophecies of oracles.

If anything the church in England was weaker and more beleaguered in the 1930s than it is today. Attendance was low and had been falling generally since the Great War, when the horrors of the battlefields had shattered the faith of many. Those who attended church were largely middle class and female. Mass Observation, the large-scale survey movement, found downright hostility to the church in some towns and cities, with only one in ten people going to church regularly in the mid-1930s. They were building community halls not churches on the new estates and holding whist drives instead of masses. The church was strongest in the affluent south and weakest in the industrial north, outside of the Catholic stronghold of Lancashire. Catholicism generally was still strong, bucking the general trend in the working towns and cities of the north. But Anglicanism and Nonconformism, the great pillars of the

Establishment and the marginalised respectively, were in decline. That *bête noire* of the Jarrow marchers, Bishop Henson, said that the church had become 'an effete establishment ... moving like a rudderless vessel over a rock haunted ocean'. Clearly, those rocks were socialism, feminism and social change, and what was needed was the enduring power of fire and brimstone.

There were no such modern uncertainties when Ripon cathedral was built. Back then, God was a very real presence in people's lives, as indeed was the devil. The flames of hell licked at one's feet at every step of life, for peasant and aristocrat alike, although of course the very rich could buy a Get Out of Hell Free pass in the form of an 'indulgence'. In the seventh century, St Wilfred put a stone roof on the wooden monastery here, thus erecting one of the first stone buildings of the Anglo-Saxon era. Soon, people came to worship here from the many surrounding hamlets and farmsteads dotted across the empty landscape.

That was 1,350 years ago, and St Wilf's place is still looking pretty impressive and certainly welcoming if you've trotted the last few miles to it in intermittent rain while being buzzed by articulated lorries. I slumped into the nearest pew and admired the décor. There's a lot of it to admire. If I were Nikolaus Pevsner I could give you the full chapter and verse on the various naves and misericords and flying buttresses, on gilts and flutings and curlicues. Lacking that kind of critical vocabulary, I'll just say that architecturally, it's a bit of a doozie.

Of course, on this autumn afternoon, what we're all really here for is the singing. Marvellous it is too. The choristers enter to the sound of the organ in full throated, eerie, *Abominable Dr Phibes* mode and proceed to match it note for note with a song that reaches to the very top bits (I told you I was no Pevsner) of the cathedral's soaring interior. Organ fans will already know that the instrument here is one of Harrison and Harrison's, the esteemed Durham family firm who also provided the sonorous beauties in King's College Cambridge, the Royal Festival Hall and Westminster Abbey.

Sermons, especially when delivered in a Yorkshire accent, always make me think of Alan Bennett's hilarious 'Take A Pew' in the *Beyond the Fringe* revue. But today the sub-Dean's was very interesting, even faintly political, with a few pointed references to Britain's ongoing national rending of garments over Brexit. 'It's worth remembering at the current time that our patron saint St George is half Greek and half Palestinian ...' There's even a wry dig at David Cameron, the departed and largely discredited former PM. 'You could say that Jesus Christ invented the Big Society, one of David Cameron's favourite ideas. Anyone remember the Big Society? Anyone remember David Cameron?' This may hardly be Lenny Bruce, but in the Tory heartlands of North Yorkshire, it's positively incendiary. (Between Ferryhill and Wakefield, the march never left Conservative-run districts.)

It's over by half four and very lovely it was too. Emboldened by the music and the general vibe of serene, sun-dappled radiance, I try and grab a few words with the Dean, who's present today. A helpful gentleman tells me that he'll go into the vestry and enquire. He disappears off 'backstage', where if the Dean were a touring rock performer he would now be sitting with a white towel around his shoulders wreathed in sweat and drinking from a bottle of Amstel. Ten minutes later, the Dean emerges in full regalia, smiling, and offers me a firm handshake. He is well aware of today's anniversary. Eighty years ago, his predecessor welcomed the Jarrow men here and offered them a tour of the cathedral. Every one of them wanted it, although some of the Catholics – Tyneside was home to a good deal of the country's three million – were worried that they might be excommunicated for even entering an Anglican church. It must have been quite a day.

'Well, of course, cathedrals are used to large numbers. But, yes, it must have been very special. They were here for a particular reason at a particular time in history and the fact that the cathedral was hospitable and welcoming would have been regarded by them as a blessing, an approval of what they were marching for. The link between the church and politics is nothing new. Politics is about how people organise themselves, how they live together and that is the business of the church too. Jesus came to make this world more like heaven. So how do we so structure our society so it more resembles heaven than it does, well, anywhere else,' he chuckles.

In 1936, Ripon was fairly well insulated from the economic downturn that was blighting the rest of the north. This is perhaps why the reception for the marchers here was so distinctly muted. Local paper the *Evening Chronicle* reported that the town had viewed them 'askance' and been 'unsympathetic'. Some youngsters had even 'tittered' at them when they arrived bedraggled and footsore. The Dean though stresses similarities, not divisions: 'Sometimes industrial areas think they have had it hard and that rural society has it easier. That's not always the case. A town like Ripon has all types, all strata of society. Life would not have been easy for everybody, not then, not now.'

The Dean has a big patch, though again I'm sure that's not the right word. 'This Episcopal area encompasses most of North Yorkshire west of the A1, right to the Cumbria and Lancashire borders and up as far as the Tees and Durham. There are lots of small rural communities; remote, isolated, and suffering real issues. There's the difficulty of trying to keep your community and society active and vibrant with small numbers of people. Younger people can't find work and have to move away.' The Dean sounds exactly like William Hague, which is disconcerting, but I concentrate hard.

'And then, also as a diocese we include West Yorkshire which is an industrial, or rather a post-industrial heartland. The north, it's seen some stuff, some changes, but this church is alive, it's full of faith, it's keen to serve the needs of this community. We see the whole breadth of life here. We're a cathedral for everyone and you can come and hear this lovely music at evensong every day. Well, not Mondays ... and not all Saturdays. Nearly every day!' and again he ends with a chuckle.

If I was expecting a firebrand revolutionary, I didn't get it. But I think I did get the Dean. He struck me as a canny, slightly guarded Yorkshireman – is there any other kind? – and he was perhaps being a little cautious and circumspect as one would with a rough-looking Lancashire cove with a flat cap and a backpack who gatecrashes your choral evensong and claims to be writing a book. 'Before you go, you must see the crypt by the way. Anglo-Saxon. Marvellous. Nearly 1,400 years old. But watch your step. And hurry up ... we're closing.'

Taking this as official blessing, I find my way to the other side of the church, unclip the velvet rope, and make my way gingerly down into a stepped descent and then along a passage of ancient rough-hewn stone. The voices above me grow quieter, and further along by a little alcove where a candle would have once burned but is now in shadow, the passage turns and gets narrower still before opening into the crypt itself. It is a small stone chamber, spectral in the half-light falling from a small window. Around the room in several more recessed alcoves are black oily stains from the candles of Saxon monks that burned more than a thousand years ago. I realise I can hear nothing now from the main church, nothing at all in fact except my own breathing and my pulse in my ears. There is something very old and very eerie about this place and after a minute or so, I turn and go quickly back up the worn, rough stone steps into the huge silent interior of the twilit chapel.

I'm the only person here, and dusk has fallen while I was in the crypt. No matter though. Someone will still be tidying up, putting away the collection box, doing whatever it is you do before locking a cathedral for the night. Except that when I get to the large vaulted front door, having met no one, I find that it is already locked. I turn around and look back down towards the altar. But it's already getting difficult to see it.

If, like me, you're a fan of Robert Aickman's ghost stories, and in particular his story 'The Cicerones' about a hapless tourist who gets lost and trapped in an ancient cathedral at night, you will know why a very real, cold ripple of panic began to run over me. This became colder and stronger when the next door I tried was locked too. And the next. I won't tell you how Aickman's story ends but I will tell you that eventually I found a small narrow wooden door hidden in the west end of the vast church and slipped out into the churchyard now bathed in yellow sodium lights, deserted and gloomy. I didn't care. Relief flooded over me, quickly followed by embarrassment and then a kind of sheepish mirth. Night was coming on over Ripon and somewhere in this lovely old town there was a pint of beer and a whisky waiting for me, and by the time I clasped it gratefully, I'm sure my hand would have stopped shaking.

STAGE SIX

RIPON TO HARROGATE

12 October, 11 miles

On 11 October 1936, as the Jarrow men enjoyed their Sabbath day of rest in Ripon, the Sunday papers they may have read would have little resembled the enormous overstuffed beasts we stagger back from the supermarket with or burden the paper boy with now. But they would have been full of an early vintage of the fizz and froth of today's news. The 1930s were the decade that pop culture properly got into its stride and what we think of as the mass media began to seed and grow. Hollywood, 'swing' and the doings of sportsmen, musicians, actors and aristocrats were staple fare of the papers, but the big media story of the weekend 80 years ago was the announcement by the BBC that they would be launching a new entertainment platform called 'television' in early November, just as the Jarrow march reached London.

By October 2016, television had grown to be a behemoth that first conquered and shrank the world and then seemed to be beginning to wane and be eclipsed by the revolutionary global power of the Internet. Nevertheless, 70 million Americans would be glued to their small screens – more probably giant screens – tonight for the second presidential debate between Hillary Clinton and Donald Trump. It would be the first encounter since the leaked tape full of lewd misogyny had shown him in his true lurid colours. I didn't think I'd be watching since I was bound for Harrogate where I could find much nicer things to do I was sure. Before I left Ripon I wanted to make a visit that couldn't be described as fun but would be salutary and very relevant to my trip.

For their part, before the Jarrow marchers left Ripon, they held a public meeting as was usual as well as a bizarre mock trial that no one has ever quite got to the bottom of. Marcher Eddie Fitzpatrick dressed as a judge in some borrowed robes and sentenced David Riley to 'bully beef' and fatigues for the rest of his life. Was it just a bit of fun and an excuse to dress up and tease the Mayor? Or a smokescreen designed to hide the real disciplinary hearing of a different marcher who had broken the strict rules by getting drunk and thereby threatened to harm the carefully managed saintly image of the marchers? That image was reinforced and restored however at the meeting. An Alderman of Ripon spoke of how the discipline and self-sacrifice of the marchers had convinced him of the march's worth after initial misgivings. David Riley gave a grim illustration of the real cost of poverty when he stunned the audience by telling them that for every stillborn child in Ripon, there were two born dead in Jarrow. Then, having been declared fit and well (apart from blistered feet and the exhaustion of one older marcher) by Mr Cargill and Miss Blake, the medical students who were part of the march, they were on their way again to the sound of the harmonica band augmented by a drum they had been given in Ripon. They were bound for another affluent Conservative town: Harrogate. Privately, the march leaders worried what kind of welcome or lack of it awaited them there.

Along the way, they were treated warmly, royally even. As they marched through the little agricultural hamlets of Wormald Green, South Stanley, Ripley and Killinghall, one newspaper said that the driver of a passing Rolls-Royce – can there have been many about, one wonders? – wound down his window to hand the men pound notes. I was to pass these villages too, some now dormitories for commuters to Harrogate or even Leeds, but no Rolls-Royces passed my way. I did get a thumbs up from a lorry delivering granary bread and seeded baps though, so this cheered me a little, and that was needed after my detour to Ripon workhouse.

It sits squat and forbidding at a quiet edge of town away from the pretty cobbled streets of bistros and bars. Standing between the pillared gates, under the curved iron arch with its cheerless lantern, one thought comes immediately to mind: what must it have felt like to see this place, to look upon this stained brickwork, those mean windows, that sinister and menacing door, arriving not as a tourist wanting diversion, but desperate and friendless at a place of last resort? 'Workhouse', like 'Means Test', is a word that still haunts working-class life. Its long, dire echo resonates far beyond its era. It's another one of those words that I can remember my nan using when I was a kid in the 1970s. Its era may have gone, but its power to frighten lived on.

The workhouse was a place of shelter and employment for those who could not support themselves, and put that way it may seem welcoming, even kindly. Without doubt, at some level the impulse behind them was to a degree benevolent. But in practice they were grim and unhappy places, frugal and basic, offering only drudgery and discomfort. Partly, this was deliberate. Conditions in the workhouse were purposely harsh to discourage anyone who could possibly avoid them. They were bleak fixtures of civic life for centuries, but by the time of the Jarrow march, they were chiefly the domain of the sick, disabled or elderly. Even so, they were still there; a shadow in every town, the bottom rung on the ladder of degradation. Several of the Jarrow marchers had spent time in them. Jarrow itself had been described as 'a workhouse without walls'.

Ripon's central workhouse, set back by the Jolly Fryer fish bar, dates to the seventeenth century and was one of two in the town. A warden manned the door, vagrants were discouraged, and, on the whim of the gatekeeper, individuals or families were admitted. Once through the entrance hall, the sexes were separated – families were broken up – and admitted to the casual wards. The new inmates were told to strip and bathe, and their clothes were fumigated in the sulphur disinfector room. Then in return for a bed and meagre rations (often stopped altogether if some minor offence were committed), inmates would perform menial, tedious tasks of physical labour such as breaking stones or picking oakum. In Ripon, they chopped wood in the small courtyard. The novelist Barbara Taylor Bradford's grandmother was born in this workhouse; when a birth occurred here the child's birthplace was simply registered as '75 Allhallowgate, Ripon' to prevent prejudice against the child later.

Ripon workhouse is a tourist attraction now, which is odd but very definitely an improvement. You tour around led by a series of information posters and an audio guide. Most of the building is exactly as it was in the Victorian era and, whilst a few effects are recreated, like the permeating odour of carbolic, the overwhelming sense of misery soaked into the walls is very real. Long drab corridors stretch away containing rows of tiny cells each bare but for a narrow, hard bed. At the end of the corridor, there is a restraining seat with leather straps and leashes. Fumigation rooms, pegs for pale, threadbare utility clothes (small versions for the children), cracked baths, bare walls. And everywhere the notices.

> RIPON POOR LAW UNION: PAUPERS SHOULD OBSERVE THE FOLLOWING. ON ENTERING THE WORKHOUSE YOU WILL BE CONFINED TO THE DAYROOMS, SLEEPING WARDS AND EXERCISE YARDS OF YOUR CLASS. YOU MUST NOT TALK WITH OR COMMUNICATE TO ANYONE OF A DIFFERENT CLASS.

It is a chilling place. Registration hall, meeting room, kitchen, laundry, dormitories, mortuary; each bleaker than the last. Stern portraits of former governors stare down from bare plaster walls and it is easy and tempting to see these men as villains, when in fact, they were probably more enlightened than many of their peers. At the end of the tour, as is obligatory these days, comments are invited on postcards which can be pinned to the wall. Like the 'below the line' comments on even the most achingly liberal newspaper's websites, they make one despair.

'People on benefits should come here to see what real poverty is.'

'Great Idea. Save us millions in benefits. Stick them in the workhouse.'

'No charging point for my iPad – Lucy, aged 44.'

Hoping that the last was at least some kind of ironic comment on the others, but still in a fairly dismal mood, I find myself back out on Ripon's drizzly and deserted streets, hoping that a late lunch at the Jolly Fryer might conjure a bit more fellow feeling and warmth towards humanity. These hopes are soon realised as I step inside the cosy little café and straight back into the 1950s, maybe the 1940s, maybe even the days of the Jarrow march itself. Wood panelling, low lighting from cute little wall mounted lamps, laminated place mats with coaching scenes; I half expect to see Trevor Howard removing some grit from Celia Johnson's eye at the next table. In fact, it's a middle-aged couple discussing last night's TV.

HER: I forgot *Emmerdale* was on at quarter to seven because of the football. I had a bath and nearly missed it. It's so daft though. I'm going to stop watching it.

HIM (shocked): It won top soap again, Helen. Third year running.

HER: Aye, by the *TV Times* … it's not gospel, is it? Anyway, I'm going to try a small portion of that special today. Bit of an unknown quantity.

Having perused the burgundy leatherette menu with its bewildering array of specials and deals (kiddies, OAPS, early birds, two-for-ones, etc) I decide to stay classic. Beef burger and chips, 'with tea and bread and butter please'. The lovely waitress, a lady of about 70, tells me, 'It comes with tea and bread and butter love, and free curry sauce as it's Wednesday. I'll give you some scissors, those packets can be tricky.' I stay here for half an hour or so, faith in humanity being restored with every friendly, tasty, happy passing minute.

The marchers needn't have worried about Harrogate, where they received the warmest welcome of the march so far. Two miles outside town, a man who had come to meet them unfurled a banner which read 'Harrogate workers welcome Jarrow workers' to initial cheers but was apparently asked to take it down when it was suspected he might be a communist. If this sounds cowardly, indeed pathetic, it should be said in mitigation that the Jarrow organisers needed the hospitality or at least support of many of the Conservative local councils that they'd be passing through. One of these, of course, was Harrogate.

A journalist from the *Guardian* joined them as they marched:

> The villagers of Ripley and Killinghall rushed to their doors to see the marchers pass; motorists waved as they went by; one shouted, 'How are you sticking it?' and a woman cried, 'Hello, Geordies.' And the 'Geordies' themselves were in great form, so that every moment I expected the band to change from 'Annie Laurie' and 'Swanee River' to 'Cheer, Boys, Cheer.' Contributions to the 'kitty' fell in as we went; here it was a pound there it was a penny, the penny specifically being the offering of an ecstatic little girl who ran across the road to meet us as if no one less than Bonnie Prince Charlie was at our head … There can be no doubt that as a gesture the march is a bounding success. I fell in with it this morning on the Ripon road. Under its

two banners ('Jarrow Crusade'), with its harmonicas, its kettledrum, and its four hundred feet, it was going strong. The marchers have with them two doctors, a barber, a group of pressmen, a Labrador dog mascot ... It is an example of civic spirit probably without parallel anywhere else in the country.

Once over the River Nidd in Nidderdsale the final three miles to Harrogate are straightforward enough. You enter the town along a lovely wide boulevard, but coming up this last pull of open road must have been tough especially when, at the brow of the hill, the road descends again – always dispiriting. As any fellwalker will tell you, the cardinal rule is 'height once gained should never be conceded easily'.

I visit WH Smith's Harrogate branch for batteries and newspapers and, just alongside the new releases table containing a *Pokemon Go* annual and a Benedict Cumberbatch mindfulness colouring book (no, really), I come across a book entitled *Harrogate in 1000 Dates*. It's a timeline of significant events in the town's history and, whilst it finds room for such landmark dates as the staging here of the 1982 Eurovision Song Contest and the opening of Betty's Tea Room in 1919, the entry for 1936 includes the opening of the town's Odeon cinema but not the arrival of the Jarrow march. This is strange, given that the town apparently embraced them warmly with collections and greetings on the street. Similarly, apart from one awful hour, I have the happiest time yet here, spending a delightful afternoon and evening walking, eating, drinking, exploring – and a long, blissful sojourn in bed.

Harrogate manages the neat trick of being smart without being prissy, and it's a town of contradictions. You can drink gourmet Ecuadorian coffee and eat artisanal cupcakes just feet from where the town drunks shout unhinged abuse at each other and dance to ghetto blasters. Hipster shops are everywhere, and the nice, chatty proprietor of a vintage clothes store tells me she likes the town but is thinking of moving as, however lovely, 'the money from selling my Harrogate place will buy me a lot elsewhere and I need a new project, as I've no pension.' I tell her that with a bit of luck I never intend to retire. I hope there'll always be someone wanting a few hundred words of my deathless prose. She laughs. 'The vintage world is a bit like that. You see these little old couples who've been in it for years, still at all the fairs and stuff.' Still, presumably, selling Jarvis Cocker his polyester peardrop-collared shirts, faded cord jeans and retro specs.

On the corner of the sweetly named Strawberry Dale Avenue, by Bridal Boutique and Commercial Road, stands the Harrogate drill hall where the town's detachment of the Army Cadet Force meet as well as the 58th Harrogate Squadron of the Air Training Corps (motto 'Venture And Adventure'). This is where the Jarrow marchers were put up in Harrogate, and though compared to some of the town's architecture, it's not a particularly impressive building, what it did have was the outrageous luxury of central heating, far from common in 1936. That would have made a world of difference to these weary men.

If any of the marchers had room in their pockets for a paperback book to curl up with on the drill hall floor, it might well have been two of the three Agatha Christie's Poirot novels that were published in the few months before they set off; *The ABC Murders* and *Murder in Mesopotamia*. Christie was at the height of her popularity in 1936, having come through a mysterious personal crisis a decade before. On the evening of Friday 3 December 1926, after kissing her sleeping seven-year-old daughter Rosalind goodnight, closing the bedroom door and going downstairs, Christie drove away from her Berkshire home into the night and simply disappeared. Days passed and one of the largest searches ever mounted was undertaken for the celebrity writer. More than a thousand policemen were assigned to the case along with aeroplanes and hundreds of civilian volunteers. Two of her peers in the crime writing fraternity, Sir Arthur Conan Doyle and Dorothy L. Sayers, were consulted. Her car was soon found abandoned near a lake close to Guildford called Silent Pool. Dark speculation swirled around the press.

Eleven days later she was found staying quietly at the Swan Hydropathic Hotel, Harrogate. In a joyous footnote, it was one of the hotel's resident banjo players who spotted her. Whilst all this did make it into that book of Harrogate's most important events, this enigmatic episode has never been fully explained. Did she lose her memory after a car crash? Was she angry or upset about her husband's ongoing affair? Or, as has been recently speculated, might she have been in a 'fugue state' with no real knowledge or control over her actions? Whatever the real story, the Old Swan revels in its Christie connection. It's one of the main venues for the Harrogate Crime Writing Festival. In a nice, if probably entirely coincidental twist, now that Nordic Noir and Scandi Crime writing have become so fashionable and successful, it's fitting that Harrogate should also now boast a Scandinavian restaurant called Norse. I had a wonderful time there and will try to refrain from eulogising the menu and the evening of eel, celeriac and general smoked, soused and pickled gorgeousness.

If your tastes run to classic British fare though, like two chicken curries, rice, naan breads, chips and a couple of pints of lager for under a tenner, head for the town's Wetherspoon which as well as being cheap is probably the most architecturally gorgeous in England. More to our point, this is where the Jarrow marchers came on the evening of 11 October 1936.

It wasn't a Wetherspoon then of course. It was the Winter Gardens Harrogate, adjacent to and part of the world-famous Royal Baths. But happily the Wetherspoon retains the famous old name, and it was here that Harrogate turned out in force to join with the Jarrow marchers at a public meeting. Harrogate loved them. The county set ladies wept openly at Paddy Scullion's tales of midwives putting their own pennies in the gas meter to deliver babies in cold, dark, impoverished Jarrow homes. Marcher Sam Rowan commented, 'By the time Paddy Scully had finished that night, the women were in tears. They were shedding buckets of tears in their fur coats, I can tell you, down in Harrogate.'

'Red' Ellen gave another witty, blistering oration. 'I know that the authorities are getting very tired of Jarrow. They are going to be even more tired of it by the time we have finished.' The Wednesday gossip column of the *Harrogate Herald* was glowing, if a little patronising. 'A petite figure with a wealth of bronze hair spoke fearlessly from the heart and as she warmed to her subject she fired the audience to frequent bursts of acclamation ... As I listened I was reminded of Joan of Arc.'

These days, the only burning steaks in the Winter Gardens are the ones that come sizzling from the grill: '8 or 14 oz Aberdeen Angus steaks from Britain and Ireland matured for 35 days then seasoned by us. With chips (add 597 Cal), peas, tomato, mushroom (add 143 Cal) and a drink.'

The J D Wetherspoon chain was founded by Tim Martin who opened the first in Muswell Hill, London, in 1979, naming it after one of his primary school teachers. It has become a modern British leisure phenomenon. Wetherspoon has been called 'the canteen of Britain', or according to the *Guardian*, 'a chain at the coalface of boozed up Britain'. A writer from webzine *Vice* actually spent a week in various Wetherspoons around the regions and whilst his resultant piece was largely fair, even affectionate, it still roped in the usual clichés: sullen, shaven-headed men getting dourly hammered, couples drinking Guinness at nine in the morning – all of which you can find in the fashionable dives of Soho. But of course if Francis Bacon does it, it's bohemian; if Wayne Rooney, or one of his lookalike spiritual brethren, does it, it's barbarian.

Into this already rich mix of social stereotyping and class mistrust, you can add the fact that Martin, founder of the budget boozer of provincial Blighty, was also one of the biggest donors to the campaign to leave the EU. Bluff and aggressively matey, with a mullet and a penchant for polo shirts, he could have come straight from central casting as the blokeish beer and burgermeister of Brexit Britain. He spent some quarter of a million pounds of his own money on backing the campaign and was rewarded by seeing millions wiped off Wetherspoon's shares in the chaotic markets after the referendum result. This was a delicious irony for many 'remainers'. But the fact certainly remains that while the English commentariat were looking elsewhere in the summer of 2016 – to the Beltway, Baltimore, Aleppo or the Chilcott enquiry – much of Wetherspoon's England was looking closer to home and, rightly or wrongly, echoing the views of Tim Martin.

To the best of my knowledge, the Harrogate Winter Gardens' Wetherspoon was my first. I liked it. As the phrase goes, what's not to like? Some people might find some callow and wearisome irony in the fact that the Winter Gardens is now a Wetherspoon but it makes perfect sense. It fulfils just the same valuable and happy function now as the Winter Gardens did back in 1936 by providing nighttime entertainment for the working folk of Harrogate. Back then it was piano recitals, plays and acrobats. Now it's big screen football and pub quizzes. It was full, and not of slavering beer monsters as I'd been led to expect, but of cheery, civilised working people having a pint and meal after work, many of them watching the World Cup qualifier between England and Slovenia on enormous screens. The match was an arid affair but it was certainly improved by a couple of large Hendrick's gin and tonics in an ice-frosted glass zesty with lemon and costing £3.80 a time. As the game ended around ten, and as I was leaving, several plates full of slathered, smothered, seared and seasoned fare arrived nearby for a table of four. Again, context is all: if you eat late at night in Madrid, you're cosmopolitan and free-spirited; if you do it in Yorkshire, you're a slob. Bon appétit, I thought.

I enjoyed Wetherspoon rather more than my other evening's outing in Harrogate. But then that was probably my fault. Although I seem to be almost alone in this in modern Britain, stand-up comedy is not really my thing. I know quite a few stand-up comics, and I like them all. But like grand opera, the circus, Formula One and many other popular and respectable diversions, it just doesn't do it for me. Perhaps it's all those panel shows. But as the Harrogate Comedy Festival was on whilst I was in town, and as comedy was certainly a popular entertainment for the average Briton of 2016 and 1936, I thought I should 'take in a show', as the genteel old phrase once went.

What would have made the Jarrow marchers laugh? The answer, by and large, was 'other northerners', chiefly ones making the transition to film fame from careers in music hall. Comedy was the decade's most successful film genre and one of its biggest stars was himself a son of the north east. Will Hay came from County Durham and was in his mid-40s when he made his first film, having been a top draw on the touring comedy circuit. His screen career was brief but glittering, making it all the more surprising that his name is nowhere to be found in the indexes of any of the major social histories of the period – surprising and disappointing since Hay's popularity reflects something in the national character. His speciality was playing a stuffy, bumptious schoolmaster, and how much we laughed at it shows how much British comedy of the time (and for decades to come) would centre around pricking the pomposity of authority figures, from Chaucer's clergymen to Captain Mainwaring. Jarrow's cinemas would have been packed for Hay's mid-1930s hits like *Boys Will Be Boys*, *Where There's a Will* and *Oh, Mr Porter*; cinema being a relatively cheap form of escapist entertainment even in poverty-stricken towns like Jarrow. Some of the comedy films of 1936 now sound like parody: *Cheer Up!*, *Excuse My Glove!*, *Keep Your Seats Please*! The last of these was a vehicle for another comic colossus of the period, George Formby. Again, Formby's schtick (if one can use that slick Americanism about a toothy banjo player from Wigan) was the cheeky little guy getting the girl and getting one over on his social betters, usually whilst strumming an upbeat, mildly obscene ditty and winking.

Hay and Formby aside, many of the other 'household names' of the period such as Leslie Fuller, Hal Gordon, Bobby Howes or Gene Gerrard are now only names in the households of real comedy buffs. You can find some of their work on DVD and YouTube and it's not noticeably funny, but then again it's not appreciably any less funny than most British TV comedy today. For the 1936 variety, it helps if you really like men dressing up, men getting into scrapes with 'coppers' or men pretending to be very drunk – or all three, as with Teesside's Jimmy James's classic 'drunk sketch' filmed in 1936 and surviving on YouTube. Though clearly a daft, northern, working-class fellow, he's dressed as impeccably formal as Fred Astaire in *Top Hat* for reasons that are never adequately explained. Perhaps you had to be there.

I was there at the middle of the 2016 Harrogate Comedy Festival and for much of the evening I wished I was pretty much anywhere else, recalling within seconds of taking my seat that I generally would feel more comfortable and relaxed at a public witch trial or the controlled explosion of a suspect package than at stand-up comedy gigs. There are about 30 or 40 of us in an upstairs 'studio' and there are a couple of comics on the bill tonight. I'm not going to name the 'turns' because my grim evening wasn't their fault, not entirely anyway. Hey, stand-up comedy! It's not you, it's me! Although it is a bit you.

It doesn't help that the chap sitting alongside me nearly recognises me. Being recognised is never a problem. It's largely a delight. But 'nearly' being recognised is always a complex and fraught social transaction, involving assuring people that I'm not their postman or Trevor from purchase ledger and culminating in having to explain why my face might be familiar and watching the blank and faintly disappointed look emerge. That's why, unless I'm going to get something particularly useful from it, like a great interview or story, a free curry, or maybe a private tour of an art gallery, haunted castle, gin distillery or secret nuclear installation, I tend to prefer to be 'a bit incognito', the better to observe and eavesdrop. I remembered exactly why when, as I got out my little notebook, my large, voluble neighbour shouted, 'Are you from the *Yorkshire Post?*' Shortly after, a sort of real recognition dawned and we engaged in difficult small talk. 'Shame about Terry Wogan, wasn't it?' he asks. 'Yes,' I reply, this being the only possible answer a person in possession of their senses could give. Nicely awkward now, I'm well set up for an hour of discomfort.

The discomfort wasn't all about the comedy, although some was, like the long, excruciating anecdote from one act about the size of her father's appendage that had not even the merciful relief of a punchline. Then there was the obligatory 'preaching to the choir' about 'issues'. Whilst she doesn't get cross about the underwhelming size of the audience she does mention it. 'I don't have a pension so I'll be doing this when I'm 90,' she said, pausing to look out. 'Playing to 17 people on a Wednesday night in Harrogate.' Then she falters and realises what that sounds like. 'Not that I don't want to. I would love that.' Wise move this; old pros have an adage: 'never have a go at the ones who've turned up.'

But, I repeat, my bad night out was not the comic's fault. No, mainly it stemmed from us, the small audience who were either 'silent smilers' (a perfectly reasonable thing to be, but terrible for a performer, who thinks they're dying) or loudly and persistently trying to get in on the act.

'Anyone in from Canada?'

My neighbour: 'YES! ... YOU!'

'Who was the best Spice Girl, do you think?'

'SCARY BECAUSE SHE'S FROM YORKSHIRE!'

Terrifyingly, the comedian notices us and leans forward into the spotlight, shading her eyes.

'Are you guys on a date?'

'HEE HEE SQUEE! HEE HEE HEE HEE!' comes the worrying, delighted squeal from my new chum.

'NO! NO, WE'RE NOT,' I shout far more quickly and loudly than is strictly necessary for someone not a raging homophobe.

Four women on the front row shriek at pretty much every word, the way that teenagers do in the street, clutching each other, in a desperate attempt to convince the world that they are 'crazy' and having fun. Is this a new thing? Maybe I did it when I was a daft kid but I don't think so. Like selfies and Facebook, it feels part of a new culture of relentless self-assertion and promotion. Eventually, the house lights come on, and before they are up to full, I am away into the night.

Later, brooding in the Bell Tavern over a small, strong craft beer, I conclude again it's no one's fault. I mentioned F1, Billy Smart and Verdi; to that I could add *The Apprentice*, rugby union and taramasalata. Stand-up is just not my thing. I repeat: it's not you, it's me. We should start seeing other people. And starting tomorrow, that could either be Claude Debussy, Jean Michel Jarre or the Chuckle Brothers, which are all possible diversions available in my next destination. Leeds awaits, as it did the Jarrow marchers, and I am going to make a part of the journey to one of my favourite cities in England in proper Yorkshire style.

HARROGATE TO LEEDS

13 October, 15 miles

Harrogate claims to be the happiest place to live in Britain, an assertion often backed up by various surveys. The Jarrow marchers and I had a lovely time here in our different ways, 80 years apart. I would have been sorrier to leave were it not that Leeds was my next stop and I was going to treat myself to a ride on the No. 36 from Ripon to Leeds via Harrogate which, from its marketing, was less of a bus, more of a lifechanging experience.

As a Lancastrian, I often say, deliberately provocatively and not entirely seriously, that Yorkshire is wasted on Yorkshiremen. Of course, I don't mean this and for reasons that are many and include Alan Bennett, Jarvis Cocker, Stan Barstow, Richard Hawley, Henry Moore, Ted Hughes, The Human League and Jake Thackray, a fabulously gifted, witty, touching, saucy singer, guitarist and songwriter from Kirkstall who was quite the celebrity in the 1970s. Inspired more by jazz, chansons, beat poetry and musicals than pop, he was the George Brassens of the South Riding, the north country Noël Coward. His song 'The Rain Upon the Mountainside' may well be the best song ever written about the north of England; spare and dark, beautiful but unsentimental. But today it was another of his tunes that I had in my head. 'Country Bus' was his tribute to the rattling antique transport of his youth that ran between the villages of remote Yorkshire and the big market towns and cities. The 'notorious ... amorous ... rumbustious ... malodorous country bus' was a vital network of commerce, adventure and romance.

The 36 provides all those functions certainly but without even a whiff of the malodorous or notorious. In fact, its website seems to promise the most sophisticated, advanced, luxurious bus ever made. Crucially, they run every fifteen minutes, so I have the leisure to catch up on the news over a cup of tea before embarking. Eighty years ago this morning, still glowing from the public meeting the night before, the marchers breakfasted on ham and beef paste sandwiches and were told by the deputy mayor as they left town, 'I don't think we let you down here. The meeting at the Winter Gardens last night was the finest I have seen in that hall in the past 30 years. It was representative of all sections of Harrogate society. That is saying a great deal as Harrogate people are difficult people to get to turn out at night.' Last night's young comic would agree, if not the staff at Norse or Wetherspoon.

I work through a pile of morning papers. 'Full steam ahead for HS2' says the *Express* on the controversial new high-speed train link. *The Times* T2 section goes with the big stuff too: 'Squeak! The Return of Leather Trousers!' The *Guardian* matches it with its splash, 'Is Spag Bol a Culinary Crime?' The *Mirror*'s 'bombshell' is 'Will Quits *Strictly*', an item about the fact that former pop singer Will Young has left a TV dancing show. Dark rumours abound with the computer tech genius behind the Amstrad emailer Lord Alan Sugar speculating that 'Will's clash with head judge Len Goodman over the weekend may have prompted him to walk away.' The *Daily Mail* has seen fit to ignore this in favour of a foam-flecked rant about Brexit that takes up most of the front page and reads like a communique from Enver Hoxha's Albania: 'Damn the unpatriotic Bremoaners and their plot to subvert the will of the British people!'

Suppressing a desire to shout 'Parklife!', I expect it to continue, 'The heads of dissidents must be smashed against the iron walls of party discipline and unity'. But they have gone with something about Fiona Bruce's shoes instead. More seriously, on various news websites there's party politics here and abroad. The BBC website reports on the toxic clashes between Trump and Clinton last night, 'The tawdriest exchanges in 56 years of televised presidential debates'. At home, a NEWS ICM *Guardian* Poll puts Labour at 26 and the Tories at 43, the second highest Tory lead in the history of polling.

I'm thankful when the next bus turns up, to be honest. I haven't been on a bus in a long while so I can't tell you whether the sleek, suave 36 with its free wifi, USB ports, plug sockets, reclining leather seats, tray tables and small library of paperback books is now the industry standard or an extravagant aberration but it was certainly a surprise to this traveller. My single to Leeds is £6. 'Do you do contactless?' I ask the driver/conductor. 'Of course,' he replies, smoothly and somewhat pityingly, as if I had asked whether the bus had wheels or an exhaust pipe. I take a front row seat upstairs and am soon joined by a lady sitting across the aisle from me. 'Hoping for a good view!' she says excitedly and takes out a tin of travel sweets. Maybe this is her first time on the 36 too. She offers me a barley sugar. I feel a little giddy.

The 36 follows the road the marchers would have taken, the A61 from North into South Yorkshire, through verdant Harrogate suburbia until it reaches the River Wharfe near Dunkeswick. This was my cue to tear myself away from the cosy reclining seats and Spotify and disembark. Just around here, halfway on the day's itinerary as the marchers crossed the broad Wharfe, a contingent of policemen led by an inspector appeared from nowhere to escort them the next few miles into the outskirts of Leeds. The reason was clear. The march was passing by Harewood House and its vast estate. Owned by Edwin Lascelles, first Baron of Harewood, it was built and sustained with money made from plantations using slave labour in the West Indies. The Lascelles first came here on a previous wave of immigration known as the Norman Conquest and by the time the Jarrow marchers passed by it belonged to Henry George Charles Lascelles. He'd gone from the merely aristocratic to the positively regal by marrying the Princess Royal, daughter of King George V and Queen Mary. Princess Mary was a shy soul, active in charity work, who for a time worked two days a week as a nurse and who did not warm to life at court. So perhaps she was in residence in her beloved Harewood when the police steered the marchers away from its grand baronial halls and nearly 30,000 acres of lush parkland.

Today there's only me, so I reckon I could have slipped in under the constables' noses at least as far as Harewood Village. I enter the village in fine rain, breath condensing in the damp air, the first real sign of approaching winter. Like so many huge and opulent homes of the aristocracy, Harewood House has now opened its doors, on its own terms, to the people of England – plantations and the slave trade not being the big earners they once were. Thanks to such generous and democratising advances, you can now get married here, stroll the gardens or peek inside the house and admire the Renaissance masterpieces. 'There are exquisite family portraits by Reynolds, Gainsborough, Lawrence and Richmond as well as a fine collection of Sèvres china, among many other delights.' You can even search the servants database and find out whether one of your family members was a footman or scullery maid here, but be warned, it might take you a while; there are several hundred former servants on the list.

I bump into a hearty, friendly group of walkers in the car park of the village hall. They've heard of the Jarrow march ('they were hungry and needed work, didn't they?') but didn't know it passed by the ancestral seat of the Earls of Harewood. They recommend a trip to the house and a circuit of the grounds. 'It's a good three miles but well worth it. It's where they film *Emmerdale*! A special purpose built set! You can't go in, but you can look at it from afar, like.' The long-running Yorkshire soap does seem to rather preoccupy folks around these parts, and I have visions of couples from Batley hiding in the undergrowth with bootblacked faces and binoculars trained on The Woolpack. I take another of their recommendations though: a mug of tea and a sit down in the village's Muddy Boots café, packed even on a damp and chilly midweek afternoon. I don't stay long. Country houses aren't really my thing and while Harewood is pleasant enough there is far better down the road, through the affluent suburbs of Moortown and Chapel Allerton and into the beating heart of one of the great cities of the north.

Leeds always gives me a heck of a thrill. With all due respect to its peers – to Manchester, Newcastle and Liverpool – and local rivals like Sheffield and Bradford, nowhere buzzes and throbs like Leeds with that feel of a grand industrial city on the make and on the move. It's a big, brash town with money in its pocket, and a ceaseless, restless appetite for enjoyment and culture found in its hundreds of pubs and restaurants, galleries and gig venues. Maybe it's a vestige of my teenage enthusiasm for Don Revie's dark and saturnine anti-heroes of 1970s football, those brooding and malevolent Heathcliffs in Admiral sportswear; Lorimer, Clarke, Giles, Bremner, Cooper. But I love this town.

In Chapel Allerton I decide to hop back onto the 36 for the last mile into Leeds and thus arrive in style. At the bus stop near the library by Gadget Exchange and Tandoori Hut, I meet the first non-white woman I've seen since leaving Jarrow, an Asian mum with little lad in tow, waiting to go shopping in Leeds. Within minutes the bus is here and I take my now regular seat, top deck front, where someone has obligingly left today's free paper. Former pop singer Lily Allen is getting 'trolled' online for apologising to the people in the Calais Jungle refugee camp about their predicament. On the next page though, something that depresses me even more. Art history A Level is being scrapped and I decide to take it personally. This leads directly to me having a brief spat in a hotel bedroom in Leeds with Michael Gove, former Education Secretary and arch Brexiteer.

He wasn't there, I should point out. Our minor contretemps was via social media, via which I angrily and it seems too hastily berated him for being responsible for the scrapping of art history A Level. But I was seething. Seething at the reductive view of education that thinks we plebs don't need to know about the finer things in life – class war conducted by stealth.

At the dawn of the 1980s in my late teens in Wigan, I found myself briefly academically becalmed before beginning my degree, and chose to fill my time with two extra A Levels chosen pretty much on a whim. One was British social and economic history, a subject I would now find fascinating but of which I now remember little except for the pioneering Speenhamland benefits system of rural Berkshire and the six demands of the Chartists. My other choice though was art history, and almost every moment of it – every languorous afternoon in the dark, hot and intimate audio visual room flipping through the slides of *Les Demoiselles d'Avignon*, *Le Déjeuner sur l'herbe*, Munch, Kandinsky, Piet Mondrian – has stayed with me ever since. Those long, absorbing hours taught me that the creation, appreciation and love of art is not just the mark of a civilised society, it is the clearest mirror you can hold up to that society, telling you more of its time than a thousand academic histories or earnest documentaries.

Picasso's *Guernica* is an astonishing piece of visual art but it's also a bulletin of blazing, angry reportage that awakened the world to the brutality of the Spanish Civil War. British war artists like Nash and Nevinson evoked the horrors of the Western Front with a dreamlike serenity that is at the same time the stuff of nightmares. But even when not reporting the actual, art brings to us vividly and pungently the authentic cultural flavour of its day. In the work of the Italian Futurists, one can see all the dangerous and muscular allure of both Fascism and Communism. Piet Mondrian's geometric grids sing with the pulsating joys of the jazz age whilst Andy Warhol both celebrates and satirises 1960s consumerism within the same gaudy frame.

Sometimes the insights of art history were more personal. Stanley Spencer's work haunted me and shaped my view of a kind of mythic, phantasmagorical England where sex, nature and religion combined in works of beauty and strangeness, like *The Resurrection*, *Cookham* and *Man Goeth to His Long Home*. The Blaue Reiter group from Germany fed my cravings for existential teen darknesses where I could brood moodily (Karl Schmidt-Rottluff's *Woman with a Bag* is, essentially, *The Scream* for cool kids; look it up). From Modigliani I learned a lot about sex. Not the act itself but the real nature of the thing. It's not just that his nudes and portraits of women are sexy – they are achingly, breathtakingly so – but they tell you everything about the nature of longing, desire and heartbreak, as well as the myth of the doomed romantic genius. Art history taught me to see the brilliance, bravery and sheer fun in the experimental in every medium, especially music and film; the need for art that challenges the dreary orthodoxies of the day. Without the revolution in the head that the study of art history fired in me, I doubt I would ever have loved or 'got' free jazz, John Cage, Webern, drone, Morton Feldman or Peter Greenaway. This was not a world I was naturally born to in seventies and eighties Wigan. But in their gentle way, my art history classes and teachers helped me storm a citadel I've lived in ever since.

So after I'd checked into my Leeds hotel, I did what any modern person would do with this righteous anger. I tweeted about it. I fired off a raging 100 characters or so condemning Michael Gove's philistinism. Then I thought nothing more of it. Instead, I took to social media again to ask for suggestions of something artistic or cultural I could do in Leeds that evening. I was determined that my Jarrow march, and this book, would show that 'ordinary' working people and their kids do appreciate art and culture and that any healthy nation provides the tools for the enjoyment of it.

The cultural delights on offer in Leeds on that one October night were many and varied. Steve Howe, the guitarist of prog rockers Yes, was playing an intimate acoustic set at the lovely old City Varieties Theatre. French electronic legend Jean Michel Jarre was at the big new arena in the city. At the theatre there was a play about the Brontës and a revival of the classic two-hander *Sleuth*, from which Morrissey pinched some of his best lines like, 'A jumped up pantry boy who never knew his place'.

After some sifting, I narrowed it down to two events which in their different ways seemed unmissable. At the old Yorkshire TV building, there was An Evening with the Chuckle Brothers, Paul and Barry, whilst at the Howard Assembly Room in the Opera House, there was a recital of early twentieth century French piano music. Now, I have a lot of time for the Chuckle Brothers; I've always enjoyed the simple comedic elegance of their 'to me, to you' exchanges. Also, at an awards ceremony 'after show', I once found myself dancing with the moustachioed siblings and the model Sophie Dahl on a podium in a London nightclub, still possibly the most glamorous few minutes of my life. But the Debussy piano preludes, which would form part of the piano recital, have a very special place in my heart. Two scratchy vinyl albums of them in a battered box set from Wigan Library were my introduction into classical music and these haunting, limpid, sensual pieces still make my head swim. I found the invitation tweet from Rowland at Opera North and hit the DM button to message him.

In the meantime, I took to the streets of Leeds to soak up its brisk vibe of brass and bravado. Leeds established itself in the late 1800s as the global capital of the wool trade. Unlike some of their kind though, the civic fathers spent their money on art, learning and fine buildings for the Leodensians as assiduously as they lined their own pockets. Whether you come via Westgate or The Headrow, down Calverley Street or up Park Row, all roads in Leeds lead eventually to its Montmartre, its Buckingham Palace, its Kremlin. The city's fabulously imposing town hall was described by historian Asa Briggs as 'a magnificent case study in Victorian civic pride'. *Architecture Today* called it 'the epitome of northern civic bombast', which sounds altogether more snidey and grudging and perhaps a little jealous.

Bombastic or magnificent, Leeds town hall welcomed the Jarrow marchers with open arms of municipal and architectural splendour. Not till they got to London and the Palace of Westminster would a building this grand open its doors to them again, and the welcome there would be ambivalent, unsatisfying and disingenuous. Leeds had no such qualms. They were treated to a reception and a slap-up feed in the hall's crypt with uniformed staff asking solicitously, 'beer or tea, Sir?' By most accounts, it was the finest night of the whole march, lingering long in the marchers' memories. Bob Maughan had worked for six months in the ten years up to October 1936. Sixty years on, he remembered their night in Leeds as, 'A bit of a holiday, a grand night. Roast beef ... Yorkshire pudding ... a bottle of pale ale ... we were well looked after.' Even Paddy the dog was served his dinner in a silver tureen.

All of this was paid for by a local Tory grandee with the blessing of the Conservative council. They even invited along officials of Leeds Trade Union council to tuck in. Quite why they did this might seem baffling. But I'd guess it was to 'show up' the lily-livered nature of the Labour Party's attitude to the march and, even more importantly, a cussed demonstration of civic pride and independence. Whatever the Tories of Westminster may have thought, the Tories of Leeds were their own men and women (though sadly mainly men).

Flanking the grand doors of the town hall are a pride of stone lions. Designed by sculptor William Day Keyworth, local legend has it that, if the town hall clock should ever strike 13, time will stand still, the people of Leeds will freeze and the lions will come to life and silently stalk the streets of the city. Call me a purist in these matters but as the lions have only been there since 1867 I baulk at that term 'legend', as I do like my folklore to at least predate, say, fridges. But if you do fancy a bit of magic, the lions will talk to you, fairly amiably, if you download the app, scan the code into your mobile phone and put your headphones on. (The voices sounded suspiciously like Brian Blessed to me.)

With only the slightest hankering for the Chuckle Brothers across town, I negotiate Leeds's early-evening throng on New Briggate and arrive at my seat in the beautifully restored Howard Assembly Room, Opera North's chamber space for Steven Osborne's piano recital. Tonight's programme is of piano works by Debussy, Ravel and Poulenc, all of whom had written masterpieces and established their enduring reputations by the time of the Jarrow march. Debussy had died two decades before, Ravel would die the year later, Poulenc in 1963. None of those names would have been known to the Jarrow men, not merely because their class or education would have kept them in ignorance, but simply because of a widespread suspicion against 'modern' music that still persists into our era. Back in the 1930s, even when enlightened ideas like subscription concerts or the Proms sought to bring classical music to the 'masses', it would inevitably be the established repertoire of various long-dead Europeans.

In the year of the Jarrow march several staples of the modern repertoire were being composed or premiered. Prokofiev's *Peter and the Wolf*, Rachmaninov's Symphony No. 3, several early pieces by the young Benjamin Britten. The premiere was held posthumously of Alban Berg's darkly brilliant Violin Concerto, still the most famous and popular piece from the 'difficult' serialist school. Perhaps most relevant, Paul Hindemith composed his Trauermusik, a plangent requiem for King George written in the single day after his death. The death of the king was a deeply felt personal human sadness that would then usher in a national crisis as the Jarrow men marched toward London.

Hearing the Debussy preludes and short pieces brings back the same thrill that I felt when I played those scratched and much borrowed editions from Wigan Library. The shivery, spectral washes of *Footprints in the Snow* and *The Drowned Cathedral*, the kooky wit of *Golliwog's Cakewalk*, the sheer loveliness of *Claire de Lune* and *The Girl with the Flaxen Hair*. My love of classical music was fostered not by my parents or through buying records (I couldn't have afforded them) but through Wigan Library, Radio 3 and the music department of Edge Hill University. Thus, like so many other joys in my life I have the state to thank for it. Or the Nanny State, as its detractors have it. In my experience, however, the people who sneer at the nanny state are usually people who had nannies.

Steven Osborne's performance is brilliant, played from memory with no sheet music and with most pieces prefaced by a little illuminating introduction putting them in context and pointing out things to listen out for. This should be standard procedure at all classical concerts; it's sheer snobbery not to do so. But for all Steven's fabulous playing it is his remarks after the interval when introducing the second half that stick in the mind. (Earlier, I had mentioned to Rowland and my friends at Opera North that I had chosen this event from a range of delights on offer in Leeds that night.)

'Thank you all for coming this evening. I hope you've enjoyed the music so far. In a moment, I'd like to carry on with Ravel's beautiful *Menuet Antique* but before that, it's come to my knowledge that there's a gentleman in the audience who had to make the difficult decision whether to come to hear me play or watch the Chuckle Brothers. Well, I can only hope you feel you've made the right decision, sir.' The hall breaks into laughter, in which I heartily join, looking around with all the rest pretending to wonder where this bloke can be and what on earth he must be like.

There is odder to come. Back in my hotel room, I scroll through texts, tweets and emails before turning in. There is a message from Michael Gove. In it, he tells me that the scrapping of art history A Level has nothing to do with him. 'I Heart Art History' he tweets, with an actual little emoji heart (rather apt

I think). So I reply to the effect that I stand corrected if he isn't to blame and I apologise. He replies, 'Thank you Stuart – a genuinely fair-minded thinker.'

'A genuinely fair-minded thinker' – Michael Gove. Is that a recommendation for the book jacket I wonder?

I look again at Twitter before turning off my phone. Someone has already seen the exchange and replied, 'Get a room, you two.'

STAGE EIGHT

LEEDS TO WAKEFIELD

14 October, 9 miles

On the morning of 14 October, with some reluctance, I pack up and check out of Leeds. In the lobby of my hotel is one of those giant screens that are permanently and silently tuned to Sky News. The image looming down at me appears to be a reanimated Douglas Fairbanks Junior with a Little Richard Pompadour and dark glasses. This turns out to be Bob Dylan, he of the asthmatic wheezing on the old mouth organ whose words, it transpires, have been considered marvellous enough to impress a group of spoony old fanboys at the Swedish Academy. The scrolling news ticker informs us that Bob Dylan has been given the Nobel Prize for literature by virtue of, as the citation has it, 'having created new poetic expressions within the great American song tradition'.

I roll my eyes and pull my 'what a world we live in today' face. Whilst acknowledging his colossal influence on popular music, I would no more give him the Nobel Prize for Literature than I would the gong for Physics or Economics. Or give Harold Pinter a grammy for *The Caretaker*. Silly old Stockholm. Leeds would never do anything as daft and soft, although they have put up a statue to Billy Bremner and they might give David Batty the Nobel Peace Prize as a black joke.

As is now customary, the day's other news is uniformly 'Brexit', an event which seems to have thrown every conversation and interaction, every normal daily event into an uncomfortable kind of relief and shine a strange, harsh new light that refracts the world differently. Packing and shouldering my rucksack draws the attention of two friendly Polish girls in the lobby, Elenya and Lana. I tell them about the Jarrow march, about how the hungry men went to find work and how (spoiler alert) the Prime Minister refused to see them. 'That is very sad but at least they had a passion, a purpose in life, and are you going to see the Prime Minister?' I tell them I hope to get into the Palace of Westminster. 'Well, we wish you luck.'

Not long after this, making my way up the unattractively named Swinegate, I have a similar conversation by the doorway of Bibi's Italian restaurant, this time with a young Russian woman called Julia who works there. She's been here three-and-a-half years and has heard of the Jarrow march as it's one of the aspects of British history her six-year-old daughter Alexandra has been studying. 'She has learned about Florence Nightingale, all the Victorian people, the *Titanic*. Do you know how many people there are on the *Titanic*? Two thousand two hundred and twenty eight people! Very sad. My daughter is expert on it.'

Julia is originally from St Petersburg, though she hasn't been back there for two years. 'It is very beautiful,' she says wistfully. 'The Hermitage. The Amber room. But very cold in winter. You should go in the summer. Oh yes, go in June. Ah, the White Nights. But –' and she gives my pack a little pat '– it is too far to walk.'

At a coffee stand in Leeds, I find myself wondering if in perhaps a year or two, or maybe ten, when the much talked of Article 50 has been long triggered and we have undergone our slow painful divorce from the rest of the continent, whether I will be having these everyday conversations with lovely people from Krakow and St Petersburg. I hope so. But there seems to be a chill wind abroad even in these happy, busy streets and I don't like the feel of it. The novelist Ian McEwan has recently been even more jittery. 'It's reminiscent of Robespierre and the terror of the French Revolution. The air in my country is very foul.'

I tear myself away from Julia and the lure of Bibi's, which is possibly my favourite restaurant in Leeds along with Tharavadu, the heavenly Keralan opposite the station. But in Leeds, the gourmet, the hedonist, the culture vulture, the epicure are all spoiled for choice. Every time I come back to Leeds it's a little more swaggering, bolder and busier, a touch more glamorous in a blousy, cheeky, 'come and get me' way, and every time I love it a little more. The city's sheer appetite for fun and profit will rock you on your heels. Every grand street is packed shoulder to shoulder these days with 'twisted street food', 'kitchens', 'canteens' or even 'cantinas', and while you may not like the words, who does not the love the thrill of a great city with an almost unseemly dedication to dressing up, getting out and having a good time.

It helps that Leeds has such a thriving student population, a number of whom come for Britain's best and most prestigious modern jazz courses, and consequently Leeds is the world capital of what's known as 'muscle jazz', a wild, technically daunting mix of rock and jazz. Four-hundred-and-eighty-three Leeds Uni students are lodged in the former Montague Burton clothing works. It's student accommodation now, but back in 1936 when its sewing machines hummed with industry, the marchers breakfasted here on porridge, bacon, sausage and tomato on the morning they left Leeds. Before they did, they were given the results of a whip-round at the factory that raised over thirty pounds, a sum that would help enormously in the days ahead. Perhaps embarrassed at the party line, some Leeds Labour Party members stitched tattered clothes and brought new boots for the marchers. Leeds RSPCA inspected Paddy the dog and declared him fit to go on (although by this time four marchers had had to be sent home due to ill health). All contemporary coverage mentions this cute canine companion, perhaps to soften any political edge to their reports. But the *Guardian* writer who'd accompanied them since the Ripon road into Harrogate did find time for some other observations too.

This is not a hunger-march, but a protest march ... There is no political aspect to this march. It is simply the town of Jarrow saying 'Send us work.' In the ranks of the marchers are Labour men, Liberals, Tories, and one or two Communists, but you cannot tell who's who. With the marchers goes, prominently carried, the Jarrow petition for work, a huge book with about 12,000 signatures, which Miss Ellen Wilkinson, M.P. for Jarrow, is to present at the bar of the House of Commons on November 4 ... It was interesting to watch motorists who passed us on the road recognise her and lean out of windows as they went by. Like us all she made friends with Paddy, the Labrador dog who accompanied the procession uninvited for five miles from Jarrow before anyone realised that he intended to go all the way. When the marshal's whistle goes he goes too and there is no holding him. It is interesting, too, to watch men employed on the road rest on their spades to watch men unemployed but also on the road go by. Their eyes spoke their thoughts ... At every stopping-place there is such a meeting so that the world shall know of Jarrow.

It would be a wild exaggeration to claim that the world knew of my march but some do, mainly friends or family or through social media. And as I'm crossing the river that bisects the city along the now fashionable Calls district, the 'wide majestic Aire' as the great song by local jazz folk rockers Trembling Bells calls it, I hear the ping of an incoming text. It's a message of good wishes from my friend Gary, a Sikh taxi driver from Manchester, filled with his usual bewildering array of emojis, hashtags and indecipherable acronyms. Gary is pushing 40 but his texts can make you feel very old. I tell him that it's going well, that I'm headed for Wakefield today and that I'll probably stop off around Hunslet or Dewsbury for an early lunch. 'Cool. Don't forget u shd go to a Gurdwara #curry licking lips emoji.'

Of course. The perfect idea. Their own cooks notwith-
standing, the Jarrow marchers relied on the hospitality of others
for food and shelter and they endeavoured to prove themselves
worthy of this by sobriety and self-discipline. One of the central
tenets of Sikhism is hospitality to strangers and travellers and
the Gurdwara and its kitchens are open 24 hours a day for the
sustenance and welcome of travellers, providing they are well
behaved and have not taken drink. If the orange flag of the
Gurdwara had fluttered over English cities in 1936, the Sikh
community would have welcomed and fed the Jarrow men. And
what a delicious change it would have made from beef paste
sandwiches and porridge.

It would have been theoretically possible too, had their
route taken them through Shepherd's Bush, site of England's
first Gurdwara established in 1911. This coincided with the first
real wave of Sikh immigration to the UK, although Britain's
links with the Punjab stretch much further back. From the
mid-nineteenth century onwards many Punjabis served in
the British army and Sikh soldiers fought in elite regiments
seeing active service in both world wars. A memorial in Sussex
honours the Sikh dead who fought for the UK in the First
World War. Partition of their homeland and labour shortages
here encouraged large scale Sikh migration from the Punjab
and by the late 1940s, there were substantial Sikh communities
settled across the land: Cardiff, Bristol, Ipswich, Peterborough,
Doncaster, Birmingham, Aberdeen, Glasgow, Edinburgh,
Leeds, Liverpool, Middlesbrough, Southampton, Portsmouth
and Manchester. In the Black Country, Sikh men formed a
large part of the workforce in the hot and physically demanding
forges and foundries. Elsewhere they went into medicine and
commerce. There are currently around half a million Sikhs in
the UK and they have become the leading ethnic minority in
business.

After a quick consultation with Google maps, I turned
through Holbeck, the rugby league heartland of once-proud

Hunslet who still play at the South Leeds Stadium. I've never been to that sporting crucible but as a kid I'd made several trips to Elland Road because of my perverse obsession with Don Revie's maligned ubermensch. This provided a heady change from the rough and guileless non-league football on offer at Wigan Athletic's Springfield Park, or the Cowshed as it was known, where muddied oafs would hack at each other in the winter twilight. It was towards Elland Road that I turned now, headed for the industrial suburb of Beeston where a small detour would take me to one of Leeds' three Sikh temples, the Guru Nanak Nishkam Sewak Jatha Gurdwara on Lady Pit Lane.

The morning was grey and damp and the walk through Leeds southern urban sprawl not the prettiest. Along the way I checked by text with Gary about the etiquette of my visit. I should simply open the door and enter, no appointment needed. I should wear long trousers and long sleeves (as if I would wear any other kind in Leeds in October), should not be drunk (he knows me so well) and should cover my head (yes, my flat cap would be fine). Around 1pm, I turned into Lady Pit Lane, a drab terrace with one dominant building – a squat Victorian structure that looked like it might have once been a mill or an old school, carrying as it did that air of old, cold hard times and unyielding officialdom and authority. 'Security cameras monitor this building twenty four hours a day' read a stern black-and-white notice. But above the door was a bold sign of eggshell blue and above that the weakly fluttering orange flag that bids welcome from miles around to Sikh and non-Sikh alike.

I stand for a long time in the street. I feel self-conscious and uncomfortable, unsure of etiquette and protocol and aware that the odd kid passing on a bike or taxi driver is wondering what I'm up to. I push the door. It won't open and I feel a mild swell of relief. Pull yourself together I think, and I push again. This time it opens and I'm in an unprepossessing vestibule strewn with a few boxes of clothes, household goods and tins of paint. On the wall is a mirror in which I can see myself looking shifty and awkward and a welcome sign which spells out the protocol for visiting the Gurdwara. I should 'wear modest attire and remove shoes when entering the congregation hall. This is a sign of respect to the sovereignty of the Guru Granth Sahib. All gurdwaras have shoe racks. You will see Sikhs bow in front of the Guru Granth Sahib upon joining the congregation. Non-Sikhs are not required to bow, but should enter and quietly join the congregation.' And I am asked to keep my head covered at all times, 'as a sign of respect to the Guru Granth Sahib. Flat caps and baseball caps are not suitable, but there are headscarves provided in the box below.'

Thanks Gary. Realising what the mirror is for, and remembering how useless I am with a bow tie, I spend the next six or seven minutes trying and failing to tie the orange scarf successfully around my head in a way that does not make me look like a bad Keith Richards impersonator or a 1940s charlady in an Arthur Askey film. This proves impossible. I try simply placing the scarf on top of my head but this makes me look like a granddad on the beach in the same 1940s Arthur Askey film or Michael Palin in his D P Gumby guise from Monty Python.

Whilst doing all this I become aware that I am being watched by a small Indian lady on my left who has peered around the partition. I start to speak but she disappears into the interior of the Gurdwara again. I wonder if there is any kind of bell I can ring or ding in the manner of a hotel reception. I'm sure there isn't, and I'm sure even thinking there is is mildly objectionable, but I'm not really sure where to go from here. Just as I am starting to think about removing the headscarf (which wouldn't take long) putting my shoes back on and sloping sheepishly back onto Lady Pit Lane, admitting failure in my adventure in multi-culturalism, a tall, young Indian with a superbly knotted turban that makes me feel distinctly inadequate comes through the door behind me carrying a bag of tools. He eyes me with mild curiosity, and my headscarf with what I think is pity. 'Can I help you?' I explain as best as I can in a couple of sentences about the march, the anniversary, the marchers' reliance on hospitality, my curiosity about the temple. He pauses, thinks for a second and then with a puzzled smile says, 'Well, you'd better come in then. Have you had any lunch?'

Inderpal turns out to be the most thorough and amiable guide to Sikhism and the Gurdwara that any traveller could have. Devout but not stuffy, he is charming and easy going, and clearly proud of his faith, his community and his temple. He indicates his bag of spanners and wrenches. 'You'll have to excuse us, we're not quite at our best. We're having work done, as you can tell.' For the first time I become aware of hammering and sawing from somewhere deep within the temple. We take a seat at one of the long benches in the kitchen area. There is one other diner, a beaming, leathery old boy missing a few teeth. He sits by the door in a long cream robe, chewing on a fresh green chilli. 'I've had ten of these today!' he says, grinning.

The Sikh kitchen or 'langar' was introduced in the sixteenth century by the founder of Sikhism, Guru Nanak. It was intended as a place where all can eat together in equality, regardless of creed, class, race or social standing. It has come to embody much of the Sikh faith's philosophy and a Sikh prayer goes 'Loh langar tapde rahin', or 'May the hot plates of the langars remain ever in service.' Today's langars are run along almost industrial catering lines. The benches we sit at are alongside several large ranges on which sit huge pots and tureens stirred by four or five Sikh ladies. Behind them, the woman who observed me struggling with my headscarf (which is proving remarkably stable if hardly stylish) is chopping bags of onions and green beans whilst chattering gaily in Punjabi to a companion. The kitchen runs 24 hours a day, its doors never close and the food is 100 per cent vegetarian.

One of the ladies comes from behind the cookers to speak to me. 'You like curry? You know Indian food?' Oh yes, I reply, and seemingly delighted with this answer, she scurries away returning with two metal trays divided into sections containing vegetable curry, chana dahl, rice and chapati. She hands one each to me and Inderpal. It's predictably delicious and as we eat Inderpal explains more about the Gurdwara.

'It is not just a kitchen and not just a temple. It is partly a school and partly a community centre. We have classes upstairs in music and dance. There is a nursery and a library and we have rooms. At the moment we have a student from the Punjab staying with us while he studies in Leeds for his degree. He will be with us for a few years. And we have the main hall of worship which is called the Dahar Sahib. In there is our holy book, the Guru Granth Sahib, which is the last of our gurus and the only one that is not a human man. We'll go there when we've eaten,' he says, scooping another mouthful of rich, aromatic yellow dahl with his folded chapatti.

'You should try one of these. Try it raw,' says the genial man at the next table, holding up a transparent plastic bag in which I would say there were 500 green chillies, gleaming as if painted and radiating latent heat and pain like mini hand grenades. 'Hand them over,' I hear myself saying and I take the bag. I grab a fistful and pass a couple to Inderpal. 'I love chillies,' I say bullishly and take a few big bites as a horse might into an apple proffered over a fence. Inderpal looks at me in a kind of horror, which turns to amusement and finally, I'd like to think, admiration. I'd like to think that but I can't really think of anything right now, much less say anything, because after a few seconds in which the mild burning sensation on my tongue was faintly pleasurable in an odd way, twin geysers of electric heat are pulsing upwards from the area of my (long gone) adenoids and threatening to burst my eardrums and eyeballs simultaneously. As a student, using some knock-off madras powder a mate's dad had got from Liverpool docks, I once made a curry so hot my flatmate Nigel went blind in one eye for several hours. That was a korma by comparison.

It's said that beer is a much better coolant after a hot curry than water, which is why Cobra, Lal Toofan and Kingfisher are so popular on the subcontinent. But clearly none of these are to hand so I content myself with drinking, in three or four draughts, the entire contents of one of those metal water jugs you used to get at school dinners. By now, I am crying a little which amuses and delights the small crowd of Sikh ladies who have gathered around me. One of them actually claps. Another pats me on the head, dislodging my headscarf. She pops it back on, as you would a bonnet back on a baby in a buggy. 'That will keep the doctor away,' says the small fellow who gave me the chillies as he takes back the bag grinning, helping himself to another couple which he proceeds to crunch his way through as blithely as if they were mini carrot batons or mint-flavour Matchmakers at Abigail's Party.

When I think I can stand unaided, I get up and Inderpal takes me up to the next floor and the main hall. Women of various ages are grouped along the walls of the room and one is seated at its head under a canopy. She is reading into a microphone in a low monotone from the holy book. Inderpal and I lurk at the entrance to the room and he whispers in my ear, 'She's reading from the Granth Sahib, our holy book. Someone is here reading from it all day and all night. Twenty-four hours a day.' The women in the room listen intently, eyes closed, some gently nodding to the recitation. 'Come on, come with me,' says Inderpal, beckoning me into the Dharbar. We pad quietly right up to the reader and the holy book. Inderpal drops to his knees, bends forward and lowers his head to the floor to kiss it. I follow suit. Then we rise and gently exit backwards. I am worried about doing something wrong, but Inderpal and the ladies smile indulgently and I get the feeling that unless I behave badly, my ignorance of Sikhism and its etiquette is no problem. I am their guest, and they are happy to have me here.

If you are used to the traditions of Christian churches, possibly synagogues too though I'm not qualified to say, a Sikh temple is almost disconcerting in its informality. No gilt, no statuary, no reliquary, no icons, no religious pictures. The most holy part of it, where the most 'sacred' things are happening, is just above what resembles at most a very basic works canteen with vats of dahl and sambar on the go. How different it feels from my altar boy days spent in a fug of perfumed incense swinging a thurible around my head in front of a burnished gold tabernacle. Although to be honest, there too the sacred and profane sat side by side. Just on the other side of the wall from the altar, they were pulling pints of Guinness and playing snooker in the Catholic Club.

We ascend another flight. There is a large room for teaching, kids' paintings adorning the walls, and there's a handwritten message of thanks for their service to local life from the local police. Inderpal opens a side door and we emerge onto a wide section of flat roof high above the cramped terraced houses of Beeston. 'This,' he says indicating a tall flagpole with its bright triangular pennant of silk, 'is the Nishan Sahib. It is the flag of the Gurdwara intended to be seen from miles around and saying that this is a place of safety, originally in time of war but now just for any who wishes to come, Sikh or otherwise.' We stand under it for a while as it flaps damply. In the distance I can see the stand at Elland Road.

I have the feeling that, just as the recitation of the holy book will continue around the clock, Inderpal would be happy, keen and capable of talking passionately about his community all day. There is something sweet and winning about this, whatever your faith or lack of it. But I have my own pilgrimage to continue with, not to Amritsar's Golden Temple, which many Sikhs aspire to one day visit, but to Wakefield, the next stage on the march's itinerary. Inderpal wants to show me one last thing though, the rehearsal rooms where one can study the classical music traditions of India. 'I don't know if there are classes there today. But I hope you can hear some.' We arrive at the door a floor below though just as a class is breaking up. Two older Sikh gentlemen are leaving, behind them a young ginger-haired British guy. His headscarf is as poorly knotted as mine and seeing each other's, we tacitly acknowledge our shared incompetence with a wan smile.

Inderpal asks one of the older gentlemen to tell me about the instrument he plays. 'It is an Indian instrument,' smiles the man, fingering a fine wiry grey beard, 'that you may never have heard of it.' Keen not to be thought a fool, but in fact being an idiot, I randomly name some Indian instruments I have heard of, such as the tabla and the sitar. Still smiling, the man shakes his head patiently. 'No, I play the santoor. It is a trapezoid instrument with 72 strings.' 'Wow,' I say, establishing my idiot credentials even more decisively. 'Is that difficult to play?' He turns to the young Western man. 'John, is it difficult?' 'Well, I've been coming here to learn for ten years and I'm still a beginner,' he says, pushing his headdress back up out of his eyes, where it has slipped down like an outsized party hat on a toddler.

We descend the stairs together, me just about persuading Inderpal that it was really not necessary for the musicians to go and get their instruments out again and play. As the Sikh men fall into conversation in Punjabi (I imagine something along the lines of, 'Who's the doofus who can't tie a headdress?'), John tugs at my sleeve to pull me back a little behind the group. 'I'm a music teacher in Bradford. I fell in love with Indian music and when I found out that he was here,' his voice drops to an awestruck sotto voce as he points at the older musician walking ahead, 'and would give me lessons ... well, I come here every week, have been doing for ten years. His name is Ustad Harjinderpal Singh, and he's one of the great virtuosi of Indian music. Look him up.'

I jot a decent approximation of this name in my black moleskin notebook for later research. John and Ustad leave and I say my goodbyes to Inderpal. It has been a fascinating couple of hours. I've been wonderfully fed, I've learned a great deal and I'm very grateful to my young host. Gauche to the end, I fumble in my pocket and pull out a fiver, wondering aloud if there's a collection plate or a community charity or, who knows, a fund for a new flag like they have for new roofs on old churches in the Cotswolds. 'No, no, no,' he waves it and me away. 'It has been a pleasure. Where are you going now? Wakefield? Well, when you have seen Wakefield, come back here. There's a wedding on tonight. We'll be here from 6.30 to 9. You must come. No drink here. But people will have drink later. You can have more food. More chillies!'

It was tempting then, and even more so after an afternoon spent trudging along the anonymous drizzly main roads of Yorkshire. I walked through quaintly named Robin Hood, past the Old Halfway House Pub (To Let), outside which a young lad in a Wakefield Trinity Wildcats replica shirt mends a puncture, past the Wakefield Diesel Centre and down Meadowgate Drive (where I sang a variant of an old Suzi Quatro hit some of you might remember) and eventually past a sign that welcomed me to Wakefield. Here the marchers enjoyed a quieter reception than in Leeds. But then that night in the grand town hall would prove the most splendid of the whole three-week trip. In Wakefield, they were given potted meat 'butties' and tea and then taken to their lodging at a disused chapel on Salem Street.

I have treated myself to accommodation that's a little nicer and lying on the bed after checking my blisters (hardly any: I was hoping for at least a few battlescars) I tap the musician's name that John gave me into Google, hoping I've got it roughly right. Hits galore pop up; links, YouTube clips, recordings. Thus it become apparent that the older, bearded gentlemen I met earlier is one of the greatest exponents in the world of the santoor, 'the hundred stringed instrument of the valleys', which I assume is poetic licence. His CV is dense with achievements and accolades. 'Born in Jabalpur, India in 1953 ... age 14 years his father sent him to learn Tabla ... made him the disciple of the santoor maestro Pandit Shiv Kumar Sharma ... toured extensively for SPICMACAY (Society for the Promotion of Indian Classical Music and Culture Amongst Youth) and gave concerts, lectures and demonstration programmes in schools and colleges ... He has toured abroad and performed in various cities around the UK.' There is a clip of him playing the santoor in Manchester's glitzy and prestigious Bridgewater Hall, home of the Halle Orchestra, and in chamber concert at Opera North's Howard Assembly Rooms, the very room where I had heard Steven Osborne play Debussy and Ravel and discuss the Chuckle Brothers.

So it was rather as if, earlier that day, I had bumped into Yo-Yo Ma in a back street near Hunslet and had him explain to me patiently and sweetly, as if to a stupid child, what a cello was. And then almost asked him to get his instrument out again and play a few of the Bach Solo Cello suites for me, there amongst the chickpeas and the bags of gram flour and the okra. It was a real shame that the Gurdwara wasn't here in 1936. The Jarrow marchers would have been welcomed with open arms, and 200 orange headscarves and a handful of glossy green chillis to make that welcome even warmer.

STAGE NINE

WAKEFIELD TO BARNSLEY

15 October, 10 miles

'Jarrow Marchers R.I.P in Ancient Wakefield City.'

It may not be quite as striking as 'Freddie Starr Ate My Hamster' or as infamous as 'Gotcha!' but the above headline in Wakefield's *Evening Chronicle* for 14 October 1936 shows how even then the British press was confidently finding its unique voice reporting gleefully and punningly how the marchers had bedded down next to a cemetery.

Even then though, independent local papers were beginning to be swallowed up by the giant national groups and chains. Circulation of newspapers boomed among the working classes in the interwar years and differences of style began to develop between low sale, upmarket publications like *The Times* and popular sensationalist dailies like the *Express*. Competitions and promotions were a major part of these papers' sales drives, some of which seem quite bizarre now. The *Daily Mail* offered certain types of free insurance to subscribers such as a hundred pounds in school fees to any child whose parent had suffered 'a fatal accident' and ten pounds to any Girl Guide who broke an arm. The popular titles would sometimes employ five times as many canvassers as editorial staff and these would tour the country offering inducements such as clothes and gifts to subscribe. One report said 'it was rumoured that a whole Welsh family could be clothed from head to toe for the price of eight weeks' reading of the *Daily Express*'. Quite why they had to be a Welsh family is not clear, but it gives an idea of the promo budgets of the new mass market press.

I could find no trace of exactly where the Jarrow marchers stayed in Wakefield, neither street nor chapel nor cemetery, and this despite the best efforts of some generous and enthusiastic help on social media from Christine Wood, Richard Earnshaw, Chris Treece, Stuart Watson and 'Kevin'. Stephen Garside even sent pictures of what we think is the now disused site with both chapel and graveyard gone. We do have a record of their stay though in the diary entry of one of the marchers, David Ramshaw. 'Wakefield. Civic reception. Menu, sandwiches and tea. Slept in pulpit of condemned church.' On waking at 6am, he then woke the other marchers with a mock sermon from the pulpit. John McNulty wouldn't have heard this. He was outside sleeping on a gravestone.

The marchers didn't stay long in Wakefield and neither did I. Not through any dislike of the city I should say, simply because I had written quite a lot about 'Wakey' in a previous book and didn't want to go over old ground. Some things are worth repeating though. Wakefield is now a national centre for modern art. The Hepworth, named for sculptor Barbara Hepworth, the town's most famous daughter and the greatest female British artist of the twentieth century, is a stylish and striking multi-million-pound venue. It had 100,000 visitors in the month following its opening in May 2011, and half a million within six. The Art House in the centre of town provides dozens of working artists with studio space and its associated venture, the Artwalk, sees those studios, as well as the shops, offices and bars of the town throw open their doors every first Wednesday of the month to become a city-wide living gallery, filled with painting, sculpture, lithographs, etchings, gouache and any other imaginable kind of art. I encourage you to make the trip one month.

When the Jarrow march passed through Wakefield, British art was in a febrile state. Hepworth, along with husband-to-be Ben Nicholson, Henry Moore, and critic Herbert Read were having a public argument with senior artistic figures like Paul Nash over whether more modern art should be allowed into the shows of the Royal Academy. Eric Gill and Jacob Epstein's sculptures were appalling the Establishment with their eroticism and modernism. Three months before the Jarrow march, the International Surrealist Exhibition opened in London, bringing Britain its first sight of Breton, Magritte and Dali.

Most intriguingly, a small but significant part of British art history was blossoming both as the Jarrow march set off and not very far away from them. The then-current *Shell Guide to Northumberland and Durham* described Ashington as a 'mining town built in the early part of this century ... dreary rows a mile long with ash pits down the middle of the streets', which makes it sound like an unlikely place for a new art movement, but that was exactly what was happening here. In 1936, the Ashington Group – 'the Pitmen Painters' as they became known – held their first exhibition in Newcastle. The group of 24 arose from a Workers Education Authority class in art in which the men had started to express themselves in striking and individual paintings. The exhibition was a huge success and the painters were acclaimed. British artists Clive Bell and Julian Trevelyan championed them and art historian Sir Anthony Blunt (later to be Keeper of the Queen's Pictures and later still exposed as a Soviet spy) said that the exhibition was 'the most important event of the year from the point of view of English art'.

So while Jarrow marched, Ashington painted, but while audiences and critics from outside the manual working class generally applauded, some within were suspicious. Wal Hannington, leader of the National Unemployed Workers Movement, grizzled that art clubs, like the BBC's morning talks for the unemployed, and occupational and recreation centres were a crafty tactic of the ruling class to 'dope' the workers.

Orwell, who was touring the north at the time for what would become *The Road to Wigan Pier*, thought such initiatives were 'simply a device to keep the unemployed quiet and give them an illusion that something is being done for them'. Whether capitalist sop or genuine liberation of the spirit, the story of Ashington's artistic movement is told in *The Pitmen Painters*, a play by Lee Hall of *Billy Elliot* fame, which addresses these conflicts and questions; after attending a modern art exhibition at the Royal Academy one painter says he realises that art teaches you 'not to put up with what you're given'.

There are some, and they may have a point, who say such proletarian defiance is as much what motivated the Brexit vote as bigotry. Wakefield is as good a place to dwell on such matters as any, and perhaps better. Put simply and factually, Wakefield voted overwhelmingly to leave the EU: 66.3 per cent on a turnout of almost 80 per cent.

The *Guardian*'s Northern Editor Helen Pidd visited the town the morning after the vote and reported finding a nervous bafflement among many, not least the town's large Eastern European community. Aneta Duchniak opened Duchniak's, the first Polish restaurant in Wakefield, two years before the vote. According to Helen's article, 'Many of her regulars are Yorkshire folk who have taken a shine to her delicate pierogi dumplings and hearty borscht soups. Lots of them wanted Britain to leave Europe, she says, and yet they made a special effort to come in afterwards to tell her it wasn't personal. "They said, 'We want to support you, it's nothing against you, it's against Brussels controlling us'."'

Some see this kind of thinking as specious and self-deluding, a mask for ingrained racism. I'm not so sure. Whilst I wouldn't claim that it's an intellectually sound position, or to be defended necessarily, I can well believe, from my conversations in towns like Wakefield or Dewsbury or Rochdale or Oldham or Wigan, that some who voted to leave bore no personal animosity to immigrants but harboured some vague and misguided grudge against the EU. This grudge was fed by the falsehoods of UKIP and the right-wing tabloids and acted on out of impotent anger.

Also, these towns have good reason to doubt the word of those infamous experts in Westminster. As Pidd points out, 'When Poland joined the EU in May 2004 – along with Cyprus, the Czech Republic, Estonia, Hungary, Latvia, Lithuania, Malta, Slovakia and Slovenia – there was little fear or fanfare about what their membership could mean for Britain. The government certainly wasn't worried. Tony Blair's administration estimated that no more than 13,000 of these new Europeans would seek a new life in Britain each year from 2004. These figures were largely based on predictions made by the academic Christian Dustmann of University College London, and worked on the (incorrect) assumption that other large countries in the EU, in particular Germany, would also open up their labour markets. It soon became clear that Dustmann's estimate was hilariously – or catastrophically, depending on your view – wrong. Between May 2004 and June 2007, 430,000 Poles applied to the Home Office worker registration scheme, joining the 69,000 Poles already in Britain, pre-EU enlargement. As the scheme was voluntary, the true figure was thought to be much higher. In July 2006, the respected Polish newspaper *Polityka* estimated that one million Poles had moved to the UK.'

That will almost certainly now change. Indeed, it is already changing. More Poles head for Germany now than the UK and that will surely increase as we slowly, wearily, raise our drawbridge against Europe. In addition, the Polish government wants its workers to come home and is luring them with a very generous child benefit system. The Polish economy suffered from the mass exodus to England by losing its youngest and brightest and experienced shortages of qualified workers in key industries. But many academics believe that some Poles will never leave, just as their forefathers came and stayed during the Second World War. Dustmann, he of the original massive underestimate, told Pidd,

'Overall migrants from Poland are very well educated, young, and have a high labour-force attachment. They easily assimilate and will be indistinguishable in the next generation.'

For now, there are still many visible signs of our new Polish communities. I pass several Polski skleps on my way out of Wakefield headed for the A61 and the route to Barnsley. I stop into one and buy a kielbasa from Milena which I munch on like a lolly as I stomp past the Hepworth and the Wildcats Belle Vue stadium. My day was very much like the marchers' was 80 years before; uneventful and benign, weak sun and cloud enlivened by the odd blustery shower. But my walk fell on a Saturday and so there was a reason to quicken my step to my next destination, the grand old South Yorkshire town of Barnsley.

Berneslai gets its first official mention in the Domesday Book, though the Saxons had a foothold here long before. Before that even, 2,000 years ago and for reasons that are unclear, the embalmed bodies of several North Africans were buried beneath the town, a discovery made by Barnsley-born Egyptologist Joann Fletcher. 'You don't think 2,000 years ago that Ancient Egyptians came to Yorkshire – but they did … in some ways it blows your mind,' she said, mind blown.

But the big significant date in the town's popular history (along with their FA Cup Triumph of 1912) occurs in 1249 when the town opened its first market. Nearly a thousand years of street marketing have not even begun to dull the locals' appetite for the notion. The market is 700 years old and has some 400 stalls indoors and outdoors, and whether coming on foot, by bus or by train, you cannot miss it; it is a huge structure, as big as the Cardington Airship Hangars in the Fens, looming over the bus station and the rail interchange. On a Saturday, from certain angles, Barnsley can feel like a vast market with a town clinging on for dear life. Once, the outdoor stalls of Barnsley were known for their wool and fish, and you can still find balls and shoals of both here. But these days, in the gigantic covered unfussy uber market, big enough to house a 747 and maybe a Saturn V, you can also find those essentials of modern life, a discount Iron Man Duvet or a bumper economy rack of vials of Black Cherry E Cig Vape. You can find handmade Loake loafers for a couple of hundred quid, a gallon of hair conditioner for coppers, plus flavours of Polish crisps that even Polish people think niche. At Vinyl Junction 42, I noticed a couple of seventies albums by John Miles; a nice coincidence in that his granddad was the cook on the Jarrow march. Flicking through I see a whole rack of second-hand albums by the dreadful right-wing rock guitarist Ted Nugent. I wonder if someone has found out about his support for Trump and flogged them all in a fit of rock pique?

The day turned bright and warm by the time I leave the market to take in the town. Just by the stalls selling discount leather belts is the Alhambra, a blue and white building that is now a bingo hall but in 1936 was one of the town's many picture palaces along with the Cudworth, the Empire, the Pavilion or the Theatre Royal. A year later, the Ritz opened its doors with William Powell in *My Man Godfrey* (and closed on 16 March 1974 with Reg Varney in *Holiday on the Buses*). It was subsequently demolished, perhaps to avoid giving the town painful memories of the latter. After a meeting in the miners' hall, the men were treated to free seats by the various cinema managements. Still proudly independent at that time, the Alhambra was taken over by the Odeon chain two years later (the fate of many independent cinemas), but only on condition that it could keep its own name. This it did to the end and still does as a shopping centre, though it closed as a cinema on 26 November 1960 with the *The Entertainer* starring Laurence Olivier, a classy but draining movie. Back in 1936, several marchers fell asleep in the Alhambra's comfy one and nines after the exertions of the day.

What did they snooze through, those weary men of Jarrow? No records were kept but it may well have been one of the

British comedies we discussed earlier. This, though, was the period when Hollywood began to establish itself as the global powerhouse of mass entertainment. In 1936 alone it produced a tranche of films that still make cineastes drool. There was Chaplin's brilliant satire on mechanisation and alienation *Modern Times* and Gary Cooper in Frank Capra's charming *Mr Deeds Goes to Town*. Ginger Rogers and Fred Astaire were paired in the delightful *Follow the Fleet*, whilst Spencer Tracy starred in a darkly intense drama about the mob titled *Fury*, the American debut of the great German expressionist Fritz Lang. He had successfully made the move to Hollywood as Europe fell under the growing shadow of Nazism and the threat of war. From Britain in this prevalent mood of futuristic paranoia, came Alexander Korda's classic *Things to Come*. This version of H G Wells's dystopian novel brought to the screen seemed even more prophetic than it did on publication three years before when the author had predicted the Second World War and the coming of a world super state.

The fact that Barnsley could host the men in four or five picture houses is testament to what a boom time this was for the cinema. Between 1934 and 1937, the cinema-going audience grew from 18 to 20 million per week on average. New cinemas were opening all the time and, like Barnsley's Ritz, were often elegant and stylish art deco entertainment temples in gilt and neon. Their appeal cut across class boundaries too. Whilst workers could enjoy Fields's and Formby's homespun cheeriness, middle-class filmgoers preferred comedies of manners and tremulous tearjerkers. Going to the cinema had none of the slightly seedy and downmarket associations of going to the pub, which would generally be a drably functional 'boozer'. This made cinema-going especially attractive to middle-class women, as well as to couples of all classes for whom it provided a warm, dark, convenient venue for 'courting'. The cinema was a profoundly democratising force at this time, offering a new range of 'celebrities' to admire for their talent, grace or beauty rather than the aloof and remote aristocracy who had been admired from afar for so long.

'Tarn' is quieting now as the market packs and folds itself back once more into the back of vans and trucks; a late bargain here, a quick sale there. The wide civic square is sunlit and almost empty, feeling like a planner's model of an imagined cityscape, a South Yorkshire Brasilia or Canberra. I stride purposefully past the Old No 7, a terrific boozer with labyrinthine depths I once spent far too much time in after a gig in Barnsley, in order to fully take in one of Barnsley's most famous and controversial sights. It's a grand thing but it very much annoyed a visitor to Barnsley called George Orwell back in the thirties.

In 1936, as plans for the Jarrow march were taking shape, Eric Blair AKA George Orwell, Old Etonian and former colonial policeman turned journalist and writer, was sent north by his publisher Victor Gollancz to research a book on the conditions of life in the depressed industrial north. Orwell thought of his trip initially as 'venturing among savages' but that didn't prevent him producing a sympathetic but unsentimental account of life in towns like Wigan, Sheffield and Barnsley that became the searing and enduring classic polemic *The Road to Wigan Pier*. For his researches he kept rough notes and a diary that you can now find in his collected works. Here is his account of his trip below ground in Barnsley's Grimethorpe Colliery:

> The place where the fillers were working was fearful beyond description ... the seam of coal is only a yard high or a bit more, the men can only kneel or crawl to their work, never stand up. The effort of constantly shovelling coal over your left shoulder and flinging it a yard or two beyond, while in a kneeling position, must be very great even to men who are used to it. Added to this there are the clouds of coal dust which are

flying down your throat all the time and which make
it difficult to see any distance. The men were all naked
except for trousers and knee-pads.

Orwell came away from his time in the mines of the north with
enormous respect and admiration for colliers. He later wrote, 'If
there is one man I feel inferior to, it is a coal miner.' I once met
someone whose family Orwell had lodged with while he was in
Wigan and it had become part of that family's lore that he was
a 'lovely young man'; thin, unfailingly polite, never snobbish,
always willing to help. In *The Road to Wigan Pier*, Orwell never
patronises the people he meets, though occasionally you can
sense a mild innate disgust at their manners, eating habits and
such. But he was on their side and they came to respect each
other. 'When I sit typing, the family, especially Mrs G. and the
kids, all gather round to watch absorbedly, and appear to admire
my prowess almost as much as I admire that of the miners.'

Perhaps this is why in the book's notorious conclusion,
Orwell excoriates the intellectual left such as George Bernard
Shaw as 'cranks' and mocks 'every fruit-juice drinker, nudist,
sandal-wearer, sex-maniac, Quaker, "Nature Cure" quack,
pacifist and feminist in England'. While this is overheated to the
point of silliness, it arises from an anger with the 'crank's' lack
of genuine empathy or solidarity with the industrial working
class Orwell had lived among and come to know. Orwell was a
socialist. But he was also a patriot and a traditionalist; he would
have loathed identity politics and Corbyn's regime I think,
seeing it as a distraction from the proper business of socialism
– the improvement of the lot of the worker, the poor and the
disadvantaged.

It was in this savage mood that Orwell turned his
considerable scorn on Barnsley town hall. The foundation stone
was laid on 21 April 1932 and it was opened by the Prince of
Wales (soon to be notorious himself) on 14 December 1933.

The cost was £188,037 12/10d. George Orwell in his book was highly critical of this expenditure, claiming that the council should have spent the money on improving the housing and living conditions of the local miners. Nonetheless, the huge, dazzling edifice, more akin to the seat of parliament of a Baltic capital than a provincial town hall, has become perhaps the town's most iconic feature – and the clichéd adjective is justified here. Built from Portland stone and designed by the architect responsible for the Northern Ireland parliament at Stormont (which it resembles), it's visible from the adjoining motorway and receives extravagant praise on TripAdvisor – 'Absolutely amazing building, a Barnsley landmark ... This is a place you step in and just think wow' – as well as the obligatory churl – 'impoverished ... a step back in time ... grubbiness of public spaces'. But as this last was posted by Toby and Bunty, perhaps we shouldn't be surprised.

The building that so irked Orwell has had a makeover in recent years. A plume of glittering spray arcs from a chic new water feature and at night the town hall glows a pale and eerie blue, turning Barnsley into the Gotham of South Yorkshire. In a tiny room high in the spire, a pale fluorescent light burns through the night, prompting local speculation that it's where the mayor keeps his sunbed. In June 2013, part of the town hall became Experience Barnsley, a museum dedicated to the history of the town and its people from the twelfth to twenty-first centuries. Outside a poster proclaims it 'a proud Yorkshire story told by the people of Barnsley'. The endless exhortations to take pride in this county can become tedious. But I liked the cut of Experience Barnsley's jib. As well as the quite proper nod to antiquity, there's much on the town's social history, coal mining and other industries, and the approach to this was robust and refreshing with no puff or blather.

That October week in 1936, the Jarrow marchers, feted at the town's new and advanced Steam Baths and fed on meat and potato pie, were not the only celebrated visitors to Barnsley.

A Wigan compatriot of mine came here too. George Formby, banjoleleist, Apartheid rebel and recipient of the Order of Lenin, came to Barnsley to support the mining community. It had suffered a terrible tragedy, the Wharncliffe mine disaster, in which 58 men were killed in an underground explosion just two months previously. Every pit village and town knew and feared these frequent reminders of the human price of coal. But King Coal itself would surely never be unseated or deposed. Surely. In fact, coal mining was one of those rooted certainties of British life that would turn out to be as evanescent as the spray from Barnsley's proud new fountain.

STAGE TEN

BARNSLEY TO SHEFFIELD

16 October, 13 miles

By day ten, the morning's packing has assumed a brisk, almost militaristic routine. There is the folding and rolling of shirts, the thrusting into spare corners of socks and unmentionables, the stowing of the 'good shoes', the meticulous stashing of the travel tooth brush, the painkillers and the plasters. Always too, when the sign has just been flipped to 'Please Make Up This Room', the trudge back along the corridor to the room for something left behind: a washbag, a contact lens case, an iPad. This last though is crucial since, thanks to this modern miracle, I'm carrying with me several volumes of literature from or about the 1930s. I have with me academic histories, memoirs, reportage. I have Orwell's first novel too, *Keep the Aspidistra Flying* as well as the collected works of the curious English Catholic writer Charles Williams and the rather less curious but equally Catholic Graham Greene. I have A J Cronin's *The Stars Look Down* – a bleak and apposite tale of a family's struggle for survival amidst a strike that the local Labour Party and Trade Union don't support in a depressed north-eastern mining town. It was written the year before the march and the echoes of Jarrow are deafening.

As well as this, I have a collection of short stories by the Welsh writer Kate Roberts that chime perfectly with my march.

Coal dust hangs thick and heavy in Roberts's writing as the ghost of it still does in the streets and pubs of Barnsley. At its peak, Barnsley district had ten deep mines and the last to go was Grimethorpe. That huge colliery was famed for its brass band and then as the setting for the film *Brassed Off*. Grimethorpe's last shift came up in 1993, having limped on for almost a decade after the defining mid-1980s strike. It's all an age ago now, but for some those days feel like yesterday.

I hop into a minicab for a short distance to pick up my route again and the driver tells me that one taxi firm, Black and White cabs (by far the most numerous on the rank) was set up by sacked miners who pooled their redundancy money after the strike. 'Some of them, they're like those Japanese soldiers who don't know the war's over. They're still fighting the fight. We wind 'em up about it. "'Ere we go, the battle of Orgreave again! Give it a rest!" Something comes over 'em when owt to do w'it strike comes up. Thatcher, Scargill, picketing ... you can feel 'em tighten up, see their expressions change. Mind you, they saw some stuff I suppose.'

Memories are long here. A friend who grew up locally told me about the working man's club in Mapplewell, the Tin Hat as it was known, where above the door was the name of one man who crossed the picket line during the miners' strike and who was never to be let in. I run this past my driver and he laughs bitterly – 'Sounds about reet'. As we drive, he points vaguely in the directions of the various pits, once employing thousands, now silent caverns brimming with dark, oily water 'Dodworth were that way ... Cortonwood ... that were a decent size ... Grimethorpe obviously. A lot of my family worked at Goldthorpe. They burned a dummy of Thatcher there on the day of her funeral. Bloody hundreds of 'em turned out. Right carry on it were.' He laughs at the grotesque memory. Later I check this story and find that at this mock funeral, where a fake coffin and effigy were burned in an atmosphere of grim celebration, the number present was actually about two thousand.

He drops me at a roadside café where I have my first cup of tea of the day and carry on with Kate Roberts's story. It's called 'Protest March' and accords completely with my Jarrow project. In it, Blodwen, living with her husband in poverty in a subterranean hovel, joins a protest march against the Means Test, that sinister, invasive scourge of towns like Jarrow. But even as she marches, she becomes disillusioned and begins to doubt that these gestures will ever change anything or that anything can be changed. 'The crowd itself was looking like something absurd to Blodwen now and depressing in its absurdity. She thought, if the government were to see them now, what they'd do was laugh at them. After all, what were they marching for?'

Marching rather than disobedience, the banner rather than the flung brick of the suffragettes, was the dominant protest mode of the 1930s. John Tanner at the Experience Barnsley Museum told me that eight Barnsley women walked to London as part of a 1930s hunger march. In 2016, whether you viewed it as energising or pointless, some of that mood seemed to be back. Just a few weeks before I began my march, supporters of Jeremy Corbyn rallied in Liverpool to show support for their leader and against Owen Smith, his rival in the Labour leadership elections. The difference in opinions even on the left about such events showed up the great open wound in the current British Labour movement. From Corbyn's camp, an enthusiastic tweet from @cameronsporkies was typical:

So Owen Smith, this is what unelectable looks like. Banking on another MSM cover up? #KeepCorbyn!

Attached was a photograph showing an enormous throng outside Liverpool's famous St George's Hall. Even to the relatively impartial, it looked an awful lot of people; it transpired that the picture actually showed the crowd for Liverpool FC's triumphant homecoming parade after winning the 2005 Champions League trophy. (Obfuscation has always been rife around 'demos' with police and activists making inflated or shrunken assessments of the numbers involved; in the 1980s, the constabulary's often spectacular underestimations of crowd size became a comic staple of satire shows like *Not the Nine O' Clock News*.) The *Guardian* reported 5,000 people at the Corbyn Liverpool rally whilst police officers estimated attendance at between 3,500 and 5,000. Organisers suggested 10,000. This size obsession has become such a contentious issue that there are now competing crowd size estimation techniques, such as the Jacobs method using grids over pictures. Gordon Arnold, a retired architect from Dallas, has created a crowd-counting app named CrowdSize which put Corbyn's rally at around 4,000 people. A team from Warwick University is working on a system that will soon be able to accurately estimate the number of people at mass gatherings by the number of mobile phones present in an area.

Quibbles about size miss the real point, however. To equate the turn-out at a rally, whether for Jeremy Corbyn or Nigel Farage, with general support in the wider population is to fundamentally misunderstand the nature of electability and indeed democracy in general. This kind of wonky thinking is a modern malaise made endemic by the internet and in particular social media, what psychologists call 'false-consensus bias'. Or as some have it, living in the 'Twitter Bubble'.

Living like this, and I've been as guilty as anyone, is to wrongly assume that everyone thinks like you do, and furthermore, that anyone who doesn't is a member of an aberrant minority. It is the tyranny of the timeline. False consensus bias is what fuelled the spluttering rage of many Remain supporters after the Brexit vote. Swapping opinions with only those people who agree with us has given us a distorted picture of what the wider world is really like. This has always been the way of things to an extent of course. We tend to gravitate to people who share our world view; we seek them out, we drink with them, eat with them, marry them. There was always an element of this in our consumption of the traditional media too. People by and large bought the newspapers that shared (or maybe shaped) their beliefs. (Interestingly, when I taught sociology, students were often shocked that newspapers were politically partisan or identified these allegiances utterly wrongly. They thought, for instance, that the *Guardian* was Tory because it was 'posh' and the *Sun* Labour because working-class men read it.) But there was always the chance still that you would see on TV news or hear on the radio a voice that challenged yours or an opinion you didn't share. As the old media gives way to the power of the new, such moments become rare. By only 'following' and 'friending' people like oneself, other, dissenting voices can almost be avoided altogether. For me, this is what undermines much of the new radical left's critique of the Mainstream Media (MSM as they would have it) and we'll come back to it.

We make Facebook friends of those who agree, we follow them on Twitter, we chat with them, and anyone who doesn't share our opinions is a troll. After Brexit, some people were forced to concede that living in the Twitter Bubble might be warm, congenial and supportive but means you have some nasty shocks in store. This is not simply an inconvenience or an interesting sociological quirk – it may well be destroying proper political discourse and debate. John West, a US journalist who's studied the phenomenon, put it powerfully if somewhat technically in a *Vice* piece about the use of Twitter in the run-up to the US election: 'All of this paints a bleak picture of online political discourse … It is one balkanized by ideology and issue-interest, with little potential for information flow between the online cocoons.' Trump versus Liberal Hollywood, Remain versus Leave; Corbyn versus the centre left, the Balkanisation, as West puts it, is ongoing and about as healthy as it was for the real Balkans. Corbyn even acknowledged it a day so after the rally when he said, not entirely convincingly, 'The idea I live in some remote bubble of adulation is frankly ridiculous.'

I finish Kate Roberts' story 'Protest March' over my lunch on the road somewhere around Tankersley. Its political message is fairly hopeless but it does at least end on a note of human consolation when the disillusioned Blodwen is welcomed home by her previously cynical husband. Roberts wrote this story during a previous 'fad' for marching as a form of political discourse, just before the Jarrow Crusade and at the height of the popular wave of protest and hunger marches. Two other marches passed through Sheffield in the same month as the Jarrow Crusade. There was the National Hunger March, a more avowedly political enterprise entirely, and the National League of the Blind March, which was supported by Sheffield's Trades and Labour council. To give an idea of the diversity and sometimes woeful disorganisation of such ventures – something the Jarrow march organisers were desperate to avoid – on the night the Crusade arrived in Jarrow, a straggling and desperate group arrived at Pomona Street School in Sheffield. They were ex-servicemen who were marching from Inverness to London to protest their meagre war pensions. Fifty had set off, but only 16 arrived in Sheffield at 3am, gaunt, exhausted 'ghost like figures' according to a local paper report, who'd badly lost their way on the moors above Sheffield.

There was no such hapless waywardness for Red Ellen, David Riley, Paddy Scullion and the Jarrow men, and hopefully none for me. Sheffield wouldn't welcome me as it had done them of course with cigarettes, tea and sandwiches and I didn't expect it to of course. I know Sheffield a little and I knew that it is not hard to find your own welcome there and make yourself at home in this compact and vibrant city. Built on seven hills (like Rome, as they will quickly tell you), and with something of the air of a mountain stronghold about it. It is its own domain, utterly unlike Bradford or Leeds or its suspicious cousins in South Yorkshire; different, individual, a unique mixture of unyielding grit and romantic softness, a city where the hardest-looking bloke in the pub is likely to call you 'love' and give you a different smacker from the one you were expecting.

Geology, topography, sociology; all contribute to the sense of a strapping, over-vigorous city bursting its banks and spilling over the hillsides. Then there's the industry. Sheffield has never had any business in wool or textiles, carding or knitting. Sheffield makes steel, and is proud of it. Some of this gets into the local character. As Graham Turner said in his splendid 1960s book *The North Country* (now sadly out of print), 'Neither [Leeds nor Bradford] can claim the virility which Sheffield's basic raw material, steel, confers; making natty gents suitings hardly compares with fashioning 300-ton ingots.'

Milling and making steel is harder work for less profit than carding wool. Sheffield likes to think itself a macho cut above Leeds for this and other reasons, even if some Sheffielders will concede that Leeds and Bradford are prettier cities because of it. In truth, despite the much-vaunted Yorkshire pride, there may even still be those who resent being lumped in with Yorkshire at all. Local industrialist Allan John Grant welcomed the Jarrow march in a speech that began, 'There is no time to discuss the principle of these marches now that the deputation from Jarrow has reached Derbyshire …' putting Sheffield in a different county altogether.

Orwell came to Sheffield just before the Jarrow march and no one could have accused him of pandering to the locals or sentimentalising their city. 'Sheffield, I suppose, could justifiably claim to be the ugliest town in the world … it has a population of half a million and it contains fewer decent buildings than the average East Anglian village of five hundred. And the stench.' This is the snobbery of the old Etonian to a degree, but even J B Priestley, a comradely rival from Bradford, described entry into Sheffield as descending through a 'murky canopy' into 'the steaming bowels of the earth'. Modern Sheffield would surely have nothing so sulphurous to show me. But on my way into the city, something terrible, suffused with misery and wickedness both pulled and repelled me.

It's an ordinary enough road, heading anonymously south from the main A61 Penistone Road in from the outer suburbs of High Green, Burncross and Grenoside. Narrowing and cutting through working class suburbia, after the brash American uberstores, the Domino Pizzas and PC Worlds, the road gathers around itself smaller, more homely, sometimes dowdier enterprises; Hing Fan's Fish and Chips and Chinese Meals To Takeaway, the Mirage E Cigarette Shop, Sybs Roofing Services, Tracey's Sandwich Bar. Next door a shop selling vintage football programmes gives a hint of where you are near. And then a small, cold feeling as you take in the street corner and wonder what it was like on that summer day in 1988. Here a tiny road leads to the West Stand of Sheffield Wednesday's famous old football ground; the A6102, better known as Leppings Lane.

Hillsborough stadium hosted five FA Cup semi-finals during the 1980s and at several there were frightening scenes and near chaos. In 1981 during the tie between Spurs and Wolves, far more spectators were crammed onto the terrace than was safe and there were 38 injuries, several involving broken limbs. Sheffield Wednesday chairman Bert McGee was sanguine, snorting at police officers who feared fatalities. 'Bollocks – no one would have been killed.' Cage-like pens were then introduced which invalidated the safety certificate and there were no more cup semi-finals at this once-regular home for such big clashes until 1987. Again there was confusion and overcrowding at the 1987 cup quarter and semi-finals. At the latter, some people were pulled up out of the crowd by fellow fans from above for their own safety. In 1988, Liverpool and Nottingham Forest met in the semi-final at Hillsborough and again there was severe overcrowding and dangerous crushes. No action was taken. The following year, the teams were drawn to meet each other again at Hillsborough. Huge crowds built up outside before kick-off with Liverpool supporters being allocated the smaller West Stand at the Leppings Lane end. With 5,000 supporters still outside minutes before kick-off (and a request to delay the start turned down), Chief Superintendent David Duckenfield ordered gate C to be opened and fans surged into the central pens on the terrace.

If you want a detailed account of the horrifying result of this decision, of what happened that afternoon, of the obscene deaths of 96 men, women and children; of the incompetence, wickedness, abuse and lies that followed from police, government and sections of the media over the next two-and-a-half decades, I urge you to read *And the Sun Shines Now* by Adrian Tempany. It is the definitive account of the disaster and its sordid aftermath by someone who was there. Tempany nearly died at Hillsborough and like many other heroic individuals, fought for justice and truth through the long decades ahead. Looking back over those last sentences, I hear a tone that could not be described as impartial. But how can one be impartial over Hillsborough? Tempany's book will make you rage and weep.

Feeling suddenly awkward and not wanting to be thought ghoulish, I walk briskly past C gate and the other blue gates of Leppings Lane with just a quick glance. I pause properly at the Hillsborough memorial at the main stand just a little further on and read the inscriptions and the dedications. It's a simple stone tablet, usually decorated with scarves and pictures, reading, 'In memory of the 96 men, women and children who tragically died and the countless lives that were changed forever... You'll Never Walk Alone'. I have no personal connection to the Hillsborough tragedy. I can't claim to be one of those countless lives directly affected by it – some who've tried this shabby trick have been rightly savaged for it, like UKIP's Paul Nuttall – and so I don't expect to find myself crying until I realise I am.

Perhaps it is because Tempany's book and Kevin Sampson's *Hillsborough Voices* are still fresh in my mind. They are hard to shake, these awful, vivid accounts of the day and the barely believable details. Police prevented fans from climbing the fence to safety, stopped friends helping other friends and allowed only one of the 44 ambulances on hand to enter the ground and so only 14 of the fatally injured ever made it to hospital. The authorities then spent the next 27 years lying or obscuring the truth about what happened and blaming the fans themselves.

This beggars belief. But there were some prepared to sink even lower. Bernard Ingham, former press chief to Mrs Thatcher, said in a letter to a victim's parent that the fault was with 'tanked up yobs' and later that people 'should shut up about Hillsborough'. Similarly, former *Sun* editor Kelvin MacKenzie lied and smeared the dead in the most vile manner in his paper for years to come, only eventually apologising partially and under duress, just before I began my walk.

That was because in April, a few months before I set off from Jarrow, a kind of victory occurred for the victims of Hillsborough and their families. Thanks to tireless and often thankless efforts, the Justice for the 96 campaign won. At the end of the longest judicial hearing in British history, a jury ruled that every single death that day was an unlawful killing. As I walked down Leppings Lane that October day, the newspapers were humming with talk that prosecutions might finally begin.

Calling Hillsborough a tragedy feels wrong. It suggests a freak occurrence such as the sinking of the *Titanic* or the downfall of Othello caused by his own flaws. Hillsborough is actually more akin to what happened at Aberfan in 1966, when negligence meant that a dangerous slag heap collapsed onto a primary school killing 116 children and 28 adults. Later, the National Coal Board was found 'wholly responsible' for those deaths. Aberfan and Hillsborough did not simply happen to working-class people; they happened to those people because they were working class. They died because richer and more powerful people than themselves did not care what became of them.

Hillsborough though has a more sinister dimension than the horror of Aberfan. Though it is little consolation, Aberfan was at least not a wilful act of enmity. It is not too lurid or sensational to see Hillsborough as the final and most terrible battle in a decade of class war, with police used as a tool of government in oppressing those it saw as the 'enemy within'. That meant essentially the left, the Labour movement and the working classes generally. As the Hillsborough enquiry ended and as I entered Sheffield, a similar event, the police actions and the violence at Orgreave coking plant in 1984, was exercising many and creating calls for an enquiry into that too. Some of the officers on duty at Hillsborough had also been at Orgreave.

There'd be more to hear about Orgreave as I neared London. For today, after Hillsborough and Leppings Lane, I loosely follow the River Don's course into the city, passing the new and fashionable Kelham Island Quarter where industrial heritage rubs shoulders with craft beer emporia and the like. If the Jarrow march passed by they'd have found it a buzzing tightly packed district of riverside mills. I say 'if' since there's some confusion about the actual route they took into the city centre. Getting slightly lost, they wrongfooted the small welcoming committee. There was a welcome but a curious one in the form of a single woman who thought they were a fascist march and hurled abuse at them.

Given the headlines of the day, this doughty lady could be forgiven for being jumpy. Mosley's Blackshirts might have been given short shrift in the East End and elsewhere but he had enough friends in high places to ensure he couldn't be discounted just yet. One such ally may well have been King Edward VIII whose close personal friendship with an American woman called Wallis Simpson was becoming very interesting to the press, Westminster and the man in the street. In Germany, the Nazis passed a law forbidding Jews from using parks or public swimming pools and from owning electrical equipment, typewriters or bicycles. Dark clouds were forming across the skies of the world as 1936 moved to a close.

In other news, as they wouldn't have said then, there was major civil unrest in India. Britain's imperial phase was ending and its relationship with the subcontinent had been volatile and problematic throughout the decade. In 1931, when the

Lancashire cotton trade was at its lowest ebb, India restricted its imports of cotton goods, hitting the north west of England hard. Gandhi himself came to Bolton to meet the workers and, while sympathetic to their plight, he reminded them that his own people were never very far from starvation. They took him for a night out to the Swan Hotel in Bolton but the ascetic Indian took only bread and water, which unsurprisingly rather dampened any party mood.

Stanley Baldwin was all for continuing the policy of liberalisation towards India, not wanting another chronic running sore like Ireland to deal with. But the UK's rule in India was still harsh and draconian. On the weekend the Jarrow march reached Sheffield, 35 people were killed in riots involving Hindus and Muslims in Bombay. All of this weighed heavy on the mind of Ellen Wilkinson who had visited India many times and was a passionate advocate of emancipation and self-rule for India and a fervent Internationalist. 'To me, the mill girls of Shanghai are as important as the mill girls of Manchester,' she said in 1936. How would that have been received in Sheffield 80 years later I wondered?

The Indian question bedevilling Stanley Baldwin in 1936 was long settled by 2016 but that night I had my own Indian question, namely at which one to eat in Sheffield. I'd not even considered other cuisine as Sheffield will always mean to me my first gleeful adventures into Indian food during friends' student days here in the early 1980s, when David Blunkett's 'People's Republic of South Yorkshire' rang to the sound of ABC and the Human League, bhajis were 10p and a 'suicide' phaal curry came free if you could manage to eat it. Happy days.

I put the question to the hive mind of Twitter naturally. Marc Webster said, 'Get yourself to Shapla for a curry. Crappy end of town, but underrated and never had a bad meal yet,' and many other correspondents agreed. Nadia Shireen suggested the Thali Café and Ian Howie told me, 'the Mogul Room on

Sharrow Vale Road is excellent. You can also have a good drink in the brilliant Lescar as well'. Shabir's gets several good reviews but in the event I choose a restaurant on Leopold Square which comes to my timeline garlanded with recommendations and testimonials, many sounding almost tearful with jealousy that I find myself nearby on Aagrah buffet night. Purists will baulk at that word 'buffet', and I take their point. Unfairly or not, the ubiquitous city-centre Chinese variety always conjures images of glutinous sweet and sours congealing under hot lamps, with pale and flaccid chips lolling unappealing nearby and, 34 times an hour, the bringing out of a small cake to a tuneless chorus of 'Happy Birthday'. Useful when strapped for cash or pushed for time perhaps, and I have often been both, but happily being neither on this Sunday evening, I make my way briskly to the £12.50 buffet at the Aagrah, the money burning a hole in my rucksack.

It has been said that I bang on a bit too much about food on my travels, so I will gloss over the gorgeousness of everything to do with the meal: the people, the staff, the tenderness and insinuating warmth of the gobhi gosht or the sweet and pungent murgh sindhi korma or even the gosht Punjabi masala, its succulent lamb steeped in a sauce bright with cardamom and sleepy with aromatic methi. Suffice to say that the whole night comes back to me often. But one comment on Twitter the next day about another Sheffield curry favourite makes me think. 'Ah ... and to think that once upon a time Mr Shabbir just had one small business in Westgate, Shipley. Corporate isn't always better.' That tells you a lot about the strangely proprietorial relationship we have with this cuisine of Empire and the people who cook it. The Indian restaurant business in Britain started with a handful of esoteric outlets and grew, in a nice reversal, to colonise us until, according to Robin Cook's famous speech on chicken tikka masala, it became our national dish. But now, some say unthinkably, it may be declining again in this new uncertain Britain.

The Jarrow marchers could have eaten Indian food if they'd really wanted to but it would have taken as much of an effort as their crusade. E P Veeraswamy published his seminal work 'Indian Cookery' in 1936, but to get it cooked home-style in anything like a restaurant setting here, one would have had to visit one of the handful of curry cafés set up by Indian sailors who'd jumped ship or were dumped at major ports like Cardiff and London. Most of these renegade seamen came from Sylhet – now a mountainous area of Bangladesh – and the 'Indian' curry house we know is really usually Bangladeshi. After the Second World War, many of these early Asian entrepreneurs bought up defunct cafés or bombed-out pubs and were the only establishments to open late. The British love of the 'after pub' curry was born.

The brilliant food writer Bee Wilson points out that the naming of British curry houses reflects their vintage:

> If you see one that is called Taj Mahal, Passage to India or Koh-i-Noor (after the famous Indian diamond), it probably dates back to the first wave of curry houses in the 1960s. These eateries appealed to retired Old India Hands, who wanted to eat hot chutney and be treated like 'sahibs' again. The names of 1970s curry houses began to shrug off the colonial past and evoke, instead, a vague sense of eastern exoticism: Lily Tandoori, Aladdin, Sheba – glamorous names to counteract longstanding British prejudices that south Asian food was malodorous and unclean.

I didn't know it, as I scooped chana and sambar on Leopold Square, but behind the scenes and the kitchen doors, the curry is in crisis. Two or three Indian restaurants are closing every week in Britain. Like the public house, it is a cherished mainstay of our social life that we are in danger of losing. A real shame this, and not just gastronomically, as for years curry houses have been rare islands of independent family enterprise in high streets dominated by chains. They played a vital role in the regeneration of many local economies in the 1980s and 1990s. Now those chains, from the cheap and carby pizza big boys to the ersatz, unconvincing curries offered by the Harvesters and, yes, Wetherspoon are forcing them out.

The price of our beloved curry has barely changed in 20 years outside of a minor trend for fine dining establishments. But costs are rising fast. The weakness of the pound has doubled the price of spices imported from India. Staples like cooking oil and rice have become more expensive and hiring costs are rising. Staffing generally is a major issue. Thousands of Indian restaurants are critically short of staff and facing a number of problems. Since the Brexit vote, economic uncertainties have hit curry houses (in fact, most independent restaurants) hard in terms of rent and overheads. Young Asians are being lured away from family curry house business into more lucrative jobs, such as in IT, medicine and finance. And of course, the climate with regard to immigration has cooled and hardened.

In April 2016, a few months before I set out, a new law was passed prohibiting Bangladeshi chefs from coming to work here unless they can earn £35,000 or more a year after living expenses. In effect, this is a ban since few Indian restaurant chefs earn that and everyone knows it. Lord Bilimoria, the Indian peer and entrepreneur behind Cobra beer, called the law 'ridiculous' and 'discriminatory' adding, 'I sometimes think we are a very ungrateful nation. You are damaging an industry that provided food your country loves.'

It's estimated that one in three British Asians voted for Brexit. Many Indian restaurateurs have told reporters that they cast their vote this way hoping that leaving Europe would bring more favourable terms for south Asian immigrants. The president of the Bangladesh Caterers Association Pasha Khandaker urged his 4,000 members to vote 'leave', sentiments echoed by rallying voices like then employment minister Priti Patel, who told British Asians that by voting leave, they could 'save our curry houses and join the rest of the world'. So far, it isn't working. You can see this for yourself tonight. Walk down your high street and look in the chain pub, look in the pizza franchise, look in the chippy even and then compare this busyness to the two occupied tables in the little independent curry house.

Happily Aagrah was still full to bursting when I left; smiling waiters weaving through tables groaning with vast, fluffy naans, chilled Indian beer, bottles of red and their laughing, ruddy drinkers. Sizzling tikkas trailed smoke through the bright and noisy room and the air was heavy with fenugreek and methi and cardamom and pleasure, for now at least.

SHEFFIELD TO CHESTERFIELD

17 October, 12 miles

According to media lore, the former TV sports host Des Lynam was so comfortable on air that his heart rate actually fell when the camera was on him. He was certainly in a relaxed frame of mind with regard to geography when he once announced on *Grandstand's Final Score*, 'Chester nil, Chesterfield nil. No goals there in the local derby.'

As I prepared to leave Sheffield on the calm, bright October morning of 17 October, I couldn't be too judgmental towards suave Des though. I too was heading out of my geographical comfort zone, away from the England I know reasonably well and headed for towns and places that are really merely names to me, if famous ones. I know the north east a little; I have travelled in Yorkshire extensively, often making nocturnal incursions over the Pennine passes of Oldham and Halifax, crawling through the moor grass by night, face daubed with mud, a dagger between my teeth and with false papers in my rucksack that claim I'm from Heckmondwike. But where exactly is Chesterfield. North? Midlands? East Midlands? All I know for sure is that from there I will head to Mansfield, through the East Midlands and into the home counties. For both the men of 1936 and for me the second half of the Jarrow march will be as much as it can be in a small, crowded island, terra incognito of a very mild kind.

Before leaving 'Sheff', I take a stroll down to Norfolk Street or at least as good an approximation of strolling as I could manage fully laden. On one side of the road is the Crucible, Sheffield's famous theatre and sports venue and home of the World Snooker Championships. The two weeks of this baize jamboree are a mainstay of BBC TV's sporting output, and moreover one of the few major sporting draws the public corporation has managed to cling onto, and it is thus guarded and boasted of fiercely. Ideologically opposed governments and commercial satellite giants like Sky and BT have steadily eroded the BBC's position as the nation's most trusted and watched sporting broadcaster, a position it held through most of the twentieth century.

Back in 1936, the World Snooker Championship was still being held in Thurston's Hall, Leicester Square, London, and was a far smaller affair than today's truly global contest of professional skill, but many of the Jarrow marchers would have followed the contest eagerly. This year proved a turning point for the sport seen previously as a more complex yet less skilful variant of billiards, and also the sign of a misspent youth. There were double the number of entrants to the world championships – which was admittedly only a rise from five to 13, but it felt a significant breakthrough. The final between the legendary Joe Davis and Horace Lindrum was the greatest yet seen and signalled snooker's arrival as a major sport. The *Daily Mail* Gold Cup switched codes from billiards to snooker and the august *Billiard Player* magazine changed its name to *Billiards and Snooker*. For many working-class men, Davis was a folk hero akin to Fred Perry or Stanley Matthews. His home town, whose Billiards Championship he won at age 13, turning pro soon after, was coincidentally where I was headed; even if I still didn't know whether Chesterfield is north, south or Midlands. All I was sure of was that it is nowhere near Chester.

Before departure though, my real reason for popping down to Norfolk Street was to visit the building across the road from the Crucible. The Victoria Hall is Sheffield's major Methodist place of worship; a Grade Two listed building that styles itself as 'the church in the middle of the city with the city at its heart'. It opens to the public every morning for coffee and I sipped mine as I wandered around the spacious commanding interior trying to visualise the events of last night, 80 years ago, when the marchers held yet another famous public meeting. Great swathes of Sheffield's citizenry came to see them, as well as the Mayor of Jarrow who'd travelled down by train, the Bishop of Sheffield and 20 other clergymen of various denominations. The Bishop of Sheffield's presence infuriated the men's own local bishop, the unsympathetic cleric Henson who had denounced the Jarrow march as 'revolutionary mob pressure'. He would have been very uncomfortable at the rhetoric warming the Victoria Hall that night. The chairman of the Sheffield branch of the Transport and General Workers Union took to the stage and was cheered mightily when he hailed his 'comrades from Jarrow' adding, 'You represent to me a tremendous tragedy, the tragedy of unemployment … There is a certain section of people who regard the unemployment problem as something to be forgotten. They do not want to think about it. But there are also those who do think of you.'

I finish my coffee and browse the second-hand books, hoping to start a conversation to divine whether anyone still thinks of them now. Affecting interest in a battered James Herriot, I ask the two older women dividing the Georgette Heyers from the Catherine Cooksons whether the Jarrow march means anything to them. Helen frowns and initially confuses it with the General Strike (understandably) but then finds her thread and knows her stuff. 'They'd closed the shipyard hadn't they and then promised them help that never came. So they marched down to tell them what for. Did they meet here? Well, that must have been something. And that's something to be proud of, isn't it? Are you a Methodist, love? No? Well, here in this church, we work with refugee families. We support them, we try and find them homes and jobs. Well, not always jobs as there are funny rules about that. They're not allowed to work some of them. But that's what we should be about. That's what the Church should do. Help the needy, help the vulnerable. I can't abide those folk who think the Church should be just clapping and holy water and—' and at this she clasps her hands and makes a wounded pious face tilted heavenward. I laugh and wonder what Hensley Henson, Bishop of Durham would have made of Nonconformist Helen of Sheffield.

The Barnsley taxi driver who'd told me about the legacy of the miners' strike also furnished me with a choice nugget of information about my destination today, namely that Chesterfield was, and I quote, 'a real ballache to get to'. For cabbies maybe. But there's a very quick and convenient train, or there's the typically luxurious, futuristic X17 bus, or if you're on Shanks's pony like me, there's the irredeemably dull waymarker of the A61 and the Chesterfield Road. I began my walk in a blaze of autumn sunshine, which made for a far more pleasant morning than the original marchers had, whipped and soaked by the worst weather of their trip so far. Robert Winship had to be left behind in the hospital with malaria which brought the total of men having to drop out to six. Slightly less than 200 men then departed the city in icy rain and buffeting winds: although morale was still high after porridge, ham, tea, toast and butter. Ellen Wilkinson left for some Labour Party business in Glasgow and the men set off on the 12 wet miles to Chesterfield.

I stride past Hallam University and along by one of the great railway pubs of England, one of my very favourites, along with the ones at Stalybridge and Huddersfield. This splendid place is the Sheffield Tap. If it were the end not the beginning of the day, I would certainly slip through the arches of the fine Grecian architecture of Sheffield Midland Railway Station for a pint or two of citrusy Jaipur IPA, or Cask Ruin from Bakewell, or most apt, Yorkshire Blackout, brewed to the 1930s recipe of a soldier who never returned from the Second World War and described as 'deliciously smooth and dark with chocolate and vanilla flavours'. But I have promises to keep and miles to go before I sleep, as the great Robert Frost once wrote. Twelve in my case.

My way leaves the city and wends down Bramall Lane. Sheffield United's home ground has none of the dark connotations that Hillsborough now sadly has, just a very distinguished past. Bramall Lane, named after an important manufacturing family, has a good claim to be the first ever football stadium. It had the first floodlights and the first sizeable capacity terraces and stands for spectators to watch in relative comfort. It hosted the final of the first ever football tournament (four years before the FA Cup). It is the oldest major stadium in the world still hosting professional football and the biggest outside the top two tiers of English football. Its proud history rather throws into awkward relief The Blades' current lowly status but their fans are still loyal and vocal. It's quiet though this morning after a very lively Saturday, which two lads in garish polyester leisurewear are discussing whilst wobbling on their bikes like circus performers on the pavement by Munchies Café, Smoketastic Vaping Shop and the tattoo parlour. Appropriately, one is vaping, the other eating a pasty. Both are copiously tattooed.

'Four nil ... and we had four disallowed. Mental.'

'We never had four disallowed, tha daft bastard.'

'We did and all. Did you not watch it on Sky? What kind of fan are thee? Part timer ...'

'So it could have been eight nil. Is that what tha's saying?'

'Well done, mastermind. Part timer. Glory hunter. Tit.'

Those 'thees' and 'thous' and 'thas', which somewhere else would smack of affected archaisms, are still common in Yorkshire and Lancashire. They are an echo of the Norsemen we once were; part of the daily natural living speech of South Yorkshire and even when it comes, as these did, amid a shower of casual obscenities that I have removed, it's still charming in a robust kind of way.

Up the road now and along one of Sheffield's many edges where after a faceless row of bookies and garages, a sudden, sublime view slides open, revealing the city cradled in a bowl of hills foregrounded before the sunlit Pennines. Sheffield's unique topography is always liable to gift you a moment like this. Step around the corner of the Washeteria or, more likely, the E Cig shop and the land will sweep away before you in a wash of green and brown, a carpet of mossy valleys and sketchy trees. After a couple of hours, I reach Dronfield, 'the place where the male bees swarm', and a hotly contested patch. Dronfield lies halfway between Sheffield and Chesterfield and a tug of love was fought over it not that long ago. Amorous, avaricious Sheffield wanted it for her own and Dronfield was almost merged into that city and hence South Yorkshire. But the local community preferred to stay true to Derbyshire and through concerted effort of will they got their way.

Around here, on the route of the old eighteenth century turnpike, maybe at Dronfield or Old Whittington something curious happens to the vowels. But working out exactly where and what is the stuff that keeps linguists up at night. Yorkshire is a huge county and there's a corresponding variation in the way people speak. If sufficiently skilled, we could guess, even if we hadn't passed by Harewood House, that *Emmerdale* is set in North Yorkshire from the gritty prettiness of its rural setting and the yellowy stone of its cottages, but also from the way they sound their 'a's in the bar of the Woolpack. It's said that the best way to tell if someone comes from Leeds or Bradford is to get them to say Bradford; a true Bradfordian says 'Bratford'.

But there's no easy way to differentiate a north Derbyshire accent from a South Yorkshire one, or to spot that you've crossed the border. You're just suddenly aware that it's happened, the change as swift and surprising as the fall of dark in early winter.

Even the people around here can't really explain the linguistic subtleties beyond a few vague generalities about 'broader vowels beyond the Trent'. Browse the local websites and you will find considerable joshing disagreement about whether Chesterfielders – Cestrefeldians if you will – are northerners or Midlanders. No consensus seems to be reached, although being annexed into the Yorkshire TV region seems to have annoyed a few. Here's a typical response: 'Probably northern I think, otherwise we would all sound like Brummies! Having said that, I would rather watch Central/Midlands TV than Yorkshire. I find it really irritating listening to *Look North* & *Calendar*, banging on about how brilliant Yorkshire is supposed to be. I think they have forgot that we are supposed to be in their TV region.'

When the marchers reached the handsome market square in Chesterfield, they were greeted by a party of communists from the nearby pit village of Normanton who were holding a public rally and offered them £20 (well over a thousand now) from the sale of flags and pamphlets. Under pressure from the Conservative councillor on the march, march marshal David Riley turned this down saying, 'This is the fourth time the communists have tried to gatecrash. They are not going to get in as easily as they think.' This seems ungrateful, even a little craven, but it does show again how desperate the Jarrow organisers were to preserve the saintly odour of being non-political. The dubiousness of this stance was underlined by the fact that the march did accept a substantial donation from a local Conservative association.

It's market day in Chesterfield and, true, the lady in the fleece and headscarf hawking mushrooms and plums sounds very different from her South Yorkshire counterparts, like the 'dee-dars' of Sheffield. But I half expected her to sound like Gina Lollabrigida and be singing out about her *zucchini e asparagi* in a lovely *bel canto*. On this warm and gentle afternoon, with stalls and tables spread across the broad piazza of the square, there is an implausibly Italianate feel to Chesterfield; appropriate since Chesterfield is home to what is, according to the council, 'The most famous architectural distortion in the world, after the leaning tower of Pisa'. You could, I think, confidently substitute the words 'most famous' with 'only' in that sentence. But then again, I may have overlooked the Tilted Chapel of Bratislava or similar. In any event, I couldn't dream of a sojourn in Chesterfield that didn't take in its most famous feature, and it shouldn't be hard to spot.

First though, I took a promenade in the square. Perhaps it's a trait of this eastern flank of the country but England seems as much a nation of market towns today as it did in 1936. Chesterfield holds one on three out of five weekdays and then again on Saturday. It looks bustling to me but one stall holder selling fruit and veg mutters about how council interference, high rates, poor parking and other strictures have made it a pale shadow of what it was. It has a friendly, unfussy, hardworking feel though, like Chesterfield itself.

Eighty years ago, Chesterfield proved admirably hospitable to the Jarrow men. The Victoria café laid on free hot food and the stall holders and townsfolk raised £19 13s (almost as generous as the Normanton commies) as well as donating clothes and bedding. Both major established churches in the town held services for the men; the Catholics were made welcome at Spencer Street's Church of the Annunciation whilst the Anglicans were taken to the parish church in the town centre, where presumably they raised their collective eyes in amusement to its spire as they doffed their caps and found a pew.

Just as the bewigged head of little Mozart brands everything in Salzburg, and that prim shot of Shakespeare with the terrible haircut can't be avoided in Stratford, so a particular example of dodgy medieval cowboy construction defines Chesterfield. It adorns everything from IT consultants to tanning salons. There's Spire Beauty Academy and Spire Insurance Brokers in a building called North Midland House (which is a clue I suppose to where Chesterfield sees itself). As for the infamous object itself, I didn't have to ask directions. I just scanned the skyline and there it was. The Church of Saint Mary and All Saints, Chesterfield has a spire which twists through 45 degrees and leans nine-and-a-half feet from plumb. That's all fairly meaningless though until you see it up close (you can glimpse it from the trains to Newcastle from the Midlands) and the only sensible reaction on seeing the spire, twisted as a Mr Whippy ice cream cone, is 'how the hell did that happen?'

Naturally, there's some unfeasible if entertaining old guff/ revered legend about just how this has occurred. According to one tale, a blacksmith from Bolsover did such a botched job of shoeing the devil's hoof that Satan jumped up enraged and kicked the spire bandy. Another explanation questions the virtue of the town's womenfolk, the spire being said to have craned its neck to look down on the rare occasion a virgin was married in the church. The truth is that they simply used crappy unseasoned wood which warped pretty quickly in Middle England's rainy climate. Also, the Black Death had made it even harder to get a decent tradesman out of Ye Olde Thomfons Local Directory than it is now. But it's the actual engineering facts of how the spire was built that proves the old adage that the truth is invariably stranger and more interesting than fiction. In a town as bristling with signage as Chesterfield, it wasn't hard to find my way down to the old mechanics' institute, now home to the museum, to get the straight dope.

Veda, Peter and Amanda at the museum are so helpful, enthusiastic and skilled at what they do that I imagine even now someone behind a desk several hundred miles away is planning to put them out of a job. They exude a quiet, firm civic pride in their town as well as provide you with lots of accurate, useful information. When I arrived just before lunch, an elderly lady was just leaving, thanking them warmly with a handshake each, whilst in the back room a party of small children was being gently corralled around some old Roman artefacts. Chesterfield has its roots in an Iron Age market town but was really founded by the Romans, whose stay here was brief but productive. When they abandoned the town to head north and subdue the ruffians up there, it grew steadily through the Saxon period, is mentioned in the Domesday Book and under the Normans developed quickly into a market town with a thriving wool and leather industry. Then in the fourteenth century, they decided to build a church.

While I am having this explained to me, there has been an elephant in the room, or more specifically a windlass. Peter notices that I've been eyeing it with some interest and so, with the same air that you might relent and let a small dog get up on the furniture, takes me over to explain exactly what a windlass is. Essentially, it's a huge, old, wooden version of those things hamsters run around on in their cage. This one is as tall as a house and would have been placed as high up as it could be during the construction of a tower. Men (and sometimes donkeys) would clamber in and walk inside it, exactly hamster-in-wheel style, and this motion would be used to pull building materials up to those constructing the tower. They have also been used to pull water from wells and in gold mines. If you were thinking of asking me how the medieval windlass differed from the Chinese or differential windlass at this point, don't.

It took 60 years to build St Mary's and thus the windlass must have been dismantled and re-assembled many times, being raised storey by storey as the tower grew higher – you can see the carved instructions on the wheel, Ikea flatpack style – until eventually it was completed. After that, the huge wheel lay forgotten on the top storey for 700 years until re-discovered after the Second World War. The wood used was a thousand years old and probably came from Sherwood Forest. I'm not an engineering buff by any means, but just standing by this tremendous and aged object was a thrilling experience. You can almost feel the hands that have run along it, the labour inside it, hear the voices raised in laughter and curses as the hard working day went on. It tells a powerful human story.

My hour in the Chesterfield museum brought home to me again that history is not just a parade of kings and queens, royal intrigues and stately homes. It's also about work, workers and engineering. Inspired by the mood, I walked just five minutes up the Newbold Road to the Holy Trinity Church. The rector here put the Jarrow men up back in 1936 and the caretaker was so thoroughly decent to them that they bought him a pipe in gratitude. I went into the churchyard in the chilly dusk, half hoping to find some kind of plaque to the march. Instead though, and just as worthwhile, I found the grave of one George Stephenson. Like the Jarrow marchers, he came down here for work from the north east, in his case to build the railway to London. He liked Chesterfield so much that he never left. He died here and his body lies in the vault of the church. 'Yes, it's not a bad old place,' said Peter at the museum and George seems to have agreed. I liked it too, but it was getting dark, and I had no kindly caretaker to help me out, so it was time to find somewhere to stay.

CHESTERFIELD TO MANSFIELD

18 October, 12 miles

As the Jarrow men walked south through County Durham, Yorkshire and Derbyshire, General Franco's Fascists were on the march, marching northwards and eastwards across Spain from their military basses in cities like Zaragoza, Valladolid, Cadiz and Cordoba. Though it was far away and in a different country, along with the Battle of Cable Street and the Jarrow Crusade itself the Spanish Civil War has become part of the doomed romantic mythology of the 1930s for the left. A democratically elected people's movement, a broad church of progressives of all kinds, helped by poets, painters and young working-class idealists and destroyed by Fascist bullies in uniform aided by Nazi bombs while the rest of their world turned their backs.

That may be the romantic view, but it is also essentially the truth. In February 1936, a Popular Front coalition won a narrow victory at the Spanish general election. Instability followed, and General Francisco Franco returned from exile on the Canary Islands to wage an appalling war against the legitimate government which, after two years of bloodshed, he won. Franco said he would 'save Spain from Marxism whatever the price' and when a journalist replied that that meant he would have to shoot half of Spain, Franco said, smiling, 'I repeat, at whatever the cost.'

In September 1936, 27 nations met in London to debate the Spanish question. They decided on a policy of non-intervention, a policy they shamefully stuck by even when Hitler began to aid Franco. The USSR was the only country to help the Republicans, along with thousands of civilian volunteers from all over the world for whom this was a defining moment of the age – one in which they were prepared to take arms for freedom against the forces of oppression. 'I suppose it's a fever in the blood of the younger generation that we can't possibly understand,' fretted Virginia Woolf in a letter to her sister. But for the younger literary generation it was really very simple. Spain and its new democracy had to be saved. It was a cause worth fighting and – if need be – dying for.

Most went to join other likeminded young people in the International Brigades. W H Auden drove an ambulance across the battlefields along with Julian Bell – Virginia Woolf's nephew – who lost his life on one. Orwell went with a gun as did Laurie Lee. Poets like Stephen Spender and David Gascoyne were supporters of this 'poets war'. But it would be wrong to think that all the artistic community were on the Republican side. T S Eliot felt 'a few men of letters should remain isolated'. And South African poet Roy Campbell was aggressively pro-fascist. Evelyn Waugh said he knew Spain 'only as a tourist ... but if I were a Spaniard I should be fighting for Franco'. Graham Greene and George Bernard Shaw dithered.

Some of the Jarrow Crusaders went to fight in Spain the year after the march. They were amongst 60 men from the north east stationed at Albacete as members of the English Battalion of the International Brigade. It would not be surprising if their experience on the Jarrow march hadn't galvanised some into more direct action, especially after the march had met with such lily-livered support from the official British left.

Ellen Wilkinson made several trips to Spain in the run up to the war, being deported to France at one point. After Jarrow, as

Franco's forces tightened their grip on the benighted country, she went again at the head of an all-woman delegation visiting hospitals and schools and meeting POWs and political leaders in Barcelona and Madrid. On her return to Britain, she appealed to the British people to support the Republican cause as a 'fight between right and wrong' and an international struggle against fascism. She set up the Milk for Spain scheme to help civilians – people bought cardboard tokens at their local Co-op to fund essential supplies – and helped transport stricken Spanish families to Britain.

Just as it did when the marchers left Chesterfield, a foreign conflict rages and preoccupies the commentariat as I set out for Mansfield. The headlines I'd scanned on the newsstands of WH Smith all talked of the start of 'the Battle of Mosul' with Iraqi state forces hoping to soon retake the stronghold of the ISIS Islamic State army. Not long after, the same headlines would be largely repeated, this time referring to the Syrian government's attempt to retake Aleppo from rebel and Islamic State troops. What was once Syria's second city was now a ruined husk of shattered buildings and lives over which the West watched in impotence, largely. But there was also clamorous contradiction and confusion. As in 1936, emotional appeals and accusations could be heard on every side. Then, some on the left like Frank Graham, active in the Newcastle branch of the National Unemployed Workers' Movement, went to fight in Spain having been scathing and dismissive of the purpose or efficacy of Jarrow's 'non-political march'.

Intractable, impenetrable, bloody. Reading the various papers of different political stripes that morning in Chesterfield brought me to only one sure conclusion, namely that the Syrian conflict is one that makes reasonable people despair and leads one to regard with suspicion anyone who claims to know right from wrong. This war appears to be one between (at least) two sets of horribly bad guys with a great many innocent people caught between their competing murky ideologies. This is my very limited understanding of it of course, but at least I acknowledge that it is limited. This puts me ahead of some I felt, as I binned the papers and set off.

There is little to say about the road from Chesterfield to Mansfield other than that the Jarrow marchers took it on 19 October 1936 and now so have I. The weather was foul as they crossed from north Derbyshire into Nottinghamshire, from agricultural land into the Nottinghamshire coalfield. Several soaked marchers became sick. This is D H Lawrence country, mining country, or at least it was. It was once a living if ravaged landscape, man intruding violently into the peace of nature, scarring it like pockmarks on a pretty face. Now that mining is gone, the land is slowly healing which is a kind of consolation. It is a green but not a pleasant land – dirty bedraggled cow parsley, unkempt hedges, tilled fields shaped and formed from slag heaps.

As with Barnsley, as with Ferryhill, even though the pits are silent and flooded and the daily routines and processes of mining are a fading memory, something of mining's hard and resilient culture still lives on. These towns and villages will never exude the same quiet contentment as a Cotswolds hamlet; the gentle hubbub of a Gloucestershire agricultural town or a Dorset port. It is not that those places haven't known hard work or hardship, but it is a different kind of work. Mining villages and towns always carried themselves differently. In their heyday, they wore a sense of hard-won self-righteousness and shared a proud collectivity. Hundreds of feet below ground, camaraderie is not merely a pleasing bonus. It may be the difference between life and death. I spent an afternoon not long ago with a group of miners from the former Bold Colliery in St Helens as they returned to the site of their old pit, now a nature park. The sense of intimacy, even physical, between them was extraordinary and quite unabashed. One of them had run the stores where the men got changed at the start of shift and picked up their safety equipment. Thirty years on, he could still remember every one of his fellow miners' pit number.

As I walk on in Nottinghamshire, past a roundabout with an angry, prescient little placard proclaiming 'Vote Leave, Sack Cameron' and over the brow of the hill, I am met by a sudden, unexpected sight, like an image from an old black and white film or flickering newsreel: a chimney and winding gear stark and proud against scattering clouds. Pleasley Colliery would have belched, roared and clanked to high heaven when the Jarrow marchers passed it in October 1936. Perhaps its winding gear and trucks would have reminded them of home.

The colliery stands above the River Meden and sits on the Top Hard seam. The first lease to mine that seam was given to William Edward Nightingale, who married into a mining fortune and was father to the famous Victorian nursing pioneer, Florence Nightingale who is said to have 'turned the first sod' when the shafts of Pleasley were sunk. For over a hundred years it produced coal in enormous tonnage and supported the local economy of the village that grew up around it. That's still here, a quiet place with neat rows of bungalows, languid cats in their windows and a pub on the river; a commuter village for Chesterfield and Mansfield I assume. Up the rise towards the country park, the houses thin out on the hillside. A woman walks her boisterous Labrador, and a man in baggy, multi-pocketed shorts leans awkwardly to mow his steeply sloping lawn.

There are two clear reminders of Pleasley's working past. The tall winding tower standing sentinel, and also the Pleasley Miners Welfare. The latter dominates the small village centre, shoulders set back on its own broad swathe of lawn. I go up the path, past the perspex shelters for the smokers, and try the door. Closed and quiet, but a few signs computer-printed on A4 sheets and taped to the window mention future concerts, a couple of talks and meetings or request members to 'please respect others when leaving the club and do so quietly'. Once the Miners Welfare and the Miners Institute were at the very heart of the community. Paid for by deductions from the men's wages, they combined library, dance hall, theatre, pub and university. Tredegar Workmen's Hall in South Wales had an 800-seat cinema and hosted celebrity concerts. None of that today in Pleasley though. There is a wildlife quiz in the bar tonight, admission one pound, and I'd have been there had Mansfield not beckoned. I retreat back down the path and find a short cut behind the Welfare, through the car park and the scrubby woods to where the mine workings crown the little hill, bold and clear against the blue sky of the fine early afternoon.

Whilst aware that I just did this very thing, it doesn't really make sense to talk about 'mining country' as a homogenous whole, even in a small nation like England. There are subtle differences in culture and attitude between fields as seen during the two big gruelling strikes of the 1970s and '80s. It might be thought, for instance, that the miners of a small Kent coalfield, far from the industry's hegemonic heartlands in the north, would be less radical and militant than those northern miners. In fact, they were amongst the most hardline. This was, in part, because some miners sacked during the General Strike could only get work in Kent, and thus a bitter radicalism was handed down father to son. Also, Kent pits like Shakespeare, Snowdown, Tilmanstone and Chislet had some of Britain's harshest working conditions. Snowdown, deepest, hottest and most humid, was known as 'Dante's Inferno' and regarded as the worst pit to work at in Britain.

By contrast, the Nottinghamshire miners appeared the least intransigent and most biddable during the 1984 strike. Sociologists and Labour historians have offered as many explanations as there were pits for this. Nottinghamshire had big underground reserves of coal, making the men feel secure. They were well-paid and without major grievance. Nottinghamshire collieries, said the NUM's David John Douglass, were often worked by miners displaced from Scotland and the north east in the 1960s. The lack of support when those mines had closed made them less concerned to stop closures of other pits in the 1980s. Nottinghamshire's large Polish mining community resented Arthur Scargill's support of the Communist government in Poland against the Solidarity union. Marxist historians like Alex Callinicos think that Nottinghamshire miners never had the case for striking adequately made to them by a complacent NUM and were alienated by the uncompromising aggression of the Yorkshire miners' stance.

I suppose I could have asked the men of Pleasley Colliery about all this since they were very much in evidence that lunchtime. But I thought better of it. Pleasley is no longer a working pit but former miners are keeping it alive as a mining museum on a nature reserve. But if that sounds twee or contrived, it is anything but. My feeling on arrival was of wandering into a working pit at change of shift. Apart from a brisk nod from a man on the gate in a sheepskin jacket, there was little in the way of welcome. No 'Is this your first time at the Pleasley Colliery experience?' or directions to the gift shop. Awkward maybe, but at least no one can accuse Pleasley of having gone soft.

Hard work has carried on here since the pit closed in the early 1980s. Sludge has been bucketed out, engines restored, shale swept away, shafts reinforced. Only this time it has all been voluntary. The men who once worked seams here are now engaged in preserving it as a piece of industrial history for their grandkids in Mansfield and Bolsover. Unsure whether it's acceptable to just wander around but doing it all the same, I take a few pictures looking up at the towering winding wheel, explore the cavernous engine house with its gleaming brass of indeterminate but virile function, all thrusting pistons and columns, and then venture into the west shaft and the workings of the pit. Three men in hard hats and dirt-streaked overalls are maintaining some kind of track and checking the glistening innards of wire along the passage walls. Noticing me ambling about, I get the now customary brisk nod and then am left with the same dilemma vis-à-vis introductions as I would be at the Finnish ambassador's cocktail reception. Eventually we fall into desultory conversation. 'Pleasley really closed as a working pit in 1983 but they kept it open as an escape hatch for Shireoaks Colliery, which were my first pit, and then of course that went too after the strike. We're here keeping it going, showing folk what it were like.' With that, he turns to his mate and they continue to prod at a junction box. The exchange wasn't unfriendly, and they weren't unhelpful, but I came away with the impression that I was keeping men from proper and more important work, which I probably was.

'Café' is far too refined and continental a term for the eating and drinking experience at Pleasley. The walls of the green corrugated-iron shed are lined with old signage from the pit, chiefly warnings and admonitions:

TREATMENT ROOM. INCIDENT ROOM. CONTROL NOTICE. ANY PERSON FOUND CAUSING A NUISANCE IN THE PIT HEAD BATHS WILL BE STOPPED FROM USING THEM.

Amongst the shift lists and the old promotional materials, framed under glass are fraying, cracked black and white pictures of men in helmets, shirtless, skin creased and grained with black, all with the dark-eyed Arabian glamour that surely contributed to the collier's status as an aristocratic prince of the working class. About a dozen of them, older now in Lonsdale hoodies, Berghaus fleeces, zip-up cardies and kagoules, are crammed into the steaming kitchen where four volunteer ladies in pinnies pirouette between microwave, griddle and toaster, bringing forth mugs of dense whirling Birds instant and bacon and egg baps. They forget mine, but I might have done that too, distracted by the constant chat, teasing and reminiscence. Dennis seemed to be holding court that morning and I wish I could have broken into the inner rank of slurping courtiers to hear him. Happily, there's an interview with him on YouTube, which for lovers of industrial history is as exotic and mesmerising as any whaler's tale or explorer's yarn. Dennis talks of the 'bright, hard coal' of the Waterloo seam hiding in the low water and, chillingly, of rationing drinking water when 'entombed in 23 seam ... that were difficult'. We should guard against romanticism though. At the time of the Jarrow march, mining was a foul, hard job that made young men old; stone dust setting like cement in the bronchia, or silica slicing the delicate tissues, or the gurgling hell of wet lung and the air heavy with methane which might ignite and bring the roof down on you, aflame.

Escape hatches. Incident Rooms. Accident Reports. The phrases and the tone speak of a working world that was once my own family's but is as alien to me now as it is to those grandkids in Mansfield. It is a world disappeared, a world apart from water coolers, hot desking and shredding. Not necessarily a better or more noble world, just one so ancient and obscure that it reminds you how much Britain has changed – and how quickly – from a country that welds and delves and builds to one that sells and advises and speculates. At the time of the Jarrow march, the national government under Baldwin were themselves puppy dog-devoted to the primacy of private enterprise and limited state interference in the economy. But that was very soon about to change, and change faster still after the convulsion of a world war. Two years after Jarrow, coal royalties would be nationalised. Immediately after the war, in a deeply symbolic act, the entire British coal industry would be taken into public ownership. Forty years after that, in what looks like belated revenge, it would be annihilated.

The three miles down the main road into Mansfield pass quickly as I have one eye on the clock, or more accurately the phone. Earlier I'd picked up a tweet from Jodie, the development officer at Mansfield museum telling me they have a present and some tea and cake for me. 'You'll always find a warm welcome in

Mansfield. We may not have much but we'll share what we have. Come any time before 4.' Jodie might not have known it but in this she echoed how Mansfield had behaved to the Jarrow men. Even the local branch of the Labour Party, perhaps ashamed of their colleagues in Chesterfield, defied the national leadership and turned out in force to greet them outside the town hall and thence to some downtime at the municipal baths and the parochial hall before giving them free cinema tickets.

I arrive with a little time to spare and so make my own little tour of the town. As I arrive, yet another market day is ending in a clatter of tubular steel and laughter. Across the emptying square and arrowing its way through Mansfield is the town's most visibly curious feature, or 'notable landmark' as the publicity blurb rather wanly describes it. This is a colossal brick railway viaduct that bisects Mansfield Berlin-wall style, although unlike that cheerless edifice this has 15 roomy arches under which carpet warehouses and kebab shops thrive, and where surely nighttime assignations occur over White Lightning and Blue WKD. Cutting up Leeming Street in the direction of the museum, I'm pulled up by the gorgeous window display of the Vinyl Lounge emporium; 12-inch albums of mod classics, Motown and psychedelic rock hung with the care of a gallery of Titians or Warhols. Inside, 'Suspect Device' by Stiff Little Fingers gives way to 'My Smile Is Just a Frown Turned Upside Down' by Carolyn Crawford. I can smell coffee. Naturally I enter.

Vinyl albums, like coal, were deemed a product consigned to the ash heap of history, an archaic irrelevance. In much the same way that we were told we need never dirty our hands with nutty slack and firelighters again (or handle another printed page in the paperless office), experts enjoined us to welcome the bright ephemeral world of digital music. But not only are market forces cold and cruel, they are often simply wrong, for they reckon without love, obsession and sheer human oddness. No one ever fell in love with CDs – those horrid little plastic coasters spilling plastic teeth everywhere. No one bought minidiscs or compact cassettes outside of a few broadcast professionals who now keep them at the backs of drawers with the Chinagraph pencils. The market simply never saw the bearded hipster coming on his sit-up-and-beg bike, or the middle-aged mod with the mid-life crisis on the new Vespa, or the teenage girl wanting the new 'old skool' fashion accessory. All these groups and more have contributed to the much-vaunted vinyl revival, and all are good news for Richard of Mansfield.

Richard looks a lot like his customers I'll bet. A rugged and genial, smart, middle-aged guy with a good crop, salt and pepper sidies and crisp white Ben Sherman. He'd worked variously around the music industry in London before coming back to Mansfield and setting up here. He's done a nice job. Moody lighting, red and black leather seating, racked vinyl, a display of rare Smiths and Bowie, a retro black and white pegboard advertising pancakes and maple syrup and espresso. 'You don't get this in HMV, do you?' he says waving a proud hand, and in truth that is exactly why shops like Richard's are thriving. They treat the customer less like a zombie consumer than an informed member of a stylish and discerning club, although without the terrifying elitism that blighted the northern soul shops of my early teenage years. Here, asking for the wrong version of 'Sliced Tomatoes' could see you cast into the outer darkness of 'uncool' for months.

'Mansfield's a big northern soul town,' says Richard, which I could have guessed. Towns like Mansfield often are; formerly built on textiles, coal or engineering with hedonistic, intense, obsessive working-class sub-cultures centred around grafting, playing hard, looking good, dancing and understated machismo. I could have spent a lot of money on northern soul 'sevens' here, but in truth I'm not the vinyl fetishist that's often supposed; my northern soul collection is now mainly zeros and ones on a hard drive the size of a pack of cards. In 1975, I could have bought a small flat with it on collectable vinyl. Also there's the matter of my rucksack. Though ample of litreage, it is no DJ bag. I wish Richard well and carry on up to the museum as dusk comes gently on.

As 80 years ago, the good people of Mansfield have turned out in force to meet me. Jodie and her team show me around 'the Tin Tabernacle', as the museum was once known. It now houses a terrific arcade exhibition called 'Made In Mansfield' that reflects the manufacturing powerhouse the town once was. The exhibition concentrates on eight famous industries that built Mansfield's reputation for manufacturing: Metal Box, Shoe Co, Mansfield Brewery, Barrs Soft Drinks and others in hosiery, precision engineering, mining and quarrying. There are artefacts, photos, film and audio featuring past and present employers of the town. Jodie is quick (understandably) to point out that modern Mansfield still has a manufacturing base, mainly light engineering and IT companies, but these are often 'hidden' in anonymous units on the outskirts of town. Made in Mansfield recalls the halcyon days of very visible commercial might when 40,000 people would have crowded these streets every morning and evening going and coming from work making shoes, speakers, metal boxes, textiles, and beer sold around the world. Even the sand from the quarry was prized for the bunkers of elite golf courses.

I'm interviewed for local radio by a young lad called Matt who asks very intelligent questions about the nature and efficacy of protest marching as a political tactic, in the news since Corbyn's re-election, whilst later Jeff and Liz the curator tell me all about Mansfield's musical pedigree which is small but fascinating. Mansfield's most famed musical son was perhaps Alvin Stardust. Born Bernard Jewry, he renamed himself Shane Fenton when he took over as lead vocalist with the Fentones from the original Shane Fenton who had recently died. If this seems a little creepy, then bear in mind that much about Alvin's seventies' image was exactly that to be honest. Even as a child I found the leather glove, the queer praying mantis stance and the line about going back to his flat to 'lay down and groove on the mat' deeply upsetting. Looking back, he was a sort of Gene Vincent for Arthur Scargill supporters I suppose, had I but known it; the Elvis Comeback Special restaged at Orgreave. He was also by all accounts a 'gentleman' who did much to support the museum.

'Oh, and we've got something for you,' says Jodie as I'm about to leave. 'Gosh, have you?' I say, pretending to have forgotten. And it's a lovely thing. Amanda, an archivist at the museum, has put together a framed front page of the local paper the *Mansfield, Sutton and Kirkby Chronicle* of 23 October 1936 (price: three halfpence) carrying a contemporary report on the march passing through.

> The Jarrow marchers, many of them drenched to the skin, who marched through here at tea time on Monday, found Mansfield's liberal hospitality a welcome contrast to pitiless rain and wind through which they had tramped from Chesterfield. True, the men were bronzed and weather-beaten, and most of them looked fit enough but then, as Miss Wilkinson, the Jarrow MP put it – no doubt with perfect truth – 'these men have been better fed during the last fortnight than they have been for years!'

This excellent present under my arm, I stop off to sip a pint in the warm, dozing snug of the Brown Cow. Mansfield Brewery closed its doors in 2002 and its remaining operations moved to Wolverhampton so I make do with a nice drop of Everard's Ascalon, a 'traditional chestnut ale brewed with British-grown Challenger and Admiral hops. Orange, zesty flavours are complemented with chocolate, earthy flavours, leaving a perfectly rounded finish,' according to the beermat. I prop up the framed front page on the bar in front of me and study that.

'There must be easier ways to read paper, lad,' says a plaster-splattered man at the other end of the bar with his folded tabloid in front of him, and, ice broken, I tell him about my day. 'Aye, we made some stuff here, beer, shoes, knickers, hats ... did they tell you they even made sand for golf bunkers here? Perhaps he buys it for his Scottish ones,' he says and points to a familiar brutish orange face on the front of the *Mirror*. It is of course Donald Trump. It's the third and final presidential debate tonight and while some are still saying 'too close to call', most reasoned analysis says that Trump will lose even despite a deep-seated antipathy towards Clinton that is hard for us Brits to really fathom. Can any reasonable, sane human being, however much they distrust the shifty and dynastic Clintons, really consider voting for a man like Trump? Surely not. Common sense and humanity will prevail, I conclude, as I take another long pull on those zesty chocolatey depths and wait for the perfect rounded finish.

STAGE THIRTEEN

MANSFIELD TO NOTTINGHAM

20 October, 14 miles

From the BBC News Website, March 2016:

> The closure of the DH Lawrence Heritage Centre in Eastwood has been described as 'tragic'... Durban House, which explored the writer's life, was closed to save £80,000 a year. The authority said the service had not stopped and would merge with Lawrence's birthplace museum in the same town. Malcolm Gray, chairman of the DH Lawrence Society, said it was a 'frustrating' decision. But Alex Khan, cultural services manager at the Conservative-led council, said: 'I actually find it quite exciting – it puts the focus of the DH Lawrence Heritage service back somewhere it has a very strong link ...' Mr Khan denied the closure was 'a slap in the face' following Nottingham's status as a Unesco City of Literature, awarded in December.

Walking the miles of the dreary Nottingham Road from Mansfield in the squalid, damp, overgrown margin of grass where there should really be something to stop foot travellers being knocked into the ditch by the backdraft of passing tankers, ankle-deep in Red Bull cans and fag packets and lord knows what unspeakable detritus flung from some passing window by a git, I remembered some words of D H Lawrence's quoted by Matt Perry that I'd read the night before:

> 'The real tragedy of England, as I see it, is the tragedy of ugliness. The country is so lovely, the man-made England is so vile. I know that the ordinary collier when I was a boy had a peculiar sense of beauty coming from his intuitive and instinctive consciousness which was awakened ... the human soul needs actual beauty more than it needs bread.'

In many ways, D H Lawrence was a pillock and there's a hint of that here. But his heart was in the right place. Whether the demise of the 'ugly' pits of Nottingham at its great human cost in community and livelihoods would have cheered the comfortably-off novelist or not is moot, since both are with us no more. But Lawrence was the first British novelist of the industrial age to have what we might call ecological consciousness, condemning mechanisation for what it did both to the human spirit and the British landscape. It did, however, help to pay the young Lawrence's family's rent as it exploited. It's a thorny one, and I'm not sure either DH or myself have any, let alone all the answers.

Until the lorries and the unnavigable undergrowth made it too risky, I had in my ears as I walked the churning road the beginning of the Second Movement of Alan Bush's *Nottingham Symphony*. Its limpid but subtly astringent loveliness turned even this dismal trudge into something vaguely meaningful and uplifting. But then my spirits were already high with the thought of an evening in Nottingham. I don't know it as well as I might but I've always liked its independent cast of mind.

From D H Lawrence to Alan Sillitoe to Ned Ludd (possibly) to Samuel Fox the philanthropic abolitionist Quaker to Games Workshop to Ray Gosling to Lord Byron to his daughter the computer pioneer Ada Lovelace to Brian Clough (adopted) to the hardcore metal label Earache Records, Nottingham produces people who do things their own way.

Alan Bush wasn't from Nottingham, but it was just like the city to ask Britain's most outspokenly Marxist composer and Communist Party stalwart to write them a symphony for the week of celebrations commemorating the quincentenary of its Royal Charter in 1949. Bush was held in real suspicion by the powers that be. When the BBC placed a ban on Bush and composers of his political persuasion, Vaughan Williams refused broadcast rights for his new work in protest. He didn't share Bush's views but he loathed such high-handed treatment, telling the BBC in a telegram 'Well, you're not having my stuff either', at which they relented. Commissioned by the Nottingham Co-operative Society, Bush's *Nottingham Symphony* was first performed on 27 June in the city's Albert Hall by the London Philharmonic Orchestra. It's a fabulous piece if, like me, you're partial to tuneful but interesting twentieth-century English music. Bush himself says the piece 'ends in a mood of purposeful optimism' and it put me in very much the same as finally, after several dreary hours, the A60, Nottingham Road, at last lived up to its name and reached Nottingham.

The day started well too. Once again, an interesting invite had pinged into my phone via social media. Whilst its undoubted popularity as a platform amongst world-class morons has made it the object of some scorn, Twitter has thus far proved an invaluable tool on my journey, which I should stress is an actual journey, and not the ones described on reality TV. I have found that social media, like the old Yellow Pages ad used to have it, is not just there for the nasty things in life. Nasty things like trolling women from behind the anonymity of your little egg avatar or perpetuating badly spelt feuds over football. It has also, in my case this trip, been about learning interesting things from interesting people; history, tips, steers – the kind of ninja knowledge that only locals have. Michael is a lecturer at West Nottinghamshire College who's been following my progress. Noting that I'm going to be stomping past his door, a mile or so out of Mansfield, he tells me he'll have the kettle on if I fancy dropping in for a cup of tea and to meet some students.

He meets me outside the bustling bright red campus which even I couldn't miss. It looks a terrific place to work. As we negotiate the throngs of students, Michael tells me that it's just had a lengthy, extensive £5 million refit. (Having spent a few happy years teaching further education in my early twenties, I always keep abreast of nice places to work that might give me a job in the future.)

'That new Health and Beauty Centre stands on the site of an old Mining and Technical College, the place where once you did day release from the pit.' He catches my smile and returns it. 'I know. It sounds ironic but it's not as strange a transition as you might think. A lot of our students, their dads used to be miners and they came to colleges like this and retrained in everything from hairdressing to IT when the mines closed.'

When I get to the refectory (or NutraStation or cantina or whatever they call them these heady days) they've made a big backdrop Image Me, with me photoshopped into the Jarrow march, which is sweet and funny. And though I suspect the students don't have the first idea who I am or what I'm up to or what the Jarrow march was, they sit behind their gleaming big screen Apple Macs and listen attentively as I tell them about the march. After listening thoughtfully, one lad asks, 'Why didn't they just get the train?' There's a lot of laughter and I join in, but it's a rather good question, given that lobbying the government for their town was the purpose of the trip to London rather than a sponsored walk. But of course that's from the pragmatic context of today. Part of the point of the long trek was the romantic endeavour of it all, the heroic endurance that was meant to convince the Establishment that these men were not idle or feckless but determined and disciplined.

Afterwards I take some questions and as usual these wander entertainingly off topic. A petite Indian girl asks me whether I'm going via Birmingham where she's originally from and I wonder for a second whether she's about to ask me to drop a parcel off at her mum's. But no, she just wants to chat about the new-ish Bull Ring and Symphony Hall. By some route that I can't recall, we establish that one young man is the nephew of the colourful late Welsh actor Victor Spinetti and we have a diverting chat about his friendship with the Beatles. Afterwards, another staff member called Liam, knowing of my interest in esoteric sounds, tells me about his PhD in children's music and we bemoan the unavailability of the crazy, educational jazz-rock numbers from *Sesame Street* on CD. More usefully perhaps, Liam thinks that there's something on in town that night that might interest me. It's an event at Rough Trade Nottingham called 'Wanted: A Real Media', which will attempt to offer alternatives from voices of the new left. Now, we donkeys live a long time, as Orwell's Benjamin said in *Animal Farm*, so I'm old and wise enough to know that this title probably translates as, 'Wanted: A Media That Agrees With Me'. But it sounds like it might chime with some of the things I've been thinking about in relation to Jarrow and now.

Of late there have arisen several websites and left-wing media pressure groups who are 'critiquing' (as the Americans say) what they call the mainstream media or 'MSM'. Since Glasgow University Media Group's groundbreaking 1976 study 'Bad News', radical sociologists have been ploughing this furrow, looking at how the structure and language of press, radio and TV news especially serves to reinforce the status quo and the

Establishment. While indisputably leftist in stance, these types of early surveys were analytical and sociological in approach. But over the last decade, the media seems to have grown, on its fringes at least, far more fissile and partisan: from Breitbart to Wikileaks to Anonymous to *The Canary*, from alt-right to new left.

Anyway, I agree to go, as it sounds like fun (of a sort) and the matter of media ownership relates very much to both today and 1936. The interwar years and especially the thirties saw a rapid growth in the mass media and a corresponding concentration of that media in only a few well-connected hands, and the subsequent creation of press empires and barons (to mix my honorifics). This was crucial, since while radio and TV were still very much in their infancy, the British press was, as historian Nick Shepley puts it, 'how the country talked to itself, its nervous system, it's arteries of discourse.'

This system, these arteries, were largely and solely in the control of a handful of wealthy and titled men. Lord Northcliffe owned *The Times*, the *Daily Mail*, the *Weekly Despatch* and the *London Evening News*. His brother Lord Rothermere owned the *Daily Mirror*, the *Sunday Pictorial*, the *Daily Record*, the *Glasgow Evening News* and the *Sunday Mail*. Another brother, Lord Harmsworth, was also a major player. Between them, they had the ear of six million readers.

Lord Beaverbrook made the *Daily Express* the most successful mass circulation newspaper in the world and used it as a mouthpiece for his personal opinions, from appeasement of Hitler (whom he greatly admired) to free trade. These few men wielded extraordinary and unprecedented political power over a mass audience of readers. They advanced their political agendas from the far right of the political spectrum in an age of uncertainty and crisis. They also did it cannily, through a diet of entertainment and a daily concentration on what would now be called celebrity culture, gossip and chat about film stars, comedians and musicians.

That said, press coverage of the Jarrow march was uniformly warm (especially in the then vigorous regional press) if bland and patronising. Put simply, the Jarrow marchers were celebrities and the march was covered as such; as a cheery human interest story involving plucky chaps, adorable dogs and that 'fistful of dynamite' Ellen Wilkinson. For her part, she was scornful of both Lord Rothermere's empire of puppet titles and the newly formed BBC. Many on the left still are 80 years later, as I was to find out.

I check in and unpack in my modern business hotel on Maid Marian Way. I like chain hotels because I know what I'm going to get with none of that unpredictable 'family run' or worrying 'funky and individual' business, where you might be expected to eat with Tiddles the cat on your lap or have a shower from a watering can. Comfortingly for us busy misanthropes on the move, my hotel is the sort of place where Phil and Jeff from head office meet Mike from the Uttoxeter branch for firm handshakes in the lobby before grabbing a beer and thrashing out rotas.

I strolled down into the town centre which is dominated by the busy, spacious Old Market Square, over which the town hall looks down in a paternalistic, aldermanly way. Here, there's the ubiquitous street food, a rasta busker playing the sax to a tinny version of 'Red, Red Wine' from a beat box and a few entertainingly incompetent skateboarders. Down an alley, I find further evidence of the city's subversive bent in the form of a properly old-school left-wing bookshop, the sort that you thought had become extinct in the nineties, where you could pick from Guy Debord's *The Society of the Spectacle*, *Women's Voice*, the Trotskyist *Spare Rib* and anarchist pamphlets which always smelt faintly of that unpleasant arrowroot herbal toothpaste.

Nottingham's Five Leaves is still thriving. Several earnest-looking students of different genders and races leaf through forbidding-looking texts and inspirational postcards expressing solidarity with various South American rebel groups. Or maybe that was my memory playing tricks on me. It was a fascinating place anyway with tons to agree and disagree with. The left has always been a place where passion and sanctimoniousness rub vigorously along together and it always will be. I'm more Bevan and Attlee these days than Corbyn or Brand. But I come out with a recycled tote bag full of stuff old and new; some miners' strike posters for dewy-eyed nostalgia, a great postcard that says 'To Make The Rich Work Harder You Pay Them More, To Make The Poor Work Harder You Pay Them Less' (which I may wave like a ref's yellow card in future arguments with free marketeers) and a cracking reprint of a 1964 Nottingham samizdat magazine called *Anarchy 38*, 'A Journal of Anarchist Ideas', which seems to be nothing of the sort but bristles with energy and brio from the young Ray Gosling on Nottingham and Alan Sillitoe on poverty. It is exactly the kind of thing the teenaged Maconie would have ensured was visible from his Oxfam overcoat pocket, chiefly to impress thoughtful girls.

I leaf through *Anarchy 38* in a big lively pub in town called the Major Oak, named after the tree where committed wealth distributor Robin Hood (who would certainly have shopped at Five Leaves) used to hang out with Maid Marian and the Merry Men. I make a few notes on a tremendous piece detailing the sundry riots that took place in Nottingham between 1754 and 1854 which confirms my impression of the city. I don't impress any girls but an Irish man comes over to me and says, 'Don't I know you? Aren't you in education?' No, I answer truthfully. 'Oh,' he replies, 'well, who'd have thought it. There's another fellow alive in the world who's as good looking as you.' I nearly bought him a pint but I have a date elsewhere.

I meet Liam along with Gordon, the college's union rep, outside Rough Trade Nottingham, one of only three branches of the successful indie. Downstairs, men with waxed moustaches and girls in black hoodies with magenta hair are leafing through racked vinyl by Laura Marling, Gil Scott-Heron and the Sleaford Mods. Upstairs, there's a large room with a spit and sawdust feel, a bar stocked from microbreweries around the world and cupcakes under glass. Beers bought, we make our way to the other end of the room where a small stage faces about 30 plastic chairs. After a short while, a man and woman appear along with a ponytailed roadie. There then ensues some mildly hilarious faffing with microphones that intermittently either do not work at all or emit earsplitting shrieks of feedback, all such as you might get in an Alan Ayckbourn portrayal of a fringe leftwing meeting. When this has been sorted to some reasonably bearable degree, Nancy Mendoza of *The Canary* tells us about the ethos of her website, which she hopes is part of a drive towards 'greater plurality within the news. Today's media has become an echo chamber to mainstream ideas and practices, which are not speaking to, or for, the range of groups in society.'

If you've looked at *The Canary*, you'll know that what this translates to is pretty straightforward left-wing agitprop but with a garish modern vibe. It's somewhere between the *Socialist Worker* and *Heat* magazine online with the clenched rectitude of the former and the relaxed chattiness of the latter ("Trump just dropped his stupidest tweet yet ... and the Internet is in stitches!') This is a neat trick if you can pull it off and should you want to. Writers give up the certainty of payment and are paid according to the traffic they generate, which seems to me about as nakedly capitalistic as you can get and might even make Rupert Murdoch let out a low whistle of admiration. It also means the quality of the writing is wildly variable and generally partisan. But it is an alternative certainly. And there are adverts for skiing holidays.

Tom from Real Media is next and starts with a few colourful anecdotes about how he used to go drinking as a youth in Nottingham city centre, this presumably to soften us up a little for the fairly indigestible stuff to come. Indigestible to me anyway. The small audience lapped it up but then I wouldn't exactly call them a 'tough crowd', as comics say. Tom makes one or two good points, such as that conspiracy websites are 'disempowering' and that the structures of the modern media concentrate power amongst the rich and the middle classes. This is certainly true, but you came all this way to tell me that? It's in paragraph one, page one of every GCSE textbook on the sociology of the media. Then there is some stuff about 'horizontalism' that I simply do not follow whatsoever, so I have to acknowledge that it might have been searing stuff.

A few phrases brought out the worst in me, it has to be said. Firstly, there's a mention of Karl Marx followed quickly by a snort of 'I'm not a Marxist of course' as if only a prize chump would have any time for the most influential and insightful economic analyst of the last 200 years. (Well, that about wraps it up for poor old Karl, I thought, now that he's been dissed above a record shop in Nottingham.) Tom also mentioned those of his kind working at 'the coal face'. Perhaps it was having spent some time around pits and miners recently but I doubted very much if anyone here with their zesty IPAs and cupcakes had ever been within a postcode of a coal face, least of all Tom, or for that matter me.

Then, in the midst of some diagnosis of the ills of the modern media, he says ' ... as much as I hate the BBC ...' Until relatively recently, I had rather innocently assumed that hatred of the BBC was the preserve of the swivel-eyed, foaming demagogues of the right. This then brings home to me how little I have in common with their rabid counterparts within the modern left. Tom is every bit as driven an ideologue as

Paul Dacre. I would say that in the end, the best, if not most passionate defence of the BBC is that it is viewed by the right and left alike as supporting the other side. I would say that such flak from both flanks means the corporation is doing a fairly decent job of being impartial, but then both Russell Brand and Guido Fawkes would probably snigger at that. Also, given my time in the BBC's employ, they may respond, 'Well, he would, wouldn't he?'

In much the same way that woolly old geezers and fresh-faced youths are forever telling me that Jeremy Corbyn is a saintly man with his heart in the right place, I will assume, if not entirely convinced, that Tom and Nancy are similarly good eggs. But I found their vision of a new, better media no great improvement on the one we have; certainly every bit as partial philosophically and theoretically. Feeble initiatives like giving a quarter of the licence fee to independent creatives (like Tom) to make their own news and documentaries are fine, as long as you acknowledge that that dosh and platform must also be given to UKIP and maybe even the EDL. Freedom is indivisible. If you don't think that, at least have the honesty to say that it isn't actually free speech you want, but your speech and paid for by people who don't agree with you.

It may seem mean but it also needs to be pointed out that there were 18 people in that room, at least one of whom was very much not in agreement. The rest definitely were but I felt this isn't a launching pad, it's an echo chamber. Like the reception at Corbyn's rallies, it may feel awfully nice to be part of, but it tells you nothing about support in the cold, wider world, where real people have to be housed, real kids have to be fed and educated, the really sick have to be cared for and sometimes real wars have to be won against some real bad guys. I don't think the people at *The Canary* or Real Media or Jeremy Corbyn or any of their ilk are bad guys themselves but I think they might be making it easier for the ones who are.

We left during the Q&As. (It's always a bad omen when you hear 'it's not so much a question, more a statement really'.) Nottingham had some venerable and famed boozers that I was keen to try and two enthusiastic guides. The people's struggle is thirsty work after all. We made our way through streets awash with students running politely riot through the streets. I couldn't work out why. It was a bit late for freshers' week, and there seemed no logic to any of the costumes but a definite lunatic gaiety about the various smurfs, zombies and cowboys; togas, bear outfits and onesies. They swarmed over Brian Clough's statue and by the time I got there, only a few girls remained snapping themselves with the bronzed figure in a tracksuit arms aloft. 'Who is this bloke?' asked a girl in a baby's bonnet to her friend taking a selfie. 'No idea,' came the reply. To the side of them, a supremely posh ginger kid in a sombrero was explaining to his upset girlfriend that, 'Look, he just bumped into you because he' s swaying because he's very, very drunk and you are just so, like so, over-reacting Daisy'.

According to the article I was reading earlier ('Riotous Times in Nottingham'), the people of Nottingham – and these are very much edited highlights – rioted in 1754 over an election, in 1755 over bread and in 1756 over the price of cheese, during which they started lobbing huge Cheddars and Stiltons about at the Goose Fair. In 1779, 1783 and 1787 they rioted over wages for knitters and in 1795 over the price of butter. It was the cost of meat that incited them in 1788 and 1792. In 1793, keen to liven up a quiet patch, Nottingham's supporters of rival sides in the French Revolution rioted. Next it was a rigged election, then bread and meat again. In 1831 they rioted over the Reform Act, and then in 1839 it was the Chartists. In between and along the way, there was generally a riot every couple of years over meat, bread, butter, cheese or knitting. Had you had a watch, you could have set it by the impressive regularity of Nottingham's riotous townsfolks appetite for disorder.

I missed out 1811, a very serious disturbance, when the Luddites smashed and burned through the city culminating in the razing of the castle itself. Their leader was Ned Ludd and in some cities, his name would be blackened and shamed forever more. In Nottingham, they named a pub after him. Since I was passing, I went in and raised a quick glass of whisky to the old troublemaker and then was on my way.

STAGE FOURTEEN

NOTTINGHAM TO LOUGHBOROUGH

21 October, 15 miles

Above the mirror in my Nottingham hotel, stylishly painted, rendered as if in the writer's flowing hand, is a quotation.

'Don't let the bastards get you down!' – Alan Sillitoe

This variant on the old wartime witticism, *Illegitimi Non Carborundum*, is one of many quotable lines uttered by Arthur Seaton in Sillitoe's brilliant *Saturday Night and Sunday Morning*, played equally brilliantly by Albert Finney in the film: Elvis-Presley-as-lathe-turner, all feral proletarian glamour. This morning, toothbrush in hand, wrapped in towel, I'm amused and irritated to see Seaton/Finney's growl of plebeian defiance turned into a motivational quote for the ambitious Midlands middle-manager.

Thursday night has become Friday morning, and a very Nottingham-style riot is sweeping through the streets of my head. We had moved on after the 'Real Media' meeting from the Ned Ludd to the Malt Cross, an old Victorian music hall still with stage and balcony, now a fashionable bar selling botanical gins, cakes and swanky porters. There we had gone over the meeting, Liam, Gordon and I, and found that we were largely of one mind. Yes, there was much wrong with the modern media, an issue that seemed to preoccupy the new left, but a little more attention paid to the future of Liam and Gordon's students, their parents' jobs and homes and the traditional working-class communities of the post-industrial north and Midlands would be nice too. A trend toward this within the Labour Party, christened 'Blue Labour' by Jon Cruddas, was influential a few years back, but this realignment seems to have been overlooked once more in favour of more theoretical concerns, such as identity politics and endless handwringing and internal wrangling, post Corbyn. Anyway, as soon as this pub closes, the revolution starts.

In truth, by closing time we were in Ye Olde Trip to Jerusalem. Many pubs in England, even several in Nottingham, lay claim to be the oldest in the land. The Porch House in Stow-on-the-Wold claims to have had the towels off since the end of the first millennium BC. Ye Olde Salutation, which we'd passed on our way here, also makes the claim as does Ye Olde Fighting Cocks in St Albans which still awaited me down what G K Chesterton called the rolling English road, made by the rolling English drunkard. But Ye Olde Trip to Jerusalem has as strong a case as any, established in AD 1189, the year Richard the Lionheart became king and responded to Pope Gregory VIII's call for a new, third crusade to the Holy Land. This is how the pub got its name. At least, that's one theory.

. The pub is literally built into Castle Rock on which Nottingham castle stands and, unsurprisingly for a pub this old, it has accrued legend and rumour like a battleship gathers a crust of barnacles. In the upstairs lounge is 'the cursed galleon', a little wooden ship that must never be dusted. All who ever made this mistake died soon after and now it is kept in a glass case, thick with inches of grime. There is a very old chair that it's claimed any woman who sits in will become pregnant and has been so well used that it is now very fragile.

The pub's queerest and best feature though is its network of caves carved out of soft sandstone, creating strange and secret chambers perfect for conspiracies, assignations, trysts, secret meetings and plotting the overthrow of the government. In one of these caverns, a young man approaches who tells me that his best friend is Matt, the radio reporter who interviewed me in Mansfield. At this stage in the evening, this astonishing coincidence is certainly reason enough to call for another round of drinks.

Attempting to leave some time later, we get sucked into a group of drinkers at the bar playing some kind of game. A chain hangs from the ceiling with a small hoop at the end and on the opposing wall a small brass spike, curved like a mini rhino horn, is fixed at about head height. The game consists simply of swinging the chain like a pendulum and attempting to hook the horn. One old boy is undisputed pub champion at this, even doing his own versions of trick shots such as swinging the chain over his shoulder. (When not thus occupied, he goes table to table doing close magic with cards and matches.) No red-blooded games fan from out of town could refuse the challenge of course, and certainly not one as deep in his cups as I am. Thus it seems important that we join in the game for another couple of halves and single malt chasers. Eventually, I succeed and it is then of course necessary for an extended analysis of my successful shot at the bar over another round. (The game by the way, I later find out, is called Ringing the Bull and has been successfully exported from Ye Olde Trip to pubs all over Britain and the Caribbean.)

A gregarious chap at the bar with a braided ponytail says that buildings like Ye Olde Trip containing labyrinthine innards are common in the city. 'Nottingham's like a piece of cheese – full of holes. They run from here straight into the castle, these tunnels, and that's how the castle was burned to the ground by Ned Ludd.' We move on to the forthcoming US election and I wonder aloud, probably waving my pint about for emphasis, how any sane person could genuinely vote for Trump instead of Hillary Clinton and why she is so mistrusted. A chap from Crewe at the bar interjects, 'Ah, well, that's because she's a mass murderer.' He then goes on to describe the international cocaine smuggling ring the Clintons were helping to run out of Mena Airport, Arkansas, and the dozens of people they have personally killed in order to keep the evildoing quiet. At this, we all fall silent, look at our shoes and shift our weight awkwardly. 'My, is that the time?' I hear myself saying, and Liam, Gordon and I head out into the night where, after some frankly ill-advised explorations of the castle's battlements, we say our farewells, and I head unsteadily up Maid Marian Way.

Next morning, a little bleary, I looked up Mena Airport online. There's quite a bit on there about the drug ring that was apparently based there, some of it exhaustive and plausible, but most of the Clinton murders stuff is on sites which also carry stories on how the moon landings were faked and the Illuminati are embarking on a mass world depopulation programme. Most of these carry a lot of scorn about 'the mainstream media', and have mottos like 'THE REAL NEWS YOU WERE NEVER SUPPOSED TO SEE'. Well, it certainly is an antidote to the mainstream media I suppose. One of the wisest things I ever read about conspiracy theorists was that they never believe just one conspiracy theory. They believe them all.

Hapless stooge and dupe that I am, I took an armful of MSM and a pack of Nurofen down to Old Market Square for a coffee and a browse of the papers. Hillary Clinton still has a slender lead in the polls, presumably amongst people who don't believe yet that she's a shape-shifting lizard. Or maybe people who do think that, but still believe her to be preferable to Donald Trump. Trump himself says that if he loses he may contest the election result.

The big 'celebrity' news story of October 1936 was certainly the subject of a cover-up. A major one too involving all of the press, the government and the royal family. But even with the best efforts at subterfuge by the most powerful in the land, a scandalous royal love affair was rapidly becoming the worst-kept secret in Britain amongst the high and mighty if not the hoi polloi. As the Jarrow marchers left Nottingham, Stanley Baldwin was meeting the new king to try to talk some sense into him about an American woman called Wallis Simpson.

Today we have a picture of King Edward VIII formed largely by his indulgent lifestyle, dandyish dress, vanity, admiration for Hitler, dereliction of duty and long, indolent, luxurious seclusion in Paris with the woman he abandoned his country for. But for most of 1936, between accession and abdication, he was regarded as a man of the people, a friend of the working class, and by government as a potential troublemaker. Throughout 1936, it was rumoured that he would soon be visiting Jarrow and though this never happened, he did take a tour of the depressed Welsh steel town of Dowlais. Here he was met by malnourished kids, unemployed men, ruined factories and a sense of desolation and misery which seemed to genuinely affect him. Some in the crowd held up banners reading 'Hunger Marchers Ask The King To Abolish The Means Test'. Edward was heard to turn to an official accompanying him and say 'something must be done'. It was an innocuous aside. But to some in government, it sounded as incendiary a revolutionary sentiment as anything being cried from a barricade in Barcelona or committee room in Moscow. Prime Minister Baldwin was not best pleased with Edward's habit of making visits to coalfields and steel towns or his sympathetic noises towards the poor and the unemployed. Perhaps this might explain why Baldwin showed little sympathy to Edward when his romantic entanglements started to become a complication for the state.

Edward Windsor had met Wallis Simpson in 1930 and soon became infatuated, calling on her for cocktails at her Bryanston Court home most evenings, whether her husband was at home or not. By May 1936, the affair between them was causing serious concern in official circles, especially when it became clear that Wallis Simpson and her husband intended to divorce. Edward wanted to charter a yacht and take her to Venice but was persuaded that this would appear to be tacit approval of the Mussolini regime. Instead, he contented himself by pootling around the Mediterranean in what fellow sailor and socialite Duff Cooper described as 'spick and span little shorts, straw sandals and two crucifixes on a chain around his neck'. On his return, he declined to open a new hospital in Aberdeen on the grounds that he was still in mourning for his father, which is a difficult look to pull off in tiny shorts, and especially when the same day he was seen collecting Mrs Simpson at Balmoral in an open-topped sports car. Tory MP Chips Channon wrote in his infamous diaries, 'Aberdeen will never forgive him'.

While the affair was common knowledge amongst Channon's circle (baffling many, as most agreed with Channon, that Mrs Simpson was 'jolly, plain and unprepossessing'), the ordinary Briton knew nothing, kept in the dark by closed ranks and the deferential, sycophantic nature of the press. American magazines carrying the story were censored, leading the indefatigable Ellen Wilkinson to ask in the Commons, 'What is this thing the British public is not allowed to know?' Even the Archbishop of Canterbury's secretary complained, 'So far our English press has been effectively muzzled by a gentleman's agreement secured by Lord Beaverbrook.'

In October, Prime Minister Baldwin went to see the King in order to try to get Simpson's divorce at least postponed if not abandoned. Edward insisted that the matter was 'the lady's private business'. Baldwin then suggested that Simpson be packed off abroad for six months to take the heat out of the current situation (and it was fervently hoped that, as historian Juliet Gardiner put it, 'in her absence his puppy dog passion would cool somewhat'). Edward was unmoved. He informed Baldwin of his intention to marry Simpson but was prepared to enter into a 'morganatic' marriage under which the couple could wed but Simpson would not become queen. This had

some support among the Establishment, not least Oswald
Mosley who thought the young and unorthodox Edward would
be 'Fascism's ideal king', but most thought it a bad idea and
an admission effectively that Simpson was not fit to be queen.
Edward replied that if he could not marry Simpson and be king,
he would abdicate.

When they learned of this a month later, in November
1936, what did the ordinary man and woman think?
Chips Channon felt that the issue had divided the nation
into Cavaliers and Roundheads again, into romantics and
puritans. Letters to national newspapers seemed to show
huge popular support for the King, but on the other hand the
singing of the national anthem at public events was markedly
less enthusiastic than normal. A women's demonstration at
Buckingham Palace carried placards reading 'God Save the
King from Baldwin', whilst at Marble Arch, a banner read,
'After South Wales You Can't Let Him Down'. The notion of
Edward being 'a people's King' with a feel for the common
man still held firm. Writer Harold Nicolson summed it up
thus: 'The upper-class mind her being American more than
they mind her being divorced. The lower class do not mind
her being American but loathe the idea that she has had two
husbands already.' Small children in the streets sang a new
version of an old carol: 'Hark, the herald angels sing/Mrs
Simpson's pinched our king!'

Back in Nottingham in October 1936, the marchers stayed
at Sneinton House, euphemistically described as a 'municipal
hostel' but in effect a workhouse. Two more men dropped out
here. One had to have all his teeth removed, a common drastic
solution to dental problems for many working-class people in the
era before the NHS. Boots the Chemists, based in Nottingham,
donated some essential medical supplies. The Co-Op gave them
32 pairs of socks and boots and 12 pairs of trousers. Two local
textile firms provided 200 pairs of fresh underwear, and thus
refreshed and emboldened, the Crusaders left the city and set

out across the flat agricultural fields of Nottinghamshire bound for Loughborough.

Even if I had not been intending to replicate their route exactly, I would certainly have been drawn to Bunny just from seeing the name on the map. The village, named by the Saxons after their word for reed ('Bune'), lies halfway between the two and here the marchers stopped for lunch and were rejoined by Ellen Wilkinson who had dashed off to Leeds on Labour Party business. I arrive a little later than they did after a fairly nondescript plod and take a look around. It is a charming spot, although clearly that's helped by the name. Everything in Bunny sounds cute: Bunny Village Hall, Bunny Primary School, even the Bunny Trading Estate (home to Fine Finish Kitchens, Appliance City UK, units available to let). An information board on the village green details local walks in the area that sound appealing – Sid's Seat, Bradmore Church, the Pineapple Gate – but which will have to wait till another day. I take a stroll down Moor Lane and Church Lane which are delightful but for the first time on the march to date I have a feeling of dislocation, homesickness even. I wonder if the marchers ever felt this way, or whether they were always buoyed by the camaraderie and adventure and the sheer selfish pleasure of getting out of Jarrow for a few weeks.

In the bar of the Rancliffe Arms the lights are coming on. A few tankards of foaming ale will be raised tonight and the issues of the day debated at the bar. Roughly 60 per cent of Nottinghamshire voted to leave the EU, although anti-EU feeling was strongest in former manufacturing towns like Mansfield rather than commuter villages like Bunny. Various signs tell me that CCTV is in operation, not anywhere in particular, just generally in the village. A man loading his Range Rover with rubbish for the tip eyes me with interest. For the first time, I get the feeling that I might be asked what exactly I'm doing snooping around here, and not entirely out of idle, genial curiosity.

Then a cheering encounter. A nice curly-haired lady with glasses and a big scarf is selling kindling by the roadside for one pound a bag. It's a family tradition. 'My father started to do it when he was 90 for something to do really. We said, "Why don't you chop some of those old trees down and sell it for kindling. You could give the money to charity." We change it around from time to time. We've done it for the church and Rainbows. You're not from Bunny are you?'

'No. I'm from the north.'

'Ah, the north,' she says, with a little mysterious laugh, as if it were Narnia. She's heard of the Jarrow march but didn't know that they stopped for lunch in Bunny. 'Oh, at the Rancliffe?' Well, no, probably a tin mug of tea and corned beef butty on the village green. 'Well, there are worse places to have lunch. I'm biased as it's my home village but I do think it's beautiful.'

I agree and though I have no need of a bag of kindling I give this kindly welcoming lady a few quid for whatever charity she's currently supporting and head off. As I go, I reflect on how very old fashioned the encounter was – the travelling fellow, the roadside stall. Once, and not that long ago, travellers on the road were much more common than today and would pitch up in villages for work or leisure. Reading Alfred Wainwright's *A Pennine Journey*, I was struck by how the author, then a young man on a walking tour two years after the Jarrow march, would simply knock on doors and ask whether the residents could put him up for the night in return for a few shillings. He even offers some advice on this matter: 'Avoid the hotels, choose the lowly homesteads. Be one of the company, do as they do. If the family goes to bed early, be the first upstairs. If the host eats with his fingers, do the same. If he repeats loudly after his meal, make the attempt. He'll love you as a brother and take you into his confidence.'

In Loughborough, the marchers stayed at another drill hall. According to the nice lady in Bunny, Loughborough's is still here and I noted its address in case I got the chance to make a visit. The skies were darkening though and I wondered again how 200 men (actually 192 by this time) often managed to make better time than me. Perhaps I needed to get myself a harmonica band. Somewhere between Bunny and Loughborough, the marchers' supply bus driver stopped to help a motorist who'd broken down on the main road. He turned out to be an ex Jarrow man himself; 20 years a resident in the town who had left to find work like so many Tynesiders had been forced to do. Between the General Strike of 1926 and the Jarrow march, South Tyneside lost almost 100,000 people. London and the home counties gained a million.

As the Nottingham road finally slides into the outskirts of Loughborough, my eye is caught by two buildings. Firstly, a city pub that promises 'Netbuster Carp Fishing Here' (which brings forth visions of men in waders splashing about struggling with slippery tench amidst girls drinking spritzers and blokes watching SkySports). Secondly, a glorious building built around the time of the Jarrow march and a fabulous example of art deco thirties architecture. Lynne Dyer, who blogs about Loughborough, tells me this would have been newly opened when the marchers passed by and is still going strong as Beacon Bingo (a great-granny won a quarter-of-a-million pounds here a few months before I set off).

It's said that when a visiting Aussie saw Loughborough on a road sign he announced 'What kind of place is Loogabarooga?' This has now become the affectionate nickname for the town, which for me will always be associated with Human Groovers. Back when I was at college in the mid-1980s, the campus was a sea of tribes. There were swots doing chemistry who liked the Alan Parsons Project and Marillion. There was a new wave of British heavy metal-heads into the Tygers of Pan Tang, who generally got kicked out after a term. There were girls who loved Rush who wore cheesecloths and girls into Dollar who wore headbands, and pale young oiks like me with a copy of Camus's

L'Etranger in his overcoat pocket and an obsession with the first Human League album.

But perhaps most noticeable of all were the PE students who would come down to the bar en masse in tracksuits at nine o'clock, put Rod Stewart on the jukebox and drink pints of 'still orange'. Their course was officially called Human Movement but we hipsters obviously renamed them Human Groovers.

One of the few things I knew about Loughborough was that it had built a worldwide reputation as a capital of excellence in the field of sport thanks to the brilliant facilities at the university. Alumni include Paula Radcliffe, Seb Coe, Monty Panesar, Tanni Grey-Thompson and former Arsenal goalie Bob Wilson. Today, the university attracts Human Groovers from all over the world. I did see a few athletic-looking types knocking around in leggings and lycra but if I was expecting to see anyone lobbing a javelin down the high street or doing squat thrusts in Pizza Hut I was disappointed.

'Loogabarooga' is now the name given to a festival of children's literature, which was in full swing when I arrived. The local Waterstones was festooned with promotional materials and classic children's books from *Black Beauty* to Judy Blume. Sometimes festivals and their host towns have only the most tenuous of links but a jamboree celebrating kids' literature makes perfect sense in Loughborough, which was for many years the home of Ladybird books. There's a green plaque in Angel Yard at the site where books were printed from 1915 to 1973. Local printers Wills & Hepworth decided to try their hand at 'pure and healthy literature for children' during the First World War, and the publishing house grew to be one of the most distinctive and best-loved British brands.

Originally Ladybird published children's fiction of a rather folksy, cutesy bent like *Tiny Tots Travels* and *Hans Andersen's Fairy Tales*. Bunnikins and Downy Duckling were very popular comfort reading during the Second World War. But following this, Ladybird took a defining decision to expand into educational non-fiction. The Learnabout books of the 1960s introduced children to everything from metalwork to heraldry. Thanks to Ladybird, I became mildly obsessed with the latter whilst still at primary school and am still fluent in terms like sable, gules, chevron, dexter, sinister and lions couchant – knowledge which has thus far proved entirely useless outside pub quizzes. Ladybird's Keywords reading scheme taught generations of British kids to read.

There were other less predictable results. 'How it Works': The Motor Car, published in 1965, was used by Thames Valley police driving school as a general introductory guide for rookie cops. Ladybird's Charles and Diana wedding book in 1981 was the first to be published and on the shelves within five days. It sold one and a half million copies. Ladybird is now an imprint of Penguin books and publishes Peppa Pig and Hello Kitty. But the classic look of Ladybird lives on in the adult versions produced by the brilliant Jason Hazeley and Joel Morris using the beautiful original illustrations and covering such topics as The Hangover, The Hipster and The Zombie Apocalypse. By happy coincidence, the second tranche of these were published on the day I arrived and piled high on the tables of Waterstones.

It is possible then that the marchers' kids would have had a Ladybird book or at least have seen them. But they would have been spoiled for choice for a good read if they'd had access to a decent library. The 1930s were a boom decade for children's literature. One might even say it was the decade in which children's literature as know it really began, in the sense of novels and stories set in a believable world or a newly minted fantastical milieu and written by contemporary writers, rather than fairy stories and folk tales. Children's authors began to move away from producing dull, adult-approved morality tales to stories that would appeal directly to children. The thirties brought us Swallows and Amazons, The Sword in the Stone, Professor Branestawm, Charlotte's Web, The Hobbit, National Velvet and Mary Poppins as well as some classics of what was almost social realism for kids: Alison Uttley's richly evocative study of rural Derbyshire life *The Country Child* and, the year after the Jarrow march and perhaps influenced by it, *The Family from One End Street*, a sentimental but sympathetic account of life among the working classes in the fictional town of Otwell.

Beyond the metaphorical and actual warmth of the bookshop, a chilly Friday night in Loughborough was warming up socially. A smart middle-aged couple meet, kiss, embrace under a street light and he says 'Shall we see what's on at the pictures?' It could be a twenty-first century *Brief Encounter*, except the huge Cineworld here has a lot more to offer than a Lyons Corner House or a rock bun in the station waiting room, including a Bella Italia, Nando's and Pizza Express.

At the big Sainsbury's, I finally met two Human Groovers, sports science students Lucy and Dawn. They wear tracksuits and their basket is definitive (smoothies, filtered water, wholegrain baps) but Dawn is wearing a t-shirt of the uber cool German jazz label ECM records. This suggests far better taste in music than the rugger buggers on my course, who were Queen fans to a man. 'They're all into hip hop now,' laughs Lucy. 'They think they're gangsta rappers. But they still take their rugby gear home to Surrey for mum to wash.'

Whether Dawn, Lucy or the sports scientists of Loughborough Uni would have approved I doubt, but I decide to take the weight (and rucksack) off in the warmth of the Nepalese curry house and the Swan in the Rushes pub, both of which had been recommended to me. The advance press was no hype; the curry was breathtaking and the range of beers in the boozer mind-boggling. But the saloon bar was raucous and crowded and I couldn't shake that feeling of being out of place and at a loose end. So I left Loogabarooga to its own Friday night devices. A good band called The Wave Pictures have a lovely, observational indie song called 'Friday Night in Loughborough' – witty, sad, pitch perfect. The line, 'With the girl from Bakers Oven holding back your hair,' is both brilliant and poignant; fans of the fast-food retail scene will know that Bakers Oven was taken over by Greggs in the mid-1990s. *Sic transit gloria mundi.*

STAGE FIFTEEN

LOUGHBOROUGH TO LEICESTER

22 October, 11 miles

With the same sense of purpose, though less sense of impending catastrophe, the Jarrow men left Loughborough bound for Leicester as the embattled Spanish Republican government moved to Barcelona, driven north before Franco's remorseless advance. Europe's other two leading Fascists, Hitler and Mussolini, were preparing to meet and sign the Rome–Berlin Axis and bring the Second World War a little nearer. If you were trying to forget all this and relaxing at home on 21 October 1936, Sherlock Holmes and Doctor Watson were attempting to solve the mystery of the Bruce-Partington plans in a new series on BBC Radio. Vying for column inches in the papers of the day was the Jarrow march itself; Scullion, Riley and Paddy the dog were becoming household names and Ellen Wilkinson one of the most famous women in Britain. The *Leicester Evening News* met the march en route and were much taken by Wilkinson's blue suede shoes. The coverage was extensive and constant but often trivial and even patronising. Five of the marchers had set up a committee specifically for dealing with the press and they were keen to maintain an upbeat, positive and non-political image of the march. It worked, but inevitably led to a lot of chattily inane columns about dogs and shoes.

The 15 footsore miles from Loughborough to Leicester as the main road are unremarkable to the point of a walking stupor. With two important appointments later this cold, bright afternoon, I make no apology for hopping on the Kinchbus No. 2 around Quorn (which is a real place) and letting it do the hard work for a few miles. Eighty years ago, when the Jarrow Crusade came to Leicester, the shoe workers of the town mended their boots overnight for them. When Ellen Wilkinson went to see them and thank them at 2am, she found them happy in the charitable work they were doing. 'There was such a gay enthusiasm for this unusual bit of help that it was fun to be among the men. One boot repairer, pulling to pieces an appalling piece of footwear remarked, "It seems sort of queer doing your own job just because you want to do it, and for someone you want to help instead of doing it because you'd starve if you didn't. I wonder if that's how the chaps in Russia feel about it, now they're running their own show".'

Sidney Sterek, one of the reporters who walked with the marchers, reported, 'If the wives and families of the Jarrow pilgrims to London could have seen their men folk last night, they might have mistaken our sturdy and well-nourished army for a huge theatrical male chorus. The Crusaders have been rigged out in new flannel trousers, new boots and underwear. If Leicester had done no more than this for the marchers, it would have been said ... that it just about topped the list of the most hospitable cities, towns and villages through which we have so far marched.' But according to the day's *North Mail*, back on Tyneside, Leicester did much more. 'It fell around our necks and hailed us as friends in dire need of assistance.'

Perhaps it could remember its own recent past and privations. While Jarrow's steelworks and shipyards were booming in 1905, Leicester's shoe and hosiery industries were being badly hit by a trade downturn and organised their own hunger march. A group of 440 men were sent on their way to Trafalgar Square by an estimated 20,000 townspeople. Many newspapers and commentators remarked on the similarities between the two marches. The Leicester men were well drilled and disciplined, much was made of their non-political and spiritual nature, and the Labour Party would have nothing to do with them.

In 1936, when the Jarrow marchers arrived in Leicester, one of the most curious aspects of the whole Crusade occurred, or rather probably didn't occur. The Church of St Marks is now, I discovered deflatingly, the Empire Conference and Banqueting Centre, having been 'decommissioned' as a place of worship in 1986. But in 1936 it was one of the main Anglican parish churches of the district and a strange, spurious tale grew up that the marchers had come here and had their feet symbolically washed in a religious blessing. They in return gave the church a crucifix made from wood hewn in Jarrow. None of this seems to be true, but the story gained credence to the degree that 52 years later, the Mayor of Leicester returned the cross (or at least, a cross) in a civic event attended by a hundred or so people including many parishioners (who said they had been at the original ceremony) and six Jarrow marchers, all of whom remembered something that seems to have been completely fictional. One marcher, Jimmy Foggon, even remarked, 'I don't remember it very well but it's part of the march and that's all there is to it.'

The resurgence of some of our modern cities often stems from some strange or unexpected seed. Manchester had the IRA bomb which kick-started a long overdue civic regeneration. When the City of Birmingham Symphony Orchestra appointed the youthful, brilliant Simon Rattle as its conductor, it gave the city new cultural clout and kudos as well as the best concert hall in Europe. Leicester has the discovery of the body of a long-dead much-maligned 'crookback' under a car park near Costa and Poundland to thank for boosting its profile and prestige. The sensational rediscovery of Richard III's burial site in the centre of Leicester, where he was unceremoniously and hastily interred after being dragged from Bosworth Field, has brought tourists and historians to the town and revitalised and smartened up a part of the city that several Leicesterians tell me was once very shady and shabby indeed. 'You would not have wanted to hang around the cathedral after dark ten years ago,' being a typical comment I heard.

Richard III, the final ruler of the Plantagenet dynasty, was killed on 22 August 1485 at the last major battle of the Wars of the Roses. Afterwards, his mutilated body, slung across the saddle of a horse, was taken to Greyfriars Friary in Leicester where it was buried in a crude, shallow grave. After Henry VIII, poster boy of the new Tudor order, dissolved the monasteries and Greyfriars was demolished, the burial place was lost and forgotten. Some said Richard's bones were tossed into the River Soar. The Richard III Society, indefatigable enthusiasts who've long campaigned to alter our negative opinion of the monarch, set in motion an archaeological project called 'Looking For Richard', which set out to find his remains on the old friary site, now a car park. On the very first day of the dig, a human skeleton was uncovered with both a severe curvature of the back and dreadful skull injuries consistent with a fatal blow from a halberd, which had sheared off the back of his skull and exposed the brain. After extensive tests, it was concluded that this poor fellow was indeed Richard III.

Leicester City Council purchased an old school building next door, empty since the grammar school moved out in 2008. This was to create a centre that would tell the story of the remarkable search for – and at that point unconfirmed discovery of – King Richard III. The resulting complex is a triumph for the city. Superbly done, it has just the right mix of gravitas and reverence with modern technological and cultural savvy. The audio-visual recreation of the battle is thrillingly impressionistic and there's a smart overview of both Richard's contentious reputation and longevity as a cultural trope, from Kevin Spacey to Laurence Olivier to Johnny Rotten, who's said to have based his onstage persona on Larry's twisted misanthrope on film. I urge you to visit it if in the area. I'd have spent longer but I had an appointment with some other guys who'd put modern Leicester on the map. Not a king this time, but King Power, the stadium where Leicester City, shock champions of English football, were playing this afternoon.

This wasn't just that I fancied a bit of footie. Honest. It was very much part of my plan to take in cultural or historical aspects along the route to compare Britain then and now; concerts, churches, restaurants, pubs, a theatre show, and very definitely a football match. Football was a vital, integral part of British culture then too, and the happy coincidence of me being in Leicester on a Saturday when the new Premier League champions were at home was simply too providential to ignore. There was just the small matter of getting a ticket for the sold-out clash with Crystal Palace. Thanks again to social media and a lovely woman called Lara (who once shared a squat with my old art editor at *NME*), I was put in touch with her friend Mark, equally terrific and equally generous. As a season ticket holder, he could get me a ticket and I was to meet him and his lad Sam at the ground. Which is how, by 2.30, I was sitting with Mark and Sam sipping a very decent IPA in the Fosse Lounge, a suite inside the splendid new stadium.

Much has changed in English football since I first went to the cowshed that was Springfield Park to watch Wigan Athletic wrestle – sometimes literally – with the likes of Goole Town and Gainsborough Trinity in the Northern Premier League back in the muddy, violent 1970s. Over the next three decades, plucky little Wigan climbed all the way up the tiers of English football to the very top of the Premier League, then won the FA Cup, and are now sliding joylessly back down again. That top tier is now called the EPL, formerly the Premiership, formerly the First Division. Times change, kick-off times change, but for some of us the thrill as three o'clock on a Saturday approaches never ages or fades.

Much of the barely believable money now sloshing around English football came in the wake of Sky's involvement and the setting up of the Premier League in the early 1990s. But even in the day of the Jarrow march, there were Cassandras and naysayers bemoaning the national obsession with football, the amounts of money in the game and the subsequent erosion of the pure ethos of amateurism. 'Shamateurism', as it was called, was rife, especially among the bigger clubs. Martin Pugh cites the case of Manchester United's Frank Barson who would routinely expect an envelope stuffed with cash waiting for him in the dressing room with his kit. 'Where's the doins? I'm not tekkin mi bloody coat off till I get it.'

The depression of the interwar years, particularly in the industrial north, made football even more popular and more important, a source of both romantic escapism and social cohesion in the face of the long dehumanising economic slump. Unfortunately, it also created an insularity. England were to go through the 1930s wrongly believing themselves to be world leaders at the sport, a notion they were to be humiliatingly disabused of after the Second World War.

When the Jarrow marchers came to their town, Leicester City, 'the Foxes', were top of the Second Division and heading back up having been relegated the year before. Many of the Jarrow men would have been able to tell you this since football was already a major part of working-class social life, much debated and discussed, if not the unhealthy, maniacal obsession it is for some now. The money involved in the game today has grown to an insane degree that no one in the 1930s would have found believable. The game's appeal now, while still strong in traditional working-class and industrial Britain, is far more classless these days. Purists and traditionalists complain the sport has become gentrified and detached from its parent culture. In 1936 though, the ravaged industrial north east was arguably the football hotbed of England, home to champions Sunderland who had just won the title for the sixth time. There'd been football at that summer's Olympics in Berlin, but it was a miserable tournament dogged by cheating and the baleful presence of

Hitler and Goebbels at some of Germany's matches. Britain sent a team who were put out by Poland but who took a principled stand by refusing to give the Nazi salute despite being told to do so by the British authorities and thus enraging the German hosts. Italy eventually won beating Austria in the final.

Mark's nine-year-old son Sam has been following football for one year, and in that year his team Leicester City became champions of the Premier League – the richest, most globally watched, most celebrated league in world football. 'I keep telling him, this isn't normal,' says his dad, ruefully. 'This isn't going to happen every year, you know. I don't think he realises quite how special and incredible it was.' Against all odds and defying the hegemony of the big glamour clubs such as Arsenal and Manchester United, or the bottomless cash reserves of Chelsea and Manchester City, Leicester City won the Premier League and the hearts of all neutrals with a brand of football that was fresh and exhilarating played by largely unknown players under the stewardship of the impish and genial Claudio Ranieri. Previously mocked in the UK as 'the tinkerman' for his ever-changing tactics when manager of Chelsea, Ranieri, smiling, bespectacled, was a refreshing contrast to the sullen, scowling self-importance of some of his managerial peers. He seemed to embody the club's self-effacing underdog charm. As Sam passed through JFK returning from his ninth birthday treat, a trip to New York (I think I got a Spirograph, by the way), one of that airport's notoriously sour immigration officials called, 'Hey, Leicester City! Well done you guys!'

Though Leicester are perhaps a more homespun club than their glitzier rivals in London and the north west, their well-travelled Italian boss still marshalled a team drawn from around the globe, from Japan to Mali and Austria to Argentina. Listening in the Fosse Lounge to a blazered Leicester City official read the team sheet and struggle with some exotic surnames, it is clear this new cosmopolitanism brings novel difficulties for the old guard.

'Number 19, Islam Salmani … Slam … Salami …'

'SLIMANI,' roar back the crowd in amused exasperation.

'Sorry, Slimani … Riyad Mah … raz.'

'MAHREZ!'

'Mahrez … and finally, the referee, Mr … ah, who cares.'

Mark runs construction companies across the Midlands and is Leicester born and bred, although he now lives in the countryside between his home city and Market Harborough (my next destination). Mark has been Leicester City through and through, since he was Sam's age. 'My first game was the old Filbert Street, late seventies, Keith Weller, Jimmy Bloomfield, sitting on the wall. Then a season ticket in the family enclosure. I was there for Gary Lineker's debut. New Year's Day 1979, Oldham Athletic in the old Second Division. But last season was something else. There was a real buzz around the place. A spring in its step.'

By dint of the Premier League victory, Leicester are now in the Champions League, Europe's biggest and most glamorous competition and have made a good start with nine points, which is more than they have managed in the League in a miserable start to their title defence.

'It'd be funny,' says Sam, 'if we won the Champions League and got relegated in the same season.'

'No, it wouldn't,' says Dad quickly.

For today's match against mid-table Palace, Sam predicts that Leicester will win three nil and the unpronounceable Slimani will get a hat trick. We drain our glasses and take our places in the stand. This is always a thrilling moment, especially if you watch most of your football on TV; the sense of space, the vivid green of the turf, the crackle of noise and expectation generated by thousands of expectant fans. Leicester decided to augment this atmosphere by giving away cardboard clappers before every home game. It was a stunt they tried at a fixture with West Ham when they were bottom of the Premier League in 2015. They won and that was the turning point from which came last year's title, so it's a talismanic 'tradition' that persists. There's one on my seat and on every seat for the 30,000 home fans. Some think this barrage of percussive noise, like the rattle of an ack-ack gun, has been Leicester's secret weapon. Others grumble that it's yet another contrivance of contemporary football. Mark says that it's rumoured that they have paid more for the clappers than they did for bargain Algerian star striker Riyad Mahrez.

Before kick-off, there's another illustration of the changed modern game. Since 2010 Leicester City have been owned by the Srivaddhanaprabha family from Thailand, who run the King Power duty-free empire. That week the Thai King Bhumibol Adulyadej had died. Where once, the booming Tannoy announcements before matches would ask the owner of the maroon Vauxhall Viva blocking the hot dog stall to move it, the one before this match goes like this:

> Can we ask that you all join us in respectful appreciation of a truly significant figure in Thai history? The directors, management, players and staff of Leicester City Football Club extend its deepest sympathies to the Thai people during this period of mourning. The world's longest-reigning monarch, his Majesty the King was widely loved, revered and admired in the homeland of the Leicester City owners and we now ask that you help us mark the occasion with a show of unity and support for our owners and the Thai people with a minute's applause.

The Palace fans are in good voice, aiming some good-naturedly abusive songs at the new Leicester faithful ('where were you when you were shit?'), who respond with a defiant, 'We know who we are, we know who we are, we're the champions of England, we know who we are.' The match itself is fast and free flowing. Leicester start poorly, with new signing Musa particularly ineffectual. Palace are clearly on top with former

England man Andros Townsend looking sharp. But after Palace's
Benteke heads powerfully against the bar, Leicester are stirred
into action. The formerly inert Musa shoots home from the
edge of the penalty area, Shinji Okazaki grabs one and a terrific
left-foot volley from Fuchs completes the Leicester tally before
Palace get a consolation goal in the last minutes. Three–one to
Leicester. On social media, my presence is jokingly seen to be as
talismanic as the clappers. 'You can come every week,' says one
Foxes fan on Twitter.

We walk back along the main road with the delirious
throng now augmented by Leicester Tigers fans leaving the
rugby union stadium. Mark has never been to the rugby union
ground and in his village pub there is a clear distinction between
the two camps; football on the telly in the bar, rugby in the
more comfortable lounge. Stacey Pope of Durham University
chose Leicester to study class differences in sporting allegiances
since the city has support fairly equally split between the two
professional football and rugby union clubs and with their
grounds barely half a mile apart. She interviewed 85 fans and
their comments were enlightening. 'It's just such a class thing.
I'm working class, that's why I go to the football. Posh people
go to the rugby … I think in this village there's an "in crowd"
that goes fox hunting and played rugby. And then there's, like,
the other people that work in petrol stations and things … Now
I look back on it I can see there is this kind of rugby and class
divide.'

Interestingly, a small number of rugby fans asserted that
their own 'local' attachment to the club was rooted much more
in the shires – to the county of Leicestershire – rather than to the
city where the Tigers played. As one put it: 'I love Leicestershire
… I hate Leicester city centre, but I love Leicestershire.' And
another, 'I don't feel as though I've got an allegiance to Leicester,
the city. I don't equate the city itself with Leicester Tigers so
much. Leicester Tigers for me is Leicestershire Tigers, not the
city … they're not just playing for the city, they're playing for

Leicestershire ... Like the cricket, it's county cricket, it's not city cricket.'

I have to say that I can't share interviewee R15's antipathy to Leicester city centre. As afternoon gave way to night, it began to throb with life and good humour. By nine it was positively jumping as I took my regular little solo promenade. A cheery East European bouncer tries to get me to come into his dingy-looking club for 'two for one shots' and 'great DJ. You like grime? Me neither. Awful. We play Katy Perry, Justin Bieber. Classy stuff'. Girls spill out of the Bossa bar on vertiginous heels and in sheer shiny tops to vape furiously, their elaborately piled hairdos wreathed in watery smoke. The Barley Mow pub is deserted though, perhaps because of the dentist-drill drum and bass music that is making the windows bulge. Two girls in micro skirts play balloon volleyball in the doorway of Fenwick's department store, in whose famous Newcastle sister outlet I bought the socks and flat cap I'm wearing. Removing the former, I have an American hot pizza and a big glass of Rioja in a restaurant down by the cathedral. The young waitress is originally from Skipton and loves Leicester but is jealous of my sojourn in North Yorkshire. 'My folks, my local, my dog ... I miss 'em all.' England is small but sometimes, she says, a hundred miles can feel a long way. I know, I say, ordering another Rioja and thinking back to Harrogate and Northallerton, and further back to Ferryhill and the dog walker, and further back, to Fenwick's on that bright morning that feels like years ago. It was three weeks.

I decided to make sure I was back in my room with a warming whisky – autumn was beginning to bite across middle England – to watch the game I'd been at on *Match of the Day*, and also to see what kind of mood presenter Gary Lineker was in. One of Leicester's favourite sons was ending a turbulent week in which he'd incurred the wrath of the *Sun* newspaper for having the unmitigated gall to show some sympathy for the refugee kids in the Jungle camp in Calais. The *Sun*, the paper that defamed and wrongly accused Liverpool fans of pick-pocketing the Hillsborough victims as they lay dying, was now calling for Gary Lineker to be sacked from the BBC.

'Getting a bit of a spanking today,' he tweeted, 'but things could be worse: Imagine, just for a second, being a refugee and having to flee from your home.' The *Sun*'s splash of the previous day, 'Out on His Ears', splurged, 'Calls for BBC to sack Lineker after he peddles migrant lies.' Of all the mendacious and slippery tricks of shoddy journalism, alleging there've been 'calls' for something or other is one of the most irritating. It means either 'we are calling for it' or 'nobody is calling for it, but our jobs depend on producing this stuff'. Or often both. It is part of the flotsam of cliché, half-truth and banality that passes for news today, it seems.

Taking a long circuitous way back, via the Jewish Museum and the railway station, I experience two different Leicesters – the same dichotomy I guess I'd see in any big English city today. On his patch between the taxi office and the station I give some cash to a guy selling *The Big Issue* who happily tells me his real name but let's call him William. He is gaunt and red-eyed; about 30 I'd say but it's never easy to tell when people live lives this precarious and draining. His story is typical I imagine. He came here from Coventry with an ex-girlfriend, struggled to get by, dabbled in heroin, became addicted, lost his job, house, girlfriend and, he says, access to his kids who've been adopted by their stepdad. 'I want to fight it in court. But there's no legal aid. So my only chance of getting access is to go on *Jeremy Kyle*.'

For a moment I think he's joking. But then I realise that William actually thinks that wretched TV freak show is some kind of court. Which I suppose it is. 'Still, I've been clean now for two months ... apart from this of course,' and he indicates the can of Red Stripe in his shaking hand. 'It's tough, because, you know, all those people who sit down and beg, the people you see on the street, they're not homeless. Eighty per cent of them have got properties. That hurts me. And the foreign people who sell *The Big Issue*, the Poles and Romanians, they shouldn't be selling it. It's British. Why don't they sell it in their country?' Blaming immigrants for our ills runs from the top to the bottom of our society, but it all feels worse when it comes from those at the bottom. 'I just want to tell my story,' says William shakily. 'Hey,' he asks, 'is that one of those machines you can record ghosts on?' No, I answer, nothing can, and shove a fistful of pound coins into his unoccupied hand. 'Come back later, I'll tell you some more,' he shouts after me, but by then I'm a few hundred yards away, in a scene typical of the new Leicester.

At the 2011 census, Leicester was widely tipped to be the British first city with a minority white population, but fell just short of this landmark with 50.6 per cent describing themselves as white. It does have one of the lowest rates of residents who identify themselves as white British, at 45 per cent, and the highest proportion of British Indians, at 28.3 per cent. Narborough Road in the city has been described by academics as the most multi-national road in Britain. The owners of the 222 shops along its one-mile length come from four continents and 23 different countries, such as Tanzania, Uganda and Zambia as well as Pakistan, Iran and Afghanistan. There are shopkeepers from eastern Europe, a fish and chip shop owner from Hong Kong and a book shop run by a Canadian couple. (The *Daily Star*'s headline read 'Foreign Nation Street', which you have to admit is good work by the subs.) Leicester is getting younger as well as more diverse. More than a quarter of Leicester's population – 27 per cent – is aged 20 or under. At Taylor Road Primary School, in Highfields, Leicester, the children speak 42 different languages.

Immigration has changed and is changing Britain. Rightly or wrongly, whether based on legitimate concerns or concocted hysteria, it informed the decision to leave Europe. It has led to the rise of certain parties and individuals, along with resentment of a perceived elite class and it is a major turbine in the engine driving the new populism. Impressions matter more than facts and statistics and as I leave behind wretched, sad, embittered

William with his can of Red Stripe and his misplaced faith in Jeremy Kyle, I pass by pavement cafés all along a neon-lit strip, where young people from India, Asia, the Middle and Far East, whose culture or faith or taste doesn't embrace alcohol, playing cards and drinking milkshakes and coffee, eating ice cream and baklava, laughing and flirting and chatting outside in what must surely be almost be zero degrees. Their presence, beautiful and lively, brings real warmth to the street and the night. This is how Leicester looks now; it has as much of the souk of Tehran or Tangiers about it as an old hosiery town of the English shires. The Jarrow marchers would not have believed it. But that doesn't necessarily mean that they wouldn't have enjoyed it.

STAGE SIXTEEN

LEICESTER TO MARKET HARBOROUGH

23 October, 14 miles

From the *Shields Gazette*, 12 November 2015:

> A Scottish company has defended its decision to sell 'Jarrow Marcher' boots for a hefty £180 price tag ... Aero Leather's website describes the boot as their 'version of the classic early twentieth century man's working boot, the type worn across the globe before WW2, made famous by such diverse and legendary characters as Charlie Chaplin and the Jarrow Marchers' ... The website also states: 'While everyone knows Charlie Chaplin, the Jarrow Marchers might not be so well known outside the UK. In 1936, a group 200 men from Jarrow marched the 300 miles to London to present a petition to Parliament, asking the government for work, as the shipyard in Jarrow had closed down in the previous year leaving local unemployment at 70%. Period photos show that almost every last man wore a pair of boots like these; it's in their honour that we remember these fine men in the naming of our boots.'

Local historian Paul Perry said that it was 'disgusting'.

Resplendent in their re-soled boots, smart new flannel trousers and clean underwear, the Jarrow march left Leicester. While the welcome had been warm, the night was less so, spent in the bare stone cells of the Swain Street Institute. I had the luxury of a bed and a bath plus hot chocolate and a complementary Hobnob but still had a bad night. At 2.30 in the morning, with the crazed, disorienting whoop that is the constant subliminal fear of the regular traveller, the fire alarm goes off. I imagine all my neighbours along the corridor making the same vague desultory attempts at dressing, wondering how little anatomical coverage is acceptable and willing the noise to stop before we all admit defeat and troop down the stairs in variously surprising nightwear to stand in the freezing car park until the fire brigade arrive. 'It'll be some drunks smoking,' comes a familiar voice behind me and thus, weirdly, I bump into my old friend the comedian Jo Caulfield, who I haven't seen for years. She is on her own kind of march, a tour of the UK, and Leicester is always a popular stop-off for comics thanks to the comedy festival here.

And so in the morning, I wake myself up with something artisanal, hot and caffeine-rich in one of the many stylish cafés of the St Martin district; a maze of little streets down which a man will never want for granola, halloumi or sourdough. Choosing one at random, I refuel cheek by jowl with yummy mummies deep in the family section of weekend papers while their offspring crayon furiously and middle-aged men in expensive knitwear drink macchiatos and earnestly read slim paperbacks. Thus fortified, I set off for Market Harborough.

London Road climbs steeply past the Lansdowne pub and various large townhouses, once the residences of mill managers and shoe barons, now converted to house financial brokers or nurseries with names like Little Acorns and Tiny Tots. Up past Victoria Park carpeted in autumn leaves with the low sun glimmering through bare trees, on past the racecourse and, after the sprawling suburb of Oadby, the city falls away behind me and the countryside opens up into Leicester's own Great Glen.

Nothing like its Scottish namesake; it would disappoint anyone who's come equipped with crampons and carabiners, being a wide open tract of flat arable countryside where pretty villages loom up every mile or so. In one, the Pug & Greyhound pub advertises an 'adults only bonfire', which seems an intriguing idea.

I spot a few early poppies blooming on some of the lapels of the villagers in Kibworth Beauchamp, who I feel sure was the handsome but cruel cavalry officer opposite Margaret Rutherford in an early *Miss Marple*. Unusually, Kibworth's village trail leaflet mentions the passing through of the Jarrow march. A local blogger comments, 'The Jarrow marchers halted here on their journey and were addressed by Ellen Wilkinson. I like to think of her standing on the mound making her speech.' It may not have been the first time inflammatory words were heard here; for all its olde worlde charm, Kibworth was known locally for the fervour of its radical knitting workers, uncommon in this leafy and docile part of England.

These lovely commuter villages with their cottages covered in ivy, old churches and well-kept gardens suggest the loaded term 'quintessentially English'. No Conrad Ritblat or Hotblack Desiato boards here. This is Fine & Country country, the estate agents of affluent rural England. I think of the marchers coming through. Was it as delicious and desirable then, or maybe just a simple cluster of agricultural workers' cottages and a few farms?

It may have been simple but it would have been a kind of paradise after Jarrow. Agriculture fared far better in the mid-1930s compared to the heavy industry staples such as steel and coal which were beginning their slow decline. The farmer and even his ploughman were more secure in their jobs than the pitmen and shipwrights of the north east, even at the price of deference and a stifling social conservatism, nowhere better seen than in the red jackets and antique traditions of the hunt.

Leicestershire is fox-hunting country and Market Harborough stands at the heart of it. It was within Rockingham Forest where William the Conqueror and his successors would chase and kill whatever was about in these royal forests: hare, boar, deer, wolves, game, foxes. In the nineteenth century, the market town became a centre for hunting the latter with dogs. Mr Tailby of Skeffington Hall established a hunt in south east Leicestershire in 1856 and Market Harborough became a centre for the 'sport'. A hunting guide of 1904 states:

> Somewhat less expensive than Melton is Market Harborough, and, although you can hunt six days if you like, yet it is not considered necessary. The Cottesmore and Mr Fernie's will be the hunts you would follow. Owing to its admirable train service it is quite possible to spend a business day in London from Market Harborough once or twice a week. It is a charming old-world town, very quiet; the hotels are comfortable, and there are some delightful houses to let in its vicinity.

Another book stashed electronically in my pack, *A Week's Fox Hunting at Market Harborough* by one Louis Dieulafait, written in the 1870s, sings the praises of the town even more fulsomely. 'It is a pleasantly situated place and a perfect picture of a homelike English market town ... a very considerable number of hunting people have made the neighbourhood their permanent home. Market Harborough is not only a pleasant town, it is a convenient one for a man who has other occupations.' The author goes on to detail how one could be up here on a Friday evening and hunt all day Saturday and Sunday before returning to town, assuming that the gentleman had the inconvenience of a job rather than a private income.

The Jarrow men would not have been familiar with the stirrup cup and the tally-ho but they would have enjoyed a good day's sport of their own with dogs. Greyhound racing, though, was never imbued with the same romantic affection as the hunt. Then and now you were unlikely to find dog track scenes on a restaurant's place mats. The 1930s were a boom time for greyhound racing, though to the consternation of some in authority. They were keen to ban betting at dog tracks but could not, since to continue to allow it at horse racing meetings would have quite blatantly been an act of class prejudice. Betting on greyhounds was legalised in 1934 but strictly controlled. It was only allowed on 104 days a year and then only for four hours a day. Its popularity continued unabashed. The number of women gambling on it was particularly worrisome to some. One Glasgow track provided a crèche. A Harringay stadium had seesaws and sand pits to occupy the little ones whilst mum gambled.

Market Harborough's idea of canine sport remains in the field though. Even as recently as October 2013 (well after the ban on hunting with dogs), a travel piece in *The Times* still found Market Harborough ringing on a Sunday morning to 'the sound of hooves and barking'. More generally though, a local shopkeeper reported that through the week the town had become very quiet, testament to its new status as a dormitory town in a commuter belt. The trains are even more convenient than they were in Louis Dieulafait's day. London is only 50 minutes away by fast train and house prices have rocketed. But for a town that was forever sounding the hunting horn, it seemed loath to blow its own trumpet to the *Times*'s reporter.

It could have been a display of East Midlands modesty, but when we asked our taciturn cab driver where we should visit in Market Harborough by way of sightseeing, his response was a ruminative silence, followed by the advice that we could always try Leicester, 15 miles away. Eminently commutable ... the town is undergoing a kind of personality shift as a result. A new development of smart modern apartments offering 'landscaped gardens and secure underground parking' sits next to Frank Hall Tailors, provider of bespoke hacking jackets to the Prince of Wales ... but in the town centre tweed-jacketed country gents and their wives now rub shoulders with city-dwellers with weekend homes and a fondness for expensive coffee.

In his magnificent survey of the nation, *English Journey*, J B Priestley showed little warmth or enthusiasm for Leicestershire's rural heartland, or Market Harborough in particular. 'I did not break my journey to have another look at Market Harborough. Hunting country and hunting people have their own literature and I have no wish to add to it. I have only now and again met hunting people and I do not understand them ... All I ask is that they should not pretend to be solemnly doing their duty when in reality they are indulging and enjoying themselves.' He went on to describe fox hunting as extravagant, cruel and antisocial, and local hunters as oafs. I probably wouldn't be giving an impromptu reading of Priestley's book in any of the local pubs where I was headed once I had taken in something of the town.

All day I've had in my head a snatch of a song by Paul Simon, an earworm in the modern parlance. It's the line in 'Graceland' that talks about travelling 'through the cradle of the civil war'. I know that Simon was singing about the bloody American conflict, but I'd felt the same as I moved along the quiet roads of Leicestershire. When we talk of middle England, we imagine something cosy and well-fed, ample and abundant, content and even self-satisfied. In fact, these shires have seen dire conflict, atrocities and bloodshed, a world turned upside down and torn apart by violence, and sleepy Market Harborough was at the centre of it.

In May 1645, the Royalists, buoyed by recent victories in the field, laid waste to Leicester, killing hundreds of civilians. News of the pillage and murder soon reached Parliament in London who were appalled and alarmed at the atrocities and by the loss of a strategically vital town in the heart of the English countryside. They set out bent on revenge. The Roundhead Thomas Fairfax lifted his siege on Oxford and the Parliamentary forces marched towards Leicester. King Charles, oblivious, was headed south to protect Oxford, his capital. Exhausted and depleted, he stopped off at Market Harborough to regroup. While here he learned that Fairfax and the Parliamentary forces were on their way. At 11pm on the night of 13 June, Charles was woken from a fitful sleep to be told that the village of Naseby, just over the border in Northamptonshire, had been captured by Parliamentary troops. Naseby thus became the site of the last great battle of the Civil War and a triumph for the Parliamentarians. Afterwards, the retreating Royalists were caught by Parliamentary troops and brutally cut down. Four hundred were killed altogether between Market Harborough and Leicester and some 5,000 infantry were taken prisoner into Harborough for the night.

It's a testament to the healing balm of time and the English capacity for turning even the direst calamity to their advantage that there is now, and here I quote the *Harborough Mail*:

An eye-catching trail highlighting the town's links with the Battle of Naseby ... The Market Harborough Civil War Trail will describe on six permanent information boards what happened in the town before and after the battle. The boards will be displayed at key sites in the town – in Church Square, Church Street, Coventry Road, Millennium Mile (near Northampton Road) and Welland Park. ... John Liddell, of the Market Harborough Civil War Committee, said: 'We believe that 1645 should rank alongside 1066 and 1940 in our nation's history. We hope that these display boards will raise awareness in local people and visitors to the town of the importance of this battle to the development of democracy in this country.'

On the quiet street in the dwindling afternoon, as a few late shoppers load wine and pizzas and loo rolls into their estate cars, I reflect again how bloodsoaked England's history is and how short memories are. We assume wrongly that human history is an unbroken journey towards peace and perfectibility; a tale of improvement and progress. But the events of 1645 – and Jarrow's march too – prove otherwise. Starving towns, fascists on the streets, decapitated kings, towns like Market Harborough and Leicester aflame and ringing to the sobs and wails of townspeople butchered by their own kinsmen. That's our history as much as thatched cottages and courtly coronations.

In a sense, the shock of the Brexit vote brought this home to many who assumed that a progressive consensus was the natural state of our democracy, and only an aberrant few dissented from this. Political analyst David Runciman remarked that the Brexit vote was a blow to 'the benign liberal idea that if you open up things to the public, they are basically OK and will come to the right decision. It's a myth.' This is hard to swallow, especially if like me you are someone who travels the country seeking to see the best in people and write about them in a positive and uplifting way. It's hard to imagine, but maybe necessary to get some kind of perspective, to imagine the Leicester streets where I ate frittata and drank mocha, ablaze, running with blood and choked with corpses. Perhaps we should be a little more calm and reflective about our current schisms and divisions. England has seen worse.

Mark Bauerlein of Emory University does see in Brexit and the rise of Donald Trump, 'a reaction against the English Majorification of politics, where there's all this meta stuff about how to express oneself and what you can say. Endless discourse obscures actual policies and emotions. Trump gets this. And he's like the fool from medieval or Elizabethan drama, an idiot who says the unthinkable and some people like him for it as an antidote.'

The musician and thinker Brian Eno in a *Guardian* interview was soberly self-reprimanding. 'My feeling about Brexit was not anger at anybody else, it was anger at myself for not realising what was going on. I thought that all those UKIP people and those National Front-y people were in a little bubble. Then I thought: "it was us, we were in the bubble, we didn't notice it." There was a revolution brewing and we didn't spot it because we didn't make it. We expected we were going to be the revolution.'

Shivering in the gathering gloom of a cold Sunday in Market Harborough, the church clock struck four sonorously and I remembered something that I had to make time for. I wish I could say that it was a civic ceremony or choral evensong or cheese rolling or well dressing or anything rooted in the deep loam of these ancient agricultural shires. But in fact it was Chelsea v Manchester United on Sky Sports 1, a top of the table clash that I was loath to miss.

I mooched about the cold darkening town looking for a likely spot to thaw out with the match. A thin, sluggish river runs through one end of the High Street and by it sat a couple of wheezing elderly men drinking from cans of cheap lager and a few kids kicking a plastic bottle around outside B&M Bargains. The church bells were still tolling and mixed in with them was the muted throb and drone of a mobility scooter, a very melancholy English evensong.

The tweedy gents and affluent commuters that *The Times* writer had found were nowhere in evidence. With my new enthusiasm, I tried the local Wetherspoon, and whilst it was warm, crowded and welcoming, it had no TV. I walked a little further up the road past a few similarly purist boozers until I found one from which the crackle and blare of televised sport with all its concomitant 'idents' and 'stings' was clearly audible above the low-level growl of male drinking. The pub was packed with loud men, most with their heads tilted upwards towards an enormous screen which had been secured to the wall just high enough to be uncomfortable. In the window, a table of drunk women was having some kind of shrieking contest. Close by, a partially demolished giant Stilton had been given a table to itself and various drinkers would weave and wobble over to it, carve off a chunk, balance it on a cracker and then return to their various perches leaving a trail of crumbs and cheese. It was like a corny comedy sketch set at a medieval banquet.

This was one of those pubs where a new face excites a surly kind of interest everywhere except behind the bar. There, a tough-looking woman with a severe ponytail studiously avoided my gaze. Eventually, by elbowing a couple of people aside and waving money ostentatiously I secured a pint as well as a hard look from a pugnacious little bloke in a tracksuit. He notices my recording device and regards it and me as if I'd brought a Luger or an egg whisk into his local.

'It's for making notes,' I explain, 'I'm researching a book. Maybe I could get a word with you. You could tell me what you think about Market Harborough.'

He nudges his mate, a tall thin chap with a shaved head.

'After a few more pints, I might tell you what I think about you.'

'Why not tell me now?' I say, way more aggressively than I intended to, and there's a weird, awkward, tense impasse broken only by loud cheering as Pedro scores for Chelsea. This confirms all my worse suspicions about the pub.

The back bar has a telly too so I decide to base myself at a table in there. It is just as unwelcoming as the main bar but in a different way. Soulless and spartan, there are two other occupied tables. At one, a mournful man with some kind of dossier is sipping an enormous glass of red wine. At the other are four young people, three lads and a girl, students I would guess, each with a different flavour of fruit cider. They are discussing British cities and the topic moves to Newcastle. 'Have I ever been to Newcastle?' says the girl. 'No. I'd get a nose bleed.' Chelsea score three more times. The Sky Sports panel begin a prolonged debate about Jose Mourinho who is pictured sulking, bottom lip thrust out like a toddler.

There was no analysis, no slo-mo, no goal-line technology or satellite television in 1936 but the boffins at Alexandra Palace were gearing up to begin the TV era. In late August of that year, 7,000 people had queued to see the first talking pictures on a television set at an exhibition at 'Ally Pally'. The broadcast featured announcer Leslie Mitchell looking sweaty and awkward and Paul Robeson singing 'Ole Man River'. The first TV sets went on sale soon after costing around a hundred pounds at a time when the average wage was three pounds a week. Even if you could afford one of these luxurious, high tech items with its walnut veneer and twelve-inch screen, you could only pick up the snowy, flickering image if you lived within roughly 20 miles of the transmitter. This led the *Spectator* to opine that it was 'a mere toy or hobby for the well to do and will make little change to social life'. It also had the dire warning that as well as being able to enjoy 'Hammond bat and Larwood bowl' you would have the comfort of your front room invaded and ruined by 'rebellions in Spain, concentration camps in Germany, misery in the depressed areas'.

The men of one of those depressed areas would probably not own a TV for another 20 years at least and they took little cheer in Market Harborough. In contrast to the new world being ushered in at Alexandra Palace, Market Harborough was the old England; hierarchical, agricultural, conservative, the domain of parson, squire, labourer where all knew their place – and I felt that a sense of that remained. The marchers got a cool welcome here; the worst of the whole journey they said. Not one member of the council or representative came to meet them. There was no reception, no public meeting and they were given the bare stone floor of an unfinished workhouse to sleep in. This was of course Market Harborough's prerogative and perhaps explicable by the fact that the industrial downturn that had blighted Jarrow had not touched them. Your child was three times more likely to die in childhood in Jarrow than in Market Harborough. The people of this market town were by comparison well off, well fed and healthy with little natural kinship with the men of the north. Local papers took offence at any slur on the town's good name and claimed the men had been warmly welcomed and shown great hospitality.

I can't say that I or the Jarrow men could claim that about our visits, although in fairness some nice people from round about did extend the hand of friendship to me via Twitter. Perhaps the marchers and I caught them on a bad day. If I were advising the marchers now, I would tell them to go to Wetherspoon, whatever their views on Brexit. Market Harborough, incidentally, voted to leave in contrast to its large urban neighbour Leicester where the majority voted to remain. A lot can change along those 14 miles of English road I had found. For the first time, I felt in a different part of England, an England I didn't know and wasn't at home in. I was reminded of a famous anecdote about the absent-minded writer G K Chesterton who once sent a telegraph to his wife: 'Am at Market Harborough. Where should I be?' To which she replied, 'Home.'

STAGE SEVENTEEN

MARKET HARBOROUGH TO NORTHAMPTON

24 October, 17 miles

At the end of yesterday's big match, the one I'd watched with the aggressive cheeseniks and forlorn vinophiles of Market Harborough, I'd spotted (along with a couple of million intrigued others) the new Manchester United manager Jose Mourinho whisper something in the ear of Chelsea boss Conte. A few minutes earlier, the latter had been visibly encouraging the crowd into making more noise at the end of their four–nil drubbing of United (drubbing, like adjudged, is one of those words only ever heard in a football context). Mourinho apparently said to him, 'You shouldn't whip them up like that at four nil. It's humiliating. You should do that at one nil.' Incredibly, Mourinho's wounded feelings took up nearly as much space in the morning papers as reports of the 'Jungle' refugee camp in Calais which was cleared by French police last night amidst flames, tear gas and violence.

Eighty years ago, the vexed question of refugee movements across a dangerous and fissile world was a global preoccupation too. British colonial powers in Kenya were dealing with a huge influx of Ethiopians as Mussolini waged modern war on a third-world country in an act of grandstanding machismo designed to distract from his incompetence domestically. Essentially, it was a conflict between modern weapons technology and men armed with spears, bows and antiquated rifles. The Ethiopians were soon overrun and Emperor Haile Selassie driven into exile as his countrymen fled into neighbouring countries.

In Jaffa, rioting and clashes between Jews and Palestinians forced 6,000 people from their homes, many reduced to camping in public parks. In Oklahoma, drought across the dustbowl displaced thousands of poor Americans, events which John Steinbeck would soon write about in *The Grapes of Wrath*. Within months of the Jarrow march, 4,000 Basque children would arrive at Southampton docks fleeing the violence of the Spanish Civil War. They were housed at the rapidly built Stoneham Camp on land donated by a local farmer.

As the horror of Nazi rule worsened and became more apparent, the first Jewish refugees began to come to England. But as Louise London showed in her book *Whitehall and the Jews 1933–1948*, the same reluctance and indifference shown by politicians and press now was prevalent at the time of the Jarrow march. The Liberal politician Viscount Samuel said, 'out of that vast reservoir of misery and murder only a tiny trickle of escape was provided'. The government feared the usual catalogue of problems, real or imagined, such as depriving the native population of jobs, and social unrest. Lord Rothermere's titles were generally most hostile to the refugees. The *Mail*, one of whose more memorable 1936 headlines was 'Hooray for the Blackshirts', said, 'the way stateless Jews are pouring in from every port in the country is becoming an outrage'. Eighty years on as I marched, the *Sun* was still giving Gary Lineker 'a spanking' for his support for refugees.

I've left some kit behind in Gary's old stamping ground of Leicester so this morning I double back the ten minutes on the train to pick them up before setting off for Northampton. (It's both amazing and slightly dispiriting how slowly the miles go on foot, and what a distorted sense of distance trains, planes and automobiles give you.) I get talking with a friendly young couple who were in Leicester last night watching a band. They're only vaguely aware of the Jarrow march ('Was there a song about it?') and when I mention Market Harborough she pulls a little face and comments merely 'Good charity shops'. Of today's destination, Northampton, they tell me to look out for one of the oldest churches in Britain and the Otis Lift Tower.

The couple came from Corby which is just down the road from here and home to the famous steelworks newly built when the marchers passed by. Ironically, it was partly the success of Corby that brought hardship to Jarrow. The plan for a new steelworks in Jarrow collapsed because competition was deliberately suppressed by the British Iron and Steel Federation to protect towns like Corby. Even worse, the BISF was part of an international cartel whose members included Germany, whose industrial strength was at this time still being propped up by some financiers and industrialists as a balance to Soviet might. All these factors conjoined to mean that in the summer before the march the Federation itself admitted, 'it is considered very unlikely that the scheme [the proposed Jarrow steelworks] will be proceeded with'.

I would be making my way to Northampton via the route of a defunct transport network where nature was slowly reclaiming the land from the technology of man. After a slightly confusing start with signage hidden in dense undergrowth around Britannia Walk and Scotland Road (where I ended up in a very surprised lady's front garden), I finally found myself on the Brampton Valley Way, which heads arrow-straight across the 14 miles between Market Harborough and Northampton. The walk literature promises pubs, local attractions like Kelmarsh Hall, Brixworth Country Park and Lamport Steam Railway but most intriguingly of all, 'two marvellously spooky tunnels' – surely a phrase that no one who has read Dickens' 'The Signalman' could possibly resist.

Many of the trails like this that you find now across the British countryside owe their origins to the infamous Doctor

Beeching 'axe'. In 1963, in cahoots with a transport minister with commercial interests in road haulage, British Rail chairman Beeching began the process of closing a third of British branch lines, becoming a bona fide folk devil in the process. But the Northampton to Market Harborough line, built by George Stephenson's nephew to ferry ironstone, survived remarkably until 1981. Then in 1993, it was opened again as what the council call 'a linear park'. After only a few hundred yards Market Harborough is left behind and the path becomes a gentle climb through open country. It's half term but even so, the way is quiet and unfrequented; the occasional family on bikes pass like a family of ducks gliding by, eyeing my enormous pack pityingly.

After the bitter, biting evening in Market Harborough, today feels like spring. The mild afternoon is full of birdsong, hazy sunshine and far-off children's laughter. I pass a small lake, and a lone fisherman raises a hand in greeting. I imagine his keep net, packed with fat carp and glistening tench, and feel suffused with well-being at the simple pleasure of being out and alive and putting one foot in front of another on a country path in England. But then in quick succession, a man in upsettingly frank lycra aimed his bike at me, and soon after in the distance comes a sight that causes a small ripple of trepidation, like the rumble in the basses in the *Jaws* theme, like something worrying glimpsed out of the corner of the eye. A few hundred yards along the path, where the embankment narrows and the trees hunch over, is a small dark hole where the path disappears into blackness beneath the hillside.

Kelmarsh is the first of two tunnels, the other being Ovenden, that will bring up short any walker on the Brampton Valley Path. They're 322 yards and 462 yards respectively, and if you really don't feel like the long, dark, slow trek along the dank and darkened first tunnel with its dripping walls, you can take a diversion that promises pleasantly, 'Kelmarsh via woods and spinneys'. That, though, would add several miles to an already long day. So, loins girded, in I went for what seemed like a dripping, echoing eternity, stumbling occasionally, cursing regularly and trying to get the torch facility of my phone to project something more useful than a pale circle of milky light the size of my hand. Every hundred yards of so, a ventilation shaft soaring up above one's head provides a pool of welcome sunlight. This though can be a mixed blessing. On YouTube I'd watched a solo walker bask in the shaft's light and film it on his phone turning slowly around as he did to get a nice shot, and then not be sure which was forward and which was back, and whether he was progressing or retreating and would have to do the whole thing again. I don't think you ever find out what happened to him. Unless you fall down, or get hit by an unlit cyclist, or perhaps snatched by a hideous formless creature lurking in the shadows, you will probably emerge from the tunnel unscathed, but it is certainly an eerie experience (or rather two) and the old adage about the 'light at the end of the tunnel' will take on new and vivid meaning when you have watched the small disc of sunlight grow from a pinprick, promising the way back out into the very welcome fresh air and sparkling light of an October early afternoon.

Between the tunnels I'd passed a middle-aged couple on a bench eating their sandwiches, sipping from their flask and clearly recovering from either Kelmarsh or Ovenden (I forget which). It was she who'd suggested I use the torch facility on my phone, unaware that my particular device possessed a weaker wattage than an ailing glow worm. As was customary now, I asked them about the Jarrow march and received the now customary response; a vague recollection of some struggle or protest. 'They came down the road, didn't they, past here? Weren't they coal miners? From Newcastle? I'm not clear as you can tell, but it was during the great Depression, wasn't it? This line would have been working then though.'

Though this is agricultural Britain, and its character 'parson and squire', heavier industry like those the Jarrow men knew had a presence here. The Midlands ironstone field stretched from Lincolnshire through Leicestershire, Rutland and Northamptonshire to Oxfordshire and the materials were moved from quarry to factories by many narrow-gauge railways like this one. The still and benign fields and pastures I'm now crossing, dotted with stiles and crossed with cow parsley hedgerows, would have once been a pitted and smoking industrial workshop. As the Nene Valley narrow gauge website has it, 'It is now hard to envisage that the pleasant rolling countryside in the East Midlands has been host to opencast ironstone mining on such a grand scale.' The quarries themselves are now nature reserves or landfill, or even suburban housing estates. Steel gave men work here for much longer than it did in Jarrow, but even here it disappeared as Britain abandoned its industries and began to lose its industrial culture.

I leave the track at Draughton Crossing bound for Maidwell village, halfway between Market Harborough and Northampton, and where the marchers took a break in 1936. It's deserted and silent; its residents all presumably hard at work at computers and counters in one of the above two towns. As it's half term, even the smart new school, built in 2000, according to its foundation stone, is shut up and quiet. There are pumpkins for sale in a neat garden but no one about to sell them. A phone rings unanswered in the rectory and the village has a newness and an unreality about it that's queer. The Old Barn is nothing of the sort, rather a newbuild a rock star might live in. Despite this, the village apparently has a long history; it has nine listed buildings and the church boasts 'interesting cupolas', but as in Bunny, I get the feeling that I'm being watched by suspicious eyes behind Laura Ashley curtains and so I pass quickly through and head along the mile or so to the main A road. It's been a good morning's walking, but a long one, and I can feel a tiredness in my legs and even a little sunburn on my face. The map shows a pint glass symbol just where I'll emerge, and I'm very much hoping that will mean a late lunch for me in a sun-dappled beer garden.

It didn't. A very apologetic young woman locking the door of the Stags Head tells me that if I'm prepared to wait for two hours, they'll be open and serving food again. But I doubt that the *Marie Celeste* Maidwell could keep me occupied that long so I dump myself and the pack on a bench dedicated to Bob Lilley ('his favourite walk') and write a couple of postcards. While I'm thinking through my next move, which may involve foraging for nuts and berries and weeing in a hedge, a passing van pulls over and stops in the layby.

Kev and Jake of Windsor Windows of Northampton have been following my progress on Twitter as they've done their daily rounds and, knowing I'm behind schedule, hungry and tired, offer to help out with a lift or a mile or two to the outskirts of Northampton. I jump in and they prove to be fine company. Kev is a 6Music fan and listens to my shows. 'This is that bloke,' he says to Jake, the younger of the two and in his early twenties I'd guess.

'I make him listen to you, educate him a bit, wean him off all that dance stuff of Radio One. His dad's the boss of the firm and it's his van. But I'm the senior worker!'

Jake smiles wanly. If I regularly ruin his day, he is too polite to say. Kev's a season ticket holder at Northampton Town. He once saw a train on the Brampton Valley Line when he was a kid in the 1970s – 'Definitely still going then'. In their working life, the pair cover all the little towns and villages hereabouts. Work is plentiful and they are kept busy. When I tell Jake that some of the Jarrow men had worked two days in ten years he looks genuinely appalled. 'Were they on benefits?' Yes, but not much. Nothing like today. 'I'd hate to be on benefits. People say it's an easy life but I'd rather be getting out and about. Even with his weird music. No offence.' Their busy schedule is a testament to how our economy has changed. We manufacture very little now, but the cash-rich, time-poor, long-hours working middle manager or teacher or IT specialist has neither the free time nor the skills to plumb in a new bathroom suite or plaster a bedroom or install double glazing. And so people who can, like Kev and Jake, tradesmen as they would once have been known, are always in work. Good, reliable ones are as rare as neurosurgeons and spoken of and recommended in the same reverential whispers. Even as we're chatting a work call comes in on the van hands-free. I keep quiet while Kev and Jake's dad discuss the scenario: 'Thing is, the client, they don't want that door going in there … what with all the wheelbarrows going backwards and forwards … and I can see their point.'

As we near Northampton, they recommend a cheese shop, the old Saxon church at Brixworth and a pint at the Malt Shovel. 'Northampton's alright. Everyone slags it off but that's the British way, isn't it? There's worse places that's for sure. And we've probably put their windows in. If you see what I mean …'

Towns always feel complicated, crowded, strange and disorienting as I march in after the quiet of country tracks or even the droning anonymity of the highway. It's late on a very ordinary Monday afternoon but there's a detectable hubbub as I negotiate the traffic islands and pelican crossings and make my way into the heart of the town to be met by flashing lights, screams, whirling machinery and the unmistakeable tang of the fair. According to a leading online encyclopaedia, 'The St Crispin Street Fair is an annual fair held the town centre of Northampton England organised by Northampton Borough Council though it is not held every year.' I like an annual event that's not actually held every year, it adds a little frisson of unpredictability. Maybe we should try it with Christmas.

The St Crispin's designation sounds nicely ancient but the fair is relatively modern, erratically staged, and not to everyone's liking. A local fancy dress shop owner complained to the local paper in 2012 that, 'there will be a tremendous amount of noise which will make it difficult to talk to customers and the smell from the food vans will get on the costumes'. The smell from the food vans was certainly making an impression on a visitor who'd walked the best part of ten miles and not eaten all day. Within minutes I had my feet up at a plastic table in the square watching terrified townspeople flung high into the air on what seemed to be a gigantic piece of knicker elastic while I set about devouring unidentifiable but delicious meat slathered in fried onions and ketchup. From the Dodgems an enormously amplified, scratchy version of the Supremes' 'Baby Love' was blasting out. So far, I was greatly enjoying the shoe capital of the Nene Valley.

St Crispin's may be a contemporary invention but autumn is the traditional season for the great British fair, some of which have achieved world renown. Scarborough Fair lasted an astonishing 45 days in its Middle Ages heyday and lured merchants from all over Britain as well as Norway, Denmark, the Baltic states and the Byzantine Empire trading wine, silk, jewellery, lace, glass and spice for wool and leather. Some fairs specialised in single commodities, like Nottingham's famously riotous Goose Fair or the impressively niche Dish Fair in York. I'm not sure what St Crispin's speciality is; bingo possibly, or Hook-A-Duck, where you can win a giant banana that looks like a Rastafarian.

I got out quickly, pushed through the crowds at the Kentucky Derby horse racing game and back into town. Professional curiosity generally drags me towards a bookshop and in this one there was an interesting conversation going on at the counter. The young goth sales assistant was talking animatedly with a wizardish-looking man of about 60 with plastic bag and grey beard. They were discussing the short stories of Edgar Allan Poe, she enthusiastically, he more analytically, and I got the feeling that this was some kind of 'catch up' between a regular, perhaps eccentric customer and a pleasant, keen member of staff. She made a few concluding remarks about 'the surreal darkness' of 'The Tell-Tale Heart' and then brightly suggested, 'OK, well, if I get you a chair and a pen and a cup of tea, maybe we could put you over there and you could start signing some stock for us, Alan.'

Slowly, realisation dawned. Alan Moore is perhaps the most eminent and critically acclaimed British writer of speculative fiction and graphic novels of our time, and I had bumped into him in a suburban branch of Waterstones on a slow Monday afternoon. Cognisance of this came to me by virtue of his distinctive appearance and the fact that we were in his home town. Northampton has haunted his work from his very first novel, *Voice of the Fire*, which consisted of connected Northampton stories from several eras of history, and the town is at the very heart of his new book *Jerusalem*, a hefty tome here stacked into piles, which he was now seated behind and signing.

Moore came to prominence in the British comic scene in publications like *2000AD* and then succeeded in the American mainstream, the first British writer to do so, with his work on Batman and Swamp Thing. Moore's fiction, whilst thrilling enough on a purely visceral level for any fan of superhero schlock and action movies, generally has a deeper dimension and darker purpose. His best work like *Watchmen* or *V for Vendetta* has always been implicitly political, anarchistic and anti-Establishment, preoccupied with the individual and the state. In the latter, a fascist regime of Mosley-style Blackshirts called Norsefire rule Britain, helped by big business and the Church, exterminating their enemies in the minorities and on the left. Ironically, the Guy Fawkes mask worn by the hero, designed by David Lloyd, has now been appropriated by the tendentious right wing blogger Guido Fawkes, which must surely gall Moore immensely.

Jerusalem is not just his most major venture yet. It is one of the biggest novels ever written. At 600,000 words, it's considerably bigger than the Bible. He considers it his crowning achievement and magnum opus, and Northampton and its people are at its centre. *Jerusalem* is not just an epic imaginative exploration of several centuries of Northampton's history, it is specifically about Spring Boroughs, the working-class area where he was born and still maintains links with. The *Guardian* described it as 'a sprawling behemoth, this teeming leviathan, this pythonic mammoth of a novel'. Some have baulked at its sheer size and ornate prose but most have agreed it is some kind of masterpiece. I haven't read it of course. Its bulk would compromise even my capacious litreage. But I decide that the coincidence of chancing upon the laureate of Northampton here in the streets he writes about, he and I the only non-employees in the shop, is too fabulous not to act upon and I go and introduce myself.

If he regarded this as an imposition or distraction, he did not show it. Gracious and genial, as anarchistic mavericks often are, he seems genuinely interested in my project ('How fantastic!') and warms to my suggestion that this centre of England, cradle of the Civil War, seems to have a secret darkness, even violence about it beneath the reassuring stereotypes about middle England.

'There's an insurrectionary tradition here. The Civil War kicked off around here, or at least came to its conclusion here at Naseby. Bedford, where you'll be going, is of course John Bunyan's home town. He was a Roundhead who spent the last 30 years of his life in Bedford prison. They'd let him out to do the odd bit of insurrectionary preaching because he was very popular. There were a lot of disenfranchised Protestant sects about round here. The Quakers, say, who were nothing like that nice man on the Oats packet. They believed in the violent overthrow of earthly monarchs to be replaced immediately by the kingdom of God, they'd tear off their clothes to make a public display.

'Yeah we had all of them. All around Northampton. I think you're right, there's a darkness beneath a lot of what are today very sedate English towns and villages, especially here around the middle of the country. This is the navel of the nation. This is where all the bad blood gathers. The main history of Northampton is of brilliant troublemakers … and that was before the Jarrow marchers turned up.'

I leave Alan to his signing. Sheepishly I admit that I don't have room to take a copy of *Jerusalem* with me, but Alan generously offers to put one by for me to collect later. Delighted by the encounter, I head back into the throng of St Crispin's fair, steeling myself against the smell of sizzling sausage and then out into the quieter streets. The Guildhall is a truly fabulous building and tonight, there's a performance of *Dracula*, more Northamptonian darkness. At the opposite emotional extreme though, Northampton has a Bar Hygge, a smart, upscale café founded on that Scandinavian notion of cosiness and wellbeing currently being simultaneously promoted and mocked in several hundred fey broadsheet articles. I like a spot of Hygge myself, but think it works best in Tromsø or Gothenburg so I pass by leaving the gravadlax, dill herring and cake untouched. A few doors down is the Saigon Vietnamese café, reminding one how cosmopolitan Britain has become in its dining. Next door to this is a vintage record shop with a collection of jazz vinyl in the window – Miles Davis, Terje Rypdal, John Surman – so achingly impeccable that it hurts. I pop in naturally just in time to overhear the long-haired owner having an involved conversation about who has shown the more genuinely experimental tendencies, Madonna or Kylie. Past the Shoe Museum, I notice a hybrid that speaks of modern Britain: a store named Sklep Na Rogu, the Polish for corner shop. I wonder how the mood behind the counter has changed since June.

Evening is coming on in the English midlands. The King Billy Rock Bar doesn't appeal with its twin connotations of sectarianism and Bon Jovi, so I make for the recommended Malt Shovel to read and make some jottings with a pint. Googling on my iPad, I seek out some of Alan Moore's recent interviews, and find one he did with his local paper the *Northampton News* about *Jerusalem*. We seem to have been thinking about much the same things.

> If people do talk about what we fondly call the working
> class then there seems to be a choice of two registers
> in which they talk about it: they either deplore it for

its vulgarity and, yes, I'm looking at you Martin Amis, and they produce spiteful parodies of the way that they perceive working class people living, behaving and thinking. The other mode is to pity these poor victims. Nobody sees themselves like that.

Jerusalem acknowledges that. It is saying these are people with lives, with histories, with stories that are as gigantic as any Royal family or bloodline. The Windsors, Bourbons, Spencers, Tudors – the aristocrats – are apparently entitled to their genetic mythologies, so this is a genetic mythology for people who have not previously had one … because when we talk about history we talk about the history of church, of state and maybe a dozen families. What about the rest of us? Weren't we doing anything while all that was going on, or were we minor players in their drama? This is insisting that everybody has their own drama and mythology and story.

Across the web, *Jerusalem* is being feted by many as the great speculative novel of 2016. At the time of the Jarrow march, similar accolades were being bestowed on the newly filmed *Things to Come*, scripted by H G Wells from his own novella, published three years earlier. This was a vision of the future clearly fuelled by the fears and hopes of 1936. Wells's story was typical of the kind of fiction and themes preoccupying the literary intelligentsia of the day; technology, war, free will, disease, propaganda and dictatorship. It is set in the British city of 'Everytown', in a world beset by a seemingly permanent global war that began at Christmas 1940 (remarkably, Wells was only three months out). The conflict drags on into the 1960s which in Wells's vision is not a blissed-out era of promiscuity, groovy sounds and kaleidoscopic kaftans but a new Dark Age of endless pointless war and a biological plague called the 'wandering sickness' which kills half of humanity and destroys the last vestiges of civilisation. By 1970, a warlord known as the

'Boss' or 'Chief' rules southern England by force and intends to conquer the 'hill people' of the north next to obtain coal and shale to fuel his machines. It's not hard to see something of the Fuhrer and Il Duce in the 'Boss', or something of Jarrow in the now-desolate hill people's tradition of mining and delving. Eventually a new world order based on a benign technocracy comes to power, and the film ends with a faintly fascistic speech about progress and conquest. Though inevitably dated now, the film's expressionist style and Arthur Bliss's strident music are hugely impressive. For a student of the thirties zeitgeist, it's invaluable. In the tremendous opening scenes, the phalanx of marching working-class men carrying placards predicting war has definite shades of the Jarrow march.

The big comic book sensation of the day was *Flash Gordon*, invented in 1934 and debuting at 'the flicks' while the Jarrow men marched. (They may well have seen it on one of their many free hospitality nights at the cinema.) Flash was basically the archetypal square-jawed, two-fisted adventurer of classic boys' adventurer yarns transplanted into the future in a somewhat unsafe-looking, cigar-shaped craft that showered sparks. Flash was a star polo player and Yale graduate, who becomes a sort of arch preppie in space. Played by the equally implausibly named Buster Crabbe in the 1936 movie, he travels to the planet Mongo where he encounters the evil Emperor Ming the Merciless, a tyrannical inhuman nutjob. Perhaps sensing a subtext, the Nazis banned the strip.

Flash Gordon was a child of the US depression and was embraced by thrill-hungry readers of 1930s Britain. In a world of shortages and murky morality, the unambiguous moral superiority of the handsome nice guy proved irresistible. And it was easy to read. Maybe even a Jarrow marcher had one stuffed in his overcoat pocket for when he dossed down on the next drill hall floor. Or, as in the case of Northampton, on straw on the floor of St James school after a rousing meeting at the town hall. Alan Moore's *Jerusalem* was going to prove less portable so thanks to the pub's free wifi I decided to download the ebook and take a look. Almost immediately, my eye was caught by a line that seemed to capture what I (and I think Moore) still see as the defining division in British society. It's the one that is still proving difficult for some to understand, the great social rift that drove the Jarrow march and may well be driving the flight into the political unknown now, away from consensus and towards demagogues and anger. 'Despite the very real continuing abuses born of antisemitism, born of racism and sexism and homophobia, there are MPs and leaders who are female, Jewish, black or gay. There are none that are poor.'

Of course, in their defence, it is hard to be poor with an income of £74,000 a year but the point holds I think. Despite a genteel nervousness about it these days, class supplied the great splintering fault line through British life in 1936 and the crack is still wide. As I ventured further south, I, and the men of Jarrow, would feel it between our feet.

STAGE EIGHTEEN

NORTHAMPTON TO BEDFORD

26 October, 21 miles

The great American cultural critic Greil Marcus came up with the resonant phrase 'the old weird America' to describe what his country was once like before the levelling and sanitising effect of modernity, before industry, homogenised culture and the mass media. America when it was still a place of dark secrets, odd corners, vast and unknowable. England is a great deal more ancient and complex than its colonial offspring. The old weird England is far older and weirder than America.

Even had I not had my conversation with Alan Moore, Northampton seemed to have very strong echoes of the old, weird England, especially on a damp, silent autumn morning. I walked through a shrouding mist up Black Lion Hill, down Chalk Lane, following the Knights Trail, a walk through the town that takes in some of its oldest and more storied crannies. Just by the railway station, there's a funny little hump with some railings around it and an information board. If you make your way up there, you'll find that this is not some old landfill or the remains of a shed for the locos. This was in fact Northampton Castle, mentioned in Shakespeare's *King John*, where turbulent priest Thomas à Becket was tried. At the parliament of 1381, the last to be held in Northampton, the hated Poll Tax was introduced. This led to the Peasants Revolt and was revived, you may recall, to similarly negative popular response by Mrs Thatcher's government in the 1990s. As Santayana said, those who forget the past are condemned to repeat it. And as Einstein said, doing the same thing over again and expecting different results is a good working definition of madness.

In 1662, the king knocked the castle down pretty much on a whim. Then the Victorians built a railway station over it. That's gone too now. So it goes. The plaque on Black Lion Hill also states that in 1349 when the Black Death came to Northampton the town was 'decimated' when 'half the town succumbed to it'. In my mind, I tried very hard not to be the sort of person who points out that this is not what 'decimates' really means. A kind of Pedants Revolt if you will.

Surrounded by dripping trees, mist hanging like lace across the Nene valley, in the heart of the old, dark weird England, it feels like it could be the fourteenth century rather than the twenty-first. If, that is, it wasn't for the National Lift Tower thrusting rudely and concretely 120 feet towards the sky just on the horizon. Even that has a strangely heraldic and Excalibur-ish feel to it, though only built in 1978 by Express Lifts, later Otis lifts for the testing of, yes, lifts. It's a Grade II listed building though, which is perhaps why the plans for a 100-seat theatre and café came to naught in what the late Terry Wogan called the 'Northamptonshire Lighthouse'. Do the people of this quiet shire look out for it as a beacon of home like Geordies look out for the Angel of the North? Twitter correspondent Phil Ashby suggested that, 'It's full magnificent grandeur is best viewed from up the road at Sixfields, from the car park by the rubbish tip'. But it looked strange and imperious enough rising in the mist from where I stood.

*

For days Ellen Wilkinson had been suffering from exhaustion and forced to convalesce. The men were publicly hugely supportive of her, but in private they worried that her insistence on leading the march was setting too slow a pace. That was a particular concern today as this would be the longest leg of the whole march, 22 miles, and the day had dawned wet, murky and freezing. My day promised to be more clement if just as long.

Once en route, the villages fall away with the miles. Yardley Hastings ('Just starting on Radio 4Extra, a classic edition of *All Pals at the Parsonage* from 1955 with Yardley Hastings as the short-sighted rector ...') has four entries in the Domesday Book as well as the new and superbly incongruous Belgian Fries outlet. The first I'd ever seen, it offered a range of exotic sauces from Andalouse to Samurai to Hannibal. Had there been world enough and time, rest assured I would have tried some in the interests of journalistic rigour, and found who knows what backstory of someone's homesickness for the snacks of Antwerp or Ghent in commuter belt, Northants.

I cross into that county over the lazy, swirling river Ouse where sleepy swans dawdle beneath a bridge and the only sound is the rasp of carrion crows across flat, churned empty fields. There seems nothing but tilled acreage and scraps of woodland between me and the low, blue bar of the Chilterns.

Possibly the most significant thing to occur to the village of Lavendon since the war-torn mid 1600s might well have occurred 80 years ago today when the Jarrow march broke for lunch here. One of the very few pictures of the march on the road was taken here as the huge group, banners aloft, rounded the bend. I come around it myself and instantly recognise the spot. Just a little further on, on the wall of the church, I found the only plaque anywhere outside Jarrow commemorating the Crusade, quite a handsome thing too, erected by local unionists of the Association of Scientific, Technical and Managerial Staff (ASTMS), Clive Jenkins's famous old white collar union, now swallowed up into the

Unite behemoth. Quite why this village rather than any other should mark an act of northern protest is not clear, but it was an excuse to pause and get a selfie, that new act of commemoration.

The miles between Lavendon and Bedford are a miserable, rough, ankle-turning trek in roadside ditches with merely the occasional pub or post office or bus shelter to break the monotony. Every pub is gearing up for Bonfire Night, 'fun nights' and 'barbecues' to commemorate a major attempted act of religious terrorism and regal assassination, its foiling by treachery and state forces and the subsequent torture and execution of those concerned. What could be more British? I revel for a while in the sheer delightfulness of Turvey with its water mill and abbey, where a district nurse waved to me as she got into her mini outside the Three Cranes. A Twitter correspondent by the name of Hazel told me that I would enter into Bedford along the Bromham Road. 'My late mother watched the marchers from outside her home Windmill Lodge on this main route into town. She never forgot the courage and dignity of so many proud impoverished and exhausted men. Her harrowing description remains with me as does the awful irony of relentless social injustice still perpetuated by shameless men in power. Good luck with your march in their memory.' I imagine that for the most part the marchers enjoyed their trek, its camaraderie and change from routine. But the days were long, tiring and hard, men got ill and they were concerned about their families left behind. Or maybe by now the harmonica band were just really getting on everyone's nerves.

Listening to the Radio 5 Live news on my headphones as I rearranged my pack in Bromham, I heard a new definition of hardship anyway. The always newsworthy Jose Mourinho blamed his team's recent poor form on him living in Manchester's five star Lowry Hotel, which he said was 'a disaster'. A sympathetic caller said he had lived in a hotel for two years and moaned that he had exhausted the restaurant menu in three weeks. I fought hard not to let glib, judgemental phrases like 'first world problem' swim into my head. We are living in the first world after all and unlikely to encounter any other kind of problem – cholera or drought, say – but I did think of the marchers bedding down on straw in drill halls and workhouses, and pressed on.

I was pleased when the road signs and the out-of-town hypermarkets began to promise an entry into Bedford. The marchers, with Ellen at their head again, were met by a Conservative Alderman and a local headteacher, H W Liddle – himself a man of the north east. He had persuaded the local Rotary Club to 'adopt' a blighted County Durham village called Eden Pit. Sixty schemes like this were set up across the prosperous south, voluntary acts of admirable civic kindness. Of course, there ought to have come state support or drastic reform, but I found myself wondering if we could count on such generosity and fellow feeling now in the land. Given the sour and bullying tone that had dominated discourse in 2016, I was far from sure.

I'd never been to Bedford before and knew little of what to expect. Inquiries about it would be met with a shrug or some vague reference to John Bunyan, pasties called Clangers or vans. Thirty-five minutes from London by commuter train, it's the 'capital' of one of England's smallest counties, but even a cursory half-hour of research on the village green in Turvey suggested there was more to Bedford than any of the above, and that the visit of the Jarrow men might be just a part of an old, strange parade of history.

'Somewhere in England'. It's an evocative phrase, pressed into service by many. It's an album by George Harrison and a song by Al Stewart, an online adventure game, a play about the US Air Force bases in Britain and a hairdressers in Farnham. But however imprecise and nebulous 'somewhere in England' might sound, make no mistake, it's Bedford. In 1942, the BBC evacuated from London and relocated here in great secrecy, and began broadcasting entertainment and propaganda from the Corn Exchange in the town. For the duration of the war, in these broadcasts, Bedford was referred to only as 'somewhere in England', a neat mixture of pragmatic secrecy and mythic symbolism.

Bedford housed the school where the Bletchley Park codebreakers were trained and the airfields from which Churchill wanted to 'set Europe aflame'. Bing Crosby, Bob Hope and Glenn Miller came here to make radio shows. The Czech government in exile ran its official radio station from here and, in perhaps the town's greatest act of wartime subterfuge and chutzpah (let's use the Yiddish word, it feels appropriate), a multinational team based in the surrounding villages of Toddington, Aspley Guise and Woburn Sands created radio programmes like 'Atlantiksender' and 'Gustav Siegfried Eins', designed to convince German civilians that they were listening to a genuine German station, playing the latest German pop hits and American jazz outlawed by the Nazis, as well as giving misleading and contradictory news and instructions. They did this so well that Goebbels raged about them and at least one German U-boat surrendered as a result of Bedfordshire's black propaganda.

There's information about all this in various places in the town such as the excellent Higgins Museum and at Holy Trinity Church, which has stood in the centre of Bedford for a thousand years. The bustle of the town goes on around, but encircled by trees and choirs of thrushes and blackbirds it's remarkably peaceful and a fine place to sip a decent coffee and watch Bedford go by. Dropping by a low green wooden hut adjacent to the churchyard to get my coffee, I was alerted to another strand of Bedford's rich story.

The name La Piazza Café needn't necessarily signify anything. Exotic, alluring, ersatz café names are commonplace in England, usually for a chain with its head office in Letchworth or Croydon or owned by a carbonated drinks giant out of Atlanta or Fort Lauderdale. But not La Piazza. Here, asking for your espresso interrupts a conversation between owner and a regular patron in quick fire Italian. A *grazie* will earn you a smiling *prego* or *ciao bella* and you can sip a strong, tiny cupful and nibble a biscotti while you take in the posters of AC Milan's great side of the late eighties – Van Basten, Gullit and Baresi – side by side with Bobby Moore lifting the World Cup. Libby Lionetti has been running the café here since that Milan heyday. He's here at six every morning for Bedford's cappuccino and macchiato devotees. He was born in Bedford's big maternity hospital but did two years' national service in Italy, and returned twice yearly to Foggia. He and his family – recently featured as typical Italians in a TV ad for Aldi pizzas – are part of a fascinating Bedford story that began soon after Jarrow's men has passed by here, coming as part of a new Europe rebuilding itself, and a story I would pick up later. First though, I wanted to check in with a son and daughter of Bedford, visionary non-conformists or troublesome zealots depending on your point of view, whose legacy lives on in buildings that face each other across staid and everyday Newnham Road.

Lynn, the lady who greets me at the door of the John Bunyan Museum, is small and twinkling and somewhere between 70 and 80 I'd say. She is wonderfully bright and nimble nonetheless, full of enthusiasm and energy and takes my arm only once at the top of a flight of steps that slowed me up too, especially after 20-or-so miles of Buckinghamshire asphalt. We've come upstairs to an exhibition about the life of Bedfordshire's most famous former resident, much-beloved of some like this lady, who keep alive his most famous book and his spiritual mission at the centre of a global branch of Protestantism. Some earlier Bedfordians weren't quite so keen on John and, perhaps with one eye on future tourism marketing opportunities, didn't run him out of town but, in 1660, threw him in Bedford nick for what turned out to be a very long if productive sojourn.

'I can show you around or you can wander at will,' chirps my guide and I think I know that the right answer is the former as she leads me gently around the upstairs room. She indicates an impressively severe mannequin of a stern puritan. 'The great man himself. He was over six foot, big for the time. Do you know his story? Born at Elstow just south of here, his father was a tinker, which meant he repaired pots and pans. John used to say he was born into poverty but he wasn't really as his father owned his own cottage and could send John to school to learn how to read and write.' There's a facsimile of John's cottage and home life. 'A fire, so you could stew but not roast and these plates—' and here a slightly pained expression crosses my guide's features at the inexactitude, '—well, these are pewter but to be honest John wouldn't have had these. You drop pewter, it bends. If it bends you have to have it repaired. John would have used wooden cups and plates I think. Drop wood, it bounces. Now these barrels ... salt fish, possibly corn ...'

We move slowly around in this delightful fashion and while there's not room here to tell it all, highlights included Bunyan's actual anvil. Like the windlass in Chesterfield, one gets a real charge from seeing an actual object – not a gilded treasure but a working tool – used physically by human hands, Bunyan's hands, four-and-a-half centuries ago. There's a violin that he made and a chair he sat on, much repaired. My guide points out on a map of Bedford the various local landmarks that made their way into *The Pilgrim's Progress*, all still there, though in various states of ruin and disrepair, such as Houghton House, 'the house beautiful' at the top of Ampthill ('the hill of difficulty') near the marshy part of Elstow that Bunyan turned into 'the slough of Despond'.

Joining the army at Newport Pagnell, Bunyan became a Roundhead. ('People are now fed up with the king, you see, so they chopped his head off' is Lynn's admirably brisk summary of the English Civil War.) 'John had been a bit of a lad in his youth, he swore, he played football on Sundays, he played tricks on neighbours. He was a thorough nuisance actually. But one time he was playing football on the green, he heard a voice saying, 'Are you going to carry on like this, young man? Are you going to go to heaven or go to hell?' and eventually, he thought he had nothing to lose so he started to go to St John's church. The rectory's still there, St John's Ambulance own it now, you can have a look in but you have to make arrangements.'

People come from all over the world to do just that. Bunyan went on to become one of the great voices of Protestantism with his sermons of 'plain piety' and force, which of course were fine while Oliver Cromwell was in charge but after the Restoration, the wilfully obtuse Puritan Bunyan was *persona non grata* in an England newly back in love with ritual and ceremony. Bunyan wrote the bulk of the great Christian allegory *The Pilgrim's Progress* whilst in prison for 12 years in Bedford.

'The gaol was at the bottom of Mill Street,' Lynn explains. 'The family were at the bottom of St Cuthbert's Street and his blind daughter Mary would walk through the town every day to take him food to the gaol. She smuggled out his books and pamphlets which a printer in London was willing to take a chance and print. An awful lot of pamphlets. I think, and I say this with great affection, John was the sort of person who had something to say about everything.' Bunyan stands thus revealed as a seventeenth century tabloid columnist forever manufacturing fake outrage and proto-Twitter storms about the irritating bendiness of pewter plates or *The Book of Common Prayer*.

The Pilgrim's Progress is still one of the world's most popular books in history with over 200 translations, making it second only to the Bible. Foreign editions are kept in a glass case here. At a quick glance I spotted Swedish, Afrikaans, Welsh, Indonesian, Hebrew, a Korean manga version and one in Dutch, the first language it was translated into. I'm not sure Bunyan would have been my sort of fellow with his dour piousness and cussed awkwardness, but finding out about him in such a charming way from gentle Bunyanite Lynn was lovely after the relentless drudgery of the road, with my own burden on my back, through underpasses of despond and flyovers of difficulty.

About a century and a half after Bunyan wrote his big seller, a woman called Joanna Southcott was working on her own, scorching religious text. This would prove much less popular, largely due to it being locked up in a sealed box for centuries and thus becoming the centre of one of the strangest of all the global cults. As I left the Bunyan Museum, the museum and headquarters of The Panacea Society was just across the pelican crossing in a comfortable suburban detached house on the other side of Newnham Road. Behind it, backing on to Albany Road, was the Garden of Eden. The actual Garden of Eden.

The lady on reception seems preoccupied in a jolly way. 'It's chaos here today I'm afraid! We're all getting ready for the Children's Book Festival tomorrow. But the museum's open. Do you know much about the Panacea Society? Would you like to watch a video? It's about eight minutes. It's quite useful.' In truth, neither an eight-minute video or the space here afforded can really do justice to the tale of Bedford's Panacea Society. But here's the bare bones of a bizarre British story.

The Panacea Society formed in Bedford in the 1920s. Mabel Barltrop and 12 female disciples were inspired by the teachings of aforementioned Devonian mystic Southcott who'd attracted some attention a century before with her apocalyptic visions and prediction of the coming of a new messiah, Shiloh. Barltrop adopted the name Octavia and believed, or at least announced herself to be the Shiloh messiah of Southcott's prophecies. The community in Bedford grew and for several decades, they lived and worshipped in relative seclusion whilst acquiring disciples across the rest of Britain and its colonies. But the Panacea Society – so named for their belief in the universal healing properties of tap water infused with Octavia's breath – gained national and international notoriety through their campaign for the Church of England to open the writings of Joanna Southcott.

Joanna had left a sealed wooden box of prophecies, usually known as Joanna Southcott's Box, with the instruction that it be opened only at a time of national crisis, and then only in the presence of the 24 bishops of the Anglican church. This became an obsession of the Bedford Panacea community, attracting international publicity and no little mirth. The Southcott Sealed Box became for a while a cherished and silly meme of English life, appearing in cartoons about Churchill and Baldwin, newspaper ads for shoes and batteries and an early Monty Python sketch.

In 1927, a psychic researcher named Harry Price claimed that he'd come into possession of the famous box and arranged for it to be opened in the presence of one reluctant Bishop. In it were a few irrelevant and random documents, a lottery ticket and a horse-pistol. Octavia and her Bedford community declared this box inauthentic and continued their campaign on billboards and national newspapers through the 1960s and '70s under the catchy, upbeat slogan, 'War, disease, crime and banditry, distress of nations and perplexity will increase until the Bishops open Joanna Southcott's box.'

But all the genteel daftness cast darker shadows. In America, rival Southcottian sects, claiming their own Shiloh messiahs, harboured sexually predatory male leaders, some of whom were jailed for sex with minors. At home, Octavia's Panacea Society, formed in the dramatic, divisive decade before the Jarrow march, were nearer to Mosley than Ellen Wilkinson, implacably right-wing and brazenly inegalitarian. Class distinctions were rigidly observed in the community. Lower-class believers were accommodated as unpaid servants with no status and little time off. Octavia believed that the monarchy, capitalist big business and empire were instruments of God and that trade unions and even the meek Labour Party were in league with Satan. In 1934 however, the society's confidence took something of a knock when Octavia died, never a good career move for an immortal daughter of God, and the community went into decline. By 1967, it numbered just 30 members and the last adherent, Ruth Klein, died in 2012. Small and marginal though it might have been, the Panacea Society was rich, owning £14million of properties in Bedford, which it was forced to sell when, no longer able to claim to be a religion, it became a charity. The museum is now run by this charitable trust and their remit is to sponsor academic research into the history and development of prophetic and millenarian movements and to support the work of groups concerned with poverty and health in the Bedford area.

The whole story is told with clarity and candour in the museum, which is genuinely fascinating. I tell the helpful trust member on reception that the Jarrow march would have passed down this very Bedford street when the Society was still a going concern, but just after Octavia's death. She laughs wryly. 'Probably just as well she wasn't around. She was very conservative in her social attitudes. She thought socialists were "reds under the bed". She did have a couple of Suffragette members but she wasn't very nice to them. She threw one of them out in fact. She wasn't very progressive at all.'

If you should find yourself in Bedford with some free time on a Thursday, Friday or Saturday between mid-February and the end of October, I can recommend the Panacea Society Museum as another peek into the old, slightly weird England. When you have taken in the wireless room where the members would listen communally in the evenings whilst knitting, or the chapel or the bedrooms and rehearsal room where the Bishops would prepare for the opening of the box (once they had seen sense and agreed), you can take a turn in the actual Garden of Eden of Book of Genesis fame, the handy Bedford location of which had been revealed to Octavia in one of her frequent communications with God. In a shady corner of the pleasant suburban lawn, you'll find an impressive tree the society believed to be 'Yggdrasil', the tree of life in Norse mythology, showing that the Panaceans were nothing if not eclectic in their outlook.

It was darkening as I left the Garden of Eden and even if there had been any forbidden apples on offer, I'd already decided in favour of a pizza and a big glass of red. In a town of 15,000 Italians (some say more), chianti and calzone are as prevalent on the menu as the much vaunted yet untasted Clanger. Why is this Bedfordshire town full of Marios and Marias, Fabios and Francescas, why as many posters for Fiorentina and Napoli than Luton or Leicester? Why is almost a fifth of Bedford's population Italian or of Italian descent? There's a short, unromantic answer: bricks.

After the war, Bedford's Marston Valley Brick Company was desperately short of the labour needed for the huge reconstruction boom and drive. A few thousand miles way, in southern Italy, they were desperate to put the ignominy of Mussolini's era behind them – and more to the point, they were shockingly poor. Unemployment was far worse than in the prosperous north, and many villagers, and even the post-war Italian government, began to see emigration as the best solution. In 1951, the Marston Valley Brick Company established an office in Naples, sending two employees to recruit 250 men. This was just the beginning. Between 1951 and 1960 over 7,500 Italians were signed up for the scheme. Each man who volunteered from the *Mezzogiorno* to work in Bedford was given a medical examination, a paid passage to England and a bed. They were lodged communally in a converted prisoner-of-war camp. The English weather and food and sheer homesickness meant that over 60 per cent returned within four years. But many stayed. They worked their contracts, bought their own houses and paid their families' passage to come and join them. By 1958 around 85 per cent of new arrivals in Bedford were married Italian women joining their husbands. An Italian/Cumbrian friend of mine Guilliano remembers visiting Bedford in the 1960s: 'It was amazing, full of delis and trattorias, like a little Italian provincial town.'

Again, social media was proving invaluable in uncovering the story of Bedford's Italians. Tweets chirruped into my devices from native or exiled Bedfordians. Tony Malone told me that at one point Bedford had its own Italian consulate. James Coyne recommended Club Prima Generazione and Amalfi cakes, adding 'virtually everyone in Bedford has one Italian relative or another'. But as I was on Newnham Street and its 6 o'clock opening time was fast approaching, I was noting hungrily the many mentions of Pizza Santaniello, 'a proper Italian family pizzeria'. In fact, I could see it. Its bright red frontage spilling enticing light on to the pavement and its white painted slogan 'Bedford's Number One Pizzeria' had a bold machismo that was irresistible. *Andiamo!*

'My parents came after the war, early 1950s,' says Antonio, whirling a disc of pizza base in his outstretched fingers. 'A four-year contract and then they were given the choice to stay or go. And we stayed. Five couples in one house, that's how close the communities were. Mostly from southern Italy – Campagna, Foggia, Sardinia.' Antonio is now head chef at what was Bedford's first pizzeria, opened by Fiorangelo and Ida Santaniello and now run by their son Geraldo, busy behind the bar as I make a nuisance of myself by the hot maw of the stone baking oven. 'There were three queues for the Italian men, my dad would say, one for Brazil, one for Venezuela and one for Bedford. We ended up here, at the brick works in Stewartby.' Geraldo's son, the younger Fiorangelo, is now the third generation to be here offering 'the best hand stretched pizzas outside of Naples, as you'll soon find out' he says as he passes by with several carafes of wine.

It's a few minutes after opening time but I still only just manage to squeeze into a corner table. It's mainly families on half term, but there are a few dining adults like me, an Indian businessman boasting to a pretty younger girl, his secretary maybe, about his friends in St Petersburg and Riga; a quartet of Scottish women swapping stories very entertainingly about their disastrous honeymoons; a white-haired man with a hefty paperback into his second carafe. It is busy, loud and hot, and by now full of delicious pizza and house red, I decide to make way for one or two of the potential diners queuing by the door, presumably being driven nearly insane by the aroma of sizzling garlic and the popping of another cork. I go to say goodbye to Antonio. He's shovelling another two pizzas into the oven's fiery recess and, pushing back his bandana, drags a forearm across his dripping brow. '*Ciao*, I hope you enjoyed it my friend … where are you from then?' I tell him I'm from the north and have been on the road for two-and-a-half weeks on the trail of the Jarrow march. Antonio hasn't heard of it, but when I tell him the story and how they came to Bedford 80 years ago tonight he cocks his head and says, 'Like my dad then, like Geraldo's parents. They just wanted work. They were desperate. They made sacrifices. Working people, you see, same all over the world. They move and they make new homes. There's still lots of Italy here. There's an Italian church that the community built. There are community centres. There's a few Italian bars …'

Really? How would they feel about a stray Lancastrian Italophile dropping by?

'Try them!' he laughs. 'Club Italia, up on Alexander Road by the railway station, bit hard to find down a back street, but if you fancy a late grappa …'

I'd been wondering how to spend the evening and had narrowed it down to the open mike music night at the Standard or the monthly meeting of Bedford Electronic Organ Club (est. 1972). Both now paled before the prospect of Club Italia. *Ciao ciao* Pizza Santaniello! *Allora*, Club Italia.

STAGE NINETEEN
BEDFORD TO LUTON

28 October, 19 miles

On a fine warm morning, or a still balmy night, should you take your *amante* or *tesoro* for a *passeggiata* down the riverside banks of the stately Great Ouse, where the ducks and rowers glide by and the lamplight ripples; you will surely find Bedford as lovely as Bath if perhaps not *Venezia*. The concrete enclave of poundshops and snack bars around the bus station, however: not so much. Although, that said, Venice's bus station is pretty grim, and Bedford's is at least brand spanking new, all curved glass and burnished chrome – 'a travel point the borough can be proud of!' – including real-time display screens, a travel centre and a new departure hub. 'A major regeneration project which has transformed the local area,' is how the leaflet trills it, and I have no reason to cavil.

It's 9am, and I'm digging out the Nurofen again at a café in Bedford's Bus Station over a mug of hot brown builder's tea. I have the address of a shop where I can find a proper Bedfordshire Clanger, and I will, as soon as my head stops banging and my vision clears. I took Antonio's advice and headed off to find Club Italia. I went across town, up Midland Road by the railway station, Bedford's own 'Via Roma', and into Alexander Road. Where Club Italia is tucked away is a parade of slightly seedy looking international drinking dens; here a Polish one, there an African, there Turkish. Across a darkened car park I glimpse an

Italian flag and, in a pool of light, two silhouetted figures lit by the orange tips of their cigarettes. I had come this far, I had expert local knowledge and I was emboldened by several glasses of slightly rough Chianti. I took my chance.

'Who you looking for mate? You wanna drink?' said one of the men. He wore a paint-spattered overall that was definitely not one of either Signor Armani, Dolce or Gabbana, and he pushed open a nondescript hardboard door to reveal a scene of frenetic drilling, hammering and sawing. The bar was open for business though and the barman beckoned so I took my place alongside a couple of other drinkers, cradling small grappas and bottles of Nastro Azzurro. 'We're having some work done as you can see,' said the barman, a doughty fellow in his late fifties with glasses and a salt and pepper moustache, 'but if you don't mind that ...' Having come this far, and feeling more foolish were I to leave, I ordered both a beer and a grappa to be on the safe side and took my place at the bar.

The welcome in Club Italia was more cautious and cagey than in Pizza Santaniello and understandably so. I doubt they get many strange northerners dropping by even if 20 days of road walking have given him a distinctly walnut complexion. Club Italia clearly had a community function but that was presumably during daytime and weekends. On a dark Monday evening, this was a place for men to drink and swap stories of the old days, play scopa and drink grappa under posters and murals of the great Italian World Cup teams and their maestros, Gianni Rivera, Luigi Riva, Paolo Rossi. It was a place to crowd round the TV on big football nights draped in the tricolore and sing on the Azzurri, shouting, '*Dai! Ma stai scherzando arbitro! Mandalo a casa!*' or 'Come on, you're having a laugh, ref, send him off!'

As we drank, we shared our stories. I told them of Jarrow and my walk in those men's footsteps. They told me of their fathers and grandfathers coming to Bedford from much further away in the ravaged post-war world. This time though, the recollections seemed less sunny and celebratory than they had in the pizzeria. 'My brother was born in 1953 and I was born in 1958 and my parents had been here a few years then and they were amongst the first ones to come. After your four years in the brickworks hostel, well, if you were good, you were allowed to stay. If not you were on the boat back. You were on probation and if you were a good worker, you were OK, but if not they could send you back at any time. They were like slaves really.'

'Yep, they were slaves,' one of the young workmen, job done and settling back with a beer, chips in. 'They were sold by Italy for 400 quid. The Italian government was paid 400 pounds for each person they exported. My dad turned 18 on the boat and because he didn't have his papers, he thought he'd be sent back. They detained him for a while. Britain was desperate for labourers though, and they were desperate for work.'

'It was exactly like the Poles and the Romanians now,' says the barman with an equivocal shrug. 'They're poor. Italy was poor. The brickworks may have been hard work but it wasn't hard compared to their lives back there. No food, no money, no decent housing, no warmth, no toilets. Italy was bad. The husbands came, the wives followed. They all came with the intention of working hard, making their money and going back. It doesn't happen, does it? You have kids. There's a good 20,000 Italians here now I reckon. Most of them have got properties over there that they built that have just gone to waste. They just stayed here.'

'Bedford has this effect on you. I came for a weekend ten years ago and I'm still here,' says a well-spoken man at the bar with a cravat and ponytail. Another voice, a young bloke in a baseball cap and tracksuit, joins in. 'My granddad was a prisoner of war, they captured him in Africa, Tripoli. Then they sent him to Yorkshire working on farms for a couple of years. After the war was all done and dusted, they let him go. He came down and joined all the Italians in Bedford.'

'Don't get me wrong,' says the barman, sliding another Nardini across the counter to me, or possibly a Fernet Branca. 'They weren't resentful. They were grateful. You and I couldn't have stuck it. We couldn't just move to another country 'cos we've got everything here. But it's like these Africans. They have nothing. Wherever they go, they're grateful even if you treat them like shit. We can't share these people's perspectives.' An old boy gets up from his card game to leave, the barman breaks off to embrace him and there follows a quickfire exchange in Italian with the odd English word standing out as if by highlighter pen: 'cooker', 'worktop', 'microwave'.

After these discussions and more like them and more grappa and Nastro Azzurro, the evening unravelled somewhat. More people, all men, came and went and gathered at the bar. 'People come here for a drink late. Not just Italians. Albanians, Rumanians, Poles ...' Brexit was discussed and there was no consensus. The well-spoken man turned out to be the grandson of an infamous Scottish writer. He had been 'in the clothing game and a GP in another life', and now he talked of his mental health problems and wondered if I could help him get some help from social services. The stocky leather-jacketed man on my left turns out to be from Albania. Tirana, I guess?

'No.'

Shkodër? I guess again. I know the names of several Albanian cities and have decided as a point of honour that this will not beat me.

'No,' replies Rudi again.

Hmm. 'Durrës?'

'Durrës! You know Durrës! Half an hour south of there!'

I've never been to Durrës, or Albania, but it was an obsession of mine during the crazed, insular, appalling regime of Enver Hoxha when it was Europe's very own North Korea. I buy him a grappa and we talk. 'Fifty years of communism my country had under a man called Enver Hoxha. What? You know of him? How?'

It's a long story, to be honest, and you'll think I'm weird.

'Well, we are small country and Enver Hoxha made it even smaller. You could say nothing. You could be arrested at school. If you did not agree with Hoxha, or you upset him, you were jailed for life … if you were lucky. You could be shot in the head. You could be hung in front of your family. I was very young. But people tell the stories. We change in 1990. We change for better. But I still come here. I came for better life. I get married. But then I get divorced, and she make a hard life for me. Now my life is over. I haven't seen my son for three years. He is 13 now. Game over. Everyone is married but not me. It is very sad.'

Rudi went on like this for some time, darker and sadder with every *slivovitz*. My head was spinning by now but even through the haze of grappa, I knew that this hard-working man was lonely; lonely enough to talk to a complete stranger for a long time while all around noisy card games were played and worktops were ordered. We had talked all night about migrants and borders but loneliness and sadness are countries without borders. My obsession with Albania's craziness and otherness now seemed very callow, even shameful.

At different times in our history, we have been very happy to allow the free movement of people to our shores when we have needed them, be it German mining engineers to the Lake District of the Elizabethan era, Nigerian cleaners to our midnight office blocks or Polish receptionists to the Malmaisons of our revitalised cities. Brexit and the reasons behind the seismic vote of the summer had cropped up in conversation but not as I thought it would, with entrenched views and clichés. Over the evening, 'somewhere in England' had proved itself the perfect description of this English town. It was both typical and utterly unique, full of the same things that we find across the modern country, the ubiquitous, the homogenous, the mass produced and, then again, full of weird secrets and stories, heroism, mystery, madness. 'Somewhere in England' was the perfect description, both prosaic and enigmatic, and echoing around my head, along with the wine and grappa, as I crossed the wide lamplit river, through reception and the bar with its change-jingling, late night business drinkers and the lift up to bed.

Before they left for Luton, the marchers went to look at Bedford's fine new brickworks at Stewartby. This was the sort of new industry their own deprived town badly needed and surely they must have looked at it with envy. They couldn't have known, however (though a few of the more gloomy might have feared it) that within three years the world would be at war, and the brickworks of Bedford would then need legions of vanquished men from the Mediterranean to help rebuild England. Bedford had been good to the marchers during their stay. The local Rotary Club and Christian charity Toc H had given them cigarettes and tobacco and put on a night's free entertainment at the town hall. So warm had been Bedford's hospitality that the Conservative mayor said that he had been accused of being 'a convert to Labour, a rigid socialist and even a communist'.

At the bus station I picked up an intriguing magazine. It was called *This England* and there was something soothing about its lovely cover of a warm russet sunset in an English wood. Being unashamedly of Attlee's patriotic leftist strain, I can be something of a sucker for this kind of thing and as the magazine seemed to consist of little else except nostalgia and anniversaries, I felt sure the autumn number would have some mention of the Jarrow march. But having scoured the magazine from cover to cover, I could find nothing – though I did find a gloating editorial about leaving the European Union, a eulogy to the late TV presenter and extreme right-winger Norris McWhirter and a fun piece condoning violence against 'atheist teachers with links to the Civil Liberties Association'. Like the Panacea Society, there was a cold meanness underneath the moist-eyed middle England niceties and a kind of ignorance too; the kind that uses Battle of Britain imagery to celebrate Brexit, forgetting that we won that with heroic help from Czech and Polish pilots; or presumes that

Vaughan Williams's music embodies their world view when the socialistic, knighthood-refusing giant of English music would have loathed them. *This England* would have probably not had much time for the Jarrow marchers and may even have thought the mayor of Bedford was a communist, embodying that particular kind of English sense of fair play, justice and tolerance that wants Rudi the Albanian builder to go home but they to be allowed to retire to Magaluf. Quite how its expatriate readership would fare in the next few years as we pulled up the drawbridge to Europe would be diverting to say the least.

I'd woken that morning with a new earworm, a song from The Clash's *Sandinista!* album called 'Something About England'. A sort of potted radical history seen through the eyes of an ageing tramp who missed out on the First World War but 'not the sorrow afterwards'. It goes, 'They say it would be wine and roses/ If England were for Englishmen again'. (An ideal strapline for *This England* magazine, I'd have thought.) I liked 'Something About England' far more than *This England*, but though The Clash meant well, they too got Jarrow wrong describing the Jarrow marchers as 'hunger strikers'. The Jarrow men weren't on hunger strike; in fact they hadn't eaten so well in years. But no matter. It was a good song to keep time to as I left town.

As I did, finally I found a Bedfordshire 'Clanger', the local pastry delicacy with savoury filling at one end and sweet at the other, thus providing both dinner and dessert for the hungry agricultural worker of yesteryear. These ones came recommended by Jamie Oliver no less and the proprietor's manner suggested I was highly honoured to be served with one. (I was once treated with similar guardedness buying 'rowies' in a back street in Aberdeen. I must bring out the worst in regional bakers.) Anyway, it was horrible. I can't remember which of the fashionable filling combos in this new artisan version I plumped for; pulled pork and banoffee must have been there and salted caramel and ricotta too I imagine. But in any event, I couldn't discern which end was which as both seemed filled with wallpaper paste mixed with Quaker Oats. As I was decanting it into a bin, the delicate, troubled writer's grandson from last night passed by with a cheery wave and a curious look as I hurriedly disappeared into the transport point/departure hub that Bedford can be proud of.

I was going to take a bus for some of the way to Luton just to buy myself a little time as I had another appointment to make, again thanks to the social media. So far I had been lucky with Twitter; only two trolls and they had been mildly useful, and lots of help, encouragements and offers to meet or walk with me. I'd been touched by many of these but had accepted few in order that I could stay flexible and agile, able to change my mind or act on a whim. But today's from Rachel Hopkins was irresistible.

'A Friday in the Brickies (by Luton Station) with a bunch of left-wing types?! A must surely?!'

I had to agree and so I took the 81 out of Bedford via Progress Way and through Elstow, Bunyan's birthplace and location of the Slough of Despond. On we went via Bunyans Mead to the 'no cold-calling zone' of Wilstead and, just after Houghton Conquest (surely the chiselled RAF hero of the wartime love story *Wings Over Waterlily Lane*) I jumped off in order to walk the A6 for a while.

The A6 café, shuttered and quiet, doesn't seem to have served a hot sausage bap or milky coffee in a good few years. Before motorway service stations and catering vans, these were the much-loved fuelling stations that broke journeys and marked the miles. I wondered if some incarnation of the A6 café had been here when the march passed by. It was just here that a contingent of Mosley's Fascists asked to join the march and were given short shrift by the men, although this should be balanced against the fact that the day before marcher Fred Harris had been rather furtively sent home for expressing 'communistic' beliefs, proving that a certain forelock tugging fear of giving offence still informed the march organisers, whatever their personal beliefs.

Having sent the Blackshirts packing, the oldest marcher, 62-year-old George Smith told the reporters, 'I'm going strong and the rest of the march is going to be a cakewalk.' As I pounded the noisy, dirty fringes of the A6, I envied George's confidence.

From time to time, my path had merged and flirted with this famous old English arterial road, one of the great north–south highways of England. But after Bedford, it generally veers and swerves left and west, thundering up through the Midlands and my patch of the industrial north west headed for Carlisle. It would make a good long walking project one day, I thought, if not a scenic one, as I negotiated the swirling confusion of the Barton-le-Clay bypass fork, a kind of whirlpool as I neared the source of this mighty, dirty river of tarmac: Luton.

Luton did not offer the marchers a grand civic welcome. This was not through any coldness or antipathy, but because the new town hall was only being opened that night by the Duke of Kent. The Duke may well have known what few ordinary Lutonians or Jarrovians did; namely that that afternoon Wallis Simpson had been granted a decree nisi at Norwich assizes and the looming constitutional stormclouds gathered ever nearer. Nothing dampened the enthusiasm of Luton towards the aristocracy that day though. Children's choirs sang, fireworks roared through the dusk, flags were unfurled and bunting draped. The crowds welcomed the Duke warmly and then many stayed in the streets to cheer the marchers into town as well in a very British display of camaraderie.

I should make clear here though that the reason Luton needed a new town hall was that the townsfolk had burned the other one down in 1919 in a quite astonishing outpouring of rage. *Luton Today*, the local newspaper website, has footage of the conflagration under the glorious headline, 'Luton Town Hall burnt down during Peace Day riots', a sentence as cherishable as the famous line from *Doctor Strangelove*, 'Gentlemen, you can't fight in here! This is the war room!' The full story is worth recounting, shedding light as it does on how England's dissenting nature has not only been shown in supplicant crusades. Sometimes we go cap in hand to our superiors. Sometimes we burn down the town hall and try to kill the mayor.

The Peace Treaty concluding the Great War was finally signed in June 1919 and Luton Town Council planned various civic celebrations followed by a sumptuous 'mayor's banquet'. This was to be paid for from the civic purse but invitations were strictly limited to the mayor, councillors and close friends, none of whom had seen active service. No ex-soldiers, sailors or airmen were included in the lavish council celebrations. This prompted various veterans groups and their supporters to boycott the council's celebrations and hold their own event in a local park. The council refused them permission, and so the ex-servicemen's groups decided to make their anger known.

At first, the protest was quiet and controlled. Maimed and disabled ex-servicemen lined the procession route under a banner that read, 'Don't pity us, give us work'. When the officials processed by unmoved, they were followed by the irate ex-servicemen. On arrival at the town hall, the soldiers barracked the mayor's platitudinous oratory and when he tried to patronise them, the mood turned really ugly. The 20,000-strong crowd suddenly surged forwards, sending the mayor scurrying into the bowels of the town hall as they tore down the doors. Once inside, the crowd wreaked havoc, hurling the contents of the town hall through the windows onto the street and trying to get at the mayor and his party who were barricaded into his parlour. Their lives were probably saved by the arrival of a contingent of police. The townspeople then turned their anger on them and fought a pitched battle with policemen in the street. By now, the rioting and looting had taken on something of carnival atmosphere and 20,000 people gathered at the town hall (with petrol stolen from Hall's garage) and razed it to the ground singing 'We'll Keep the Home Fires Burning Here'. The mayor was spirited away and the police turned savagely on the crowd, beating women and children with sticks. Four days and nights of rioting followed before order was restored leaving the town centre in ruins and looking like a war zone.

The Bricklayers Arms was nothing like this lively, but it was packed and noisy even for a late Friday afternoon. Some kind of speech was being made, and pictures of a smiling man adorned the pub walls. It was evidently some kind of wake and the young woman who pushed her way through the throng to appear at my elbow, explained more. She was crying a little as she indicated another picture of the man, this time above a stool at the end of the bar. 'My friend Steve. That was his seat. A lot of these people here have come to pay respects to him because of his work and his art. But he was just my mate Steve. I met him five years ago when I first started coming in here. He was just your classic decent bloke.'

Steve Dillon, a Lutonian born and bred, was one of the biggest British names in the field of comic book art. He began his professional career at the age of 16 on Marvel's *Hulk Weekly* before moving on to *Nick Fury, Warrior, Doctor Who* and *2000AD*. He co-founded the influential *Deadline* magazine in 1988 which brought comics to the attention of many an indie kid thanks to its pop cultural savvy and hip *NME*-style credentials. In recent years, he had invented the series *Preacher* which had transferred successfully to TV and was in New York doing some work for a comics charity when he died suddenly from a ruptured appendix. 'He was cremated today at 10.30 in New York, which is why we all came here at 3.30 our time to raise a glass to him.' The pub is full of colleagues, friends and fans, and the range of t-shirts, adornments, hair styles and piercings is impressive.

I might have felt something of an interloper into other people's grief but Rachel, who'd been following my progress on Twitter, had wanted us to meet up anyway. She's a Labour councillor, her dad is Luton's Labour MP – one of only two in Bedfordshire – and she had a Jarrow tale for me. 'As an idealistic 14-year-old, I went down to the drill hall in 1986 when a group of unemployed marchers were passing through Luton recreating the march and I made them their breakfast. The week after, we were visiting my granddad and I told him this proudly and he smiled and said, "Well, guess what, I did the very same thing for the original marchers when they passed though Leicester".

I'm liking 'The Brickies' very much. It's an old-school boozer in Luton's 'High Town', a favourite with football fans, real ale drinkers and lefties alike. Rachel's boyfriend, a cheery soul and I think a little less political than her, nudges me and says, 'All the politburo are in here,' with a grin. I fall into a conversation about progressive rock with a genial man in a well-filled t-shirt featuring the cover of Emerson, Lake and Palmer's *Tarkus* – the concept album about the war between the robot scorpion and the giant mechanised armadillo. I feel I am amongst friends.

Another local councillor, Mark, offers the thought that, 'Luton is essentially a northern industrial town in the south of England'. Politically it has never been as conservative as the rest of the home counties, although it did return Tory MPs at the high imperial phase of Thatcherism. Drawn to work in the town's Vauxhall car factories, it has a Kashmiri population of 40,000, a quarter of its population, and is sometimes cited as officially 'hyperdiverse', i.e. more than 50 per cent of its population are black or minority ethnic, although definitions of the term seem to differ. Rachel checks her phone. 'There's a reception for the Kashmiri consul tonight and my dad's going to be there. He says he'll pop in here and have a beer if you can hang around for a while.' It would be rude not to, I say, as the chap in the *Tarkus* t-shirt goes to get me another pint of Centurion.

Not long after, I am in the quieter back bar with the only man in the pub wearing a suit. Rachel's dad Kelvin has been the Labour MP for Luton since 1997. 'There were 22 of us from the region then but we've declined ever since ... till now. There were a lot more socialists then. That was exceptional but at each election since then we've been cut back, we nearly only had me. The Margaret Moran scandal cost us lots of votes.' (The former MP for Luton South was convicted of fraud in 2012. Moran's claims for expenses 2004–05 were £73,198 higher than Kelvin's.) 'But we go on. Jeremy's been elected leader by the membership not by Parliament, thousands of people are joining the party, tens if not hundreds of thousands left because of New Labour. But that's all history now. I'm in a progressive mood and I think there's a real chance we can have a progressive Labour government next time round.'

I'm forced to say that I don't agree, even though I find Kelvin's positivity and optimism laudable. I also don't share Kelvin's view – a widespread one admittedly – that Blair was an enemy of the people and his leadership a toxic one. The Iraq War was a dire misadventure but making mistakes in war situations is not, I suggest, a problem Jeremy Corbyn will ever have. Didn't Kelvin concede that the Blair administration did a lot of good – like Sure Start schemes and the minimum wage – and that 1997 seemed for a while to mark the rise of the forces of good? He sighs.

'I have to say I didn't believe that myself. I felt that the people wanted a Labour government and wanted progressive change but they didn't get that. What they got was another version of Conservatism. Blair and Mandelson were free marketeers who wanted to privatise and carry on with the neo-liberal revolution. I know many people welcomed it. My wife in fact said, "Isn't it wonderful, now we can do all the socialist things we've always wanted," and I said, "No dear it won't happen." The day I was elected, at the count just down the road, people kept asking me, "Why are you looking so sombre and reserved?" And I said, "Well, I'm very happy to be in Parliament, thanks to all these wonderful people and their votes but I'm contemplating the struggles to come against the forces of darkness in our party," and now people know what I was talking about.'

Kelvin's optimism for Jeremy Corbyn's new left-wing agenda was tempered by one thing. 'The boundary changes are going to ruin us. We'll lose 20–25 seats before you even talk about swings. But Scotland's the real problem. We have to win back Scotland to stand any chance of a majority government. You would hope that the Scottish Nationalists wouldn't want to sustain a Tory government. But we shall see. That's four years away.' (It wasn't.)

Kelvin's clearly a man of principle but I put it to him that a jolt of pragmatism is also needed on the left. Competency and power is a precursor of change, and the metropolitan left has lost touch with its working-class base, just as it did in 1936. Marches and rallies are good for the soul, but they change nothing. Ask the Jarrow marchers. 'But Jarrow resonates still,' counters Kelvin. 'It may not have achieved anything directly back then but it has echoes and meaning. Sometimes even a defeat can inspire; the miners' strike, the general strike, the split in 1931 when we were sold down the river by Ramsay MacDonald who joined the Tories. All those things remind us that we have to fight. Things do change. Take South Africa; I was a campaigner in my youth and we often thought that nothing could ever really be done. But eventually things change although there will always be forces of darkness and conservatism in the world.'

He give me a wry smile. 'When I was a student I worked in Potters Bar, 1962 it would have been. At the works there was an old man who said, "When those Jarrow marchers came past our town, I went out and jeered at them, the communist bastards." I could never believe that, that a working-class man could do that.' Britain's first troll, maybe, I suggest and remember the statistic that I used to pass on to my sociology students back in Skelmersdale. A third of the working class routinely vote Conservative. Without those working-class Tories, there would never be Tory governments. It is not a peculiarly British condition or even delusion either. John Steinbeck once said, 'Socialism never took root in America because the poor see themselves not as an exploited proletariat, but as temporarily embarrassed millionaires.'

I take my leave amongst much kissing, handshaking and laughter. I liked Luton's rugged individualism, fierce sense of self and ornery distinctiveness. I liked the Brickies and its draught Centurion. Rachel shows me to the door and I thank her, her dad and her friends for a lovely afternoon. I ask her if she'd like to follow in her dad's footsteps and become an MP. She smiles coyly. 'Maybe, who knows? It'd be nice to do something for people, ordinary people,' she says and there's another hug or two and then I have to be on my way, onward to St Albans.

'We have to look after our own Stuart,' she calls to me as I head purposefully up the darkening street.

'Oh and by the way, Stuart, you're going the wrong way. St Albans is that way,' she points behind her and, laughing, disappears into the happy cauldron of warm companionship that is the Brickies.

STAGE TWENTY

LUTON TO ST ALBANS

29 October, 10 miles

As autumn hardens into winter, and the dark nights close in, so the mother of Parliaments finally has to go back after the mother of all summer holidays, now as in 1936. On the morning that the marchers left Luton for St Albans, Ellen Wilkinson headed for the Commons and the reconvening of Parliament after the recess. When she got there, she asked Prime Minister Baldwin how many resolutions and messages he had received about the Jarrow march. Quite a few, he grudgingly acknowledged, but he was still refusing to receive them when they reached London. Historian Dominic Sandbrook has said of Baldwin that his 'emollient and media-friendly' manner make him in some ways the first modern prime minister. Possibly so, but surely his pointed refusal to meet the men was a PR disaster that a contemporary spin doctor would have advised against, however distasteful he might have found it.

Over the last week or so of trekking, I had decided that I should like to try and succeed where the Jarrow men had failed and be met and taken to the Commons, if not by the Prime Minister herself, Theresa May (elevated unelected after David Cameron's resignation in the wake of his Brexit humiliation), Jeremy Corbyn, Tim Farron or whoever was UKIP leader on the day I arrived, then at least by an MP. I tweeted to this effect asking if any Member of Parliament would care to meet me.

Almost immediately I had received a charming reply from a new MP Tracy Brabin saying that she'd be delighted to meet me when I arrived on 31 October, and to get in touch when I was approaching Marble Arch.

When I mentioned this in the pub in Luton, Rachel, Kelvin and the councillors had been impressed, delighted and a little moved I thought. 'That's fantastic. Do you know her from the media?' No, not at all, I replied a little confused. 'She's an actress,' laughed Rachel. 'Didn't you know? She was in *Coronation Street*. She's just become an MP because, well, it felt right. It was a brilliant, amazing thing for her to …'

'Sorry?' I say. Maybe it was the three pints of Centurion but I genuinely wasn't following this.

Rachel looked closely at me. 'You haven't realised, have you? Tracy was a friend of Jo Cox. Tracy Brabin is the new MP for Batley and Spen.'

Batley and Spen is a political constituency in West Yorkshire created in 1983 and unremarkable until the summer of 2016 when a far-right extremist killed its MP, Jo Cox, outside her office. Thomas Mair, 52, stabbed and shot Jo, a Batley girl and the mother of two young children, whilst yelling 'Britain First'. There was no doubt what Mair's motivation was, nor his affiliations to white supremacist and neo-Nazi groups, or his fascist sympathies, but the majority of the British press chose to ignore these, describing him as a lone lunatic. This was an approach in sharp contrast to these papers' treatment of murders by Asians and Muslims, who were uniformly presented as radical Islamists. No newspaper called it an act of fascist or extreme right terrorism, which it quite plainly was; one presumably perpetrated in twisted response to Jo's support for the Remain side in the EU referendum. While the immediate reaction was dismal, there was worse to come from spokesmen of the far right. Nigel Farage attacked Jo's widower in a radio interview saying, 'Well, of course, he would know more about extremists than me, Mr Cox …'

Others of a similar cast of mind soon joined in. 'When are we allowed to say that Brendan Cox is a total arse?' tweeted *Spectator* and Breitbart fulminator James Delingpole. UKIP bankroller Arron Banks contributed, 'I'm sorry about his wife but he chose to massively politicise it. Who does that?' Even in the enormously debased political discourse of 2016, these remarks represented a new low. It took either monumental stupidity or sheer wickedness to not acknowledge that the murder of a Member of Parliament by a neo Nazi shouting 'Britain first' seemed to have quite a political dimension already. So it was with a mixture of anger and pride that I picked up the pace as I left Luton. Whatever happened in the next few days, I would be there to meet Tracy at the Houses of Parliament on 31 October.

That Farage, Delingpole and Banks's remarks were contemptible was beyond doubt. But beyond that given, the situation in Batley and Spen was complex, awkward and revealed much about the chaotic and febrile state of our political culture in 2016. At Jo's memorial service in London, husband Brendan Cox's words were broadcast live back to Batley.

> Across the world we're seeing forces of division playing on people's worst fears, rather than their best instincts, trying to divide our communities, to exploit insecurities, and emphasise not what unites us but what divides us. Jo's killing was political, it was an act of terror designed to advance an agenda of hatred towards others. What a beautiful irony it is that an act designed to advance hatred has instead generated such an outpouring of love. Jo lived for her beliefs, and on Thursday she died for them, and for the rest of our lives we will fight for them in her name.

In a brilliant piece in the *New Yorker* though, British writer Ed Caesar went to Batley to gauge the response. Many wept in the streets at the mention of Jo's name, but in the main room of the Conservative Club,

Two members, named Darren and Stuart (they declined to offer their surnames), sat at the bar discussing how they had both voted Leave. Darren knew Jo Cox from school and said she was 'a lovely lass'. But both men spoke repeatedly about how they had been let down by politicians, particularly on the issue of immigration. Their complaint did not just concern the recent migrants from the E.U. but the older Muslim residents of Batley. Darren put his wish to leave the E.U. partly down to 'the change in the town and the feeling in the town. There are certain people who don't integrate.' Stuart said that, 'it's a sad thing what happened last week,' but added, 'we just want our country back.'

Both drinkers thought that the 'Jo Cox thing' would have some influence on the result. But both thought, unlike the professional pollsters and commentators, that Batley's region of Kirklees would vote to leave the EU. They were right, professional informed opinion was wrong, and as I walked along old Luton's streets of its famous blue Victorian brick – now highly desirable for the townhouses of Hampstead and St John's Wood – the fallout from that detonation was still settling gently on Britain, a cloud of unknowing that obscured the familiar and made the way ahead difficult to see.

The Jarrow marchers and I were now crossing over in the heart of the home counties, from one England to the next. The stretch between Luton and St Albans is only ten miles but it feels more, at least culturally, as the polyglot urban sprawl of a railway and car town falls away and a different England comes into view; older, leafier, smarter, richer. My drinking mate in the *Tarkus* t-shirt had said that most people thought Luton was 'a hellhole', which was not strictly true and certainly not the impression I had taken away. But no one would ever say it of St Albans, rightly or wrongly. We are not quite in Betjeman's Metroland yet, but we are moving into the ample bosom of the affluent commuter belt: golf courses, tankards, roses, stripped-pine gastropubs and garden offices.

Betjeman wrote some of his defining verses in the mid-1930s often rooted in very English locales, as in 'Death in Leamington', 'Distant View of a Provincial Town' and 'Slough'. The latter shows something of how untouched and untroubled by hardship some lives were. Drafted while the marchers were on the road, it says much of Betjeman's privilege and pursed lip that while the Jarrow Crusade held the attention of most, bringing the plight of workless men and their towns to the nation's conscience, Betjeman's major poem of the period was an etiolated sneer at one town's drab aesthetic and lack of pastoral charm. 'Come friendly bombs and fall on Slough, it isn't fit for humans now,' he pleaded; not because of slums, hunger or poor sanitation, but because he didn't like the vulgarity of its Tudor houses, sports cars and hairdos. It is snobbery – much anthologised snobbery, but snobbery none the less. If any town deserved friendly bombs to fall on it because it wasn't fit for humans, it was Jarrow, not Slough.

Fortunately, Betjeman in this unappealing register was far from being the typical voice of the most exciting decade of the twentieth century for British poetry. Those voices belonged to writers who were altogether tougher, more colloquial, more engaged. 'Even before they were quite over, the thirties took on the appearance of myth,' as critic Robin Skelton put it. The architects of that mythic significance were young poets like Stephen Spender, Louis MacNeice, Cecil Day Lewis, William Empson and Wystan Hugh Auden.

I have my battered copy of Skelton's classic paperback Penguin anthology *Poetry of the Thirties* in front of me for reference now as I write, but I could probably quote accurately from memory. This 1971 edition of the 1964 original with its striking red and white modernist cover design by Stephen Russ carries a recommended retail price of 35p, but I am ashamed to say that it cost me nothing as I stole it from an English

Lit store cupboard at St John Rigby Grammar School when I was 12. It has come with me to college, back home again and through every flat and house move over four decades. It fired my love of poetry and in particular the poetry of the thirties. I'd go on to love the poetry of Larkin, Gunn and Hughes and the generation of poets who followed after the Second World War, but I'd never have got there without Skelton's slim, dense volume, as packed with explosive force as a hand grenade.

To the best of my knowledge, there are no poems of the period specifically about Jarrow, but the best of them address and explore the world and the systems that made Jarrow poor and the world more dangerous. This was a time when, as Skelton remarks, 'mass movements were in the air and quite explicably. Hunger marchers were out in England. The militant unemployed were reading the *Daily Worker*. There was a need and a clamour for social justice'.

The media loves a movement; from Bright Young People to Britpop. They fill supplements and make good copy in high art as well as low culture, in the salon as well as the streets. The 'Auden Group' was something of a journalistic creation but there was something meaningful there too. The poets who have come to embody the spirit of the 1930s were of roughly the same Oxbridge generation and shared a demotic, forceful style and a vaguely left-wing outlook. Four poets were central to the 'group': MacNeice, Auden, Spender and Day Lewis, satirically lumped together as a single fictitious hydra-headed beast called MacSpaunday by the Franco-sympathiser Roy Campbell, who was no friend of the group. (Campbell is an interesting figure; one of the few poets of the time to support the fascists. Some apologists like Joseph Pearce and Roger Scruton deny that he was one himself and say that he merely loathed Marxism. But a line like 'The chill, webbed handclasp of the Jew' suggests a deeper, darker affiliation to the far right.) MacSpaunday was a sardonic dig of course, and in truth the 'Auden' group never held meetings, were probably never even under the same roof and had no shared agenda beyond making poetry more vital and connected with the world. But there were connections between individual writers, as friends, travellers and collaborators. They had something else to bind them too. What shocks me now about Skelton's collection is that while many of the writers were gay, not one was a woman.

Spain loomed large in the lives and work of this group as it did in the newspapers of late October 1936. The Civil War caught the romantic imagination and fired the verse of the thirties poets but it spurred some to more direct action as part of the International Brigade. Auden and Spender both went, the former as an ambulance driver and stretcher bearer, the latter as a radio reporter, and Auden returned from Spain more philosophical and nuanced in his views than he had gone. His poem 'Spain' – which Orwell described as 'one of the few decent things to be written about the war' – with its notorious line about 'the necessary murder', later fell out of favour with its writer. He removed it from future anthologies on the grounds that it was 'dishonest', espousing views for effect that he did not really hold. But many of his poems from this time and later do embody the period and stand as brilliant individual works. He had begun 1936 with the celebrated 'Night Mail', a poem written to the music of Benjamin Britten and the visuals of Humphrey Jennings. He would end the decade with the doom-laden and valedictory '1st September 1939', written at the fag end 'of a low dishonest decade' and on the eve of a devastating war.

That was a few years away still though. On 26 October 1936, as Franco's troops approached the southern and western suburbs of Madrid, the Jarrow marchers neared the rather more placid outskirts of St Albans. As I made the same progress, uneventfully (with all due respect to Harpenden) following the old Roman road of Watling Street through Hertfordshire's undulating chalk downs and vales, flat pastures, and eventually its well-tended gardens and neat hedges, I wondered if the change in the country had been as apparent to the Jarrow marchers as it was to me.

A journey south through England via the route I've taken at least is one through increasing prosperity and growing attractiveness. St Albans greets you with the contentedness of a town in the heart of comfortable shires. At least it looks that way if you've walked from Jarrow. Perhaps it felt like that in 1936 too, although the enormous, swirling, centrifugal pull of London, its wealth, privilege and real estate, was less powerful then. But I could feel it as a real presence now. For all St Albans's distinct character and independence, its fine visage is tilted towards the capital, as if turning its face gratefully to the sun.

Once though, when Watling Street was a new transport project, London wasn't even in St Albans's league. Osbert Lancaster in his curious 1961 travel guide *Here's England* wrote, 'If you have a pleasant day for the journey to St Albans, you can stand on the bank of the little river and suddenly feel yourself touched, saddened by the great passage of time – Romans and Saxons and Normans and Lancastrians rode across the stream. Galloped up that hill and disappeared into the centuries.'

How steeped in, how packed with history every cranny of this nation is; sometimes the least likely, most prosaic or overlooked crannies. I spent the first 18 years of my life in Wigan but never noticed until a few years back that there's a chunk of old Roman wall down by a discount store on a town centre back street, or that in the door frame by the bar of the Grand Hotel, there are two bullet holes from a Civil War skirmish (or was it the Jacobite one?) When I walk into Manchester down the Ship Canal from the BBC in Salford, just before the fantastic chip shop on Liverpool Street, I pass a small Roman amphitheatre. As opposed to America, where the Trump Tower counts as an ancient monument, in Britain, we have history to burn, and we often do.

Unruly ancient Brits razed St Albans to the ground in AD 61. But eventually the Romans subdued them and rebuilt it. This time they wisely did this in stone not timber and named it Verulamium, one of the first places in Britain to be identified by its own name. The titular Alban is thought to have been a Roman-Briton of the third century who gave shelter to a Christian priest on the run, the religion still being outlawed then. When the authorities came for the refugee priest, Alban changed places with him, which turned out to be a bad move in every respect – except for his claim on posterity. Alban in disguise offered himself to the authorities and was taken to the pagan temple at Verulamium and presented to the judge. Enraged, the judge demanded that Alban renounce Christianity and offer sacrifices to the gods. At this, Alban spoke the words quoted in the prayer still used at St Albans Abbey: 'I worship and adore the true and living God who created all things.' Again, not the wisest of responses. Alban was scourged and sentenced to death. On his way to the place of execution, Alban had to cross the River Ver and, to speed things along, prayed for a quick death. At this the river dried up, allowing Alban and his guards to cross on dry land. When Alban's executioner witnessed this he baulked at carrying out the deed, so both he and Alban were beheaded. But as Alban's head fell to the ground, the eyes of the second executioner fell out too. The judge was so moved by all this – it must have been quite a morning after all – that he ended the persecution of Christians and began honouring saints. In perhaps the only nice touch to this grisly tale, the fullest and most definitive account of Alban's life and death was recounted by a famous son of Jarrow, the Venerable Bede.

St Albans Cathedral now stands on the very site of these gory and outlandish events, and is still the big draw in town, even if it is surprisingly easy to lose or never find, shyly hiding behind obscuring thickets of the everyday; cafés, pubs, delis. Prince Charles once opined that the clutter around St Paul's was like a carbuncle on the face of a much-loved friend. The architecture of St Albans is not a carbuncle but it is a fairly effective mask. I approach listlessly, summoned by bells through the town's back streets, which are fine as back streets go, but confusing. I pass Empire Records and Chaos City Comics – which amuses me since whatever St Albans may be, Chaos City it certainly isn't – until there it is, suddenly and gloriously. Osbert Lancaster was a little sniffy and backhanded in his compliments: 'St Albans is interesting, if not as grand as some of the other more famous English cathedrals.' Well, Osbert, I thought it was tremendously impressive and so it appeared did the genial babel of German, Dutch, Spanish, Italian tourists who had flocked to it.

In a little basement room, a choir was rehearsing a lovely version of 'Amazing Grace'. Inside the cathedral itself, a clearly supremely gifted organist was playing one heck of a flashy toccata (my notes read 'this dude can play') and the effect was cumulatively amazing. Of course, there will be some who say that this tremendous edifice is built on nothing but fairy stories and superstition. But, and I speak here as an agnostic, the mischievous part of me thinks that might make it all the more magnificent. Here are layered centuries upon centuries of history, human stories, politics, hubris, layered like geological strata, or the butter cream and jam in a Victoria sponge; Briton, Roman, Viking, Anglo-Saxon, Norman, Tudor, Civil War, Regency, Georgian, industrial, technological.

The marchers arriving in chill, heavy rain must have been cheered by the warmth of the welcome. A civic delegation was there waiting on the steps of the grand white town hall, including the Chief Constable and the mayor, eager to show the king Saint Alban's shrine, even then the town's main tourist attraction. Though the people of St Albans shared little of Jarrow's plight and discomfort, they knew of it and even the sceptical changed their minds and were moved by the men's testimony. The porter at the town's workhouse said, 'I had heard about Jarrow but quite frankly I was inclined to put the stories down to exaggerations. Now I know that what I thought could not possibly be true does in fact exist. If you can only convince everyone of those terrible conditions, as you have convinced me, I do not think that anyone can refuse you the work you ask.'

Also in the crowd was an old woman who had lived in Jarrow 20 years earlier and had come here with her son to find work. 'I have visited the old town several times in the last few years and I have tried to tell my friends how terrible things are in Jarrow but it's no use. They can't understand.' Much debated and pored over today, the 'north/south divide' was as real and unbreachable as the walls of St Albans Abbey in 1936. Baldwin was no 'one nation' Tory and he presided over a shockingly divided Britain.

When I arrive at the town hall I find a solitary man in his 60s loitering in the disused entrance of what looks to be an abandoned building. 'Is this … was this … the town hall?' I ask. 'I reckon so,' he says in an accent forged many miles north of St Albans, 'but they've 'ad for't close it darn cos it's full of asbestos'. It turned out he and his wife come down to watch the big NFL American football game at Wembley every year, staying somewhere on the outskirts of the capital. 'Last year it was Hemel Hempstead. This year we're in Tring,' he says morosely, suggesting Tring has not been all he might have hoped.

St Albans's Saturday market is as busy as Barnsley's but of a different character. Less cheap Spider-Man duvets and *Fast and Furious* DVDs, more military memorabilia and varieties of marinated olives. An enthusiastic Asian lady approaches me waving a leaflet. 'When you've carved your pumpkin, don't throw it away. We have lots of ideas here! Sustainable St Albans! Can I interest you in some pumpkin soup?' Noting that the marchers would certainly have availed themselves of this generosity, and it looking and smelling delicious, I readily accept and someone takes a picture of my benefactor ladling out the pungent, gingery soup into a styrofoam cup for me.

I've been on the road for three weeks now, and as night comes on in the home counties, colder and rawer than expected, it begins to feel like it. Maybe it was the unfamiliar town, or a low-level cold threatening to come on, scratching at the back of my eyes and throat. Maybe it was just the relentless miles with the pack. Perhaps it was the long, full, satisfying but exhausting days, the constant note taking, negotiating and route finding, or the nights at hotel desks or on beds, reading and tapping at the laptop. Whatever it was, as I sprawled in my room at the top of Holywell Hill, (down which St Alban's head had once rolled, causing the well to spring) I felt weary and disoriented. I wonder how the marchers were feeling at this stage. Was it still a great adventure? Or just cold, hard, tiring graft? They walked every inch of the way, unlike me, and unlike me they couldn't text, tweet, call or email. Some will say of course that that's a good thing but I wouldn't agree. For all its potential for abuse, I know without it my trip would have been harder and less rewarding, and this book would have been thinner, and less well-informed.

With a supreme effort of will, since the room was warm, the bed soft and the newscaster's voice on the TV lulling, I got up, showered and headed up Holywell Hill to sample the weekend nightlife of St Albans, or a section thereof. If your name is Victoria, you get a free prosecco every Friday at the Victoria pub St Albans. Mine isn't and I don't think I could pretend otherwise, so I push on. I'd actually heard about the Horn when in Luton. It is known locally for its live music, and since I hadn't heard any of that since choral evensong at Ripon and Debussy at Leeds, I decided to try a new experience on my route. The Jarrow march had an 'embedded' three-piece mouth organ and, however keen one is on the braying of the harmonica, by St Albans that must surely have been a pleasure that was wearing thin.

The Horn is a big, solid pub on the bridge by the station, the one adorned with the mural of St Albans's favourite sons. This includes Alban himself (still with head), sole English pope Nicholas Brakespear, Stephen Hawking and Stanley Kubrick, the latter represented by a stylised 'Hal' and 'Dave' interchange from *2001: A Space Odyssey*. On the way there, I was delighted to see that St Albans can also boast one of those lovely traditional sewing machine and telescope shops.

Whilst the Horn is 'just' a pub, the back room plays host to bigger names than I'd have guessed. Upcoming attractions included The Bluetones and China Crisis (both sold out) who will be familiar names to any reader who knows their 1980s and '90s British pop. Tonight though, it's the turn of Maxwell Hammer Smith, a covers band whose name is a rather convoluted pun on an old Beatles novelty track. They promise 'harmony rock … Fleetwood Mac, Eagles, Queen' which to me (and this is personal and subjective of course) is a selection that in turn appeals and terrifies.

A common refrain of the last few years has been the valedictory lament for the English pub. We are losing them in droves across the land it appears, and the pub is now threatened with extinction. But even in the 1930s, a period one might assume was a golden age of the English local, some 1,500 pubs were closing every year and another modern malaise, that of binge drinking, was causing concern then too. In the poorest areas, mothers left their prams outside the pub while they drank, nipping out to placate the baby with a shot of whisky. At the very bottom of the drinking ladder, desperate folk drank Red Biddy, a potent, lethal mixture of cheap red wine and meths. At the top of the social order, Churchill was bet £120,000 by his chum Lord Rothermere that he could not go through 1936 without a drink. He refused the wager, probably sensibly on balance, as Winnie's drinking day began at 9am with a whisky and soda, continued with a pint of champagne at lunch and then would be topped up with amontillado, gin and brandy through the evening, often ending with the best part of a bottle of cognac at three in the morning.

English popular music in 1936 was dominated by the sentimental or the humorous in various different registers of class and region. George Formby was cleaning windows with lubricious intent while Noël Coward was picking his way daintily though several arch ditties. But the most illustrative hit song of late 1936 was Sam Coslow's 'If You Can't Sing It, You'll Have to Swing It, Mr Paganini'. All forms of music, popular and highbrow, were starting to feel the heat of a new music coming out of America. As Jarrow marched, America swung.

'Swing cannot be defined,' said the American jazz magazine *Metronome* in 1936. Fats Waller tried though: 'two thirds rhythm and one third soul' – which is more impressionistic than useful. Swing was more than just music anyway; it suggested a whole generational culture at least among the leisured and affluent with its own dances, tunes and clothing styles. But while audiences in the States (and increasingly Europe) were being wowed by the new offbeat rhythms and irresistible energy of Benny Goodman and the constantly touring, pioneering bandleaders of the new idiom, not everyone was keen. Novelist Compton Mackenzie said it was 'the wriggling of a child with an overcharged tummy'. Others were more savage; 'Musical Hitlerism' read one review, ironic since jazz, swing and associated music had been banned across all German radio since 12 October 1935. That day, Eugen Hadamovsky, conductor and Third Reich official, announced, 'As of today, I am placing a definitive ban on the negro jazz for the entire German Radio.' Swing was unstoppable though, and would have been the music most enjoyed by the Jarrow marchers and their dancing partners had they had time for music. I doubt music was laid on at St Albans's workhouse that October night in 1936, but the men got a hot meal from the sympathetic master of the institution.

I treated myself to a big glass of red wine at the bar of the Horn. The band weren't scheduled to be on till half ten, which felt very late for someone beginning to feel the fatigue of his journey. When they took to the stage of the back room though, there were still only a few of us in there, though I assume things filled up later. I stuck around for the first 20 to get me to stay in the same room as the music for the entirety of 'Somebody to Love' by Queen, something no one has ever managed before.

That's unworthy perhaps, but tonight I was feeling more road weary than battle hardened. I trooped back up the hill into the centre of St Albans. There were a couple of police cars outside the Slug and Lettuce and a young PC in a body armour gilet was gently trying to keep apart two women in sparkly dresses. A shaven-headed man with a short-sleeved white shirt, presumably the cause of this physical and emotional exchange, sat on the kerb with his head in his hands. My night, like my march, was ending, but there was certainly still some life in theirs.

ST ALBANS TO EDGWARE

30 October, 11 miles

On the morning of 30 October 1936, two days away from journey's end, the Jarrow marchers woke to find that they were the victim of Fake News or perhaps 'alternate facts', or as they called them then, lies. Even in 1936 though, the pure and simple truth was, as Oscar Wilde pointed out, rarely pure and never simple.

A phone call to the St Albans workhouse where they were lodged claimed that two marchers, Jos Bradley and Ralph Smith, had actually spent the night in the Barnet workhouse. This came as something of a surprise, not least to the two men concerned who were in fact with their comrades in St Albans. There may well have been a perfectly innocent explanation for all this: the two men in Barnet may have belonged to a different hunger march or were merely tramps who thought that claiming to be Jarrow men would give them better treatment or celebrity. But, typically fearful and suspicious, David Riley assumed yet another secret plot by communists to infiltrate the Crusade. 'If anyone attempts to crash in on the march, he will be met with the boot,' he told the press. There may have been a similarly reasonable explanation for the arrival of a taxi whose driver said he'd been booked to take a marcher to hospital. A simple case of crossed wires, perhaps. But the marchers suspected a plot to kidnap one of them, and both of these sinister explanations were widely featured in the press.

We don't know what the word or phrase of 1936 was. They didn't guess or vote on such things but if they did then, globally, it may well have been one of the words that have echoed through this book; 'Spain' or 'Swing' or 'Nazi'. In Britain specifically, perhaps it would have been 'Abdication' or 'Blackshirt' or 'Formby' or even 'Jarrow'. But in 2016, Oxford Dictionaries chose 'post-truth' as the international word of the year, after the contentious Brexit referendum and an equally divisive US presidential election saw the word gain global currency. As the *Washington Post* put it, 'in this case, the "post-" prefix doesn't mean "after" so much as it implies an atmosphere in which a notion is irrelevant.'

I read or heard the phrase almost every day as I walked and initially it gained purchase in the States, during the last days of the gruelling and vindictive presidential campaign. 'We concede all politicians lie,' wrote the conservative *Washington Post* columnist Jennifer Rubin. 'Nevertheless, Donald Trump is in a class by himself.'

'Post-truth' was selected after Oxford's dictionary editors noted a roughly 2,000 per cent increase in its usage over 2015 and 2016. But not just in the States. They also talked of the enormous increase in the frequency of mentions in news articles and on social media in the United Kingdom. British intellectuals and commentators, of the right and left if truth be known, still tend to exhibit a snooty, paternalistic high-handedness towards the supposed crassness of American taste and mores. The rise of Donald Trump could support such an attitude, but only as long as one was prepared to overlook the similar ascent to prominence of his friend Nigel Farage. The events of summer 2016 showed that Britain had moved as far 'post-truth' as anywhere in the world.

Take, for instance, one of the most visible and emotive central planks of the Leave campaign: a trumpeted promise that the supposed £350 million a week the EU was costing us would be spent on the NHS if we voted out. Both ends of this statement were lies; the figure was imaginary, and the NHS stood to gain nothing. But still it was emblazoned on the sides of buses – buses paid for by millionaire donors – and supposedly respectable politicians such Boris Johnson, Kate Hoey, Michael Gove and Nigel Farage were happy to stand alongside and peddle that untruth. Once the Leave vote was won, all instantly acknowledged that the figures and claim were false and that nothing of the sort would be done. Even by the standards of modern politics, there as something in this brazenness that was new and quite breathtaking.

By 2016, the word 'lie' had all but disappeared from our political lexicon. But extinction had loomed since as long ago as 1759, when Edmund Burke wrote instead of being 'economical with the truth'. Winston Churchill may be many an Englishman's idea of a straight-talker, but it was he who invented the euphemism 'terminological inexactitude' to cover his own porkies. Lyndon B Johnson was guilty of a 'credibility gap' and then with Richard Nixon we enter a new golden age of slippery deceit, of 'inoperative statements' and 'strategic misrepresentation'. Alan Clark wrote shiftily in his diaries about being 'economical with the actualité'. Hillary Clinton 'misspoke', rather than 'invented', coming under gunfire on a trip to Bosnia. But in late 2016, Carl Bernstein, who along with Bob Woodward had exposed the lies of Watergate, said that 'Nixon had nothing on Trump'.

In Britain, barefaced and gleeful lies like the one about the £350million for the NHS promised by the Brexit lobby are rarer than a kind of 'building of one's part', as actors say. This is often to claim purchase on some romantic and emotive element of our shared past. Thus as I was writing this book, the then-UKIP leader Paul Nuttall got into hot water over claims on his website that he had been at the Hillsborough disaster and 'lost good friends there'. These claims turned out as resistant to verification as the one about him having been a professional footballer with Tranmere Rovers.

'Jarrow' has its own murky legacy of half-truth, partial truth and downright falsehoods. The old northern term 'romancing' seems appropriate here, as most of these myths are attempts to appropriate the teary romance and sentiment of the Crusade. Brexit minister David Davies said in 2005 that his grandfather had led the Jarrow march from York to Aldermaston. His grandfather was not part of the Jarrow march, which in any case never visited those towns. The *Guardian* claimed that the left-wing folksinger father of UB40's Ali and Robin Campbell had been on the Jarrow march. He hadn't. There's the incident of the cross in Leicester and the disputed whereabouts of the Jarrow Crusade banners today. It's easy to judge, or even mock, but as I found as I walked and talked and read, something as drenched in significance and emotion as the Jarrow march will inevitably create false memory, Chinese whisper and hyperbole, and not all of it ill-intentioned.

*

Upon reaching Radlett, halfway to Edgware from St Albans, the town council provided the marchers with a crate of oranges and some welcome, hot mugs of tea at the Congregational Hall. Even then Radlett was comfortable. Now it's one of the most prosperous towns in the south of England. Lovely too, although we are now deep into that part of the country where the dizzying, lung-grasping, vertiginous height of the house prices make your head swim. A five-bedroom house here will cost you £2.5million, although a little place in Letchmore is a snip at £600,000. But this for a solid suburban house, not a gravel-drived country seat, which I still dozily expect for that kind of money. At the time of the Jarrow march, only a quarter of the British population owned their own home, and whilst sometimes this might have put them at the mercy of unscrupulous landlords or living in hostels, it meant we didn't have the uniquely toxic obsession with property we have today. From here until London, I will wonder at every estate agent's window I pass, and there are many, how any ordinary working person can live here, whether they're a carpenter, a cook, a nurse, a teacher, a roofer, or any of the jobs without which society can't function but seems to view as valueless rather than invaluable.

Dusk now, chilly too, and as the lights come on down the main drag, I'm envious of the late stragglers in the well-lit bakeries and bookshops, the milkshake bars and delis. In the Red Lion pub, at a scrubbed and notched faux-rustic table filled with food, young Mum and Dad are happily plying their little girl in a high chair with french fries from a battered metal cone. They look cosy, happy and presumably mortgaged to the hilt. The Radlett Centre has a colourful, enticing and diverse list of forthcoming attractions: Mark Steel, Think Floyd, Annie, an H P Lovecraft adaptation, *The Wiz* and Psychic Sally (Feefo Gold Trusted Service Award; 'deluded but essentially harmless' – *Guardian*).

On the garage forecourt, a Middle Eastern cabbie called Kerem notes both my huge pack and weary tread and astutely makes the connection. 'Hey, my friend, you look tired, man. Where you headed, London? I'll give you good price. You off to find your fortune?' I tell him that that would be cheating and why, but he is so convivial and funny, and I am so comprehensively knackered, that I accept his offer of a lift to 'the best kebab shop in Edgware, I should know. I worked there, my friend. There are many, but this is best. Also cleanest.' Fireworks streak across the sky as we ride the few, dark, hibernal miles to Edgware, a gentle profound reminder of how Britain has changed since 1936. Then those fiery trails could only have meant Bonfire Night. Now they might augur Diwali too.

'Ecgi's weir' is the pond where Ecgi the Saxon and his people would fish. By 1422 it had become 'Eggeswere' and by 1489, the Tudors had added a T, making it almost the name we have today. There's no Domesday Book mention but we know that the Edgware Road follows the same line as ancient Watling Street, an important Roman road later used in the medieval period by pilgrims headed to Canterbury. One of Dick Turpin's most infamous crimes was carried out here on 4 February 1735, when he and five of his gang broke into a farmhouse owned by elderly Joseph Lawrence. Turpin and his gang stripped, beat, scalded and burned the old man before threatening to cut off his legs. During this ordeal, one of the gang forced a servant girl upstairs and raped her. This is vile stuff, and I include the details for one reason only, to make a point about our national culture. While bemoaning the lawlessness and incivility of the modern world, we've sanitised and glorified Dick Turpin, turning a brutal, murderous thug into a *Carry On* film rogue, a dandy highwayman of pop songs and a tea towel icon. The British capacity for forgetting, let alone forgiving, is boundless. I expect a rosy, joshing article on Dick in *This England* magazine soon. Perhaps they've already done the Krays.

The coming of the railways and trams transformed Edgware from a hay-producing rural backwater into a crowded adjunct of London itself. In 1932 the parish became a part of Hendon, and Station Road rapidly developed in the early 1930s, with cinemas and stores opening all along a busy thoroughfare.

Born the year after the Jarrow march, a resident called Brenda Franklin told the BBC People's War site, 'Our address was 7 Millais Gardens, Mollison Way, Edgware. Edgware was right on the edge of London then – a sizeable sprawl of the mid-thirties house building explosion. Miles of mostly terraced, Bauhaus-influenced, wide-windowed houses occupied by respectable upper working class families with aspirations. I think that most were quite happy in their brand new easy-to-run houses in the leafy suburbs.'

The marchers would have walked down some of these new streets and emerged along burgeoning Station Road, finding Edgware in the grip of its feverish transformation from outlying village into London's maddening vital edge itself. It must have made them wonder what Jarrow would feel like when they returned, as they soon would. Homesick as they may well might have been, this was a prospect that still evoked dread. One confided to a journalist, 'The first morning is what I'm afraid of. It'll be getting up and looking out of the window on the same old sight – Jarrow – knowing that there's nothing, nothing at all to do. My feet hurt terribly, but all the same it's been a holiday. While you're marching, you don't think.'

After quietly comfortable Radlett, Edgware feels hardier, edgier, noisier. There's no pretty, languid sedate Sunday mood here. This could be any day in the rough hinterland of the city, the buses and cabs elbowing for space, honking and revving; the cheap convenience stores fluorescent and crowded. I realise that I've never felt entirely at home in the London suburbs, affluent or otherwise. Perhaps it was my bad experiences at the eastern extremities of the Central Line during a glum, brief sojourn there in the late 1980s but I'll think I'll always feel unmoored and out of sorts here in the transient, fragmentary, ad hoc nature of these places, by the crowded streets of people who always appear stressed and unhappy and just passing through. Or is that the three weeks on the road talking, in a tired, whiny little voice? Possibly.

Happily, the distinctive neon outline of a rotating kebab tells me that I have found Keren's old alma mater, the cleanest kebab shop in Edgware, which shall diplomatically remain nameless of course. I find a table in the midst of the diverse urban bustle of teenage couples, Turkish cabbies and the odd solo oddball like me, shoving his massive rucksack awkwardly under the table and ordering expansively, randomly, hungrily in a way that makes the small dark-eyed girl behind the counter laugh as she repeats it, 'OK, so that's large doner, kacik, sucuk sausage, patlican, large Efes beer, pitta, salad ...'

These are always strange but nicely meditative moments, these, becalmed somewhere new after the relentlessness of the road. I cover the table in books and notes, devices and maps but end up paying attention to none of them, drinking in the changing atmosphere of the café instead. A smart, neat older woman comes in slightly diffidently, one hand on her pearls and the other dipping her glasses as she peers at the laminated menu on the wall as uncomprehendingly as if it were the shattered frozen landscape of a Jovian moon. Her awkwardness is not assuaged by the large, burly, moustachioed Middle Eastern proprietor behind the counter asking, 'Do you live nearby then, love?' as he sharpens and wipes a huge, glistening blade of obscure function, entirely innocently but unnervingly. A little girl and her dad, clearly regulars, enter and are welcomed warmly by all ('Hello Princess! Give us a kiss!'). They begin an order of great length and complexity with much discussion. Princess turns out to be boisterous, wildly voluble and just the charming side of irritating.

'This door is rubbish [swinging on door] – you need to get a new door,' she pouts.

'Will you give me the money, Princess?' says the blade-wielding owner, sweetly.

'No! Ask your mummy and daddy for the money!'

'Ah, [sadly but tenderly] my mummy and daddy are in Turkey. Do you know what Turkey is?'

'Yes, it's like a chicken you can eat.'

Leaving some time later, I find the White Hart hotel where the Rotary Club of Edgware treated the marchers to tomato soup, steak and kidney pud and apple pie. It's still there though it has changed its name. To the Change of Hart. Whether this is hilarious or dreadful, I find myself no longer able to tell. But I do know that tomorrow, Halloween, will mean the end of my long, strange trip and that London, tricking or treating, awaits.

STAGE TWENTY-TWO

EDGWARE TO MARBLE ARCH

31 October, 9 miles

London is the most dynamic city in the world today. Sure, it has always been an international hub … but it has never sizzled like it sizzles today. Other cities in the UK make grand claims and have their devotees and champions but Manchester, Edinburgh, Leeds etc pale before the might, sight, sounds, churn and fire of London. And those who disagree are just expressing the politics of envy.

Dylan Jones, *London Rules*

The thing is, most people in London are tired of life. You've only got to witness the queues in the Westfield multistorey or the reaction to a crying baby on the Tube to realise that this is a city that exists permanently at the end of its rope … It's the last metropolis in a sinking country on a starving continent, an island within an island oozing out into the Home Counties like an unstoppable concrete oil spill.

Clive Martin, 'Reasons London is the Worst Place Ever', *Vice*

I'm in a bagel shop in Cricklewood on the hottest Halloween since records began, reading up on my iPad about London, whose swaggering presence has been waiting for me like an unpaid bill since Jarrow. I feel that this might be the strangest day of a long, strange trip. The bagel shop promised free wifi and air conditioning, and, fair enough, you might not normally need the latter on the last day of October in England, but it can deliver neither. So having walked from Edgware already this morning, I sit, a glaze of damp across my chest, arms and forehead, having emerged out of the maze of dead residential backstreets, onto Cricklewood Broadway (formerly Watling Street).

I like the difference in tone of the above quotes, the second from Clive Martin in *Vice* magazine, sour and sharply truthful, the former from *London Rules* by Dylan Jones (who I know and like, if rarely completely agree with) full of the breezy superiority that so annoys us troglodytes of the north. Almost 200 of those came stomping through Cricklewood 80 years ago this morning, and now I follow belatedly in their wake; hot, sweaty, thirsty but not I think, *pace* Dylan Jones, envious.

Of all the queasy, weaselly, mealy-mouthed lickspittle dismissals in modern English, nothing compares to that phrase the 'politics of envy'. Effectively, it reduces people's desire for proper schools, houses, jobs and health care to no more than a jealousy for some nice brogues they once saw in *GQ*. It is both smug and vacuous and it is, of course, partly why Brexit Britain gave Islington a bloody nose though Islington still doesn't have the common sense or humility to see it.

Today is the last day of the Jarrow march. I was up and off early because I had a date at Westminster. If I could be there before noon, Tracy Brabin had very kindly agreed to meet me at the Commons and for this last day, I wanted the feel of the Jarrow marchers' entry into London, albeit that theirs was in the torrential rain and murk of a thirties Halloween and mine is in shirt sleeves, perspiring, under a freakish late October sun on the warmest morning of my 22 so far. I wash down the last of the salt beef and dill pickle with some sweet, scorching black coffee and push through the door into simmering Cricklewood.

Like Balls Pond Road, Golders Green, Surbiton or East Cheam, Cricklewood is one of those London locales that were once staples of British radio and TV comedy. *The Two Ronnies, The Goodies, Hello Cheeky*, all would regularly use these venerable names as handy ciphers as suggestive of tedious, drab London suburbia as Cleckheaton, Wigan and Goole were of northern bleakness when used by Les Dawson or Norman Collier. Cricklewood: is it the sound of the name with its evocative English tweeness, or could it be the place itself that has made this commuter backwater a synonym for genteel nothingness?

Peter Capaldi made a spoof documentary about British cinema called *Cricklewood Greats*, but its comic laureate was undoubtedly Alan Coren, writer, TV and radio panellist, former editor of *Punch* and *The Listener* and father of the modern media personalities Victoria and Giles. Coren styled himself 'The Sage of Cricklewood' and used the unloved area as a neglected eyrie from which to view the foibles of the world in hundreds of columns and parodic books such as *The Cricklewood Tapestry, The Cricklewood Diet, A Year in Cricklewood* and more. In their tribute to him, website *This Is Local London* said, 'Coren almost did for his childhood home what the Brontes did for Haworth'. The London *Evening Standard*'s obituary writer made plain that finding out that Coren actually lived in Cricklewood had to be 'a joke, I thought; so eminent a man could not possibly live in this mocked corner of north-west London, this nowhere between Kilburn and Colindale'.

Cricklewood follows the same spatial arrangement that's been common on the last, southern leg of the journey, one that's very different from northern towns. There the shops and offices and enterprise cluster haphazardly around a market square or town centre. Cricklewood, like Edgware and St Albans, comprises a single parade of commerce stretched out for a mile or two along the sides of an arrow-straight major road. It's linear rather than ganglia, with terraced streets stacking up behind in a residential hinterland. Apart from its very heart, nowhere in London feels like a town to me in the way that northern towns do, confirming my (not entirely negative) view that Greater London is 50 or so little hamlets held together by a tube train system.

Perhaps it was the heat, or our old friend the pack, but it was hard to tell where Cricklewood ended and Kilburn began. There was no greeting sign, no border patrol, just an elision from one unremarkable bit of the capital to another and one prevalent old ethnic tradition to the next. From the late nineteenth century onwards there was an influx of Jewish immigrants to the area and by the time the Jarrow march passed through, three new synagogues had been built in a district which even acquired the jokey cod-Yiddish name Cricklevitch.

Kilburn though is, or was, the raucous heartland of London's Irish community. They may now represent just 5 per cent of the population, much less than the Italians of Bedford, but their influence still permeates the district. Kilburn was prosperous briefly in the late 1860s and '70s when handsome villas abounded and a private school founded by A A Milne's father was attended by both his son and H G Wells. But then the area faltered and became much poorer later in the century. The posh schools closed and the large villas were broken up into flats or took in lodgers, mainly Irishmen coming to work as labourers. These new Kilburnians were pouring in when the Jarrow men marched by and continued to do so for the next four decades. Their story is essentially that of the Bedford Italians and a thousand immigrant communities around the world; young men (and women) come to a new land desperate for work intending to make money and take it home. Instead they work hard, build lives and families here and keep alive a dream of the old country while bringing colour and energy to the new.

Those days seemed to have gone. A reporter from the *Irish Times* had visited over the summer and found the same surly resentments that were making themselves felt everywhere. Kerryman John O'Sullivan told him, 'You go up the road there now and you don't see one English, Irish, Welsh or Scottish face working.' Kilburn's dominant ethnic minority groups were once Irish and West Indian; now it is Somali and Polish. Almost all of the Kilburn Irish interviewed in the piece had voted to leave the EU. This ran contrary to the perceived geographical split over Brexit, the one that said that London was an island of internationalist liberalism while the north and Midlands had been lured towards UKIP and the right. The opinions of Kilburn, whose parent constituency Brent actually voted to remain by 60 per cent, showed what I had long thought to be the case, that class not region was the significant variable, and that the commentators of the metropolis had little notion of life or the mood of depressed, post-industrial England. I might have popped into the offices of Hampstead and Kilburn Labour Party to chat about this, but as I passed it was closed and shuttered.

With all due respect to Dylan Jones, this didn't feel like any kind of international hub to me. Perhaps that ritzy marketing speak applies to a few postal codes around W1 or the City, but there was nothing here of the upscale vibrancy of Leeds. It was a dull plod from the fringes of London's grubby urban edges to its congested heart, though of course with a certain ragged liveliness and colour. But no hills or rivers, no views nor trees, no stone-deep history, just a long strip of commerce, cheap and tatty. That can't be helped of course; the same applies to

Smethwick or Levenshulme or Hebburn. But none of those places make claims for themselves as London does or seeks to mythologise itself quite so desperately, dismissing everywhere else as envious and 'chippy'. In fairness, novelist Zadie Smith, a former Kilburn resident who set her book *NW* here, wrote proudly but candidly of its unprepossessing nature when she wrote, 'Kilburn bloody High Road. Not everyone wants to be a national treasure, after all, nor to be knighted, and not every building longs for a blue plaque or to be held up as a shining example of the "Best of British". Not everything has to be part of the "national conversation".'

There are a few memorable highlights of my late morning in Kilburn though. Jessica, a long-standing Kilburnian of Jamaican descent, spots me marvelling at a grand art deco building across the road, shielding my eyes from the dazzling sun to take in its impressive white tower.

'Great isn't it? Ian Dury and Kilburn and the High Roads played there a lot.' It is the Gaumont State Cinema and for Jessica it has memories not just of late 1970s funk punk but 'Saturday morning cinema for ten pence. It's got one of those amazing pop up organs and a gorgeous art deco staircase that's all curving brass. Every now and then they open it up to the public and let you have a look.'

They, I ask?

Jessica rolls her eyes. 'The Happy Clappies, they've had it for about 15 years.'

More properly, 'they' are the Ruach City Church who offer 'lively, multicultural evangelical ministry with faith and bible classes'. Had I known it then, I would have impressed Jessica, who had by now gone into the Al Rouche Super Market to do some shopping, by telling her that you could add to Ian and his Blockheads, Larry Adler, Gracie Fields and George Formby, who all played at the Kilburn State on its opening night of 30 December 1937 in a concert broadcast by the BBC. When it opened it was one of the largest auditoriums in the world, a colossal piece of Italianate architecture whose art deco skyscraper frontage was designed to ape that of the Empire State Building. ('Ape' I think is a good King Kong joke here. No? Oh, please yourself, as Frankie Howerd would say. He played here too by the way.)

Kilburn was once renowned across the capital as a lively and popular place for public entertainment. Entrepreneurs established several variety theatres and the High Road rang with a good-natured rowdiness that it became famed for. Ian Dury's first band were named Kilburn and the High Roads in its honour.

It is quieter now. In the noughties, the London Tourist Board tried to brand Kilburn High Road 'Music Mile', specialising in Irish and country music played live. But most of the famous pubs, like the legendary Biddy Mulligans, are now gone, reborn as discount stores, gyms or computer repair shops.

The A5 London to Holyhead trunk road winds on to Maida Vale. When the marchers passed along this road, the BBC had not long acquired the Maida Vale skating rink a few blocks away for orchestral purposes and it is now the home to the BBC Symphony Orchestra. It was where most of John Peel's radio sessions were recorded and every significant talent (and quite a few insignificant ones) in British alternative and progressive music recorded such sessions here. A blue plaque above a studio door will tell you that this is where Bing Crosby recorded his last session in 1977. I was once showing rock superstars REM around the studios and pointed this plaque out. Mike Mills and Peter Buck were genuinely interested but singer Michael Stipe barked, 'Can we just get on please!' Buck and Mills gave me a collective apologetic look that suggested to me the band was not long for this world, and it wasn't.

On the other side of the A5, you will find perhaps the world's most famous zebra crossing outside the EMI studios on Abbey Road in St John's Wood. As the marchers passed, Pablo Casals was headed here to record Bach's Cello Suites. Four years before, Elgar had conducted the teen prodigy Yehudi Menuhin in a performance of his own violin concerto. Over the next few years, everyone from Fats Waller to Vaughan Williams would beat a path to this corner of north London. Had I time, I would have taken a detour to see what bizarre, touching, inappropriate new graffiti had been written on its low white wall. This is a place of pilgrimage for Beatle obsessives from around the world who come from São Paulo and Tromsø and Lagos to have their pictures taken walking in step on the crossing as featured on the Beatles' *Abbey Road* sleeve. They then normally write something quite odd. 'John! Happiness is a Warm Gun, from Mexico!' was particularly unforgettable. I'm not sure even the language barrier accounts for thinking a gun reference an appropriate tribute to the shot and slain Beatle.

Those few miles along the A road take you, if you'll allow some poetic licence, from the Holy Land through the Emerald Isle to the Levant. Soon after Maida Vale, in appropriate temperatures, I reached the bustle and sizzle and scents of the lower Edgware Road, its sudden exoticism a thrill. Three hundred years ago, it provided refuge for Huguenots fleeing persecution under Louis XV. Later it became a destination for successive waves of Middle Eastern immigrants. New trade with the Ottomans brought an influx though the late nineteenth century.

In the 1950s, many Egyptians moved to the area to establish businesses, but it was conflict and unrest that drove or drew people here from the seventies onwards; the Lebanese Civil War, the Soviet Invasion of Afghanistan, the Iran–Iraq War, violence in Algeria, the Gulf Wars. Some call it Little Cairo or Little Beirut. Less charmingly, a *Spectator* piece I read as I dallied over a thick Syrian coffee called it 'The Arab Street'.

Quite a few of those refugees had held skilled professional posts in their home countries such as teachers, programmers or doctors. But denied the same opportunities here, many went into catering or started businesses in the food industry. This may have been a tribulation to them but, from a selfish point of view, for me it has made the Edgware Road the best place to eat in the whole of London. The food of a whole diverse but connected swathe of the world is here from the Dardanelles to the Khyber Pass – Damascene cuisine, Kurdish cuisine, Afghan cuisine, shawarma, Arabic dates, labnah yogurt cheese, tangy zaatar bread, oozing baklava. But I have mentioned food enough and I had a pressing date (not that kind). Tracy Brabin, the MP who had so kindly agreed to meet me at the Commons, had a debate in the afternoon and so I had promised to be there by noon. Damp with sweat and steeling myself against the sizzling and incense of 'Arab Street', I pounded down the Edgware Road until the familiar shape of Marble Arch swam before my eyes.

Technically, Marble Arch was the end. The end of mine and the marchers' journey. They arrived here in teeming rain to be met by large crowds and the assembled press. The harmonica band played some of the tunes that had kept them going over the last three-and-a-half weeks: 'The Long, Long Trail', 'Tipperary', 'Annie Laurie'. I arrived to the sound of a passing boy racer playing grime and some construction work, took a selfie and grabbed a black cab by the swanky hotels of Park Lane. In my time, I've been to these scores of times for various awards do's. I wouldn't be dropping in this morning I didn't think, in my battered walking trainers, flat cap and gigantic rucksack. I was going to look odd enough in the palace of Westminster.

The Jarrow marchers carried a petition of 10,000 signatures from the north east in a wooden box the 300 miles from their home town to London. Each night it would be placed under lock and key in the council offices and drill halls of Ripon or

Mansfield, Darlington or Bedford. The petition asked very politely for a new steelworks to be built in their town; for anything to alleviate their dire, workless situation. Prime Minister Stanley Baldwin refused to see them. Later they trudged in their sodden capes to the Houses of Parliament to see the King in a Royal Procession to Parliament. Because of the rain though, the procession was cancelled and the marchers, standing four deep in the downpour, watched him swish by in his chauffeured car into the House. The mood of the capital's elites is brilliantly captured in a painting by Thomas Cantrell Dugdale, titled 'The Arrival of the Jarrow Marchers in London', in which a young woman with a cigarette holder eyes the Crusaders languidly from a salon window whilst her foppish male companion looks elsewhere. I had no petition, no request, no axe to grind or whet on my 'politics of envy'. But I had decided not long after setting off that I should try to do what the marchers failed to do. Get inside the House of Parliament and speak to a Member of Parliament.

Tony Benn, one of the great Parliamentarians whatever one thinks of his politics, said of the last stage of his life that it was being lived 'in a blaze of autumn sunshine'. It's a lovely phrase, something to hope for and it was very literally what had brought hundreds to Westminster that lunchtime. There are always crowds at the Houses of Parliament but there were more than usual that morning; smiling groups from Tokyo and Tampa having their pictures taken beneath the huge cliffs and crenulations of the palace and the imperious gaze of Big Ben. Again, whatever your politics, it's hard not to feel a little shiver of pride at moments like these. We do palaver well, and the Houses of Parliament are pure palaver, writ large in gilt and honey-coloured Rutland limestone.

It takes an age to get in, even with George, Tracy's assistant, at my side. There are security checks and re-checks to be queued for, but who could baulk at that after the events of Batley this summer. George is a lovely young man about a foot taller than me, as is customary amongst the youth of today. It's his first day in this job and I am his first official duty. He and I both pale a little when I realise I have a Swiss Army knife in my pocket, essential for my march but less welcome here. But we sort this out with the guards just as the new MP for Batley and Spen comes down the hall to meet us, beaming, blonde and sunny in a bright red tunic.

'Well, day five in the Big Brother house,' she laughs 'and all is going well.' It's Tracy's first week and I wonder whether, to try another analogy, it's like first term at big school. 'It's pretty full on. I've sharpened a lot of pencils, and I do keep getting lost which is what happens when you go to a new school, isn't it? But no one's flushed my head down the toilet yet ...'

She was born in Batley, West Yorkshire, in the constituency she now represents, and educated at Heckmondwike Grammar School. She studied drama and then did a Master of Arts degree in screenwriting. She had a long-running nineties role in *Coronation Street*, also appearing in *Holby*, *EastEnders* and *Emmerdale*. She's a writer too, and has written episodes for *Heartbeat*, *Family Affairs*, *Crossroads*, *Tracy Beaker*, *Hollyoaks* and *Shameless*. But in parallel with this she has long been politically active.

'There'll be people thinking, oh, you're just some actor off the telly, but I've been a campaigner and activist for 30 years, initially for the Writers Guild and Equity. I spoke at the European Parliament about gender, I've campaigned for refugee rights. I've done a lot of stuff which people wouldn't know about, but they do know about *Coronation Street*, which is fine. Nobody wanted this obviously. I wouldn't have wanted to be here under these circumstances. But I'm from the area and Jo was a friend and I campaigned with her over closures of libraries and the like. So when the Labour Party asked me to do it, to stand as MP, I thought I can't say no, I have to step up.'

We sit beneath a bush in the lobby and famous faces pass by, politicians, journalists, TV presenters. If the Jarrow march arrived today, would they be interested? Would anyone be clamouring for a soundbite from Ellen or Marshal Riley? A quick woof from Paddy the dog? Apart from the crowds in Trafalgar Square and the press, Westminster itself was cool and awkward toward the Jarrow men. Some thought it 'a bolshie show' but others surely knew that these 200 sodden men from the north were a painfully visible sign of their own failure. I ask Tracy what that word Jarrow means to her.

'It means working-class protest. It may have been in the end just a gesture but it was a gesture that says together we're stronger. But it's about poverty too. Batley food bank has given out 8,000 meals and that's not going to get any better. Are we not on the verge of a Jarrow again, with the poor literally having to choose between heating and food?'

I liked Tracy a lot. She is bright, brave and passionate and I could have stayed a lot longer. But to be honest, my journey was over now and after the long miles and the procession of towns and cities and days, I felt slightly overwhelmed in the vast lobby with its busy chatter. Staying around to eat cake at Westminster felt like prolonging the inevitable, which was turning around, making my way to Euston and heading back north, home. Tracy was going to be busy this afternoon too. 'The Orgreave debate is today, we'll get some kind of conclusion.'

Orgreave is a place like Jarrow that casts a long shadow and tolls like a bell in the political history of Britain, in particular the story of the English industrial working class. In the summer of 1984, at the combustible height of the national miners' strike, members of the National Union of Mineworkers picketed a coking plant at Orgreave, South Yorkshire. When they tried to persuade lorries not to leave or enter, a force of around 6,000 policemen turned on them savagely. A former officer present that day, who asked to be anonymous, told the BBC that the police were told to use 'as much force as possible' against the miners and that the police 'were anticipating trouble and in some ways relishing it'.

After Hillsborough, Orgreave was seen as another open wound in the British, or at least northern psyche. The behaviour of the police and the role of government in the attacks on the miners is something many still want proper answers about and satisfactory explanations for. South Yorkshire Police had told the BBC they would 'fully participate' in any enquiry. The day that I arrived in London, Amber Rudd, the Conservative Home Secretary, was to announce whether there would be a public enquiry or not. There was a definite feeling in the air that, with the truth about Hillsborough slowly emerging, the other great symbolic attack on the working class, Orgreave would be next to be opened up to the light of scrutiny and the fresh air of honesty. We would know in a matter of hours.

I walked back into central London via the House of Commons souvenir shop to pick up some postcards as souvenirs. As I walked past the Cenotaph I bumped into another Labour MP, Alison McGovern, who I recognised from her Twitter picture. She too was rushing back for the Orgreave verdict but she'd been following my progress and we had a congratulatory hug and picture ('I wouldn't normally do this with no make-up on, you know') before she dashed away back to Westminster. Around Leicester Square, the heat and tiredness finally became too much and I flagged down a black cab to take me the last few miles of London's clogged streets to Euston.

'You look done in, mate,' said the cabbie cheerily into his rear view mirror, surveying my slumped figure. 'You come far?'

'Jarrow,' I said, eyes closed

'Jarrow? As in the march? From Newcastle?!'

'That's right.'

'Bloody 'ell, mate. No wonder you're knackered. What was all that actually about then? Was it something to do with the General Strike, or later? I seen pictures and you hear the name. But what was the protest? What did they want? Were they miners? Who were they?'

I pause. It's a good question. But I can't summon either the energy or expertise to answer it fully or properly.

'They were just some bloody left wingers coming down here to make trouble.'

The driver gives me a long, amused look in the mirror, trying to work out if I'm serious or not. He's wondering what response to give when I suddenly ask him to turn the radio up, as there's breaking news crackling through and a familiar name. Orgreave.

The Home Secretary Amber Rudd has just told the house that there will not be a public enquiry into the Orgreave clashes between police and miners during the 1984 miners' strike. The announcement will come as a bitter disappointment to campaigners. She said, 'This has been a difficult decision to make, and one which I have thought about very carefully. But I have now concluded that there is no case for either a statutory inquiry or an independent review.' Ms Rudd added that 'policing is very different' now to what it was 30 years ago.

It was a perfectly proper, fitting and bitter end to the trip. On arrival in London 80 years ago, the crowds were large and warm. Even Rothermere's right wing mouthpiece newspapers gave 'Three Cheers for Jarrow'. The harmonica band were offered a recording contract. But Parliament largely ignored them. As Ellen Wilkinson reported, despite many MPs being bombarded with requests for support for Jarrow from their constituencies, 'A few questions were asked … and the house moved on to consideration of other things.'

Sir John Jarvis MP did announce, however, that he was negotiating for a new steel tubes mill on the Palmer's site. But this was largely a ruse. Jarvis paid for a boat trip for the men on the Thames, ostensibly as a reward for their efforts, but actually to avoid any ugly scenes in the House. When they returned, they were told by the Special Branch that the petition they had carried 300 miles had been 'presented in their absence'. They were sickened. No one knows where this piece of people's history is: lost, burned, discarded, perhaps at the bottom of a cupboard in New Scotland Yard.

No new steelworks was ever built in Jarrow. The tube works opened a year later and the brief, fleeting hope that it sparked in the men is sad and touching. When Ellen Wilkinson walked through the site when the men were laying the concrete foundations of the rolling mill, she was greeted with, 'This is what we marched to get.' But the pathos and irony was not lost on her. She commented: 'The grim reality is that the workers have no share in these mills. When the works are built they will still be subject to the toll of profit, the exigencies of a system where they can be closed at the will of people far away to suit a financial policy.' In any event, the tube mill, dreamed up primarily as a face-saving ruse by Runciman, employed only 200 men and then only briefly.

When the money from their various collections was totted up that day, there was a profit of £100. It was decided to buy all the men a new suit with this since, if it were given in cash, the Unemployment Assistance Board would probably take it out of their benefits. As well as the suit, there was enough for each for a train ticket home. Otherwise who knows? Maybe they'd have been expected to walk back too.

My train was leaving in eight minutes. I gave the cabbie a handful of pound coins and, on a whim, a postcard of the Mother of Parliaments, floodlit and grand against an indigo night. Then I hauled my pack onto the escalator and thought about what the marchers Billy McShane and Con Whalen, the last surviving marcher, had said many decades on. 'When we were turned down at the House of Commons … that was it, you knew you were finished. It was a waste of time … but I enjoyed every step.'

The youngest marcher never came back. John Farndale stayed in London to work as a baker's assistant. But the harmonica band didn't get that record deal. They went back to Jarrow and waited for the call from London that never came, and then quietly broke up.

POSTSCRIPT

October's a blink of the eye, the apples weighing down the tree a minute ago are gone and the tree's leaves are yellow and thinning ... the days are unexpectedly mild ... but the nights are cool to cold ...

Ali Smith *Autumn*

Thou watchest the last oozings hours by hours ...
sinking as the light wind lives or dies ...
... And gathering swallows twitter in the skies.

John Keats 'Ode to Autumn'

October 2016 seems a long time ago. St Albans seems a long time ago; Bedford, Luton, Market Harborough, Ripon, Ferryhill, Jarrow, all of them, long ago and miles away. Autumn froze and hardened into winter, and with each passing season, the unthinkable became the norm.

Do the Chinese really have a curse that goes 'may you live in interesting times'? It might well be one of those fictitious pub 'facts' like the Great Wall of China being the only man-made structure visible from space. (It isn't. You can see lots of stuff from the moon, from Bedouin campfires to power stations to football stadia.) But the few months since I retraced the march have been about as interesting as we could bear, interesting to the point of fevered insanity.

Nothing felt quite as seismic and surreal as Trump's astonishing and frightening elevation to the White House. Trump won the US election, though not the popular vote, and within days, mad and unprincipled executive orders were fired off from the White House where our Prime Minister scurried to curtsey and hold his hand. He appointed several far-right demagogues and white supremacists into his closest circle of advisers. One of his friends and supporters in the media called Alex Jones has a radio/TV show *Info Wars* that Trump often appears on. Jones said that both Hillary Clinton and Barack Obama were literally demons from hell who wreaked of sulphur and who were haloed with a ring of flies indoors at all times of year. David Icke, wearing a turquoise tracksuit, used to say these kinds of things on the Terry Wogan show in the 1980s and we would chortle, perhaps uncharitably, at how the ex-goalkeeper and *Nationwide* presenter had gone so demonstrably and spectacularly nuts. Now such people are in the spheres of influence of the most powerful man on earth. As of early 2017, Icke is mildly resurgent with a quarter of a million subscribers to his YouTube channel. He has wisely toned down the stuff about Blair and Bush being pan-dimensional lizard overlords in favour of much raging about, naturally, 'the mainstream media'.

One of the things I like about the mainstream media, for all its undoubted faults, is that it uncovers, say, the Watergate scandal – which is why Trump fears and loathes it – rather than disseminating some juvenile garbage about the Queen being a super intelligent reptile in a rubber mask. But that kind of abject nonsense is thriving like a poisonous mushroom in the dampest, darkest corners of the Net. Technology and politics writer John Naughton says that the rise of the new angry populism, of Trump and to a degree Farage, is perhaps because 'once upon a time people angry about globalisation, cultural change, immigration or whatever had to fume impotently in small local circles, but now can crowd-source their indignation'.

Just as in 1936, the world seems to have fallen in thrall to 'strong men' again, all promising action as an end in itself however rash or backward. For Franco, Mussolini and Hitler read Trump, Erdogan and Putin. The far right in France is in the ascendant again. The engineer of this has been a young thinker called Florian Phillipot. He has had the ear of *Front National* leader Marine Le Pen for several years now and his two main strategies, both successful, have been to move the far-right party away from taints of racism and anti-semitism (to the extent of expelling Marine's father Jean Marie Le Pen) and making it a populist party appealing to the ignored and discounted working class of the northern French rust belt. Its English collorary, the post-industrial north and Midlands, similarly abandoned by liberals and globalists, is exactly the heartland Labour have lost and must regain if they are ever to become electable again. This is less an opinion than simple psephological truth, however unpalatable it might be to the north London caucus. Unpalatable, that is, if you are of the opinion that Corbyn and Momentum actually want to win elections. This is a serious point; I suspect that there are some now at the ideological helm of Labour who find the purity of permanent opposition far more attractive than the messy, difficult compromised business of government.

The romance that I felt in the stands at the King Power stadium that Saturday afternoon, dissipated swiftly in February when eight months after the greatest achievement in club football, manager Claudio Ranieri was sacked by Leicester City's billionaire Thai owners. These are the ones whose royal family we had dutifully clapped in October like the saps we are amidst some homily about respect and tradition. Fenwick's in Leicester closed too, though the one in Newcastle where I bought gin, socks and a flat cap still thrives. The happy and hardworking Santaniello family of Bedford have appeared on the *Hairy Bikers*, cooking spaghetti bolognese and touring the Stewartby brickworks. Perhaps emboldened by our Twitter exchange, Michael Gove was granted an audience with the new US President. Rupert Murdoch sat in, just visible in the shadows, baleful as the Mekon.

Three-and-a-half weeks. Three hundred miles. Roaring arterial highways that arrowed to the horizon, B roads that snaked down the shallow tray of a valley; up ahead, the bulk of a city or the silence of trees; the growl of haulage, silent lanes under canopies of leaves, abandoned railway lines, village inns lighting up at four, market days, candlelit cathedrals, darkened tunnels, steamy restaurants, the bright lights of the fairground, blue remembered hills, angry men in bad pubs, limpid French impressionist music in intimate salons, vast flat fields haunted by rooks. Britain in 1936 was a land of beef paste sandwiches and drill halls. Now we are a nation of vaping and nail salons, pulled pork and salted caramel. Some things have returned though; old-fashioned barber shops and hot towel shaves, allotments and baking.

I walked from the top to the bottom and into the heart of England. I looked it in the eye from morning till night and I never grew tired of it. Like the marchers, I learned something from those long days, evenings and nights that no amount of TV news or opinion pieces or well-meant documentaries could have given me. I learned about England now, about England then, and about England's secrets, its scraps and footnotes. I hope I have done it justice. Sometimes it baffled me, sometimes it irritated. But I came to know that, to quote that old maxim, yes, it is my country right or wrong. It seems to be wrong about something almost every day now, but I understand some of its discontent, its bristling dissatisfaction with how it has been ignored, patronised and marginalised.

When it is right, it is still cheery and industrious, generous and tough, patient and dependable, rugged and gentle, mysterious and fascinating, charming and funny. It is not yet become solely the ruddy faced, shouting, unpleasant enclave of *This England* magazine, Piers Morgan and Nigel Farage. No, it is still the England of the warm, lovely Santaniellos and Inderpal the earnest, decent young Sikh in Beeston. It's the England of generous Mark and his little lad Sam in the stands at Leicester and kindly ladies like Lynn in the Bunyan Museum.

On leaving choral evensong at Ripon, after a few glasses of good Italian red, I took a turn around the town in the gathering gloom and found myself down by the bus station where I recognised two members of the congregation. They had seemed incongruous among the Barbours and tweeds and headscarves then; his raincoat too shabby and trousers too short, her coat too thin. He had pushed her out of the cathedral in a wheelchair, a worn plastic supermarket bag dangling from the arm. Now they were sheltering from fine drizzle under the plastic roof of the shelter. She was coughing violently and he was crouching to comfort her. They both peered at the illuminated yellow ticker that told them to 'await further information' about their bus home.

Seeing that couple, not young, not strong, ill-looking and sad in a chilly bus shelter as dusk began to fall, made me wonder: who is speaking for them? Who is fighting their corner, the weak and insecure and vulnerable? Who will make their lives better? Not bullies and narcissists like Farage or Trump for sure, nor Corbyn, scuttling in fear from every journalist's question. Maybe it is no bad thing if that consensus has been shattered if that is what makes the comfortable of left and right easy in their superiority. Maybe it might make them wonder what the lives of others are really like, whether they like them or not.

That last full marcher Con Whalen said that the Jarrow march had made 'not a ha'porth of difference' to the town's fortunes or its people and had been 'a waste of time'. But, according to Tom Pickard in his book *Jarrow*, a Sir Charles Allison, a politician of the north east, was asked about the Depression and the Jarrow march in 1965. He said, 'It's not bloody well going to happen again. There is a feeling, yes, a feeling in the minds of those who have experienced it that it could happen again. But if it did, there would be an armed revolt. Men would not go in supplication to the lord. They would take what they wanted.' Perhaps next time then, Geordie actually will go and burn them down.

Was 2016 like 1936? Will 2017 be like 1937? And so on and so on until disaster awaits a few years down the line. I saw and heard chilling echoes, not from the Jarrow march route but not too far away, that made me think. Domineering men telling lies, big lies, and snarling at the judges and journalists who try to hold them to account. Contempt for women. Contempt for decency. Banter instead of wit. Cruelty in place of compassion. The age of the troll and the snowflake, people reduced to stereotypes, and the newspapers once again denouncing 'enemies of the people' and printing their names and pictures. In 2016, for the first time for me, it was not glib chatter or student drivel to think that something very like fascism was arising again out of the depths of history, a rough beast slouching towards Bethlehem to be born.

Looking at the toxic venom and gainsaying between right and left today, you might despair. But don't. In 1936, Mosley's Fascists moved comfortably around the towns of England assisted by the police, championed by the press and tacitly supported by the aristocrats and royals. The Jarrow marchers, now fabled and romanticised, were spied on and bullied by the police, abandoned by the Labour Party and the TUC and mocked by the church. They were lied to and cheated and eventually ignored. It was ever thus. There may well always be people who lord it loudmouthed and self-satisfied: whether leering bullies or dreary puritans, over-entitled man-babies, privileged pub bores or ineffectual commissars, they are brothers under the skin, self-absorbed and impervious.

But they are not the best of us. The Jarrow men and Red Ellen were. Like her, like them, we are a mess of contradictions, a desperate, striving hotch-potch who are flawed and human and try our best to make the best of things. I'm not sure I want a nation entirely at ease with itself. We're not altogether the peaceful and compliant land we appear. We've cut the heads off kings and taken axes to each other in the streets and pastures. We've done wicked things to ourselves and to others. So no, not a nation at ease with itself. Better a nation always arguing amongst itself, civilly but passionately and endlessly restless in brilliant, angry, loving, vital cities and hard, defiant little towns, in market squares in the long afternoons and empty fields at evening under a huge, darkening sky of clustering, darting swallows or teeming with starlings. And in the distance, out of the past, the ghostly clatter of boots coming again down the long English road.

March 2017

POST POSTSCRIPT

The Met Office overview for October 2016 calls it a 'benign' month, and so it felt to a traveller on the road. Long, still afternoons of calm weather and mild temperatures, plump and ripe and russet, the kind of autumn that poets love. But out there in darkest England, there was also an undertow of the unreal, a febrile, apocalyptic feeling abroad, a weirdness in the air and in the news. Donald Trump growing daily crazier and more infantile. Brexit still bubbling like a fever through the national bloodstream. Terror and fear on the streets. There was the occasional biblical portent too: flash floods in Cornwall; thick, unexpected banks of fog closing airports and making the English Channel unnavigable (heavy symbolism there); sudden storms; a lightning strike razing a barn in Northamptonshire; and at the close, the warmest, clammiest Halloween in living memory.

That Halloween found me sweltering in smart casuals in the lobby of Portcullis House, Westminster, ill at ease and sticky amongst the American tourists, the Japanese hipsters, the coach parties. I had been on the road for three weeks and walked 300 miles. I had thrown my 'good' pair of trousers in a bin in Northallerton and worn my lightweight Meindls down at the outside of the heel because of that weird thing I do when I walk. I was still shaving daily but the trudge along the Edgware Road that balmy morning had left me gritty-eyed and glazed with sweat like a doughnut.

The thin trickle of perspiration that ran down from between my shoulder blades along the length of my spine between shirt and backpack was not entirely down to exertion and temperature though. Just as I was about to pass through the security scanners with George – assistant to Tracy Brabin, the MP for Batley and Spen, who'd kindly agreed to meet me at journey's end – I realised that in my pocket I had a knife: the Swiss Army knife

I'd carried the whole journey, boy scout-like, and never had occasion to use. Now I was about to try to enter Parliament with it, to meet the MP whose friend and predecessor had been stabbed to death by a deranged fascist in the street. Panicking, I managed to ditch it, quickly and at the very last moment, just before I was surely and rightly pinned to the floor, cuffed and bundled roughly away.

I didn't include this detail in the first edition of this book. By then, like much else about that long, difficult, fascinating, rich and strange October, details like that had taken on the gauzy quality of a nagging dream. It was a dream that still comes back unexpectedly at the mention of a town's name or a sign whizzing by on a train platform, then solidifies into a memory of huge moons on cloudless nights over quiet northern towns, or trancelike miles across England's flat, quiet shires. Looking back, it has that unreality and the footsore ache of real life; real as the blisters and paracetamol, the greasy roadside pasties and the wonky hotel-room showers.

One of the central thrusts of *Long Road from Jarrow*, one of the reasons I wanted to make the trip and write the book, was my contention that 2016 felt very much like 1936, the year that the Jarrow men made their trek to London. I soon realised that others perhaps more qualified and eminent than I were having the same thoughts. American political writer Timothy Snyder wrote a bestseller later that year called *On Tyranny*, comparing the climate here and in the United States to the one that fostered the Blackshirts and the Nazis, and concluding that if we forget the lessons of the 1930s, we will be forced to repeat them. Martin Amis though, waspish and smart as ever, rejected all the comparisons between Trump and Hitler, stating in an interview in the *Guardian* that the President was clearly Mussolini, a pompous, vainglorious, essentially stupid bully. Historical novelist C W Gortner asserted bleakly that the thirties were certainly back but sadly 'without the fabulous fashions'.

Both countries, the England of 1936 and 2016, seemed to be in state of seizure, of quiet, twitchy convulsion, and jittery anticipation – dread even – of the next chapter in our national story. Both times, both moods, reflected our vexed relationship with the continent of Europe. In 1936, Oswald Mosley was trying and failing to ape the ubermensch posturings of the equally risible but chillingly more successful fascist bullies in Italy, Germany and Spain. Their poison would soon plunge the Jarrow men and their community and the whole of Britain and the world into a dreadful, protracted war. In 2016, our far right – some more clubbable and chummy, others more nasty and squalid – was having rather more success this time in abandoning Europe altogether and turning sourly in on ourselves.

A quote I often return to – and like Churchill, I think that 'it is a good thing for an uneducated man to read books of quotations' – is Rudyard Kipling's penetrating 'What do they know of England who only England know?' But as writer John Lanchester has pointed out, it's now as pertinent to ask after the Brexit vote: 'What do they know of the UK who only London know?' When, before embarking, I told metropolitan friends of the route of my journey and the places it would take me, many mentioned that I'd be in 'Brexit country'; a 'here be dragons' wilderness of crippled industries, troglodytic racists and poor quality restaurants. It was refreshing to find then that in the months after I'd written the book, some writers and pieces seemed to be emerging who shared my dismay at this. The *Times* columnist Janice Turner has written with angry brilliance about how 'Brexity' has become a loose, glib term of abuse used to denote and dismiss towns, cities, people, music, even foods associated with the benighted and ignorant post-industrial wastes or possibly the 'reactionary' market towns of middle England. When people do this they are talking about the places I walked through, ate and drank and talked in. They are talking about the curry houses of Ferryhill and the pie shops of Framwellgate Moor, the pubs of Wakefield and the cafés of Kibworth. They are talking about Jarrow. G K Chesterton was, I think, rather better disposed to them when he talked of these places and people, this unfashionable and overlooked England, in his dark, sad poem 'The Secret People'. 'Smile at us, pay us, pass us; but do not quite forget; / For we are the people of England, that never have spoken yet.' In 2016, for better or worse, they spoke.

I think they made a bad mistake, one they will come to regret in the cold months and years ahead. But I still had little time for the scornful, superior way their feelings were dismissed by the commentariat within the Beltway of the M25. A second referendum was bayed for, on the wonky, spurious logic that we simply would have to ask these serfs the same question over and over again until we got an answer we liked.

The American academic, Mark Lilla, was addressing American liberalism's failure to prevent the rise of Trump or even decently give battle with it when he wrote the following, but the echoes of the Remain lobby's abject failings and superciliousness were clear:

> You need to visit, if only with your mind's eye, places where wifi is non-existent, the coffee is weak, and you will have no desire to post a photo of your dinner on Instagram. And where you'll be eating with people who give genuine thanks for that dinner in prayer. Don't look down on them.

Beverly Gage, a *New York Times* reviewer, called this 'trolling disguised as erudition', suggesting that a dim, wounded preciousness and snobbery are not just confined to the British intelligentsia. If Lilla were English, his passion for a broad-based inclusivity and his sympathy for the old working class would doubtless see him mocked as a 'centrist dad', a popular fey rebuke of 2017.

'Centrist', like 'Blairite', had become a standard insult applied by the nouveau left, especially the more high-profile arrivistes, for anyone who didn't share their unqualified enthusiasm for Jeremy Corbyn or sometimes those who had been politically engaged or aware for more than a year or two. They sometimes reminded me, ironically, of those Sky Sports campaigns (and fans at large) that assume football was invented in 1992 with the coming of the Premier League. As I was planning the walk, Jeremy Corbyn was widely regarded as the most incompetent and divisive leader the Labour Party had suffered since the Jarrow march era and the aloof and uninspiring Ramsay MacDonald. Those of us whose natural initial inclination was to regard Corbyn similarly were increasingly surprised, amused, delighted by how this changed and by how great sections of the electorate warmed to him and Labour, not just his dogged long-term ideological kinsmen like John McDonnell and Diane Abbott but ordinary young people new to politics ('youthquake', as applied to the cult of Jeremy, was the *Oxford English Dictionary*'s word of 2017) and older voters sick of the stage-managed banality of the Westminster bubble.

This groundswell continued until, by the summer of 2017, he was, as I would jokingly put it on the tour and shows I did around the book's first publication, 'now widely accepted as the greatest statesman the world has ever seen or will ever see, a transformation effected by the brilliant tactic of losing a general election'. That was a gag of course, but it contained a kernel of truth. The elation surrounding Labour's unexpectedly good showing at the ballot box and the disarray of the Tories was palpable and widespread, though it was salutary to keep in mind that Labour had actually lost. I was reminded of the now hugely unacceptable old Goffin and King song 'He Hit Me (And It Felt Like a Kiss)': they beat us but it felt like a win.

Part of that was down to the incumbent, Theresa May, and the Conservative Party campaign in general, a lumbering zombie of rank arrogance and crass ineptitude. Mostly the Tories were invisible over the five weeks of the campaign and when they did take centre stage, they would generally say something stupid, announce something unpopular like the so-called dementia tax on older voters, and conduct themselves with a complacency and high-handedness that turned out to be almost entirely misplaced. The electorate gave them the short shrift they deserved, if not quite short enough.

But credit where it is due. On that Jarrow book tour (which took me again to many of the towns and cities on the route such as Nottingham, Barnsley, Mansfield and Leicester) I would sometimes be asked whether I had changed my mind about Corbyn. I would answer, truthfully, that yes I had. But I'd add that, for me, that change had been significantly due to a colossal improvement in his performance and Labour strategy. Buoyed by genuine popular enthusiasm and a new mood of (perhaps grudging) solidarity in the Parliamentary Labour Party, he grew more confident, to the extent that he seemed at times to be almost enjoying the rough and tumble of realpolitik of which he and his team had once seemed so disdainful.

With noses held perhaps, both wings of the party – old-school Labour apparatchiks and Corbynistas – put aside deep-seated suspicions and worked together, knowing that each needed the other. Old and New Labour both had to acknowledge and harness that genuine passion and momentum (with a capital M and without) of the Corbyn movement. Conversely, as Heather Stewart wrote in the *Guardian*, 'None of Corbyn's high command supporters had run anything on the scale of a nationwide general election campaign. They needed Labour's party machine, with its spreadsheets and budgets and cumulative wisdom of campaigns gone by. Both sides ... harboured deep suspicions of each other, and there were bitter battles, over resources and tactics. But ultimately both tribes played their part.' Labour recruited political strategists who knew about both doorstepping and Facebook, and hired some of Bernie Sanders's team from the States. (He lost too, of course, but he did better than anyone could have predicted, which turned out to be prophetic.)

Labour's 2017 election manifesto was also exemplary; passionate, clear, candid and full of ideas that chimed with actual voters, especially the young. The gulf between the old guard (as typified emblematically by Murdoch, Dacre and the ageing, fearful dinosaurs of the print media) and the newly engaged was exposed brilliantly and hilariously in a BBC *Question Time* edition from York just before the election. Ruddy-faced, angry middle-aged and elderly men on the panel and in the audience frothed and fulminated on about Trident, the unions and the IRA, unaware that such straw men belonged these days on *I Love the '70s* rather than the BBC's flagship political debate show. The rest of the audience – the young, the women, those of the BAME community – rolled their eyes, smiled and shook their heads. Their pressing concerns and daily struggles were about getting a mortgage, a decent wage, child care and ending discrimination, not what happened at British Leyland in 1975. A newly alert electorate had no problem with full grants, nationalisation of key industries, a properly funded welfare state or strong unions, no matter how much the Conservative press tried, rather pathetically, to drape these ancient bogeymen in moth-eaten white sheets and parade them on their front pages. Younger voters, quite rightly, were not in the least frightened by these chimeras. Indeed, they found it rather baffling and pathetic. They were not entirely sure what the Nanny State was and certainly could not see what was so terrible about it.

But that's another book. The next one, I think. This one should end with a final tribute to those great men and women, and how they seared their name and their town into history and became a byword for working-class pride, dignity and resolve and possibly heroic failure. Mark Lilla also wrote that, to defeat the far right and the untrammelled force of capital, we needed 'less marches and more mayors'. Jarrow had both.

On my Jarrow talks, I would always get a laugh when, after discussing the laureate of the 1930s, W H Auden, I'd show a slide of his leathery, prune-like 'late' face and repeat that line of my old English teacher's: 'What must his balls be like?' But I would also talk of how Auden's genius was to turn the political into the poetical, to see men for what they are despite their humbug and cant, behind their rhetoric and beyond their competing ideologies.

Auden became as much of a British 'centrist dad' as a gay communist poet dividing his time between Istria, New York and Austria probably could. Once, in the poem 'Spain', he had written effectively, if chillingly, of 'the necessary murder': the ruthlessness often required to get what one wanted politically, especially in the dark and savage 1930s. But by the time he came to write 'September 1, 1939', at the end of that 'low dishonest decade', he had seen through the lies and inhumanity of every kind of extremist and denounced them all. It ends with a plea and an admonition to everyone: liberal, totalitarian, strong man, bully, snowflake; to the shrill and eager denouncers, the moralists of left and right, the self-satisfied, self-absorbed, self-obsessed of every stripe. It sounds disarmingly, shockingly direct and emotional now but Auden and the Jarrow marchers dealt in strong feelings in hard times.

Those times are back. Auden and Jarrow were right.

'We must love one another or die.'

Manchester, Christmas 2017

THANK YOU...

...to the following generous and lovely people, largely in order of appearance:

Matt Perry
Tom Kelly
Joanne Hackett-Smith, all at Jarrow Council Fun Day
Rowland at Opera North
Clare Hudson
Inderpal and all at the Gurdwara, Beeston
Nadia Shireen
Rowland at Opera North
Dan Jackson
Ian Stringer
Lara Skinner and Foxes fans Mark and Sam Pausey
Peter, Veda and Amanda at Chesterfield Museum
Mansfield Museum
Kev and Jake at Windsor Windows
The Chuckle Brothers
Tracy Brabin and George

And everyone who kept me company and made valuable suggestions via my blog of the journey or social media.

FURTHER READING

Jarrow Protest and Legend, Matt Perry, University of Sunderland Press (2005)

Jarrow, Tom Pickard, Alison & Busby (1981)

The Thirties: An Intimate History, Juliet Gardiner, Harper (2011)

We Danced All Night: A Social History of Britain Between the Wars, Martin Pugh, Vintage (2009)

The People, Selina Todd, John Murray (2015)

Britain in the 1930s, Andrew Thorpe, Historical Association (1992)

Britain in the 1930s, Noreen Branson and Margot Heinemann, Panther (1973)

CHAPTER ONE

Something happened at the balloon debate. Freya had no idea what it was, but over the next four months, she was increasingly convinced that whatever it was that *had* happened, started there.

She hadn't even wanted to take part. Vanity had been her downfall. When she turned down the invitation, Dulcie Makepeace had lowered her voice to a confidential whisper. 'We need some star quality on the panel,' she explained, 'and I immediately thought of you.'

Later, Freya grumbled to Felix that the only reason Dulcie approached her was because she needed a token woman.

'In that case,' Felix said, 'make a virtue of it. Choose someone who can make a rousing feminist argument for staying in the balloon.'

It was a good idea and there were any number of admirable role models. She could be Florence Nightingale or Boudicca or that woman who pioneered birth control whose name she could never remember. But they were predictable choices. They were precisely the sort of women her audience would expect her to choose.

Freya did not want to be predictable. She was queuing at the post office when the idea came to her. It would be difficult, it would be unexpected, and it would be more high-brow than Dulcie anticipated or wanted. So much the better, Freya thought. She still smarted from the ease with which Dulcie had persuaded her to perform.

1

She decided not to tell Felix beforehand. It would be hard to explain what she was trying to do; Felix would offer a number of sensible suggestions as to why she shouldn't do it; she would be discouraged and she didn't *want* to be. She felt she was creating something difficult and fragile and fascinating. The slightest criticism would blow it all away.

On the evening of the event she left Felix eating chicken salad – she was far too nervous to eat a thing – and went upstairs to change. She put on what she called her Glamour Outfit – a figure-hugging black dress and a matching bolero jacket with a fake-fur collar. She made up her face, sprayed her neck liberally with perfume and stared at herself in the mirror. At her age there was a fine line between dressing to make an impression and looking like a Joan Collins wannabe. She had forgotten how short the dress was.

She applied a final coating of lip gloss to her mouth and went back down to the kitchen where Felix was loading the dishwasher. She put her hands on her hips, extended one leg in front of the other and adopted her Lauren Bacall look, a stance she had frequently plagiarised in her modelling days. 'What do you think?' she asked.

Felix straightened his back and scrutinised her. 'I think,' he said thoughtfully, 'that every man in the room will want to take you home tonight. I know I will.'

'Seriously. You don't think I'm mutton dressed as lamb?'

'If you are,' Felix said, 'then you're very sexy mutton. You look beautiful.'

'Oh Felix!' Freya smiled. She *had*, long ago, been beautiful. Now that she was middle-aged she could see that.

When she looked at old photos, she admired the tiny waist, the long legs, the blonde hair and the cheekbones. The waist had long since thickened, the legs were defaced by gristle-like knees and thin blue veins, and the blonde hair posed a constant dilemma: should any woman over fifty have long hair?

The miracle was that Felix saw none of this. When they first got together, he described them as Beauty and the Beast. He had had tiny green eyes, a large if indeterminate nose, untidy short hair and a small scruffy beard and moustache. All of these features, apart from the beard and moustache, were still in evidence. The addition of laughter lines around the eyes, broadened shoulders and a bulkier chest provoked an irresistible comparison with a rumpled teddy bear. If Felix was a Beast, he was an endearingly attractive one.

In the car, Freya checked she had her notes in her bag, took a few deep breaths and gazed out of the window. She loved the woods at this time of year. The green leaves on the trees continued to be a novelty and, even though it was almost June, there was a still-flourishing carpet of bluebells and pale primroses.

The first time Felix had brought her to see the cottage, she had been taken aback by its rural solitude. Now she couldn't imagine living in London again. Here, their nearest neighbours were a quarter of a mile down the lane and, as they passed Pam's house, Freya noticed that her red Renault Clio was gone. Freya felt a slight easing of tension. Pam was one of the best by-products of moving here. She was loyal, kind, and utterly reliable.

'She must have left already,' Freya said. 'I asked her to

sit near the front. I need a friendly face to look at.'

'I'm a friendly face,' Felix said.

'You're *too* friendly. You'll be nervous for me and that'll make *me* nervous.'

'Rubbish. You're brilliant at these things.'

They were coming into Darrowbridge now. Felix drove past the railway station and then the garage. Freya stared into her bag to check she had her phone. 'I told the twins I was dreading this,' she said. 'I thought they might have rung.' She felt a little hollow-chested. She should have eaten something earlier.

Her phone gave two little bleats and Freya took it out of her bag and studied it.

'Let me guess,' Felix said. 'It's from one of the girls?'

'"Off to Scotland tomorrow! Hurrah! Good luck tonight, love Tess." Now I feel bad.'

'Oh, ye of little faith,' Felix murmured.

Freya sighed. 'Tess does love Scotland. She'd move there like a shot if a job came up.'

'I rang Ma to wish her happy birthday the other night. She's so excited about Tess's visit.'

'They've always been close. I hope I'll be close to *my* grandchildren. If I ever get any.'

'Of course you will. People take longer to settle down these days, that's all.'

'Most twenty-seven-year-old women have at least had a *few* long-term relationships.' Freya swallowed hard as Felix turned into the town hall car park. 'Oh God, it's almost full.' She watched him slide the car into one of the few remaining places. 'I wish it was all over.' She opened her door. 'Dulcie told me to go in by the side entrance. Wish me luck.'

'You don't need it,' Felix told her. 'You'll be terrific. You look terrific.' He switched off the engine and reached across to kiss her mouth. 'I'm very proud of you.'

'Tell me that when it's finished,' she said. She climbed out of the car, straightened her dress, hoisted her bag over her shoulder and went through the side door into a room with walls covered in alphabet posters. Her four fellow-panellists were there and, as she accepted a glass of wine from Dulcie, one of them, an ex-editor of the *Darrowbridge Gazette*, came over and kissed her cheek.

'Freya, my darling, you look good enough to eat!'

If the girls were here they would roll their eyes but Freya could never resist a compliment.

'Thank you, Roland, I hope I've not overdone the party look.'

'I love your party look,' he assured her. He enjoyed his reputation as a ladies' man and took great care of his teeth, which were now fully in evidence, in all their radiant regularity.

Dulcie's phone let out a shrill screech and she clapped her hands together. 'That's my alarm. It's time we went in.'

And so, in they went. Freya felt a flutter of apprehension as she took her seat and noted with gratitude that Pam sat right in the middle of the front row. The hall was almost full, a testament to the formidable organizational powers of Dulcie, who stood up and waited for the excited chatter to subside.

'Tonight,' she proclaimed, 'we have five local celebrities who have given up their time to bring you this entertainment. Each of them will take on the role of someone they admire. Each will give a brief talk in which he or she will try to persuade you to keep him or her in the balloon. Your job is to vote one of them off. The remaining four will then speak again, you will vote another one off and so it goes on until only the victor remains. So, without further ado, we will begin the proceedings with our first celebrity. Most of you will know her as Freya Eliza Cameron, one of *Darrowbridge Life*'s favourite columnists. Every month, she gives us regular insights into the complexities of ancestral research. An experienced genealogist, her website, *RevealingFamilies.co.uk* is extremely popular and I would recommend it to you all. Ladies and gentlemen, I give you Freya Eliza Cameron!'

Freya stood up and acknowledged the applause with a modest smile. She was aware of the adrenalin charging round her brain, firing up synapses and sharpening her memory. This happened every time she spoke in public. Beforehand, she would feel nervous and unwell, but as soon as she started to perform she'd put aside her notes and enjoy herself.

'Before I start,' she said, 'I have an admission to make.' She shut her eyes for a few seconds. 'I am . . .' she paused for dramatic effect '. . . an unfaithful wife.'

There was a slight, nervous rattle of laughter, a reaction Freya had anticipated. 'I am Madame Bovary,' she continued, 'and I want you to keep me in the balloon despite my reputation as a fallen woman. Some of you may have read my story as told by Gustave Flaubert. He is famous for his insights into the female mind and for his compassion towards me. I can tell you now: his reputation is undeserved. I am the victim of a stitch-up!'

6

A mobile in the front row exploded into action. Its ringtone, the first few chords of 'Under My Thumb', provoked a ripple of laughter in the audience. The owner, a middle-aged man with a limp ponytail, muttered an apology and turned off his phone. Freya threw him an understanding smile, an Oscar-winning performance in itself, and took a deep breath.

'Flaubert begins the story – *my* story – with a description of my husband as a little boy, jeered at by his schoolmates because he has been given a ridiculous hat to wear by his mother.' She stopped to glance around the room. 'Do you see what Flaubert does? Despite the fact that Charles grows up to be a dangerously inadequate doctor and an oafish husband and lover, he remains a figure of sympathy because of that first childish episode. The odds are stacked against me from the start!'

Freya's idea had seemed so clever when she'd planned it. Now she was aware of a big, shimmering question mark hovering over the heads of the audience and, worse, it was hovering over her head too. She had wanted to reclaim Madame Bovary as a victim, a woman trapped in a loveless marriage and starved of romance. She knew as she stood on the stage that she'd lost her audience with the story of little Charles in his ridiculous hat. Everyone felt sorry for children who were bullied. *She* felt sorry for children who were bullied. Felix was right. She should have gone for an obvious heroine, someone like Florence Nightingale or Boudicca or the woman who pioneered birth control.

She struggled on, trying to paint Madame Bovary as a universal symbol of downtrodden women, but when she finally finished she knew she was as confused as everyone

7

else. She had wanted to portray Flaubert as a misogynist and instead, she had ended up supporting his silly, self-absorbed creation. She felt she could weep.

The applause was polite. Freya attached a calm smile to her face and let her eyes wander over the audience, her expression only faltering when they settled on her husband. Felix was not clapping, he was not even looking at her. He was staring down at his phone, his attention fully engaged on the small screen in his hands. Freya wanted to wave her arms and shout out, 'Felix, what are you doing? I'm here! I'm humiliated! I need your support!'

The rest of the evening was a gruelling ordeal. Freya listened to a wise-cracking Casanova, a sing-along Walt Disney, an unlikely Sir Winston Churchill and a hip-swerving Elvis Presley. Freya was the first to get voted off by a large majority. Elvis Presley won. Freya knew she had entirely misjudged the nature of the evening. She had come across as humourless, inarticulate and, worst of all, dull.

When the event finished at last, Freya made her excuses, found Felix and murmured that she had to go *now*. In the car, as he negotiated his way out of the car park, she broke the silence with a loud groan. 'I was a disaster,' she said.

She waited for Felix to do what he did so well: reassure her, make her laugh, put things into some sort of perspective. When he didn't respond, she glanced across at him. 'Was I really terrible?'

He kept his eyes fixed on the road. 'Perhaps your speech was a little too subtle. I couldn't understand what you were trying to say.'

She waved a hand in the air. 'Oh I can't bear to think

about it. I totally failed to get my point across.' The truth was, Freya could no longer remember what her point was supposed to be. She folded her arms together. 'And *you* were looking at your phone. You hate people looking at their phones!'

'I'd forgotten to turn it off,' Felix said. 'I had a text and I was trying to switch it off.'

'Did you even listen to my speech?'

'Yes. Yes, of course I did.'

'I feel so stupid,' Freya raged. 'That's the last time I will ever take part in one of Dulcie's fundraising evenings. Not that she'll ask me again after this.'

In her bag, her phone made itself heard. Freya read out the message. '"Good luck, Mum, love Anna."' She shuddered. 'At least the girls weren't here to witness my humiliation.'

'Freya,' Felix protested. 'You're being melodramatic. You weren't *that* bad.'

'Thank you,' Freya said. 'That's very encouraging.'

Back at home, she stood in the hall and made a face at her reflection in the mirror. She turned in time to catch Felix staring at her with an expression of almost clinical disinterest, as if he wasn't sure who she was. It disconcerted her. It was unnerving. She said, uncertainly, 'I can see what you're thinking.'

'Can you?' He seemed surprised, almost guilty.

'I could see it in your face. *How could Freya get it so wrong?*'

'Don't be silly.' He took off his jacket and hung it on the coat-stand. 'I think I'll watch the news. Do you want some tea?'

'Only if you're making some. I shall go to bed and read my book.'

When she woke in the morning, Felix had already left. She couldn't remember a time when he'd set off to Bristol without first saying goodbye to her. She presumed he must be preoccupied by something at work.

She had planned to spend the morning at her laptop but it was impossible to study dusty old census records when she felt so frazzled. She had made a fool of herself last night and she had no one to blame but herself. She should try to stop thinking about it. She was aware that, these days, her emotions were dangerously incontinent. A brief, bland call from Anna could reduce her to tears followed by an afternoon's soul-search as to how she had failed her children. A new liver spot on her hand plunged her into a gloom accompanied by sinister presentiments of mortality. Middle age was a frightening place for anyone cursed with the sin of vanity.

Vanity, she thought suddenly, had been responsible for Felix. How could she resist a man whose first glance was one of startled adoration, particularly since his shyness had forced *her* to do the running? She remembered the odd way he'd looked at her last night, and then rolled her eyes. She would get nothing done if she carried on like this.

Freya opened her top left-hand drawer and pulled out her perfect displacement-activity project. In just over three months, she and Felix would celebrate their thirtieth wedding anniversary. Six weeks ago, demoralised by an inconclusive trip to the National Archives in Kew, she had brought out a new pink folder and labelled it 'Anniversary Stuff'. She had selected a possible date for a party, one close to Christmas when Felix's mother would be with them. This morning she would spend a half-hour composing a speech.

She pushed her laptop away, reached for her pad of A4 paper and picked up her pen. She imagined the sitting room, full of family and friends all staring expectantly at her . . .

Thank you for coming here tonight. Thank you for helping Felix and me to celebrate our anniversary. And forgive me for making a speech. I know it's self-indulgent but you are *a captive audience and I'd like to say a few words about marriage.*

First of all, I like it, obviously. Otherwise, we wouldn't be having this party. But actually, now I'm so old, I do find it odd that I went into marriage and motherhood with such blithe optimism.

Motherhood is easier to understand. You feel broody. You have a baby – in my case you have two at once – and you love them. They love you. And then they're teenagers and they want nothing to do with you. Even when they're adults, you're still low on their list of priorities.

Marriage seems equally straightforward at first. You fall in love with a man, he falls for you and you marry. Then you discover there are times when he irritates you. Even more outrageous, you know there are times when you *irritate* him. *You can catch him staring at you like you're a stranger and . . .*

Oh dear God! What a load of self-pitying, pompous rubbish! Freya wrote in big capitals 'DO NOT TRY TO WRITE SOMETHING POSITIVE WHEN YOU FEEL NEGATIVE!' Then, reaching for her felt-tip pen, she drew thick lines over everything she'd written. She tore out the piece of paper and put it in the folder which she returned at once to her drawer. What was wrong with her today?

Action was imperative. No to census records; no to anniversary speeches; and double no to Madame Bovary. She glanced at the window. The weather was lovely. She would go into the garden, which at this time of year had exploded into its usual overwhelming fecundity. She would arm herself with her trowel and her fork and she would decimate the weeds. On her return to the house, she would go back to her census records in the happy knowledge that the balloon debate would soon be forgotten. And as for Felix's odd expression last night, it was ridiculous to dwell on something so silly. He was probably just tired and fed up. She couldn't blame him for that.

CHAPTER TWO

'We need 2 talk.'

When had Richard learnt to *text*?

Tess Cameron sat on the steps of the stone Mercat Cross, the hood of her anorak tied tightly under her chin, her hands already cold without their gloves. She stared intently at the small screen as if it would provide an answer. Richard was the only man she knew who didn't have a smartphone or a tablet. She wasn't even sure he knew about Facebook. The text was so incongruous, like Prince Charles wearing leather trousers.

'We need 2 talk,' he said, but no, they absolutely didn't. They – *he* – had talked for England. He had been devastated, apologetic and awkward, and then defensive, angry and outraged. The words had kept coming and she'd tried to apologise – it was *her* fault, she'd been taken by surprise, she'd lashed out in panic when he lunged at her. He *had* lunged – she would always think of him now as Richard the Lunger – but she hadn't meant to hit him; his chin had got in the way of her fist and she was *sorry*. He hadn't tried to listen, his words kept crushing her like a steamroller: *violent, disproportionate, extraordinary, psychotic, aberration*.

And yes, she supposed, her reaction had been disproportionate. She was sufficiently aware of her oddness only ever to have confided in three people, two of whom she no longer saw. Rachel, the first, had been her flatmate and a close friend since university days in Durham. At first,

Rachel had compared Tess's problem to a fear of death. Her sister, she said, had been obsessed with her own mortality since early childhood but could now go for at least three days without dwelling on it. Rachel's conclusion was that Tess would grow out of her fear of sex. In the months after that first conversation, Rachel would occasionally ask, 'How's the fear of sex coming along?' and Tess would say, 'It's still there, thanks for asking.'

Rachel, ever the optimist, assured Tess that one day she'd meet a man who would be so right that Tess would *want* to have sex. This seemed highly unlikely. She was extremely fond of Richard, but when he lunged at her on Thursday evening, she'd felt nothing but terror. And now, as a result, she had lost a good friend.

Her long-planned trip to Scotland could not have come at a better time. Tess had cherished for some years a secret fantasy, a glorious scenario that, in her more positive moments, she really believed might come true. She would finish her PhD in London, turn it into a biography of Sir Walter Scott which, for reasons currently unclear, the whole world would wish to buy. Every university in the country would clamour for her services and she would graciously bestow them on Edinburgh. She would move up to Scotland, buy a small terraced cottage in Melrose and commute to Edinburgh in her new little car – a Mini or a convertible Golf, either would be more than acceptable.

The cottage was so real she could see it. It was on a short cobbled lane that led nowhere. It had one of those front doors that were horizontally partitioned across the middle, and the top part would be fully opened in order to let in the streaming sunlight. On dark winter days, she would sit by her fire, sipping cocoa – a dubious detail since she didn't even *like* cocoa but it was a word that evoked warmth and safety and comfort. On the long summer evenings, she would roam across the hills, absorbing the peace and the beauty of the place, so at odds with its history of battles and massacres. London would soon be a memory and the Border country would be her home.

In the meantime, she had to make do with the occasional visit. It had taken her nine hours and ten minutes to travel up on the coach from Victoria Station to Melrose and as far as she was concerned it was worth every minute. At nine o'clock that morning she had left London with its chaotic traffic, its anxious commuters, its grimy buildings and its billboards promoting the increasingly unreachable rewards of financial success. And now here she was, in her black jeans, her polo-neck jumper and her red anorak, sitting on the steps of the ancient stone cross in the wide market square at Melrose. She dropped her phone in her bag, put on her gloves, and watched two elderly women chatting with great animation while their pets – identical white poodles – circled busily in impotent attempts to sniff each other's rear end.

Melrose was as different from London as Heaven was from Hell. Melrose was a small town with no traffic jams and no taxi drivers hooting angrily at wayward cyclists and lumbering buses. Melrose had no tower blocks or huge, anonymous offices with sad, anonymous employees. Melrose had slow, sedate cars that stopped unquestioningly to let the women with their poodles cross the road. It had the soft sandstone ruins of Melrose Abbey with its seemingly random foundation stones scattered on the lawn around it. It had a friendly high street that opened into the generous square where Tess now waited. It had rugby fields and trees and quiet streets with terraced houses, and bungalows with fenced gardens. It had, on every horizon, undulating green hills dappled with purple heather and darker green copses and, best of all, it had pure Scottish air. Tess could almost feel it purging her pores of the last vestiges of London.

Her phone went and, pulling off her gloves again, she took it out of her bag.

'Hi, Tess.' Her sister's voice sounded breathless. 'Is it today you're in Scotland?'

Anna's voice always sounded breathless on the phone. She was not the sort of person who liked long, chatty calls – at least, she didn't like them with Tess – and therefore tended to ring while on the move: going into or out of her hospital, in which case her words competed with the sound of ambulance sirens; or walking from one part of the building to another, in which case there would be constant interruptions while she exchanged information with other members of staff.

'I arrived a few minutes ago,' Tess told her. 'It's very cold. I'm sitting in the square waiting for Grandma.'

'That's why I rang. I forgot her birthday was on Wednesday. Will you tell her I'm sorry?'

'Can't you tell her yourself?'

'Have you called the Commune lately? I've tried three times this week and it just rings and rings. Give her my love and tell her as soon as I can get hold of a car, I'll come up and see her.'

'I'm sure she'll be impressed.'

'Don't be sarcastic, Tess, it doesn't suit you. You know coaches make me sick and train fares are exorbitant. It's Grandma's fault for living somewhere that's insanely inaccessible. I must go. Have a good holiday.'

'I'm not here for a holiday. I'm here to do research.'

'Yeah, right. Have a good time and kiss Sir Walter for me.'

Tess put her phone back in her bag. She could imagine Anna scurrying after a patient or hailing colleagues and engaging them in earnest conversation about some diagnosis. Anna had phenomenal energy. Tess supposed it must be an essential requirement for a doctor.

The fact that she and Anna were twins was a never-ending mystery to Tess. She knew the science. They were the result of two different eggs and two different sperm. It was therefore no surprise that Anna should have big breasts, blue eyes and straight blonde hair while she had what might be politely described as an androgynous figure with green eyes and auburn curls. To be honest, Tess thought, they had little in common apart from once sharing a womb.

At school, Tess excelled in English and History and Art while Anna came top in Science. They were extraordinarily different, no more so than in their attitude to the Borders. For Anna, the place was cold and dull and, 'It doesn't even have a proper cinema!' Tess must ask her sometime what an improper one might look like.

She saw Grandma approaching the square in her antique Ford Escort, sitting bolt upright with her face a little too close to the windscreen. Tess stood up and waved.

Grandma was out of her car in a moment. No one would think she was now eighty-three.

'Darling girl, I'm so sorry I'm late, there was a stupid sheep in the middle of the road and I hooted and hooted and it just stared at me! I had to get out and virtually push it back into the field. You must have thought I'd forgotten you...'

'I wasn't worried for a moment...'

'That's sweet of you to say so, you must be freezing. I can't believe we're in June next week. Let's get you home. Katherine's made one of her casseroles in your honour.'

Tess put her case in the boot and climbed into the car. As always, Grandma had to turn the key in the ignition twice before the engine started, and, as always, she swore under her breath as she did so. Her short wiry hair still had the rogue lock at the back that refused to lie flat. She wore her corduroy trousers, her puffa jacket and one of her Guernsey jumpers. They were almost a uniform.

Tess stretched her arms in front of her. 'Oh Grandma,' she said, 'it is *so* good to be here again! I wish I could get here more often!'

'Felix rang me on my birthday. He and Freya are definitely coming in October. You should cadge a lift up with them.'

'I will, if it's during my autumn break. I'll talk to Dad. What about this week? Am I all right to borrow your car?'

'Of course. Will you have to go to Edinburgh every day?'

'I might be able to take Friday off. How are all the Communards?'

'They're fine. Sheila had another story published two weeks ago.'

'That's great. What's it about?'

'Two lonely people are brought together by their love of a homeless kitten.' Grandma spoke without expression

'Oh.' Tess thought for a moment. 'I read that one at Easter.'

'No,' Grandma said. 'In that one, two lonely people are united by their love for a bird with a broken wing. Sheila is a great believer in recycling.' She braked as they reached the crossroads and then turned left out of the town centre. 'You might notice a change in Linda. She has problems with her memory. It's not easy for her or for Derek.'

'I'm so sorry,' Tess said.

'Well.' Grandma shrugged. 'It's one of the perils of getting older.'

Her tone and her body language indicated that the subject was closed. Forthright in so many ways, she had never been a woman to welcome sympathy over matters that truly upset her. Grandpa Philip's great idea had never fully addressed this problem, Tess thought. It was all very well for a group of old friends and relatives to set up house together, but what was to happen when members began to grow frail and die?

Grandpa Philip had been so confident. Retirement had made him restless, he was bored with Surrey and he began to pine for his homeland. On a visit to his brother and sister-in-law in Scotland, he introduced the idea of a commune.

Four years later, the plan came to fruition and nine Communards moved into a house outside Melrose. Grandpa Philip and Grandma brought with them Grandma's oldest friend, Sheila, and their neighbours from Surrey, Linda and Derek. Great-uncle Andrew and Great-aunt Katherine arrived with their friends, the Knoxes. On their first evening in their new home, Grandpa Philip, apparently hale and hearty, celebrated his seventy-fourth birthday.

Three years later, Grandpa Philip was buried in the nearby churchyard. Two years after that, Great-uncle Andrew and Mrs Knox died within four months of each other. For a time, it looked as if the Commune would fall apart. Great-aunt Katherine accepted an invitation to move in with her daughter and son-in-law. Doctor Knox toyed with the idea of renting a small bungalow in Melrose. After a bracing discussion with Grandma, Doctor Knox decided to stay put. Great-aunt Katherine spent two months with her daughter and came to the conclusion that she preferred the company of her peers to that of her son-in-law. No one was told what the son-in-law thought.

And so, like a dignified old ship, battered and buffeted by storms, the Commune slowly righted itself. These days, the six remaining pensioners employed a gardener and a cleaner, and at least three of them continued to drive regularly. But every day they grew older. Tess couldn't bear to think that Linda, who was always so sensible and kind, could be brought down by dementia

Grandma, clearly determined to change the subject, said, 'I hope you remembered to bring a dress with you.'

'Of course I did. You didn't tell me why I needed to bring one.'

'Our friend, Flora, is having an eighty-fifth birthday party next Friday. Her late husband was a great pal of your grandpa's. I told her it was your last night with us and she said she'd be delighted if you came along too.'

'That's very kind but quite unnecessary. I'm more than happy to stay behind.'

'That's what your great-aunt said.' Grandma paused in order to let the full significance of that statement sink in. 'Of course if you don't want to go, there is no pressure on you to accompany us. Katherine has assured me you'd find the event very dull.'

'I see.' Tess knew what was expected of her. 'Well, I'll be delighted to prove Great-aunt Katherine wrong.'

Grandma released a small, satisfied smile. 'Good girl! Now tell me: how's the PhD coming along?'

This was one of many reasons why Tess loved her grandmother. There were never any coy enquiries about possible boyfriends. Grandma, in her time a probation officer and then a JP, had always believed that it was work that defined a life. The Communard women had all had careers. Great-aunt Katherine had been a teacher; Sheila had been the indispensable secretary to a brilliant but highly strung businessman. Linda had been a highly regarded crossword compiler. Grandma always said she was the cleverest person she knew.

In many ways, Tess thought, their generation had been truer to feminist principles than her own. They'd lived through tough times and valued their independence. Certainly, they never viewed romantic love as an excuse to sidestep careers.

Tess was fond of all of them. She had a number of good friends in London, most of whom discussed their love lives with her. She did sometimes feel like the sole vegetarian in a burger restaurant. The Communards

21

might be vegetarians due to age and circumstance rather than by choice, but at least they proved it was possible to get by without meat.

CHAPTER THREE

Anna's consultant was small and slight with smooth brown hair neatly tied in a chignon. There were many stories about Miss Diamond, the latest only two months old. She had looked into the labour ward before going out to a dinner party. In a matter of seconds, she took in the distinctive aroma of panic, pulled off her diamond bracelet, calmly called a crash team and performed a Caesarean section before the husband returned from the vending machine. She was a genuine star. Her cool rational tones could often be heard on the *Today* programme and *Woman's Hour.* Her book, *How to Love Your Labour*, was invariably recommended to mothers and midwives.

Miss Diamond was easily the most terrifying person Anna had ever encountered. Her smile could freeze a desert. The first time it was directed at Anna was after Anna's suggestions concerning a pregnant patient's diabetes. Miss Diamond had exposed her pearly white teeth and gazed at Anna with apparent amusement before falling on the diagnosis like a lion feasting on an antelope. After months of continuous put-downs, Anna was beginning to wonder if she was deliberately singled out for regular doses of vitriol.

Today, Miss Diamond, surrounded by her disciples, stood beside the bed of a grossly obese patient whose layers of fat made a palpation of the foetus almost impossible. She gave a little sigh and requested Anna's opinion. Anna took a deep breath and ran through the systematic procedure, to no avail. The baby's cushion was, unsurprisingly, of the extra-large variety.

When she finished, Miss Diamond proceeded, in her quiet, gentle voice, to demolish entirely the medical technique that Anna had set out. 'I wonder, Dr Cameron,' she concluded, 'if you are sure this is where you want to be.'

If this was a film, possibly one starring Kristen Wiig – Anna would *love* to be played by Kristen Wiig – Anna would respond with a scathing, 'What do *you* think, Miss Diamond?' She would turn on her heel and stride out of the hospital, backed by the awestruck, if silent, respect of her peers. Unfortunately, it wasn't a film, Anna wanted to keep her job, and Miss Diamond held all the aces.

It was possible that Miss Diamond genuinely thought Anna was a hopeless, ignorant, misguided and potentially dangerous doctor. It was also possible that within Miss Diamond's sylph-like body, there existed the corrosive soul of a bully who sought out potential victims and tried to reduce them to gibbering wrecks. On balance, Anna was inclined to believe the second hypothesis was the correct one.

Fortunately, her timetable left little time for self-pity, however justified it might be. As she hurried along the corridor, she caught sight of William Niarchos, her good friend and true confidant.

'I'm off at five,' he called out. 'Do you fancy seeing the new X-Men film?'

She had only time to nod before speeding on to her destination. Just the thought of recounting Miss Diamond's latest put-down helped to lessen its poison.

At the gynaecology outpatient clinic, she attended to patients with menstrual disorders, utero-vaginal prolapses and stress incontinence, all of which helped to put her problems with her consultant into some sort of perspective. In the afternoon, stopping only to have a leathery sandwich, she made her way to the maternity ward.

The visitors' hour was coming to a close when she arrived. She exchanged notes at the desk with Andrea Arnold, the specialist nurse, and watched the usual procession of shell-shocked young fathers and overexcited new grandparents file out through the doors. Then her eyes focused on a man in denim jeans and a red and green checked shirt.

She hadn't seen Patrick for fourteen years but she recognised him at once. There were some people whose good looks made them permanently memorable. In Patrick's case, ash-blond hair, dark eyebrows and eyelashes, along with perfect bone structure, ensured his inclusion in this tiny elite.

'Patrick?' she said.

'That's me.' He stared back at her, his demeanour expressing surprise at being accosted by a strange doctor. His eyes hovered over her hospital ID badge and then widened with disbelief. 'Anna? Anna Cameron! Is it really you? I don't believe it!' He reached for her hand and shook it vigorously with both of his. 'After all this time! You look so different. You've got short hair and you're...'

'Slimmer? I hope I'm slimmer. You look exactly the same.'

'How long is it since...? It must be at least fifteen years.'

25

'It's fourteen. Not that I've been counting.' She laughed and he grinned back at her with no hint of awkwardness or embarrassment. He was genuinely delighted to see her. She wondered if he'd forgotten the circumstances of their last meeting. It *was* fourteen years ago. She said briskly, 'I must get on. Do give my regards to your parents.' She put a hand to her forehead and nodded towards the new mothers in the ward. 'Oh Lord, I'm sorry, I didn't think. Presumably, I should be congratulating you...'

'What? Oh I see... No, I've been visiting a friend. Look, this is ridiculous. You can't just walk away.' He reached into the pocket of his jeans and pulled out a card. 'We have so much to talk about. Are you working next weekend? Can you come over to lunch? Where do you live?'

'I have a flat in Deptford. But I'm afraid I will be working.'

'This is so weird! We're virtually neighbours. You *have* to come round. What about the weekend after? Come to lunch. I'll introduce you to Fizz and Lola.' He scribbled a few words on the back of his card and kissed her cheek before handing it to her. His skin smelt of wood-shavings. 'It is so amazing to see you! And you look... you look fantastic!' He gave her a final smile. She restrained herself – with difficulty – from staring at him as he left.

A rather less attractive smell of well-worn scrubs heralded the close proximity of Andrea Arnold.

'Well,' Andrea said, '*he's* very easy on the eye.'

'He's quite beautiful, isn't he? We were at school together. I haven't seen him in years.'

The last time she'd seen him she was thirteen. Thirteen! It seemed like a lifetime ago. She couldn't resist looking at his card. The words *Furniture Repairs and Fine Upholstery* were emblazoned in red. There was a phone number and a business address in Blackheath. His parents had had an upholstery business in Wimbledon. Perhaps they'd moved it to Blackheath or perhaps Patrick had set up on his own. At school, everyone, including Patrick, had assumed he'd become an actor.

Anna turned the card over and noted a Lewisham address he'd written for her. He *was* almost a neighbour. He certainly only lived a short bus ride away. She wondered who Fizz and Lola might be. They could be flatmates or a wife and daughter. They could be cats or dogs. Patrick had always liked dogs. She hoped they were dogs.

She finished at five and breathed a sigh of relief. It had been a long, long day and if she was sensible she would probably go home and have an early night. But the X-Men film would help to exorcise the most recent memory of Miss Diamond and, if that didn't work, William was the perfect friend for the situation. He rarely allowed himself to be upset by scathing superiors. When a senior doctor once threw his stethoscope at him, William simply assumed he was having problems at home. (In fact he'd been right on that occasion. The doctor had apologised to him the following morning and confessed that his daughter had recently announced her engagement to a very unpleasant boyfriend.)

They both enjoyed the film. Afterwards, she and William sat in a pizza place, united by a mutual adoration of Jennifer Lawrence, while disagreeing about the charms of James McAvoy. They had an interesting conversation about the strange alchemy of charisma which reminded her of Patrick. She told William about their meeting.

'I was in the maternity ward and I bumped into him. He was my first boyfriend. I haven't seen him since I was thirteen. He hasn't changed at all.'

'He looks like he's thirteen still?'

'No, stupid, I mean he's as beautiful as he always was. He's asked me to lunch. He wants to introduce me to Fizz and Lola. Do you think they're his wife and daughter?'

'They could be dogs.'

'That's what I thought. They *sound* like dogs.'

'They sound like lapdogs. If they *are*, he's probably gay.'

'Trust me, William, Patrick isn't gay.'

'My first girlfriend found me through Facebook last year,' William said. 'We went for a drink. It didn't end well.'

'What happened?'

'She wanted to tell me why she broke up with me. We were both thirteen too. She said she watched me dancing with a girl and saw me stroke the girl's bottom.'

'Did you?'

'I have no idea. Who can remember what happened fourteen years ago?'

Anna could. Anna remembered everything: the excitement and passion of first love; the fury she'd felt towards her mother; the despair when they moved to Darrowbridge; and, with a sudden ray of clarity, the fact that at thirteen she had stopped liking herself.

William had been finishing the remains of her pizza. He hated waste. 'I'd better go,' he said. 'I'm on at seven tomorrow.'

Anna could picture him as a thirteen-year-old, with the same untidy dark curls and wicked grin. She bet he *had* stroked that girl's bottom. 'William,' she said, 'do you think it's unhealthy to dwell on the past?'

William wiped his hands with his paper napkin and downed the last of his wine. He gave the question some thought before pushing back his chair and putting on his jacket. 'Only,' he said, 'if it makes you fall in love with a man who has lapdogs.'

Freya did wonder, at first, if Felix had succumbed to one of his depressions. The first of them occurred fourteen years ago, a month after they moved to Darrowbridge. Felix described it as a mental migraine and, when Freya said she didn't understand, he said he didn't either. It had lasted three days. He continued to go to work but each evening he came home late and then took off on his bike for a couple of hours. At night he retired to the spare room because he claimed he slept fitfully and didn't want to keep Freya awake. That first time, Freya had been bewildered and alarmed by the change in Felix. After it was over, he apologised, blamed stresses at work and assured her it would never happen again.

Freya had her own theory. She suspected he missed his London colleagues and felt guilty about dragging his reluctant family down to Somerset. In the circumstances, he would find it difficult to confess he'd made a mistake.

In fact, Cameron & West Financial Services soon began to flourish as Felix collected a loyal team around him. Yet the 'sessions', as he came to call them, continued to recur once or twice a year. Felix didn't like talking about them and neither did Freya. The fact that her devoted husband could, if only sporadically, metamorphose into an aloof individual who barely noticed her was a frightening reminder that one could never take security for granted. As a child, Freya had grown up with this knowledge but ever since she'd met Felix she'd done her best to forget it.

This time, she wasn't even sure he *was* depressed. He didn't go for long bike rides or retreat into silence. He came home from the office and chatted to Freya while she cooked their supper. He expressed interest in her caseloads and... That was it, she thought, he *expressed interest*. He was polite in the same way that Anna was polite on her fortnightly calls. Surely, it wasn't right for a man to be polite to his wife? She had had to accept the formality of her relationship with Anna, but Felix was a different matter.

Possibly, she was imagining all this. She was fifty-three, an age that was invariably tricky for women. She wasn't sure it was particularly healthy to hope she was physiologically unstable or at least unstable enough to conjure up problems where none existed. But it was far easier to have concerns about herself than to have concerns about Felix.

In the meantime, she had work to do. On Monday, she drove down to Dorset in her canary-coloured Beetle – a best-ever present from Felix on her fiftieth birthday. A client – Henry Riley – had commissioned her to explore his family's history as a surprise for his father's seventy-fifth birthday in the autumn. It was the sort of assignment Freya loved: a generous amount of time in which to collect and collate information, and a specific geographic location that wasn't too far away. None of the Rileys had ventured far beyond the south-west of the country.

At midday she stood in an overgrown churchyard in a tiny Dorset village, looking down at the gravestone of Henry Riley's three times great-grandmother. Freya knelt down to brush aside the cow parsley before taking a photograph. On the gravestone was written *Mary Riley, aged 32, wife of Samuel Riley*. So far, so expected. Underneath these words there were more: *Also Martin Riley, aged 8 and Edward Riley aged 8*.

This was strange. Freya knew that Mary had a son called James. He was a direct ancestor of her client. Until now she'd known nothing of any other children. The fact that Mary and her twins died in the same year seemed to indicate that they'd fallen victim to one of the many infectious diseases that plagued society before the advent of penicillin and a national health service. But why was there no mention of twins on any of the documents she had read? It was a mystery and Freya loved mysteries.

On Tuesday, she cancelled her hair appointment and drove to Taunton to examine the Register of Burials. It was here that she unearthed one of those rare discoveries that made her job so enthralling. She found the names of Mary and her twin sons. Next to the name *Mary Jane Riley* the vicar had inserted in brackets '*suicide after murder*'. And then, underneath, next to the names of Edward and Martin, he had added '*murdered by the above*'.

Freya felt a little giddy. In her imagination she had visualised Mary and her small sons gently fading away together. Now, Mary was a child killer. Why? She had brought up her older son, James, who was eighteen when

31

she died. There was no documentary evidence of maternal mistreatment.

It seemed to Freya that Henry Riley might soon come to regret his choice of birthday gift for his father. Freya had already discovered that the grandson of Mary's oldest son had gone to prison for a year after killing someone in a fight. But then, no one was exempt from bad impulses or errors of judgement. As Freya often said, every family had its secrets.

CHAPTER FOUR

On Tess's last full day in Scotland, she treated herself to a trip to Abbotsford. The walled garden was as beautiful as ever, its wide herbaceous borders a profusion of pastel colours. She walked down to the river and felt the peace steal over her. Sunlight scudded across the water, illuminating trailing ribbons of greenery and shiny black pebbles below the surface. She turned and let her eyes travel across the lawn, up the steep bank and along the formal terrace, before settling on the vast, sprawling house that, with its towers and turrets and gables, was the ultimate embodiment of Sir Walter Scott's romantic vision.

Grandma had brought her here six years ago. It was while gazing at a marble bust of the great writer that Tess had been smitten. He looked so approachable: a sense of warmth and kindness and humour seemed to emanate from his eyes. A sketch of him in the house endorsed her first impression. He held a walking stick at a jaunty angle and had a scarf tied a little untidily round his neck. Were he to come to life, Tess could imagine him saying to her: *How very nice to meet you! Do tell me what you are thinking.*

Tess could not remember her state of mind on that afternoon. She suspected she'd been preoccupied with her personal failings. She'd spent far too much time at university dwelling on this topic. How she managed to make any friends was a mystery.

She still didn't quite understand what had happened to her on that first visit. She and Grandma had returned to the

Commune and, over supper, Tess had talked hesitantly at first and then with gathering enthusiasm about Sir Walter. Doctor Knox, still mourning the loss of his wife, had risen abruptly from his chair and left the room, causing the other residents to cast worried glances at the open door. A few minutes later, he'd returned with a well-thumbed copy of *Waverley*.

'Start with this,' he'd said. 'Let me know what you think.'

Everything had followed on from that. Tess had arrived at the Commune as a dejected, self-absorbed streak of misery and left it as an eager student who knew exactly what she wanted to do. And now, six years later, here she was, a fully fledged academic armed with a first-class degree, a teaching post at a good university in London and well on her way to finishing a PhD on the lasting legacy of Sir Walter Scott. These days, she felt quite at home when she walked through the entrance hall with its suits of armour and relics from Waterloo, its armoury stuffed with swords and guns, including Rob Roy's very own pistol. Sir Walter had been an avid collector of historical paraphernalia and he also loved spending money, a weakness that would cost him dearly in the last years of his life.

Each time she entered the rose-coloured dining room she remembered it was here that he died while listening to the sound of the River Tweed outside. In the drawing room, there was a painting of Sir Walter with his dogs. One of them stared longingly up at him and Tess knew just how he felt.

She checked her watch and hastily pulled her car keys

from her pocket. It was time to return to the Commune and get ready for the party. Three of the inmates were going and all of them were sticklers for punctuality. Tess drove back along the narrow roads as fast as she dared. Arriving at the house, she raced up the wide staircase, clutching her anorak in her arms.

Twenty minutes later, she walked down the stairs in her black dress. She could hear laughter coming from the kitchen and went through to find Sheila and Linda chopping vegetables at the table while Derek stood, rolling pastry.

'Hi, Tess.' Sheila smiled up at her. 'We're making a mushroom quiche for the three of us. Derek, show Tess your pastry!'

'I don't know why they find it so funny,' Derek said. He held up a vast thin circle of pastry for Tess's inspection. 'I think it looks rather good.'

'Derek,' Sheila said, 'it's just for the three of us!'

As she and Linda started laughing again, Tess kissed Derek's cheek and said, 'It looks very professional. If there's any left over, I'll eat it later!' She hastened through to the hall and found Grandma, Doctor Knox and her great-aunt waiting for her.

Doctor Knox wore a tartan tie with his tweed suit. Grandma's short figure was well served by the brown velvet dress she always wore to parties. Great-aunt Katherine, her short grey hair newly permed for the occasion, wore a long black skirt and a silk shirt, its material festooned with purple flowers. She cast a meaningful glance at the grandfather clock. 'We should go right away. It's a long way to Kelso.'

35

'It's half an hour,' Grandma protested. 'And we don't want to be the first to arrive.' She smiled at Tess. 'You look lovely, darling. I'm so glad you're coming with us. Robert has something exciting to tell you.'

'I do,' Doctor Knox said, 'but let's get going first.'

In fact, most of the journey was taken up by Grandma's discovery that they had left their hostess's birthday present behind. Doctor Knox was happy to turn round but Great-aunt Katherine wouldn't hear of it, arguing that it was better to be punctual and present-less than to be late with a gift, particularly as the gift was a nondescript scarf. Since Grandma had chosen it, a heated altercation between the sisters-in-law ensued and was only terminated by Doctor Knox's timely reminder that he had news for Tess.

'I met an old friend for lunch yesterday,' he said. 'His wife has a clothes shop in Gasterlethen.'

'I don't think I know it,' Tess said.

'Not many people do,' Great-aunt Katherine said. 'Gasterlethen is very unmemorable.'

'I don't think that's fair,' Doctor Knox said. 'It has a quiet sort of charm...'

Great-aunt Katherine sniffed. '*Very* quiet.'

'It is a small village,' Doctor Knox conceded. 'It's on the road between Galashiels and Peebles. My friend wants his wife to take on some help over the summer. And I thought of you, Tess.'

'Me?' Tess leant forward. 'That's very kind of you but I'm already sorted. I'll be working at a restaurant and...'

'You don't *have* to do that, do you?' Grandma asked. 'You could come here instead, borrow my car, do your research on days off. Of course you might prefer to spend the summer in London. You might think Gasterlethen would be extremely dull.'

'Grandma,' Tess said, 'you're as subtle as a sledgehammer.'

'Well,' Grandma said, 'I've never had much time for subtlety.'

Great-aunt Katherine grunted. 'That's true.'

'It's not just the restaurant,' Tess said. 'I'll be doing tutoring work too.'

'I quite understand,' Great-aunt Katherine said. 'You can't let people down.' She breathed a sigh of relief. 'Here we are in Kelso at last!'

Unlike most of the Border towns, Kelso was rather grand. It possessed not just a ruined abbey and a river but also a racecourse and a genuine fairy-tale castle, occupied by the current Duke and Duchess of Roxburghe. Doctor Knox parked in the impressive cobbled square and nodded across at one of the elegant Georgian houses. 'Let's go,' he said.

The pale blue door was opened by a cheerful mop-haired teenager who took their coats and suggested they help themselves to drinks from the trestle table behind him. Doctor Knox took an orange juice for himself and poured wine for the ladies.

Tess followed her companions upstairs to a long drawing room with two high windows, framed by heavy, maroon-coloured drapes. On the walls there were paintings of men and women in silks and satins who stared down at the festivities with grim distaste. At one end of the room, a group of people stood chatting to a regal old lady who sat in a high-backed chair in a long grey skirt and a lilac-coloured jersey.

Tess was aware that two young men were following her entrance with interest. She glanced fleetingly at them. One was dark-haired and wore a suit. The other had red hair and wore a kilt and stared so blatantly at her that she turned away quickly. There had to be about thirty people here, all talking in hushed voices as if in church. The few teenagers in evidence were busy taking round canapés. This was a very well-behaved party.

In the next half-hour Tess was introduced to a variety of guests, most of them seemingly related to Flora Macdonald, the eighty-five-year-old birthday girl in her high-backed chair. The old lady patted Tess's hand and told her she *must* meet her grand-daughter, Susan. She beckoned to Susan and told her to take Tess off for a chat.

Susan was a red-faced woman of indeterminate age, with a very short neck and two thick plaits fixed together on top of her head like an old-fashioned German hausfrau. As soon as Susan heard Tess's English vowels, her eyes narrowed with scorn and she settled her arms on her well-endowed chest.

'We attract foreigners like flies, particularly in this part of the country. I suppose you're here for a holiday?' The last word was spoken with a contemptuous flourish.

'I'm here for work,' Tess assured her. 'I'm writing a PhD on Sir Walter Scott.'

'Are you indeed?' Susan gave a mirthless smile. 'He's certainly an appropriate subject for an English girl, particularly one who is conservative by inclination which I presume you must be, given your choice of subject.'

'Actually,' Tess said, 'my grandfather was Scottish and

38

I'm sure many Scots are impressed by the author of *Ivanhoe* and *Waverley*.'

Susan's small eyes narrowed into dangerous slits. 'Most Scots would rather read a Latin dictionary than plough through a novel by Sir Walter Scott. Have you ever tried to read one?'

'Well, of course I have and...'

'They are unreadable. The man himself was an abomination. He was a Tory who did his best to turn Scotland into a playground for the English aristocracy. He rewrote our history and invited to Edinburgh one of your most dissolute kings...'

'In fact,' Tess told her, 'George the Fourth probably inherited his dissolute habits from his *Scottish* ancestor, James the Sixth of Scotland, who unfortunately became James the First of England.' She made an effort to rein in her indignation. 'I know that Scott romanticised elements of Scottish history but...'

'Romanticised?' Susan's florid complexion had taken on the colour of a tomato. 'The man *fabricated*, he didn't romanticise! He made up a false history to please his posh English friends and he thought the pernicious Act of Union was a good and noble law. Well...' Susan's head nodded violently '...our time has come. This year is *our* year and you and your Sir Walter will have to accept Scotland's independence...'

'*I* support independence...'

'And I'll tell you something else about your precious Sir Walter! He encouraged the royal family to wear kilts! To this day they wear kilts! They are German, they don't have an ounce of Scottish blood in their veins...'

'Well, actually,' Tess said, 'as I think I pointed out, that's not quite true. George the First was the great-great-grandson of James the First on his mother's side...'

'He was German! He never spoke a word of English!'

'Yes, but he did have Scottish blood in him and I don't think you can condemn Scott for persuading the royal family to appreciate his homeland. A lot of people accept that if it weren't for him, Scotland would have no tourist industry and...'

'I'm supposed to be grateful for that? I'm supposed to be grateful for your caravan parks and your holiday homes?'

'They aren't *my* caravan parks...'

'Let me tell you about Sir Walterrrr.' Susan's accent was becoming ever more pronounced. 'He built a preposterous house at Abbotsford which was his idea of what a great Scottish house should be despite the fact that it bore no resemblance to any other great house in the country. He wrote ridiculous novels...'

'He was the first *ever* international bestseller who influenced the great writers of his day! Byron, Goethe, Hugo and Austen all thought he was brilliant. And even today there are people like A. N. Wilson and Alan Massie who revere him...'

Susan gave a laugh that sounded like a steam engine in full throttle. 'In England, you had a hideous programme called *Big Brother* that had more viewers than any other. That doesn't mean it was commendable. In England, your most famous celebrity is an anorexic airhead called Victoria Beckham. That doesn't mean she's commendable...'

40

'She *is* commendable. She's a very successful businesswoman and a widely respected clothes designer.'

Susan dismissed this with a wave of her hand. 'In England you have a plastic-breasted woman called Katie Price who changes her men and her body every few months and whose books sell in their thousands. Just because the English are obsessed with the base and the vulgar, should *we* have to follow your lamentable example?'

'Who has plastic breasts?'

Both women turned to register the newcomer. He seemed to have appeared from nowhere. Tess recognised him at once as the friend of the red-haired man. Susan gave a loud sniff. 'I was talking,' she said coldly, 'about Katie Price.'

'I can't say I know her,' the man said. He looked expectantly at Susan and then turned to Tess. 'I don't think she's going to introduce us. I'm Susan's cousin: Jamie Lockhart.'

'I'm Tess Cameron,' Tess said, 'and...'

'And *you*, Jamie Lockhart, are my *second* cousin,' Susan said, 'and since I'm aware you didn't come over here to talk to *me*, I shall leave the two of you together. I'm sure you will find you have similar views.'

Susan turned and, moving like a stately battleship, set off in search of more congenial company. 'I think you should know,' Jamie murmured, 'that her last comment was not a compliment.'

Susan's voice resembled a hard-bristled broom being dragged across a stone floor. Jamie's soft Scottish tones were far more melodic. Tess had never seen anyone quite like him. He wore an unexceptional black suit and a white

41

shirt. He was of average height and slim build. It was his colouring that was so unusual. He had jet black hair that was pushed back from his forehead and his skin was pale as alabaster. It reminded her of Sir Walter's marble bust at Abbotsford and there was something statue-like about him. He didn't fidget or glance round the room. He kept his hands on his empty wine glass and his eyes fixed on Tess. His face was remarkably inexpressive. The immobility of his features together with the quiet tone of his voice suggested a certain gravity of mind. On the other hand, Tess had a strong suspicion that he had enjoyed baiting his cousin.

'Susan doesn't seem to like you very much.'

'She doesn't seem to like *you* either. What did you do to upset such a sweet, unassuming woman?'

Tess smiled. 'I told her I was doing a PhD on Sir Walter Scott.'

'He's not very fashionable these days. Are you looking to restore his popularity?'

'That's the idea.'

'Trust me, you'll need to add some salacious details.'

'He was a faithful husband, a loyal friend and an honourable businessman. There are no salacious details.'

'Make them up.'

'I happen to believe in academic integrity.'

'The problem with academic integrity,' Jamie said, 'is that it doesn't sell. Are you doing your work in Edinburgh?'

'No. I live in London. I'm staying with my grandmother. I go home tomorrow.'

'Ah.' Jamie opened his mouth and then shut it again.

'You were about to say something?'

Jamie nodded. 'I didn't want to be rude.'

'Please,' Tess said politely, 'feel free.'

'Well then. You choose to focus on a Scottish writer and you decide to study him in *London*. It's odd.'

'Now you sound like your cousin.'

'She's my *second* cousin and I do not. Susan is a bigoted, bad-tempered nationalist who refuses to believe there's any merit in the world outside Scotland. She's also a closet psychopath.'

'A moment ago you said she was sweet and unassuming.'

'I have a tendency to change my mind quite quickly. If I'm honest, it may be unfair to call her a psychopath. As far as I know she hasn't killed anyone yet.' He caught the eye of the mop-haired teenager who was currently refilling glasses a few feet away. 'Hey, Rollo! Come here.'

The boy sauntered over. 'Do you want another drink?'

'We do indeed. And then I want you to do something for me.'

'I might,' Rollo said. 'You may remember, Jamie, I asked you three weeks ago about a holiday job in the summer? You said you'd get back to me?' He attended to the empty glasses and then stood and waited.

'You strike a hard bargain, Rollo,' Jamie said. '*If* – and only if – you do it properly, I'll see what I can do. You notice Andy over there talking to Susan?' He nodded towards the red-haired man. 'Your mission – if you choose to accept it – is to go across and engage him in conversation.'

'What about?'

'Rollo, you are a resourceful young man. You can talk for Scotland. Look, he's poised to come over. Off you go.'

Tess watched Rollo hurry off. 'Why don't you want your friend to join us?'

Jamie shrugged. 'Where women are concerned, Andy is not to be trusted. He is in point of fact unscrupulous. Susan will have told him about Sir Walter and you. He'll pretend he loves Scott's books when I happen to know he's never read a novel in his life. I am trying to protect you.'

'That's very considerate of you.'

Across the room, Rollo had made contact with Andy and was making animated gestures with his bottle of wine. It was clear that Rollo was very keen to get a holiday job with Jamie. Tess's mouth twitched. She was enjoying herself. It was impossible not to be amused by Jamie. He was an attractive man, who was flirting with her. She could enjoy such attentions in the happy knowledge that there would be no complications.

'I'm sorry you leave tomorrow,' Jamie said. 'I would have liked to invite you to my castle. Sir Walter was a regular visitor.'

'You have a castle? Scott went there?'

'Well, he visited once, in 1801. At least we think he did. We think he went with his friend William Wordsworth so that counts for something.'

Tess eyed him suspiciously. 'Are you telling me the truth? Do you really own a castle?'

Jamie reached into the inside pocket of his jacket, took out his wallet and extracted a business card which he gave to Tess.

On one side there was a photo of a genuine castle. On

44

the other were the words: *Jamie Lockhart, custodian of Reidfern Castle*. Underneath there were his contact details. She tried to return the card to him but he shook his head. 'Keep it. Next time you're in Scotland, get in touch. I'll show you around.'

'Is it a real castle or is it just a ruin?'

'It is *very* real,' Jamie assured her. 'We have weddings and business functions there.'

Tess looked down at the card. 'Sir Walter's son-in-law was called Sir John Lockhart. They were the greatest of friends. I wonder if your family is related to him.'

Jamie gave an authoritative nod of his head. 'I'm pretty sure we are.'

Tess smiled. 'You'd never heard of him until this moment!'

'That might be true but I feel in my bones we must be. My grandfather's name was John.'

'We should have my mother here. She's a genealogist. She reads family trees like other people read newspapers. It would be quite something to be descended from the son-in-law of Sir Walter Scott.'

'It would,' Jamie said gravely. 'I must tell my father. He's been saying for years that he means to explore our family history.'

'Tell him to google Freya Eliza Cameron. Her website will tell him how to go about it.'

'I'll do that.' The red-haired man had extricated himself from Rollo and was now bearing down on them. 'Andy,' Jamie said, 'I was about to tell Tess here I ought to introduce you.'

Andy ignored Jamie. 'It's a pleasure to meet you. Susan

45

has told me you're a fan of Sir Walter Scott. I have to tell you I *love* his books.'

For a brief moment, Jamie's eyes met those of Tess. 'That's very interesting, Andy. I never knew that. Tell us: which is your favourite novel and why?'

On the journey home, the hot gossip was that Susan was walking out with her local SNP agent.

'I found Susan rather difficult,' Tess confessed. 'She's such an *angry* person.'

'She's not easy,' her great-aunt agreed. 'As far as I could see, you spent most of the evening with Jamie Lockhart. He couldn't keep his eyes off you.'

'He was just being friendly,' Tess said.

'We have a saying in the family,' Great-aunt Katherine said. 'When a Lockhart befriends a woman, she should pack her case and run.'

'That's not a saying *I've* ever heard,' Grandma retorted. 'I think Jamie's charming.'

'The Lockharts are always charming,' Great-aunt Katherine intoned. 'You don't know them, Maggie. I was at school with Flora when her sister married into the family. Flora told me her mother cried all night.'

'Her mother sounds very silly,' Grandma said.

'She had her reasons,' Great-aunt Katherine said. 'I will only say that John Lockhart had a *reputation*. And his son is no better. He's left behind a long trail of broken marriages.'

'I don't know about that,' Grandma said, 'but...'

Doctor Knox made one of his rare interventions. 'I do. The Lockharts were patients of mine. Jamie's father was a delightful young man. I remember visiting him when he was almost beside himself with pain from an acute ear infection. He still took the time to thank me for calling on him. As far as I know he's only on his third wife and I'm told they're very happy.'

'"*He's only on his third wife*",' Great-Aunt Katherine repeated with heavy sarcasm. 'That says it all.'

'I'm glad to hear it,' Grandma responded, 'because you've said quite enough already.'

CHAPTER FIVE

Eliza Sample kissed her friend and agreed they must meet again soon, though, as she walked out into Piccadilly, she decided it wouldn't be as soon as all *that*. She was fond of Jean but she did have a tendency to go on about her aches and pains and, really, what was the *point*? Aches and pains were an essential part of the ageing process and a pretty reasonable price for survival when one thought of all the friends and acquaintances who had succumbed to fatal illnesses and falls.

And to be perfectly honest – and while Eliza might sometimes be a little *veiled* in her dealing with others, she believed in being stringently honest with herself – it was not terribly fascinating to listen to Jean's gossip about her family when *she* had no family of her own with which to contribute and compare. It wasn't as if Jean's family were particularly interesting anyway. Her daughters seemed to live tiresomely exemplary lives with useful careers in the civil service and education, husbands who remained their husbands, and children who were good at sports and exams and joined youth orchestras and ran marathons.

There had been one special moment. Jean's daughter-in-law was trying to unearth the mystery of her great-grandfather, a man who had disappeared one day, never to be seen again. Eliza had said, 'There's a very good website I've found. It's called *Revealing Families.co.uk*. It's run by a woman called Freya Eliza Cameron. You should tell your daughter-in-law about it.' Eliza had enjoyed passing that on.

She was glad she'd chosen to have coffee with Jean rather than afternoon tea because now she could look forward to her twice-weekly treat, knowing she had performed her social duty. The weather, while not exactly warm, was at least dry and she enjoyed walking along Piccadilly and down Regent Street into Pall Mall. It wasn't just the shops and the architecture, it was the people. She couldn't understand why so many of them felt compelled to talk into their phones as they walked; it meant they missed out on so many fascinating little scenes and conversations. Only last week she had heard one snippet of dialogue that kept her happily occupied for days. A couple were walking together and, as they passed by her, the man said, 'So we tell our spouses at six and we meet at seven. All right?'

Eliza had been enthralled. Were they going to announce their departure to their unfortunate spouses and, if so, weren't they allowing rather too little time to break such traumatic news? And how would they broach the subject? Would they suddenly, on the hour of six, break into a robot-like delivery of execution? Fascinating, absolutely fascinating.

And now, two stunning girls in short white dresses were walking towards her in the company of a less stunning young man. 'I hate Megan,' one of the girls said as they walked past her. 'She's such a whore.'

Was Megan a whore? It was an unusually censorious term to issue from the mouth of one who didn't look particularly virginal herself, despite the white dress. Was the word a routine insult these days and, if so, what had happened to feminine solidarity? What had happened to

49

feminism? Eliza often wondered what had happened to feminism. Why did so many girls spend so many boring hours every day counting their calories? Why did so many women spend so much money having unnecessary, dangerous operations in order to attain a mythical approximation of contemporary beauty? In her thirties, Eliza had read books extolling the liberation of women and now, all these years later, the daughters and grand-daughters of those thoughtful writers shaved their pubic hair and called each other whores. It was a little depressing.

Her spirits lifted as she reached the National Gallery. As long as she could keep coming here, life was worth living. Eliza knew only too well that in order to sustain a heady love affair one must restrict exposure to the object of one's passion. She never visited the gallery more than twice a week, even though she was often tempted. And with each visit she would only look at one room, or occasionally two. Sometimes she would only look at one painting. She knew what she wanted to do today. She had just finished reading Hilary Mantel's *Wolf Hall* and had been delighted by the appearance of Hans Holbein in the story. Today, she intended to look at some of his paintings and she might as well start with the biggest.

The Ambassadors dominated the room in which it was hung, taking up the whole of the end wall. Eliza sat on the bench opposite it with a little sigh of pleasure. She put her bag down beside her and adjusted her skirt.

The two diplomats in the painting were dressed sumptuously and stood on either side of a table packed with artefacts – a globe, books, scientific instruments. The man on the left was quite handsome in an arrogant sort of way.

He wore a black cap, black hose and black undercoat, all of which emphasised the dazzling pinkness of his satin doublet. He stood with his coat deliberately exposed to reveal an extravagant ermine lining. He had a long gold chain round his neck that would be the envy of any of those rappers Eliza occasionally glimpsed on television. He also carried a gold dagger with a ridiculous green tassel.

His friend was *not* attractive. His costume, while less flashy, showed signs of opulence, since his coat was lined with fur. Both men looked out at Eliza – or rather, she supposed, they looked out at Holbein – with expressions of serene confidence in their position in the world.

But what excited Eliza was the fact that amid the conventional portrait of two powerful men there was something so surreal, so contemporary in its deliberate attempt to shock it made her want to laugh. In the foreground of the painting was a sprawling, diagonal shape. It looked like a UFO that had crash-landed onto the rich carpet. On further examination, it turned out to be a skull. Did the two men know that in front of all the pomp and wealth so lovingly reproduced by the artist, a crazy skull would intrude, a V-sign to all that they presumably held so dear?

This was why Eliza loved the National Gallery. How could one be lonely when one visited this place? At the age of eighty-one she no longer had many friends. She rarely left London now. There was only her sister-in-law in Bath who continued to invite her to stay. Yet here, across the centuries, she had made a connection. She was, she felt, talking to an artist who felt as she did about life: that it was a game in which money and position were mere diversions

51

in the face of inevitable death. Life was fragile, death was random, and the best way to live was to regard one's continued existence with sceptical amusement and plenty of gratitude.

A voice said, 'Do you mind if I join you?'

Eliza looked up into possibly the ugliest face she had ever encountered. The man was like an ape. The gap between his nose and his protuberant mouth was excessive and it didn't help that his chin had apparently collapsed into his neck. He was bald, apart from a crescent-shaped rim of grey stringy hair round the back of his head, and he wore a baggy, shabby, brown suit that would have been loose on a man twice his size. She refrained from pointing out that he had already joined her and instead said coldly, 'This bench is public property.'

He sat down and, taking out an enormous handkerchief, blew his nose noisily. 'I love this painting,' he said, pointing his walking stick at Holbein's picture. 'Do you see the ambassador on the left has a badge on his cap? If you look at it carefully, you can see there's the image of a skull on it.'

Eliza nodded but said nothing since she had no wish to let the little man know she hadn't noticed the badge.

'And if you look on the top left corner, you can see a crucifix, almost hidden in the folds of those curtains. Why is it there? The painting is full of clues and puzzles. Look at the table for a start.' He carried on pontificating about the symbolism of each object on the table and she rather grudgingly conceded – if only to herself – that he knew far more than she did. When he eventually stood up, however, she remained stubbornly seated. He glanced at his watch.

'I'm afraid I have to go. Do you often come here?'

'I do,' Eliza said. 'It is,' she added with some deliberation, 'very peaceful.'

'It is, it is,' the man agreed, failing to notice the implied rebuke. 'I'll be here next Thursday. I thought I'd look at the Impressionists. Come along at midday and we'll look at them together. I'll wait for you by Pissarro's *The Avenue, Sydenham*. Goodbye now.'

The little man nodded and walked away without giving time for her to respond, which was just as well since he'd irritated her so much she'd been tempted to forget her manners. Why would she care if he were here next Thursday? Why would he think she would want to look at paintings with him? And why would he assume, as she was sure that he *did*, that he knew far more than she did about art? She had no intention of waiting for him by the Pissarro next week, in fact she would go out of her way *not* to be waiting by the Pissarro.

She gave a slow and careful glance round the room and, having assured herself that he had well and truly gone, rose and walked up to the painting. She felt an almost reluctant surge of interest. There was the badge on the ambassador's cap with what indeed looked like a skull engraved on it. And there was the small crucifix on the top left-hand corner. Her eyes flickered over to the face of the ambassador on the left. It seemed to her that he stared at her with a rather mocking expression. But that was just fancy.

CHAPTER SIX

Anna supposed that Patrick must be doing well. Lewisham Hill was a pleasant tree-lined road with substantial Victorian houses on either side. Genteel Blackheath was a little further up the hill and Lewisham Station was conveniently situated down at the bottom. His housing block, more or less midway between them, had a big communal lawn, and there was no sign of litter anywhere.

His maisonette was on the first floor and when she spoke into the machine, his voice shot out with unabashed warmth. 'Anna! Come on up!' He was waiting for her on the landing. When he kissed her cheek, he smelt of basil. 'Come in, come in,' he said. 'Meet Fizz and Lola.'

Fizz and Lola were not dogs. Fizz was an attractive woman in leggings and a lumberjack shirt, with a wide mouth and glossy brown hair. Lola was a grave-faced toddler with enormous blue eyes and shoulder-length blonde hair. The child stretched out her arms towards her father and he gathered her up in his arms with practised ease. 'Take Anna through to the sitting room, Fizz. Lola can help me finish the cooking.'

The sitting room was modest in size but full of light, with green walls and a pink carpet. There was a two-seater sofa, a floor cushion and a simple wooden chair. Behind the sofa was a short table with a laptop, a tray with glasses and a bottle in an ice bucket. Underneath the table was a red plastic box stuffed with toys.

Having settled Anna on the sofa with a large glass of wine,

Fizz took the floor cushion and said, 'I've heard all about you, you know. Don't you love being called Dr Cameron?'

It was impossible not to like her and indeed, Anna thought, why should she not? Fizz had a low husky voice and a throaty laugh. She was self-deprecatory to a fault – 'I don't want to talk about my job. If you want to freeze a conversation instantly, just try saying you're an industrial land lawyer.' She confessed she was not a natural mother – 'I adore Lola but if I'm on my own with her for more than a few hours I start climbing up the wall.' She admitted she'd find motherhood impossible without a partner like Patrick. 'When I met him he was an actor and thank God he was unsuccessful because he was quite happy to give it up when Lola came along. His parents had bought larger premises in Blackheath and then they bought a house there. That's why we came to Lewisham. Patrick's joined the family upholstery business. He looks after Lola and takes her to work with him. He has ten times more patience with her than I do and his parents are brilliant too. I'm very lucky.'

Fizz *was* lucky. When Patrick called them into lunch, there was a tomato tart along with a Niçoise salad awaiting them. While Fizz helped him serve out, Anna took a seat next to Lola and gave her an uncertain smile. She had no idea how to address such a small and solemn infant.

Lola pointed to her feet. 'I have purple shoes,' she said.

Anna studied Lola's purple trainers. 'They're very nice,' she said.

Lola nodded and gave a little sigh. 'Do you like purple?' she asked.

The child was making polite conversation. Anna had

55

no idea that small children could even begin to do that. 'I quite like purple,' she said, 'though I have to say it's not my favourite colour.'

Lola regarded Anna with a hint of disappointment in her eyes. '*I* like purple. Purple is my favourite colour. I like alpacas too.'

Anna was even more impressed. 'I don't think I've ever *seen* an alpaca.'

Lola's face dissolved into laughter. '*I* have. I see them all the time. I *love* alpacas.'

Lola was lovely, if a little frustrating. Anna doubted she would ever have the patience to cope with small children. Having conversations in their presence was like driving in a traffic jam. Over lunch, Fizz told Anna that she tried to learn something new every six months which meant that on Wednesday evenings she now went straight from work to something called dynamic yoga. Dynamic yoga sounded like a contradiction in terms. How could yoga – all deep breathing and slow motion movements – ever be dynamic? Anna was intrigued but the subject was terminally derailed by Lola who wanted Anna to know that her friend Jonah liked eating buttons from his shirt. And then when Patrick mentioned that Anna's childhood tormentor, Felicity Eggins, was already on her second marriage, Lola said she didn't like tomatoes now and that was the end of Felicity Eggins. Fizz and Patrick were fascinated by Lola's revelation. Anna couldn't imagine a time when she would be more interested in a child's dislike of tomatoes than in Felicity Eggins' love life.

When she said goodbye, she walked down the stairs and turned when Lola called her name. There were the three of them, Fizz, and Patrick, and Lola blowing a kiss at her. She blew one back and went on her way. On the bus back to Deptford, she rang William to tell him Fizz and Lola weren't lapdogs.

'I like Fizz,' she told William. 'You would too.'

'You sound a bit down,' William said.

'Oh well... You know...' Anna's voice tailed off. She knew William would understand.

'Who was it who said the past is another country?' William asked.

'I haven't a clue. I expect Tess would know.'

'Well, it's true,' William said. 'And if I were you I'd keep well away from it.'

Anna laughed and said goodbye. Almost immediately she had a text from Olivia. 'I'm back!'

Anna's spirits lifted at once. Olivia was back!

Fourteen years ago, Anna and her family moved from London to Somerset. Their mother had dropped her and Tess off on their first day at their new school. 'You'll be fine,' she said brightly. 'After all you have each other.' Which only went to show that her mother knew nothing about anything since Tess was no help at all. Tess's passive acquiescence towards the move had remained as incomprehensible as it was infuriating.

They found themselves in a class united by old allegiances and shared primary-school experiences. There was only one pupil there who interested Anna and by the end of the day she knew why. She and Olivia were both exiles who were consumed with rage.

Olivia, half Ghanaian and half Italian, had spent all her life in Shoreditch where she had a tight-knit group of friends. Now her parents – just like Anna's – had made an arbitrary decision to move their family away from all that was familiar. Olivia found herself in a class where she was the only black pupil in a room of white teenagers who had never even heard of Shoreditch.

Meanwhile Anna had been forcibly uprooted from Wimbledon, her friends, and Patrick. Her new home was a rural cottage that was nearly half a mile from anywhere of interest. Not that Darrowbridge *was* interesting but at least it offered more than fields and trees and the faint smells of the pig farm down the road.

By the end of that first week, Anna and Olivia were best friends and had remained so ever since. These days the two of them shared a small flat in Deptford. For the last two weeks Olivia had been away in Manchester, working on a programme about a family called the Balderstones whose domestic life was impeded by a ghost in their sitting room. Thus far, the ghost had failed to materialise and the team was forced to rely on ever more lurid accounts from Mrs Balderstone, who relished her moment in the spotlight. The only breath of sanity came from a local builder called Jim who assured Olivia that the entire story was a load of old rubbish. Such lucid common sense meant that Jim had to be discounted as a witness, which was a pity since Olivia said he was extremely easy on the eye which was more than could be said for Mrs Balderstone.

Olivia's job often took her away from home. Each time she went away, Anna expected to enjoy the chance to tidy the flat and have the place to herself and each time she soon remembered that she hated being alone. Anna's sister had once voiced the hope of, some day, buying a small cottage of her own in the country. Tess's dream was Anna's nightmare. She couldn't imagine anything worse than living on her own.

In the flat there were the welcome signs of Olivia's return: the open rucksack on the sofa, the carrier bags on the rug and the signs of culinary debris on the kitchen bar. Anna could hear her on the phone in her bedroom, having what sounded like a heated discussion.

Anna filled the kettle with water and had just located the box of teabags when Olivia came in, looking effortlessly cool in a sludge-green boiler suit that on anyone else would look horrendous.

'Welcome home,' Anna said. 'We can share the last teabag.'

'Just what I need,' Olivia breathed. 'I am *so* pissed off. My brother and his wife have invited us all to Cambridge for Christmas.'

'It's the middle of June. They're making plans for *Christmas*?'

'I know. That's what they do. I can't believe Mum's even considering it. I've just reminded her, "Do you remember what we said last time? *Never again!*"'

'I thought you adored your nephews.'

'I do. I adore them all through the day but there should be a cast-iron rule that children under six should be in bed by six. And meanwhile we have to eat my sister-in-law's disgusting veggie food and, if we don't praise it to the skies, my brother looks anxiously at *her* and then gazes desperately at us and I am *not* going there and... Oh, let's not talk about it. It only makes me cross. Shall I tell you the latest about the Balderstones' ghost?'

'You didn't *see* it?'

'Oh, we saw it all right. We saw it yesterday. We'd packed everything away so we could make an early start this morning. We were about to go to the pub when Mrs Balderstone rang and told us to come over at once. We dashed over, she let us in and we tiptoed towards the sitting room. We all heard the noises. Steve and Tom set up the equipment in the hall. I opened the door and felt something furry brush past my leg and I screamed. And then we saw him leap up the stairs. It was a squirrel. I nearly had a heart attack over a frigging squirrel.'

'I can't believe you screamed. How can you make a documentary about a ghost that turned out to be a squirrel?'

'Easy. It will become a witty exposé of human gullibility. I suspect Mrs Balderstone will not be amused. Anyway, I'm already thinking about the next project.'

'Do you have any ideas?' A silly question. Olivia always had ideas.

'I bought a stack of magazines the other day and I've identified two possible subjects. One is a woman whose husband walked out on her and their three children. He went on to marry again and had another child. His new wife died and now the first one's taken him back and is bringing up the new baby.'

'That is depressing on so many levels.'

'The other's a very dishy bloke who runs a holistic garden-design business. He's bringing a book out and he has a great name too: Xander Bullen… Why are you staring at me like that? Anna?'

Anna was aware she had the kettle in her hand. She put it down. 'Do you still have the magazine? Can I see it?'

Olivia stood up and went across to one of the carrier bags. She pulled out a folder and brought it back to Anna. 'I tore it out this morning. He's very photogenic, don't you think?'

Anna stared down at the photograph and swallowed hard. 'Olivia,' she said, 'if you make a programme about this man I will never speak to you again.'

CHAPTER SEVEN

Felix was about to leave the office when he had a call from Freya.

'I need some Parmesan,' she said, 'and *good* red wine! We are *celebrating*!'

He bought a bottle of Fleurie near Bristol Temple Meads and had to run to get the train. He was lucky: five more seconds and he'd have missed it. He was even luckier to find a seat. The young woman beside him was engrossed in a magazine. The words *SALLY CHEATS ON RICK!* were emblazoned above a photo of – presumably – soap-opera Sally on the phone in a quite ridiculously furtive pose; behind her, a man – presumably Rick – sat reading a paper in blissful ignorance.

He would buy the Parmesan at Darrowbridge. He wondered what it was they were celebrating. Oh God, he thought, it couldn't be the anniversary yet? But, of course, it couldn't. They'd married in September. At some point in July, it would be thirty-one years since he'd first met Freya. He couldn't recall the exact date but he could picture the occasion as if it were yesterday.

He'd gone to a friend's wedding. He had sat in the church, keeping a place for his sister who, as usual, was late. And then this beautiful girl had walked down the aisle in a little pink suit which showed off her tiny waist and hips and her long slender legs to perfection. She stopped by his pew, pushed back her blonde hair and asked, 'Is this seat taken?'

'I was saving it for you,' he'd said, which was totally out of character and quite absurd but he felt as if it was true.

At the reception he stood talking to the bride and glanced across the room. The girl was surrounded by a trio of male guests vying for her attention and she smiled suddenly at him. At the time he couldn't believe he had been the intended recipient. She was way out of his league. But then, later still, she came up to him and asked, 'Shall we see each other again?' and that was it. He was done for.

Alighting from the train, he put the Fleurie in his car and walked on towards the small supermarket. He bought the Parmesan and was about to head back to the station car park when he saw Pam's next-door neighbour, Percy Jenner, along with his small pug, Serge. They made an incongruous pair and the sight of them together always made Felix smile. Percy, a skilled plasterer before his retirement, was a thin, wiry man with curly grey hair. His pet was a tiny, dainty little animal who looked like the perfect lapdog. Percy's wife, Elaine, had acquired him four years ago and – mistaking him for a French bulldog – given him a suitably foreign name. Three months later, she died of heart failure while undergoing what was supposed to be a routine operation.

Felix had a lot of time for Percy. After his wife's death, he had taught himself to cook and kept their cottage spotless. He and Elaine were childless and had been devoted to each other. Now Percy was devoted to Serge. Tonight, he told Felix, he and Serge had walked along the river and spotted a heron.

'Do you want a lift back?' Felix asked. 'I have my car at the station.'

Serge looked up at Felix. Serge looked as if he'd very much like a lift.

'We're going to the graveyard,' Percy said, 'but thank you for the offer. It's a good evening for a walk. Will you thank Freya for the broad beans? She dropped them in yesterday. Tell her I had some last night. Your wife's a very kind lady.'

'She is,' Felix said. 'And I'll be sure to pass on the message.'

Percy was right, he thought, it *was* a good evening for a walk. On an impulse he turned and walked on to the path by the river. He didn't see a heron but he spotted a very unusual bird on the water. It was small and black with a bright orange beak and tiny beady eyes.

He sat down on the bench and wondered what it was about water that was so soothing. Perhaps it was the fact that its inhabitants – the ducks, the elusive heron and the funny little black bird – all had such a simple life, paddling along, foraging for food, enjoying the sunlight. Of course, for all he knew, their lives weren't simple at all. Just now, for instance, the funny little black bird was squawked at by two hostile green and white ducks and emitted a surprisingly guttural squawk of his own. For all Felix knew, the funny little black bird was a lonely creature desperate for friends.

He should get back. Freya would be waiting for him. The truth was that Felix didn't want to go home. The truth was that Felix would like to stay here, open the Fleurie, drink the whole bottle and watch the ducks and the poor little black bird.

'What do u think?'

Tess stared at the hopeful text and knew she was not yet ready to answer it. She should never have left it to Rachel. She had only herself to blame. As she entered her house – her house for another two weeks – she greeted the cats and said, 'Yes, hello, you two, I'll feed you now!'

She went through to the kitchen and gazed at the royal blue tiles, the double sink and the wide breakfast bar. She felt like Eve taking a last look at Eden before being thrown out into the wilderness.

She knew she had been exceptionally lucky to live here. Eight months ago, Rachel's brother, an insanely successful actor, had invited her and Rachel to move in, for a tiny rent, on condition they looked after his cats while he was filming in the States. The small terraced house was a stone's throw from London Fields with its collection of artisan food shops and cool little coffee bars. She and Rachel had felt as if they'd died and gone to Heaven. And now Rachel's brother was coming home and Hell was on its way.

This afternoon Tess had gone to see the flat that would soon be her home. The building was in an unexceptional if noisy street near Fulham Broadway. As soon as Tess unlocked the front door she was hit by the pungent aroma of cat. She liked cats, she enjoyed looking after Rachel's brother's two, but the smell here was something else, this was the smell of a very sick cat, possibly one on the verge of decomposition. She walked up the first lot of stairs and let herself in through the mud-coloured door. Inside there was a narrow corridor with a small, dark kitchen on the left and a small, dark bedroom on the right. A little further along, there was a small, dark bathroom on one side and a tiny bedroom on the right. And that was it.

She couldn't help wondering if Rachel would have seized on this place so readily if it weren't for the fact that she spent a great deal of time with her boyfriend who had a far more salubrious flat in Putney. To be fair to Rachel, given their budget, it was always going to be difficult to find pleasant accommodation in central London. Tess's income was modest and Rachel had had to take a drop in salary since she worked for an events company that had too few events to organise. The rent here was remarkably cheap, though now Tess had seen it, it seemed not remarkable enough.

Less than a fortnight ago, Tess had stood with her back to the River Tweed, gazing at the enormous majesty of Abbotsford. Already, that seemed like another life. Now, sitting in Rachel's brother's kitchen with the cats down at her feet, she made a decision. She took out her phone and called up a number. After what seemed like an eternity a familiar voice said, 'This is Maggie Cameron speaking.'

'Oh, Grandma,' Tess said, 'I'm so glad it's you. I just thought I'd ask: I don't suppose that job's still going in the summer?'

Freya opened the door and beamed at Pam. 'What a nice surprise!' she said. 'I thought you were Felix. He should have been here ages ago.'

'I'm sure you're cooking supper. I'm on the scrounge. I need three eggs…'

Pam was wearing her green dress today. She had three work dresses: green, grey and black, which she wore in strict rotation, in order to save time otherwise wasted on choosing what to wear. When her beloved Henry died eighteen months ago, she lost a great deal of weight and her dresses looked like tents blowing in the wind. Freya had suggested a belt and gave her a leather one with a brass buckle. It became an essential part of Pam's working wardrobe and these days she looked rather Bohemian.

'Come on through,' Freya said. 'Let's have a drink. Felix is late and I'm dying to tell someone my news.'

'Just half a glass,' Pam said. 'I have a lot of cooking to do tonight.'

Freya sat her down at the table while she sorted out eggs and wine. 'I've been investigating a client's ancestor,' she said. 'Her name was Mary. She had an eighteen-year-old son and eight-year-old twin boys. And then…Are you happy with Chardonnay?…I discovered that she murdered her twins and then killed herself. But there seemed to be no motive. Why would a woman who's brought up one strapping great son want to kill her small twins? And, by the way, she doesn't just kill them in a nice, gentle way…'

'Can you kill someone in a nice, gentle way? Freya, that's enough. I need to be sober.'

'I suppose you could wait till they're sleeping and put pillows on their faces. That would be quite gentle, don't you think? Whereas Mary poisons her boys with prussic acid and then takes it herself. The question is: Why?'

'She had to be mad.'

Freya shook her head. 'Eight years after Mary died, her husband, Samuel, still employed his long-standing housekeeper, Maud Harries. According to the records I found today, he also had a sixteen-year-old stable boy called Peter Riley Harries. He was born in the same year as the twins. Do you see what I mean?'

'I'm sorry. You've lost me.'

'He had to be the illegitimate son of Samuel. Why else would he be given the name of Riley? I reckon Mary found out and killed herself and her twins in a fit of jealous fury.'

'She had to be mad. No one would do such a thing otherwise.'

'I know. But it fits, you see, it really fits.' She heard the front door slam and called out, 'Felix! We're in here!'

When Felix saw Pam, he beamed. 'Pam! This is a treat!' He came over and kissed her cheek. 'Are you staying for supper?'

'No, no, I came over to borrow some eggs. I had a call from Simon this afternoon.'

Simon was Pam's only child and could do no wrong. Felix put the Parmesan and the red wine on the table. 'How *is* Simon?' he asked. 'I haven't seen him for months.'

'He's very well. He rang me at work this afternoon and asked if he and Naomi could come down tomorrow night. He says they have something to tell me. It has to be wedding bells, don't you think? So I thought I'd make a special cake tonight and then I saw I had no eggs.'

Felix accepted a glass of wine from Freya and took a seat by Pam. 'You approve of Naomi, don't you?'

'She's perfect for Simon. They climbed Kilimanjaro

last year. Naomi got altitude sickness and vomited for hours but she still said she adored every minute of it. I loved Henry with all my heart but if he'd ever asked *me* to climb Mount Kilimanjaro I'd have told him I couldn't do it. Fortunately, he was quite happy with Swanage.'

Felix laughed. 'It *is* good to see you. Won't you stay to supper?'

'There's quite enough,' Freya assured her.

'No, really, I have so much to do.' Pam finished her drink and stood up. 'Thank you for the wine, Freya, and the eggs. I'll let you know what Simon has to tell me.'

'I'll see you out,' Felix said.

Freya heard the two of them chatting in the hall and then a low rumble of laughter from Felix. When he came back to the kitchen, he reached for his wine and said, 'I'm sorry Pam couldn't stay.'

'I could see that,' Freya said lightly. 'Now you'll have to make do with me.'

'Freya!' Felix protested.

She put the water on for the pasta and then turned. 'I'm not stupid, Felix. I know you're not happy at the moment.'

'No,' he agreed, 'but I'm working on it.'

'Can I help?'

'No, I don't think so.'

She began tearing up pieces of lettuce for the salad. She'd known the answer before she asked the question. He never liked discussing the strange moods that settled on him like ash.

'So tell me,' he said, 'what exactly are we celebrating?'

For a moment she had no idea and then she nodded and told him about Mary Riley and if he wasn't really interested he made an adequate job of appearing to be.

* * *

Way back in the Surrey days, long before Maggie had even heard the word 'commune', she and Philip lived in a street of solid suburban houses. Each one had a long rectangular garden at the back. One morning Maggie had woken at six. Going across to the window, she spotted Linda next door, dressed in jeans and jumper, digging up a clump of stinging nettles. Two days earlier, Linda and Derek had welcomed back their pale-faced son from university. Within a few hours he'd been rushed off to hospital with acute peritonitis. Maggie was not overly surprised to see Linda out working at such an early hour. When Linda was troubled, she always found solace in her garden.

Thirty-five years later, she continued to do so. Tonight, Maggie joined her on a slow perambulation round the lawn at the back of their house. Sheila and Derek were cooking tonight and had announced that dinner would be ready within the next half-hour. It had taken Maggie and Linda nearly ten minutes to put on their coats and their gloves but then, as Maggie told Linda, it didn't really matter since Sheila would almost certainly forget to put the greens on until Derek was ready to serve up.

Maggie was in a good mood. 'I had a call from Tess this evening,' she said. 'Robert had found her a holiday job in Gasterlethen and now she's decided to take it. So she'll be up here with us through August.'

'I'm so glad,' Linda said. 'I always enjoy her visits. Are there any men on the... the...?'

'On the horizon? No. There never do seem to be any men on Tess's horizon.'

70

'Perhaps she doesn't like men.'

'I suppose it's possible. I'm not sure she's interested in women either.'

Linda stopped to point her walking stick at the rose bushes. 'They need spraying,' she said. 'We must talk...We must talk to the gardener.'

Maggie nodded. 'I'm sure Gordon mentioned it a few weeks ago. I'll be sure to remind him.'

They set off again. 'How is... Tess's sister?' Linda asked.

This was what Linda did these days. Names eluded her and she would use deceptively formal language to refer to individuals she had known for years. All through the Surrey decades, she and Maggie had been in and out of each other's house, sharing children and then grandchildren. Linda had seen almost as much of Tess and Anna as she had of her own grandsons. And now Anna was 'Tess's sister'.

'Anna's fine,' Maggie said. 'She's a very busy doctor. She was always such a funny little girl. Do you remember a time I brought her and Tess to tea with you? It was the day you and Derek had your old beech tree cut down and you told them it had died. Anna looked at you and me with immense gravity and said, "I expect you'll die soon." I said something like I very much hoped we wouldn't and she looked at us with great sweetness and said, "Don't worry. I'm sure it won't hurt." She was only four and she said that! Do you remember her saying that?'

'No,' Linda said. 'I don't remember. Is Felix coming here soon? I am so fond of Felix. I haven't seen him for a very long time.'

Felix and Freya had been there with Tess only two months ago for Easter. Maggie said, 'He and Freya are coming in October. It's a long drive for them and Felix works so hard.'

Linda nodded. 'This morning,' she said, 'I sat up in bed and I thought: I don't know how to switch on my bedside lamp. Derek was awake and I told him. I said, "I feel as if all the lights in my head are slowly going out." And do you know what he said?'

'No.' Maggie reached out for her friend's hand. 'Tell me.'

'He said I shouldn't worry. He said he'd be my torch.' Linda smiled and for a moment the old Linda was there, with the usual spark of mischief in her eyes. 'I told him,' she said, 'he'd need to stock up on batteries.'

CHAPTER EIGHT

Anna met William Niarchos when they were both at medical school. At the time she was seeing a charming but complicated boy who shared a flat with William. Her friendship with William had lasted far longer than the relationship with his flatmate. She and William both loved the cinema and he was a non-judgemental and easy-going companion; they were impressive characteristics given the peculiarities of his upbringing. His brother was called Trevor and, as he pointed out to Anna, one only had to consider their names to indicate that there was something dysfunctional about the family. Their father was proudly Greek, their mother was stubbornly English and their favourite pastime was to argue ferociously as to whether England or Greece deserved to be known as the cradle of democracy.

The brothers had grown up witnessing dramatic conflagrations on a regular basis. William had once acted out to Anna one particular family breakfast. He and his brother were eating cereal with their mother when his father burst into the kitchen and emptied the contents of a plastic bag over his wife. It transpired he had cut into pieces the dress she had worn to a party the night before at which, so their father told them, their mother had done her best to seduce the host.

'What did you say?' Anna asked. 'What did you do?'

'We carried on eating our cereal,' William said. 'They started rolling about on the floor trying to hit each other and so I threw a jug of water over them.'

Anna was fascinated by these stories. In her own family, she and Tess had always been encouraged to 'respect' the opinions of others, which as far as she could see meant accepting them without complaint. She told an incredulous William that she had never heard her parents raise their voices at each other.

After medical school, Anna had gone on to Bangor and Bristol and now London whereas William had trained at Durham and Sheffield. His stint in Durham overlapped briefly with Tess's time at Durham University and Anna had put them in contact with each other. They'd only seen each other a couple of times but Tess had reported back her approval.

And then William arrived at St Peter's. His parents had divorced three years ago which, he told Anna, had been a source of great relief to their children. Their mother had married a UKIP activist and lived in Margate, while his father remained in the family home in Reigate where he lived in exhausted contentment with a mild-mannered librarian.

For Anna, the return of her old friend was particularly welcome. Any time Miss Diamond was horrendous, she would seek out William and he would be ready with a cinematic comparison. One day, Miss Diamond was like Bette Davis in *All About Eve*, desperately insecure about a stunning young doctor with the look of Jean Seberg. 'I doubt if Miss Diamond's ever heard of Jean Seberg,' Anna said. Another time, William would compare the consultant to Julia Roberts in *August: Osage County*, unable to keep the malice from spilling out because that was the way *her* mother talked. Whenever Anna discussed her nemesis with William, he had the great gift of reducing her power to that of a sadly disturbed woman whose dislike of Anna was completely bound up with her own malfunction. Presumably, the years he'd spent listening to his parents' quarrels had immunised him against the sulphurous behaviour of others.

Tonight, they were back eating pizza, discussing their latest cinematic outing, *Edge of Tomorrow*, a film that William dismissed as a *Groundhog Day* remake without the laughs or the brilliance of Bill Murray.

'I know you're right,' Anna said, 'but I still liked it. I like the idea that you can keep going back to refine and improve your life until you get it right.' She took a bite of her pizza and chewed thoughtfully. 'I'm going to have supper with Patrick and Fizz on Friday.'

William blinked. 'I'm sorry? Is that piece of information connected to the film? Do you hope to refine and improve your relationship with Patrick?'

'I just thought you'd be interested.'

'Two weeks ago you had lunch with them and now you're going over to dinner. Patrick must be keen. Perhaps Fizz is too.'

'Sometimes, William, you just have to accept there aren't always hidden motives.'

'Do you still find Patrick outstandingly desirable?'

'Well, I suppose…'

'I rest my case. Let's not talk about it now, it's too depressing…Are you going to eat that crust?'

'You know I don't like the outside bits.'

William whipped the offending piece from her plate.

'My brother rang me last night. He's got engaged to his girlfriend.'

'Do you like her?'

'She's beautiful and brilliant and she adores Trevor.'

'Lucky Trevor.'

'He knows he is. He's very smug. He's having a small party for her next month. Will you come with me?'

'Do I have to pretend to be your girlfriend?'

'Certainly not. Just look at me occasionally as if you'd *like* to be. There'll be food. And champagne.'

'All right. I'll come.'

'That's very generous of you,' William said. 'It can be our farewell date together.'

She wished William hadn't brought that up. He was moving on to Reading at the beginning of August, a prospect she found depressing.

'Reading's hardly the Outer Hebrides,' she said. Her phone bleeped and she picked it up. 'It's Tess. We're going down for Dad's birthday on Saturday. I don't know why she thinks I'd forget.'

'How *is* Tess?'

'I don't know. I think she's all right.'

'Next time you talk to her, tell her Marnie says hello and thank you.'

'Who's Marnie?'

'She's my cousin. She met Tess in Durham. She thinks Tess is very wise. Which is more than I can say about Tess's sister.'

'For God's sake, William, I'm just going to *supper*!'

'Right,' William said. 'Of course you are.'

* * *

There were two other guests besides Anna, a fact she would pass on to William. Cleo was an old actress friend of Patrick and 'Unlike certain people I could mention,' Cleo said, jabbing an accusing finger at their host, 'I have not given up on the dream.' Cleo was tall and slim with a mane of red hair, a thin pointed nose and a mobile mouth. She had not actually done any acting for fourteen months, she told Anna, and was currently working as a receptionist. She had done three auditions in the last six months and had been recalled four times after the last one. The casting director had virtually promised her the part until a young actress from *Hollyoaks* had expressed an interest and 'That was it. I was out. They wanted a name, even if the name had as much talent as a rotten potato. So I went home and cried for an hour or two. Then my flatmate reminded me that Kristin Scott Thomas lost Hugh Grant to Andie MacDowell in *Four Weddings and a Funeral* and now Kristin's an international film star and Andie does adverts for hairspray. You have to keep going, don't you?'

The other guest was a broad-shouldered man with a slightly pockmarked face and rather cold green eyes. He looked like Richard Burton in *Where Eagles Dare*. It was easy to imagine him in military uniform barking out orders to his terrified subordinates.

'This is Matthew,' Fizz said. 'He's only here because he's a partner in my firm and I'm hoping if I'm nice to him, he'll make me one too.'

'It's so good to feel needed,' Matthew murmured. He smiled at Anna and instantly looked a lot less like Richard

77

Burton because his eyes were no longer icy but simply amused.

Over supper, the abundant white wine, so generously provided by Matthew, produced different reactions. Anna, after a punishing week at St Peter's, was happy to sit back and observe the verbal fireworks around her. Patrick, perhaps equally tired by the production of the meal, was also content to make only the odd interjection. Cleo charged in with instant opinions which confusingly changed when challenged by an increasingly animated Fizz. Occasionally, Patrick would catch Anna's eye and smile across at her.

Matthew, Anna noticed, liked to throw a topic onto the table and then watch while it was grappled with by his companions. Cleo had been telling them all about a photo her ex-boyfriend had sent her in which he lay naked on his bed. Matthew said, 'Do you remember that poor congressman in the States a year or so ago. He did the same sort of thing'

'Excuse me?' Cleo asked incredulously. 'Did you use the word "poor"? Are you saying you feel sorry for him? The man had a stellar career and decided to derail it by sending lewd photos of himself to women he met online. You feel sorry for him?'

Matthew shrugged. 'He sent an inappropriate photo to a female follower on Twitter. It's hardly a hanging offence.'

'It's why he did it that's interesting,' Fizz said. 'You read about this sort of thing all the time. Why would someone who has a good career and a happy marriage want to risk ruining everything?'

Matthew shrugged again. 'Perhaps his marriage wasn't

as happy as he thought.'

'Excuse me?' Cleo said again. 'Are we therefore supposed to make excuses for him? He was a successful politician and therefore...'

'Therefore,' Matthew said, 'we are all entitled to have a go at him. We don't like successful people.'

Patrick shook his head. 'It's not that we don't like successful people. It's that we don't like successful people who abuse their position.'

'Quite right,' Anna said. 'My consultant makes my life a misery.'

'That's different,' Matthew said. 'It's quite healthy to wish disaster on bullies.' He nodded sagely at Anna. 'Your consultant will get her comeuppance one day.'

'I doubt it,' Anna said. 'Unfortunately, she's very good at her job.'

Matthew settled back in his chair and folded his arms. 'Let me tell you a story,' he said. 'My older sister, Tina, was tormented throughout her schooldays by a girl called Jocasta Kale. Tina grew up to be a dentist and last year she had an emergency patient – one Jocasta Kale. So Jocasta comes in and she doesn't recognise Tina, and Tina gets her in the chair and starts probing her mouth and making polite conversation. "Did you ever see *Marathon Man*?" she asks and Jocasta nods because she can't say anything at the moment. And then Tina says, "I love that bit where Laurence Olivier starts torturing Dustin Hoffman by extracting Hoffman's teeth." And she can see Jocasta's eyes widen a bit and then she says, "It's so funny to see you after all these years. Do you remember filling my lunch box with used tampons? That was *so* funny!" And now sweat is

79

pouring down Jocasta's face and Tina proceeds to do a skilful and gentle job on Jocasta's teeth and afterwards Jocasta rushes out with a face as pale as milk.'

There was a short silence while the company digested Matthew's account. Fizz gave a theatrical shudder. 'Matthew, that's a really horrid story, if a strangely satisfying one.'

Anna left soon after, not because she wasn't enjoying herself, but because the long day had finally caught up with her. On the bus back home, she remembered Patrick smiling across at her. She caught sight of her reflection in the mirror and discovered she was smiling too.

Her good mood was enhanced when she found a message on her bed from Olivia. 'Back tomorrow. Thought you'd like to know I've managed to bury the Xander Bullen proposal. We're doing Battersea Dogs' Home instead.'

Anna took out her laptop and googled his name. Under *Images of Xander Bullen*, there were four photos. In two of them he gazed at the camera, his forehead slightly furrowed, his eyes exuding thoughtful sincerity. In the other two he smiled out at Anna.

'Back to the drawing board, Xander,' she murmured but even as she said it she knew she was a King Canute trying to hold back the waves. Men such as Xander would always rise effortlessly like scum. He was handsome, he knew how to charm and he was not held back by scruples of any kind.

CHAPTER NINE

It was wonderful to have the girls with her. Anna was so positive about her work and Tess was thrilled to be going back to Scotland at the end of her term, particularly since she'd moved with Rachel into a dark little flat on a very noisy road.

Best of all was the change in Felix. When he came back from the station with them both, his eyes sparkled and Freya dared to hope he'd returned to his old self. Over lunch, he sat at the head of the table, accepting his daughters' jokes about his age with great good humour, assuring them he'd be leaping around the tennis courts this very afternoon.

'What about you three?' he asked. He cut a large wedge of Brie and transferred it to his plate. 'Are you going off to Ivy straight after lunch?'

'We'll go at half three,' Freya said. 'We don't want to tire her.' She glanced at her daughters. 'I do hope Ivy remembers you.'

'Last time,' Anna said, 'she thought I was you.'

'It's the blonde hair,' Felix said. 'Last time *I* saw her, she thought I was the cook.'

'That was because you kept going on about her chocolate bourbons,' Freya noted. 'You ended up eating all of them.'

Tess put an arm round her father's shoulder. 'I'm sorry you're not coming with us.'

'I would,' Felix said, 'but unfortunately I have to play tennis.'

81

'Very unfortunate,' Anna murmured.

'It is my birthday after all,' Felix said. 'But I'm glad you girls are going with your mother. She visits Ivy twice a week and it's not easy.'

In fact, Freya felt guilty that she only visited her stepmother twice a week. There wasn't a mother alive who could be as fiercely loyal and loving as Ivy had proved to be.

Freya and her father had been on their own for seven years when he married again. Freya was, for nearly a year, the stepdaughter from Hell. At fourteen, she was accustomed to being the centre of her father's world and had no intention of surrendering her position to an interloper, particularly when that interloper was a mousey young academic whose love for her new husband was as embarrassing as it was irritating. Freya ignored her when her father was around and was devastatingly rude to her when he wasn't.

And then one evening, everything changed.

Ivy and Freya's father went out to a dinner at which her father was speaking. Freya went to the cinema with a boy she'd been seeing for a couple of months. Afterwards, Russell walked her home and, on the way, he laughed at something she said and she realised for the first time that he had a peculiar laugh. When they got home, she invited him in for coffee and noticed for the first time that his fingernails were unpleasantly long. These revelations forced Freya to tell him she was sorry but she no longer wished to go out with him. Freya had already had similar revelations with her first two boyfriends. Graham had walked out of the house in

82

dignified silence which had been bad enough. Paul had started crying which had been worse. This time was a whole new level of awfulness. Russell sat back in his chair, narrowed his eyes and launched into a lacerating attack on her character. He told her she was conceited and selfish and only ever talked about herself. Reflecting in later years, Freya thought he'd probably been right. He said her looks wouldn't last and now that he was used to them they no longer interested him. All that remained was her character and her character was actually pretty boring.

If he wanted to hurt her – which obviously he did – he was brilliantly successful. Freya knew she was pretty and if he'd tried to convince her otherwise, would have known he was lying. When he told her she was boring, she burst into tears.

And then Ivy appeared in the doorway in her red quilted dressing gown and a nose the same colour. A bad cold and blocked sinuses had precipitated her early return. She stepped into the kitchen and told Russell she had heard all he'd said and felt forced to intervene. She knew he was hurt but she couldn't allow him to voice such wicked untruths. He should accept that part of being a teenager was learning how to reject and how to be rejected. It wasn't Freya's fault that she no longer wished to go out with him. These things happened. If he really thought Freya was boring, he wouldn't be upset at the prospect of losing her and he quite clearly *was* upset. And finally, she said, drawing herself up to her full five feet and two inches, she couldn't allow him to talk to her stepdaughter like that and she would like him to leave.

Russell opened his mouth to speak, thought better of it and left without another word. Freya burst into tears again, flung herself at Ivy, cried, 'Oh, Ivy, I'm sorry, I'm sorry, I'm sorry!' and had loved her ever since.

So naturally, she visited her twice a week and even more naturally she felt guilty she didn't visit her every day. But Felix was right: it *wasn't* easy. Ivy's mind had started showing signs of wear and tear two years ago. When Freya's father died, Ivy didn't cry once, even though everyone knew she'd adored him. She neglected the home she'd always kept so neat and so trim and, more dangerously, she neglected her diet and her appearance. Within a few weeks, she was talking obsessively about her friend, Marilyn. It was as if she had bounced herself out of her real life and into another one of her own making. When it became apparent that she was incapable of living on her own, Freya moved her into a nursing home a few miles away. It was a converted manor house, clean and comfortable and set in delightful gardens, but Freya continued to feel she had let Ivy down by putting her there.

Today was one of her good days. She was delighted to see Anna and Tess and received their embraces with enthusiasm. The girls took chairs on either side of her and she beamed at them both and said, 'You two have such hair! You have such beautiful hair!'

'You're looking well, Gran,' Tess said. 'I haven't seen you in that dress before.'

Ivy's voice sank to a conspiratorial whisper. 'Marilyn gave it to me. She keeps on at me to visit her in Hollywood. I tell her, Marilyn, I can't, I'm needed *here*. She's such a sweet girl but has no luck with men.' She gripped Tess's hand. 'Do you have a young man?'

Tess shook her head. 'No, Gran, I don't.'

'I think that's sensible,' Ivy said. 'You never know what will happen.'

On the opposite side of the room, a frail old lady, with skin like parchment, sat gently weeping. Anna went over to see if she could help and returned a minute or so later. 'The poor woman's wet herself,' she murmured. 'She reeks of urine. I'll go and find someone.'

Anna, action woman incarnate in her blue jeans and black leather jacket, marched out of the sitting room. Freya turned back to Ivy and said brightly, 'Tess is studying very hard these days. She's quite in love with Sir Walter Scott.'

Ivy nodded politely. 'I didn't know she had a young man.'

'Walter Scott was a writer,' Freya said. 'He's dead now.'

'That doesn't mean anything,' Ivy said. Which, actually, Freya thought, in relation to Tess, was probably true.

'He wrote some famous novels,' Tess explained. 'He wrote *Ivanhoe*.'

'I saw Ivanhoe,' Ivy said. 'I saw him on television.'

'She did!' Freya cried. She felt absurdly pleased that her stepmother had at last said something that was sane and true. 'It used to be on television every week. The man who played Ivanhoe was an assistant to the very first Doctor Who.'

'Who, dear?' Ivy asked, and smiled when Freya laughed.

Anna came back in a state of high indignation. 'I found a member of staff and he said he'd have to find someone to help him. How difficult can it be to help an old lady to change her clothes?'

'I don't want to change my clothes,' Ivy said.

'*You* don't need to, Gran,' Anna said, returning to her seat. 'You look so pretty in your dress.'

'Marilyn gave it to me,' Ivy said. 'She's in love with Tony Curtis at the moment.'

Anna nodded. 'I bet that will end in tears.'

'You're right,' Ivy said. 'I said to her, Marilyn, don't do it. Read a book instead.'

'I quite agree,' Anna said. 'Books are better than men any day.'

Three members of staff came in and bore down on the frail old lady who was whimpering quite loudly now. One of the men said, 'Hello, Iris, let's sort you out, shall we?'

What followed was straight out of a horror film. The gentle old lady turned instantly into a snarling, biting dervish. She kicked and scratched and yelled and was eventually carried out by the three now battered and bruised carers.

Freya and her daughters exchanged horrified glances. Ivy gave them all an understanding smile. 'Don't worry about her,' she said. 'She likes to make a fuss.'

Afterwards, they walked out to the car in silence. Anna looked at her mother and said, 'Are you all right, Mum?'

Freya swallowed a large lump in her throat and said, 'I feel so ashamed that I've put her in a place like that.'

Anna grasped her mother's hand. 'It's clean, the staff

are kind and, quite honestly, Gran has no idea how awful it is.'

'I know,' Freya said. 'It just seems so unfair. And I can't understand how a woman who was an expert on Anglo-Saxon literature can spend all her waking hours talking to Marilyn Monroe.'

'It could be worse,' Anna said. 'Imagine if she were talking to Mother Teresa or Margaret Thatcher.'

They arrived home at six. Felix took one look at Freya and announced he wanted presents and champagne *now*. Freya protested it was far too early for alcohol but Felix said, too bad, it was *his* birthday.

Later, as they sat outside eating his favourite meal – steak, new potatoes and spinach – Felix told himself he was truly blessed. He did that a lot these days but tonight he almost believed it. It was a perfect summer's evening with no sound other than the distant hum of a plane in the sky. And there around him were the three most important people in his life: Anna, with Freya's heart-stopping eyes and the easy assurance he used to long for, little Tess whose infectious laugh he heard too rarely these days and, lastly, Freya, so beautiful in her floral dress and pale pink cardigan, and so full of energy and a determination to extract every last bit of experience from each and every day. He hated what he was doing to her, he hated that she tried so hard to be calm and understanding. He worried about all of them. Both his daughters were troubled. He had no idea why but he recognised the signs. He'd say nothing to Freya of course. Heaven knew, she had enough on her plate at the moment. But now, tonight, he could almost convince himself that all was well. Perhaps if he tried hard enough, it would be.

He raised his glass and cleared his throat. 'This has been a quite spectacularly satisfactory birthday. Thank you, girls, for making the effort to come here this weekend.'

'We wouldn't miss your birthday,' Tess said.

'I appreciate that,' Felix told her. 'I feel very happy.'

Freya felt happy too, happy and full of love for Felix and their daughters. She beamed at them all.

'We have another celebration soon,' she said. 'On September the sixth, we'll have been married for thirty years.'

'Will you have a party?' Anna asked. 'You'll have to have a party.'

Freya glanced expectantly at Felix and just for a moment he looked back at her. He looked...How did he look? Awkward? Defensive? Taken aback? Then he turned away and reached for the wine.

'We don't want a party,' he said. 'There's nothing more smug or sanctimonious than inviting one's friends and family to marvel at one's perfect marriage. A quiet dinner at home will do very well.'

'Sounds dull to me,' Anna said. 'What do you think, Mum?'

So nothing had changed. Or rather, everything had changed. This wasn't one of Felix's sessions, this was something different, something permanent, and she had no idea how to deal with it. Felix didn't want a party, because he didn't want to celebrate his marriage. For the first time, Freya felt scared. She forced a smile to her lips.

'I certainly don't want a party if Felix doesn't. That wouldn't be fun at all.'

CHAPTER TEN

Eliza had been determined not to meet the ugly little man again. Curiosity was her downfall. She wanted to know if he really would turn up at his self-appointed position in front of the Pissarro in Room 44. She couldn't believe that any man, especially a diminutive monkey-like man, would seriously expect a woman he'd only just met to agree to meet him in a place and time of his choice.

She had intended to slip into Room 44 and slip straight out again. Her plan was immediately derailed. No sooner had she stepped into the room than a surprisingly loud voice rang out from the other end, 'I'm here!'

Everyone looked at her as if it were *her* fault that the cathedral-like calm of the place had been interrupted. In the circumstances she felt duty bound to walk quickly over to the man before he shouted again. She did murmur in a fierce whisper that it was quite unnecessary to yell at her.

'Never mind that,' he said. 'Just look at this painting! Isn't it beautiful?'

Behind him was a picture of a wide country road under a wide blue sky. She had to admit it was special. It was called *The Avenue, Sydenham* and she could almost imagine she was standing by the artist, gazing beside him at the rural lane and the ancient church. It looked singularly enticing, and enticing was not an adjective she would use about most parts of south London.

'Why did he come *here*?' she asked. 'He was a great Impressionist painter. Why come to Sydenham?'

'I presume he thought it was more congenial than eating rats in Paris. He fled to England when the Prussians decided to invade France in 1870. They laid siege to the capital and, within months, people were reduced to eating their household pets. Even the two elephants at the Paris zoo were made into elephant cutlets. I'm sure you know all the stories.'

Eliza gave a neutral sort of nod. She was irritated by his easy assumption that she knew as much as he did. She gazed at the painting. 'It looks so real,' she said.

'Pissarro was one of the first artists to leave his studio and set up his easel in the open air. But you knew that already, I expect.'

'No,' Eliza said. 'I didn't know.' The man's knowledge about everything was one reason why she had vowed she wouldn't see him again. It was also the reason why in fact she returned for more. He was infuriating and interesting in equal measures.

And so now here she was on her way to her fourth assignation with him. Assignation was hardly the right word to use since it implied something furtive and sexually suggestive and there was nothing even remotely sexy about the man at the National Gallery. Eliza supposed it was a sign of her great age that given the choice between a romantic lover and her annoyingly bumptious art expert she would definitely go for the latter.

In fact, there was little sign of bumptiousness today. He was unusually subdued, possibly because the painting they were looking at clearly moved him. It depicted Gainsborough's young daughters chasing a butterfly. For once it was Eliza who did most of the talking. She commented on the discrepancy between the somewhat sinister backdrop of a dark forest and the almost unearthly radiance of the two children. She mused on the title – *The Painter's Daughters chasing a Butterfly* – and wondered if Gainsborough was trying to make a comment on the fleeting nature of childhood and innocence.

Her companion made an effort to rouse himself. 'I don't know. Perhaps it was simply a literal record of an incident he observed. It's interesting though: it's almost as if he knew what lay in store for them.'

'What *did* lie in store for them?'

'Their lives were difficult. They were daughters of one of the most fashionable artists in the eighteenth century. He regularly carried out commissions for the royal family. So the girls had access to high society without being properly accepted by it. Mary married a musician but the marriage broke down and the sisters ended up living together. I believe Mary suffered from prolonged bouts of mental instability.'

'That's so sad.'

'Yes, it is.'

Eliza waited for him to say more but he had lapsed into silence again. She was worried. It upset her to see him without his usual energy and enthusiasm. She could see she had been wrong to find him conceited and patronising. He was simply a man who loved art and had a wish to share that love with others. Today, that had gone. Something wasn't right. She said hesitantly, 'I know you have to rush off. Please don't...'

'I don't have to rush off any more.'

The statement was all the bleaker for being made without expression. She made a sudden decision. 'In that case, will you allow me to buy us both a coffee?'

She took him to the espresso bar and bought coffee and a flapjack. They sat opposite each other and she was at a loss as to how to proceed with the silent, preoccupied stranger in front of her. She cut the flapjack in half and offered him a piece but he shook his head.

'This is our fourth meeting,' she said. 'I really think we should introduce ourselves. My name is Eliza Sample.'

He gave a formal nod of his head. 'I am Dennis Woodward.'

'Now that we are introduced,' Eliza said, 'I hope you won't mind if I say that you seem a little sad today. It's so unlike you.'

Dennis took a sip of his coffee and then set his cup down on its saucer. 'My sister died three days ago. She's been ill for some time. Every Thursday for some months now I've gone to Bromley to visit her after coming here. Of course, at my age, I am used to the deaths of relatives and friends. But Barbara and I were close and today I feel a little lonely as a result of her absence.'

'I'm sorry.'

'I am grieving for me not my sister. She was always frightened of death. Last week she told me she welcomed it. She told me she was impressed by the cleverness of Nature. "I feel sick all the time," she said. "Why should I want to go on living when I feel sick all the time? You don't need to feel sorry for me when I die." So I don't. I just feel sorry for *me*.'

'That is quite understandable.'

'Thank you. I'm afraid I am not very good company at the moment.'

93

Eliza nodded. 'Let us talk about next week. I think we need to see something that will rouse your spirits and I know exactly the picture that will do it.'

'If you are thinking of one of the religious paintings, I should tell you...'

'Certainly not.' Eliza took one of the flapjack halves and bit into it, aware that she had at last won his complete attention. 'We shall see *The Execution of Lady Jane Grey* by Paul Delaroche. It never fails to lift my spirits.'

'You *like* that painting?'

'I love that painting. Why? Don't *you* like it?'

'No, I do not. Do you want to know why?'

'I would very much like to know why.'

'I'll tell you. Apart from the fact that it's sentimental tosh ...' Dennis proceeded to give a withering assessment of the qualities of Delaroche and, as he did so, Eliza observed with great satisfaction that he picked up and ate the other half of the flapjack.

Maggie left Sheila at the surgery after agreeing to meet later for coffee. Sheila had given up driving after a minor collision with a parked car in Galashiels, and Maggie was happy to act as chauffeur this morning. Katherine had offered to come too but had been diverted by a phone call from her sister in Fife.

Maggie always enjoyed coming to Melrose. In their first year in Scotland she had found communal life difficult. She and Philip would escape to Melrose for lunch together. Philip would sit her down with a large glass of red wine and listen while she ranted about Katherine's tactlessness and Derek's tendency to take an hour to load the dishwasher. After Philip's death she had thought she could never face Melrose again. In fact, she discovered it was here she felt closest to him.

Today, she spent a pleasant half-hour perusing knitting patterns in the fabric place and picture frames in the antiques shop before making her way up to the market square.

She saw Jamie Lockhart walk into the bank. The last time she'd seen him was at Flora Macdonald's birthday party in Kelso, almost a month ago. For a moment she thought about calling out to him. By the time she decided she would, it was too late. He had already gone in. She walked on across the wide square, past the Mercat Cross and entered the distinctive green door of Randall's coffee shop.

Sheila sat at a table by the window, her glasses halfway down her nose, her ever-present notebook in front of her, ready to receive ideas for poems or stories. Maggie had known Sheila for sixty-eight years. They had helped each other through teenage crushes, miscarriage (Maggie), extra-marital temptations (Sheila), career disappointments, maternal worries and bereavement. Now they helped each other through their final years.

'I'm sorry I'm late,' Maggie said, sitting down opposite her and unbuttoning her jacket. 'Have you been here long?'

'Only a few minutes. I've ordered coffee and shortbread. You look a little discombobulated.'

'I suppose I am. How was the doctor?'

'I have to stay on the blood pressure pills. Are you going to tell me what's wrong? Were you worried I might keel over in the surgery?'

'I've just seen Jamie Lockhart go into the bank,' she said.

'He's Tess's admirer?'

Maggie nodded. 'I nearly called out to him.'

'Why didn't you?'

'Well…' Maggie hesitated, already aware that Sheila would find her response pathetic. 'It would look so odd.'

'I don't see why.'

'There's a great difference between striking up a friendly conversation on the pavement and yelling from halfway down the street. He must know that I watched him monopolise my grand-daughter at the party. I would hate him to think I wanted to interfere in some way.'

The waitress arrived with their order and made a point of admiring Sheila's earrings. While Sheila began one of her interminable direction speeches – the earrings had been purchased in a small shop in Edinburgh and if the waitress could follow Sheila's instructions she was a brighter woman than Maggie – Maggie glanced across at the bank and berated herself for her indecisive attitude towards the Jamie question.

Once the waitress had gone, Sheila put her elbows on the table and rested her chin on her hands. 'I've often thought that where your family is concerned, you don't interfere *enough*. And besides, in this case you would be intervening rather than interfering. And anyway, why is it so bad to interfere? Why are we so rude about busybodies and do-gooders? They are busy bodies and they do good. If there were more of them we wouldn't need social workers or dating agencies or therapists. Why is it wrong to want to improve someone's life?'

'Because,' said Maggie, 'I'm not sure I *would* improve it. Suppose I encouraged Jamie to see Tess in the summer and suppose she fell in love with him and suppose he broke her heart – I'd never forgive myself.'

'Suppose Jamie is her soulmate and you do nothing to help them? I think you were *meant* to see Jamie this morning. You think about that while I go to the Ladies'.'

Maggie *did* think about it. She cut her piece of shortbread into four neat columns and took a sip of her coffee. Sheila was a great believer in Fate. Fate was a regular participant in her short stories. As far as Fate was concerned, Maggie was an agnostic. She could not believe her meeting with Jamie was written in the stars. She often saw Jamie in Melrose. He lived in Melrose after all. She sighed and looked out onto the Mercat Cross. A woman sat on the octagonal base with a little girl. The little girl reminded Maggie of Tess. She had the same wild auburn curls and thin little legs and was laughing. Tess used to tell Maggie long, involved jokes that she could never finish because she'd start giggling helplessly and Maggie would laugh too and feel quite weak. It had been a long time since Maggie had seen Tess laugh like that.

'Maggie?' Sheila had returned. 'You were miles away.'

Maggie looked up and, as she did so, she caught sight of Jamie Lockhart talking into his phone by the Cross. 'Sheila,' she whispered, 'that's him!'

The two women stared across at him and then, as he met their eyes, they both waved sheepishly in unison.

'Well, that was embarrassing,' Maggie said. 'For God's sake, Sheila, stop staring at him, he'll think we're both completely mad.'

'Perhaps he likes mad people,' Sheila said, 'because I'm

pretty sure he's coming over to see us.'

Sheila was right. In a matter of seconds, the young man had entered the café and was telling Maggie how very nice it was to see her again.

'It's very nice to see you too,' Maggie said. 'This is my friend, Sheila. Sheila, this is Jamie Lockhart.'

Jamie reached across to shake Sheila's hand. 'Mrs Cameron and I were at the same party a few weeks ago. I met her grand-daughter there.'

'We're all so fond of Tess,' Sheila said. 'We're so thrilled she'll be up here for the summer.'

'Will she? Is she coming up to do research?'

She's got a holiday job in Gasterlethen,' Sheila said. 'She's going to work in a clothes shop there. I'm sure she'll fit in some research though.'

'That's nice,' Jamie said. 'I shall try to call in on her. Do you know when she starts her job?'

'I believe,' Maggie said carelessly, 'it's July the twenty-first.'

Sheila smiled. 'Tess does love Scotland.'

'She obviously has excellent taste.' He glanced at his watch. 'I'd better get on. I'm supposed to be in Edinburgh for lunch. It's been very nice to see you both.'

They watched him run across the square. 'That was interesting,' Sheila said. 'He was very keen to say hello.' She looked across at Maggie and frowned. 'You're quiet. Should I not have mentioned Tess's plans for the summer?'

'I'm glad you did,' Maggie said. 'It meant that I didn't have to. If Jamie does call on Tess...'

'And he will,' Sheila said. 'I guarantee it.'

'If he does,' Maggie continued, 'and Tess asks how he

knew she'd be there, I can look her in the eye and say that *you* mentioned it.'

Sheila sighed. 'Do you ever think it might be a lot simpler if you just talked to Tess about all this?'

Maggie picked up a piece of shortbread. 'Yes,' she said, 'but I'm rather keen that Tess wants to keep coming up here.'

CHAPTER ELEVEN

The supermarket was busy today. The schools had broken up and parents were buying extra rations for the long summer holiday. Freya, negotiating her trolley round children and harassed mothers, came to a halt when she reached the magazine aisle. The covers were like siren voices: pick *me* to find out what Tom Cruise thinks about love; choose *me* to discover the secrets of a perfect complexion; buy *me* to learn the ten steps to lasting happiness.

Now her eyes were caught by a children's magazine. It was the price that shocked her: £4.99 for what was essentially a comic. The cover had a picture of an obviously female mouse since it had a pink tutu, a pink ribbon between its ears and big vertical eyelashes. The magazine promised *One hundred stickers inside!* It exhorted children to *Make a cake-stand!* Who would have thought that all these years after *The Female Eunuch* and a female prime minister, there would be girls' comics for sale, busily encouraging their small readers to make a cake-stand?

A little girl and her mother turned into the aisle. The mother was in her mid-thirties, Freya judged, an attractive woman with light brown hair caught up in a ponytail. She wore faded blue jeans and a sleeveless floral tunic. Her daughter had neatly plaited blonde hair; she wore red trousers and a matching T-shirt and her eyes went straight to the mouse magazine.

She picked it up and looked up at her mother with

pleading eyes. 'Can I have this?' she asked. 'Please, can I have this?'

Her mother gave it a quick glance. 'No way,' she said, 'it's nearly five pounds!'

'Please!' her daughter begged. 'I want this so much! I really, really want it! I *love* it!'

'I'm sorry, Chloe,' her mother said. 'We can't afford it and anyway it's a lovely day. You don't want to spend it doing sticking and stuff. We'll go to the playground later.'

'I don't want to go to the playground,' the little girl cried. 'I want *this*!'

The woman stared impassively at her. 'No, Chloe,' she said.

'I hate you, Mummy. I really hate you!'

For a moment her mother glanced at Freya and rolled her eyes. Then she looked down at Chloe and said, 'The only way I can afford to buy that magazine is if I don't buy Friday treats this week and if I don't buy them you'll have to explain why to Martha when we pick her up from playgroup, and then Martha will be quite justified in wanting to share the magazine with you...'

'I don't want to share it with Martha. She always puts the stickers in the wrong places!'

'Fine. So the choice is clear. You either get to share the magazine with Martha and she gets to put half the stickers wherever she likes, or we don't buy the magazine and you both get your Friday treats. It's quite simple. The choice is yours.'

'That's *so* unfair!'

'No, it isn't. I'm trying very hard to be fair to both of you.'

'Oh all *right*.' Chloe threw out her arms in a gesture of tragic surrender. 'We'll get the Friday treats!'

Freya was impressed. The mother's tactics had been exemplary: calm, rational arguments followed by careful negotiations. The woman should be in the diplomatic service.

It was only when Freya had loaded her boot with her groceries and was sitting in the car with the key in the ignition that the memory arrived in her mind like the ping of an email. She was in the garden making a den underneath the rhododendron bush. She had swept up the leaves and was serving out tea to Lady Arabella who sat on the ground in her beautiful dress with red roses, her stiff legs splayed out diagonally. Freya passed her a plate with three rhododendron flowers on it. Lady Arabella said they were delicious.

Freya heard her mother calling her and she yelled, 'I'm over here!'

She saw her mother's feet first. They were encased in white sandals and her toes were painted with gold nail varnish. 'Freya,' she said, 'it's time for your bath.'

'Lady Arabella and I are having tea,' Freya said. 'You can join us if you like.'

Her mother didn't want to join her. Her mother wanted her to have a bath right away and when Freya demurred she became very cross and told her to stop being naughty. And then Freya got cross and said, 'I hate you! I want Daddy to bath me!'

And then her mother did something quite extraordinary. She burst into tears and ran away and Freya sat frozen and scared and didn't dare move. A little while later her father came out to collect her and he bathed her and put her to bed. Later still, Freya heard her mother come into her bedroom. Freya pretended to be asleep and when her mother kissed her cheek she could feel the salty tears on her skin. When Freya's mother left the room, all that was left of her was her rose-scented perfume hanging in the air.

And the next morning, she had gone. Her father told her she'd left them, it was just the two of them now and they'd never see or mention her again. And Freya had nodded and said nothing because she knew it was her fault they were on their own.

Freya blinked and, as she did so, saw the mother come out of the supermarket, a basket in one hand and her daughter's hand in the other. The little girl was skipping. The mouse magazine was clearly forgotten.

Stepping down from her coach after a long, weary day of travel, Tess sat waiting for Grandma in the centre of Melrose. Two boys – and they *were* boys, they had to be a good five years younger than her – came up and started chatting to her. Tess was impressed by their confidence. One of them had acne and the other had a very unpleasant styc by his left eye. But they seemed quite undaunted by their physical blemishes and began firing questions in fast Scottish voices that were difficult to understand. She was relieved when Grandma showed up in her car.

It was only a ten-minute journey to the Commune by car and at least half of that time was spent in an argument as to whether Tess should pay rent during her stay.

Grandma was adamant. 'Our house has its rules and one is that we share our guests. If any of them are irksome to at least three of the residents, then we ask them to go.'

'I bet *that's* never happened,' Tess said. 'I can't imagine you standing by the door, demanding someone leaves.'

'It happened a few months ago when Robert's brother, Angus, came to stay. He is one of those men who are so sure they know the answer to everything that you almost believe they do but the longer you talk to them – or rather the longer they talk to *you* – you know that they don't. And the reason why Angus knows so little is because he is so keen to air his own views that he never listens to those of anyone else. We could cope with that most of the time, but then we caught him upsetting Linda, telling her she should make more of an effort to exercise her brain. You may recall that Linda has trouble remembering things these days and she's sensitive about that. So we called a special meeting and the first resident to call for the ejection of Angus was his brother.'

'How did you tell him to leave?'

'Robert told him we didn't like the way he treated Linda and he tried to dig his heels in and insist that he'd been cruel-to-be-kind which is always such a dubious argument, I think. And then Sheila told him he had to go as her children were coming up for her seventieth birthday and there would be no room for other guests. That put Sheila in a good mood for weeks because Angus never even questioned the fact that she was nearly seventy when in fact she is fully six months older than I am.' Grandma turned into the drive of the Commune. 'Now here we are!'

'Grandma,' Tess said. 'Before we go in, can I point out I'm up here for well over a month? I can't – I really can't –

stay here so long without making some financial contribution.'

Grandma turned off the engine and fixed Tess with steely eyes. 'When we settled here, my main worry was that we would see less of our children and grandchildren. So it is an undiluted joy to have you staying here. It only becomes diluted when you go on about paying rent. Do you understand?'

Tess's father had always been easy-going where his children were concerned. Just occasionally, he would look at them in a way that made them understand there was a line beyond which they could not cross. Grandma had that same look now.

On Monday, Tess borrowed a bicycle from the Commune and set off to work. If she were in London, she would be boarding an overcrowded bus now, trying to find an empty seat and avoid breathing in other people's germs and stale sweat. Instead, she was cycling along roads lined by trees, with the company of a buzzard soaring in the sky above her. She'd been given careful instructions by Dr Knox, which were hardly necessary. All she had to do once she joined the main road was cycle in the direction of Peebles until she came to Gasterlethen.

It turned out to be an odd sort of place. Perhaps early American frontier towns had been like this. There was a wide main street, edged on either side by sober grey terraced housing interspersed with the odd shop. It possessed an equally sober church, a grim-looking primary school and very little else. The place seemed to be deserted apart from two elderly men coming out of the newsagent who gazed open-mouthed at her as she cycled past.

It was not difficult to find Mrs Talbot's shop. It had a bright red door, its glass window frames almost obliterated by posters advertising various entertainments: a production of *Oklahoma!* in Peebles, a meeting of the Horticultural Association in Galashiels and an excursion to Scotland's oldest private house in Traquair. Presumably, interesting events and places were few and far between in Gasterlethen.

Mrs Talbot's shop window had a couple of mannequins who looked like they'd been modelled on the young Doris Day. Certainly they wore clothes that might appeal to the old Doris Day: well-cut slacks, sensible skirts and cashmere twinsets. Scattered around their feet were slim packs of fifteen denier stockings. Tess had no idea that women still wore them and wondered if this was an example of the North/South divide. She must ask Grandma.

She parked her bicycle, as instructed, in a little courtyard behind the shop. She took off her mac and put it over the bicycle while she tried to tie her hair back, a task that took some patience since her curls had become more Medusa-like than ever during the ride from the Commune. She wore the black skirt and white shirt she had always worn when working at the Italian restaurant in London and she smoothed them into shape, collected her mac and went round to the front of the shop.

Mrs Talbot was a small, thin, bird-like woman with grey hair and a soft Scottish voice that rose and fell along with the hand gestures that accompanied it. She had just made a pot of tea, and after checking Tess's particular requirements – milk and no sugar – disappeared behind a brown door, giving Tess a chance to inspect the shop.

The wall to the left of the high counter was covered in shelves on which the knitwear was stacked by colour. On the other side, clothes rails on castors were packed with skirts and trousers. There was a small stiff armchair by the changing room which looked hideously uncomfortable. Tess noted with pleasure the high counter with the burnished wooden surface. There was a pleasing smell of wax polish about the place and the wine-coloured carpet had been newly vacuumed.

Mrs Talbot came back with a tray on which sat two cups and saucers. She directed Tess to one of the two stools behind the counter and set the tray of tea in front of her, before pulling out the second stool for herself.

'So,' she said, 'Dr Knox speaks very highly of you and that's more than good enough for me. I should tell you that your employment is a trial, not for you, of course – at least, I'm sure I hope it isn't – but it is a trial for me. My husband retired a year ago and wants to see more of me, which is very nice, but I have to tell you, I'm not completely convinced that *I* would like to spend more time with *him*. Don't get me wrong; he's a very good man. But I've had this shop for nearly nineteen years and I said to Archie – Archie's my husband – "Archie," I said, "I just can't hand it over and say goodbye, I need to feel the water before taking the plunge," and that's why you're here, Tess. When Doctor Knox told me about you, I thought you would be just what I need and I shall *endeavour* to stay out of your way and see if I like spending more time at home. As regards our customers, Tess, I have *always* believed my job is to be a peaceful presence amongst the bustle of everyday life. I am ready to offer advice if asked, but otherwise I sit and I smile and I do *not* push myself forward. Quiet discretion is what I do, Tess, quiet discretion. Do you have any questions before I continue?'

'Well, I did wonder,' Tess said with a fleeting glance at the empty street, 'how busy you are.'

'You would be surprised,' Mrs Talbot told her, 'how many people beat a path to this door. We have quite a few foreigners stopping off here and I always like to point out that unlike certain neighbouring factory shops, the standard of our cashmere is second to none.' She stopped to take a sip of her tea. 'Now what I suggest is that, after our tea, I show you the ropes as it were and then I'll leave you on your own. If you have any problems, you can reach me at home and if, by any chance, you can't reach me you can always rely on Mr McTavish at the butcher's three doors away.'

Within the next half-hour Tess learnt how to use the till and record sales, how to fold jumpers and lock up the shop. When Mrs Talbot left, it was with visible reluctance and only after she extracted a promise from Tess to ring her in event of even the slightest difficulty.

The next two hours weren't difficult at all. Tess brought out her much fingered copy of Sir Walter Scott's journal and marvelled once more at his stoicism and good sense. Here he was in 1827, mourning the death of his wife and crippled by debts he was determined to pay back: *'Some things of the black dog still hanging about me but I will shake him off. I generally affect good spirits in company of my family whether I am enjoying them or not. It is too severe to sadden the harmless mirth of others by suffering your own causeless melancholy to be seen. And this species of exertion is like virtue its own reward for the good spirits which are at first simulated become at length real.'*

She could imagine him greeting his many illustrious visitors, chatting to his daughter or his gamekeeper, all the time concealing the fact that his health and his business were falling apart. What a man he was!

At midday Tess had her first customer of the day, a middle-aged woman in a deerstalker hat and brown corduroy trousers. She bought two pairs of stockings and seemed most put out that Tess had replaced Mrs Talbot. Mrs Talbot rang shortly after to check on Tess's progress and Tess described the customer.

'That'll be Edna Murdoch,' Mrs Talbot told her. 'She buys the stockings for her mother.'

'She was not at all happy that you weren't here,' Tess confessed.

'I'm sure that's not true,' Mrs Talbot said, but she was obviously pleased.

At two, an American couple came in and within twenty minutes had bought a total of eight cashmere jerseys and three silk scarves. Tess was thrilled, and when Mrs Talbot rang at three, could barely contain her excitement.

'Didn't I tell you?' Mrs Talbot said. 'You never know who'll come popping by.'

Mrs Talbot was right. Half an hour later, Tess raised her head at the sound of the bell and instantly recognised the young man with pale skin and dark black hair. He appeared not to notice her, focusing with great concentration on the packets of stockings in the window. He wore navy jeans and a navy blue jersey over a white T-shirt, all of which emphasised the slightness of his build. Great-aunt Katherine would probably say that he needed feeding up. Though actually, Tess thought, remembering her strictures on the Lockhart family, she would probably tell Tess to have nothing to do with him. The cuffs of his jersey were beginning to unravel. Tess cleared her throat and said, 'Hello there!'

He raised his eyes, took one of the stocking packets and went over to the counter. 'You're here in Scotland!' he said.

She nodded. 'I am. Do you want to buy those?'

He nodded. 'They're for my mother,' he said. 'So you are here and you haven't rung me. I gave you my card.'

She had forgotten this about him, the disparity between what he said and the way he said it. His voice was soft and gentle, there were no expressive gestures and yet his words expressed an outraged indignation that made her want to laugh.

She opened the till and took out his change. 'I've only been in Scotland a couple of days. To be fair, it's not easy to ring a man who once randomly suggested that I ring him some time.'

'I don't remember making a *random* suggestion.'

'You might have forgotten me and then...'

'I couldn't forget you even if I wanted to. Thanks to you, Rollo began his first shift on Thursday and dropped a tray of glasses within twenty minutes.'

'You *did* give him a job. I'm so glad.'

'Well, that's all right then.'

She folded her arms and stared back at him. 'If you don't mind my saying so, you seem very... very truculent.'

110

'I don't mind at all. I like the word truculent. Truculent suits my mood very well. Do you still want to visit my castle?'

'That would be very interesting, but...'

'What time do you finish work on Friday?'

'I'm supposed to lock up at five but I have my bike and...'

'That's all right. We can put it in the back of my car. I'll pick you up at five fifteen. I have to go now.'

And that was it. He left the shop before she could raise any objections or even have time to work out if she *had* any objections. She noticed too late that he'd left his stockings on the counter. She did run out after him but he'd already gone.

CHAPTER TWELVE

On Wednesday evening, Anna was on her way out of St Peter's as William was on his way in. She called out, 'William!' and watched with glowering eyes as he came across to her. 'I heard this morning,' she said, 'that you had a farewell do at the pub last night.'

'That's right,' he said. 'It was good.'

'I'm sure it was. Did you not think to ask me to come along?'

William frowned. 'I did. I asked you last week if you were free and you said you were working.'

'You didn't say what you were planning. I might have been able to change my shift.'

'You didn't need to,' William said, 'I knew I'd see you at Trevor's party. Which reminds me, it's quite a smart do, so wear a dress.'

She stared at him with mounting irritation. 'I do know what to wear to engagement parties.'

'Great. I'll see you Saturday. And by the way, have you given Marnie's message to Tess?'

'Do you mean the message, *Marnie says hello*?'

'"*Marnie says hello and thank you*."'

'I haven't seen Tess recently. She's in Scotland now.'

'Can't you call her?'

'The reception is terrible up there. Can't the message keep? Is Tess so important to Marnie?'

'The thing is…' William hesitated. 'Tess was very good to her.'

'In what way?'

He shrugged. 'I can't say.'

'I don't understand. You can't say or you won't say?'

William looked at his pager – which hadn't beeped – and said, 'It's odd you speak to your sister so rarely.' And then he looked at his pager again and said, 'I have to go.'

As Anna cycled home, she felt increasingly indignant. Who was he to stand in judgement on her sisterly responsibilities? Tess was as bad as she was about keeping in touch. And if Marnie's anodyne message was so important, William could at least explain *why*. And actually, a man who was taking a pretend girlfriend to his brother's engagement party was in no state to sit in judgement on the sibling relationships of others. She would tell him that on Saturday.

She arrived home to an empty flat and remembered that Olivia was going out to dinner with a man called Jason. She wished she could haul herself out of her black cloud. Her whole psyche seemed to be soaked in bile and her future looked bleak. Her career, as far as Miss Diamond was concerned, was a joke. So was her social life. In the last ten months she had had two fleeting and dismally unsatisfactory relationships. Here she was, in her youthful prime, on her own, jealous of Olivia and a man called Jason.

Her phone went and, picking it up, she felt instantly better. 'Hello, Patrick,' she said. She went across to the sofa and settled down with her feet tucked under her. 'How nice to hear from you. How are you?'

'In need of sympathy. Lola threw up over me and the carpet. Fizz is at dynamic yoga and I'm sitting here smelling of sick. How about you?'

113

'Oh, I'm all right. Work wasn't great today. At least I've had no one throw up over me.'

'That's a perk of parenthood. Fizz is going to Glasgow for the weekend. I know it's work but two nights in a hotel beats spending a weekend with a sick child. I hope you're feeling sorry for me.'

'Yes, Patrick, I am.'

'Good, because I want support. Come and join me on Saturday evening. We could talk about Wimbledon days without boring anyone else. I need you to save me from terminal self-pity.'

'I'm supposed to be going to a party with a friend…'

'I can't say I'm surprised, I knew you'd probably have plans…'

She heard herself say, 'I could probably get out of it.'

'Oh, Anna, could you? Already I feel better. If you come at eight you won't have to help with putting Lola to bed. You're welcome to come earlier of course.'

'I don't know a great deal about putting children to bed. I'll come at eight. See you then.'

She felt quite breathless. She was letting William down, she knew that. He'd asked her to come to Trevor's party over a month ago. *And* he was moving on to Reading. How to explain that as soon as Patrick asked her, she knew it was imperative to go? I'm a case of arrested development, she could say, I need Patrick to kick me forward. She could imagine William's response. He'd say she was mad, but she was used to that.

She rang him before she could change her mind. He sounded as if he were in the middle of a football scrum.

'Where are you?' she asked.

'At a farewell party.' William raised his voice. 'Not my own.'

'It's all right, I'm not angry now.'

'I can't hear you, I'll go to the other end of the bar... What did you say?'

'William, I can't come with you to Trevor's party, I'm sorry. Something's come up and I feel I have to go. First time you're back in London, I'll take you out to make up.'

'It's Patrick, isn't it?'

'It's difficult to explain. I'll tell you when I see you.'

Someone called his name and he said, 'I have to go.'

She felt bad about William. She honestly felt she had no choice.

Jamie was waiting for Tess on Friday, leaning against a battered old Land Rover. He took her bike, lifted it effortlessly into the boot and went round to open the passenger door for her. This was probably the first time that a man had opened a car door for her. Grandma would be impressed by his manners. She watched him climb into the car and start it up. She asked, 'How is your mood today? Are you still feeling truculent?'

'On the contrary,' Jamie said, 'I'm feeling quite benevolent. I'm always benevolent when showing people round my castle.'

This was not the first time he had referred to 'my castle'. The use of the possessive pronoun triggered a distant memory. When they were children, whenever there were visitors, Anna would ask them, 'Would you like to see my guinea pig?' with the same combination of pride and affection.

They drove out of the small town and on into the open countryside, only to be stopped by a farmer crossing the road with his sheep. Jamie spoke for the first time since he'd got into his car. 'It's rush hour,' he murmured.

She laughed. There was only one other car on the road. She was struck again by how still and patient he was. He didn't drum his fingers on the steering wheel, he simply sat and watched the sheep as they made their leisurely way across to the other side. 'You left your stockings behind,' she told him and, encountering a blank look, added, 'You bought them on Monday for your mother. I've got them here. I'll put them on the back seat.'

'Of course,' he said. 'Thank you.'

'Does your mother live round here?'

'No. She re-married some time ago and moved up near Oban. She and her husband run a small country hotel.'

'Do you see her often?'

'They work very hard. I go up when I can.'

'You must miss her.'

'Well,' Jamie murmured, 'I have my castle.'

He was, she suspected, only half joking. 'Tell me about it,' she said. 'Tell me the history.'

'Are you sure?' he asked. 'It might take some time.'

'I want to know. I'm interested.'

'Well then.' Jamie took a deep breath. 'It was built in the fourteenth century and owned by Sir Richard Palmer, a friend of the English king, Edward the First.' The road was finally clear. Jamie drove on. 'There've been many unpleasant English kings but Edward the First was one of the nastiest.'

'You're sounding like your cousin again.'

116

'She's my *second* cousin and any history book will confirm what I say. He was a very nasty man and he deserved a friend like Sir Richard.'

'Why? What did Richard do?'

'He stole the king's horses and weapons from time to time. When William Wallace began his rebellion, Richard deserted to William's side. He must have been a smooth-talking charmer. Wallace was captured and hung, drawn and quartered but Sir Richard was forgiven until he made the mistake of deserting again, this time to the side of Robert the Bruce. That wasn't a great career move. Richard was captured and Edward had him brought down to London where he was castrated and disembowelled with his entrails burnt before him while he was still alive.'

'That is disgusting.'

'And *then*,' Jamie continued, 'he was hung, drawn, quartered and, finally, despatched into the hereafter. They didn't leave things to chance in those days. Most of the castle was burnt down and a few years later it was taken over by another family and rebuilt and all was peaceful.' He paused. 'Then it was burnt down by the English again after the Battle of Flodden.'

'There is a distinct edge to your voice when you mention "the English".'

'I'm sorry. I find this quite emotional.'

She smiled. 'I feel for you. So what happened then? Was it rebuilt *again*?'

'It is that sort of castle. It refused to die. It remained more or less intact until the Civil War when Cromwell's forces did their worst. What you are about to see was mostly built in the eighteenth century by a family who converted it into a tower house. They held on to it until 1901. That was when it was sold to my family. They lived there for a while but it finally defeated them. It was leaking everywhere and they had no money for repairs. Look over there.' He pointed to the only sign of human habitation: a solitary grey tower in the distance. 'That's my castle,' he said. 'By the time my grandfather inherited it, it was in a terrible state and he vowed to restore it. I can remember as a child helping to clear rubble from pathways.'

'So the castle was saved?'

'It was. Grandfather built up a successful legal practice in Edinburgh and he even established a branch in London; in fact, he bought a flat there. But every available penny went to the castle and so, thanks to him, it rose like a phoenix from the ashes.'

They turned into a narrow tree-lined lane and Jamie lapsed into silence. Tess had told the Commune on Monday evening of her chance encounter with Jamie, and Great-aunt Katherine had launched once more into a diatribe against his family. She could remember his grandfather, she said, he'd been a very stubborn man. Tess told Jamie this now and he gave a slight smile.

'People often accuse *me* of being stubborn,' he said, 'when what they really mean is that I'm determined.'

'Sometimes,' Tess said, 'they might just mean you're stubborn.'

'To be honest, I can't see the difference.' He pointed to two neat little cottages on the left. 'I lived in the first one for fourteen months while I did them up.'

'They're lovely.'

'They are *now*. I nearly froze to death at the time. I

started renting them out last year. They're both occupied at the moment.'

They drove through an imposing stone arch and suddenly they were there and Tess caught her breath. Perched on the edge of a lush, tree-covered valley was Jamie's castle, standing to attention like a grizzled old soldier guarding Paradise. It was an L-shaped tower rather than a castle, albeit one with rounded corners, battlements and a balustraded balcony. To its left, the hill fell steeply down to meet the River Tweed, to the right was dense woodland. The place was like something out of a horror film or a medieval fairy tale. Tess breathed, 'Oh Jamie, I *love* it!'

He gave a careless nod but she could see he was pleased. 'It is rather fine. Come on, I'll show you around.'

For Tess, entering the castle was like walking into one of Scott's novels. She had feared its spirit might be neutered by all the functions that took place there. She needn't have worried: the place was made of sterner stuff. The Great Hall was full of trestle tables laid out for a wedding the next day but the lighting was muted, there were candlesticks on the tables and Tess could easily imagine banquets in years gone by when weary soldiers would meet to discuss the day's fighting. There was so much to take in – the hall with its vaulted ceiling and its walls decorated with ancient shields, the spiral staircase leading to a small room with a pit dungeon which was supposed to be haunted, a bedroom which Jamie assured her had definitely been slept in by Mary Queen of Scots and another that had seen a tragic murder. And everywhere they went, Jamie told stories and anecdotes in his soft level

119

voice, love of his castle showing through with every word.

When they finally climbed up to the battlements, they stood in the open air, the wind brushing Tess's hair against her face. She buttoned up her thin black jacket and gazed about her, taking in the sharp grassy incline, the dark blue river below and beyond it the equally steep hillside with its clusters of trees and grassy spaces. To be here, she thought, was to elevate the soul. She smiled at Jamie with shining eyes. 'It's so dramatic and yet so calm. I've been to Glencoe and one can feel the violence of its past, but here, it's just... glorious.'

'It's like the Border Country,' Jamie said, 'grand and wild and very romantic.' He saw her shiver and said, 'It's also rather cold. I'll take you back now.'

On the way home, he talked about his efforts to turn the castle into a profit-making concern and the plans he had to repair the outbuildings if only he could find the money. 'The trouble is, the Borders are awash with castles. We're all vying with each other for tourists.'

'You really ought to read Scott's novels,' Tess told Jamie. 'Your castle is so like the one described in *The Bride of Lammermoor*. That would be a good tourist angle for you. You still haven't told me why it belongs to you. Did your father give it to you?'

'My father left my mother when I was ten and moved down to England. My grandfather was not pleased. When he died he left the London flat to my brother, and the castle to me.'

'It seems a bit hard on your father. Didn't he mind?'

'He's never been a man to worry too much about possessions. And he always thought my grandfather's obsession with the castle was crazy. Now he thinks I'm crazy too. So does my brother.'

'My mother and sister think the same about me. They think I'm obsessed by Sir Walter Scott.'

Jamie shrugged. 'Speaking as one obsessive to another, I'd rather spend my life caring too much about something than caring too little about anything.'

They were approaching Melrose now and Tess gave him the directions to the Commune. She was conscious of the fact that she wished to see him again. She was also concerned that this simple wish might bring with it a trail of possible complications.

Jamie said, 'Tess, can I take you out to dinner next week?' just as if he'd read her mind, and then he said something so outrageous that she almost gasped. 'I will of course expect something in return.' He absolutely *had* read her mind.

Tess kept her voice admirably level. 'Would you like to tell me what it is you expect?'

If he noticed that the atmosphere in the car had dropped to freezing point, he didn't show it. 'It happened at the party,' he said, 'I've been thinking of you ever since.'

She folded her arms. 'Have you?'

'I have. And now, after this evening, I'm more convinced than ever. I can't think why I didn't think about him before. You're right. I should use Scott to sell the castle. So this is the deal: I take you out to supper and *you* tell me how to do it. Is that a fair transaction?' He gave her a fleeting glance and said, 'I'm sorry. It's not the most exciting way to spend an evening. I shouldn't have asked you. I always forget that other people aren't as fascinated by my castle as I am.'

And Tess, ashamed of her unfounded suspicions, found herself in the unusual position of persuading a man that she wanted to go out to dinner with him.

CHAPTER THIRTEEN

Anna kissed Patrick's cheek. 'You smell nice,' she said.

'I've done my best. Lola's still not well. She threw up again tonight. I've showered and slapped the cologne on but I still smell of sick.'

'Seriously, you don't.'

She sat at the table while Patrick cooked, and they drank the Rioja she'd bought. She asked about former schoolmates and was struck by the inability of men to show interest or even mild curiosity about the personal details of people they knew. He could tell her that Felicity Eggins' second husband seemed a nice guy but had no information as to why her first marriage had failed. Richard Graham – a rather sweet loner at school – was earning a fortune in the City but Patrick had no idea where he lived or whether he had friends now. Most extraordinary of all was the fact that Gavin Millar had joined the Army.

'We went to a party in Wimbledon last year,' Patrick said. 'Gavin was there. He'd just got back from a long stint in Afghanistan.' Patrick might have been telling her Gavin was an estate agent for all the excitement he showed. To be fair, he was busy squeezing cooked garlic cloves out of their skins which looked like a difficult operation.

'Gavin was in Afghanistan?' Anna said. 'I don't understand. Gavin loathed sport at school. What happened to him? Did he change after I left?'

Patrick frowned as if this question had only just occurred to him. 'I don't know that he did. He started going to the gym in the sixth form.'

'Did you *ask* why he'd joined up? What did you talk about?'

'I can't remember.' Patrick's face cleared. 'I think we talked about Andy Murray. He'd been there for the final game.'

Anna sat back in her chair and folded her arms. 'You're a great disappointment. You see Gavin Millar and he tells you he's in the Army and you don't ask him *why*! How could he change so much?'

Patrick set his chicken dish on the table and handed Anna a serving spoon. 'People do change. I wasn't interested in cooking when I was a boy. Now I love it.'

'I don't think people do change that much. Most people learn how to cook when they leave home. I must say this does look amazing.' She took a small helping. She had no appetite tonight.

Patrick topped up their glasses. 'To old friends,' he said.

'To old friends.' Anna clicked her glass against his.

'Tell me about Tess. What's she doing now?'

'She's a university lecturer in London. She teaches English Literature.'

'That doesn't surprise me. She always understood things before the rest of us did. I remember her talking about *Tom's Midnight Garden* in class. She was like you. She had great confidence.'

'I don't remember that. I don't recall Tess being unusually confident.'

'Well, she was.' Patrick shook his head. 'I can't believe you didn't notice that.'

Anna put down her knife and fork. 'I know what you're

124

doing,' she said. 'I've exposed your indifference to the lives of old friends. So now you accuse me of not knowing my own sister...'

'If the cap fits...' Patrick murmured.

'I'll tell you something,' she said. 'You really haven't changed. Do you remember suggesting we meet for a walk on the common after rehearsal? I rushed home to get ready and was there at four, and you were half an hour late and...'

'That was entirely your fault. I'd expected you to wait while I did my scene with Mercutio.'

'Why would I wait? I wanted to get changed and look nice.'

'You already *did* look nice. I was blameless.'

'You were very lucky I waited.'

'I was. Do you remember that walk? It was the first time I kissed you.'

Anna picked up her glass. 'Of course I remember. It was the first time *anyone* kissed me.'

'Was it? I wish I'd known. I'd have been less nervous.'

'I'm sorry, you were *not* nervous.'

'You have no idea. You were so lovely. You still are.'

Their eyes met for a moment. She looked away first and he asked after her parents. She talked about her mother's website for a bit and then asked after *his* parents. They were happy, he said, they liked living in Blackheath. 'I'm sure they'd like to see you again. I know Mum was fond of you.'

She nearly choked on her wine. 'I can't believe you said that! Do you *remember* the last time I saw her?'

'Anna, that was fifteen years ago...'

'It was fourteen. I still shudder at the memory. The way she burst into your room and saw me half-undressed and then she drove me home and I couldn't stop crying. Oh, it was terrible... Patrick, stop grinning! It was one of the worst moments of my life!'

'I know,' Patrick said, 'but it was so like a farce. Mum comes into my room and her mouth drops and then *she* starts shrieking and *you* start apologising while I try desperately to cover my rapidly shrinking erection... It *was* funny!'

'You didn't have to share a car with her afterwards.'

'No, but I faced a full-scale grilling when she got back. And the next morning we all drove off to France for a happy family holiday and she would hardly look at me. What happened when she dropped you back home? Did your mother say anything?'

'I was lucky. She came home a few minutes after me. She'd been given a farewell party at her shop and was far too merry to notice I'd been crying. And then later Dad came back with blood all over his shirt.'

'Why? What happened?'

'Someone tried to mug him and he put up a fight. It was all very dramatic and rather lucky for me. I looked like a tragedy queen and no one noticed.'

'It was a rotten way to break up. When we got back from France, you'd moved down to Somerset. I walked over to your house and imagined you were there. I did miss you.' He grinned again. 'You and I were the Romeo and Juliet of Wimbledon.'

'Possibly. I never wanted to kill myself. I wanted to kill *Mum*. It was her fault we moved away.'

'I always liked your mum. She was very nice to me.'

'She's always nice to handsome young men.' Anna put

126

her knife and fork together. 'That was lovely.'

'You haven't eaten much. Can I offer you cheese or fruit?'

'I couldn't eat another thing.'

'Then let's take our glasses through to the sitting room. I have something to show you.'

It turned out to be the sofa. 'It was my first proper effort at upholstery. Sit down. See how it feels.'

She sat down. 'It is quite extraordinarily comfortable.'

'Now you're making fun of me.'

She laughed. 'It *is* nice to see you again.'

He watched her finish her wine. 'Would you like another glass? I have a bottle in the fridge.'

'Thanks, but I'd like to be able to walk back to the bus stop without falling over.'

Patrick joined her on the sofa. 'Do you ever wonder,' he asked, 'what we'd have done if Mum hadn't burst in on us that evening?'

'We'd have been sensible and stopped. At least, *I'd* have been sensible. At least I think I would.'

'I was crazy about you. You do know that?'

'Well,' Anna said. 'I was crazy about *you*.'

'It still seems unfair. One minute you were there and then you weren't. It always felt unfinished. You know what people say? You never get over your first love.' He leant forward and kissed her lightly on the mouth. 'You make me feel like I'm thirteen again.'

They both knew what would happen next. This time, his kiss was long and easy like the resumption of a long-delayed conversation between old friends. She felt she'd been waiting for this forever. She let her head fall back

127

against the cushions, then arched her back as his hand moved up to unhook her bra.

And then Lola started crying.

Patrick was a good father. 'I won't be long,' he promised. She watched him go upstairs and she heard his voice, soft and gentle as he reassured his child.

So, she thought, first his mother and now his daughter. Someone was trying to tell her something. She stood up and fastened her bra. For a few moments she hesitated and then she picked up her bag and left.

On the journey home she had a text from him. '*Sorry. Sorry about me. Mostly, sorry about Lola.*'

She sent back a jaunty text. '*Just as well! Thanks for supper!*' Already she knew she wouldn't see him again. All she'd wanted, she told herself, was closure. She remembered something William had said a long time ago concerning a difficult relationship from which he was trying to extract himself. 'She says she wants closure,' he'd cried. 'I never trust people who say they want closure.'

And now William was on his own at his brother's engagement party and he'd been right all along. She should have kept away from Patrick. She'd told herself she needed to lay old ghosts and actually all she wanted was to get laid. Patrick was struggling with a sick child and open to temptation. She'd rolled up to his flat like a present waiting to be opened. And the worst of it was she had no one to blame but herself.

Freya was at the dentist and feeling quite cheerful. August was turning out to be rather good. Felix's colleague, Ted Davies, had had a heart attack and of course that was *not* good but at least he'd survived and was now taking a well-earned rest. His misfortune had galvanised Felix. He was working all hours but when he did come home he talked to Freya about the pressures on Ted and problems at work. And meanwhile she'd had lovely phone calls from both the girls. Anna had rung last week and been unusually forthcoming, talking about Olivia's new boyfriend, and a dinner date she was about to have with some gorgeous doctor. And Tess sounded so happy in Scotland. She enjoyed her holiday job and was helping some friend of Maggie to promote his tourist business. All in all, life seemed more hopeful than it had for some time.

Freya's eyes drifted towards the magazines on the table and she reached abruptly for one of them. A stunning flower arrangement was displayed on the cover. On either side of it there were allusions to the delights within: *How to get the best out of your allotment!... See our sensational herbaceous borders...* And then the extraordinary words: *Meet gardener Xander Bullen: dishy and different!*

There couldn't be another Xander Bullen. She rifled impatiently through the pages and there he was. His shoulder-length hair was now short but it was most definitely Xander, in faded jeans and a white T-shirt, one foot poised ready to push his spade into the soil. Fourteen years had actually improved his looks. He'd been a little too thin before, whereas now his T-shirt displayed to flattering effect his rather more solid chest. He looked more confident, too, his eyes staring out at the camera with a hint of amusement. She turned the page and gazed at another photo of him on a bench with a baby on his lap and a pretty girl beside him. The caption below said, *Xander in his garden with his wife, Poppy, and his daughter, Georgie.*

Poopy looked very young. Freya started reading the interview. *'"There is nothing airy-fairy about holistic gardening," Xander told me. There is nothing airy-fairy about Xander full stop. Forget the gym, boys. If you want a six-pack like his, maintain a successful garden... "Holistic gardening," Xander says, "is simply an understanding that everything is a question of balance. So, for example, if you plant horseradish near new potatoes, you'll be doing your bit to deter potato bugs. If you grow thyme near your cabbages, you'll reduce the number of cabbage worm and whitefly. You know how some people bring out the best in you? It's the same for plants. Respect your garden and your garden will respect you."'*

Apparently, he had a book out this month. Who would have thought it? The dentist came through and told Freya he was ready for her. She put the magazine down and resolved to buy a copy for herself as soon as possible.

Eliza had invited Dennis to tea.

Such an invitation was quite out of character and Eliza still wasn't certain why she had made it. She had moved into her present flat twelve years ago and had never welcomed guests. If she wished to see friends, she went out to meet them for coffee or lunch or tea. She neither accepted nor proffered dinner invitations on the grounds that she went early to bed.

The fact that she never invited guests to her flat only occurred to her after she extended the invitation to Dennis. She assumed it was because she was lazy, and there was an

130

element of truth in that. It wasn't that she was ashamed of her home. It was very pleasant and ideally situated, being just a stone's throw from Harrods. It had no garden, of course, but it was on the ground floor so there were no wearisome stairs. She kept all her books in the spare room and her living quarters were cool and uncluttered. In fact, should anyone ask her to describe her home in one word, 'uncluttered' would be the word she would choose.

It was also the reason why she had never entertained here. She was, she could see now, a little embarrassed and possibly even ashamed by this aspect of the place. There were no photographs, no family portraits of husbands or gap-toothed children or lanky teenagers. Anyone could see that Eliza Sample was a woman who had left no mark on the world in which she lived. It was not that Eliza regretted the absence of children or grandchildren. She had made her choices and, having made them, saw no point in indulging in pointless hypothetical fantasies about what might have been. She knew she was lucky. She lived in comfort, she had her health and her mental faculties – touch wood – and she had no reason to feel sorry for herself. What she found difficult to tolerate was the idea that others *might* feel sorry for her. She liked her cool, uncluttered flat. She kept people away from it because she didn't want to see it through their eyes.

But Dennis was different. Dennis had never once asked her for any personal details. He had never asked about husbands or children or grandchildren. He was motivated by a passion for art. At first, she had mistaken his passion for an arrogant, pushy desire to show off his knowledge and his erudition, but it wasn't that at all. He wanted her to share his enthusiasm and his excitement. He wanted her to share the fascination he felt when he looked at a painting and the secrets it revealed about individuals who were long dead but not forgotten. He showed her that a passion shared and discussed was ten times more powerful and satisfying than one digested in solitude. Dennis made her happy and that was why she invited him to tea.

She had suggested he come at half past three. She had thought about producing scones but she hadn't made them for years and decided it was safer to prepare egg sandwiches. She did make a cake – a simple sponge, sandwiched with jam and fresh cream – and she was glad she had done so because its aroma filled the flat with a welcoming warmth.

At twenty past three she went into her bedroom and checked her appearance. She wore grey trousers and a crisp pale pink shirt with her usual pearl necklace. Her white hair, cut in a smooth, sleek bob, was as disciplined as ever. She applied a little perfume and smiled at her vanity because she knew her visitor would almost certainly appear in his same, badly fitted brown suit.

Checking her watch, she went through to the kitchen to boil the kettle and warm the teapot. She took out from her cupboard two porcelain cups and saucers and a small matching jug which she filled with milk. At a quarter to four she moved to the sitting room and glanced round at the small desk in the corner with her laptop and her brass lamp, the two-seater sofa with its abundance of cushions, and the coffee table on which sat her latest acquisition, a book about Velasquez's paintings. She was looking forward to showing it to Dennis. She went over to the window and stared out into the street.

An hour later she knew he wouldn't come. She went into her kitchen and considered the food on the table. She wasn't sure what to do about the cake. If she put it in a tin, the cream would go off. She put it in the fridge and turned her attention to the egg sandwiches. She could have some of them for her supper. The rest would keep till tomorrow.

It was more than a fortnight since the evening with Patrick. Anna had done her best to rouse herself from her pit of self-loathing. She had been ultra-kind to her patients, she had accepted a dinner invitation from a doctor acquaintance, she had rung her mother and made an effort to be nice. She'd even told her about the dinner date, a big mistake since the evening revealed they had nothing in common except a mild mutual attraction.

Still her dark mood persisted and she knew the reason why. William – kind, easy-going, best pal William – had expunged her from his life with a ruthlessness that shocked her. When she rang, he wouldn't pick up. He responded to none of her texts or voicemail messages. For the time being she'd stopped trying. There was nothing more she could add to the apologies she'd made. Of course she'd been wrong to cancel Trevor's party but if he'd been so upset about it, he should have told her at the time. It wasn't like William to sulk and she felt stunned by his silence. Now she was beginning to be angry with him. If all their years of friendship meant so little to him then, fine, she'd be fine. Eventually.

CHAPTER FOURTEEN

The job of castle custodian was far more complex than Tess had realised. For a start, there were a fair number of castles in the area and Jamie did not have the monopoly in romantic wedding locations. In fact, he told her, weddings provided only a small part of the castle's income. In the last year alone, there'd been a Burns supper for fifty, a marmalade festival, office parties, business lunches, school tours and the hiring of the castle for a four-minute scene in a BBC serial drama.

Tess was convinced that Sir Walter Scott could be a huge draw. She had discovered that he and Wordsworth had indeed visited the place. 'The timing is perfect,' she said. 'There's this huge debate about Scotland's relationship with England. We have the referendum in September. Scott was a huge supporter of the Union but he was also fiercely proud of being Scottish. He was the great reconciler. He couldn't *be* more contemporary.'

'To be honest,' Jamie said, 'his only connection with the castle is that he once spent an afternoon here.'

'There's your name,' Tess said.

'To be honest again,' Jamie said, 'I'm not absolutely sure that I *am* related to his son-in-law.'

Tess frowned. 'You don't need to say you are. You can just talk in your literature about Scott and his great friend and son-in-law, John *Lockhart*. People will see your name and make the obvious assumption.'

'Tess,' Jamie murmured, 'I'm worried I'm corrupting

you. Whatever happened to academic integrity?'

Tess wasn't sure. In the last few weeks she had spent so much time with Jamie that it was impossible not to share his enthusiasm. As an academic, she did sometimes feel she led a rarefied existence; it was exhilarating to find she could apply her skills and knowledge in the development of a sound business project. She and Jamie had spent evenings in pubs pouring over competitors' brochures. She agreed with him that Reidfern Castle was superior to all of them.

Tonight, for the first time, she was driving over to his house in Melrose. Intent on following his instructions, she turned into a small lane near the famous Melrose ruins and parked the car by the green litter bin on the bank. She reached for her bag, climbed out of Grandma's car and locked it before turning round to check that she was indeed opposite Number Two.

For a moment she stared blankly at the small terraced cottage opposite her. She took a sharp intake of breath, felt quite light-headed, and let her back slump against the car. It was her house. It was *her house*. She gazed down at her feet. Here was the cobbled lane and, as she looked up to the left, she could see that it ended in a small clearing a few yards further on. She swallowed and fixed her eyes on the white door with its horizontal partition. She shut her eyes and put her hand to her forehead.

A voice said, 'Tess?' and she opened her eyes. Jamie was there, looking anxiously at her. 'Are you all right?' he asked. 'Is something wrong?'

'It's just that…' Her throat felt dry, it was difficult to speak. 'I know this place. I've seen it. I don't understand.'

He put an arm round her waist and guided her across the lane, through the door and into a small sitting room. He took her to the sofa and sat her down. 'I'll get you some water,' he said. 'Don't move.'

As soon as he left, she sat back, her eyes travelling round the room. A small pine table by the window carried Jamie's laptop and printer. The walls were painted in a soft chalky colour; they were empty of pictures apart from a large black and white print of Reidfern Castle on the wall to the right of the fireplace. On the mantelpiece above the wood-burning stove there were a couple of framed photos. The grey carpet looked like it might once have been white or cream. The sofa on which Tess sat was comfortable though the material was worn, particularly on its arms. Only the curtains, resplendent tartan green and red, looked new. It was easy for Tess to imagine herself sitting here, reading her book and sipping her cocoa.

'Here we are.' Jamie was back with a tray containing a tumbler of water and two glasses of red wine. He put them down on the pine table. 'I prescribe water first and then wine. You do look pale.'

'I'm fine. It was rather a shock seeing your house. I know it sounds weird but I feel I know it. I must have walked here once with Grandma or something. It's a lovely place. If you could see my horrible, poky little flat in London... Seriously, you have no idea how lucky you are. Have you been here long?'

'I moved in two years ago. I'd been camping out in the castle cottages while I did them up. It was a great pleasure to move into a place with a working bathroom and kitchen.'

'I can imagine it would be.'

136

'Are you sure you're...?'

'I'm fine. Tell me about the photos on the mantelpiece.'

Jamie brought them over to her and put them on the table. He nodded towards the first one, a black and white picture of a fierce-looking man with a strong jaw and piercing eyes. 'That's my grandfather. You'd have liked him. He was a great fan of Scott. Every time he drank a little too much whisky he would declaim Scott's words: *Breathes there a man with a soul so dead, Who never to himself hath said This is my own, my native land!* He drank a little too much whisky quite often so that's how I know those words by heart.'

'And what about the other one? They must be your parents. The man looks so like you.'

'Now he would tell you I look like *him*.' He took his wine and joined her on the sofa. 'You're not going to faint on me, are you? When I saw you out by the car, I was convinced you were going to faint. We had a wedding at the castle three months ago and the bride's mother did just that...'

It was a pleasure to sit listening to Jamie's soft, lilting voice. She was aware that her first stunned amazement was settling into a sort of dazed acceptance that there was something almost magical about this evening.

When Jamie suggested it was time to eat, she followed him through to the kitchen and again, it was as she'd imagined: a small, immaculate galley kitchen. Either Jamie had impressively high standards of cleanliness or he had made a huge effort. On the table there was a bowl of salad, with places for two and napkins to the side. Tess watched Jamie take the lasagne out of the oven. 'You've gone to so much trouble,' she said.

'I owe you,' he told her. 'I think we make an excellent team and I'm very grateful for all your help.'

'I'm enjoying myself. I think I might be getting slightly obsessive. I woke up this morning with ideas for castle worksheets for schools. You could find out what people ate and wore, you could bring in the Battle of Flodden and Mary, Queen of Scots. The possibilities are endless.'

'I know,' Jamie said, 'but I need someone who knows about that sort of thing to organise it. I need someone who's good at research and academic work. I'd pay her, of course, and I'd be happy to give her free board and lodging here. I'd even cook her lasagne from time to time.'

Tess smiled. 'That sounds nice.'

'I hoped you'd think so.' Jamie began to serve out the lasagne. 'I'm serious by the way.'

'I'm sure you are.' She took the plate from him. 'This smells good.'

'Help yourself to salad. Would you like dressing?'

'Please.'

He placed a small jug on the table. He sat down beside her and then stood up again. 'Do you want salt and pepper?'

'Jamie, I'm fine. Please. Sit down. You're making me nervous.'

'I'm sorry. I *am* nervous.'

She stared at him. 'Why? Is there something wrong?'

'I don't know. That's the problem. I have absolutely no idea.' His voice was as level as ever but his eyes never left her face.

Tess wasn't naïve. She had suspected his interest in her was not just professional. She had even been ready to politely deflect any advances tonight. But the sight of his house – *her* house – had thrown her. She had a queer impression that she was in some parallel universe in which she could contemplate with a degree of curiosity the idea of kissing the man sitting next to her at the table.

She had a sudden conviction that she was at a crossroads. Tonight – this moment – she was ready to be kissed. She leant forward. 'Do you want to explain?'

'The thing is…' Jamie murmured, and now, very slowly, he brought his face towards her own. She felt a wave of panic but she didn't turn away.

And that was when the doorbell rang.

Freya should have been preparing supper. Instead, she was re-reading an intriguing email.

'Dear Mrs Cameron,

I heard about your website from my son, Jamie, who lives in the Borders and has been seeing quite a lot of your daughter. For some time now, I have had the idea of researching my family tree. We're quite an interesting bunch. One of my ancestors on my mother's side was Lord Chancellor. I have a picture of him in our library. My mother maintained that we're descended from the half-brother of Mary, Queen of Scots. By all accounts, he was not a very nice man so perhaps I shouldn't boast of the connection.

Having studied your website, I would love to engage your services. I also have a rather cheeky suggestion. On 6 September, my wife and I are throwing a party to celebrate our tenth wedding anniversary. I've been trying, so far without success, to persuade Jamie to come down for it. I have a strong suspicion that if he knew Tess and her parents were invited, he'd make the effort to do so. Would you and your husband and Tess care to join us? I quite understand if you can't but I'd be delighted to meet you all. Yours, very sincerely, Neil Lockhart.

His son had been seeing 'a lot' of Tess! Freya felt a surge of excitement. Was it possible that Tess had at last found a man who appealed to her? The fact that Jamie had told his father about her seemed to indicate a level of confidence on his part. Neil Lockhart obviously believed there was a serious romance. Why else would he want to meet Tess and her parents? Freya read through the email again. The man had a library! She picked up the phone.

The trouble with ringing the Commune was that one had no control over who answered. At the moment it looked as if no one would. She couldn't believe that all of the inmates were currently out on the town. She drummed her fingers on her desk and then stopped as she heard sounds of life from the receiver.

'Hello?' The voice was tentative.

'Linda? Linda!' Freya's voice increased in volume and enthusiasm. 'Hello there! It's Freya!'

'Oh.' There was a pause followed by a cautious 'Hello.'

'It's Freya,' Freya said again, 'Felix's wife.'

'Felix!' Linda said, with more enthusiasm. 'How is he?'

'He's very well! We're both looking forward to seeing you all in October. Linda, could I have a word with Tess… or with Maggie?'

'Right,' Linda said, 'I'll go and see.'

'Thank you,' Freya said. If she ever ended up in a commune she would make sure that each of the residents had mobiles. It was ridiculous for all of them to share just one house phone. She glanced at her watch: half past seven. She had no idea it was so late. Keeping her phone clamped to her left ear, she went through to the kitchen and poured a large glass of Sauvignon. The fact that Tess had at the very least a *possible* boyfriend was definitely a cause for celebration. Felix might say – Felix *often* said – that Tess would find a partner in her own good time but there was no denying that it was odd for a pretty young woman to be resigned to celibacy at twenty-seven and Freya was as sure as she could be that Tess *was* resigned. Freya used to believe that all she wanted for her daughters was that they were happy. But actually, she wanted them to be normal as well. She didn't mind if Tess proved to be gay. She just wanted to know that she was capable of loving *someone*, because if she wasn't, Freya felt that somehow *she* must be to blame.

She went back to the study with her wine in one hand and her phone in the other. She took her place in front of the computer. Linda was taking a very long time. Freya shouted, 'Hello,' into the silence. Linda was clearly losing the plot and sooner or later so would the others and eventually no one would answer the phone, and concerned relatives would be left hurling out greetings into the ether.

And now at last a voice responded. 'Hello? Is anyone there?'

'Aunt Katherine! Hello there! It's Freya.'

'The receiver was lying on the hall table.' Aunt Katherine sounded quite aggrieved as if this was Freya's fault.

'I spoke to Linda. She said she'd go and find Tess and

141

Maggie for me. I've been waiting some time.'

'Tess is out, I'm afraid. She's very rarely *in*. How is Felix?'

'He's very well.'

'I'm glad to hear it. We're about to have supper. I'll go and get Maggie for you.'

'Thank you, that's very kind. I'm sorry to ring now. I only want...' But Aunt Katherine had gone. It was interesting that both she and Linda had asked after Felix and had shown no interest in *her* at all. She had another sip of wine and hoped Aunt Katherine's attention span was sharper than Linda's.

It was. A familiar voice came to the phone and said, 'Freya, how nice! We were having our sherry in the garden. It's the most beautiful evening up here.'

'It's lovely down here too. Maggie, I'm ringing about an email I've received. It's from a man called Neil Lockhart.'

'Oh.'

There was a rather odd intonation in her mother-in-law's voice. Freya asked, 'Do you know him?'

'I know his *son*.'

'I gather Tess does too. According to the email, they've been spending a great deal of time together.'

'That's true. Jamie owns a castle. He hires it out for functions and weddings. He wants to expand the tourist side. I gather Sir Walter Scott went there and...'

'How *fascinating*! Tess told me she was helping one of your friends promote his business and I imagined some sweet old gentleman and instead he's a young man with a castle! Are he and Tess close?'

'I have no idea. Why did his father write to you?'

'He seems to think there might be a romance. He's invited Felix and me and Tess to a party in London.'

'Has he? How extraordinary.'

'Jamie has told him about my website and he wants me to research his roots.'

'His what?'

'His roots, Maggie. He wants me to look into his roots. Could you ask Tess to ring me sometime soon? I've tried her mobile once or twice but there doesn't seem to be a signal.'

'That doesn't surprise me. It's not easy ringing people up here.'

'So I've discovered,' Freya said with feeling.

'Now tell me, Freya, how is Felix?'

'He's very well.' Freya could hear Aunt Katherine calling Maggie to supper and added quickly, 'I must let you go. We'll speak soon.' She put the phone down and wondered, not for the first time, why Tess had to be so secretive. Why had she said so little about the mysterious man? A man with a castle known to Walter Scott had to be perfect for her. She was aware she was being watched and saw her husband in the doorway.

'You were miles away,' he said, 'staring up at the ceiling like it was about to fall down on you.'

Freya pointed at the computer screen. 'Read that,' she said.

His face looked increasingly bewildered as his eyes scanned the text. 'Has Tess talked to you about this man?'

'She said he was a friend of Maggie. I rang Maggie just now and she says she knows him but... you know what

Maggie's like. She's not very forthcoming.'

'Well... I don't know what to say. I suppose you and Tess might find it fun.'

'Don't be silly, Felix. September the sixth is our *own* wedding anniversary.'

'I know.' Felix pushed back his chair. 'I'm afraid I'll be in Spain for it.' He rose to his feet and put his hands in his pockets. 'It's because of Ted. We're opening up a new office in Madrid. Ted was in charge and of course now he can't go...'

'And so *you* have to go?'

'There's no one else. I'm sorry. I only found out today. It'll be fine. We'll celebrate when I get back. I know it's an important anniversary...'

'I thought it was.' Freya turned off the laptop. 'I suppose if I'm not having my own, it might be fun to go to someone else's.'

'Freya, I've told you I'm...'

'It's all right, Felix, I'll have fun in London. I'd like to go to the party. The truth is I'm curious. We've been worried about Tess for years...'

'*You've* been worried. I'm not.'

'Well, of course, it suits you very well to have Tess all to yourself without any annoying boyfriends in tow.'

'What does *that* mean?'

'Oh I don't know.' She picked up her wine glass. 'I suppose I'm fed up with the fact that we keep pedalling along as if everything's great and now I have an email from a man who seems to think that our younger daughter might at last be interested in a flesh and blood male and you're saying we're fine and I don't think we are, Felix, really I

144

don't.' She stared at him, almost out of breath. If he laughed at her she would cry.

Felix didn't laugh. He looked down at the floor and then back up at her. 'Go to the party. Stay at a hotel and buy a new dress. You'll be the belle of the ball. You always are.'

Fortunately, there was more than enough lasagne for the three of them.

Jamie's brother was every inch the actor. Rory was very good-looking, he *knew* he was good-looking, he loved to be centre stage and he took it for granted his audience was thrilled to see him.

'I cannot believe,' he said, helping himself to more lasagne, 'that my big brother would *forget* that I was coming to stay with him. Do you want to know something, Tess? The last time I saw Jamie was at Christmas – *Christmas*! That was over half a year ago. A couple of months ago, anxious to pay my fraternal respects, I went out of my way to suggest a fortnight when we could see each other and now, I wend my weary way to his house and...'

'Rory, you are such a bullshitter,' Jamie said. 'The only reason you're here is because you've been performing at the Edinburgh Festival and you wanted an easy, inexpensive holiday afterwards. How *was* your play?'

'Thank you for asking, Jamie, particularly since you failed to turn up even though I got you a ticket. There I was on stage, peering out into the audience, trying in vain to spot my brother and all I saw was an empty seat. The play, I have to tell you, was a dog's breakfast. Mona – and never was a name more aptly given – Mona wrote it herself and if I'd known what an appalling director she'd be, I'd have turned it down at once. The rehearsals were a joke. And then, when we get to Edinburgh, it's clear she's shagging Bernie Root. If I tell you that Bernie is the most repulsive actor in the world, you should know that I am being kind to him. At the first rehearsal in Edinburgh, Bernie has to rape Ruthie and Bernie gets carried away and throws her down so hard that we have to call an ambulance and she has to have an X-ray on her head or her neck, I can't remember which, and then, just before we start again, without poor Ruthie of course, we see Mona bend over for something – and you have to know that Mona has started wearing very short skirts – and Mona bends down and we all see Bernie push his hand up her legs and we all try our hardest not to puke. Trust me, if you could *see* Bernie, you would puke. He refuses to wear shoes on his feet and they are quite disgusting; he doesn't approve of alcohol and he sits around eating revolting food. His favourite snack is bread smeared with vinegar. He and Mona both have partners but they spend their time slipping, very subtly, into the conversation that they don't believe in monogamy. And none of this would matter if the play had been any good but it was supposed to be sexy and meaningful and it was about as sexy as a fart in a lavatory.'

'In that case,' Jamie said, 'it was just as well I didn't see it.'

'I'm sorry, but that is no excuse.' Rory turned to Tess. 'The trouble with Jamie is he's a workaholic. He lives and breathes his stupid castle. He can talk about nothing else. He can *do* nothing else. He is, I'm afraid, a complete bore about it.'

'It's quite a beautiful castle,' Tess said. 'It's easy to be obsessed by it.'

146

Rory looked at her as if she were mad. 'Do you work for him?'

'No. I know a little about the Borders...'

'She's being modest,' Jamie said. 'She's an authority on Sir Walter Scott. She thinks I could use him to promote Reidfern. She has some amazing ideas.'

'I see.' Rory looked at Tess and then at Jamie. 'I haven't interrupted a romantic evening, have I?'

'Not at all,' Jamie said. 'We are both thrilled beyond words to have your company.'

'In that case,' Rory said, 'I'll finish off the lasagne.'

CHAPTER FIFTEEN

Everything had gone wrong. With every smutty story Rory told, Tess was freshly aware of her own humourless, sexless self. She tried to smile politely but her facial muscles were frozen. She was like one of those actresses who overdose on Botox. How had she possibly imagined she might have a proper relationship with Jamie? As soon as she could, she made her excuses and left.

The horrors did not let up. The next day she got back from work and her mother rang with some weird story about Jamie's father who had apparently heard all about her and wanted Tess and her parents to come to some party in London which her mother thought would be fun. Tess said she was expecting a call and rang off. And then, as if to punish her for that lie, the phone *did* ring and it was Jamie who asked if she'd like to meet up that night. He and Rory were off to see their mother in Oban the following day and would be away for most of the week. He did not seem surprised when she made an excuse and he made no effort to suggest a future date.

In Tess's less rational moments she wondered if Fate hadn't led Rory to his brother's door at that particular moment, thus preventing her from leaping into the void. But she was bereft without Jamie's company. In the last few weeks they had seen so much of each other. Without Rory, their friendship might possibly have ended abruptly. Now it seemed to have ended anyway. As the days went by, she knew Jamie had spoilt Scotland for her. In the evenings she played backgammon with Dr Knox, and Scrabble with Grandma and Sheila, her ears alert to the sound of the telephone. Whenever it did ring and turned out not to be Jamie she was torn between relief and disappointment.

And then at last she had a rather formal call from him. Could he take her out to dinner on Thursday? He knew she'd be going home on Saturday and it would be nice to say goodbye. She said primly that that would be fine.

She was ready and waiting by seven. Jamie was twenty minutes late and full of apologies. There'd been a crisis at the castle, something had short-circuited; she wasn't sure what. She barely listened to his explanation, she was simply glad to be in his car with him again.

He had chosen Burt's Hotel in the centre of Melrose. It was an elegant place that was gloriously old-fashioned. Its walls were full of gilt-framed paintings, patterned carpets, impeccably starched white tablecloths and napkins, and staff who were unfailingly courteous.

They were led to a table for two and after Jamie had ordered wine and water, he stared at her in that disconcertingly blank way of his. 'I wasn't sure you'd agree to come.'

His candour and his shrewd understanding of her character shocked her. She could feel her face blush red. 'I wanted to say goodbye.'

'How was your last day in Gasterlethen?'

She was grateful for the change of subject. 'I think Mrs Talbot's quite happy to see me go. She's discovered she definitely doesn't want to spend more time with her husband. She can't wait to have the shop to herself again.'

'Are you glad to be going home?'

She swallowed. 'No.'

'I'm pleased to hear it. Tess?'

He had put his hands on the table. She noticed a plaster round his index finger. She raised her eyes. 'Yes?'

'I think…' He looked away and then reached for the menus. 'I think we should decide what we want to order.'

They both studied their menus with careful deliberation. Tess chose the chicken; Jamie went for the venison. The waitress arrived with their drinks. Jamie gave their choices. When the waitress left them, he poured out the wine. 'I have some news,' he said. 'Next Sunday evening, I have a Very Important Person coming to inspect the castle. If she likes it – and it will be a very big If – it will be the focus point for a documentary series on England and Scotland. The provisional title is *Intimate Enemies*. Thanks to the referendum, it's a hot topic.'

'Jamie, that's amazing!'

'It *will* be if I can sell it to her. I'll be working flat out till I see her. It's a pity you can't be there. You could impress her with the Walter Scott angle.'

'I wish I could be. To think I'll be back in London and…' she stopped. 'In fact I'm supposed to be at your father's anniversary party next Saturday. He contacted my mother. I hear you told him all about me.'

'I actually told him about your mother. I said he should use her services to research our ancestors. He's invited you all, has he? He does things like that.'

'My mother is determined we go. I think she's making a point to Dad. It's *their* wedding anniversary and he'll be abroad on business.'

'You should go. I'm sorry I can't be there. You'll like my father. People always do. His wife's a nice woman.'

She gave a little shrug. 'Well, if we do go, I'll let you know what it's like.'

He raised his eyebrows. 'Are we to keep in touch then?'

He seemed determined to wrong foot her. 'Don't you want to?'

He sighed. 'I have a confession to make. It's an embarrassing one. You may well decide as a result that you don't wish to see me again. The trouble is, if I *don't* tell you, I don't think I'll want to see *you*. It would be too difficult.'

Tess had the weirdest sensation that her brain had been taken over by two voices. One cheered Jamie on, the other advised her to shut him up now before he got any further. 'In that case,' she said slowly, 'you'd better tell me.'

'Right.' He glanced round at the other guests as if seeking their approval. Then he put his elbows on the table and stared at her. 'The first evening we met, you came into the room surrounded by your three elderly companions and... I was transfixed. That doesn't happen very often. I told myself, Jamie, you do not walk up to a strange woman and assure her she should spend the rest of her life with you. I was cool. I refrained from going over to you for at least thirty minutes and when I *did*...' He smiled slightly. 'You have a beautiful voice, you know. It's quite husky and every now and then you sound as if you're going to cough but you don't. It sounds like it's wrapped in caramel and sometimes you get near the nut in the middle... I'm sorry, this must be very boring for you.'

'How can it be boring to hear I have a nice voice?'

151

'Well. I chatted away and you were charming and gave no indication that you had any idea of the momentous event that had taken place. And then you went back to London and I spent long, bitter hours thinking that being cool was overrated.'

The waitress came back. The venison was off, she said apologetically. Jamie ordered the fish and followed her departure with a slight cough. The voices in Tess's brain had gone silent. For now, all that mattered was to hear the rest of Jamie's confession.

He pressed his palms together. 'The miracle happened and you came back. I'd been given a second chance. Eventually, I invited you to supper to express my feelings and then Rory arrived – and by the way I could cheerfully have killed him in any number of ways. I noticed that you ate very little and left as soon as you could with what I could only observe was almost indecent speed. She doesn't like me, I thought, I will keep away. So I do but then I think: if I tell you what I feel, at least I'll have tried and if I don't try I might spend the rest of my life wondering what might have happened and so…'

'Listen, Jamie…'

'Please, I have to finish this. If you find it all excruciating and embarrassing, you only have to say so and I'll tell you I understand and we'll have dinner and talk about castle worksheets or something and at the end of the meal I'll take you home and I will thank you for being honest with me.'

When she said nothing, he threw up his hands. 'Actually,' he said. 'I can see I *have* finished. Tell me what you think. Please take as long as you like. I'll just sit here.'

He gazed at the wall on their left and began to study with apparent fascination a painting of a stag on the hillside. Tess drank her wine, aware that her heart was racing. 'This is silly,' she said at last. 'I'm not even sure what you expect me to say. The idea of a... a romantic relationship is totally impractical. You live up here and I live in London. You must see that.'

He shook his head. 'It's only impractical if you don't *want* a romantic relationship.'

'What if I were to tell you I *do* find this excruciating and embarrassing?'

'I would ask you very politely to tell me why.'

'That's not what you said before.'

'I know,' Jamie said. 'Sorry.'

She had never felt so helpless. 'Jamie,' she said. 'I like you so much. I'm incredibly fond of you.'

Jamie nodded. 'Oh dear,' he said.

'I mean it. You've become a good friend but...'

'Thank you,' he said. 'I understand now.' He gave a short, polite smile. 'I'd like to say thank you for all your hard work this month. You've been the best of good company and I... I shan't forget you.'

'So this is it?' she asked. 'We say goodbye tonight?'

'I'm sorry.' He shook his head. 'I can't do the friends thing with you. It wouldn't work. I wish it could.'

It wasn't fair and it wasn't right. She was overcome by an acute case of panic. Life without Jamie would be dullness incarnate. She said, 'I think I'm going to have to tell you something. You see you're not the only one who has a confession to make.'

153

Freya supposed she should be feeling aggrieved about the coming weekend. Felix had, after all, chosen to be away for their thirtieth wedding anniversary. But actually, she was looking forward to her own small adventure. She had rung Tess earlier this evening and they'd had a nice chat. Tess said she loathed being back in London and was looking forward to being cheered up by her mother. Which was lovely since Freya often felt uncertain about her daughters' feelings towards her. Pam had a theory that the whole point of children was to bring uncertainty and self-doubt into one's life. Pam maintained this was a good thing since one should guard against complacency as one grew older. As Freya pointed out at the time, she had quite enough self-doubt without her children adding more.

She put her hands on her hips and surveyed the clothes on the spare-room bed. She had selected her black trousers and silk shirt for tomorrow and Sunday and her shirt dress for Saturday. The Glamour Dress would do for Neil Lockhart's party. She had not taken up Felix's offers of a brand new outfit and two nights in a hotel. She had told him they were an unnecessary expense. She wanted him to know she could not be bought off so easily.

She had planned her London trip with care. Tomorrow she would visit the Society of Genealogists and the London Metropolitan Archives. She would arrive at her friend Sylvie's in time for a large gin and tonic. On Saturday she would attack Oxford Street and find a gorgeous dress for Tess who would otherwise, almost certainly, turn up to the party in one of her black sacks. On Sunday she would take the girls out to celebrate her wedding anniversary. They would drink champagne and later, back at home, she would take great delight in calling Felix and telling him what an enjoyable anniversary weekend she'd had.

On the other side of the bed she had set out Felix's clothes: six freshly ironed shirts, the linen suit he had bought two years ago, underwear, pyjama bottoms and a couple of T-shirts. He was catching a plane from Bristol this evening and even as she thought he was cutting it a bit fine she heard his key in the door and she called out, 'I'm upstairs!'

When he joined her in the room, he was already taking off his tie. His eyes registered the neat piles on the bed and he said, 'You've been busy.'

'Do you want me to help you pack?'

'No, no, you've done quite enough. It won't take me long. Give me twenty minutes and then we'll have some tea together.'

'Do you want something to eat?'

'I'll grab a sandwich at the airport.'

There was a febrile energy about him today. He was not a fan of modern air travel and was always stressed before a journey. It was best to leave him alone to sort himself out.

When he came downstairs he had changed into cotton trousers and a polo shirt. He said, 'I'm ready.'

'Passport? Boarding card? Book for the plane? Reading glasses?'

'All present and correct.'

'Come and have some tea then.'

'They sat at the table. She poured him a cup. 'Can you relax for a while? You have almost twenty minutes before you have to go.'

He glanced at the kitchen clock. 'Freya,' he said,

'there's something I have to tell you.'

She smiled. 'You sound very serious.'

'I am. There isn't a good way of saying this. I want us to separate.' His tone was quiet, almost conversational. 'I want to stop living with you. I'm so sorry.'

Freya had the weirdest sensation that the world – the literal world – was crumbling about her. She gripped the table with her hands. Her eyes filled with tears, obscuring her vision. She wanted to say something but she couldn't. Her stomach felt as if it were falling away but in fact her entire body was shocked into a frozen stillness.

'I was going to wait until I came back but I think it's better to tell you now.'

His eyes were sympathetic and he sounded apologetic, as if he'd forgotten to buy some ingredient she needed for a recipe. Still, she couldn't speak. If she simply sat and waited, perhaps he would tell her she had misunderstood what he was trying to say.

'What I suggest,' he said, 'is that when I come back next Wednesday we discuss what to do. I've looked at our finances. You can stay here and I'll rent a flat in Bristol until we sort ourselves out.'

She found her voice at last. 'Why have you stopped loving me? Is there someone else?' Even then, she hoped he would assure her he *did* love her and offer some unimaginable explanation that they could sort out together.

He looked down at his feet. 'No. No, there isn't. I suppose it's been a gradual understanding. We'll talk about this when I come back.'

'Is this why you arranged the Spanish trip?'

'No, but…' He rose to his feet. 'I was happy to go along

with it.' He glanced at his watch. 'I'm sorry. I must go now.'

She didn't move. She watched him walk out of the kitchen. She remained in her chair until she heard his car drive away. Then she stood up. He hadn't touched his tea. She took his cup and saucer and threw the warm liquid down the sink. She felt she'd been thrown into some terrible nightmare. Felix, kind, gentle, loving Felix had taken less than a minute to tell her he was leaving her. She held up the cup and, hurling it across the room, watched it splinter into pieces.

CHAPTER SIXTEEN

Anna had chosen obstetrics for the very good reason that it was the one area of medicine where the majority of patients weren't ill. They had interesting conditions which, most of the time, led to euphoric conclusions in which doctors were showered with praise. There were the occasional desperately sad tragedies, just as there were more frequently difficult mothers-to-be and mothers.

Mrs Halligan was one of these. A pale-faced woman with bottle-black hair and intense brown eyes, she had, she told Anna, a low pain-threshold which in her case meant she was a self-indulgent prima donna. This morning she'd cried that there was no way she could be allowed to go home tomorrow. Anna thought she could detect a trace of real fear in Mrs Halligan's eyes and agreed that perhaps she could stay at St Peter's for a further two days.

And now Miss Diamond stood at Mrs Halligan's bed, surrounded by her usual tribe of medical students and fellow trainees. When Mrs Halligan announced that Doctor Cameron had said she could stay on, Miss Diamond sighed. She then launched into a clear, concise and extremely graphic account of the Caesarean procedure. 'You see, Mrs Halligan,' she concluded, 'it would be very odd if you did *not* feel sore after an operation like this. Indeed, if you weren't sore, I would be extremely worried about you. It is far better for you to leave us this afternoon and begin your convalescence in your own home where you can relax and be comfortable. You are a lucky woman. You have a beautiful baby boy. Go home and enjoy him.'

In the face of her consultant's comprehensive display of professional expertise, Mrs Halligan was silenced. Anna's admiration lasted up until the moment Miss Diamond gathered her acolytes round the nurses' station. In a light, clear voice that Anna knew could be heard by the nurses behind them, she said, 'I have tried for some time to work out what is the point of Doctor Cameron. I think she must exist in order to show the rest of you what *not* to do. The NHS has very little money and we cannot afford to fill our beds with nervous hypochondriacs. Mrs Halligan is easily frightened and ready to tumble into hysterics at any moment. By concurring with her entirely unnecessary demand to stay here, Doctor Cameron simply proved to Mrs Halligan that she was right to want to do so. If we all behaved like Doctor Cameron, the NHS would be bankrupt within the year.'

Anna did not try to defend herself. Miss Diamond was right to rebuke her but wrong to take such pleasure in doing so. When she finally got away, she wished she had William here to do his usual brilliant magic of transforming a demoralising experience into an interesting one. Well, she thought, she was not going to give up on medicine, however much Miss Diamond might want her to. She was not going to give up on William either. She had maintained a lofty silence for over two weeks now and it had got her nowhere. For a moment, as she walked down the corridor, she thought she saw William coming towards her but it was just a man with curly dark hair. Anna came to a stop. She pulled out her phone and looked at it. Then she sent William a text: PLEASE CAN WE TALK?

* * *

Freya woke late the next morning after a troubled night. She limped downstairs at midday and put the empty bottle of Merlot in the recycling bin. She was glad she hadn't cancelled Sylvie. She couldn't bear to stay in a house full of happy family photos on the walls. If she didn't leave soon, she would pull them all down and destroy the lot of them. She would tell Sylvie everything. Sylvie would be furious. They would spend the whole evening assassinating Felix's character. And then, on Saturday, she would see Tess and would tell her *nothing*. She would leave to Felix the pleasure of telling his daughters what he had done. She and Tess would go to the party in the evening and have *fun*.

It took three cups of coffee, a long bath and strong painkillers to repair the excesses of the night before. She took her case through to the spare room and slowly packed the clothes she'd put out on the bed.

When Freya boarded the train, she fell asleep almost at once and only woke when it reached its final destination. As she walked towards the Tube she glanced around her and wondered how many jettisoned wives there were on the concourse. She felt a new, strange rage well up in her. If Felix were to come up to her now, she would hit him. She had been a good wife, especially in the last few years. She had responded to his moods with sympathy and understanding and where had it got her? Didn't Jesus say that the meek would inherit the earth? Boy, did he get that wrong! Meek people just got trampled on! Freya felt better already. She wanted to embrace her rage. It was better than self-pity any day.

She arrived in Putney at six and was greeted with a hug by Sylvie who said it had been far too long, they must have a drink at once and how *was* she? Freya was about to tell her but was distracted by a book on the coffee table – *How to Make your Life (and your Garden) Happy*. The cover showed Xander sitting serenely on a bench, his long legs stretched out in front of him. On either side of him there were wide herbaceous borders full of lupins, delphiniums, Michaelmas daisies and gypsophila. Xander, dressed in jeans and a grey T-shirt, appeared to be the embodiment of masculine perfection: a strong man at peace with his spiritual side.

Sylvie noticed her interest and smiled. 'It was an impulse buy. He looks so gorgeous, don't you think?'

'I happen to know he *is* gorgeous,' Freya said. 'Xander Bullen was our gardener in Wimbledon!'

'No! Really? You lucky woman! What was he like?'

'Well, actually,' Freya said, 'he had quite a crush on me.'

'Men always have crushes on you,' Sylvie said. 'It's very boring for the rest of us.'

'Oh Sylvie,' Freya sighed, 'you have no idea…'

But Sylvie's phone had started ringing and it was clear within seconds that something was very wrong. When she came off the phone, she stared anxiously at Freya. 'We have a family crisis, I'm afraid. Candy and Amelia are on their way. Candy's in a terrible state.'

Candy was in a terrible state. The last time Freya had seen Candy was two years ago. Freya had gone to Putney for lunch and Candy and her daughter arrived. For the rest of Freya's visit, the conversation had been exclusively concerned with the state of Candy's marriage and the all-round brilliance of Amelia who was an unprepossessing two-year-old with a nose that produced unlimited quantities of green slime. Freya had been unsurprised when Sylvie told her a few months later that the marriage had collapsed. Now, according to Sylvie, the husband had suggested a marital resuscitation and Candy was distraught.

This was not the time to confide in Sylvie about her *own* marriage. Freya took on the preparation of the potato salad while Sylvie made a watercress soup and agonised over her daughter's state of mind.

Candy and Amelia arrived at seven. Amelia was half-asleep and Candy took her straight upstairs.

'How do you think Candy looks?' Sylvie asked in a hushed whisper.

'She looks rather good,' Freya said. 'She's lost weight.'

'I know. I'm terrified she'll get anorexia.'

'I'd say she has a long way to go before she looks anorexic.' Already, Freya regretted her decision to come here.

Candy came downstairs and attempted a tremulous smile. 'Magnus says…' She took a deep breath. 'I am trying so hard not to cry…'

She wasn't trying that hard, Freya thought, watching Candy burst into tears.

The entire evening was given over to Candy's dilemma: should she take Magnus back? Who would believe that such a simple question could produce four hours of soul-searching? Freya never wanted to hear the name Magnus again. It was a stupid name, designed for a Roman soldier not a chartered surveyor who'd just left a girl called

Tamsin. As they sat drinking coffee, she said in a bracing tone that it was really quite simple. Did Candy still love him?

'I don't know,' Candy sniffed. 'He's made me so unhappy, he's had at least two affairs to my certain knowledge and now this one with Tamsin...'

'Stop there,' Freya said. 'You've answered the question. He's made you miserable. It's far better to end it now and find someone else while you're still young and attractive. And you *are* attractive. You look so slim.'

Candy gave a mournful nod. 'I can't eat a thing at the moment.'

'Well,' Freya said, 'that's not so bad...'

'Freya,' Sylvie protested, 'it really is...We don't want Candy to get too thin.'

'I'm sure that won't happen,' Freya said briskly. 'And if you want my advice, you should cut Magnum ('Magnus,' Sylvie murmured.) out of your life. Take control!'

For a moment it seemed that her confident assertion had settled the argument but then Candy's eyes started watering again and Sylvie protested that it wasn't that simple. 'Amelia misses her daddy,' she said.

Freya made her excuses and went to bed. She was awestruck by Candy's monumental self-absorption. Not once in the evening had she asked Freya how *she* was or how her girls were doing. To be fair, they had never had much time for Candy but even so she might have managed at least one polite query.

The next morning was even worse since Freya had to share the breakfast table with Amelia who'd been unpleasant enough at two and was even more charmless now she was four. They sat in Sylvie's pleasant little dining room and Amelia complained about the cereals. 'I don't like Rice Crispies, I want granola and blueberries.' She complained about her drink. 'I don't like orange juice, I like apple juice.' She even complained about the sun in her eyes and they all had to move places to accommodate her.

When Sylvie and Candy went off to the kitchen to produce something the child *might* like, Amelia stared at Freya and stuck her tongue out at her.

Freya leant forward. 'Have you ever heard of the Rude Old Woman in the Cave?'

Amelia stuck out her lower lip.

'She loves children like you,' Freya told her. 'Every time you say, "I want", instead of, "Please can I have..." the Rude Old Woman jumps with joy. Every time she sees you make that extremely ugly face, she laughs again. She laughs because she knows that once you've been rude one hundred times, you will turn into a Rude Old Woman too and you'll spend the rest of your life in her dark, cold cave.'

Amelia's lower lip wobbled. 'That's not true,' she said.

Freya gave an eloquent shrug of her shoulders.

Amelia stared uncertainly at Freya. 'I don't have my daddy,' she said.

'Neither do I,' Freya said. 'Get used to it.'

Sylvie came back with her latest offering. 'There you are, darling,' she said. 'Scrambled egg on toast with two little tomatoes.'

Amelia pointed an accusing finger at Freya. 'She's been horrible,' she cried and burst into tears.

Freya had behaved appallingly and she knew it. Sylvie and Candy were horrified and had every right to be. Freya

164

apologised before making a speedy exit. There was no question of her staying another night with Sylvie and her ghastly family. How could she be polite to pathetic Candy and awful Amelia when she was consumed by an ever-increasing fury at her husband? She walked with a beating heart down the street, cursing him as she did so.

She found a bench on Putney Heath and sat down with her phone. In a few minutes she had found a hotel in Kensington, a short walk away from the party. She booked a room and then rang Tess to tell her the change of plan. Then, she consulted her *A to Z*. Felix had told her to buy a dress and enjoy the party. She fully intended to do so.

Her energy was failing by the time she found the small shop in Knightsbridge. It reminded her of the one she used to manage in Wimbledon. She stared at the shop window and her heart leapt. Discretion was not a word one would use to describe the dress on the mannequin.

As soon as she went through the door she was approached by a young woman in high heels and a grey dress. 'Hi, there,' she said. 'Can I be of any help?'

'I hope so,' Freya said, 'it's my thirtieth wedding anniversary today. I'm looking for two dresses for tonight, one for me and one for my daughter. We're both the same size and I know what she likes. That pink dress in the window...'

'Isn't it heaven?' The girl gave a conspiratorial laugh. 'It just shouts sex appeal! If my mother bought that for me, I'd love her forever!'

'That's a pretty good endorsement,' Freya said. 'Perhaps I'd better try it on.'

When she finally stepped out of the changing room, the

girl let out a little cry. 'Isn't it fabulous? You see how the black stripes down the sides emphasise your waist and your hips? And that black zip down the back is so perfect! It's a complete showstopper. Your daughter will love it!'

'I'll take it,' Freya said. She noticed that the girl had a second dress draped over her arm and said hopefully, 'That looks nice.'

The girl held it up. 'It's deceptively simple,' she said. 'It looks great when it's on.'

The girl proved to be right. When she saw Freya in it she clapped her hands. The dress was perfect: sheerest green silk with a black under-slip.

'I'll have that one too,' Freya said. She hadn't enquired the price of either of them and when the nice girl accepted her credit card and handed her the receipt, Freya did feel a momentary sense of guilt. She consoled herself with the thought that if she and Felix had had the anniversary party she had originally assumed they would have, he'd have had to spend far more.

As she picked up her carrier bags, the girl said, 'Have a wonderful party tonight. I know your daughter will love her dress!'

'She will,' Freya assured her. 'Green is her favourite colour.'

She checked into her hotel in the late afternoon. The continuing silence from Felix – she must *stop* checking her phone – had lowered her spirits but it was impossible not to be cheered by her room with its enormous bed, the walk-in shower and the outstanding views of Kensington Gardens.

The shower was heaven. As the water rained down on

her she could feel it washing away her anger. Tonight she would refuse to think about Felix and her frightening future. Tonight, she would enjoy the party, flirt outrageously, laugh with Tess and enjoy the luxury of her hotel room.

At six, she eased herself into her dress and performed a twirl in front of the mirror. It was not a dress for the faint-hearted. Shocking pink, with the ostentatious black zip that went all the way down to the base of her spine, it fitted her like a glove. She had at least paid lip-service to her age with her hair, putting it up into a neat roll at the back of her head.

When Tess arrived her reaction was – possibly – reassuring. 'Oh my God, Mum!'

'Is it too much?' Freya asked. 'Do you think it's too obvious?'

'It's very obvious,' Tess said, 'but you can take it.'

'I've bought you one too,' Freya said, picking up one of the bags from the floor.

'No offence, Mum, but…'

'It's not like this one. Look.' As Freya had suspected, Tess was dressed in her calf-length black dress that made her look like a girl who's come straight from the convent.

For Freya, the evening began once Tess put on her dress. 'You look like an autumn nymph,' she breathed. 'You should always wear green.'

'I love it,' Tess said. 'It must have cost…'

'Never mind that.' Freya picked up her bag. 'There is a very sophisticated bar downstairs. I think we should try it out.'

She ordered margaritas and, while they waited, gave a quick murmured assessment of the clientele. 'The man in the corner is fascinated. He can't stop staring at you, Tess. He's pretending to look for his companion. I suspect, she doesn't exist and that actually he's plucking up courage to come over but of course he won't, and over near the bar there's a romantic couple who have both noticed us…'

'You're smiling at him,' Tess protested.

'He smiled first.'

'It doesn't matter. You'll get her coming over to have words if you don't behave.'

'Nonsense, I'm just being friendly. This is such fun and we owe it to your friend, Jamie. Did you have a lovely time in Scotland with him? What did the two of you do together?'

Tess shrugged. 'We visited Scott's home and his graveyard and…'

Freya rolled her eyes. 'Poor Jamie. You do remind me of my father, you know. The two of us spent one holiday traipsing round the Elwy Valley in Wales because Gerald Manley Hopkins had written some verses about it. I was ten at the time and far too young to appreciate his poems – to be honest, I still don't – but dear Daddy stomped around, declaiming away and gazing at me with such happy expectation that I had to pretend to enjoy it. I wish he were here now. I do miss him.'

'I know you do,' Tess said. 'I'm not sure you would want him here at the moment. I don't know what he'd make of your dress.'

'He'd rest his head in his hands,' Freya said, 'and he'd say, "Freya, oh Freya, you will be the death of me!" Oh look, here are our drinks!'

The rims of the cocktail glasses were frosted with salt

and the liquid was a pale cloudy green. Mother and daughter took tentative sips and Tess murmured, 'That is *good*!'

'It's the only way to drink tequila,' Freya said. 'If the party is dull we can come back for more.'

'I don't know why we're going,' Tess said. 'I'd be quite happy to celebrate your anniversary here.'

'Oh,' Freya said, 'I'd forgotten that.'

Tess raised her glass. 'I haven't. Here's to you and to Dad. Cheers, Mum!'

'Thank you.' The margarita slipped down Freya's throat like nectar.

'I still don't understand why we've been invited. It seems so random.'

'I told you. Jamie's father hoped to use us as bait to get his son down here.' Already the margarita was giving her confidence. This was no time for tact. Freya was not at all sure that tact was a particularly sensible quality anyway. She said, 'Tess, can you look me in the eye and assure me the young man has no interest in you?'

Tess raised her eyes to meet those of her mother and faltered. 'He *did*,' she conceded at last, 'but I... I discouraged him.'

'Poor Jamie. Is he ugly?'

'No! No, of course he isn't.'

Freya gave a sympathetic nod. 'Is he boring?'

'No!' Tess took a reckless gulp of her drink. 'The fact is I... I didn't want to have the sort of relationship... *that* sort of relationship.'

'Why not? What is wrong with him?'

'There is nothing wrong with him! I just... I don't need

169

a boyfriend in my life right now, especially one who lives in Scotland. I'm sure you think that's very dull but…'

'To be honest,' Freya said, 'I think romantic love is a minefield. Perhaps you're right to leave it alone.'

'Really? That doesn't sound like you.'

'Well, perhaps I don't feel like me at the moment…'

'Oh my God!' Tess clutched her mother's hand. 'Don't look now but the romantic man has left the room and now the romantic wife is coming over here. I *told* you she'd be cross.'

The woman stopped in front of Freya. 'I'm sorry to bother you,' she said, 'but my husband's taking a phone call and I thought I'd ask you… He loves your dress, you see, and I wondered… Would it be very cheeky to ask you where you bought it?'

CHAPTER SEVENTEEN

Their destination was a gleaming white three-storey townhouse, minutes away from the hotel and with views over Kensington Gardens. Tess was taken aback by the grandeur of the place and even Freya was a little apprehensive although, 'I don't see why you're so surprised,' she told Tess. 'If Jamie Lockhart owns a castle, it stands to reason that his father must be wealthy.'

'Yes, but Jamie's castle isn't a grand sort of castle. It's used for business parties and weddings. It's not as if Jamie lives there.' Tess cast glanced at her mother. 'Are we going in?'

'Of course we are. I've spent a small fortune on our party dresses.' Freya mounted the steps and rang the bell.

The door was opened by a young man in a maroon shirt and black trousers. He welcomed them into a high-ceilinged hall with grey walls and a charcoal carpet and took Freya's jacket and Tess's mac, hanging them with great care on the coat rail behind them. Freya's attention was caught by a gilt-framed painting on the left of the staircase. It depicted a wild-haired man in a kilt looking out at the world with a gun in his hand and what looked like a slaughtered stag behind him.

They were directed up the stairs to a large drawing room with elegant windows and a vast ornate chandelier. There was an enormous antique mirror at one end of the room and a huge landscape painting at the other. It had its own little light above it and must therefore be very, very expensive.

The deep pile carpet, the vast Chesterfield sofa, the Chinese table lamps by each window all spoke of barely restrained opulence.

Mother and daughter gazed at the group in front of them. 'Look at the women,' Freya murmured. 'They're all dressed in fifty shades of grey. I look like a firework at a funeral.'

'Everyone likes fireworks,' Tess said.

'*You* never did,' Freya reminded her. She beamed at a young waiter who handed them thin flutes of champagne. 'Dutch courage,' Freya murmured and downed a third of it at once. She was aware she was being watched and found herself locking eyes with a slim, dark-haired man in the far corner of the room. He was tieless, with a black suit and white shirt. He was also quite extraordinarily handsome, a rare phenomenon in mid-life men who weren't famous actors. She knew, even as he turned his attention back to his companion, a voluble, pinstripe-suited male with gesticulating hands, that he wanted to come over to her. She rather hoped he would do.

The next moment she thought she was dreaming. An identical man, his eyes fixed on Tess, was walking towards them from another part of the room. As he drew nearer she could see he was considerably younger. She glanced enquiringly at Tess whose face was a portrait of stunned bewilderment.

'Jamie?' Tess sounded almost angry. 'What are you *doing* here? You should be at home. You have a serious meeting tomorrow.'

'I'm getting a plane back later tonight,' he said. 'It's under control.'

172

'You must be mad. You have to prepare for it, you need to be alert and awake. I can't believe you thought this was a good idea!'

The young man offered his hand to Freya. 'She's not going to introduce us, is she? I'm Jamie Lockhart and you must be Tess's mother.'

'Please call me Freya.' The man was lovely, she thought. His soft Scottish accent could melt an ice-cube. How could Tess not be impressed by him? She really must be a lost cause. Freya gave him an encouraging smile. 'I gather my daughter's been dragging you round graveyards and museums all August.'

'She did me a great favour. I'm revising my entire marketing strategy thanks to Tess.'

And now another gorgeous young man came up to them. He took Freya's hand and kissed it. 'You must be Tess's mother. I'm Jamie's brother, Rory.'

Unlike Jamie, his voice held no trace of a Scottish accent. He had his brother's dark eyes but was otherwise quite unlike him: reddish hair, not black, and an altogether more muscular and rugged type with a great deal of confidence. He had a bottle of champagne in one hand and caught her eyes drifting towards it. 'If you finish your glasses,' he said, 'I'll fill them up now. The waiters here are very slow to do it.'

'Oh, why not?' Tess said. 'The whole world seems mad tonight.'

If Tess felt it all right to do so, who was she to disagree? Freya swallowed her champagne and held out her glass, murmuring without much conviction, 'I really shouldn't.'

'I'm delighted to meet you,' Rory told her. 'I've been staying with my brother in Scotland. I must tell you from

173

bitter experience that if we stay with these two, they'll talk about nothing but musty castles and dead writers. Let me take you away, Mrs Cameron...'

'Please call me Freya.'

'I love that name! Now if we go over to the piano, we can hog the canapés.'

Freya said gaily, 'I do love canapés!' It was quite obvious that Jamie wanted to talk to Tess.

Having emptied the bottle, Rory put it down, took her hand and walked purposefully towards the piano. He told Freya he refused to believe she was old enough to be Tess's mother. His curse, he said, was that he found women of his own age dull. Older women were far more fun. He was an outrageous flirt and Freya was quite disappointed when they were joined by someone else.

'This is my stepmother, Eva,' Rory said. 'Eva, this is Freya Cameron, mother of Jamie's friend, Tess.'

'You're the genealogist,' Eva said. 'I'm so glad you could come tonight. Rory, will you go and talk to my aunt? She's over there in the corner. You know she adores you and she's all on her own.'

'I'd be delighted,' Rory said, making a face of silent horror at Freya as he went away.

Freya cast a critical, if veiled, eye on her hostess. She would be far more attractive if she weren't so thin and it was a pity she had chosen to wear a low-cut dress. Thin women should never wear low-cut dresses. Despite these handicaps, she was an excellent hostess, asking Freya various questions about her career and seeming genuinely interested in her answers.

A couple came up to greet Eva who introduced them as,

'our very dear friends, Harry and Nicola'. They couldn't be *that* dear since Eva lost no time in slipping away to join another group. Harry, an overweight man with a puce-coloured complexion, seemed pleased to meet Freya, his plump wife Nicola less so. Harry was halfway through a long explanation as to how he had first met their hosts when a hand touched Freya's elbow and a voice said, 'Nicola and Harry, how lovely to see you. May I ask you to do me a favour? We've invited some new friends. They've recently moved to Marylebone and I know they'll get on with you. Would you go and say hello to them? They're over there with Charlie and Charlie is on his seventh glass of champagne so they need rescuing. I'll catch up with you both later.'

It was the man who had smiled at her. It was like looking at Jamie Lockhart twenty years on. The man had the same dark hair, eyebrows and eyes and the same pale skin. But whereas Jamie's face was curiously immobile, this man had an easy laugh and a winning smile with which he was currently seeing off poor Harry and Nicola.

He turned to Freya. 'The trouble with being a host is that too many of your guests want to talk to you. I've been trying to meet you forever. My name's...'

'You have to be Neil Lockhart,' Freya said. 'You look very like Jamie. I'm...'

'You are Freya Cameron. I recognise you from the picture on your website. It doesn't do you justice.'

'Thank you.' His eyes seemed to bore into her soul, firing every nerve-end in her body. There was an almost tangible electric current between them. This was turning into a very good party. 'You shouldn't stare at me, you know,' she said. 'It's a little off-putting.'

'I'm sorry. I've been trying not to stare at you ever since you arrived.' He nodded towards Tess and Jamie who were listening politely to a man with a beard. 'Look at our children. I suspect my son has lost his heart. Is there any hope for him?'

'To be honest,' Freya said, 'I doubt it. My daughter's only interest is her work.'

'Jamie's a very persistent man. Let's go and help them out. Once Julian starts talking, he never stops.'

He was very impressive, she thought, apologising to his friend Julian but insisting that he needed Jamie and Tess to find Eva. 'I think you'll find her in the study, Jamie. Tell her I need to show Freya the Lord Chancellor and then I'll be back for the speeches. And, Julian, I have a request for you too. Eva's aunt is desperate to talk to you. She's sitting by the fireplace. Can you go and have a word? Thanks so much.'

He led Freya out of the drawing room, one hand lightly resting on the small of her back. She had to fight against the urge to lean into him. As they walked down the stairs, she asked, 'Is Eva's aunt really desperate to talk to him?'

'Eva's aunt is desperate, full stop.'

'And is Eva really in the study?'

'I very much doubt it but Jamie needs some privacy with your daughter. He's come all the way from Scotland to see her.'

Freya sighed. 'She's a funny girl.'

'He's a funny man. They are clearly made for each other. Jamie says you live in Somerset. I occasionally come to Bath on business.'

'We live outside Darrowbridge. Bath is only a half-hour drive.'

'I must come and see you sometime.'

Freya said primly, 'That would be nice.'

Neil opened a door on his right and said, 'Here we are.'

Oh!' She put her hand to her throat. 'This is a lovely room. It is just what a library should be.'

She could imagine her father in a room like this: book-lined walls, chocolate-brown carpet, sturdy oak desk. There was even a fire in the grate. She noticed a wide, ornate frame above the mantelpiece and asked, 'Is this your Lord Chancellor?'

He nodded. He stood in the middle of the room with his hands in his pockets. She wondered if he knew how attractive he was.

She walked across to the fireplace and studied the pen and ink print of a good-looking man in army uniform, with short curly hair and dark, brooding eyes. The inscription beneath told her that he was Lord High Chancellor of Great Britain to His Royal Highness, George, Prince of Wales. 'It would be fun to find out about him,' she said. 'Do you still want me to research your family?' She turned. 'You're staring at me again, you know.'

'I can't help it. I've wanted to be alone with you from the moment you arrived. To be honest, at the moment, I don't give a damn about my ancestors. If they give me an excuse to see you again, I shall be most grateful to them.'

Freya wondered if the margarita had been a good idea. It was wildly exciting to be alone with this man in this library but she had no idea how to respond to him. Her heart pounded. She should probably tell him to behave himself.

She should possibly walk out now and go back to the party. This man was dangerous. She stalled. 'We've only just met.'

'This has been the longest evening of my life. Every moment's been an hour.' He took his hands from his pockets and walked over to her. 'You have no idea how beautiful you are.'

This was crazy. She felt as if she were on fire. She stared up at him and tried to tell him he was being absurd but he stopped her with a kiss and she thought: tomorrow, I will go back to my husbandless home and I shall never forget this moment.

'Freya Cameron,' he said, 'can I see you again?'

And now she took a step back. 'No,' she said. 'You absolutely can't.'

For Tess, the evening was like a dream during which she seemed to be an entirely different person from the Tess she had always known herself to be.

The new Tess appeared briefly when she put on her new dress in her mother's hotel bedroom and saw her reflection in the mirror. Then, when she saw Jamie walking towards her at the party, she felt a rush of such joy that she thought she might faint. And when he looked at her, she could see in his eyes that he thought she was beautiful. That was when the new Tess elbowed the old to one side. She wanted to hug Rory when he offered to take her mother away.

'I hope she'll be all right with him,' Jamie said. 'He's definitely trying it on with her.'

'Mum will love that,' Tess assured him. 'I can't believe

you've come all this way for such a short time. You must be mad.'

'I wanted to see you.'

The old Tess would have been tongue-tied, confused, unsure how to proceed. The new Tess looked up at him and said, 'I'm glad you came.'

'I was afraid you might be angry. You did seem so certain our situation was hopeless.'

She said, 'Well, actually...'

And that was when the first of a stream of guests came up and said, 'Jamie, I'm so pleased you're here! Are you going to introduce me to your lovely companion?'

It had never occurred to Tess that she might be more than averagely attractive. She had a beautiful mother and a blonde sister with breasts. She was long accustomed to playing third fiddle in the family. But tonight, she *did* feel lovely. Confidence was a new sensation and she enjoyed it, although she would have preferred to enjoy it in Jamie's exclusive company. Jamie's manners were impeccable but she could sense he was as impatient as she was with the fact that they were spending their precious time in party talk with random guests.

And then, while they were listening to probably the most boring man in England telling them exactly why the congestion charge in London was doomed to fail, the cavalry arrived in the unlikely forms of her mother and Jamie's father.

The presence of Jamie's father only added to the dreamlike quality of the evening. He looked so very like Jamie: like Jamie with a face whose features had been shaken and stirred. He even wore an identical dark suit and white shirt.

He came over with her mother and asked, a little apologetically, if she and Jamie would go and find Eva. Even more apologetically, he asked the boring man to go away and talk to someone else. It was impossible not to like him, even if he did guide her mother away with what seemed to be a rather proprietorial hand on her back.

The boring man said, 'That's so typical of Neil. He wafts up here with the most beautiful woman in the room – apart from you of course, my dear – and tells *me* to go and talk to Eva's hideous aunt. I'll catch up with you two later...'

'Not if I can help it,' Jamie murmured, ushering Tess away. 'Another two minutes and I might have had to kill him. Let's go to the study.'

The study was downstairs. It was half the size of the drawing room, with pale green walls and primrose-coloured curtains. There was a small sofa opposite a long table of palest ash on which sat an impressive amount of computer hardware. Behind the table was a tall, elegant chair. Tess thought that if she had a room like this in which to work, she would finish her thesis in no time at all.

'Well,' she said, 'Eva's not here.'

Jamie shut the door behind him. 'I know she's not. I saw her in the sitting room.'

'Jamie! We should go and tell her what your father said.'

'My father knew very well where she was. He also knew I wanted to be alone with you. In a few hours' time I'll be back in Scotland. You and I need to talk. Come and sit down.'

On the wall behind the desk, there was a framed Marc

Chagall print of a man in a black suit, holding the hand of his partner who was flying in the air above him. Tess felt as if she were flying too. She walked over to the sofa and sat down.

Jamie remained standing. He put his hands in his pockets and cleared his throat. 'I came here tonight to prove that distance, at least, isn't a problem. I live in Scotland and you live in London but I'm here now and it hasn't been difficult.'

'You won't think that tomorrow,' Tess said. 'You'll be exhausted.'

'I'd rather be exhausted and happy than not exhausted and unhappy. I don't mind waiting till October to see you as long as I know you *will* come up in October. I want to say that, as far as I'm concerned, it's all very simple. I don't want to say goodbye to you. And if you feel the same, then nothing else matters. I appreciate you have a problem with... with physical intimacy but I've thought about that. If *you* have a problem, then it's my problem too. We can work it out together... There are people we can see for that sort of thing. I'll wait, I'll wait as long as it takes.'

Tess stood up and walked across to Jamie. He had made the most monumentally romantic gesture in coming here and she felt it was time to make an effort of similar magnitude. She took a deep breath and raised her face to his. 'Jamie,' she said, 'will you kiss me?' There was the ticking of a clock from somewhere in the room and for a few moments its sound seemed to get louder and louder.

His response was unexpected. 'To be honest,' he said, 'I'm not sure I want to. Call me old-fashioned, but I don't normally kiss women who have to clench their fists in anticipation of the experience.'

'I'm sorry.' She unclenched her hands. 'I didn't know I was doing it. Please. I want you to kiss me.'

He approached her warily, stared at her unhappily and gave her a brief, fleeting kiss. 'How was that?'

'Well,' Tess said, 'I didn't hate it.'

He gave a polite nod. 'Thank you. That's most encouraging.'

She laughed. 'Actually, it is.'

A head appeared round the door and Jamie said, 'Oh, Eva, we were looking for you. Dad thought you might be in here.'

Eva did not point out, as she was fully entitled to do, that it was fairly obvious she hadn't been. A flicker of amusement did cross her face but she only said, 'I was looking for him. We ought to get on with the speeches.'

'He's gone to the library to show Tess's mother the Lord Chancellor.' Jamie looked purposeful. 'Tess and I will go and get them.'

'I'll come with you,' Eva said. 'It will be nice to get away from the noise for a moment or two.' She smiled at Tess. 'I'm so glad you could come tonight. We don't see enough of Jamie. I'm sure you're the only reason he's here this evening.'

'I don't see enough of you and Dad,' Jamie said, opening the door for the two women. 'I feel quite ashamed. I must make more of an effort to see you both in the future.'

'That would be nice,' Eva said, adding pointedly, 'you live in London, don't you, Tess?'

They walked across the hall. 'I do hope Neil isn't boring your mother,' Eva said. 'He's so proud of his Lord

Chancellor.' She opened a door and that was when the dream ended and the nightmare began.

For a split second Tess was conscious of a large, comfortable, brown room but almost immediately her attention was drawn to the entwined couple in the middle of it. It was the outrageous black zip – half undone – that alerted her to the fact that the woman with her arms round Jamie's father's neck was her mother.

CHAPTER EIGHTEEN

It was almost comical, though Tess had never felt less like laughing. As Jamie's father registered the fact that he had an audience, he froze and for a few moments his face was devoid of expression. There was a terrible silence while everyone took in what was happening.

Her mother was the first to move. She turned sideways and spoke with commendable control. 'Neil,' she asked, 'would you mind doing up my zip?'

He did so immediately and she walked over to the sofa, picked up her bag and went straight across to Eva.

'I am so very sorry,' she said. 'This is entirely my fault. I'm afraid I drank far too much champagne. I shall go back to my hotel and drink gallons of water.' She glanced at Tess, murmured, 'I'll see you tomorrow, darling,' and walked out of the library, shutting the door behind her.

Neil stirred at last. 'Eva,' he said, 'I'm so sorry you had to see that.'

'I'm sure you are.' Eva's face was deathly pale.

'It was the act of a moment. I was showing her the picture...'

'I'm sure you showed her all sorts of things. I think, in the circumstances, we will keep the speeches as short as possible.'

'Eva,' Neil said, 'you have to believe me. It was nothing but a drunken grope. You know I have no head for alcohol...'

'We can talk about it later,' Eva said. 'Right now, we need to return to our tenth wedding-anniversary celebration. Perhaps,' she added, 'you might like to tuck your shirt in.'

She turned on her heel. Neil attended to his clothes, glanced briefly at Tess and Jamie, murmured, 'I'm so sorry,' and then went to the door. 'Jamie,' he said, 'you won't be long, will you? I would appreciate some support up there. Perhaps you could speak instead of me?'

'You want *me* to say something? For God's sake, Dad...'

'Please.' Neil said, 'you're good at speeches.' He opened the door. They could hear him calling to Eva in the hall.

'Can you believe them?' Jamie asked. 'They both still want *speeches*!'

'I must go after Mum,' Tess said. 'Ring me tomorrow evening. I'd like to know how the meeting goes.' She hesitated, then gave him an awkward kiss on the cheek before racing across the hall. She only just remembered to collect her mac before going out into the night. She could see her mother in the distance, an elegant figure in her grey jacket, pink dress and heels. Tess couldn't help admiring the way she'd handled her exit. It had been a lot more dignified than that of Jamie's father.

She caught up with her on the corner of the road and said breathlessly, 'Mum, can we stop for a moment?'

Her mother halted. 'Go back to the party, Tess. I think I need my bed.'

'I wouldn't go back to that party if you paid me a million pounds. Mum, what were you *doing*?'

185

Freya started walking again. 'You could see what I was doing.'

'You know what I mean. How could…? You'd only just met him!'

'I know.' They were almost at the hotel now. 'I need to go to my room and have a very large glass of water.' She put a hand to her forehead. 'Would you care to join me?'

'Yes,' Tess said. 'Yes, I would. But I don't…'

'Tess, I'm sorry but I can't say any more until I get that water. My throat feels like sandpaper.'

A woman in a cocktail dress stood at the reception desk, quizzing the man behind it about a message he'd received from her husband. 'Are you sure he said he'd arrive in the morning? Did he not say what *time* he'd arrive?'

The receptionist said he hadn't and the woman shook her head with impatience before going over to consult her male companion. 'You see, we're all at it,' Freya murmured to Tess, before asking the man behind the desk for her room key.

In the lift, it was Freya who broke the silence. 'What happened when I left?'

Tess made a face. 'Eva was an ice queen and returned to the party. Jamie's father looked like he wanted to die. He asked Jamie to make his speech for him…'

'Speech?' Freya murmured.

'It's their tenth wedding-anniversary party. They were all supposed to be making speeches.'

'Of course! Oh God!' Freya hit her forehead with her hand. For a moment her eyes sparkled. 'I'd love to be a fly on the wall when they start.'

'You wouldn't,' Tess said. 'Eva would swat you with one blow.'

Once in her room, Freya kicked off her shoes and made for the water bottles. She poured out a big glass of water and drank long and hard. Tess walked over to the window and looked out towards the big houses on the edge of Kensington Gardens. She wondered if Jamie *was* making a speech. What would he say? Here's to the happy couple?

Behind her, Freya said, 'Felix has left me.'

Tess turned at once. Her mother sat at the end of the bed, hands round her glass. Tess stared at her in blank incomprehension. 'He's left you? What do you mean?'

Freya shook her head, as if trying to dislodge a fly from her hair. 'He's left me. He wants us to live apart.'

'He loves you!' Tess protested. 'He's always loved you!'

'And now he's stopped,' Freya said. 'He told me before he went to Spain. He hasn't rung, he hasn't made any contact at all. He said he'd find somewhere else to live when he came back.'

'But...' Tess felt she had been hurled into some strange alien landscape. 'It's ridiculous. He must have a reason. Has anything happened lately? Perhaps he's unhappy at work, perhaps he's depressed...'

'He does get depressed. I always thought it was a sort of illness but now I wonder if he hasn't felt like this for ages. He should have said something before. It's not fair. He just announced it and then he left for the airport. I don't... I don't deserve this.' She finished her water and went over to the dressing table to refill her glass. 'After tonight, you probably think I *do* deserve it but...'

187

'Of course I don't.'

Freya shrugged. 'There's no excuse. I mean I drank too much but then I set out to drink too much. And Neil Lockhart is a very good-looking man and I thought at least there's someone who still finds me attractive...' She took a deep breath. 'I shall write to Eva tomorrow, I shall explain about Felix and tell her I jumped on Neil, which by the way isn't true...'

'I didn't think it was, and anyway, none of that matters. What matters is you and Dad. You should ring him. Would you like *me* to ring him?'

'Absolutely not.' The words shot out. 'Felix would hate that. You can talk to him once we've talked to each other. You never know, he might feel quite different when he comes home.'

'I bet he does. I bet he'll come back and you'll find it's all some huge misunderstanding.'

'He as good as told me he'd stopped loving me. It's pretty difficult to misunderstand that.'

'Look,' Tess said, 'you've drunk a lot, you've had a traumatic evening and... Perhaps you should go to bed now and we can discuss things in the morning. I'll come over and...'

'Tess?' Freya held out a hand. 'This bed is huge. Would you like to stay the night?'

'Would you like me to stay?'

'Yes,' Freya said, 'I'd like that very much.'

Anna was meeting Tess and her mother at a place near Embankment. She had decided against cycling. Knowing her mother, there'd be wine and champagne which suited

Anna just fine. She was crossing Waterloo Bridge when her phone rang. She pulled it out of her bag and clamped it to her ear. 'William! Thank you for calling!'

He said, 'I don't see the point in...'

'William, listen!' She was terrified he'd change his mind and ring off. 'I want you to know, I hate myself for letting you down over Trevor's engagement party. I shouldn't have done it, I don't know why I did, I had some stupid idea I needed to sort out stuff and I truly regret it. You're such a good friend, I can't afford to lose you. Please say you forgive me and let us be friends again. Please?'

'Look,' he said, 'I'm only ringing to explain. I was hurt about the Trevor thing, I admit I was hurt. But when I thought about it, I knew it was because I'd got you wrong, I hadn't understood you...'

'You *do* understand me, you understand me better than anyone!'

'No, no I don't, or rather, I didn't. You're not who I thought you were and – I don't know how to say this but the truth is, I don't like you now.'

He might as well have hit her. She felt her eyes sting, and she bit her lip hard.

'I appreciate your apologies.' His voice was careful and deliberate. 'I'm sorry I haven't rung you before. I hoped you'd give up calling me. I'm sorry, Anna, but I don't want to see you again.'

She swallowed hard and took a deep breath. 'Right. I won't bother you again. Goodbye.'

He didn't like her. William didn't like her. She started crying now and stumbled along the bridge, aware of curious glances from those about her. She found a Ladies' at the station and washed her face and put on new make-up. William said he didn't know her. Well, she didn't know *him*. She'd messed up once, just once, and he'd showed himself to be a pious, judgemental prick. She wouldn't be his friend if he paid her. *And* he'd made her late for the anniversary lunch.

When she arrived at the restaurant, she stood on the pavement for a few moments, trying to catch her breath. She caught a glimpse of her mother and sister through the window. They were the only customers and sat at a table in the centre, their heads close together. Tess talked earnestly and Freya listened. Anna stood, unseen, and watched them with rising curiosity. Tess never talked earnestly to Freya and Freya was not a natural listener. She was one of those people who wait with barely suppressed impatience for a brief hiatus in which to interpose her own opinion. Possibly, Anna thought, that was a little unfair, but certainly she could not recall an occasion in which her mother had ever behaved with such apparently mute docility. When Anna walked in, they both sat up straight as if they'd been told off for slouching.

She glanced at their tumblers of mineral water. 'Where's the champagne?' she asked. 'I thought this was supposed to be a celebration.'

Her mother stood up and kissed her cheek. 'Tess and I rather overdid the alcohol last night.' She did indeed look grim, with puffy eyes and a pale complexion.

'That's all very well but while you two were partying I was saving babies...'

'*Were* you, darling?'

'Not exactly, but I'm ready for wine even if you aren't.'

Anna took her seat and raised an arm to the waiter who'd been standing listlessly by the aspidistra plant; he seemed grateful to be called.

'Please,' Anna told him, 'I'd like a glass of house white. In fact, bring a bottle. I can always take it home with me.'

'Certainly,' the waiter said. 'Would you like to hear our specials?' Encouraged by Anna's nod, he rattled off a choice of four dishes.

'Have you two already decided?' Anna asked. 'Are we having starters?'

'Do have one if you like but…' Her mother's voice faded into nothing.

'We're not terribly hungry,' Tess said. 'We're having spaghetti Bolognese.'

'Some celebration this is turning out to be,' Anna said. She glanced up at the waiter. 'I'll have the seafood special, please.'

He nodded with apparent satisfaction at the excellence of her judgement and walked through to the kitchen. For a moment as he opened the door, there was a burst of laughter from one of the staff and then the place returned to its quiet, hushed atmosphere.

'So,' Freya said, 'how are you, Anna?'

'I've had a rubbish week, thanks for asking, but at least I don't have a hangover. You both look like zombies. I presume the party last night was a success?' She caught a brief, fleeting glance between the two of them which annoyed her – but then, everything annoyed her at the moment. 'Did your friend come?' she asked Tess.

'Jamie? Yes, he did.'

'That was nice. Did you meet him, Mum?'

'Yes. He was charming.'

'And what was the party like?'

'It was in a very grand house in Kensington.' Freya made a visible effort. 'Tess and I had margaritas before the party. That was probably a bad idea but they were delicious, weren't they, Tess?'

Tess nodded.

The waiter brought Anna's wine, opened the bottle and poured a little into her glass, waiting expectantly for her approval.

'I'm sure it's fine,' she said, and then took a quick sip. 'It's very nice,' she murmured and he nodded his pleasure before going off to greet three newcomers. Anna raised her glass. 'I suppose I should make a toast, Mum. Happy anniversary and here's to the next thirty years!' She caught another of those odd conspiratorial glances. 'Is something wrong?' she asked. 'I mean I was expecting a jolly party and you two act like someone's died.'

'There's something I should tell you.' Freya took a sip of her water and then tried to speak. She opened her mouth, shut it again, and bit her lip.

Tess spoke for her. 'Dad has left Mum,' she said.

It was, literally, an incredible statement. Anna must have misheard it. She stared first at her mother, then her sister. Tess sat biting her fingernails. Freya's face looked tight and taut.

'I don't understand,' Anna said.

Freya gave a small shrug of her shoulders. 'Join the club. He told me on Thursday afternoon.'

'Why?' Anna asked. 'What did you do?'

The words were out before she could stop them. They were gratuitously offensive and she didn't need Tess's furious protest – 'For God's sake, Anna,' – to point that out.

Freya took her hands from the table. She bent down to pick up her bag, took some notes from her wallet and placed them on the table.

'Mum,' Tess said, 'what are you doing?'

'The money should cover your meal. I have to go home now. I don't feel well and I can't face Anna today...'

'Mum, please,' Anna said, 'I shouldn't have said that. It just came out. Please sit down.'

'I don't want to sit down. Tess, I'll talk to you soon. Goodbye, Anna.'

'Look, I'm sorry,' Anna said. 'It's all such a bombshell. I didn't mean...'

'Of course you did.' Freya's voice was hard and certain. She walked across to have a word with the waiter before collecting her small suitcase from its place by the coats. Anna watched her mother walk out onto the pavement, head held high and her face carefully devoid of expression.

Tess sat back and folded her arms. 'Well, that was amazing. Even by *your* standards that was amazing.'

'I said it before I could think. I swear I didn't mean to upset her. It was shock, that's all. I can't believe she's just *left* us. Do you think I should go after her?'

'Multiply your shock by ten and you'll have some idea how Mum feels. And no, I think you should leave her alone. You've done quite enough.'

'I know. You don't need to tell me. I feel terrible. I just don't understand. Dad adores Mum. He'd only leave her if she'd done something…'

'Right. So it would never be *his* fault…'

'That's not what I'm saying. But…' Anna glanced rather warily at her sister. 'Mum loves to be admired. I know she loves Dad but… She does have a weakness. We were never given a good reason for the move to Darrowbridge. You know that's true.'

Tess threw up her hands. 'I knew you'd bring that up. Elephants and Anna never forget. In your case, you never forget things you only *think* might have happened.'

'That's not fair. I have every reason to believe that Xander Bullen…'

'I don't want to talk about Xander Bullen…'

'You never *do* want to talk about him.'

'He has nothing to do with this. I stayed at the hotel with Mum last night. I woke up at three and found her sitting by the window. I don't know how long she'd been crying. She kept asking me why Dad's left her. She's devastated. You must have seen how ill she looks…'

'I was wrong to say what I did and I'm sorry I said it. I'll ring Mum later and grovel. Have you spoken to Dad?'

'No. Mum is very keen that we keep out of it for the time being. He hasn't contacted her since he left. He gets back from Spain on Wednesday evening.' Tess stared levelly at her sister. 'He is not behaving well here.'

'I agree,' Anna said. 'Of course I agree!' She felt cross. She resented the fact that she had to play *mea culpa* to Tess's righteous sister act. It was easy for Tess to be reasonable and rational. She'd had a night to get used to the news. 'Did Mum want to go to the party last night? It seems such an odd thing to do in the circumstances. How could

194

she possibly expect to enjoy it?' She watched Tess reach across for the bottle. 'I thought you said you drank too much last night.'

'I didn't drink as much as Mum.'

'So… How was the evening?'

Tess poured wine into her glass.

Anna raised her eyebrows. 'Tess? How was it?'

'I don't want to tell you. You wouldn't understand.'

'Now you're being seriously annoying. You have to tell me. What happened?'

'There was an…incident. I was with Jamie and his stepmother. We went into the library. We saw Jamie's father kiss Mum.'

'Oh my God! And you tell me Dad's behaved badly!'

'You see? Instant condemnation! You have no idea! She was in a state about Dad. She drank far too much. Jamie's father comes on to her and she lets him kiss her.'

'Oh well, that's all right then. It's quite understandable.'

Tess put down her fork and knife. 'Why are you in such a foul mood?'

'Possibly because I've just learnt that my parents are splitting up.'

'You were in a foul mood when you got here.'

The two of them stared at each other and Anna was the first to speak. 'You're right. I'm sorry. It all seems so unimportant now. William and I have fallen out. I had a horrendous call from him on the way here. That's why I was late. He was quite cruel.'

'That doesn't sound like William.'

Anna waved an impatient hand. 'He was transferred to South Reading Hospital at the beginning of August. He'd asked me to go with him to his brother's engagement party just before he left... I said I would but... But then I didn't.'

'Why not?'

'It was silly. I'd bumped into Patrick Wainwright in May... Do you remember Patrick?'

'Of course I do. How is he?'

'He's married with a daughter. They live a mile or so away from me which is weird.' Anna took a large gulp of her wine. 'Anyway, Patrick invited me over to supper and I suppose I thought William would understand.'

'You went to supper with Patrick and his wife?'

'Well, actually, his wife was away.' She caught Tess's eye and blushed. 'I don't even know why we're talking about this.' She let her eyes wander restlessly round the restaurant. 'Nothing happened. Patrick kissed me and I realised I should leave. So I did.' She finished her wine and stared defiantly at her sister. 'Why are you looking at me like that?'

Tess raised her eyebrows. 'It's interesting, that's all. You're very quick to judge Mum...'

'I'm not judging her.'

'It sounded like it to me. And meanwhile...'

'All right.' Anna bit her lip and stared up at the ceiling. She said stiffly, 'I do regret going over to see Patrick. And I regret letting William down.'

'I take it he's still upset.'

'I keep saying I'm sorry. And now he says he doesn't want to be my friend. It's so childish.' She glared at her sister. 'So that's why I was a cow to Mum and I know that's no excuse and I'm sorry. Can we talk about our parents now? I've tried to give you *my* theory. Why do *you* think

196

Dad's acted totally out of character?'

Tess put her hands to her face. 'I haven't a clue,' she said.

CHAPTER NINETEEN

It was Sunday evening and Eliza was still in a state of shock. Yesterday morning she had picked up her copy of *The Times* and, as was her habit, had gone straight to the obituaries page.

And there it was: *WOODWARD Dennis, passed away peacefully on 26ᵗʰ August 2014 after a short illness, aged 87 years. Beloved husband of Vera (deceased) and father of George. A good friend to many, he will be sadly missed.*

She had cut it out and put it on her noticeboard in the kitchen. She sat looking at it now. It seemed absurd that Dennis Woodward had spent eighty-seven years on the planet and now that he was dead his life had been reduced to three lines. He had been a beloved husband to Vera, a father to George and a friend to many. And now he was dead.

What would *she* have written? 'Dennis Woodward, husband to Vera and father to George, was an exceptionally ugly man whose physical shortcomings were utterly irrelevant in the face of his infectious passion for art. He will be greatly missed by his many friends and most particularly by Eliza Sample whose life will not be the same without him.'

That was true. It might be melodramatic but it *was* true. There were times in her life when a cocktail of events led her to view herself and her life in a new and radical manner. There was the day when, still a teenager, she realised that her mother's intemperate rages were motivated by marital unhappiness rather than by Eliza's failings. Years later, there was the night she went downstairs to find the husband

198

she adored asleep on the sofa. Stephen was a complex, fascinating man who worked too hard and cared too much. She had often come downstairs to find him sprawled against the cushions, reeking of whisky, his mouth wide open and a thin line of spittle trailing down his chin. On this particular occasion, she stared at him with a strange, almost detached understanding that her passion and her sacrifices had been wasted on a weak alcoholic whose charisma and charm, still evident in public, had diminished and would continue to diminish at home.

The notice of Dennis's death had triggered another revelation. She was lonely. She saw old friends like June so rarely not because they were dull but because she was jealous, jealous of their husbands if they had them, and jealous of their children and their grandchildren.

Dennis was the first true companion she had made in years. At a stage in her life when friends seemed to die with worrying regularity, a new one was a prize indeed. She had known he would have come to tea if he could. Every Thursday since, she had haunted the National Gallery, drifting through the rooms like a disembodied ghost, unable to settle in any of them, waiting for him to appear so he could tell her he'd lost her address or had been struck down with flu, hoping he would take her arm, ready to show her some new ancient glory.

After each of their mornings together, she had gone home with a renewed sense of purpose to open her laptop and attempt to keep up with him. She had prepared with great care for her choice of the Lady Jane Grey picture. 'Do you know,' she had told him, 'that this is one of the most viewed pictures in the gallery? Do you know that the floor in front of it has to be re-varnished regularly?'

She had expected him to tell her that popular pictures weren't necessarily great pictures. But he had surprised her again. He had looked at it carefully, told her it was historically inaccurate, for poor Jane had been executed outside rather than in a dungeon, and then he had looked at her and said, 'It *does* move me. You were right to bring us here.' She had felt as proud as if she'd won the Turner Prize. And now he was dead.

She was glad at least that his illness had been short. She remembered what he had said about his sister. And he was right: it was selfish to mourn, but since he was dead he couldn't tell her so and she *would* mourn him. She would keep his sad little obituary on her board until she ceased to miss him. She would go back to the gallery, if only because he would have been cross if she didn't.

He would, she thought, be unimpressed by her current decline into self-pity and introspection. He had been a man of joyous enthusiasm. She poured her nightly glass of red wine and stood to attention. 'Dennis Woodward,' she said, holding her glass in front of her, 'I salute you.' She felt a little foolish but that was stupid. There was, after all, no one here to see her.

On Monday morning, Freya was cleaning the kitchen floor when the telephone rang. She supposed this was what it would be like for the next three days. The phone would ring and it would be the outside world or Anna or Tess and she had no wish to speak to any of them. Or it would be Felix. She felt a surge of relief as she heard Pam's customary way of announcing herself. She could

200

just about manage to speak to Pam.

'Freya, I'm not interrupting your work, am I?'

'No, of course not.' Freya tiptoed across the wet floor and went out onto the patio.

'I'm at the office so I can't talk for long. It's about Percy. He had a funny turn on Saturday. I checked on him last night and he was fine but... If you have a moment today, could you call on him? He shouldn't be living on his own but I suppose I'd feel the same. The idea of an institution terrifies him.'

'Of course it does. I'll go round in an hour or so.'

'Thank you. You and Felix must come over to supper. I want to tell you all about Simon's plans. He and Naomi want a March wedding. What are you doing on Saturday?'

I don't know, Pam. Felix has decided he wants to end our marriage and I'm not sure either of us would be great company at the moment...

'I'm pretty sure we're busy,' Freya said. 'I'll ring you later in the week.'

Perhaps if Pam had been at home she might have said something, though in fact she preferred to postpone the predictable sympathy for as long as possible. She could only hold herself together by refusing to think beyond Wednesday evening.

She took round some homemade soup – leek and potato, Percy's favourite – and rang the doorbell. She could hear little Serge barking furiously. She should have rung Percy first. But now he appeared and seemed as pleased to see her as Serge was.

'Can I offer you tea?' he asked. 'Or would you like coffee?'

'I'm all right, thank you.' The coffee would be instant and the tea would taste like dishwater. Normally, Freya accepted either with good grace. Now she felt she was in no state to see anyone, least of all provide comfort and care.

The kitchen was not as spotless as usual. The pine dresser had a patina of dust across its surface. There was a half-empty pack of sliced brown bread on the table and a small carton of milk without its lid.

Freya took a chair by the table and bent down to stroke Serge. 'Pam told me you've been unwell,' she said.

'I blacked out,' Percy told her. 'One moment I was watching the News and the next I felt Serge licking my face. I've promised Pam I'll keep this by me.' He held up the pendant he had round his neck.

'Quite right,' Freya said. 'You have my number on it, don't you?'

'Pam's number one and you're number two. The thing is...' Percy's eyes drifted down to Serge who was now draped across Freya's feet. 'I'm worried about Serge – if something happens to me. Pam said she'd take him but she has to go to work every day and he hates being on his own. He's always loved you and I wondered...'

'Of course I'd take him. But Percy, nothing is going to happen. You're tough as old boots.'

'I'm not scared of being dead,' Percy said. 'I feel I'm on borrowed time anyway to tell the truth. I watched Elaine die. One moment she was there and the next she wasn't. Her body was there but Elaine had gone.'

'Oh Percy!' Freya reached for his hand.

'I tried to feel her presence but no, it was just me... me and Serge. So I know what to expect and I'm not scared.

202

But I worry about Serge. He's not good on his own.'

'Neither am I,' Freya said. 'I'm with Serge on that. I promise, you don't have to worry about him.'

'Thank you, Freya. You've eased my mind.' He glanced at her hopefully. 'Are you sure you won't have a coffee?'

'Just a quick one then.' She glanced at the carton of milk. 'I think I'll have it black.'

In the evening, her phone rang and a voice said, 'Freya?'

It was him! She couldn't believe it. Her hands tightened round the handset. 'Hello, Neil.'

'I hope you don't mind me calling you,' he said, 'I want to apologise for my appalling behaviour the other night.'

'It was my fault, too.' She hesitated. 'You might as well know – I've told your wife about it in a letter. My husband's in Madrid this week on business. Just before he left on Thursday, he told me he wanted to leave me. So I'm afraid I was a bit of a loose cannon at your party.'

'You were a very beautiful loose cannon.'

She smiled. 'Thank you.'

'When does he come back from Madrid?'

She stood by the window, gazing out at the dusky sky. 'Wednesday.'

'Do you want to see him?'

'What do you think? He hasn't been in touch since he left. He knows I'm just sitting here waiting. It's pretty humiliating really.'

'Then don't wait. Come and stay with me.'

That made her laugh. 'That's very kind. I've spent all this morning composing a long and very contrite letter to your wife. I'm not sure I can face the idea of swapping small talk with her.'

'You wouldn't need to,' Neil said. 'I've moved out. I'm staying with Rory in Chelsea.'

'Oh, I'm so sorry! Now *I* feel guilty.'

'It's not your fault. We should never have had the party. Things haven't been right for a long time. So, there you are. Come to London.'

'You *are* joking, aren't you? I've known you for five minutes! Can you imagine what your children would say, what *my* children would say? And Felix would come home and…'

'Exactly. He'd come home and find you gone which would serve him right.'

'There is that,' Freya conceded. 'I suppose your son's flat doesn't run to a spare room?'

'It does and I would be delighted to share it. The bed is very comfortable.'

She couldn't help smiling. 'You are a very wicked man.'

'You have only to ring and I'll meet you off the train.'

'Thank you. It's out of the question but you've made me feel better.'

'I could make you feel all sorts of things if only you'd let me.'

'Neil! I'm ringing off now.'

'Can I talk to you again soon?'

She said, 'This is silly! You know nothing about me.'

'I'd like to rectify that. Ring me if you change your mind.'

She wouldn't, of course, but she *did* feel better. As

Felix had often said, she was a sucker for flattery. She wondered what Neil would say if she took him up on his offer. She suspected he'd be appalled.

Whenever she could, Freya set aside Tuesday mornings for Ivy. Today, Ivy was in an odd mood: fretful, easily distracted. There was no talk of Marilyn. She'd had some phone calls, she said, but she couldn't remember why. At breakfast she'd eaten sausages and they'd disagreed with her. Freya talked brightly about favourite breakfasts: fresh fruit salad, she suggested, with homemade yoghurt and strong black coffee. And then Ivy said quite suddenly, 'Where is Felix? He should be here!'

Freya was surprised into silence and then her eyes began to smart and all she could do was to press Ivy's hand and agree that, 'Yes, he should be!'

On the drive home, she marvelled at Ivy's extraordinary lapse into her old perceptive sanity. But of course it was no such thing. From time to time Ivy's brain flared into life like a brief, beautiful firework, offering a tormenting glimpse of what had been lost.

Freya had planned to stop in Darrowbridge for eggs but Dulcie Makepeace stood on the pavement, chatting to a friend; she was in no mood to make conversation so she drove on. She hadn't seen Dulcie since the balloon-debate fiasco. That had been a terrible evening and Felix hadn't helped afterwards, shutting himself away with the television and going off to work the next morning without saying goodbye. He hadn't been himself ever since. They used to go for an Indian meal fairly regularly. The last time had been a few days before the debate. And their sex life was virtually non-existent. The only times he'd shown any interest was when he'd had a few drinks.

Freya turned into her drive and stopped the car. She sat, frowning at the windscreen. The memory was sharp as ice. She was on the platform, accepting with faked confidence the half-hearted applause for her Bovary speech. Her eyes scanned the audience and there was Felix – Felix who regularly decried the use of mobiles in inappropriate occasions – staring down at his screen while his wife was dying onstage.

Everything fell into place. How had she been so blind to all the signs? There *was* no mystery. Felix was a walking cliché. He had met someone else.

In the kitchen, the answerphone flashed and she hit the button. *'Freya, it's Felix. I'm sorry I've missed you. I should be home about eight tomorrow evening. I've been in touch with Harry from work and he says I can stay with him until I find a place of my own. Anyway, we'll talk plans tomorrow.'*

She played the message over and over and each time her anger increased. He had had no intention of talking to her. He knew she visited Ivy on Tuesday mornings. And now he had told Harry from work that he'd left her. There was no apology, no explanation, just a brief, curt message. He couldn't wait to get shot of her. Well that was fine. If he expected her to wait at home in order to hear his 'plans' for their future, if he really expected that, he didn't know Freya.

In the evening, she honed the letter she had spent the entire afternoon composing. Finally, she read it through for the last time.

'Felix, I have gone to stay with a friend in London.

206

There is no need for you to move out since I have no wish to stay in this house on my own. Once I've worked out what I wish to do, I'll let you know. For the time being, I think it's best if we don't communicate. I doubt you would tell me the truth anyway. Freya.'

The letter had originally run to four pages and into it Freya had poured all her bitterness and rage. But actually, brevity was far more effective and dignified. He didn't want her. A four-line farewell was all he deserved.

On the train the next day she sat in the Quiet Carriage, only too happy to switch off her phone. She had the sense that her life was spiralling out of control and she had neither the will nor the energy to do anything about it. Felix had pushed her off her planet and now she floated in space with no idea of her destination. She was Anna Karenina setting off to meet Vronsky though Anna Karenina's husband loved her and Freya's husband didn't.

She remembered a silly argument she'd had with her own Anna, who must have been sixteen because it was then that she started going on about her legal right to have sex when she wanted. On this particular night, she hadn't come home till the early hours of the morning and Freya waited up for her. When Anna eventually returned, very much the worse for wear, she did what she always did in these circumstances and plunged into a pre-emptive attack. 'Why did you call us after women who *died*?' she demanded. 'It's like you wanted us to fail or something...' And she had ranted on and on, her pronouncements growing ever more incoherent until Freya lost her patience and told her to go to bed.

207

The girls would be horrified by her flight to London. She would have to tell them soon. She'd had a number of missed calls from them in the last few days. And what would she do if Neil was not there to greet her? Why had she ever thought this was a good idea? A man who could flirt with such enthusiasm while his marriage fell apart could hardly be expected to be a safe port in a storm. He'd sounded – understandably – taken aback when she rang him. What would she do if he didn't turn up?

There were any number of friends on whom she could call. There was no one to whom she could face telling the truth. The trouble with being part of a couple for such a long time was that one was totally unprepared for life as a soloist. Most of her friends were Felix's friends too. What would they do with a Felix-less Freya? *Their* Freya was a successful woman with a fascinating career, a loving husband and two clever daughters. The truth was that Freya's career provided her with just enough income to buy nice dresses and good haircuts. The truth was that her husband didn't love her and her daughters never talked to her about anything remotely personal. The truth was that Freya was an abject failure. She couldn't even indulge her misery by crying since a young woman with plaits sat opposite her. The woman was reading *Anna Karenina* and was directly responsible for the thoughts in Freya's head. Freya hoped she'd get off soon. She did, at the next station, smiling at Freya as she did so, which made Freya feel bad.

By the time she got off the train she had formulated a plan. If Neil wasn't there – and she was now pretty sure he wouldn't be – she would find a B&B for the night and send a message to Felix. Why *should* she move out of her own home? She'd done nothing wrong. He could go and live with his new woman in some horrid flat in Bristol. She would go home tomorrow and insist that he sit down and tell her the truth.

A kind man helped her get her suitcase out of the train. She wheeled it along the platform and through the ticket barrier. She planted herself near the stationery kiosk and scanned the people on the concourse. She tried to school her expression into one of calm and ease and slight amusement.

And then she saw him. Neil stood, checking his watch, impossibly handsome, his thin raincoat over his suit. His face broke into a beautiful smile when he saw her. He strode straight across to her and put his arms round her. As romantic gestures went, it was up there with *Anna Karenina*.

CHAPTER TWENTY

Tess had had a disturbing dream on Sunday night. She was in the library at the party. Her mother was in the arms of Neil Lockhart. As she stepped towards them, the couple raised their faces and they were no longer her mother and Mr Lockhart, they were Tess and Jamie. Tess could feel Jamie's breath on her face and his body pressed against her own.

The memory made her feel awkward when Jamie rang her on Monday evening and their conversation was difficult enough without it. He assumed everything was settled. She'd told him she'd come back to Scotland for her October Reading Week. As far as he was concerned, the week was already set aside. She was beginning to see that life for Jamie was quite clear-cut. He loved *her* and she'd kissed *him*. Ergo, there was nothing to worry about. All was well.

And he seemed almost indifferent to the actions of his father and her mother.

'Did Mum strike you as drunk at the party?' she persisted. 'She didn't seem to be. At the time she seemed far more composed than the rest of us.'

'Different people act in different ways,' Jamie said. 'I have a friend. When he's had a few drinks he speaks with huge passion about the state of the planet. When he's sober he doesn't give a damn. How does your mother usually act in that situation?'

'I don't know. She gets quite merry after a few glasses of wine. What's your father like when *he* gets drunk?'

'I have no idea. I don't see him very often. I expect he

210

goes round kissing strange women.'

She couldn't understand his flippancy. She couldn't understand his family. 'Has he said anything to you about it? He must have said something.'

'He did send me a text. He said he'd been an idiot.'

'What did you do?'

'I sent one back to say I agreed with him.'

Tess sighed. 'And that's it? Has he been in touch since?'

'Rory rang last night. He wants me to invite Dad up to Scotland.'

'Well, that's thoughtful of him.'

'No, it isn't. Dad's moved into Rory's spare room. Rory's worried it might prove permanent.'

'He and Eva have split up? That's terrible!'

Jamie sounded unconcerned. 'I don't blame Eva for throwing Dad out. I don't know why she ever took him *in*. You'd think his marital track record would raise alarm bells. Don't worry about him.'

'*I'm* not worried about him. I'd have thought that you might be. I just keep going back to that night.' Tess hesitated. 'It was very unnerving to see my mother in the arms of a strange man especially when...'

'When what?'

She said, almost apologetically, 'He does look so very like you.'

'He's fifty-five!' Jamie was outraged.

'Well, he looks much younger.'

'Right,' Jamie said. 'Is that supposed to make me feel better?'

She smiled. 'I'm not trying to make you feel better.'

'No,' Jamie said wistfully. 'I didn't think you were.'

She almost laughed but she said sternly, 'Jamie, this is important! Do you think your father and Eva will get back together?'

'I have no idea and I don't care.'

'You should do. We're talking about your father. You should ring him.'

'You're right. I will. I have things on my mind at the moment. The TV lady has got back to me. She wants to do it!'

'Oh, Jamie, that's brilliant!'

'It's better than that,' Jamie said. 'I might just have got you a job.'

'What do you mean?'

'I told her I have a beautiful, photogenic castle with a violent, dramatic history and that I also have a beautiful, photogenic girlfriend who is an authority on Sir Walter Scott and the Borders.'

There were various disconcerting assumptions in his response. For now, Tess focused on the last of them. 'I'm not an authority on the Borders! Why did you say that? Why did you even mention me?'

'I wanted to impress her. I *did* impress her. I showed her that photo of you with Sir Walter at Abbotsford. She likes it. She likes *you*. When I told her you were a natural speaker...'

'Jamie, I'm *not* a natural speaker. How can you possibly *know* if I'm a natural speaker?'

'You have a great voice and, to be honest, if you can make *me* interested in Walter Scott, you are clearly a born teacher. I know you'd be brilliant. Don't start worrying yet, though, the whole idea may well fall to dust. She's sending one of her minions to look at the castle. I'll give you a ring afterwards. I think we can afford to be a little excited about this.'

'I'm glad it went well. At least, I think I am.'

'You'd be mad not to be. Imagine if you could go on television and talk about Sir Walter. You'd have publishers queuing up to commission books from you.'

'What would your cousin Susan say if she saw me pontificating on television about Border history?'

'She'd be incandescent. If for no other reason, we must make sure you do it.'

'I can't think about this now. I'm way behind on my marking. I'd better go.'

'All right. I miss you. I'll see you in October.'

I'll see you in October. It was like a mantra. It reminded her of Chekhov's three doomed sisters forever going on about moving to Moscow. She felt almost nostalgic about her life pre-Jamie and pre-party. It seemed so simple and straightforward. Now, her emotions were all over the place and she felt like a rudderless boat, veering first one way, then the other.

Jamie rang again on Thursday evening. 'The minion is keen,' he told her. 'They want to do a series of documentaries. Thank heavens for the referendum. "Scotland is hot," she said. She said that a lot. Your Sir Walter was a great fan of the Union. Did you know that?'

'Well, of course I did. I told you that...'

'You see? You're an expert. You'd be on hand to provide the scholarly context. You could wear some floaty dress and sit with your hand caressing that marble bust of Sir Walter in Abbotsford...'

'I wouldn't be seen caressing Scott's head for a million pounds. And I certainly wouldn't wear a floaty dress, it would be quite unsuitable.'

'You're right. Perhaps you should wear a suit and have some glasses. You'd look terrific in a suit...'

'I don't *have* a suit. Why are you obsessing about my wardrobe?'

'It stops me obsessing about *you*. October seems too far away. Incidentally...'

She loved the way he pronounced every syllable. 'Incidentally what?'

There was a new awkward tone in his voice. 'Have you spoken to your mother today?'

'She won't pick up the phone. Why?'

'I tried to ring my father last night. You made me feel guilty. I couldn't get him so I rang Rory. He said Dad met your mother off the train and took her out to dinner. Rory seemed to think she was coming up to stay in the flat.'

'But that's crazy. She knew Dad was coming back. Why would she do that? Why would she want to stay there?'

'I have no idea. Rory treats the place like a dustbin. He might be wrong, of course. Rory often *is* wrong.'

'I'd better make some calls. I don't understand anything. This is all such a *mess*!'

Rory had to be mistaken. She tried ringing her mother again and left a number of questions on voicemail. 'Where are you, Mum? What's going on? Can you ring me?'

She put the phone down and almost immediately it whirred into action. She picked it up and took a deep breath. It was her father.

'Tess,' he said, 'how are you?'

'I'm *well*! *Hi*!' She sounded like a children's TV presenter, her voice ready to explode with enthusiasm, while she desperately played for time. 'How was Madrid?'

'It's a lovely city. There's so much to see. Unfortunately, I was holed up in conference rooms most of the time. Tess, I'm trying to get hold of your mother. She's not at home and I can't seem to get her on the phone. Do you know where she is?'

'I'm not quite sure.' Tess picked up the pack of spaghetti she'd bought and then put it down again. 'I think she might be in London. She might be staying with... She might be with the Lockharts.'

'The Lockharts? They're the couple who had the party on Saturday? So you both went along to it?'

'Yes. Yes, we did.'

'That's nice. And your mother stayed on with them?'

'No. I'm pretty sure she did go back home. But I think she might be with Mr Lockhart now, with him and his son.'

'That would be your friend from the Borders?'

'No. That would be Jamie's younger brother, Rory.'

'I see. So Mrs Lockhart's gone away?'

'Not exactly. Mr Lockhart's moved into Rory's flat.' Tess sat down at the table. She had no idea what to say. 'There was a disagreement at the party. Between Mr and Mrs Lockhart.'

Her father sounded understandably confused. 'I thought it was their wedding anniversary.'

'It was. But they had an argument.'

'That was unfortunate.'

'Yes,' Tess said feebly. 'It was rather.'

215

'So why would…?'

'Dad, I don't know much more than you. Jamie told me on the phone that he thought Mum might be at Rory's, that's all.'

'I see. Well, it's a great mystery but…'

'Dad, I think I should tell you… Mum told me what you said to her before you went to Spain.'

'Did she?' There was a brief silence and then, 'I'd better get on, Tess, I have some soup boiling on the cooker. If you hear from your mother, tell her I'd love to know what she's been doing. Goodbye now!'

Tess put the phone down and pushed her fingers through her hair. What was it with her parents? They were both as mad as each other. She prepared her supper and flung saucepans on the hob in a frenzy of frustration. How could either of them get anywhere when they wouldn't talk to her or each other? On the whole, she preferred her mother's silence to her father's jolly conversation.

She was eating her meal when her mother rang.

'I thought I'd left my charger at home,' she said. 'I found it in my case and now I'm listening to my messages. How are you, Tess?'

'Dad rang. He wants to know where you are. He's tried to ring you but…'

'He has *not*! You may tell him I'm staying with Neil Lockhart.'

'Can't you tell him yourself? He wants you to ring him…'

'I wanted him to ring *me*!'

'But, Mum, what do I tell him? Are you… Are you *with* Mr Lockhart?'

'He's collecting a takeaway at present.'

'You know what I mean.'

'I don't think I do, Tess. I know you and your sister hate intrusive personal questions. You may tell Felix I'm happy. If he wishes to know anything else, he can ring me.'

The phone went dead. Tess stared at it in stupefaction. She had never heard her mother talk to her like that before and, actually, she felt she deserved the rebuke. 'One last call,' she said aloud, 'and then that's it.'

Her father picked up almost at once. 'Hi there, Tess.'

'I've spoken to Mum.' Tess spoke with brisk efficiency. 'She says you *haven't* rung her. She *is* staying with Mr Lockhart and Rory. She says she's well. If you want to know more, I suggest you ring her. I can't keep acting as go-between.'

'Of course you can't. I only wanted to know where she was. That's all I needed to know. I won't bother you again.'

'It's not that but... Look, why don't I come and see you? I can't make this weekend but I could come down the next.'

'That's very kind but I'm visiting a friend...'

'I could come the weekend after.'

'Can I ring you next week? We can sort out something then. I'd better sign off now. I have some soup boiling on the stove. I'll speak to you soon.'

The mixer tap was dripping slightly and Tess walked over to the sink and tightened it. She wondered where he was going and who his friend might be. Surely he couldn't be seeing someone else? It was inconceivable. But then, everything about him at the moment was inconceivable. She took her half-eaten pasta and tipped it into the kitchen bin. She felt in need of caffeine and put the kettle on. How could he sound so normal when he knew that *she* knew what he'd done? Perhaps he *was* normal. And yet, if he hadn't tried to ring her mother why would he pretend he *had*? She spooned coffee into her mug and frowned as she remembered his soup. It had been boiling on the cooker for a long time.

On Friday evening, Tess met Anna for a conference over a pizza. The weather had been beautiful all day and the evening air still retained its warmth. They sat at a pavement table. Anna was at her most business-like. 'Let's lay out the situation. Mum's moved in with her new boyfriend...'

'We don't actually *know* he's her boyfriend...'

'His wife throws him out because he's all over Mum. Then he invites Mum to stay so she can sleep on the sofa?'

'If you put it like that...'

'Good. We agree. And meanwhile Dad is quite happy.'

'Or he wants us to *think* he's happy.'

'I offered to go down this weekend but he's visiting a friend.'

'I offered to go down *next* weekend. He said the same thing.' Tess picked up her glass. 'I think his friend might be a woman.'

Anna shook her head. 'I don't believe it. There's something very odd going on. I think we should both go down tomorrow, whatever he says. I bet you he's there.'

'I can't do that. Rachel is moving out.'

'Is she? Why?'

'She's moving in with her boyfriend and the new flatmate arrives in the afternoon. I have to be there.'

'What's the new one like?'

Tess shrugged. 'I have no idea. We advertised on Gumtree.'

'She might be horrific. Then what would you do?'

'I'd move somewhere else, I suppose.'

'I'm sorry. I'd hate it if Olivia left. How long have you known?'

'About Rachel? It's been on the cards for weeks. I can't say I blame her. Our flat's dark and depressing. Her boyfriend's place is lovely.'

Anna stared at Tess. 'We should see each other more often.'

'I'm all right,' Tess said. She was touched by her sister's comment. 'Will you go down to see Dad on your own? What would you do if he *is* away?'

'I have a key. If the weather continues like this, I'll sit out in the garden all day. It'll be good to get away. I'm fed up with London at the moment.'

A couple walked past them, their arms slung carelessly round each other's waist. 'So I told her,' the man said, 'if that's the way you feel, I couldn't agree more!' Their laughter hung in the air. Tess said, 'Are you still not talking to William?'

'William's still not talking to *me*. I didn't think I'd miss him so much. Isn't that pathetic?'

'No, not at all.' Tess raised her glass and smiled at her sister. 'Here's to *us*,' she said. 'We *should* see each other more often.'

CHAPTER TWENTY-ONE

It was quite something to be a sex-goddess at fifty-three, especially when one's husband had gone elsewhere for physical satisfaction. On her first night with Neil, they made love three times. *Three times!* She and Felix had always prided themselves on their thriving sex life. They would usually manage it twice a week, though in the last few months… Don't go there, she told herself, don't even think of going there.

Neil said he could not get enough of her. On Thursday, she was in Cromwell Road, outside the Society of Genealogists, when he rang. 'Freya,' he told her, 'you've bewitched me. I had a client this morning. We discussed a complex land search and all I could see was my head between your silky white thighs…'

'Neil, stop it!' she laughed. 'How can I concentrate on anything when you talk like that? I hope none of your colleagues can hear you.'

'I'm out on the pavement,' he assured her. 'And I ache for you. Don't imagine you'll sleep tonight.'

That suited Freya. It had been a week since Felix dropped his bombshell and bombshells were not conducive to nocturnal tranquillity. Sex with Neil was the perfect antidote. When they'd finally fallen apart, spent and exhausted, she had slept like a child. In the morning, she woke at dawn and was consumed by panic. Why was she here? Why hadn't she waited to hear what Felix would have to say? What would become of her? And then there was

Neil, his hand tracing her breasts and then moving down, his fingers touching, probing, stroking. He was like a magician, deleting her fears with each caress until all that mattered was this moment, this ecstasy.

She barely needed his wicked midday phone call. Every time she thought of Felix she had only to recall Neil's love-making to recover his magic. Felix had torn apart her sanity and now Neil kept it together.

On Friday evening, he drove her to a small country hotel just outside Oxford. Rory was hosting a party on Saturday and escape, Neil said, was imperative. The next morning, they missed breakfast. They walked along the river and stopped for lunch at a pub with wooden floors and pine tables. The weather was perfect – it was more like summer than autumn – and they sat outside, their eyes squinting in the sun.

'I can't believe I'm here,' she said. 'This time last week, I was walking in London, an abandoned, angry wife and now I'm...'

'You're here with your red-hot lover,' he said. 'Feel free to agree with me.'

'I do. But it's so odd. We know nothing about each other.'

'Ask me anything you like,' Neil said. 'I lay my life before you.'

She gazed at the river. Two ducks bobbed primly along the surface, occasionally dipping their beaks in the water. She said, 'Tell me the worst moment of your life.'

'Oh Lord,' he said, 'I've had a fair share of those. The very worst would be a long time ago. I was fifteen. You know what it's like when you're that age. The whole world revolves around *you*. My mother had been ill for months and that made me cross. She'd always wanted more children and it just never happened so she spoilt me rotten. And then she got ill and was too tired to humour me and I didn't understand. And then she died.'

'Oh Neil!' Her eyes pricked with tears. So many things made her cry at the moment.

'Are *your* parents still alive?'

'My father died two years ago. I adored him. He was a professor of English Literature at Oxford and the cleverest man I've ever known. Most people were terrified of him. I sometimes think I'm the only person who *wasn't* terrified of him. He always made me feel important. I miss him very much.'

'And what about your mother?'

'I have no idea whether she's alive or dead. I'm an only child like you. My mother left Daddy and me when I was seven. I can hardly remember her. She had blonde hair. I remember her scent: she smelt of rose petals.'

'So it was just you and your father?'

'He married again six years later. She was lovely. She's still alive but she's away with the fairies now.' Her eyes drifted back to the river. She must go down to Darrowbridge soon and see Ivy. She shivered. She didn't want to think of Darrowbridge.

Neil reached for her hand. 'It's my turn to ask a question. I want you to confess something. Give me a confession, the juicier the better.'

'I don't know you well enough for that,' she said. 'I can give you one but you'll think it silly. When you met me at the station, I didn't think you'd be there. You took me out to dinner. And I drank too much. I have to confess that that was deliberate. I was nervous as hell. I could barely remember the last time I slept with a man who wasn't my husband.'

'May I say, Mrs Cameron, that when I finally got you into bed that night, you gave no indication of any nerves whatsoever?'

'It was all that wine. It made me forget.' She lowered her voice. 'And actually, Mr Lockhart, you gave me no time to remember.'

'You bet I didn't. I'd been thinking of nothing else for days.'

'You weren't apprehensive? You didn't feel even a little uncomfortable at the restaurant?'

'Oh God, yes. It was the most uncomfortable evening of my life. I was in an almost permanent state of arousal. Thank heaven for the very large napkin on my lap.'

'You are quite outrageous,' she murmured, casting a furtive glance towards the elderly couple two tables away. Either they were deaf or they were very broad-minded. 'Now *you* have to confess something. And keep it clean.'

He sat back and folded his arms. 'This is a big one. When Jamie told me about your website, I was curious. I am genuinely interested in finding out about my ancestors but actually I was more interested in *you*. Jamie was obviously smitten by your daughter and I thought I'd better find out about her mother.'

'I'm afraid,' Freya said, 'Jamie doesn't have a chance. Tess is very single-minded about her career. She's not interested in romantic complications.'

'You don't know Jamie,' Neil said. 'He's like my father.

When he wants something, he won't be deflected until he gets it. If he wants her, *she* won't stand a chance.'

'That's all very well,' Freya said, 'but *you* don't know Tess. Anyway, I interrupted you. You were looking at my website…'

'That's right. I saw your photo and I'm afraid I forgot all about ancestors and Jamie and your daughter. You seemed to smile straight at me and I knew I had to meet you. Hence the invitation.'

It took a moment to grasp what he'd said. 'You asked me to the party because you fancied me?' She was genuinely shocked. 'It was your *anniversary* party!'

'I told you it was a big confession. It was bad. I do feel bad.'

'I should think so. Neil, that is terrible!'

'I know, I know. Can we please move on before you decide I'm beyond redemption? Ask me another question.'

'I can't think of one. I'm too shocked by your confession.'

'All right. Here's one for free. Shall I tell you about the best moment of my life?'

She felt she should ask about Eva – at least find out if his marriage was bad enough to justify his invitation to a strange woman. But if she did, he might ask about Felix and she didn't want to bring him into this setting and this occasion. She had the company of Neil – so much better-looking than her husband – she had the sun on her back and she had the Oxfordshire countryside. 'Yes,' she said, 'I'd like to hear that.'

'The memory's quite clear. I was at a party. A friend was telling me about his plans to build a conservatory. He's a very dear friend but I'm afraid my attention was wandering. I've never quite understood the point of conservatories. As far as I can see, you either want to be outside or in. And then a woman walked into the room. She wore a tight pink dress with the most suggestive zip I have ever seen and I knew straight away that I'd met the woman of my dreams.'

Freya smiled. 'That's so romantic. I don't believe it for a minute.'

'What about you? What has been the best moment of your life?'

'Oh,' Freya said, 'that's easy.' She raised her glass and smiled at him. 'That's now.' When she looked into his rich, dark eyes, she could almost believe it.

Anna had planned to get a taxi from the station but it was such a beautiful morning that she decided to walk. She stopped off at the supermarket to buy rations: eggs, pasta, tomatoes and bread. As she made her way up the lane she tried to work out a plan. She had not rung her father to say she was coming. He had, after all, told her he'd be away. If he *was*, she supposed she'd have to consider the possibility that he had indeed met some new woman, though she wouldn't believe it until she'd seen it with her own eyes. If he was at home, she could then, legitimately, confront him. 'Dad,' she'd say, 'I insist that you tell me what is going on.'

She could no more imagine herself insisting than she could him see him responding. He had always been a private man where his emotions were concerned. He was like his mother. Grandpa Philip's funeral had been a perfect example of their self-control. The family were out in force and everyone was crying. Only her father and Grandma were dry-eyed, their faces still as stone. Afterwards at the wake, the two of them were assiduous hosts, passing round sandwiches, consoling lachrymose relatives, maintaining a constant flow of conversation. And yet, Anna knew, they'd both adored Grandpa Philip.

She turned into the drive and came to an abrupt stop. Her father's car was there. For the first time, Anna had qualms about her presence here. It was quite possible – it was very likely – that her father had made up an excuse because he wanted to be alone. Worse, he might want to be alone with some woman. Why hadn't that occurred to her before? He might regard her visit as a colossal invasion of his privacy. She was almost tempted to turn round and go back to the station. On the other hand, she had a right to want to know how he was and why he wanted to split the family. She went up to the front door and her fingers hovered over the bell before pressing it. She heard it ringing inside the house. She waited and then rang again. She opened the letter flap and peered through it into the hall. She could see a vase of dead roses on the table. There were crimson petals on the flagstones. There wasn't a sound from anywhere.

She took out her key and pushed at the reluctant door. The obstacle proved to be a small collection of bills, circulars and letters. She picked them up and put them on the hall table. The house smelt airless, empty, abandoned. 'Dad, where the hell are you?' she murmured.

She froze. She could swear she heard a slight cough from the spare bedroom. She quelled the urge to turn tail and run and tiptoed into the sitting room. Her eyes fell on

226

the poker in the fireplace. She picked it up and went back to the hall. The house was silent again. If there was an intruder up there, he was a very *still* intruder. She took off her shoes and left them in the hall before creeping upstairs and along the landing to the spare room. The door was ajar. She took a deep breath, tightened her grasp on the poker and sidled into the room.

There was someone in the bed and he must have sensed her presence since he turned to look at her. She would never forget the expression on his face. For just a moment there was a glimmer of hope in his eyes. Then he saw it was her and the light dulled and he said, 'Anna? What are you doing here?'

She hardly recognised him. He had a rough growth of beard on his chin, his eyelids were red and puffy and his hair was a mess.

'I nearly brained you with this,' she said, waving her poker above her head. 'It's just as well you showed your face to me!' He made no attempt to pretend to be entertained by her feeble attempt at levity. She put the poker on the chest of drawers and went round to his side of the bed. 'Dad? What's going on? And why are you in the spare room?'

He hauled himself up by his elbows and sat back against his pillow. His pyjama buttons were in the wrong holes, giving his chest an oddly misshapen appearance. There was a sour smell of alcohol mixed with sweat in the room.

'I'm a little out of sorts,' he said. 'I'm not very well.' He reached for the glass of water by his bedside table and drank deeply from it. He put it back and stared up at her as if he hardly knew her. 'I thought I told you not to come this weekend.'

'I was worried about you. With good reasons as it turns out. Tell Dr Cameron. What are the symptoms?'

'I...' He looked out of the window as if trying to remember. 'I'm not exactly sure.'

She frowned. 'I'm not surprised you feel ill. There's no air in here.' In a few quick movements she opened the curtains and then the windows. 'It's a lovely day out there,' she said.

'Anna,' he protested, 'this is very kind but...'

'...You wish I was back in London? I'm sorry, Dad, but this isn't good enough. I tell you what we're going to do. You are going to have a shower, wash your hair and have a shave. And I am going to make some lunch for us. Is that clear?'

'I'm really not hungry...'

'See how you feel after your shower.' She picked up the poker and then stopped by the door. 'Promise me you'll wash your hair.'

'Nag, nag...' he murmured. For a moment a smile hovered. 'I promise,' he said.

Freya and Neil returned to London in the early hours of Sunday evening and almost immediately wished they hadn't. As they opened the door of Rory's flat they were greeted by the stale smells of smoke and alcohol. In their room, the bed was a mess and on the floor around it there were empty beer cans, a black lace bra and one high-heeled black shoe.

'For God's sake...' Neil murmured.

They heard the sound of flushing water from the bathroom and went out to see Rory emerge with a white face and red eyes. He wore pyjama bottoms and a dirty white T-shirt and looked like death would be welcome.

'Hi there,' he said weakly. 'I've been trying to clear up but I don't feel too well.'

'Rory,' Neil said, 'there've been people in our bedroom. You could have spared our bedroom.'

'I'm sorry.' Rory put a hand to his stomach. 'I thought I'd do the kitchen first...'

'Neil,' Freya said, 'the poor boy's *ill*...'

'The poor boy,' Neil said, 'has had the whole day to sort this out.'

'I was celebrating,' Rory said. 'I have a recall in the morning. It could be a breakthrough.'

'I very much doubt it,' Neil said. 'If you look like you do now, they'll...'

'He'll be fine,' Freya said. 'What time is the audition?'

Rory frowned. 'I think... It's half past ten.'

'Good,' Freya said. 'Go to bed. I'll bring you water and you must try to drink it. In the morning I'll give you a big breakfast. I'll sort out the flat tomorrow. Do you have clean sheets?'

Rory nodded. 'In your room. In the cupboard.'

'Excellent. Off you go now.'

'Freya,' Rory said, 'you are a total angel. Please never leave.' He turned and walked with great care to his bedroom.

Neil shook his head. 'I don't believe this.'

'At least he's done the kitchen,' Freya said.

It was difficult to see what it was that Rory had done.

The vinyl floor was sticky and damp. Every available surface was covered with glasses, ashtrays, pieces of baguette, bottles and cans. On the cooker, a big saucepan had the remains of a noxious-looking curry. Another pan had congealed wads of rice.

'I'll tell you what we'll do,' Freya said. 'If you change the sheets in our room, I'll make a start in here. I'll tackle the rest of the place tomorrow.'

Neil went across to her and took her hands in his. 'I don't deserve you,' he said. 'And Rory *certainly* doesn't.'

CHAPTER TWENTY-TWO

'So what exactly is wrong with him?' Tess sounded bemused.

A woman and her child wanted the lavatory and Anna moved away towards the door of the train. 'He *says* it's flu but it didn't look like that to me. I think it's a case of acute depression. I made him promise he'd call the doctor first thing tomorrow'

'Anyone would think it was Mum who left *him*,' Tess said. 'Did he talk about it?'

'Only to say it was his decision. He seems exhausted. He got up this morning but had to go back to bed. I took a taxi to the station. Oh and, by the way, I called in on Pam today. I told her what's happened.'

'Oh, Anna…'

'I felt I had to. There's Dad on his own and he's in no state to go to work at the moment. Someone needs to keep an eye on him.'

'That's all very well but if Dad won't even talk to *us*…'

'I told him Pam would drop by on Wednesday evening and he wasn't very happy. So I said it was Pam or Grandma, and on balance he preferred Pam. I had to promise we wouldn't tell Grandma.'

'I have no intention of telling Grandma. She left a message the other day and I daren't call her back. It's all so difficult…'

'I know. And, by the way, I asked him if he'd like you to come down next weekend and he said he wouldn't. He wasn't exactly thrilled to see me. Have you spoken to Mum yet?'

'I've tried. I'm not going to keep hounding her.'

'All right. Let me know if you *do* hear from her. How's your new flatmate?'

'Oh, fine… In fact…' Anna could hear a voice in the background. 'I'd better go. Emily wants us to rearrange the fridge.' Tess spoke in a voice of faded resignation.

'Good luck,' Anna said. She went back to her seat. Poor Tess, she thought. Emily was obviously going to be a disaster. There was one point in her favour. She'd saved Anna from having to relay the lowest point of the weekend. She liked to think she *would* have told Tess.

It had happened on Saturday night. She'd made a risotto for supper and her father had barely touched it, although he'd assured her it was very good.

'So good you only managed two mouthfuls.' She couldn't bear it any longer. 'What's happened to you, Dad? What has Mum done to make you like this? Was she seeing someone else?'

She knew at once she'd gone too far. It was actually quite frightening. He took his plate to the sink and then stood with his back to her. Finally, he turned and stared at her with blazing eyes. 'Let me tell you something,' he said. 'At some stage your mother and I will have a talk. And when we *do*, I have no intention of confessing to her that I chose to indulge your taste for *gossip* and *tittle-tattle*.'

'That is totally unfair.' She tried to keep her voice steady. 'I'm trying to help you. How can I help if you won't say what's wrong?'

'I don't *know* what is wrong. If I find I need help I'll

seek it from a professional therapist not from my *very* junior doctor daughter. I didn't ask you to come here. I didn't want you to come here. And now I'm going to bed.'

She felt like she'd been attacked by a thunderstorm. She'd been wrong to push him. On balance, she thought as she made her way back to her train seat, she was glad she hadn't told Tess.

When she got home, Olivia was sitting with her laptop on the sofa. She looked up at Anna and put it to one side. 'How was your dad? Was it as bad as you thought it would be?'

'Worse. He didn't want to talk to me. He didn't want me there. I shouldn't have gone down without telling him. He's always hated surprises. I felt... I felt like an intruder.'

'Have you had any supper? There's some ham in the fridge.'

'I had a sandwich on the train.'

'I'm sorry you're having such a rotten time.' Olivia put her laptop to one side. 'I'm about to make it worse, I'm afraid.'

'Why? Has something happened?'

Olivia sighed. 'I had Jason round last night. You know he works for Corkscrew Productions? They're planning a short series on holistic gardening and they've found a very hot presenter.'

Anna put her hands to her aching head. 'It's not who I think it is?'

Olivia nodded. 'Xander Bullen. Apparently he has a huge, perfect garden and a telegenic family. Jason says he'll be a star.'

* * *

Rory came back on Monday evening, bearing gifts: flowers, wine and chocolates.

'Rory!' Freya said. 'This is too much!'

'It's not enough but I want you to know how much I appreciate you. You gave me a five-star breakfast this morning and I bet it took you all day to clear up the place. I feel abjectly humble.'

'I was happy to do it. I like to be busy.' This was true. Pam had rung this morning. She'd been quite wonderful really. She'd been short and to the point. 'Freya, Anna came to see me yesterday. She told me about you and Felix. If at any time you need to talk or want my help, you have only to call. I'm going now but don't forget.' And that had been that. She'd been kind and tactful and Freya had almost fallen apart. And then she'd looked at the sitting room with its crumbs and its glasses and its mess and she'd got to work.

'I have to tell you,' Rory said, 'this flat has never looked this good. You are a miracle worker. Can I have a hug?'

Freya smiled. 'You can!'

Rory put his arms round her and embraced her tightly. 'You even smell perfect,' he said.

A voice came from the doorway behind them. 'Get your hands off my woman, you libidinous toad. I can't leave you alone for a minute.'

Rory grinned and released Freya. 'I'm showing my appreciation. Do you even know what libidinous means?'

'It means over-sexed and as far as you're concerned that's an understatement.'

234

'It takes one to know one. If... *when* Freya sees that you're way past your sell-by date, I'll be waiting in the wings.' He sniffed suddenly. 'Is that chicken in the oven?'

'Yes. I didn't know if you'd be in but...'

'Of course I will be! I *adore* chicken. I shall never go out while you're here! Shall we open the wine?'

Neil cast a despairing look at Freya. 'Do you see what you've done? We'll have him round our necks forever!'

Freya laughed. She felt she was in some Noël Coward play with two gorgeous men on hand to amuse her. Who needed Felix when there were Neil and Rory?

Lunch with Flora was always very civilised. There were crisp white napkins on the polished table, cut-glass tumblers of water – with a thimbleful of sherry beforehand. Flora's housekeeper was an excellent cook. For first course there was tomato soup, followed by fish pie and then trifle.

The conversation focused on the referendum. Katherine and Maggie – for once in agreement – both supported the Union while Flora backed independence. 'It's a leap of faith,' she conceded, 'but sometimes one needs to be brave. A vote for Union is a vote for England and the Tories.'

'You've been talking to Susan,' Katherine said.

Flora acknowledged the truth with a sheepish smile. 'She is indefatigable. She's out every night, pounding the streets. If the vote goes against us, I don't know what she'll do.'

'I wouldn't worry about Susan,' Katherine said. 'She's a very strong woman. Are all of your family with the two of you on this?'

'Of course. Jamie's hoisted the Scottish flag on his

castle. And down in London, poor Archie is beside himself because he can't vote. It doesn't help that Susan rings him up to berate him for leaving his homeland in its hour of need, even though he left eight years ago and would have lost his job if he hadn't. Poor Archie feels quite marooned. At least he has his cousin down there, though he has *not* been behaving well.'

Katherine's shoulders rippled with anticipation. 'Are we talking about Neil Lockhart?'

Flora nodded. 'He and Eva threw a party to celebrate their tenth wedding anniversary. Eva's only been up here once which doesn't surprise me. She was so cold all the time. Eventually she bought a thick cardigan. She was a nice young woman. I told her to get her circulation checked.'

'But Flora,' Katherine urged, 'what happened at the party?'

'Archie said it was all very odd. There was a woman at the party, very glamorous, Archie said, but quite *obvious* if you take my meaning. He said Neil couldn't keep his eyes off her and then the two of them disappeared for a *considerable* period of time.'

'On his wedding anniversary?' Katherine's eyes sparkled. 'Can you believe it?'

'Knowing my nephew,' Flora said, 'I can believe it too well.'

'So did they come back?' Katherine asked. 'Did Eva notice?'

'Neil came back. Eva and the woman were conspicuous by their absence. Neil made a short speech in which he thanked everyone for coming. Then Jamie stepped forward and announced that his stepmother had been taken ill and that in the circumstances it might be better if everyone left.'

'Perhaps she *was* ill,' Maggie said.

'Archie rang her a few days later. He told me she sounded very strange.'

'Well!' Katherine said. 'Well!'

On the drive back to the Commune, Katherine talked knowingly about the Lockhart bad blood. Aware that her strictures were received without comment, she said a little tetchily, 'You're very quiet.'

'I've been trying to remember something,' Maggie confessed, 'and now I have. When Tess was with us she told me she and Freya had been invited to the party. Jamie's father wanted to pick Freya's brains about family research. I don't know if they went but...'

'You must find out,' Katherine said. 'They would have seen it all. Maggie, you must ring them.'

'I don't believe any of it,' Maggie said. 'It sounds very far-fetched.'

'Where the Lockharts are concerned, nothing is beyond belief.' Katherine nodded wisely. 'I did warn you about them.'

That settled it, Maggie thought. She would ring Freya who would tell her what had really happened, which Maggie would, with great satisfaction, relay to her sister-in-law.

The washing-machine had stopped mid-cycle. The only clue was the red light that kept blinking the letter D at him.

Freya kept her household file in her desk. Felix took it out and rifled through the various documents until he found the instructions he wanted.

It proved to be quite simple but Felix felt childishly pleased that he'd sorted it out. The D stood for drain and the relevant compartment was blocked by a hard knot of tissue. Well, he thought, he was not completely useless.

He took the file back to the study and opened the drawer. It was then that he saw the folder. Written across its cover was 'Anniversary Stuff'. He was tempted to leave it alone. He knew he could not.

The first page had a title, 'Speech', and then below it a few paragraphs and notes, all of which had been covered with Freya's thick black felt-tip. The second page contained a list of guests – fifty all told – and a sample invitation: *Felix and Freya want you to join them in a celebration of their thirtieth wedding anniversary. Dress informal. Food provided!*

Finally, Felix found a few cuttings kept together with a paper clip. There were adverts for weekends in Rome and Venice, membership to an exclusive wine society, a trip 'of a lifetime' to the Arctic, a place Felix had always hoped to visit one day.

He'd had no idea she'd planned any of this. When he dismissed the idea of a party, she'd seemed unconcerned. Why hadn't she said anything? He knew the answer to that one. Felix didn't want a party. Therefore, there would be no party. He felt unbearably selfish. He didn't deserve her. He had never deserved her.

The phone on Freya's desk rang and, without thinking, Felix picked it up and said, 'Hello?'

'Felix? I thought you'd be Freya. Why aren't you at your office?'

238

It was his mother. Felix stood up and walked to the window. 'Hi, Ma. I'm working from home today. I'm afraid Freya's not here. Can I help?'

'Well, you might. I'm ringing out of rampant curiosity. Katherine and I had lunch with a friend today. Flora Macdonald. She told us a strange story about a party in London. Her nephew, Neil Lockhart, and his wife were hosting it and I remembered that Tess said she and Freya might go to it. Do you know if they did?'

'Yes,' Felix said. 'Yes, they both went.'

'What did Freya say about it afterwards? On second thoughts, get Freya to ring me. You were always hopeless at relaying good gossip. I've tried to ring Tess but I suppose she's working. In fact, I rang her last week – Robert's grandson is thinking of applying to her university – and she never got back to me. She hasn't changed her number, has she?'

'I don't think so.' Felix swallowed. 'Tell me about the party. It might jog my memory.'

'Well, all this is courtesy of Flora's son, Archie, who I suspect is blessed with a vivid imagination. According to him, a sensational lady appeared at the party and entranced the host. The host and the lady disappeared for a while. Then the host returned – without the woman – and announced that the party must finish since his wife had been taken ill. According to Archie, it's all very sinister...'

Felix cleared his throat. 'I wish I could enlighten you but...'

'I knew you'd be useless. Your father was just the same. I remember when...'

'Ma, I'm sorry, I have a client calling me on my mobile.

239

I'd better take it.. I'll talk to you soon…'

Felix turned off the phone and put it down on the desk. Tess had told him Freya was staying with Neil Lockhart. Her vagueness as to the reason was now explained. Freya wasn't staying with the man. She was living with him.

He sat at Freya's desk, staring at all the clutter she kept there: the calendar notepad, frozen on the day she'd left, the jar of pens and pencils, her dictionary and thesaurus, the photo of Tess and Anna on their tenth birthday… And then he saw it: a pink envelope propped up against the picture frame, labelled 'FELIX'. Inside, he found a voucher for a balloon ride over Bath. There was a small sheet of paper inside the envelope and Felix took it out. *'Felix, I bought this for you for your anniversary present. It seemed mean not to give it to you. I'm sorry you've stopped loving me.'*

This was a different Freya from the woman who had left the short, bitter farewell note. *'I'm sorry you've stopped loving me.'* Felix could imagine her sitting at her desk as she wrote it.

He sat and stared through the window at the drive and front garden. But what he saw was a different garden, the one they'd had in Wimbledon, and Xander Bullen in his red hat, pulling up weeds and then smiling as Felix approached him.

'Xander,' Felix said, 'I have something I need to say. It isn't easy. I know how fond Tess is of you and…'

'It's all right.' Xander sprang to his feet. His face was white as a sheet. 'I know what you're going to say. I admit it. I'm in love with your wife. I've made a fool of myself. Freya's been very kind and generous but… You want me to go.'

240

'Yes,' Felix said. 'But not because of that. I had no idea...' Felix was out of his depth and knew it. He could think of no suitable response. Xander looked utterly miserable. Felix actually felt sorry for him. 'We're moving in a couple of months and there's no need to keep a gardener. I'll give your details to our successors here. I have to say though – given what you've told me – I do feel it's best if you leave us today.'

'Right. Of course. I'll get my things together.'

Felix handed him an envelope. 'There's a bonus in there along with your wages. Goodbye, Xander. I hope things go well for you.'

And then, as Felix left, Xander called after him, 'It only happened the once.'

Felix nodded and walked back into the house. He assumed Xander meant that he'd only once revealed his feelings to Freya.

But then as the days went by, the words took on a new and scarcely credible significance. At odd times, Xander's words would break into his thoughts: *It only happened the once.*

CHAPTER TWENTY-THREE

Tess wondered if she might be getting Emily out of proportion. Certainly, the labels were an irritant. The fridge was now full of them. Emily had even labelled her soya milk though Tess assured her she had no desire to use it. Yesterday, Emily brought home four apples, put them into Tess's papier-mâché bowl and labelled *each* of them. Tess had been very inclined to label the bowl, 'Tess's property'.

On both Monday *and* Tuesday evening Emily had colonised the kitchen. She sat at the table, pouring over Facebook like it was the Holy Grail, and chatting on her phone to her mother or her sister or her boyfriend. Worse, she would look quite affronted whenever Tess came in to make a sandwich or a coffee.

When her father rang on Wednesday to ask if she'd come down after all, Tess's first reaction was one of heartfelt gratitude at escaping from Emily. Her second was to question why he'd changed his mind. 'Are you sure you want me to come?' she asked. 'I'm not offended if you don't. Anna said you needed time on your own.'

'Well…' There was a long pause. 'I'm afraid I was very unfair to poor Anna. I was out of sorts but that's no excuse. I'll try to do better this time. Let me know when your train gets in…'

And then, just a few minutes later, her mother rang, which Tess found a little bit spooky. Freya, like Felix, was anxious to tell her she was very well and would love to see her. 'Are you free tomorrow evening? Come over after work and we'll have a drink on our own before the boys get back.'

Presumably the 'boys' were Neil and Rory. Tess accepted at once and prepared to cancel Rachel who'd invited her over to see her new love-nest. Tess felt no compunction about doing this. If it weren't for Rachel, there'd be no Emily.

She arrived the next evening at a smart red-brick building in Chelsea, opposite the Thames. The intercom had five names with corresponding buzzers. Tess was trying to identify Rory's name when a woman with stiff hair and a shiny handbag came up behind her. 'Are you looking for Rory?' she asked. 'He's on the first floor in Flat Two.'

She unlocked the door and Tess, following her in, asked, 'How did you know I wanted Rory's flat?'

The woman smiled. 'It's always pretty young women who want to see Rory,' she said.

'I see.' Tess laughed, though she rather resented being seen as one of his groupies. She climbed the first flight of stairs and stood on the landing, admiring the tasteful wallpaper and the grey carpet. Rory, she thought, was a very lucky young man. She knocked on the door and within moments it was flung open.

'Wow,' she said.

Her mother wore an apron – now, Tess could see it was an apron – with the imprint of a woman's naked torso. Freya laughed and took it off at once. 'Isn't it dreadful? It's Rory's, of course!'

Tess stepped into the narrow hallway. She caught a glimpse of the room on her left. Her mother's silk nightdress lay on the double bed. She turned away quickly and followed her mother into the sitting room. There were signs of a bachelor owner: a poster of Marilyn Monroe pouting at the camera, a vast television, a framed collage of photos of glamorous blondes and inebriated males draped over each other, a big, squashy, leather foot-cushion. But there were also signs of her mother's influence: a jug of roses stood on the mantelpiece, the three cushions were positioned neatly on the sofa and the coffee-coloured carpet bore signs of a recent vacuum.

'It's very nice,' Tess said. She walked across to the window and stared out at the river. 'It's a great location.'

'It *is* nice, isn't it? Let's have a glass of bubbly. It's only cheap but still...'

The kitchen was in need of re-decorating. The vinyl, patterned floor was worn and the laminated covering on the beige units was curling in corners, exposing the cheap plywood beneath. A colander full of washed spinach stood on the draining board, a jug of rice was ready for action and there were rich smells from the oven. 'I can see you've been busy,' Tess said. Last time she'd asked about Neil, her mother had bitten her head off. Tess watched Freya open the bottle and said cautiously, 'So, how's it all going?'

'Well, of course, it's rather odd.' Freya gave a smile that went on a little too long. 'I'm staying with two men I hardly know for a start! But I think it's good for me. I was in a very cosy rut down in Darrowbridge. And the boys are such fun. They insult each other all the time but they do make me laugh. You'd think it might be difficult but Rory seems quite happy to have us here.'

'You're in no hurry to leave then?'

Freya poured out the drinks and led the way back to the sitting room. 'To be honest,' she said, 'I don't know what I want. I mean obviously, soon, I must talk to Felix, and Neil must talk to Eva and we'll have to sort things out. For now, I'm quite happy to take one day at a time. But how are you, Tess? Tell me about *you*.'

'I have a new flatmate. I don't like her much. Mum … Anna went down to see Dad on Saturday. She's worried about him. He looks really ill. Anna thinks he's seriously depressed.'

Her mother flicked her hair back with her hand. 'That's nothing to do with me. He said he wanted *out* and so I *moved* out. It's a little late for him to have second thoughts. Do you know he hasn't rung me once since he came back from Spain?'

'Have you rung *him*?'

'It's not my place to do so. I wasn't the one who wanted to change everything. If I think about Felix, it makes me miserable, and I am trying…' Freya moved towards the window and brushed her eyes with her hand. 'I'm trying very hard not to be.'

'I'm going down to see him on Friday. Can I give him a message?'

'I can't think of anything. You could be an angel and bring back my black mac. It's hanging in the hall.'

'Of course.' Tess took a sip from her glass. 'I thought I'd go and see Ivy.'

'Oh darling, would you? I've been in touch with the home and I plan to go down in a week or two…' They heard the sound of men's voices and then the key turning in the door. Freya brightened at once. 'That will be them,' she said. 'This is such *fun*!'

Neil was charming and showed no sign of awkwardness while Rory greeted Tess like an old friend. She did her best to be responsive but it was difficult to be comfortable with them. She felt disloyal to her father just by being there. It was painful to watch her mother lapping up compliments, laughing at every not terribly funny joke, gazing up at Neil as if he were the answer to every woman's prayer. And Rory's florid praise of her mother's culinary and cleaning achievements soon began to grate. Tess wondered how long she'd be content to be the perfect housewife.

Rory went out after supper, apologising profusely for breaking up the party. After he'd gone, Neil asked Tess about Jamie. 'Have you heard from him recently? I seem to remember he said something about a TV show?'

'The signs seem to be good,' Tess said. 'You should ring him.'

'I know.' Neil smiled and took her mother's hand. 'I've been a little… preoccupied lately.'

That was it. Tess couldn't take any more. She rose to her feet and said, 'I'm afraid I shall have to leave the party too. I have a lecture to prepare.'

'May I say something?' Neil's eyes stared straight at her. 'I know this evening can't have been easy for you. It's not easy for any of us. It was good of you to come and it's meant a lot to your mother.'

'Well…' Tess said feebly, 'I'm glad.'

'All this must seem so crazy.' He flashed Tess a smile. 'I met your mother and… I adore her. I'm a lucky man, I know that. But we've done nothing wrong. Your father no longer wants your mother and I do. I want her very much.'

'Oh Neil!' Her mother leant against his shoulder and put her hand to his chest.

No question. It was definitely time to go. Only later did it occur to Tess that Neil's poor wife had been airbrushed out of the equation. The party had happened less than a fortnight ago and already he'd forgotten his wife of ten years. He wasn't the only one to be behaving strangely. Freya Eliza Cameron had always been proud of her feminist credentials and yet now she simpered and smiled every time her 'boys' praised her housework and cooking abilities. Tess's father's behaviour was incomprehensible and *she* was having sex dreams. Nothing and nobody made sense.

On Friday, Tess was half-asleep throughout the day, the result of a long night spent following the course of the Scottish Referendum. She only just made the train to Darrowbridge and it was standing room only. She was forced to stand in between the carriages, her rucksack between her feet, her body swaying gently against a sharp-suited young man who seemed to think she was touching him up.

'What's your name then?' he asked.

She sighed. 'Tess.'

'I'm Gideon. It's a crap name, don't you think?'

'No. I like it.' She shouldn't have said that.

'You have beautiful hair.'

'Thank you.'

'Some people hate red hair. I don't.'

'My hair's auburn not red but…'

'Don't take offence. Didn't I say I liked it?'

'Well, thanks again.' Her phone rang and she had to lean against Gideon in order to dig it out of her pocket. 'Jamie,' she said with exaggerated enthusiasm. 'Hi!'

He sounded downcast. 'Have you heard the news from Scotland?'

'I'd have to be blind and deaf not to. I'm so sorry.'

'Well, I'll keep the flag flying.'

'Look at it this way. Now the Union's safe, you'll keep attracting English visitors. And it might be good for the programme.'

'That's why I rang. You're on your way to see your father?'

'Yes. The train's packed.'

'I won't keep you long. I thought I'd better warn you that you'll get an email this evening. It'll offer you a provisional plan of what you might want to talk about...'

'But I haven't a clue...'

'I know. Don't worry. Don't answer it. We'll talk about it Sunday evening. I've got a big wedding on tomorrow.'

'All right. I'll speak to you then. Bye now.'

She managed to put her phone away without bumping into Gideon.

'Is that your boyfriend?' he asked.

She nodded. 'We get married next month.'

'Oh.' Gideon shifted slightly.

'He likes my hair too,' Tess said.

'Good,' Gideon said. 'I'm very happy for you.' He said nothing for the rest of the journey.

When Tess arrived at the station there was no sign of Felix. Instead, Geoff, the local taxi driver, stood by his

248

cab waving to her.

'Geoff,' she said, 'is there something wrong with Dad?'

'He sounded fine two hours ago. He asked me to collect you. He probably fancied a beer or two.'

Her father was a past master at sounding fine when he wasn't. As they drove through Darrowbridge, she half-listened to Geoff while he aired his extremely suspect views on the Scots and their referendum. When he finally stopped the car, he told her that Felix had sorted out the bill.

'I'll see you on Sunday,' he said. 'Can you remember the train you're getting?'

'It's the four thirty but...'

'Good, I'll pick you up at four ten. It's always better to be early.'

He drove off before she could question him further. She picked up her rucksack and waved as she saw Felix in the doorway. Anna had led her to believe he'd resemble a tramp. He looked thinner and pale but his clothes were respectable and his hair was clean. He was touchingly keen to show how well he was managing. 'I went online today and learnt how to make pastry and so tonight we have ham and mushroom pie made with my own fair hands. I was about to start work on the beans.'

'I can help with them,' Tess said. The house was aired – 'It's like the Black Hole of Calcutta,' Anna had warned – and in the kitchen the beans were ready and waiting.

The house phone rang and Tess could have sworn that Felix flinched. She picked it up and rather quickly wished she had not.

Grandma was in no mood for small talk. 'I presume

you're with your father,' she said. 'At least I have the chance to speak to you at last.'

'Grandma, I'm so sorry. I have meant to ring you...' She threw a glance at her father who reacted by shaking his head vehemently and pulling a bottle of wine from the fridge. 'The thing is we're about to eat supper.'

Grandma was implacable. 'It can wait. This afternoon, Katherine spoke to Archie's wife, Sally.'

'Who's Archie?' Tess asked. 'And who's Sally?'

'They are relatives of Neil Lockhart and they were guests at his anniversary party... Are you still there?'

'Yes, Grandma.'

'Sally told Katherine that Neil has left his wife to go off with a woman called Freya Cameron. Now I hope I'm wrong, but am I right to assume she was talking about your mother?'

'Well yes, I suppose she was...'

'But I don't understand. I thought she'd never met him before the party.'

'That's right. You see... She was in a bit of a state...'

'*Why?*'

Tess gave up. 'I have Dad right here. I think you'd better ask *him.*'

Felix had just poured two very large glasses of wine and he looked at Tess in horror. She didn't care. She handed him the phone and picked up her glass.

'Ma,' Felix said, 'how nice to talk to you again...' He stood up and began pacing the kitchen, pushing his hands through his hair. 'No, of course I mean it... I didn't want to worry you... No, I'm fine. I told Freya before the party that I wanted us to separate... Of course I'm telling you the truth... I really can't explain it now... No, absolutely not, I'm deluged with work which I'm trying to do, so I can get up to Scotland to see you in a few weeks' time... Yes of course I still want to come. I'm very much looking forward to it. We can talk about things then... You mustn't be cross with Tess. I asked her not to tell you. I wanted... I wanted to tell you in my own time and to be perfectly honest this isn't it. Tess has just come down from London, dinner's getting cold and I'd rather talk to you about this, face to face... I'm sure you're concerned and I appreciate that but both Tess and I know very little about Freya's movements at present and... Ma, I do *not* want to talk at the moment, I'll see you soon.'

Tess had begun preparing the beans. When her father finished his call, she put down her knife for a few moments before taking it up again and continuing with her job.

Felix picked up a saucepan and then slammed it down on the hob. He said, 'I can't cope with my mother at the moment.'

Tess raised her eyebrows. 'You made that pretty obvious.'

'The rumour-mills are working overtime up there.' Felix pulled up a chair beside Tess. 'Can you leave the beans for a moment? I would be grateful if you could tell me exactly what *did* happen at the party?'

Tess put down her knife. She wondered if her father had asked her down here in order to ask her that question. 'Mr Lockhart wanted to show Mum a picture of his ancestor in his library. Mrs Lockhart asked Jamie and me to tell them to come back to the party and then she came with us, which was a pity because we found Mr Lockhart kissing Mum.'

'I see.' Felix gave a rough laugh. 'Your mother is amazing. A week after she despatches her husband, she moves in with another man.'

'Mum didn't despatch you. *You* despatched *her*. I had supper with her and Mr Lockhart on Wednesday. Mr Lockhart said that you didn't want Mum and he did. He has a point.'

Felix pushed his hands in the pockets of his trousers. 'What's he like? Tall, dark and handsome?'

'Yes to all three,' Tess said. She was in no mood to be gentle with him. He was being quite irrational and she hated upsetting Grandma.

'Is your mother happy?'

'What do *you* think, Dad?'

'I mean, do you think she's happy with *him*?'

'She says she is.'

'Well.' Felix stood up and walked across to the window.

'Dad, you can hardly blame her for…'

'I don't.'

'Good.' Tess picked up her knife and began again to cut the beans. 'I thought I'd go and see Ivy in the morning. Will you drive me over there?'

'You can take your mother's car. I'm not in the right mood to see Ivy.'

'It's supposed to be sunny tomorrow. We could go for a walk in the afternoon.'

'No.' Still he had his back to her.

'Why not? It'll do you good to get out. Anna said you wouldn't leave the house last weekend.' She stared at his back. 'Why did you ask Geoff to come and get me? And why is Geoff driving me to the station on Sunday?'

And now at last, Felix did turn. 'I can't leave the house. That's why I'm on sick leave.'

Tess frowned. 'I don't understand.'

'That makes two of us.'

'You mean you literally cannot walk out of the house?'

'Correct. Don't look so worried. It's a symptom of stress or something. The doctor came over on Tuesday. He says it will pass.'

'But, Dad, that's terrible. How do you manage for food and stuff?'

'Believe it or not, Tess, I do know how to order groceries online.'

'But…'

'I'm dealing with it, Tess. Tell me about Lockhart's son. The one you met up in Scotland. What's his name…?'

'He's called Jamie.'

'Are you and he just friends or…?'

'We're just friends.'

'Thank God for that.' For the first time that evening, Felix gave a genuine smile. 'One Lockhart in the family is more than enough.'

CHAPTER TWENTY-FOUR

Maggie had been deeply upset by her call to Felix. Tess sounded unhappy and uncomfortable while Felix sounded positively unhinged. Maggie had a restless night. This afternoon she had taken herself off to the cinema and watched – if that was the word – a film called *Guardians of the Galaxy* that she had completely failed to follow.

This evening, she and Katherine were washing up after dinner. Katherine had cleared away the plates and Maggie had loaded them into the dishwasher. Now Katherine had donned her yellow gloves and was washing the remaining pans while Maggie dried.

'Maggie!' Katherine said, and then again with more volume, 'Maggie!'

Maggie blinked, 'Yes?'

'You've spent the last five minutes drying up that one Pyrex bowl. I know you're upset by all the rumours but…'

'I'm a silly old woman,' Maggie said. She put the bowl down on the table with an air of heavy finality. 'You were right and I was wrong.'

'Well, that's a first! What was I right about?'

'The Lockharts.' Henry the Second had ordered monks to whip him after the murder of Thomas à Becket. In the same way it seemed only right to Maggie that it should be Katherine to whom she should break the latest news.

'Oh dear,' Katherine said. 'Are we talking about Jamie or Neil?'

'Why would I talk about Jamie?' Maggie strove to

254

subdue her irritation and recall her impulse towards humility. 'I rang Felix last night. The rumours are true. Freya's moved up to London to be with Neil Lockhart.'

'Oh!' Katherine's hands stood suspended above the frothy bubbles. This was another first. Katherine had no idea what to say.

'Felix pretends he's all right,' Maggie said. 'He even told me he'd asked Freya for a divorce before the party. I don't believe that for a second. He's always adored Freya.'

'Of course he has. Do you remember their wedding? Freya was the most beautiful bride I've ever seen. When she walked up the aisle with her father, Felix turned round and he looked...' Katherine dropped her hands at last and began to wash the casserole lid. 'I shall never forget how he looked.'

Maggie shook her head. 'The first time I met her I thought she'd be trouble. She was far too beautiful. I couldn't understand what a glamorous model would do with Felix.'

'I don't see that at all. Everyone likes Felix.'

'I know but he's no Cary Grant. She could have had her pick of any number of beautiful young men.'

'But she wanted *him*,' Katherine said. 'And they've always seemed so happy. Why would she leave her marriage to go off with a stranger? It doesn't make sense. Perhaps Felix *did* say something to her beforehand. It's not like him to tell lies.'

'You didn't hear him on the phone. He was absolutely fine. He was very happy. He was busy with work. He did promise he'd come up here soon but I'm not even sure he meant *that*. I feel so guilty. If I hadn't pressed Tess to come with us to Flora's party in May, she'd not have met Jamie, and Freya wouldn't have met his father.'

'That's ridiculous,' Katherine said. 'No one could predict this would happen.'

'You did.'

'I did no such thing. If Freya ran off with Neil Lockhart, she must have had some compelling reason to do so. A woman in her fifties does not walk out of a happy marriage in order to follow a stranger to London.'

'She might if he were very... desirable.'

'Nonsense. Can you imagine either of us doing that?'

'No,' Maggie said, 'but then we weren't deluged with offers by gorgeous admirers.'

Katherine sniffed. 'Speak for yourself,' she said.

Tess would never forget saying goodbye to her father. He stood impotently in the doorway while she climbed into Geoff's taxi. He gave a buoyant wave that was utterly at odds with the frustration in his eyes. She was going back to London while he was literally imprisoned in his house.

On the train, she sat trying to digest everything that had happened. She still didn't know why he'd created this mess. She wasn't even sure that *he* knew. None of it made sense. If he wanted to leave his wife, why would he care so deeply – and he obviously *did* – about the fact that she had moved in with someone else? And, meanwhile, here was she, stuck in a no-man's land, aware that she was deeply attached to Jamie, which was in itself an impossible state of affairs and now made more so by the undeniable fact that her father hated all men called Lockhart.

She began to flick through her emails and found the one

Jamie had told her about. A woman called Geraldine wanted – '*asap please!*' – a five-hundred-word analysis of Scott's influence on Scotland. She also wanted to meet Tess in person, presumably to see if she was as perfect as Jamie had told her. There was an email from Jamie to say he'd met a local historian who Tess would like. He ended with a cheery *See you soon!*

Her phone went. She pulled it from her bag and answered it without checking the caller, which was a big mistake since of all the people in the world she least wanted to talk to right now, Richard the Lunger was probably top of her list.

'Thank you for not hanging up.' His voice was stiff and formal.

'Hi, Richard, how are you?'

And now the words came out in a torrent. 'I want to talk to you. Actually, I want to talk *at* you, if that's all right with you. You see I've been thinking about you for quite a long time and I feel – I do feel quite sincerely – that you need to know a few things. You and I saw each other for over a year. We went out together, we rang each other, you were pleased to see me, I was pleased to see you and then, when I eventually do the obvious next step, which any other man would have done long before by the way, you treat me like I'm some sort of pervert and I am *not* a pervert...'

'I never thought you were...'

'Yes, you did, or if you didn't you looked as if you did and I honestly think you're quite fucked up or else you have no idea how a man might feel when a woman he cares for can't bear him to show even the slightest display of affection. You hit me! I mean, you really hit me! The point

257

is, Tess, if you don't like men you should stay away from them because it's not fair to make them feel guilty when they've done nothing wrong and… That's all I wanted to say. I just wanted you to know.'

'Can I speak now?' Tess glanced round the carriage. The only other occupants were an elderly couple in the aisle opposite her and they were both absorbed by their magazines. 'One: we saw each other a lot because I thought we were friends. Two: I never knew that friendship between a man and a woman had to include sex as well. Three: if you thought it did, you should have told me long before you lunged at me. Four: next time you meet a girl you like, don't blame her if she doesn't want to have sex with you. It isn't obligatory. I'm sorry you're so angry but I refuse to let you make *me* feel guilty because I don't happen to want to go to bed with you.'

There was a long silence and then Richard said, 'All right. I'm going now.'

Tess put the phone down. Her eyes were drawn across the aisle. The woman smiled at Tess, gave her a thumbs-up sign and continued to read her magazine. Tess gazed out of the window. She meant what she'd said to Richard. She had never given him any indication that she'd wanted more than a platonic relationship. And that pious comment – if you don't like men you should stay away from them – was just pathetic. As the train continued on its way, the words *stay away* seemed to merge with the rhythmic sound of the engine and continued to beat inside her head like a gentle hammer against her skull.

Freya and Neil sat finishing their bottle of wine while

watching the first episode of the new *Downton Abbey* series. This was Freya's choice and one that Neil found incomprehensible; he kept pointing out anachronisms of speech and the excessive use of pauses. When they heard voices in the hall, he sat up immediately, his eyes bright with curiosity. Rory had not returned home from a party last night.

Now, he came into the sitting room, radiating smells of beer and tobacco. 'Hello, lovebirds. Can I introduce you to Hayley? Hayley, this is Neil, my dad, and this is his beautiful lady, Freya, who looks after us both.'

Hayley raised a hand and waved it without much enthusiasm. 'Hi, Neil. Hi, Freya.' Hayley had long black hair and a spiky fringe which finished just above her kohl-lined eyes. She had a small nose, an enormous mouth and, Freya thought, a rather weak chin. She wore a small black leather mini-skirt and a long-sleeved close-fitting black top under which a pair of generous-sized breasts strove to escape.

Rory said carelessly, 'We're tired so we're going straight to bed. Goodnight.' As they went out of the room, his hand caressed Hayley's backside.

Neil's eyes followed Hayley out of the room. 'I have to say,' he murmured, 'I have never seen Rory look *less* tired. I can't say I blame him.'

Freya thought about pointing out the girl's weak chin but decided that Neil might misconstrue what was simply an interested observation. Instead, she agreed a little stiffly that Hayley was very striking and then suggested that, since *Downton Abbey* had just this moment ended, Neil might like to help her wash up the dinner things.

Neil downed the rest of his wine, put the glass down on the table and took Freya's face in his hands. 'Hayley doesn't have what you have.'

'That's true,' Freya said. 'She doesn't have my years.' She felt quite sad: sad and old.

'If I were a wine expert, I'd say she's like a young, transparent little Riesling. Personally, I prefer a mature red Rioja anytime.'

Freya finished the last of her wine. 'You're a smooth-talking bastard, Mr Lockhart.'

'I mean it.' Neil took her glass from her hand and put it down beside his own. 'Personally, I feel like a taste of my mature, red Rioja right away. The washing-up can wait.'

Over breakfast the next morning, Freya asked if she should make scrambled eggs for Hayley, but Rory said she was still asleep. 'She's doing an audition at two,' he said, 'so she'll probably spend the morning in bed. You just carry on as usual. She can let herself out.' He finished his coffee, stood up and kissed Freya's cheek. 'How do you always look so lovely at this time of the morning?'

'Because she *is* lovely,' Neil said. He kissed Freya's other cheek. 'Thank you for a fabulous breakfast, have a great day and remember I love you.'

'I love you too,' Freya said, her good humour thoroughly restored after last night's temporary blip. It had been silly to feel so discomfited by Hayley's presence. She was just a girl, after all, who would go the way of all the pretty girls in Rory's life. It had been ridiculous to expect Neil *not* to notice Hayley's breasts. He had given delightfully satisfying evidence last night that she, rather than Hayley, was the object of his love and his lust.

She spent longer than usual clearing up after breakfast and the night before, and it was some time before she settled down to write an article she had been commissioned to write for a Sunday magazine supplement. Her subject was the difficulties thrown up by discovering new relatives when researching one's ancestors, and she wanted to create something punchy as well as informative.

She had finally thought of a good opening sentence when Hayley entered the sitting room, dressed in one of Rory's T-shirts, and raised a hand to give the same sort of vague wave she'd given the night before. 'Is it all right if I have a shower?'

'Of course,' Freya said. 'You'll find towels in the cupboard in the hall. Did you sleep well?'

'When you share a bed with Rory,' Hayley said, 'you don't do a lot of sleeping.'

Freya wasn't sure whether to give a knowing laugh or a sympathetic smile. She didn't feel like giving either. Fortunately, Hayley didn't seem to expect a response since she drifted out of the room as lifelessly as she'd drifted into it and a few minutes later, Freya heard the sound of the shower. She turned her attention back to her laptop and realised she had now forgotten the brilliant first sentence she'd been about to put down. After deleting at least eight alternatives, she finally thought of one that was a little pedestrian but would have to do: 'All relationships should be handled with care, new ones as much as old.' She glanced at her watch. Hayley had been in the shower for ages. At this rate there would be no hot water left. Only when she heard the shower stop and the consequent opening of the bathroom door did she return to her article.

There was something about Hayley's presence in the flat that made concentration difficult. She had only written a couple of paragraphs when she heard Hayley banging around in the kitchen, presumably preparing herself either a late breakfast or an early lunch. Freya felt very strongly that she should not intervene. It wasn't as if Hayley had asked for help. Eventually the noise in the kitchen stopped and then some time later, Hayley emerged in her clothes from the night before and said, 'I'm off now. See you soon,' and left without waiting for a response, almost as if she had already forgotten her.

As soon as the door closed behind her, Freya went through to the bathroom and pursed her lips. There were little pools of water on the floor and the wet towel had been thrown in a heap in the corner. The kitchen was even worse. It was clear that, in Hayley's eyes at least, Freya was just a housekeeper. There was a dirty frying pan on the hob and a sink full of dirty plates, cups and cutlery. A half-empty bag of mushrooms sat on the chopping board along with the innards of the green pepper Freya had been reserving for the evening supper. On close examination of the fridge, she noted that the last of her fruit yoghurts had gone. It was too bad and Freya very much hoped she'd never see her again.

Her hope was dashed later that evening when Rory turned up with Hayley while she and Neil were watching a film. Rory disappeared into the kitchen and came into the sitting room a few minutes later with a couple of generous-sized bacon sandwiches. He yelled to Hayley who came in, wearing Rory's T-shirt. Hayley sat next to Neil and put her long bare legs up on the coffee table while she ate.

Later, in bed with Neil, Freya told him that Rory and Hayley had left a big mess in the kitchen. Neil sighed and said Rory was hopeless. She should leave him to do his own clearing up. The trouble was, as Neil knew very well, Freya cared far more about a clean kitchen than Rory did.

The next morning, over breakfast, she did say a little playfully to Rory that he and Hayley had forgotten to wash their things up the night before and that if he washed up as he went along, he would find that it only took half the time to do.

'You sound like my mother,' Rory told her good-naturedly. 'I know I'm a slob. So is Hayley. I'll tell her we have to do better in future.'

Freya didn't know which part of Rory's response was the more annoying, the comment that she was like his mother or the implication that Hayley was going to be around for a while. She and Neil went out for dinner that night and the main subject of conversation was a result of the unwelcome discovery Freya had made before they left the flat. She had spent some time getting changed and had emerged from the bedroom to find Neil, Hayley and Rory on the sofa, watching television. Rory and Hayley were eating a fry-up on trays. Slipping into the kitchen for a quick glass of water, she had taken one look at the sink and blanched.

As they ate their meal, she tried to make Neil see the delicacy of her situation. 'I am living in Rory's flat,' she said. 'I can't nag him about cleaning his kitchen when it *is* his kitchen. I'm not even paying any rent. I was happy to clear up after him when he was on his own because I felt it was my contribution. But it's different if I'm going to be cleaning up after him *and* Hayley. It doesn't seem fair.'

'I'll have a talk with him,' Neil said. 'Not that he listens to anything I say.'

Freya sighed. 'It's been fun to stay here, but it can't go on. I have to start thinking about my future. Felix said I could keep the house in Darrowbridge and...'

'Freya,' Neil said, 'I don't want you to go back to Darrowbridge. I want us to be together.'

'That's very sweet but not terribly practical.'

'Why not? We'll rent a small little love-nest of our own.'

'Well, if you're serious, perhaps it's time you talked to Eva. I mean, there she is, on her own in that great big house while you and I are tucked into your son's spare room. It's crazy. She can't be happy there. Perhaps it's time for you to consider selling the place.'

Neil looked startled. 'That house belongs to Eva. Her father left it to her years ago. I could never afford a house like that.'

'Oh!'

'But you're right about Rory's flat. We ought to find a place of our own. Perhaps you should start doing some research.' Neil reached across for her hand. 'Let's face it: as long as we have each other, it doesn't matter where we live. I'd be happy in a shoebox in Whitechapel if I was with you.'

It was on the tip of her tongue to remind him that she hadn't left behind a lovely old house and garden in order to live in some poky little flat. Then she remembered that Neil had given up a beautiful mansion in Kensington in order to be with her. It was a shock to find that Neil's wife, rather than Neil, seemed to be the owner of the beautiful mansion, but after all, Neil was a solicitor and must therefore be fairly affluent in his own right. Besides, Neil was right. They had each other. She would be happy with him anywhere. And at least in a shoebox in Whitechapel, she wouldn't have to clear up after Hayley.

CHAPTER TWENTY-FIVE

Tess's new flatmate had gone home for the night in order to attend her grandmother's funeral. This was a sad occasion for Emily and her family but great for Tess who had the flat to herself for an entire evening. She poured herself a large glass of water and placed her phone on the kitchen table. She took a deep breath, picked it up and rang Jamie.

He sounded tired. 'Hi, Tess. How was your father?'

'That's why I'm ringing.' Tess straightened her back and curled one hand round her glass. 'He's bad. He gets panic attacks if he tries to leave the house. The doctor's signed him off for a couple of months. And then… he found out about the party. I had to tell him about Mum and your father. I don't understand him. He seems so angry with them both. It's like he's totally forgotten what he said to Mum the last time he saw her.'

'I see.' She could hear him sigh down the phone. 'I don't pretend to understand your father's thought processes but I can see why he might feel hostile towards my family…'

He understood. She knew he would. 'It's awful to see him like that. And I realise…' She took a deep breath. 'I realise I can't see you again.'

'All right...?'

His voice dropped and then rose, waiting for her to explain her decision and she wasn't sure she could. She felt she held a tangled ball of wool in her hands and when she tried to extract a strand, the knot simply tightened. She said, 'It's all hopeless, I mean, if things were different, to be honest, I'm not even sure if they *were* different… but anyway, everything's such a mess and I can't deal with you and me and… I'm sorry, Jamie, but I feel, I really do feel, it's better just to say goodbye.'

There was silence and then he said again, 'All right,' but this time there was no question mark, just a weary sort of acceptance.

She said, 'As far as the TV series is concerned, I'll email Geraldine and tell her I can't…'

'You'll do no such thing. It's a great opportunity for you and probably for the castle, too.'

'It seems wrong, that's all, when…'

'Why? Just because we're no longer going to see each other? You'll do a brilliant job.'

'I wish I had your confidence. I wish things could be different.'

'Well. Perhaps it's my fault. Perhaps, I let myself get carried away. Look… if there's nothing else, I'd better get on. I have Martha coming round and…'

'Martha?'

'I think I mentioned her. She's our local historian. We have a lot to discuss, so…'

'Of course. I'll let you go. I suppose there's nothing else to say.'

'I don't think there is. I can't bully you into wanting to see me. Goodbye, Tess.'

She put the phone down. She had expected to feel relief but she felt a sort of dead numbness. She was grateful to him for not trying to push her further. She bit her lip and knew that most of this had nothing to do with her parents' troubles. For weeks she had sensed she was wandering into a strange new country for which she was totally unprepared. Like all normal people, Jamie wanted sex. She supposed that a very small part of her – the sleeping, subconscious, sex-obsessed part – wanted it too. The trouble was that the having-sex-with-Jamie thoughts cast ever-darker shadows over the lovely Jamie thoughts. However patient he promised he would be, there would come a time when he'd tire of his fucked-up, or rather *not* wanting-to-be-fucked-up girlfriend. She was frightened of failing him but far more scared of the alternative. It was easier to take the simplest path of action: run away.

There were times when the sheer randomness of her memory startled Anna. Months ago, William had asked her to give Tess a message, a simple task she had signally failed to carry out. If it weren't for the Riddlers, it would have remained buried in the back of her mind, along with goodness knew how many urgent but neglected requests.

John and Amy Riddler had arrived at St Peter's in the early hours of the morning. When Anna saw them in the afternoon, Amy was distraught and exhausted. She'd had strong contractions all day but the cervix was still hardly dilated. Her husband was barely holding together his supportive, grimly positive demeanour. When Anna examined her, she discovered the baby was stuck behind the cervix. 'I'm going to try to dislodge him,' she said.

'Her,' Amy breathed. 'She's a girl. We're going to call her Marnie – if she ever comes out.'

Two hours later, Anna was with them when Marnie

decided to enter the world: a girl with dramatic eyebrows, a full head of black hair and a pugnacious little face. While Amy, weary but happy, smiled down at her daughter, her husband embraced first the midwife then Anna, fervently singing their praises and that of the hospital.

As Anna cycled home, the name of Marnie ran like a river through her mind, prompting a memory that remained frustratingly out of reach. This was not surprising, since her brain was simultaneously conducting a non-stop interrogation into the possible reasons for her father's extraordinary behaviour. It was Tuesday night and she still hadn't heard from Tess, which could either mean that the weekend in Darrowbridge had been a disaster or that it was utterly uneventful which actually, Anna thought, would in the current circumstances be a positive piece of news. Back at the flat, she made a mug of tea and picked up her phone.

'Tess? How was the weekend? You said you'd ring me.'

'Oh yes…' Tess's voice trailed away as if she'd already forgotten about it.

'Did you manage to get Dad to talk?'

'A little. He can't leave the house at the moment. He says it's agoraphobia.'

'Oh God, poor Dad!'

'He didn't seem too upset about it. His doctor assures him it'll go soon.'

'That explains a lot about last weekend. Why didn't he tell me when I was with him?'

'Perhaps he didn't know. Perhaps he came home from Madrid and stayed in bed till you surprised him. I only found out because he'd hired a taxi to collect me even though he was up and about. It was obvious something was wrong.'

'He needs to get help. I'll ring him and…'

'I think you should leave it for the present. He's on anti-depressants and he's got two months' sick leave. He doesn't want us to fuss.'

'Did he talk about Mum?'

'A little. He asked about the party. He still makes no sense. The way he talks about Neil Lockhart, you'd think Mum had left *him*. He hates Neil Lockhart.' Tess gave a little laugh. 'He hates all Lockharts.'

'That can't be easy for you. He must know you're friends with Jamie.'

'Well, I can't be. Not now.'

'Can't you? Would you mind a lot if you didn't see him again?'

'It's sad to lose a friend. You know how you miss William.'

To retrieve a wayward memory was like a long-awaited sneeze. Anna felt all the better for it. 'I've just remembered something,' she said, 'and I must tell you before I forget it again. William asked me to give you a message ages ago and I've only just remembered. He said you were nice to his cousin, Marnie. He said she wanted to say hello. Hello and thank you. He obviously felt it was important to pass it on, but it wasn't exactly riveting and I forgot.'

'I remember her. I liked her a lot.'

'I'm so glad I remembered. It was really bugging me…' Anna went on to explain about the Riddlers and baby Marnie and it became obvious that Tess was paying no attention because she suddenly broke in in mid-sentence.

'Could you do something for me? I don't think I have

270

William's number. Could you ask him to give me Marnie's?'

'I suppose so. Given his glacial silence, I can't promise he'll talk to me but...'

'If you prefer I can call William myself.'

'No, I'll do it. It's a good excuse to try again with him.'

'You won't forget?'

'Of course not. Tess, are you all right?'

There was a long silence before her sister responded, and the silence was a revelation to Anna. Tess was on the verge of telling her something deeply important. That fact alone showed how far they had come in the last few weeks. The fact that Tess decided not to tell Anna showed how far they still had to go.

'I'm fine,' she said at last. 'I have marking to do. I'd better...'

'Tess, I'm on my own here next week. Olivia's going away on Tuesday. Come over to supper and stay the night. In fact, you could take a long break from your delightful flatmate and stay three nights if you like. What do you think?'

'I'm not sure. I have...'

'Oh, do say yes. I hate being on my own and we could come up with a concerted plan for Mum and Dad...'

'Well... All right. Thank you.'

Anna felt quite energised by her conversation with Tess. She would get in some wine and plan a few good meals for next week. She'd enjoy that. She heated a can of baked beans and put bread in the toaster. All she had to do now was to work out how best to help her increasingly mad parents, persuade William to like her again, and be a better sister to her twin. No problem.

She spread the hot beans over her toast and sat down at the kitchen bar. She wondered what it was that Tess had almost told her. She wondered when they'd stopped talking to each other and why. It was probably her fault. She'd been a horrible teenager, she knew, angry with her mother and angry with Tess for not sharing that anger. She'd hung out with bad boys and despised Tess for not doing the same. And then they'd left home and they'd both been busy, living in different parts of the country. Even when Anna came to London, it was difficult to meet up. Or rather, it was difficult to make an effort. They were like two juggernauts steaming purposefully away in different directions.

And now their parents had their meltdown and she and Tess had talked more in the last few weeks than they had done in years. She wasn't sure why it was now so important to get through to Tess. She supposed that amid the shipwreck of their parents' marriage, she was anxious to find some part of the family to which she could still cling. Whatever the reason, it was a weird discovery to make: more than anything in the world, right now, she wanted to turn her vast juggernaut around and find her sister again.

Felix had been on his own for three weeks. He still found it impossible to step out of his front door. He could, however, venture into the garden at the back. On good days, he dug up weeds, looked at emails, cleaned the house and watched TV. He had begun to take an interest in cooking, if only to confound his daughters who asked him regularly what he was eating. Tonight he had made a casserole with diced pork and olives. It had been rather good. Felix put what was left of it into a small bowl and covered it with cling-film. Freya would have been impressed. She loved anything with olives.

He was about to wash up the casserole dish but he made a quick diversion to the radio and turned it on, pushing up the volume. Two men talked earnestly about workplace *issues* and *best practice* and the *bottom line*. Felix found them both irritating but at least they drowned out thoughts of Freya.

He could hear what sounded like a steady thumping on the front door and switched off the radio. He couldn't imagine who would call at ten to ten on a cold autumn evening. He went through to the hall and flung open the door. Pam, dressed in her voluminous grey mac, held a bulging bin bag in one hand and a lead in the other. Percy's little pug, Serge, was at the end of the lead and looked unhappily up at Felix.

'I'm sorry to bother you,' Pam spoke in little gasps. 'I rang your doorbell but you didn't hear me.'

'Come on in. Would you like coffee, or something stronger? You look as if you need it.'

Pam gave a long shuddering sigh and set the bin bag down on the floor. 'A glass of wine would be very nice.'

Felix settled them in the sitting room. Serge and Pam both seemed to be as tense as each other. Serge sat on his haunches, his face raised towards the ceiling as if waiting for a starting gun. Pam perched herself on the edge of her armchair, her back straight, her hands cupped round her glass.

'Percy's not been well,' she told Felix. 'I called round as

273

soon as I got back from work. I went upstairs and could hear Serge whimpering. I went into Percy's bedroom and he…' She took a quick gulp from her glass. 'He was dead. I could see right away he was dead. Serge lay beside him. It was so sad…'

'Pam, I'm so sorry. What about Percy? Is he…?'

'I made some calls. They've taken him away. The thing is… I can't take Serge with me to the office tomorrow. My job's on a knife-edge as it is. People keep talking about voluntary redundancies. Would you mind looking after him until Friday evening? I can't leave him on his own during the day. He's used to being with Percy. I'll try to sort something out. I might be able to take him to my aunt in Cardiff at the weekend. He's a good little dog, he's housetrained and everything. I've brought his dog food and his basket and…'

'Pam, of course, I'll look after him. Finish your wine and go home to bed. You look white as a sheet. Don't worry about Serge.'

'Thank you.' Pam swallowed hard. 'You're very kind.'

When Pam had gone, Felix picked up the bin bag and went through to the kitchen. He took out the dog cushion, the food and the two dog bowls. He filled one with water and set it down near the fridge. Serge padded over to the French windows and whimpered.

'Right,' Felix said in an overly cheerful voice, 'let's take you outside, shall we, Serge?'

In the garden, Serge sniffed around the lawn before finding a place in the flower bed. He looked up at Felix and then, with some reluctance, lowered his backside.

'Well done, Serge!' Felix said. 'Who's a clever boy?'

274

Serge looked as pleased as a dog with a squashed-in, wrinkled face *could* look, and gave an expectant, breathy pant. He followed Felix back into the kitchen and sat staring at him as he finished the washing-up. When Felix had finished he said cheerfully, 'Bed time now, Serge! Come to bed!' He bent down and patted Serge's cushion.

'Good boy!' Felix said. 'See you in the morning!' He shut the door and went up to bed. He thought of poor Percy taking his last-ever breaths with only Serge for company. Felix wished he'd been a better neighbour.

The howling started almost as soon as he switched off his bedroom light. He went down to the kitchen and opened the door. Serge stood, one ear up, the other down, his unblinking eyes fixed hopefully on Felix.

'Poor old boy,' Felix said. 'Do you miss Percy?'

Serge looked up at him as if he knew Felix would make everything all right. Felix couldn't resist those enormous, sad, trusting eyes. He picked up the dog cushion and said, 'Just for tonight, you can sleep in my room.' He went back upstairs with a delighted Serge breathing heavily behind him. He placed the cushion on the floor, watched Serge climbed onto it and went to bed.

As was usual at the moment, Felix slept fitfully. In the morning he reached out for Freya. Each morning he woke surprised to find he was alone. Today was different. This time, he touched her soft, smooth hair. He thought he was at last going mad. When he opened his eyes, he found himself staring into the bulbous eyes and nasally challenged features of Percy's dog. Felix heard a strange sound in the bedroom and realised that for the first time in three weeks he was laughing.

CHAPTER TWENTY-SIX

Eliza approached the gallery like a bullfighter sizing up his opponent. There were to be no more listless meanderings round the place. Today, she was determined, would be different. Today, she would recover her enthusiasm for beautiful paintings. Something would catch her eye if she had the right attitude. She ascended the big staircase slowly.

Twenty minutes later, she found it, or rather she found *him*. The portrait was so big that she had to crane her head back to take it all in. She took a few steps back. The painting was called *Lord Ribblesdale* and the artist was John Singer Sargent.

She was sure she would have loved Lord Ribblesdale. He was tall and slender and very elegant in his Edwardian hunting clothes. They were far more fetching than the present-day uniform of red coat and white breeches. One hand held his riding crop and the other was in the pocket of his buff-coloured trousers, pushing back the calf-length coat to expose his smart cream waistcoat. His top hat was worn at a jaunty angle and he exuded confidence and humour. She stood and imagined the conversations she could have had with him.

Before she left the gallery, Eliza went to the shop and bought a postcard of her gentleman. Could he have imagined that over a century later he would still be arousing the imagination of visitors? She suspected he could have.

At home, after lunch, she sat down at her laptop and

investigated her lord. He had been a Liberal politician and a trustee of the National Gallery. Years after his portrait was painted, Virginia Woolf met him and wrote to a friend that he was very like his portrait, 'only obviously seedy and dissolute'. Eliza brushed that aside. Virginia Woolf was not renowned for her appreciation of men.

She went onto another website and discovered with pleasure that he was generally well liked. It appeared that he was one of those Edwardian aristocrats who were bright and intelligent and knew how to enjoy life.

And then she scrolled on down and read that his father had killed himself, his two sons had been killed in action and his first wife had died of consumption.

Eliza began to cry. It was only after she stopped crying that she understood she was crying for herself rather than for poor Lord Ribblesdale. She made a cup of tea and sat sipping it in the kitchen, trying to quell the small insistent voice inside her head. But still it continued. *I want to see my daughter*, it said. *I want to see Freya.*

On Friday morning, the postman asked Felix to sign for a parcel. Felix liked the postman; he always had interesting ailments – the current one was a dodgy knee that necessitated a snail-like walking pace – and invariably made Felix feel young and healthy.

Felix had just finished signing his name when Serge slipped between his legs and made a dash for freedom. At the same time, Felix could hear the sound of a car and he knew – he had no idea why he knew – that that car was destined to flatten Serge. And then he heard a voice – which of course he knew later was his imagination or his subconscious or just possibly the postman – and it said, 'Save him.' And that was what Felix did.

He flew down the path and grabbed hold of Serge just before he was about to career onto the road and just before the green Vauxhall drove past, going faster than it had any right to in a lane with a thirty mile per hour speed limit. Felix stood by the gate, clutching Serge to his heaving chest and murmuring, 'It's all right, boy, it's all right,' though whether he was speaking to Serge or to himself he wasn't sure.

The postman walked up to him and said, 'That was a close shave. You look quite pale. You should go and have a cup of sweet tea. Add a bit of brandy if you have any.'

'I'm well.' Felix nodded. 'I'm well. Thank you.' He wanted to ask the postman if he had told him to save Serge but if he *hadn't*, the postman would think he was insane and he would probably be right.

'Bloody motorists,' said the postman. 'If I were Prime Minister, I'd ban anyone under thirty-five from driving. That'd sort them out.' He gave Serge a pat, hauled his sack onto his shoulder and walked on down the road.

Felix turned and looked at his door. He put his left foot forward and then his right. Then he turned again and stood, still clutching Serge, smiling out at the world.

On Monday evening, Anna had a call from her mother. It was the first time they'd spoken since the abortive anniversary lunch. 'Anna?' she said. 'I can't get hold of Tess. How are you?'

'I'm fine,' Anna said. Adding pointedly, 'It's nice to hear you.'

278

'I thought I could take you both out to dinner on Wednesday if you're free. I have something to tell you and… Have you spoken to your father lately?'

'I rang him yesterday. He's looking after Percy's dog. Did you hear that Percy had died?'

'Yes. Pam told me. I'm going down to Darrowbridge to stay the night with her on Thursday. Felix suggested I call in on him. Anyway…Talk to Tess and get back to me. It would be nice to see you both.'

'It would be nice to see you both.' Had she even noticed that she'd failed to answer any of Anna's calls? Tess said that Freya was on a permanent adrenalin rush and yet just now she sounded abstracted, distracted, almost as if she didn't know who or where she was. It was impossible to keep up with the vagaries of her parents. Yesterday, Anna had rung her father and could hardly get a word in edgeways while he told her about the long walk he'd forced poor Serge to do that morning. She hadn't dared mention the word agoraphobia.

Her phone went again and she blinked at the sight of Patrick's name on the screen. Her hand hovered over the phone. *They* hadn't spoken since the evening she'd had supper with him. She picked it up and said briskly, 'Hi, Patrick!'

'I'm outside your flat,' he said. 'Can I see you?'

It seemed silly to say no. She told him to come on up and then rushed over to the mirror above the mantelpiece, hating herself for the instant need to check her appearance. When she opened the door, he held out a bottle of red wine. 'Please,' he said, 'accept this as a peace offering.'

She smiled. 'There's really no need. Come on in. Do

you fancy a glass?'

'Yeah, all right.' He looked tired. His T-shirt and denim jeans smelt of paint. His black jacket was worn, with slivers of lining appearing round his cuffs. He still looked like a film star. 'Can we talk? I need a friend at the moment.' His face twisted a little. '*Are* we still friends?'

'Of course we are.' While she opened the wine and found glasses, Patrick roamed round the room, picking up things and putting them down. He went across to the window on the far side of the sitting room and picked at the broken blind. 'How can you bear this? It would be easy to fix it.'

'I've tried, twice,' Anna said, opening his bottle. 'It's not as if it hides a beautiful view.'

'I could do it for you. It might take a bit of time.'

'That's very kind but it can wait.' Anna set the glasses down on the tea chest and sat down on the sofa. 'So what's wrong? I take it something *is* wrong?'

Patrick collected his glass and stood, staring at the unfortunate blind. 'It's Fizz,' he said. 'She's been having an affair.'

'Fizz?' Anna's voice exploded with disbelief. 'That's ridiculous. Who told you?'

'She did. Do you remember coming round to supper with all our "friends"? Do you remember Matthew?'

'He worked with her. He had a sister who was a dentist.'

'She's been sleeping with him.'

'I don't believe it.' She was shocked. How could lovely Fizz, who spoke so warmly about her husband, even contemplate having an affair? 'You must be mistaken,' she said but even as she said it she thought back to that jolly evening they'd all spent together and saw it through new eyes. Matthew was an attractive man and apparently single and yet it had never once occurred to her to flirt with him, probably because it was quite obvious that he had no interest in flirting with *her*. Matthew's sexual antennae, she thought, were waving furiously in another direction.

Patrick finished his wine. 'She's been going out every Wednesday evening for months now. She *said* she was going to yoga classes with her friend, Abbie Spencer. So on Wednesday she goes off to work as usual and I take Lola to work with me as usual, though I'm a little late because I can't find my phone and then in the evening I put Lola to bed and I find my phone in her room and I take it downstairs and then the phone rings and I pick up and it's Abbie Spencer expecting to speak to Fizz and I realise I've got her phone and Fizz has probably got mine – it's happened before – and Abbie asks me to tell Fizz she can't make lunch the next day and I ask her why she's not at yoga with Fizz and she says she's never done yoga in her life and I must be confusing her with another Abbie, and I say that's probably what it is and then I sit down and wait for Fizz to come home and while I'm waiting I look at some of her messages...'

Patrick took a gulp of his wine and then set the glass on the mantelpiece before digging his hands in his pockets. 'So Fizz comes home at half past ten and at first she tries to pretend it's all been a misunderstanding but she knows it's no good, so then she starts crying and says I don't know how difficult it is for her to come home and see Lola wanting me rather than her. She says she can't help resenting me because she's the one who's earning all the money but I'm the one who gets to be with Lola and she says she thinks that's why she started an affair with Matthew and I tell you, Anna, I am standing there listening to all this self-righteous, self-pitying crap and then I tell her what it's really like to be a house-husband. I tell her how hard it is to take Lola to nursery and have the other parents – who are all mothers by the way apart from one sad man in his fifties – and they all look at me in a way that is virtually shouting out: why can't you get a proper job, you loser? And then I tell her there are some days I'm so bored I want to scream, days when Lola and I do the old Postman Pat jigsaw for at least the twentieth time or when I'm walking in Greenwich Park with her and she won't go in the buggy so we're walking at the speed of a tortoise. I remind her I gave up my acting career so that she could pursue all her high-flying legal ambitions, I remind her that she *wanted* me to look after Lola and if she resents me for doing that then she has no one to blame but herself. And finally I tell her that if she ever again tries to make me feel I'm responsible for her squalid little affair then I'll see to it that she never spends another day with her daughter. Can you beat the sheer hypocrisy of the woman? She tells anyone who listens that she's so lucky to have a husband who's prepared to look after the baby and then the moment I find out what's been going on, she uses it to excuse what she's done. I mean, can you believe it?'

There was something terrible about watching Patrick unravel in front of her. It was as if he were tearing at his skin, revealing his raw, naked heart and she was sure he would later regret it. 'Patrick,' she said, 'I'm so sorry. Does she want to leave you? Does she want to go off with Matthew?'

Patrick gave a laugh. 'No. She knows I'd get Lola. She's terrified of losing her.'

'Then in that case you can work things out. I totally understand why you're angry but...'

'You don't understand. I don't *want* Fizz to stay. She's like some alien being. I don't know who she is. I don't recognise her. She revolts me. And that means I'm free. *Now* do you understand?'

'No,' Anna said. 'I'm not sure I do.'

'Way back in May, when you came up to me in that maternity ward, you introduced yourself and it felt like I'd got my oldest friend back. And then you were so good with Lola and *she* liked *you*, which means a lot with Lola. What I'm saying is: you and I are meant to be together. I really believe that. And now we can be. I want you to help me start again. We'd be so good. You know we would. Can't you see us together?'

For almost a moment, Anna *could* see. She could see her and Patrick playing with Lola in the playground, smiling at each other over Lola's head. They'd all live together in that nice clean mansion block and on Sundays they'd go to lunch with Patrick's parents who had always liked her apart from that one last time when his mother had treated her like Delilah about to cut Samson's hair off. And in the evenings she'd come back from a hard day at hospital and Patrick would be waiting with a tomato and basil tart and afterwards they'd sit hand in hand watching a bit of television before going to bed.

Patrick's phone went. He glanced at it and said, 'I'd better take this,' and his voice was hard as steel. 'What is it?... I'm with Anna... because right now I need to see a sympathetic face and Anna is sympathetic... I have no idea... You must see you've forfeited any rights to ask a question like that and I'm sure as hell not going to answer it.' He switched off his phone and put it in his pocket. He came over to the sofa and sat down beside Anna. 'Do you know what I want to do now?'

'I have a pretty good idea.'

He leant forward and kissed her and when she pulled away, he gave her a quizzical glance. 'Don't you want me?'

Anna took hold of his hands and held them hard. 'Patrick, why did you answer Fizz's call just now? You could easily have left it.'

'I knew she'd be worried. She wanted to know where I was. I stormed out of the flat in rather a hurry.'

'But you more or less told me you don't care about her any more so why should you worry if *she's* worried? You answered her call because you wanted her to know you were here. You wanted her to know you were here with me. You don't want to have sex with me because you love me or even because you fancy me, you want to have sex so you can get back at *her*.'

'You've got it all wrong. I told you I've been crazy about you for months.'

'Oh Patrick!' Anna released his hands. 'You fancied me. And you knew I fancied you. You're angry and bitter and at the moment you hate your wife. I'd probably be the same. Except, I'm not sure if you can afford to be very angry. You invited me to supper and we both know what would have happened if Lola hadn't woken up. Neither of us is in a position to cast stones at Fizz.'

'That's totally different. Fizz has been lying to me for

284

months. You and I got carried away on one single evening…'

'Patrick, you know that's not true. You didn't invite me over to discuss Felicity Eggins' second marriage. You wanted to have sex. So did I.'

'But that's what I'm saying. This time there's no Lola and there's no guilt…'

'It doesn't work like that though. I wanted you *then* and afterwards I felt guilty. Patrick, I *hate* feeling guilty. You and Fizz produced Lola who's confident and happy and has single-handedly converted me to the idea of having children sometime in the future. The two of you have made her what she is. I'm not sure you have the right to indulge your very natural wish for revenge by... by wilfully dismantling your family. At the very least, you need to count to ten, or maybe one million, before you decide to cast Fizz into the wilderness.'

Patrick had been sitting forward with his hands gripped together. Now he sprang to his feet and started pacing round the room again, like a lion in a cage. 'She put herself there! She wants to be with Matthew!'

'It doesn't sound like that to me. There may be all sorts of reasons why Fizz had an affair with Matthew but I bet you love isn't one of them. If she loved Matthew she wouldn't be so desperate to stay with you, however much she adores Lola. Perhaps she was flattered – he's a partner in her firm, isn't he? Perhaps she *did* resent the fact that you are the primary parent and I know that's not fair but I've noticed that fairness doesn't seem to count for a lot in these cases. So go home, rage at Fizz – but do it quietly in case you wake Lola – and talk to her and go on talking until you fix things.'

285

'How can I trust her after this?'

'If she knew about you and me she'd probably say the same. Go home and talk to your wife. You're a brilliant father. Do you want to undo all the great work you've done and break up Lola's world? Fizz has been an idiot but at least it sounds like she *knows* she's been an idiot.' Anna stood up and went across to him. 'You need your family.' She kissed his cheek. 'Go home.'

Patrick pushed his fingers through his hair. 'I don't want to go home.'

'Well, tough.' Anna strove to keep her rising impatience out of her voice. 'We all have to do things we don't want to do.'

'All right. I'll go.' Patrick threw up his hands in a gesture of surrender. 'Thank you for your diagnosis, Doctor Cameron.'

'It's a pleasure.' She gave him a push towards the door. 'Go on, Patrick. Go back to your wife.'

'What about you and me? Are we still friends?'

'Of course we are. But perhaps we won't see each other for a while.'

'Perhaps we won't. I'll see myself out.'

After he'd gone, Anna went over to the offending blind. Patrick was right, she thought, it was very unsightly, she really must mend it. She would like to believe she had been very noble in renouncing Patrick. In fact, it was easy to turn down a man who only wanted to sleep with her in order to get back at his wife. It helped that she no longer found him so desperately attractive. She'd realised that as soon as he started talking about the sacrifices he'd made. She didn't blame him of course, but there was something very unattractive about self-pity.

There was also the William factor. She'd left a message last week on his phone: 'Hi, William, Tess asked me to ask you for the phone number of your friend Marnie, so here I am. Get back to me. I'd love to see you. Any time…' She wouldn't ring again. He'd responded with a text comprising a phone number and nothing else.

It was neither fair nor rational to blame Patrick for the end of her friendship with William but she couldn't help herself. Irrational feelings were invariably more powerful than rational ones.

CHAPTER TWENTY-SEVEN

It was touching to see how much trouble Anna had taken. There were clean sheets on Olivia's bed and flowers on the dressing table. There were fillets of salmon and a splendid salad for supper along with a bottle of cold white wine. As they sat talking about Anna's morning set-to with her terrifying consultant, Tess felt her own dramas of the afternoon loosen their hold on her and when Anna asked her what *she'd* done today, she was surprised to discover that she actually wanted to tell her.

'I had a Skype audition,' she said. 'It's all down to Jamie. He'd told them I was a natural in front of the camera so of course I was terrified.'

'Of course you were. What did you talk about?'

'Who else but Sir Walter? I spent a few minutes describing the traditional view of him as a committed old Tory Unionist and then I brought out my copy of *Waverley* – I have it in my bag, I'll lend it to you. Waverley's a hero who keeps changing sides. He can't decide whether he's a Hanoverian or a Jacobite. It's almost as if Scott can't make up his *own* mind. Anyway, that's what I talked about.'

'And how did it go? Did you get any feedback?'

'That's why I was late coming over. Geraldine rang me back at six.'

'And you've let me rabbit on about Miss Diamond! What did she say?'

'She liked me.'

'Tess, that's brilliant! We should be drinking champagne.'

'Yes,' Tess said. 'Yes, it's good. She thinks Martha and I would make a good team. We both have the same hair apparently. I don't know why that's so important.'

'Have you told me about Martha? Who is she?'

'Well,' Tess said, 'she's an expert on Borders history.' She hesitated. 'She's a friend of Jamie.'

'This is all quite brilliant. Why do you look so very unexcited?'

'I suppose... I suppose I'm a little jealous of Martha.'

It was only now she said it she knew it was true. Anna looked as surprised as she was.

'When you were thirteen,' Anna said, 'you had a crush on Xander Bullen. Since then... I've always assumed you didn't really care for men.'

'So did I. I miss Jamie, that's all. I'll get over it.'

'Why *should* you? If you want to see him again, you should do so. You don't need to tell Dad.'

'I couldn't do that.' Already, Tess regretted her admission. She tried to smile. 'I do feel sorry for Mum sometimes. She named her daughters after the most romantic heroines she could find and look how we've turned out!'

'Speak for yourself! I've always found Mum's choice of names for us rather sinister. She once tried to convince me there was some sound feminist reason, but look at the facts! She called her daughters after Anna Karenina and Tess of the D'Urbervilles: two women who comprehensively messed up their lives. A psychoanalyst would have a field day with that one.'

289

'You've always been hard on her.'

'She's taking us out to supper tomorrow. I said we'd meet her at half six.'

'Oh Anna, I can't. I'm meeting someone. I can't get out of it.'

'That's all right. I'd like to have Mum to myself for a bit. I have a lot to say to her.'

'Do you?' Tess eyed her warily.

'I think I know why Dad left her. Do you remember the week before we moved to Darrowbridge? Dad came back late with a black eye. He *said* he'd been mugged and had put up a fight. I think he'd confronted Xander Bullen.'

Xander Bullen. Tess reached for the bottle and filled her glass. 'Do you want some?'

'Oh, go on then,' Anna said. 'Can you finish the salad?'

'No, that was lovely.'

'The thing is,' Anna said, 'I know you always liked Xander but... I've never told you this before... Xander told me once that... He didn't actually tell me but he *implied* that he and Mum were very close. I think that's why Dad moved us all to Somerset. He knew they were having an affair.'

It was too much to take in. The full enormity of Anna's conclusions hit Tess like a tidal wave. She sat, aware some response was expected. All she could manage was to mutter feebly that she thought Anna was wrong. She reached for her wine and hoped it would dull her sensibilities before the tidal wave submerged her.

Anna was the first to arrive which pleased Freya. It was ridiculous to sulk about ill-timed remarks she'd made

290

nearly a month ago. Ill-timed remarks were part of Anna, and a good mother should embrace the bad along with the good. Far better to forget past unpleasantness and concentrate on the here and now. She couldn't wait to tell the girls her news.

'Anna,' she said, 'how lovely to see you. I've ordered wine and olives.'

'Great,' Anna said, taking off her leather jacket to reveal a low-cut black top that Freya would have coveted even five years ago. 'It's good to be here.'

'Rory promised me we'd love this place. To be exact, his words were, "cheap but good". I told him that was my sort of restaurant!'

The waiter arrived with her order and invited Freya to try the wine which she assured him was unnecessary. Now Anna was here, she couldn't wait for Tess to arrive. What would they say? What would they think?

Anna reached for an olive. 'Do you remember Xander Bullen?'

'Of course I do! He's got a gardening book out. Did you know that?'

'A friend of Olivia works for a TV production company. He and his boss are going to see him on Friday. They want to give him his own gardening programme.'

'Do they? How extraordinary. But of course he'll be perfect for television. He's so good-looking and he has such charm. I'm glad he's doing well.'

Anna reached for her glass and took a gulp. 'You were very mysterious on the phone. You said you had some news.'

'I do but I'll tell you when Tess comes.'

'I'm sorry. I meant to tell you. She sends her love. She can't make it. She's meeting someone.'

'Really? Do you know who the someone is?'

Anna gave Freya one of those appraising glances that had accompanied most of her teenage years. 'Mum,' she said, 'you do know she's in love with Jamie Lockhart?'

Freya shook her head. 'No,' she said, 'she isn't. I asked Tess most particularly about him. She assured me she had no feelings for him.'

'I can see why you'd want to believe that.'

This was what always happened when she and Anna were alone together. Why had she thought it would be different this time? Anna would make some gnomic utterance designed to make her feel smaller than an atom and so on it would go. Freya pressed her hands tightly together. 'I think that's a little unfair. You weren't at the party in Kensington. Tess had no idea Jamie would be there. I could see he was keen on her but she looked rather irritated to see *him*.'

'I imagine she felt a little uncomfortable given that you were standing next to her. She spent the whole summer getting to know him. Then you meet his father and in a matter of minutes you fall into his arms. Last week Tess told Jamie she couldn't see him again. She said it wasn't fair on Dad.'

'I don't see what your father has to do with any of this.'

'Well, funnily enough, he's not too keen on the Lockhart family.'

'I see.' Freya took a sip of her wine and then folded her arms. 'And of course this is my fault. Can I just remind you that it's your father who wants a divorce? Felix has no right to have any thoughts about the Lockharts. He made it very clear he didn't give a damn what I did with my life as long as he wasn't involved in it.'

'Dad's always loved you. I'm pretty sure he still does. I think he's spent fourteen years trying to cope with what happened and in the end he just couldn't.'

'Anna,' Freya said, 'I have no idea what you're talking about.'

'Xander Bullen,' Anna said. 'I'm talking about Xander Bullen.'

Freya stared at her daughter. 'What does Xander have to do with this?'

'Mum,' Anna said, 'Xander told me.'

'Xander told you? Xander told you *what*?'

'He told me you loved each other. And I think he told Dad. I think that's why Dad came home with a black eye the week before we moved. I've always known that Xander was the reason we moved to Darrowbridge. Dad wanted to get you away from him. So *we* had to leave Wimbledon.'

For a few moments Freya sat staring blankly at Anna, trying to work out what she was saying. It was crazy, it was incomprehensible, but what was important was that Anna was convinced of its truth and in fact there was a horrible twisted logic to it. Freya shook her head, too stunned to refute any of it. Even if she tried, Anna wouldn't believe her. 'So I'm the villain in all this,' she said. 'How you must hate me.'

'Mum, of course I don't hate you. I'm simply trying to work out why Dad, of all people, would want to break up his marriage.'

'If you knew how hard I have tried, year in, year out, to

be calm and understanding and make excuses for your moods and your nasty little barbs and your cold, polite phone calls and all the time you felt these things and you never said. Why *didn't* you say anything?'

'I don't know... I should have done... I wasn't sure and...'

'I'll tell you what I think. I think you didn't *want* to find out you might be wrong. I think it suited you very well to make *me* responsible for everything wrong in your life. You're a very good hater, Anna. You know that phrase "passive aggression"*?* It could have been made for you.'

'That's not fair...'

'You know that it is. I can see it in your face. I am so fed up with being patient and careful with you and with Felix. I've had enough, Anna. I don't care any more. I give up on you both.' She bit her bottom lip hard and reached down for her bag.

'Mum, what are you doing? You wanted me to talk to you and now when I *do* talk, you won't listen. You can't just walk away every time we disagree.'

'Watch me.' Freya threw a note down on the table. 'That's for the wine. I won't pay for your meal this time. It's impossible for the two of us to be alone together. I can't stay here. I don't know you, I don't know my husband, I don't know anyone.' She pushed her chair back, stood up and then glared at Anna as she tried to do the same. 'Sit down! Don't you dare try to follow me! I have *nothing* to say to you.'

She went out into the dusk, almost tripping over her heels. Oh it was terrible, terrible. She had been so proud of her family, she had loved and nurtured and cared for them and this was the result. It had all been false, it had all been one huge messy failure. She would never see any of them again. And was it true about Tess? Did she really love Jamie? She must talk to Neil, they must talk to Jamie, she must talk to Felix. Felix! She was so sure he'd met someone else. But if he hadn't, if Anna was right, it was even worse. She could never, she would never forgive him. A sob escaped her throat and she shook her head hard. She would not cry. She would go home and talk to Neil.

She was almost at the flat when she heard her name being called and turned to see Rory running towards her. He was carrying a large bouquet of red roses. She stopped and waited for him to catch up with her. She said, 'What beautiful roses!'

'They're for Hayley.' He kissed her cheek. 'We had a little argument the other night. She caught me fooling around with someone. And then this evening we were supposed to be going out with friends. And I got to the pub and she sent me a text to say she was tired and I thought: Rory, you must take action. One, buy flowers. Two, return home. Three, grovel. What are *you* doing here? I thought you were taking your daughters out to dinner.'

'There was a change of plan.'

'We could have a takeaway,' Rory said, 'unless you feel like cooking something.'

'I don't, I'm afraid. I shall make your father take me out.'

'That might be a good idea. I'll rustle up something for Hayley and tell her I love her.'

'I'm sure that will impress her.'

He took his door keys from his pocket. 'Now we must

creep into the flat and surprise her. I want to overwhelm her with my romantic gesture.'

In the event, it was Rory and Freya who were surprised. At first they thought the flat was empty, but then they heard a sound. The door into the sitting room was wide open. For at least a moment – or at least until Rory cried, 'Hayley, what the fuck are you doing?' – Freya didn't understand what was happening. For at least a moment she thought that Hayley might be kneeling in front of Neil because she was trying to find a contact lens or something.

Then Neil said, 'Oh fuck!' and Rory said, 'Fuck you!' and Hayley got to her feet, adjusted the shirt that as usual seemed to be her only item of clothing, pushed back her hair and turned to face Rory. 'I was only doing what your friend did to you on Saturday.'

Rory gave an extravagant grimace. 'That is *so* gross. You were doing it to my *father*. He's my father and he's *old*.'

'Freya's old too. That doesn't stop you flirting with her.'

'I always flirt with older women. It's polite and it cheers them up. I can't believe you would do this.'

'I couldn't believe what you did on Saturday. So there you are. We're quits. Now I'm going to pack.' She walked out of the room, brushing Freya's arm in the process.

Neil sat with his hands held in front of his crotch. 'Rory,' he said. 'I'm so sorry.'

Rory didn't even look at him. He thrust his roses into Freya's arms and went off after Hayley.

'Freya,' Neil pleaded. 'Freya...'

'Do you have any idea how ridiculous you look?' She

296

threw the flowers onto his lap, turned on her heel and stormed into their bedroom, flinging open drawers and pulling out her clothes.

Neil came in and looked at the suitcase on the bed. 'Freya, will you at least let me try to explain?'

That stopped her. She straightened her back and put her hands on her hips. 'I would *love* to hear your explanation, Neil, I really would. Explain away!'

'I came home from work. Hayley was here. She said Rory was out and I knew you were too so I offered to cook and she offered to help and we couldn't find anything so we had a drink and then we had another and she started to... It was a moment of madness, it meant nothing. You mean everything to me...'

'If I mean everything to you, why did you let that girl even touch you?'

'I was a little bit drunk and she's young and she's beautiful and she was very persuasive. It's like...' He scratched his head and narrowed his eyes. 'Imagine you're on a diet and someone offers you a chocolate truffle...'

'Are you saying that being with me is like being on a *diet*?'

'No, no, of course not, you're perfect, you're utterly perfect. It's only that Hayley's so young and she seemed so eager and...'

'And you are disgusting and pathetic and amoral and I never want to see you again because you make me feel quite sick, so feel free to go and eat as many chocolate truffles as you like, though perhaps in future you should stay away from those belonging to your son. Now get out and let me pack.'

'Freya,' Neil said, 'this hasn't been easy for me, you know. I fell in love with you and almost at once we were living together in a cramped flat with Rory...'

'You said you wanted me to live with you!'

'I know and I don't regret it for a moment but it all happened so quickly and tonight, I suppose, was just me letting off steam and...'

Freya put her hands on her hips. 'Let me tell you something. I am giving you the benefit of the doubt here and assuming you *are* drunk because if you aren't you are even worse than I think you are. Let me tell you something else. From now on, you won't have to let off steam because I won't be here.'

'That's not what I meant. I love you!'

'Well, all I can say is that your idea of love is very different from mine. Now get out of this room before I start to scream.'

Neil looked at her for a moment before displaying, if belatedly, some prudence, and left the room.

She marched round the bed and slammed the door shut. It didn't take her very long to finish her packing. She shut her case and wheeled it across to the door. She found Neil waiting for her on the other side. From Rory's room came the unmistakable sound of lovemaking.

Neil tried a weak smile. 'Rory's obviously forgiven Hayley,' he said. 'Can't you forgive me?'

Freya raised her chin. 'I think the three of you are made for each other. I want to forget I ever met any of you. Goodbye, Neil.'

'I can't let you walk out like this. Where will you go?'

'That is not your concern. Step aside.' She hesitated and

then turned and went to the bathroom to retrieve her toothbrush. When she came out, Neil said, 'Freya, please...'

She ignored him. In the lift down to the ground floor, she stared at her reflection in the mirror and saw a mad woman with thin streaks of mascara running down her cheeks. She struggled out of the lift and then struggled again down the steps of the building. Finally, she reached the pavement and began to walk, pulling her case behind her. She stopped after about ten minutes, aware she was on the Embankment.

She stared down at the Thames. What a fool she had been! Neil was not Prince Charming, he never had been. He was a man who was ruled by his penis. He had wanted to have sex with her and *she* had wanted to erase the appalling fact that the husband she loved did not love *her*. She had wilfully disregarded Neil's obvious flaws, she had run into his arms to get back at Felix, she had, in short, made a monumental fool of herself. What was it Rory had said? *'I always flirt with older women. It's polite and it cheers them up.'* Oh God, Freya thought, how she hated herself. She was selfish and silly and worthless.

The water was as black as the night sky above it. It would not be difficult to tip herself over the edge and let the water cover her. If she were Emma Bovary or Anna Karenina she wouldn't hesitate to throw herself in. But she was Freya Eliza Cameron and she would hate Neil to think she had killed herself on his account and there was no pleasure in envisaging her husband and her daughters crying at her funeral as she wasn't at all sure they'd bother to come. For now, she had to think practicalities. There was

only one option. She saw a taxi coming her way and she
hailed it.

CHAPTER TWENTY-EIGHT

Anna had continued to sit at the table, occasionally sipping her wine. When she caught sight of the waiter staring at her, he looked embarrassed. He came over at once and asked if she was ready to order.

'My mother's been called away,' Anna said. 'Will you bring me the bill for the wine? And a cork so I may take the bottle away with me?'

It was ironic that her mother, such a stickler for appearances, should be the one to erupt from the restaurant while she stayed stubbornly here, resolutely ignoring the whispered asides of other clients, determined to act as if all was well. Once she paid her bill, she walked out with her head held high.

As she unlocked the padlock of her bicycle, she was aware she'd drunk a little too much. She cycled back with extra care, concentrating on the traffic around her. It was a relief to impose an embargo, if only temporarily, on all thoughts about the evening.

Tess was still out when Anna got home. For once, she was glad to be on her own. She sat on her bed, her arms hugging her knees. There was no point in trying to defend herself. She had been clumsy, tactless and unfair tonight. And as for the rest, she thought bleakly, her mother's brutal assessment of her character was spot on. When Anna thought back to her teenage self, she saw only resentment, bitterness and bile. As she grew up, she had assumed she'd taken on a new maturity, taking care to ring home with punctilious regularity. Who was she kidding? Her *grown-up* behaviour had been worse than her earlier sulks and tantrums. How could she blame Freya for lashing out at her this evening? She certainly hadn't acted like a mother found out in a fourteen-year-old affair.

Anna's eyes focused on the chest of drawers opposite her but what she saw was the road outside their old house in Wimbledon, and Xander walking towards her along the pavement. He'd waved and asked her where she was going.

'I'm meeting a friend in town,' she said. 'Where are *you* going?'

'I have a fossilised stone for Tess. Is she in?'

'You do know we finished our fossil project weeks ago?'

'Yes, but Tess likes collecting them.'

'Xander,' Anna said, 'you come over a lot, and Tess... Tess really likes you.'

'The feeling's mutual. It's impossible *not* to like Tess.'

'Yes,' Anna said. She wished she hadn't started this now. She was aware that her motives for doing so were mixed. It was true she was concerned that Xander might just enjoy being the focus of one girl's adoration, but it had always irked her that he was so much more interested in Tess than he was in *her*. Doggedly, she stumbled on. 'You know what I mean. And she's thirteen and you're nearly thirty.'

He'd stared at her for a few unsettling moments and then he laughed. 'I'm not sure what you're getting at,' he said. 'It's not just Tess I come to see.'

'Yes, but you don't garden for us now.'

'No. That's true.' He gave her a speculative sort of

302

smile. 'You have a very beautiful mother, you know. Has it never occurred to you to wonder why your dad's so keen to carry her away from Wimbledon?' He laughed again and then patted her arm before walking on and calling out, 'See you, Anna. Take care now.'

Freya paid off the taxi and stared up at the grand old mansion block. There were five steps up to the entrance. She pushed down the detachable handle of her case and struggled up to the big black door with it. She took a few deep breaths and then pressed the button next to the word 'SAMPLE'. A clear voice answered almost immediately. 'Come on in, Freya.'

She went through to the hall and pushed up the handle. A door on the right opened and a small, thin woman stood silhouetted against the light. Her white hair was cut in a short, elegant bob. She wore grey slacks, a green ribbed jersey and a pendant. Her face, despite its network of thin wrinkles, was still beautiful. Her eyes were Freya's eyes but she was a stranger. Freya had hoped she might experience a waterfall of memories and recollections but there was nothing. She felt embarrassed to be here, in this state, with this elegant old lady.

'I'm sorry,' Freya said. 'I had nowhere else to go. It's only for one night.'

Her hostess stepped aside to let her into the flat. 'I'm glad you rang me. I've made up your bed. Would you like a glass of wine? I have only red, I'm afraid.'

'That would be nice.' Freya moved her case to one side of the door. 'Do you mind if I use your bathroom first?'

As soon as she had shut the door behind her, she pressed

303

her back against it and raised her eyes to the ceiling. It was just one night. She would leave first thing in the morning. She glanced round at the white floor tiles and white walls. She went to the basin and stared at her reflection in the mirror. She saw a wild-looking woman with dishevelled hair, swollen eyes and a face streaked like a zebra. There was a glass jar full of cotton wool balls on the small wicker chest of drawers. She took one of them out and began to clean her face.

When she finally emerged from the bathroom, Eliza came out of the kitchen with a silver tray containing two long-stemmed glasses generously filled with red wine, and a bowl of cashew nuts.

Freya took a seat on the sofa. 'You're very kind. I do apologise for my dramatic intrusion. I think I owe you an explanation.'

Eliza settled into the armchair and picked up her glass. 'You don't owe me anything.'

'I'll keep it short. I had a disagreeable encounter with one of my daughters and returned home early. I found my partner in a compromising position with his son's girlfriend, so I packed and left. I'm going down to Somerset to stay with a friend tomorrow.'

Eliza nodded as if Freya's explanation was quite normal. 'I'm sorry about your daughter and your unsatisfactory lover but I'm glad you came to me.'

The word 'lover' issued from her mouth with no trace of affectation or awkwardness. This was not a woman who would be easily shocked. Freya took a sip of her wine and then attempted a smile. 'I couldn't believe it when I got your email. I'm sure you must regret sending it.'

304

'I don't regret it for a moment. I'm pleased you're here. I wasn't sure you'd want to reply. I spent a great deal of time composing it.'

Freya reached for the nuts. She was, she realised, hungry. 'It seemed so odd to hear from you after all this time. I meant to tell my girls tonight. What made you do it?'

'Very selfish motives, I'm afraid. I'm old and discovered I was lonely.' She regarded Freya with unblinking blue eyes. 'I suppose you've had no supper. I can offer you an omelette.'

'That would be marvellous. Can I help?'

'No. I won't be long.' Eliza looked almost amused. 'Finish the nuts.'

Freya had already emptied half the bowl. Once Eliza had gone, she took another gulp of wine. It seemed surreal to be sitting in this stranger's flat but at least she had found the one place in the world that could distract her from the horrors of the last few hours. She had not seen her mother for forty-six years and now she could hear her in the kitchen making an omelette.

Already, the wine was relaxing her. She glanced around at her surroundings, admiring the soft grey carpet and long rose-coloured curtains. There was a small desk in the corner on which sat a laptop and a brass lamp. On one side of the mantelpiece, a modest-sized television sat on an antique chest of drawers. The only lighting came from the standard lamp behind the sofa. The whole effect was one of calm tranquillity.

Freya's eyes wandered over to the mantelpiece above the gas fire. She put down her glass and walked across the room, feeling suddenly giddy as she took in the collection of framed photographs. There was a toddler sitting on the lap of a laughing young woman with long blonde hair falling over one eye. The next showed a small child with plaits and a steady, serious expression. She recognised the third: it was a professional photo in which she modelled a black cocktail dress with her usual Lauren Bacall expression. And now she and Felix came down the aisle together, both of them beaming as if they'd just discovered the Holy Grail. Another had the two of them sitting together. Felix held Anna and she had Tess. And finally there was one taken by her father only a few years ago. It had been Christmas. She and Felix stood with the girls and all of them stood behind Ivy who sat holding a cracker. It was incredible to see her life played out in this sitting room.

Eventually, Freya went through to the kitchen, another pristine room with a cork floor, shiny black surfaces and a bright pink fridge.

'Do sit down,' Eliza said. She served up the omelette and refilled Freya's glass.

'Won't you join me?' Freya asked.

'I've already had two this evening and at my age that's one too many. Do you want any salt?'

'No, this is perfect.' Freya watched the old lady squirt washing-up liquid into the sink. 'When you left home,' she said, 'I thought it was because I'd been horrid to you.'

Eliza put on a pair of plastic yellow gloves and dropped her frying pan into the water. 'I'm afraid your father and I handled it all very badly.' She cleaned the pan and put it on the draining board. 'I fell in love with Stephen. He was your father's best friend and a diplomat. He'd been posted to

Argentina. I decided to go with him.'

'And you left me behind.'

'Yes.' Eliza began work on a small Pyrex bowl. 'Your father wanted to keep you with him. I felt, in the circumstances, it was unfair to take you.'

'He would never talk about you. He removed all the photos. I have none of you.'

'Well,' Eliza said, 'I can see why he would do that.'

'Were you happy with Stephen?'

'We had our moments. It's difficult to be happy when you both feel guilty. He missed his old friend and I missed you.'

'I don't understand,' Freya said. 'I don't understand the photos on the mantelpiece.'

'Your father promised to keep me informed of your progress. For a long time, I kept the pictures in a folder and then, a short time ago, I bought frames for them.' She took off her gloves and took a seat opposite Freya. 'I don't expect – or deserve – anything from you. I do want you to know that not a day has gone by in the last forty-six years when I haven't thought of you. I have a friend – Stephen's sister – I visit in Bath. Every time I stay with her, I'm aware you live nearby. I'm an avid reader of your blog on your website. It's very good.'

'Thank you.' Freya had wolfed the omelette in seconds and now she put her knife and fork together.

Eliza fixed her eyes on those of Freya. 'May I ask you something? On your website you call yourself Freya *Eliza* Cameron. Why did you do that?'

'I suppose…' Freya hesitated. 'I wanted to remember I once had a mother.'

Eliza tried to speak and failed. She took out a tissue and blew her nose. Freya watched her try to recover her composure. She reached out for her mother's hand. 'Eliza?' She smiled. 'It's *very* nice to meet you.'

At midday, the next morning, Freya sat on the train to Darrowbridge, gazing out of the window and thinking about Eliza Sample. Eliza was elegant and sophisticated. She'd abandoned her seven-year-old daughter to live a glamorous life with a man she loved. Yet when she told Freya she'd never once stopped thinking about her, Freya believed her.

Freya could still remember the strong conviction that had sustained her throughout her own pregnancy: the belief that motherhood would be her crowning achievement. And when the twins were born, she was exalted, giddy with the knowledge that these tiny girls were why she was here.

They were supposed to be boys. Sylvie, a self-styled foetal diviner, had assured her they were boys. Their names were already chosen. They were going to be Peter, after Freya's father, and Philip, after Felix's, though as Freya told Felix, she had never cared for the name of Philip and liked the idea of shortening it to Pip. Pip and Peter. They would grow up to be gorgeous young men with the twinkling eyes of their father and the intellectual brilliance of their paternal grandfather.

She had never forgotten the moment when the doctor – who seemed to delight in telling Freya *not* to push – finally told her to push now this minute. Freya, duly obliging despite the fact she felt she was giving birth to an elephant, released into the world the first of her babies and asked faintly, 'Is Peter all right?'

She barely had time to register Felix's odd response, 'I'm not sure about Peter, but the baby is beautiful,' before the officious doctor told her to push for England and, four minutes later, Pip followed Peter into the world.

Only they weren't Peter and Pip. Sylvie had made a big mistake and Freya didn't mind at all. She sat cradling her baby daughters while Felix talked to the midwife. She gazed down at their little heads and imagined talking to them about life and love.

They had been such sweet little girls. Anna had been far sturdier and more confident, organising endless games in which Tess, always so pliant, was happy to join. And then, about the time they left Wimbledon, adolescence kicked in and Freya felt quite at sea with them. Tess took to spending long periods in her room, while Anna spent most of her free time with her terrifyingly confident new friend, Olivia. Sometimes Anna would return from meals with Olivia's family and talk admiringly of the heated discussions that took place round their kitchen table, ignoring the fact that it was difficult to have heated discussions with daughters who were so very unforthcoming.

It went without saying that she was proud of them. Freya was the first to admit that it had taken her a long time to work out what she wanted to do with her life, apart from being a wife and mother, of course. She had already tired of modelling by the time she met Felix and, despite her protestations, found it remarkably easy to leave the clothes shop in Wimbledon. She was delighted that the girls were so focused on their chosen careers. It was possible that they were quite contented with their lives. She didn't *know* because she never had those sorts of conversations with them.

But she should have done. She should have tried harder. It was the same with Felix. All these months, she'd known something was wrong and she'd just paddled along, waiting for things to get better. It was too late for her and Felix. It wouldn't be, it mustn't be, for her and her daughters.

Felix spent the afternoon cleaning the house. Freya rang at three. Her voice on the phone sounded cold and clear. She was running late, she said. She intended to go straight to Ivy's home before checking in with Pam. She thought she would be with him a little after six.

The last time he'd seen Freya, he told her he wanted a divorce before scurrying off like a frightened rabbit. He had no idea what he would say to her.

The doorbell rang at six twenty-five and there she was in her jeans and long black jumper.

'Freya,' he said, 'come into the sitting room.'

'This isn't a social call. The kitchen will be fine.'

And then her face changed as Serge, huffing and puffing, pushed his way through Felix's legs to get to her. She knelt down to greet him. 'Hello there, little Serge! How are *you*? Let's go into the kitchen, shall we?'

Serge was happy to go wherever Freya wanted. In the kitchen, he stood up on his hind legs, waiting to be lifted onto her lap. She said gently, 'Not now,' and brought her chair right up to the table, clasping her hands together, her face cold and pale.

'Would you like a glass of wine?' Felix asked

'I'd prefer water.'

'Well, I shall have wine.' He attended to their drinks, hating the silence, unable to speak. He joined her at the table and cleared his throat. 'Freya,' he said, 'before we get down to business, I wanted to say, I am fully aware... I have behaved...'

'I stayed with my mother last night,' she said.

'Your *mother*?'

'Yes. She got in touch with me at last. She's rather good fun. I always thought she didn't love me but she did. You'd like her. She said something that made me think. She said she and Dad had never been good at talking to each other. It seems that you and I are the same. So I'm talking to you now, Felix, and I want you to listen very carefully and then talk back to me. Do you understand?'

Felix nodded. 'Yes.'

'I saw Anna yesterday. She thinks – and she thinks *you* think – that fourteen years ago I had an affair with Xander Bullen. Is that true?'

He was shocked to his core. He took a swig of his wine and then nodded.

'So all this time – *all this time* – you believed I was unfaithful and you kept it to yourself. You know, I look back at our married life and I wonder if there was anything real about it at all. All these years you've thought these things about me and you never felt I deserved to hear them? You believe Xander and I had an affair. Why? Where's your evidence? Tell me. Tell me *now*.'

Felix's mouth was dry as dust. He took his glass to his lips again, had a sip and put it down again. 'It was after we put the house on the market. I went out to the garden to tell Xander we no longer needed him. I think he must have thought… Well, I don't know what he thought but he told me he was in love with you. He said he'd told you and you'd been kind to him.'

'Why didn't you tell me this at the time?'

'I rather hoped that *you'd* tell *me*.'

'I thought you'd be cross with him. He needed the work and…' She frowned. 'You said you believed him. So what's this about? He had a crush on me. I told him not to be silly. He got over it. So why…?'

'He told me it only happened once.'

'It did. He never brought the subject up again.'

'Freya,' Felix said, 'I *heard* you.'

'I don't understand. What did you hear?'

'You remember that night I came home with a black eye? I'd been home before that. I came back at six. Xander's red hat was lying on the hall table. I stood in the hall and I heard the two of you making love in our bedroom.'

Freya sat and stared at him. 'I don't believe… Felix, this is rubbish!'

'I know what I heard. It was unmistakable.'

'I don't know what you heard but it wasn't *me*. I wasn't there. At six o'clock, I was at the shop. They'd thrown a surprise farewell party for me. What with all the excitement over your mugging I forgot to tell you. Do you understand, Felix? I wasn't *there*.' She pushed her hands through her hair and he noticed for the first time how tired she looked. 'I'd like that wine now.'

'Right,' he said. 'Right.' He rose and went to the fridge.

He heard Freya's voice, sharp and worried, behind him.

'The question is: who exactly *was* upstairs?'

Felix gave Freya her wine and sat down beside her. 'What time did you get back from your party at the shop?'

'About seven, I suppose.'

'And were the girls there?'

'I think Tess was out, or she might have been in her room, I can't remember. Anna was in the kitchen making a sandwich. She said she didn't want dinner. She wouldn't talk to me. I don't know why…'

Felix swallowed hard. 'There must have been something she said to you. Did she look upset? What did she *say*?'

'I've told you, she wouldn't say anything to me. I do remember her eyes were very red. I wanted to tell her about my party but she took off with her sandwich and I…' She put a hand to her mouth and rubbed her index finger along her lower lip. 'You should have seen her last night. She was so angry with me. She actually brought up Xander. She accused me of sleeping with him and… Why would she do that? Unless…' She pushed her chair back. 'I can't believe it. She was a child. It doesn't make sense.' She stood up and pushed her hair back from her face.

Felix felt a little sick. 'The alternative,' he said, 'is that Xander brought a girl to our house, took her upstairs, made love in our bedroom, while Anna made tea in the kitchen.' He reached across for his tablet and opened the cover.

'Felix?' Freya came back to the table. 'What are you doing?'

'I'm going to try to talk to Anna,' Felix said.

He pressed the Skype button. His eyes remained fixed

313

on the screen as a photo of Anna's face came up along with the word 'connecting'. Freya moved her chair away from Felix.

And now at last Anna herself appeared, sitting on her sofa, smiling and waving. 'Hi, Dad. I've got Tess here with me. She's in the shower. She'll be out soon.'

'Anna,' Felix said. 'I want to ask you something. I won't be angry or shocked but I need you to tell me the truth.'

'Are you all right, Dad? You sound very serious.' She leant forward, concerned, and then her face changed. 'Is Mum with you?'

Freya moved closer to Felix. 'Yes,' she said, 'I'm here.'

'Mum, if this is…'

'Do you remember the evening I got mugged?' Felix asked. 'That afternoon, when you finished at school, what did you do?'

They both watched her eyes veer away from the screen. Guilt was written all over her face. Felix couldn't bear it. She folded her arms and asked warily, 'Why?'

'Anna, Xander Bullen told me he had an affair with your mother. One reason why I believed him was because on that particular evening I came home at six and heard two people making love in our bedroom.'

There was a strange expression on Anna's face: half relief and half straightforward bewilderment. 'Dad, I went back with Patrick after school. His mother gave me a lift back. I got home a few minutes before Mum. I don't know what you're talking about. If you did hear a noise upstairs, it wasn't anything to do with *me*.'

Felix could see Tess in the background, draped in a

314

towel with her hair hanging wet around her shoulders. He wondered how long she'd been there. She came forward now and sat down beside her sister.

'It wasn't Anna,' she said. 'And it wasn't Mum. It was me.'

Freya stifled a cry and Felix gripped the edge of the table with his hands. He forced himself to sound calm and measured. 'Tess... just tell us what happened.'

'I've been meaning to tell you... I just didn't know how to... I hadn't realised you thought... Xander came over to say goodbye. I was on my own in the house. He said he loved me. I was so happy he loved me. He took me upstairs and we kissed on the landing. He wanted me to show him I loved him. He took me into your room and he kissed me again and then he sort of lost control and I got scared and tried to get him to stop but he didn't seem to hear me and we made love and it hurt and I hated it.' She stared out at them with great haunted eyes.

Felix felt physically sick. He had been in the house when his daughter was being raped in his bedroom. He could have raced up the stairs and saved her. Instead, he had assumed his wife was making love and he'd been too much of a coward to confront her. He could have pulled the bastard off Tess but he had walked away and got drunk. He could scarcely take in the full extent of his culpability. He felt a hand on his arm and moved aside to let Freya speak.

'Tess,' she said, 'of course you hated it. That wasn't making love. That was rape.'

They saw Anna's face crumple and then Tess cried out, 'I'm so sorry. This is all my fault. I never thought... I never meant... I'm so sorry... I've ruined everything!'

'Darling Tess.' Freya's voice was soft and urgent. 'Darling sweetheart, this is *not* your fault, this is not your fault at all. You were thirteen, you were a child. That man was twenty-nine! He was *sixteen* years older than you. If I had him here now, I would kill him for what he did to you. Nothing matters but you. You are *not* to blame yourself. I *forbid* you to blame yourself! Do you understand? I forbid you!'

Tess was half-smiling, half-crying, but she nodded and then she nodded again.

'That's my good Tess. Now I tell you what I want you to do. Go and get dressed and dry your hair before you catch pneumonia. Go now. I want to have a few words with your sister but I'll talk to you tomorrow evening. Do you know that we love you? Do you know we love you very much?'

'Yes. I know. I love you too. And I'm so sorry, Mum, I'm…'

'I know you are. I'm sorry too. Now go and get some clothes on and dry your hair. Go now!'

They watched her turn and disappear from the screen. They waited a few moments and then Anna whispered, 'She's gone.'

'Good.' Freya's voice was brisk now. 'Listen carefully. I want Xander Bullen's address. You told me yesterday that Olivia's friend was going to visit him. I need his address and I need you to find it out this evening and text me the details. I don't mind how late it is but I want the address tonight. Will you do that?'

'Yes, all right. Mum, those things I said…'

'There's no time for that now. Get me that information

316

and look after your sister.' Freya reached for the tablet and switched off the connection.

Felix slammed the table with his hand. 'Oh God,' he said. 'That fucking bastard!'

'She was thirteen,' Freya whispered. 'She was thirteen and I never realised.'

'You were brilliant with her. You did everything right. I couldn't speak. I wanted to but I couldn't.'

He walked over to the wall and kicked it.

'That won't help,' Freya said.

'It helps *me*. I should have seen what sort of man he was. Tess was always hanging around him. She idolised him. I remember thinking he was very kind to her. You see what he did? I went out to tell him I had something serious to say and he...'

'He used me as his smokescreen. I was just as bad. When he professed his love for me, it seemed very sweet and rather flattering. I remember telling him he should look for younger women.' She took a tissue from her bag and blew her nose. 'It makes my flesh creep to think about it.'

'Do you realise I was *there*? I stood there in the hall, listening to those sounds, hating myself and hating you and all the time I could have stopped it. I could have stopped it.'

'We're both to blame. I should have told you what Xander said to *me*. You should have told me what Xander said to *you*. If we'd had a halfway healthy marriage, none of this would have happened. I enjoyed his attention. I should have seen that he was only fully engaged when he was with Tess.'

Felix kicked the wall again.

'Felix!'

'I'm sorry. I don't care if he lives in the Outer Hebrides. I'll drive off tomorrow and find him.'

'We'll both find him.'

'I'll kill him.'

'That wouldn't help Tess. Feel free to beat him up. I'll beat him up too.' Freya bent down to pick up her bag and stood up. 'I need some fresh air. I'll walk down to Pam's. I told her I wouldn't be long.'

Felix put a hand to his forehead. 'I'll come with you.'

'No. I need to be on my own. I need to think. I'll ring you as soon as I hear from Anna.'

Felix thrust his hands through his hair. 'I could have saved her...'

'We can talk about that later. Don't dwell on it now. We'll sort out Xander tomorrow and then we'll sort out Tess.'

He nodded and followed her through to the front door. There were huge questions to ask and huge decisions to make but they would wait. As he opened the door, he said, 'Freya, I'm sorry I doubted you.'

She stared at him without expression. 'You should be,' she said. 'I take responsibility for lots of things, but it was you who killed our marriage. Goodnight, Felix.'

CHAPTER TWENTY-NINE

They were lucky and, realising this, set out with an odd sense of exhilaration. Xander Bullen did not live in the Outer Hebrides, he lived in Hampshire, an easy journey along the motorway and down the A34. Freya had brought her case with her. Felix would drop her off in Andover later and she would go back to London and see Tess. For now, all that mattered was the meeting with Xander.

In the car, Felix and Freya discussed strategy. Felix, they agreed, would do most of the talking. Once they'd worked out their tactics they lapsed into a silence occasionally broken by Serge who lay at Freya's feet.

As they turned off the motorway, Felix asked, 'Did you tell Pam what we were doing today?'

'No.' Freya stared out at the green fields on either side of the dual carriageway. 'Mostly, we talked about my future.'

'I see.' Felix hesitated. 'Did you reach any conclusions?'

'I think so. Did you know that Percy left Pam his house?'

'No. I'm glad. She was always so good to him.'

'I suggested I could rent it from her.'

Felix threw her a startled glance. 'You'd move there with Lockhart?'

'Oh... I didn't tell you. I left him.' She sounded unconcerned, almost as if it meant nothing at all.

Felix struggled to equate her calm, careless tone with

319

the enormity of what she was saying. He threw a fleeting glance at her. He could see she had no idea what that casual, small statement meant to him. In his mind's eye, he watched tall, dark, handsome Neil Lockhart fall into the quicksand and disappear slowly from view.

'I see,' he said at last in a deliberately neutral sort of tone. 'As far as Percy's house is concerned, I think it's an excellent idea. But it makes more sense if I'm the one to live there. You're the one who works from home. Serge should stay with you. It would only confuse him, being in Percy's house without Percy. And if you really imagine I would let you stay down the road while I swan about in comfort in our home, then you don't know me very well.'

'I don't think I do know you,' Freya said, in that same detached manner. 'I don't think I ever did.' She glanced at the satnav. 'We turn off soon. I feel nervous now.'

'We're not the ones who should be nervous,' Felix said, but he didn't talk again. He came off the dual carriageway and negotiated his way through a series of ever-narrowing country lanes on either side of which were large country houses with big gardens and paddocks. Twice, Felix had to slow down for ladies on horseback.

'Of course we're in *Downton Abbey* country,' Freya murmured. 'The big house they use is in this area.' Her fingers drummed on the window. Serge, sensing her discomfort, tried without success to climb on her lap.

And now, finally, the satnav's perky little flag appeared and they arrived at their destination. They sat and stared at the old wooden gate and the drive that led to a Hampshire cottage: red-brick walls, tiled roof, wisteria trailing across the front. Traversing the front of the house was a big stone patio with garden chairs and a table. On the right of the drive, there was a square lawn with silver birches in the far corner and a variety of shrubs and flowers along the borders.

Felix said at last, 'He's done well for himself.'

They walked down the drive without talking. Freya held Serge's lead. Felix rang the doorbell.

'Do you realise we're both dressed in black?' Freya murmured. 'We look like Jehovah's Witnesses.'

A voice called, 'I'm coming!' and the door was flung open. A pretty girl in red trousers and a cream top said, 'Hi, there! You're early! Do come in and... Oh, isn't your dog beautiful?'

'He's called Serge,' Freya said, 'after Serge Gainsbourg.'

'Right.' They could see she'd never heard of him but was too polite to say so. 'I'll let Xander know you're here. He's just changing. I won't be a moment.'

They watched her run upstairs and heard a brief murmured exchange. Then down she came and invited them into the kitchen. They followed her through the corridor into a big airy room with wooden floors, white-painted furniture and red gingham curtains. A quiche and a bowl of coleslaw covered in cling-film sat on one of the work surfaces. On the middle of the pine table stood a small vase with four white roses. There was a mint-green high chair in the corner and on the wall there was a big noticeboard plastered with photos of a plump smiling baby and various adoring helpers, the most frequent of whom was Xander.

The girl smiled. 'I'm Poppy,' she said, 'but I guess you worked that out!'

'It's nice to meet you, Poppy,' Freya said. 'You have a lovely home.'

'I know. We're very lucky. My gran left it to me.' Her voice trembled for a moment. 'She died three years ago.'

Freya walked over to the photo collection. 'And that's your baby?'

'Yes, that's our little Georgie. She'll wake up soon and then you can meet her. We called her after my gran.'

Freya smiled. 'You look too young to be a mother.'

'I'm twenty-three! Most days I feel very old. Georgie doesn't sleep too well.'

'I remember that feeling! Have you known Xander long?'

'We've been together forever! My parents live in the village. Xander's looked after their garden for years and he used to help out Gran. In fact, he's been amazing...' They heard his footsteps in the corridor and his voice ringing out, 'Hi, there, I'm sorry I wasn't...' He stopped in the doorway and looked blankly at his visitors. His clean hair gleamed as did his crisp white shirt, his sleeves rolled up to the elbows. 'Poppy,' he said, 'I thought you said they were Nina and Jason...'

'Oh.' Poppy was embarrassed. 'I assumed they *were* Nina and Jason.'

'No,' Felix said, 'we're Felix and Freya.'

Poppy gazed a little uncertainly at Xander.

'Well,' Xander began, 'it's fantastic to see you both.' He smiled at Poppy. 'A long, long time ago I used to work for these people. They were very good to me.' He scratched his head. 'This is rotten timing, I'm afraid. I'd so love to catch up on all your news, but we're expecting guests.

322

They're rather important. They want to talk about a TV series. Can you believe it? And they'll be here any minute so...'

'That's all right.' Felix folded his arms. 'We won't take much of your time. I needed to ask you something.' His eyes rested briefly on Poppy. 'I can say it right now if you like.'

Xander hesitated. 'I think I heard Georgie stirring. Poppy will want to get lunch ready before she wakes. We'd better get out of her hair. Come and look at our pond before you leave. We're rather proud of it.' He strode across to the back door. 'Come this way then.'

It was a beautiful garden. They stepped out onto a stone path, lined on either side with lavender bushes, beyond which were raised vegetable beds. 'We suffer from rabbits,' Xander said. Further on to the left, was a large old garden shed, its roof and walls covered in a cascade of small, starry white flowers – '*Clematis flammula*,' Xander said. 'It begins to bloom in August.' He sounded like a tourist guide anxious to herd his clients through the exhibits as quickly as possible. And now, finally, they reached Xander's pond, an oasis of calm tranquillity. Beyond it a wooden fence separated the garden from a large meadow.

'I do love water in a garden,' Freya said.

Xander put a hand to the back of his neck. 'I'm afraid I'm rather an evangelist where ponds are concerned. I could go on forever about them.'

'We mustn't let you do that,' Felix said. 'We know how busy you are.'

'That's true.' Xander glanced briefly at his watch. 'This is very frustrating. As I said, I would love to chat but...'

'I'll be brief,' Felix assured him. His voice sounded friendly and relaxed but his eyes never left Xander's face. 'You see, Freya and I are getting a divorce.'

'Oh.' Xander's expression was one of bewildered concern. 'I'm so sorry to hear that. Is that what you came to tell me? I don't quite see why...'

'It was my decision,' Felix said. 'I told her I knew she had an affair with you in Wimbledon.'

'Oh.' Xander's eyes drifted back to the house as if seeking help. 'I'm sure you must be very upset but...'

'Freya refuses to admit her guilt. So I suggested we came together to see you.'

Xander gave an incredulous smile. 'I assure you, Felix, there was nothing to...'

'The thing is,' Felix said, 'a couple of days before we moved, I came home early from work. I saw your hat in the hall and I thought I heard the two of you making love in our bedroom.'

'Oh dear.' Xander stared out at the meadow. A thin patina of sweat glistened on his forehead. He put his hands on his hips, stared down at the ground and then fixed his eyes on Felix. 'This is all rather embarrassing. It was a long time ago. I was young. I admit I had a... a crush on your wife. I do remember telling you that and, on that one occasion, we did get carried away. I felt very bad about it. I still do. It was never meant to happen. I regretted it almost at once. I know Freya did too...'

'Which is odd,' Felix persisted, 'since Freya wasn't there at the time. Tess was. She was the one in our room with you.'

Xander wiped his forehead with his hand and began

324

rubbing his chin. 'Look,' he said, 'I didn't want to tell you the truth but I'm going to have to tell you now. The thing is… Tess had been pestering me for months. To be honest, I was embarrassed by her persistence. I came round that afternoon to ask Freya for a reference. Tess was there on her own. She… she told me there was an intruder in your bedroom. I went upstairs to investigate and then she shut the door and started to undress. I told her to stop. She said if I didn't make love to her she'd pretend I'd assaulted her. I was scared. I didn't know what to do. I suppose I panicked.'

'And so you felt obliged to have sex with her?'

'Look, it was the last thing I wanted to do. I was terrified. She was getting hysterical…'

'Liar!' Felix leapt forward and punched Xander in the face. Xander lost his footing and fell into the water and Felix waded in after him.

Xander struggled to his feet, shouted, 'You fucking lunatic,' and lashed out at Felix, directing a stinging blow at his face. Felix stumbled, rose again like a deranged leviathan and then lost his footing as Xander hit him again. Felix tried to get up. Xander raised a clenched fist and Freya shouted, 'Don't you dare!'

She'd released her hold on Serge's lead and made straight for Xander, plunging into the pond, throwing back her shoulder bag and hitting him hard on the side of his head with it.

'*That's* for hurting my family,' she yelled. She hit him again. '*That's* for raping my Tess,' and then again, 'And *that's* for raping her too!'

Xander, his arms flailing in a desperate attempt to

defend himself, yelled, 'All right, I had sex with her. I didn't mean to hurt her! I thought she wanted it!'

'She was thirteen!' Freya cried. 'She was only thirteen!'

Xander lunged at Freya and now she too fell into the water. Xander pushed his way out onto dry land and was set upon by a frenzied Serge, barking in a high-pitched fury and pushing his teeth into Xander's ankles. Xander shouted, 'Get off, you fucking animal... Get off...'

'Xander?' Poppy's voice stunned them all, even Serge. Freya ploughed across to Felix who was trying with obvious difficulty to get up on his feet. She helped him out of the pond, picked up the lead and called out, 'Serge, come here.' Serge issued an impressive growl at Xander but did as he was told and allowed Freya to fix his lead to his collar.

Xander seemed to be rooted to the spot. Felix pushed the wet hair back from his face and limped up to the group of onlookers. Poppy stood clutching baby Georgie. Beside her stood a young couple. They both wore sunglasses and they both held mobiles. The young man appeared to be videoing Xander.

Felix wiped blood from his lip and nodded at Poppy. 'We were just leaving,' he said. 'We can see ourselves out.'

'Come along, Serge,' Freya murmured. She took Felix's arm and they made a slow progress up the path and through the house, their shoes squelching as they did so, a thin trail of water marking their progress.

'I think,' Felix gasped, as they shut the front door behind them, 'I've done something to my ankle.' He winced with pain. 'Would you be able to drive?'

'Of course. Lean on me.' Freya's black shirt clung to her skin like glue. 'We could stop somewhere if you like.

We could go into Andover.'

'I am not walking through Andover looking like this.'

They stood by the car, doing their best to shake off the excess water. 'Thank God I have my case in the boot,' Freya said. 'I'll find some dry clothes. We'd better get your trousers off before your ankle starts swelling.'

It took time to pull them off. Freya helped him exchange his wet shirt for her black polo-neck jersey and it stretched with visible protest over his chest. At least Freya could change into her own clothes. She found clean underwear and her blue shirt dress and sandals. Finally, she helped Felix into the car and Serge leapt in after him. She went round to the driver's seat, looked at Felix and smiled. 'I shall never be able to wear that jumper again. How do you feel?'

He nodded. 'I'm all right.'

'You've split your lip,' she said. 'It's bleeding.'

'There was a big stone in the pond. If I hadn't tripped over it, I'd...'

'I'm glad you did. I got to join in the fight. He'd have hit you when you were down. I did enjoy hitting him. He did look scared.'

'So he should be. I know how much stuff you keep in your bag.'

She turned on the ignition and cast another quick glance at him. 'You look like you've been hit by a steamroller.'

'I *feel* like I've been hit by a steamroller.'

Freya put a hand to his mouth and brushed away the thin streak of blood. 'Are you sure you don't want to stop for...'

'I don't want to stop for anything.' Felix tried to shift his position and then winced with pain. 'I'd just like to go home.' He put a hand to his mouth. 'I know you wanted to get to London today. If we can...'

'I can go back to London tomorrow. I'll make up a bed in the spare room.'

'That won't be necessary.' Felix shifted his stricken ankle with difficulty. 'You can have your own room. I've been in the spare room since you left me.'

Freya put her foot on the accelerator. 'You mean, since you told me *you* wanted to leave *me*.'

Felix shut his eyes. 'I don't know what I mean,' he said.

Olivia came home at ten and stopped dead at the sight of Anna. 'Oh my God,' she said, 'what have you done?'

Anna was making a mug of tea. She put the kettle down. 'Are you referring to my hair?'

'It's auburn. You've dyed it. Why've you dyed it?'

'Solidarity with my sister,' Anna said. 'She's left you some chocolates on your bed.'

'She didn't have to do that.'

'I know. I told her. I don't suppose you've been able to talk to Jason yet?'

'No, I haven't had a moment.'

'Oh but...'

Olivia grinned. 'Of course I've talked to him. He says as long as he lives he will never forget this afternoon.'

'Oh my God, what happened? I've been thinking about it all day. Did Jason get my text? I know my parents wanted to confront Xander. I wanted Jason to know they weren't mad. I wanted Jason to know Xander raped Tess.'

'He got your text when they drove back to London. He couldn't get back to you because he had a call from his boss. He'd sent him the film and...'

'Jason sent him a film? What film? Tell me. Tell me what happened.'

'I can *show* you.' Olivia pulled her phone from her bag. 'Jason managed to get most of the fight on his mobile. You know you said you'd like to beat the crap out of Xander Bullen? Well, your parents got there first.'

'Jason won't make it public, will he? The last thing Tess needs is…'

'Of course he won't. He knew I'd want to see it, that's all.' Olivia leant over the kitchen bar, her hands holding her mobile. 'Watch this and see Xander's hopes of TV stardom die a very, very watery death.'

There was no question of going back to London. Felix was not well. He made a brave but unsuccessful attempt to eat the supper Freya made and she insisted he go to bed. She took him up a hot drink at ten. He was in his pyjamas but was hobbling about, laying out clothes on the floor.

'Felix,' she said, 'what on earth are you doing?'

'I'm packing. If I can get to Percy's house in the morning…'

'You're crazy,' she told him. 'You have a fever. Your left eye is almost completely closed. Your face looks like someone's thrown a paint-box over it. You're not going anywhere. I'll stay on for a bit…'

His voice was unexpectedly fierce. 'That's not fair on you. I can't ask you to do that.'

'No,' she agreed, 'you can't. This is my decision. I will stay here until your fever's gone and your face looks halfway normal. Now get into bed.' She stood and watched him struggle onto the mattress. She put down the mug and helped to lift his injured ankle up and under the duvet. 'Good. Now have your drink and try to sleep. Did you take the painkillers I gave you?'

'Yes. Thank you. Freya, I need to say...'

'No. You don't need to say anything. Not tonight. Go to sleep.'

She went downstairs and accompanied Serge into the garden, watching him make a fastidious study of the flower bed until he found the right place in which to lower his haunches. She took him back to the kitchen, said goodnight and went upstairs with a glass of water.

In bed, she lay looking out at the stars, revelling in the silence of the countryside. She could hear Felix sneeze and, a few moments later, she sneezed too. She had thought she would find it difficult to sleep tonight but it was easy. All she had to do was to close her eyes.

CHAPTER THIRTY

Anna had suggested to Tess that they meet for a brunch on Saturday, a fortuitous idea since she'd stayed up late with Olivia on Friday night and needed a lie-in. She arrived at the café in Fulham at ten thirty and ordered strong black coffee.

She was sipping it with deep appreciation when she saw her sister walk straight pass her. She called out after her and grinned at her reaction.

'Your lovely blonde hair…' Tess said. She took a chair opposite Anna. 'I can't believe it.'

'Oh.' Anna waved a careless hand. 'I fancied a change.'

'You've succeeded. You look totally different.'

'I want to look different. I want to *be* different.'

Tess rolled her eyes and took a seat opposite Anna. 'This guilt trip you have is ridiculous and… This is typical of you. It's so extreme…' She stopped as the waitress came towards them and asked for coffee. Anna ordered scrambled eggs, smoked salmon and toast for them both.

Tess leant forward. 'Just so you know, brunch is *not* on you. I'm not sure I can cope with you being so nice to me all the time. It's a little unnerving.'

'I'd take advantage of it while you can. You know what I'm like. Normal service will soon resume. How did you get on at work yesterday? I was lucky not to kill any patients. I kept falling asleep.'

'Me too.' Tess rested her elbows on the table. 'I've some news. Mum rang me on the way here.'

Anna had a brief vision of her mother wading into the water and laying into Xander Bullen. 'How is she?'

'She's still at home. Dad has flu and she's looking after him. She sounds pretty ill herself but she says it's just a cold. She plans to come back to London later this week. I'm not sure where she'll stay.'

'Won't Neil be waiting for her?'

'No. He's off the scene. Mum broke up with him on Wednesday evening.'

'But...' Anna stared at Tess. 'I saw her Wednesday evening.' She could remember everything she'd said. She'd been, even by her own standards, spectacularly unpleasant. And her mother had run off, in order presumably to break up with the man who might have made her happy. There is no way, Anna thought, I can begin to make things up with her.

'It must have happened after she saw you,' Tess mused. 'Did she say anything about him to you?'

'No,' Anna said. 'Not a thing.'

'It's all very odd. I asked her if there was any chance of her and Dad getting back together...'

'Well?' Anna prompted. 'What did she say?'

Tess shook her head. 'The way she sees it, Dad chose to believe in Xander rather than in her... Oh, Anna, don't look like that, it's different for you.'

'No,' Anna said, 'it really isn't.' She clasped her hands round her hot mug. 'So what will happen when Dad's better?'

'Mum's moving back to Darrowbridge. Dad plans to rent Percy's house. She said she'll tell us all about it on Thursday evening.'

'I'll be on duty then.' She was almost relieved.

The waitress arrived with Tess's coffee. 'You two sisters?' she asked.

Anna nodded. 'How can you tell?'

'The hair, of course. You don't see hair like that very often. Your breakfast won't be long.'

Anna caught Tess's eye and grinned. She put her mug to one side and leant forward. 'So Mum sounded all right then?'

'She was great,' Tess said. 'She wants to pay for me to have counselling. I told her I've organised it.'

'Have you?'

Tess nodded. 'Marnie's put me onto her lady. She says she's great.'

'Marnie?'

'William's cousin. That's why I couldn't come with you on Wednesday. I rang her as soon as you gave me her number. When she visited Durham, she'd just finished her A-levels and was unsure about her university choices. William had invited me to supper and then had to dash off to his hospital. So Marnie and I spent most of the evening together and we got talking...'

'About university choices?'

'We dealt with them quite quickly. And then she told me something terrible. She'd been raped by one of her school-friends a few months earlier. She said he didn't seem to think he'd done anything wrong. She said that sometimes she wondered if he *had*. When William eventually got back he found two very emotional women. He was great actually but... the next morning I felt so embarrassed. Apart from Rachel, I'd never talked to

333

anyone about Xander. I couldn't face seeing him after that.'

'So William knew…'

'He promised he wouldn't tell you. I felt so ashamed.'

'But you could see what Marnie went through. Why couldn't you…?'

'It's quite easy to give advice to other people. It's taken me a while to believe I could be different if I wanted to be. Anyway, at least I'm going to try. Marnie was very encouraging.'

Their meal arrived and, as they tucked into their eggs, Tess had more good news to impart. 'I had supper with Rachel last night. I was so tired I nearly cancelled but I'm so glad that I didn't. Her brother was there. He's landed another great part in some Hollywood blockbuster. In six weeks' time he's off to the States for at least seven months. He wants me to look after his house again. Same rent as before but with two extra responsibilities. Besides the cats, he's now acquired some goldfish and a Bonsai tree. I'll be back in London Fields. I can't wait.'

Her sister, Anna thought, had acquired a whole new energy. Tess had a meeting with Geraldine in a couple of weeks and more work to be done on Sir Walter. Anna felt she did a good job of hiding her own feelings but it obviously wasn't *that* good. When they said goodbye, Tess hugged her and murmured, 'Don't worry too much about Mum. You'll sort it out.'

Anna had no such confidence. It wasn't just her mother. It was William too. His past tentative attempts to get her to spend more time with Tess now took on a whole new meaning. She had, she felt, let down all those she loved.

And then on Sunday she had an email from him.

'*Here's a photo of one our hospital admin staff. Wife of Miss Diamond's ex. See the resemblance?*' Attached was a photo of a woman with blonde hair in a smart grey suit. She was older and slimmer than Anna but she had the same short haircut and blue eyes. Anna couldn't believe that Miss Diamond's dislike of her was fuelled by a vague similarity with her ex-husband's partner. Even so, she felt warmed that William had cared enough to suggest it.

On Tuesday, Anna carried out a Caesarean section. This was only her second and she took care to arrive in good time. At least there were no complications to worry about. This was Harriet Arnold's first baby; it had proved to be breech and a Caesarean had been advised. Harriet's husband, Ed, a giant of a man, stood clutching his wife's hand while Anna and the rest of the team worked. His features only relaxed when Anna pulled out the baby and he said, 'Oh Harry, you lovely lady, we have a son and he's beautiful. Oh Harry, he's beautiful!'

And that was when everything went wrong. Harriet began to haemorrhage. The baby was placed with the neonatologist. As the red and seemingly endless flow of blood oozed out, the anaesthetist said sharply that he'd have to put Harriet to sleep for a while. Harriet's husband stared desperately at Anna who told him gently he'd have to leave. The anaesthetist moved in, the husband was moved out and Anna tried to ignore the scared faces around her.

She began to massage Harriet's womb but still the blood flowed. She asked for a drip to firm up the uterus and help reduce the bleeding and then, trying to keep her voice firm, asked the anaesthetist to help with more drugs. Nothing was working. Anna's brow was drenched with sweat and she called out desperately, 'Can someone find Miss Diamond?'

After what seemed an eternity, Miss Diamond arrived. She pushed Anna to one side and barked orders for instruments, blood and further doses of drugs. Then she placed a B-Lynch suture round the womb. Anna held her breath and watched as the womb at last fell into line and began to contract; slowly, but surely, the blood settled.

There was an awestruck silence, broken only by the sound of Miss Diamond's heels on the hard floor as she left the theatre.

The anaesthetist looked across at Anna. He said slowly, 'The last woman I saw in this situation had to have a hysterectomy.'

Anna nodded. 'I think Miss Diamond might just be a genius.'

An hour later she went to see her. She knocked on the door of her office and went in. Miss Diamond sat behind her desk, sipping her coffee, cool as a cucumber, just as if she performed life-transforming surgery every day of her life. Perhaps she *did* perform life-transforming surgery every day of her life.

'Miss Diamond,' Anna said, 'I wanted to thank you. What you did for Mrs Arnold was magnificent. I felt so useless. I tried everything I could; I didn't know what to do next.'

Miss Diamond put down her cup. 'Of course you didn't. You're a junior doctor. You're here to learn from people like me. For the record, you did everything correctly.'

'Thank you,' Anna said. She turned and went to the door.

'Doctor Cameron?'

Anna waited for the inevitable killer comment. 'Yes?'

'I like the hair,' Miss Diamond said. 'It suits you.'

Freya rang Tess on Wednesday night and said she'd be staying in Darrowbridge for the time being. Felix's flu had turned into bronchitis. She suggested Tess came down to them for the weekend.

Stepping down from the train on Friday night, she could see her mother waving and was attacked by nerves. She wasn't sure what she dreaded most – the thought that Freya might want to talk about Xander or, the more likely scenario, a weekend of careful, tactful avoidance.

It appeared that Freya had no time for tact. As she drove them away from the station, she said briskly, 'Let's deal with Xander Bullen right away, shall we? I should tell you that Felix and I called on him the day after we Skyped you.'

'What? How did you…?'

'He lives in Hampshire,' Freya said as if this explained everything. 'The journey was easy. We confronted him and he more or less admitted he'd pretended to be interested in *me* in order to conceal the fact that he was targeting *you*.'

'Oh.' Tess swallowed. 'What's he like now?'

'He's a creep,' Freya said. 'His wife is young enough to be his daughter so, as the French would say, *plus ça change*. You were the victim of a very nasty man and Felix and I will never forgive ourselves for failing to keep you safe.'

'Mum, if Dad hadn't believed you were having an affair with him, he'd never have left you.'

'That's something else I need to deal with. If your

337

father and I had had a healthy relationship, he would never have fallen for Xander's lies and he certainly wouldn't have kept them to himself for so many years. Your father and I broke up because our relationship was wrong. None of this is your fault.'

'I can't believe you went to see Xander. He must have been terrified.'

Freya gave a small, tight smile. 'I don't think it was the best day of his life.'

'Right.' Tess lapsed into a brief silence. 'How is Dad?'

'He's a little better. The doctor's put him on antibiotics and he's bored stiff with being an invalid. I left him getting dressed. He's determined to join us for supper. I should tell you his face looks a little battered. He fell and hurt himself last weekend. He's so looking forward to seeing you.'

'Me too.' She glanced at her mother. 'Anna sends her love.'

'That's nice.' Freya turned into the drive and stopped the car. 'Here we are,' she said.

Tess gave a long sigh. 'It's good to be home.'

Any diffidence Tess felt as she entered the house was soon overturned by the eruption of Serge, who barked furiously at her for a good three minutes until deciding she might be a friend. She had thought it would be difficult to be together with her parents but they made it very easy. There was a slight formality between them, a new diffidence in her father's tone whenever he addressed her mother. But, almost, one could believe things were as they should be.

Freya had excelled herself with roast chicken and all the trimmings, followed by apple crumble. Over supper, Felix put a hand on Tess's arm and said gravely, 'I have something to say.'

Tess reddened. 'If it's about Xander Bullen…'

'It isn't. I wouldn't dream of blighting this evening by mentioning him. It's Scotland. I believe you start your Reading Week in a fortnight?'

'Yes, but…'

'Hear me out, Tess. You and I did at one point talk about travelling up to Scotland together. Now in fact… What is it, Serge?'

Serge's paw was scratching at the French windows and he uttered urgent little whining noises.

'I expect he can smell a fox,' Freya said. 'I'll let him out.'

Felix watched Freya rise from the table. 'I've promised Ma I'll go up to the Commune for a few days. She'll never forgive me if I don't go. You can come down here on the Thursday evening and then we can drive off together in the morning.'

Freya returned to her seat. 'You can get the night train down from Edinburgh on the following Saturday and be back in London on the Sunday.'

'It's my treat,' Felix said. 'Your mother has gone online and done the sums. I want you to go and I want you to see your friend, Jamie.'

'I would love to go with you,' Tess said, 'but I don't even know if Jamie *wants* to see me.'

'Then you'd better go and find out. Do you like him?'

'Yes. Very much. But…'

'In that case, go, Tess. I rarely give you advice but I know of what I speak. If you're lucky enough to find someone who can make you happy, don't mess it up. Do your best to make it work or you'll always regret it.'

In the silence that followed they could all hear Serge barking somewhere in the garden. Freya pushed her chair back. 'I'd better go and see what he's doing.' She went across to the French windows and disappeared into the darkness.

'Dad?' Tess reached for his hand. 'If you really believe all that, why are you planning to move into Percy's house? Why aren't you doing your best to get Mum back?'

Felix gazed out after his wife. 'Believe me,' he said, 'I'm working on it.'

By the end of the following week, Felix was better. He was determined to go back to work after Scotland. He would spend the next week organising Percy's house, he said. When he came back from his holiday he'd spend one last night at home and then move in the next day.

He assured Freya he could sort out Percy's house on his own. Freya announced they would do it together. In fact, it was a relief to them both to spend the days sorting out cupboards, packing up boxes and cleaning floors. In the evenings, they collapsed in front of the television.

When Tess arrived on the Thursday night, she seemed to be alight with anticipation. The next morning, Freya stood in the doorway with Serge and waved goodbye to the travellers. Tess gave one last dazzling smile before the car disappeared round the corner. Freya hoped they'd been right to encourage a meeting with Jamie. It was ironic to think that it was only now when she and Felix were splitting up that Tess was at last confiding in them.

She went back into the house and put Serge down. She felt dispirited about the weekend ahead of her. She'd planned something special for Saturday and on Sunday morning there'd be a visit to Ivy. It still left the evenings to get through. She squared her shoulders and went to the kitchen to find her shopping list. Serge followed her and sat down on his back legs, his head to one side, his protuberant eyes gravely regarding her.

'I know,' she told him, 'I try to be positive. I'm off to the supermarket. The weekend will be fun.'

Serge regarded her with a sceptical expression.

She got back at eleven to find the postman had visited. She put the letters on the hall table and then brought in the food bags, flowers and wine carrier. Serge barked ecstatically at her return. Already she couldn't imagine life without him. She put the kettle on for coffee and went through to the hall to collect her post. There was a handwritten envelope addressed to Freya Cameron, c/o Felix Cameron. She opened it, raised her eyebrows and took it through to the kitchen.

'Dearest Freya, I am writing to let you know that Eva has been most gracious and taken me back. I want to apologise for my extraordinary behaviour the last time I saw you. As I said at the time, I was thoroughly inebriated but that is no excuse. I hope you will find it in your heart to forgive me. I shall always remember you with love and affection. I hope that one day we can meet for a meal and laugh about all this. I think about you every day and shall always treasure our time together. Neil.'

Freya found matches in the kitchen drawer. She dropped the letter in the sink and set fire to it. It made a bright, brief flame but left a black mark on the sink that took some time to eradicate.

She spent the rest of the day making up beds, cleaning the house and preparing the evening meal, stopping only to take Serge for a walk in the woods. At seven, she realised she had no idea which train to meet. She was about to make a call when the doorbell rang.

'All right, Serge,' she said. 'Keep calm.'

Anna stood in the doorway, clutching a huge bouquet of red roses. She looked as nervous as Freya felt.

'Hello, Mum,' Anna said, and then her voice broke. 'Please... can we start again, please?'

CHAPTER THIRTY-ONE

All three of them were nervous. In the front of the car her father and grandmother maintained a dogged conversation about the weather while Tess sat in the back, twiddling her hair with her little finger and telling herself that she hadn't *asked* Jamie to have her over today.

They dropped her off by the Abbey ruins. 'I'll keep my phone on,' Felix told her. 'If you decide you want to join us, we'll be at Burt's Hotel for at least the next hour or so. And then after that, we'll be enjoying the delights of the Autumn Fair so...'

'I'll let you know what I'm doing. Don't worry. Have a good lunch.' Tess got out of the car, gave a cheerful wave and crossed the road. She walked up the lane and stopped outside Jamie's house. Once again, she was struck by its familiarity. Almost, she felt, it expected her to be here. It gave her courage. She knocked firmly on the front door.

She waited for what was probably less than a minute but seemed like a lifetime. Then he opened the door and stood aside to let her in. She smiled but he didn't smile back. He wore black jeans and a black jersey. She wondered if his choice of colour was a subconscious statement.

'Thank you for inviting me to lunch,' she said.

'Thank you for getting in touch with me.' His tone was unnervingly formal. He closed the door and moved towards the fireplace.

'I was coming up to Scotland to see Grandma. It seemed wrong not to contact you, especially now...' She stumbled but she had to mention it for why else was she here? '…Especially now my mother and your father are no longer together.'

'You must be pleased by that.'

'Of course I am. I still hope she and Dad might get back together.' She had forgotten the way in which his face could remain so resolutely unreadable. But his eyes, dark, wary, possibly hostile, never left her face. She attempted a smile. 'I did think you might ring me once you heard. But you didn't. I thought perhaps you'd transferred your affections to your local historian.'

'*Martha?*'

'Then I googled her and discovered she's a sixty-five-year-old grandmother.'

'She has your auburn hair,' Jamie conceded. 'In her case, I'm not sure it's natural. She's an extraordinary woman. You would like her.'

'I hope I get the chance to meet her.'

'I'm forgetting my manners,' he said. 'Let's go to the kitchen. I have wine in the fridge.'

She followed him through. His politeness lowered her spirits. She sat at the table while he attended to their drinks. The kitchen was as neat as it had been the last time she was here.

He took a seat beside her and considered her gravely. 'I'm confused,' he said at last.

There was to be no small talk then. 'I can't say I blame you,' she said.

'Why would you expect me to ring you? You said you didn't want to see me again.'

'I said I felt I *couldn't* see you again.'

'I really can't see the difference. I can't force you to care about me. If you *had* cared, you'd have made a small effort to make it work. Our parents' affair was a convenient excuse for you.'

His perception was impressive and also off-putting. 'Jamie, I don't blame you for giving up. I'm hard work, I know that. Most men would run a mile. I'm seeing a counsellor now, by the way, but... I don't blame you for giving up.'

'That's very gracious of you.' There was a slight glint in his eye. 'At least... I'm not sure if it *is* gracious. Are you suggesting I *shouldn't* give up?'

'I'm not saying one thing or the other.'

'Tess,' he said, 'I find it very difficult to know what you want me to do.'

'I can see you're a little angry and I sort of understand but...' This was proving impossible. It was like wading through mud. 'Can I just say that it's very difficult sitting here trying to tell you how I feel when you look at me like I'm some crazy alien? It's not easy to admit I'm in love with you. You can ask me to go or say you don't want me...'

'Wait a moment.' Jamie frowned. 'Did you say you were in love with me?'

'Isn't it obvious?'

'Where you're concerned, nothing is obvious.'

She looked at him steadily. 'Well, I do. I love you. Now do you want me to go or stay?'

Jamie put his glass to one side. 'I don't want to be rude,' he said, 'but that is possibly the stupidest question you've ever asked.'

She let out a sigh of exquisite relief. 'I thought you might have lost patience.'

'You should have known better. I was attempting to conduct a strategic retreat.'

'Was that what it was?' She smiled. 'It was very effective.'

They sat looking at each other. 'Just so you know,' he said, 'if the doorbell rings I intend to ignore it.'

'Good,' she said gravely, 'so will I.'

He looked at her again. Then, slowly, tentatively, he kissed her. It was longer than last time. Tess had the oddest feeling that Jamie's house was holding its breath.

His eyes went down to her hands and he broke into one of his rare, sudden smiles. 'Hey, Tess,' he cried, 'you weren't clenching your fists!'

Felix and his mother sat opposite each other on a table by the window at Burt's Hotel. Their fish and chips had arrived at last and Felix commented on the unusual number of guests in the restaurant.

'It *is* busy,' Maggie agreed. 'Perhaps they're all coming to the fair this afternoon.'

'Perhaps they are. Do you hope to buy some Christmas presents there?'

'I may do. We'll have to see.' She poured out a glass of water from the jug on the table. 'Now, what were we talking about before the food arrived? We've covered Tess and the little dog you've been looking after and you gave me a detailed description of your journey up here.'

Felix nodded. 'I thought you'd be interested to hear

346

about the pub we found in Lancashire. The lunch was excellent.'

'It sounds delightful. But I would like to change the subject now, just in case Tess comes back earlier than expected. I think I should tell you that Neil Lockhart has gone back to his wife.'

Felix put down his knife and fork. 'Has he? That was quick. Freya only left him a few weeks ago.'

'So you know that.' Maggie took a sip of her wine. 'Felix, I don't want to pry…'

'That's what I love about you, Ma,' Felix said. 'Other mothers would be desperate to interfere. You understand that it's not your place.' He raised his glass. 'I salute your dignity and… your reticence. It's wholly admirable.'

Maggie gave him a withering stare. 'I presume you are *trying* to annoy me? Of course I want to pry. I'm your mother. Are you taking Freya back?'

'I'd take her back tomorrow. Unfortunately, she shows no wish to be taken.'

'I don't understand any of this. I thought you loved her.'

'I did. I do.'

'So why did you tell her to leave you?'

'It's very simple. I thought she'd been unfaithful. I was wrong.'

'That doesn't sound simple at all.'

'Those are the facts. I gave her no chance to explain her side of things. I told her very brutally that I wanted to leave her. And then I found out she was blameless. Why would she want to come back to me?'

'I wouldn't say Freya is *blameless*… Let's not forget Neil Lockhart.'

'He'd never have happened if I hadn't done what I did. The fault is all mine. I won't have you condemn her.'

Maggie threw up her hands. 'I don't. I feel sorry for her. Felix, I'm your mother. I know you. You must be intolerable to live with. You never say what you mean. Look at you now here with me! I don't believe for one moment you'll accept defeat. You know you'd be miserable without her. You can tell me, you know. Stoicism is a very overrated virtue.'

Felix laughed. 'Ma, you are such a hypocrite. Twelve years ago you had breast cancer and cancelled a visit without saying why. We only discovered the reason six months later. If I'm a stoic, I learnt from an expert.' His phone rang and he picked it up at once. 'It's Tess,' he murmured, his eyes stiff with anxiety.

Maggie watched him sit back and assume a calm, easy manner. 'Hi, Tess, how's it going? ... Good... No, that's fine... Tell him to call in. Tell him I'd like to say hello.'

He put the phone down and took a gulp of his wine. Maggie watched him bite his lip and saw his face contort in an effort to control himself. She cut a piece of her fish and ate it with great concentration. Finally, she said lightly, 'Is Tess all right?'

He nodded. 'She's exceptionally all right. They're going out to the castle later this afternoon. There's some function going on and she wants to help. She won't be in for supper. He'll bring her back at ten. He'll call and say hello before he goes home... She sounds happy. She sounds so very happy.'

They all waited up for them. Katherine and Robert sat

348

playing backgammon. Maggie knitted. Sheila and Derek argued amiably about the referendum. Felix chatted to Linda. At a quarter past ten, they all heard the car pull up outside. Katherine went over to the window.

'They'll see you pulling the curtains back,' Maggie protested. 'What are they doing?'

'They're talking,' Katherine said. She moved away from the window. 'Now they're coming in.' Katherine returned hastily to her chair. 'I think we should all try to look natural.'

Maggie raised her eyebrows but resumed her knitting. Katherine and Robert stared intently at the backgammon board. They heard voices in the hall and now Tess came into the sitting room with Jamie who, understandably, looked a little taken aback by the reception awaiting him.

Felix was the first to move. He sprang from his chair and strode over to Tess's young man. 'Good evening, Jamie,' he said. 'I'm Felix. It's so very nice to meet you.'

On Tuesday afternoon, Anna sat in the impressive glass foyer of South Reading Hospital, flicking through the messages on her phone. William had been told she was here. He was working. He'd be with her as soon as he could. That was twenty minutes ago. All right, she thought. As long as it takes.

Another fifteen minutes went by and then there he was. She hadn't seen him for three months and he looked pretty much the same except that there was no welcoming warmth in his eyes, and that hurt. 'Anna,' he said, 'your hair.'

She smiled. 'Hi, William.'

'Is this because of the photo I sent you?'

'I'd already done it. I must say Miss Diamond seems to like the new me.'

He sat down beside her. He seemed to be at a loss as to what to say. 'So… How are you?'

'I'm well. I spent last weekend with my mum. On Saturday we went to Bath and I met my grandma for the first time.'

'Really? How did *that* go?'

'I didn't think I'd like her. She walked out on her family when Mum was a child. The two of them met up again a few weeks ago. This weekend, she was staying in Bath with her sister-in-law. She took Mum and me to the Pump Rooms for lunch. She greeted me by asking if I was the clever academic daughter or the one who was horrible to her daughter. I told her I was the horrible one and after that we got on well.'

Briefly, William's face relaxed. 'She sounds fun,' he said. '*Have* you been horrible to your mother?'

'Yes. It's something I'm trying to change. It's one of many things I'm trying to change.'

'Look…' William seemed to be at a loss as to how to reply. 'Why are you here, Anna? I can't stay long and…'

'I wanted to see you. I wanted to tell you, to your face, that I know I let you down and I'm sorry. But I think – I really do think – you're being unfair. Can you look me in the eye and swear you've never done something you wish you hadn't? Can you sit there and promise you've never been ashamed of your behaviour?'

William sighed. 'No,' he said, 'of course I can't.'

'So how come I get the cast-out-of Eden treatment? I miss you.'

'I miss you too. But…'

'You said you didn't want to see me again. Ever. That's quite harsh, William. I apologised. I transgressed. Am I not to be forgiven? You said you didn't like me now. Is that true?'

'Look,' William said, 'you don't… The main reason I said that was to stop you calling me again.'

'Why? If you really don't like me, then I understand. But if you don't, why did you take the trouble to send me that photo?'

He murmured, 'I don't know how to put this. I was upset when you rang that evening to cancel me but…' He stopped and gave a half-smile. 'The thing is, I wasn't just upset. I was jealous. I was properly jealous and that made me see… When I joined St Peter's, I enjoyed spending time with you. I enjoyed it too much. I liked you too much, which meant my love life was rubbish. I don't want to be on my own for the rest of my life. I'm going on dates now. I am getting over you and…'

'That's the problem. William, look at me. I don't want you to get over me.'

'I'm sure you don't but…'

'William, are you being deliberately obtuse? Do you really want to make me spell it out?'

The left corner of his mouth lifted slightly. 'I think you're going to have to.'

'Oh William!' She squared her shoulders. 'I like you. I like you a lot. I want to be with you. In the biblical sense. In every sense.'

'Anna,' William said, 'I know what you're like. I walk out of your life and suddenly you miss me. How do I know that if I walk back in, you won't …?'

'You don't know. Neither do I. I do know I've never missed anyone like I miss you. When do you finish today?'

'I'm off at six.'

'I can be here at six. If you want me to. I can go and look at the high life of Reading for a couple of hours. Or I can go home and agree that I'll never bother you again. It's up to you.'

'I don't know what to say. It's a lot to take in.' William glanced at his watch and stood up. 'I have to go.' He glanced down at her doubtfully. 'I suppose we could have a pizza together.'

'Great.' Anna nodded. 'I'd like that. I'll see you here at six.' She sat and watched him walk back across the concourse. Her hands were trembling and she gripped them tightly. He was about to go through the swing doors when he turned and smiled at her. A moment later, he disappeared.

Anna relaxed her hands. He smiled, she thought, he smiled. She rose to her feet. It was time to go and explore Reading. Whatever it was like, she knew she would love it.

On Saturday afternoon, for the first time since her return to Darrowbridge, Freya sat down at her desk, able at last to concentrate on her November column. She had lit the wood-burning stove. Serge lay at her feet. All was calm. Tomorrow evening, Felix would come back and on Monday, her new life would begin.

She sat staring at the screen, waiting for inspiration to arrive. It didn't. She opened her left-hand drawer in order to find her IDEAS FOLDER, a name that promised far more than it tended to deliver.

Her Anniversary folder sat at the top which was odd since it had lain at the bottom of the drawer for months now. She picked it up. 'Anniversary Stuff', it said, and then, underneath, in Felix's writing, was the word, 'Amended'.

She opened it up and took out the guest list. Felix had made various comments in the margin, alongside certain names: '*Really? ... Must we? ... No!!!! ... Oh God!*'

When had he done this? *Why* had he done this? She was about to put the list back when she found a new sheet of paper. There was a heading: *FELIX'S SPEECH – heavy editing required.* At her feet, Serge began to snore. Freya began to read.

'*We are here to celebrate my huge good fortune in having Freya for my wife. The first time I met her was at a wedding. I can tell you nothing about the bride since I had eyes only for Freya. I was sitting in a church pew when this vision came up and asked if she could sit next to me. Imagine an ornithologist exploring some remote part of the country. Imagine his reaction when the rarest bird in the world flies up to him and lands on his wrist. Imagine that and you will understand how I felt when Freya asked if she could share my seat.*

She was – and continues to be – the most beautiful woman I have ever encountered. As I grew to know her I found that her personality was as fascinating as her appearance. She was energetic, enthusiastic, funny and bright and endlessly curious about the world. Somehow, I persuaded her to marry me.

Three years later, we became parents to twin girls.

353

Freya had read Anna Karenina *and* Tess of the d'Urbervilles *while she was pregnant. She burned with indignation at their tragic ends. She wanted to call the children Anna and Tess in order to remind herself what was important. She wanted them to grow up to be confident, clever and independent, to be answerable to no one but themselves. They've turned out pretty well. Inevitably, with a mother like Freya, they have beauty as well. I should warn any men foolish enough to try to hurt them that they will have Freya to deal with.*

We lived in Wimbledon throughout the girls' childhood and we were happy. Freya had given up modelling when the girls came along and she used her savings to start up a clothes shop which she ran with great success. As time went on her enthusiasm became a little muted. She seemed restless. In retrospect, I think she was bored with the shop and needed new mountains to climb. Her mood was infectious. At work, I'd been offered the chance to head a new office in Bristol. I decided to take up the challenge.

And now we come to my downfall. We had a gardener who was everything I wasn't: young, strong and exceptionally good-looking. He adored Freya but then most people did. Once we'd decided to move, I told him we'd have to let him go. His response was unexpected. He told me he loved Freya and implied they were having an affair.

Now, you're all sensible people and you're presumably making two obvious suppositions: one, that I would of course assume there was something odd about the young man's wish to give me such explosive information and, secondly, that I would naturally tell Freya about it. Let me try to explain why I didn't show such natural common sense myself.

The young man seemed open and honest and genuinely apologetic. I wanted to talk to Freya about him. I refrained. When apparent new evidence came my way I was terrified. If I confronted her, she might admit she loved him? Suppose she left me? That was unthinkable. We were moving away. She'd forget him. It was too dangerous to rock the boat.

And so we came to Darrowbridge. The girls settled down. Freya found a new and lasting interest in genealogy. I tried to forget the gardener and some of the time I succeeded.

A few months ago, Freya took part in a balloon debate. If you ask her about it she will tell you it wasn't her finest hour. She took on the role of Madame Bovary. At the beginning of her speech she proclaimed to the audience that she was an unfaithful wife. It was like a shotgun going off in my brain.

We have since discovered that the gardener was a twisted individual who told me a pack of lies. Since you are sensible people, this won't surprise you, and, in a way, that's not important. What mattered was that I believed him. In the months after the balloon debate I decided I could no longer live with what I assumed was Freya's infidelity. I arranged to go on a work trip to Spain on the weekend of our thirtieth wedding anniversary. The night I left, I told Freya I no longer wanted to live with her. I gave no explanation. I went off to Spain. Freya being Freya went off to London and found a new admirer almost at once. I came home to an empty house and knew I had ruined my life.

By this time you will all say I deserved everything I got. I agree. Why would Freya ever take me back? Well, I have to tell you this is my *speech and* my *fantasy. So yes, Freya has forgiven me and this is why:*

She knows I love her. She knows I will always love her. She knows I will devote the rest of my life to making her happy. She knows I will never forgive myself for my past behaviour. I am far too high-minded to resort to emotional blackmail so I have restrained from pointing out to her that our girls would like nothing better than for us to be together again. What I have told her – and since this is my fantasy, she instantly agreed – is that I firmly believe that our best years are yet to come. On our fortieth anniversary, I look forward to telling you all that we have a strong marriage based on honesty, respect, affection, tolerance on her part and boundless love on mine.'

Freya raised her eyes from the document and gazed at her screensaver: a photo of the family at the wedding of Felix's nephew in Cardiff in March. There was Felix in his best suit surrounded by Freya and their daughters, all of them smiling at the camera, blissfully unaware of the dramas waiting to engulf them.

Felix arrived home at six on Sunday evening. He turned off the ignition and climbed slowly out of the car. His muscles ached. He stared at his home. All the lights were on and smoke was rising from the chimney which meant that Freya had lit the fire. This was his last evening with her and he was determined to be positive. He would talk about Tess. He would not dwell on his imminent exile. He would refrain for the time being from trying to persuade her to take him back.

He took his hold-all from the boot and let himself into the house. He could hear Freya in the kitchen and called, 'I'm back! I'll just take my case upstairs.'

When he got to his room, he stopped and then slowly put his bag down on the floor. His bed had been stripped. His clothes lay on neat piles on the mattress. He couldn't believe it.

When he went downstairs, he took his bag back down with him. In the hall, he took out the present he'd bought and went through to the kitchen. Freya was at the sink. He could smell chicken cooking in the Aga, so presumably he'd be given dinner. It was easier to attend to Serge who gave him a rapturous welcome. At last, he looked at his wife.

'Hello, there,' he said. 'I've bought something for you.'

She took it without speaking, opened the paper and pulled out the jersey.

'It's cashmere,' he said. 'Tess took me to her shop in Gasterlethen. We chose it together.'

'It's lovely,' she said. 'Thank you.'

He said, 'I saw the bed. Do I take it I am leaving tonight?'

Freya pulled off her plastic gloves. 'I have something to show you. Won't you sit down?'

'I've been sitting in the car all day. I'd rather stand.'

She went across to the dresser and held up the anniversary folder. 'I found this.'

He put his hands in his pockets. 'Ah.'

'Did you mean me to see it?'

'I hoped you might.'

357

'Well, I did. And it made me angry. Even now, after everything that's happened, you still couldn't bring yourself to look me in the eye and explain it all to me. You had to write it down.' She threw the folder on the table.

'I wanted to...'

'I know what you wanted to do. Why couldn't you just *tell* me? If there's to be any hope for us, you have to start talking. If you get depressed, you tell me. No more painful silences. No more long, lonely cycle rides into the darkness. I can't take that now. I love you, Felix, but I *will* walk if you shut me out. I don't deserve that. I'm better than that. It's taken me a long time to see it but I *do* deserve better.'

'Freya...'

'How can I trust you if you don't change? How do I know that in another fourteen years you won't tell me you're leaving because I slept with Neil Lockhart? We haven't talked about him. I've been here for weeks and we still haven't talked about him.'

'I didn't feel it was my place to bring him up. I quite understand why you went with him. I've lost any right to be jealous.' He took his car keys from his pocket and put them on the table. 'I did ask Tess about him.'

'What did she say?'

'He told me he was tall, dark and handsome. I think she was quite cross with me at the time.'

'He was all those. He was also an idiot. I think I've told you that already.'

'It's great to hear it again though.' Their eyes met for a second and then she looked away.

'I'll tell you about him sometime. Felix, we've spent

358

fourteen years living a lie. Secrets in a family are… they're like moths in cashmere. They dig themselves in and eat their way out. Our family has been torn to shreds because of secrecy. In future, if you have anything… anything at all on your mind… then you tell me. Do you understand?'

'Yes.' He nodded. He didn't understand anything except for the extraordinary possibility that she might take him back.

'And there's something else. If we are to get back together, we *will* have an anniversary party and I want the speech. You'd have to edit it, in fact you'd have to rewrite nearly all of it, but I want the speech and I want champagne and I want some fun. But most of all, Felix, I refuse to go back to how we were. If you can't accept that, I'll give you supper and then I'll drive you down to Percy's.' She unfolded her arms and went over to the fridge. 'Although, actually, *you'll* have to drive, because I need a large drink.'

He watched her take out a half-empty bottle of wine. He walked across to the cupboard and took out two glasses. 'Fill them up,' he said.

She stared at him. Then, very deliberately, she filled them to the brim.

Later, he would tell Freya – and he *would* tell her – that this had a profound effect on him, that – and he would struggle to describe it – he felt as if his heart shook off the last embers of doubt and jealousy and self-flagellation But, now, at the moment, all he could do was to smile and smile. He was where he should be. He felt as he *should* feel. He was home.

How far would you go to feel safe again?

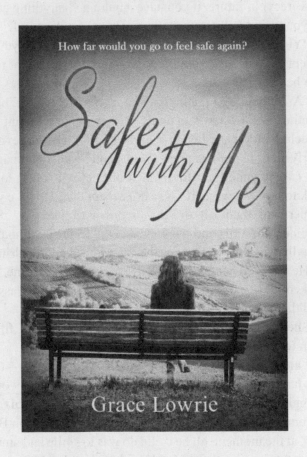

An emotional and evocative story about the deepest bonds of friendship.